BOB HOPE

A LIFE IN COMEDY

WILLIAM ROBERT FAITH

BOB HOPE

A LIFE IN COMEDY

DA CAPO PRESS

A Member of the
Perseus Books Group

Cataloging-in-Publication data for this book is available from the Library of Congress.

ISBN 0-306-81207-X
Published by Da Capo Press
A Member of the Perseus Books Group
http://www.dacapopress.com

Da Capo Press books are available at special discounts for bulk purchases in the U.S. by corporations, institutions, and other organizations. For more information, please contact the Special Markets Department at the Perseus Books Group, 11 Cambridge Center, Cambridge, MA 02142, or call (800)255-1514 or (617)252-5298, or e-mail j.mccrary@perseusbooks.com.

1 2 3 4 5 6 7 8 9—06 05 04 03

To Bob Hope —

the man
the talent
the legend.

"Hope" is the thing with feathers —
That perches in the soul —
And sings the tune without the words —
And never stops — at all —

Emily Dickinson

CONTENTS

⌇ Clown Hero: 1942 to 1945 ⌇

⌇ Comic Drummer: 1946 to 1951 ⌇

⌇ Court Jester: 1952 to 1963 ⌇

⌇ The Patriot: 1964 to 1970 ⌇

⌇ The Loyalist: 1971 to 1972 ⌇

CUE IN: NINETY IN THE SUN

"I left England when I was four because I found out I could never be king."

Late in the afternoon of one of California's breathtaking spring days, a crowd of three thousand people—invited guests, celebrity seekers, network employees, and curious onlookers—were packed into metal bleachers set up adjacent to the National Broadcasting Company's Burbank studio complex waiting for a living legend.

A long black limo approached the scene and rolled to a stop. The doors opened and out stepped the guest of honor with his broadly smiling wife. The *Tonight Show* host Jay Leno appeared from out of the crowd to escort the couple toward a makeshift stage. Then two NBC executives, West Coast President Don Ohlmeyer and Entertainment President Warren Littlefield, made a presentation of a plaque that read NBC STUDIOS. DEDICATED TO BOB HOPE, MAY 1, 1993. THANKS FOR THE MEMORIES. In his inimitable manner, their longtime big moneymaker quipped, "I wonder if this makes me a part owner."

Ironically, Hope had not yet been asked to sign a new contract with his network for the first time in 55 years.

As Bob and Dolores sat in the bleachers with other guests and spectators, Jay Leno took up the duties as host. "NBC *should* rename its studios after Hope. It's the only piece of real estate in Burbank he doesn't own." And then he added, "You know, it wasn't hard for this man to get to the Bob Hope Studios today. All he had to do was take the Bob Hope off-ramp from the freeway (which somehow he does not own) and just follow Bob Hope Drive."

Gesturing toward the dedication plaque, Leno depicted Hope's career in show business history with a due sense of import. "It's kind of like the Rosetta Stone," he said. Suddenly there was a roar from up above as six Air Force jets flew overhead, tipping their wings in a loving military salute. The Hopes shaded their eyes against the late-afternoon sun as they pointed their fingers toward the passing planes; the audience was delighted and applauded enthusiastically. A few moments later, just as dusk approached, fireworks burst into the sky and sprayed multicolor blossoms through the air. Trailing sparks began to fall over the crowd a little too close for comfort, and Bob quickly led Dolores off the bleachers. Later, as the honored couple was leaving, the guests rose to their feet for more cheers and applause.

Thus began, on that late May afternoon in 1993, one of the biggest, longest, and most expensive birthday bashes in Hollywood history.

This long, long party was being thrown for a 90-year-old man who had performed in literally every decade of the twentieth century and had conquered all the major show business media the century had invented. After a tentative start as a childhood show-off and then as a youthful hoofer in short musical comedies called tabloid shows, he got to be a headliner in vaudeville and played Manhattan's storied Palace, starred on Broadway in the *Ziegfeld Follies,* and was voted best radio comedian in America in 1941. He became one of the country's most beloved film stars and more recently, to judge by his ratings, an undisputed television superstar. Undeniably, he was a man who had lived his entertainment career publicly. There were no secrets—well, maybe a few. . .

His legendary reputation for both speed and patriotism was indelibly traced in the American consciousness because he flew millions of miles to entertain millions of GIs in both wartime and peacetime. This trajectory began with the airmen at March Field in 1941 and ended, several hot and cold wars later, with the jet fliers of Desert Shield in 1991. As a result of this extraordinary journey, Hope has had everything imaginable named for him, including roses and ferns, theaters, schools, hospitals, a freeway off-ramp, a golf tournament, several city streets, a C–17 Air Force plane, named *The Spirit of Bob Hope,* and one naval vessel, the USNS *Bob Hope.* Perhaps the most singular military honor ever paid him was in 1996, when Congress declared him the first and only honorary veteran of the U.S. armed forces.

A Senate resolution declared Bob Hope "a part of American folklore." The *Guinness Book of Records* says he is the most honored entertainer ever. Countless writers have referred to him as *peripatetic* (Greek: "one who travels") because he has spent more days *away* from his home in California than *in* it.

Having a studio complex dedicated to him was a pretty nice gift, but so was the colossal cellophane-wrapped entertainment package that arrived the very next afternoon at around five o'clock. Hundreds of people, dressy women and men wearing black ties even if they were technicians, paraded grandly over red carpets into NBC's cavernous Studio 11. These folks were much more than a mere studio audience having drinks and hors d'oeuvres as they watched a three-hour "blockbusting" show. They were drawn to this ceremony and would not be found any place else at this moment because they were partners, in all their different ways and degrees, with Hope and his life in comedy.

Johnny Carson—who had bantered with him many times on his late-night show—came out of retirement to introduce a kind of "this is your life" friendly roast, the kind that is suitable for family television viewing in mid-May. Other hosts included Roseanne and Tom Arnold, Walter Cronkite, Angela Lansbury, Paul Reiser, Brooke Shields, Garry Shandling, Tom Selleck, and Betty White— extremely successful and popular performers all, who took turns recalling Hope's roots in vaudeville and his subsequent successes on Broadway, reflecting on his mythic radio years, conjuring up anew the *Road* pictures with Bing Crosby and Dorothy Lamour (Lamour would join him onstage), and with the help of some other leading ladies—also aging but there in the audience—reviving the magic of his film persona and replaying some very funny sequences from five hundred TV specials. And each host somehow reflected Hope's legacy in their lives.

There were the singing, dancing, and comedic talents of Rosemary Clooney, Whoopi Goldberg, Ann Jillian, Donald O'Connor, and Michael Richards, and there was as always "Thanks for the Memory," played for the thousandth time by Les Brown and His Band of Renown.

Probably the most touching moments of the evening came after General Colin Powell saluted Hope for his tireless USO (United Service Organizations) trouping, followed by several onstage tributes by all branches of the armed forces and eye-witness accounts by servicemen and -women who had been in Hope's overseas audiences. One of the most telling came from a Marine veteran who said to Hope, "My father saw you in the South Pacific the year I was born. My son saw you two years ago in Desert Storm. And I saw you in 1965 during the first of my three tours of duty in Vietnam."

There were standing ovations for both George Burns and Milton Berle, and nostalgia for people like Bing Crosby, Jack Benny, Judy Garland, Lucille Ball, Ethel Merman, Jimmy Durante, and Sammy Davis Jr., who had all departed this life but who were heard or glimpsed on the screen singing, dancing, and clowning with Hope in comic episodes from his radio days, his movies, and TV. But no standing ovation was louder and longer than the one for Dolores Hope, 84, when she sang "It's Only a Paper Moon," the song she was singing when Bob walked into Manhattan's Vogue Club with George Murphy on a December night in 1933.

Stars such as Humphrey Bogart and Ginger Rogers were present only on film or tape; others—Gene Autry, Candice Bergen, Garth Brooks, Carol Burnett, Chevy Chase, Phyllis Diller, John Forsythe, Gregory Hines, Jack Klugman, Tony Randall, Phylicia Rashad, Roy and Dale Rogers, Jane Russell, Telly Savalas, Raquel Welch, and Vanna White—stood up at their tables at the big party and blew kisses or offered birthday wishes.

But equally important invitees were industry people from every aspect of show business who had worked for, and with, the man during his professional life. In a segment called "Stagehands to Presidents," Hope's production staff and technical crew—friends such as Al Borden, his propman since *Roberta* in 1934; Barney McNulty, his cue-card man since 1953; *Daily Variety*'s Army Archerd, who was an office boy at Paramount in the 1940s; Ward Grant, his public relations man of 25 years—all got to say things that had been on their minds for years, all amusing or revealing. Some filed long-held complaints while others wanted to finally confess affection for their boss, and Hope managed a comedic spar with all of them. Even for his presidential golf buddy Jerry Ford, who appeared live on stage, Hope quipped, "It's not hard to find him on a golf course—you just follow the wounded." It also wasn't so shabby that this one-time scrawny kid from

Cleveland, Ohio, received verbal gifts from four other former presidents—Richard Nixon, Jimmy Carter, Ronald Reagan, and George Bush, Sr.—as well as one from the man then occupying the Oval Office, Bill Clinton.

How did this televised extravaganza of a party happen? Not by chance but also not without a dilemma or two. Linda Theresa Lande Hope, vice president and director of Hope Enterprises, Inc., and on-and-off producer of her father's television shows since the late 1970s, had originally come up with the idea. She simply wanted to have her father's extraordinary contributions to the entertainment world remembered, or at least recognized and appreciated by a new generation as he turned 90. "He's my dad and I grew up with him," she said. "It was never a big deal to me. But I must say, going back [Linda undertook six months of research, on both coasts] and looking at the enormity, the volume of work this man has done, I was blown away by the excellence of it. And I said, we just have to let people see how this man has witnessed the century."

"No way," Hope grumbled. "Why don't you do an *Around the World with Bob Hope* special using all that travel footage we've shot over the years that's still sitting on the shelf." But he lost that battle when NBC liked Linda's idea for a ninetieth-birthday telecast, although they strongly advised her to hire an award-winning producer-director. She was able to get an Emmy winner, Don Mischer, on board.

Hope was still fussing even after he agreed to the big telebiography. He sensed the possibility of an Emmy award in his future and he liked the idea. But then he heard that they wanted to call it *Ninety Years with Bob Hope* or something like that. "I wanted 'ninety years' taken out of the special's title," he said. "But NBC took over and it wound up *Bob Hope: The First Ninety Years*. Sometimes you win and sometimes you lose." What he *did* win was important. NBC decided to give Hope three hours of prime evening time for the show, just as they had done for his seventy-fifth–birthday show.

Although he was officially the co-executive producer (with Linda), he really didn't have a lot to do with the production of the show itself. He did, however, play an important role in publicizing the birthday telecast. Invitations were issued to all the national and local columnists and reporters to attend the big party. He expected that a dozen or so of them would want personal interviews with either Bob or Linda. Hope was increasingly in a reminiscent mood, now that he was turning 90, although what he said often was anchored in favorite stories and familiar jokes from the past. Hope was a born publicist. He could make every interview seem exclusive. The veteran newsman Vernon Scott of United Press International said, "In my thousand or so interviews with Hollywood stars over the years, my favorite has to be Hope. He was the best, and do you know why—he was the brightest."

Both Linda and Ward Grant were pleased, if only for archival reasons but certainly for audience-building purposes, that Hope wanted to blanket the media, just so long as it didn't interfere with his golf game. He and Dolores tried to play nine holes at Lakeside Country Club four or five times a week, usually in the midafternoon. Twenty interviews were set up with major entertainment editors; eight of them were invited to come to the Hopes' house in Toluca Lake, adjacent to Burbank, for lunch, and the others had appointments for late-morning telephone chats while the comedian was still in bed.

True to his word, the morning after the big party at NBC, upstairs in the bedroom suite of the Hopes' 18-room Tudor-style mansion, Bob had his eyes partly open even before his wake-up call. Actually, Dolores opened the door of her adjoining bedroom to rouse him just as his telephone rang. And since he didn't react to the ring (having become hard of hearing, sometimes he didn't know it was ringing), Dolores picked up the phone. It was Patrick MacDonald of the *Seattle Times*; he said he was supposed to speak to Bob Hope.

"Oh, I suppose so," Dolores said, then yelled, "Bob, it's for you."

Hope picked up his amplified phone. "Who? Oh yeah, sure, I remember. . . Ward told me you were going to call. . . Oh, that was Dolores—she comes in every morning to turn on my applause machine. . . Where? Oh, on the golf course. No, I'm not out there yet, but I will be. I try to get out there every day. And if I don't play, I practice. You know, it's my exercise."

MacDonald adjusted to Hope's asking him to repeat his questions, and they talked some more about golf, the times he and Bing played in celebrity matches at the Broadmoor resort hotel in Seattle. Then MacDonald said he was surprised to read in Hope's official press biography that he had once been a newspaperman.

"Not really," Hope said laughing. "I did a daily column called 'It Says Here' for [Randolph] Hearst for a couple of years. But finally I couldn't handle it anymore because I was doing so many things. You know, I had my radio show and I was starting in movies, which is what I really wanted to do."

Hope told MacDonald that Hearst didn't want him to quit and the powerful news tycoon was a man who got his way. So he kept offering more and more money, and when Hope still refused, Hearst asked him if he would come up to see him in his palatial residence, San Simeon. Hope said he went because he was curious about the place. "It was a kick," Hope recalled. "Marion Davies [Hearst's mistress] was knitting in this huge room and he was in this little alcove where he had his office. And he said, 'We like your column, we're gong to put it in bold type this way,' and so on and so on. All I did was nod my head and say 'yes—yes—yes.'"

MacDonald asked Hope when he was finally going to slow down, take a vacation. Hope said, "Me? Oh, no. I can't. I'm booked for six months and there'll be more after that." MacDonald was surprised to hear the comedian say near the conversation's end, "I should really write my autobiography. I've been meaning to for years. . . I just have to find the time." The official publicity material MacDonald had been sent by Ward Grant listed eight autobiographical books Hope had coauthored. Undoubtedly the journalist could only wonder what this very public comedian could mean—what could he yet reveal about his life?

Shortly after noon of the same day, Bob, dressed in tan slacks and a white golf sweater emblazoned with a DWIGHT D. EISENHOWER AIR FORCE ONE insignia, welcomed the syndicated writer Eirik Knutzen, the first of a series of journalists who would sit down with him for lunch. They met in the Hopes' spacious sunlit playroom with its huge bay windows that looked out over the swimming pool and regulation three-par golf hole. On a wall nearby was a portrait of Hope by Norman Rockwell, and near that a now priceless winter scene by Grandma Moses, which Hope said he had bought in 1946 for $1,700.

Knutzen found that Hope tended to jump from subject to subject while ignoring some the writer's more probing questions, but he attributed this to Hope's hearing loss and suspected that for media interviews Hope was adept at setting the agenda. Hope, trying hard to cool the steaming chicken pot pie in front of him, observed, "The hardest thing about being ninety years old is answering all the questions about being ninety years old."

Knutzen thought that Hope's physical condition was amazingly good, despite the fact that he had put on some weight and had several liver spots and thinning hair. "I've been damn lucky with my health," Hope said. "At my age it's just unbelievable. I walk a couple of miles every day. . . . Exercise and laughter keep me going. . . . Yeah, I've been lucky."

About the future of comedy he said, "I'm always looking for talent on cable TV. . . . Comedy hasn't changed much over the years. It still comes down to timing and delivery. But I don't think we'll find another George Burns or Phyllis Diller." When Knutzen reminded him that Roseanne was appearing on his show, Hope asked why she had to use so much foul language. The Hopes had watched Roseanne's last pay-TV special on HBO. "She used the f-word thirty or forty times during a solid hour. My wife and I just sat there and said, 'What's going on?' We still can't figure it out."

The next face-to-face encounter was a relaxed and congenial lunch with John McDonough of *The Wall Street Journal,* during which Dolores walked into the playroom. The topic of the Hopes' impending fifty-ninth wedding anniversary came up. "We're staying together for the children," Hope said laughing. "We're waiting for them to die," he continued, still laughing. McDonough wanted to know how Dolores managed her life with Hope traveling so much and she said, "I let him know on our fiftieth anniversary. I gave him a gold paperweight with the inscription: 1934 TO 1984: DON'T THINK THESE THREE WEEKS HAVEN'T BEEN GREAT."

McDonough observed that Dolores had resumed the career she had cut short when as the singer Dolores Reade she had married Bob. He asked if she was enjoying her new celebrity, a reference to the fact that Dolores had just completed an album of songs, *Then and Now,* that she described as "romantic and gentle" and that had just been released to record stores. Moreover, it had just been announced that she would be performing with Skitch Henderson at Carnegie Hall later in the month. Hope said, "Now when I come down to breakfast she's sitting in my key-light."

The following day, Bob Thomas, the dean of syndicated journalists and coauthor of Hope's book *The Road to Hollywood*, came to lunch. Because he had interviewed Hope so many times in the past and had such a reservoir of material, he did not need to do much more than update. Thomas noted that six presidents would be taking part in the big 1993 broadcast and Hope had entertained five others, including Franklin Roosevelt. So, had Hope ever met a president he didn't like?

"I sure didn't. I liked them all—and if I didn't like them, I made believe I did—because they're in a pretty good spot, you know."

"What about our new President—Clinton?" Thomas asked.

"I met him a few years ago in Little Rock. He was governor then and he took me to his house and introduced me to Hillary. That night when I was doing the show he sat in the front row, so I asked him to stand up and take a bow. He stood up and waved to the crowd, came over and climbed up on the stage and made a speech—a long one. He was rehearsing then. I don't know what he does besides go to McDonald's and play the saxophone—but that will come in handy if we ever have a recession and people start singing the blues, he can play along."

"How do you feel, Bob?" Thomas asked loudly.

"My grandfather lived to be nearly one hundred. We have good genes. I used to have a hemorrhage in my left eye and now I have one in the right eye. I'm a walking hemorrhage."

"He takes his ailments beautifully," said Dolores to Thomas in a normal voice that Hope did not seem to hear. "He is a model of acceptance. The toughest thing for him is the eye problem. He doesn't seem to understand it. Otherwise he's a prizefighter. He rolls with the punches." Then she added that Dr. Howard House, of the noted House Ear Clinic in Los Angeles, describes Bob as his only failure. "Bob has a brand-new $1,200 hearing device in his drawer, but he refuses to wear it."

Thomas then made his farewells and started for the door. "Bob, will you ever stop performing?"

"I'm a kid. I won't quit as long as I feel good. I'm lucky. I'm so lucky."

Hope's next noon lunch partner was John Stanley of the *San Francisco Chronicle*, who shared with his readers that "breaking bread with Bob Hope in his Toluca Lake mansion has to be the American equivalent of taking four o'clock tea with Queen Elizabeth in an opulent little nook at Windsor Castle."

Stanley was in the playroom when Hope entered wearing a white cotton golf shirt, tan slacks, and white Reeboks. They sat at the table before the big windows as a gardener sheared hedges outside. Hope waved his hand out at the wide expanse of lawn and said, "One time I was rehearsing a show with Claudette Colbert and she was sitting in the same chair you're in now. She looked out and asked, 'How can you afford *all that lawn*?'" He laughs and raises his fork to attack their light lunch of chicken in a white sauce and a simple lettuce and tomato salad, followed by a custard dessert topped with a single strawberry. To the inevitable "age" question, Hope says, "I never thought when I was young that I should be old. Now that I'm old I wonder when I'm supposed to be decrepit."

When they had finished the easy questions, Stanley asked Hope about his hawk-ish attitudes in the early days of the Vietnam War, the unpleasant image of Crosby that had emerged since his death, and his differences with conservationists over the development of some of his land holdings in southern Ventura County. These top-ics all seemed to wash over him as if none of it had happened—he heard the ques-tions clearly enough. "Naw, none of those things upset me. I made nine trips to Vietnam. A small minority thought I was supporting the Vietnam War. I was anti-war—who wouldn't after seeing those boys. As for the land, I gave some of it away in 1990. And I donated sixty-six acres for the Eisenhower Medical Center in Palm Desert in 1966." Hope looked out over the green expanse of his one-hole golf course and then back at Stanley and said, "You know, money means one thing to me—doing what I want to do and helping people."

Hope invited Stanley to visit his upstairs office to see some photographs; celebrities, presidents, generals, all posing with the comedian. Before leaving Stanley asked, "With so many milestones in your life, is there anything left to conquer?" Hope looked out the window and then back at Stanley and said, "Yeah, two and they're both impossible now. I'd like to win a golf tournament—and an Oscar."

For another six days Hope continued to do phone and lunch interviews with a lighthearted, positive attitude, showing no evidence that doing this kind of self-promotion on the eve of his ninetieth birthday was any less important than what he would have done to plug the debut of his Pepsodent radio show, or his first film role in *The Big Broadcast of 1938.* Hope had never ceased to believe in the neces-sity of constantly reminding the fickle public who he was, what he was doing then, and what he would be doing next.

He made sure the media knew that midday on Thursday (the day before the big birthday telecast) he was getting yet another gift—his fourth star on the Hollywood Walk of Fame. Once the star was set in place it would be one more sidewalk icon to Hope that pedestrians and tourists could walk over and gawk at and photograph. This latest star represented his work in the area he loved most, live stage performance. He already had three stars on the boulevard, one each for his work in radio, movies, and television. And this time, unlike the other place-ments, he would be there in person with a big crowd of onlookers and special guests.

Leading the ceremonies was Johnny Grant, the honorary mayor of Hollywood and an architect of the Hollywood Walk of Fame. Along with Grant, who made gentle gags about Hope, were other famous stand-up comics: Steve Allen, Milton Berle, Pat Butram, Red Buttons, Norm Crosby, Phyllis Diller, Louis Nye, Gary Owens, and an old vaudeville pal of Hope's, Eddie Rio. Fans and the curious had caught the item on the news and had come to watch. The star was placed across the street from the Hotel Roosevelt, where they would go for lunch afterward. The new star was quite close to the spot where Dolores Hope would get her first star on the Boulevard four years later for her work on the stage. The timing of this gift to Hope could not have been better engineered to help maximize the TV audience for the following night.

The next morning, he and Dolores flew to Noblesville, Indiana, in his Jetstar for a benefit show in which he would do a few jokes and Dolores would sing a few songs to boost the sales of *Then and Now*. On Saturday afternoon they flew from Noblesville to New Jersey's private-jet airport at Teterboro, and then continued on into Manhattan by limousine. This trip was really for Dolores because she had to rehearse for her Carnegie Hall concert with Skitch Henderson.

After dinner in their hotel, the Waldorf Towers, they planned to take their usual late-night walk along Park Avenue for an hour or so. But just as they headed for the door of the suite to go down to the lobby, their door buzzer sounded. Bob's valet and companion, Michael, opened the door and there stood a surprise visitor, President Bill Clinton. Dolores reached out her hand and said, "Good evening, Mr. President. Won't you please come in?" Clinton smiled broadly and said, "I was in the neighborhood and thought I'd stop in and say hello." He introduced his two bodyguards, who remained outside in the hallway. The President put his arm around Hope and walked him toward the living-room area, congratulated him on his birthday tribute, and continued to chat about how much he and Hillary had enjoyed the program. Finally he told Hope he could use some golf tips. Hope thanked Clinton for his cameo segment of the telecast. The President stayed for about 15 minutes and then said he had to go.

The Hopes then set out for their walk along Park Avenue, exchanging words of surprise and pleasure at their "presidential drop-in." Truth is, Ward Grant had heard that President Clinton was to be in New York on Saturday for a function and was probably staying at the Waldorf Towers. So he alerted the White House that Hope would also be in the Towers just on the off chance that there could be a meeting.

At this advanced stage of the Hopes' life together, they had accumulated a huge galaxy of friends and acquaintances in and out of show business and had socialized so much in high places, mixed with so many presidents and royalty and the famous and celebrated from different walks of life that it was unlikely that they could be overly impressed with position, pomp, or circumstance. They both insisted that at their ages they did only the things they wanted to do. And Dolores, in these later years, had finally gotten to have what she wanted—to be her husband's most frequent companion.

What had happened was that at last Bob was willing to let her begin running the show and to let her feel, by default to be sure, in charge. She was singing as well as she had ever sung in her life, which had given her the confidence to think about restarting her career and she was also newly confident about her role as Mrs. Bob Hope. Being asked to sing at Carnegie Hall and later at the Rainbow and Stars cabaret room was a further boost.

On top of all this, Dolores was "producing" her own star-studded birthday party for her husband in their own home. Of course, she knew it was not going to be a surprise to Bob (as usual, he had been tipped off), but he didn't know the guest list or the theme of the party or any of the details. He just knew he had to attend.

And if the more public party thrown by Linda Hope and Don Mischer and NBC was all red carpet and black-tie, this one thrown by Dolores in the sprawling backyard of their home on Moorpark Street in Toluca Lake was laid out on sawdust. It would be a bustling garden carnival where a troupe of 50 performers would greet the partygoers as they entered a "circus midway" featuring games of chance and games of skill, all with prizes, a fortune teller, a caricaturist, clowns, and look-alikes of legendary comics such as Charlie Chaplin, W. C. Fields, and the Marx Brothers. Dolores wanted in 1993 to give her husband the kind of spectacular birthday party that a ten-year-old Leslie Towns Hope could only have fantasized about 80 years earlier. For Bob, a party of this scale was like having Cleveland's famous Luna Park become his private domain for a day.

The Hopes' backyard was dominated by a huge circus big top inside which was a 1920s soda fountain and candy store, thousands of balloons and flowers, and historic Bob Hope photos. Later the famed celebrity hangout Chasen's would cater dinner for 370 Hope well-wishers.

The guest list was very carefully drawn up by Dolores to include her husband's closest friends at this stage of his life. It was an extraordinary turnout of big names in comedy: Milton Berle, Joey Bishop, George Burns, Red Buttons, Sid Caesar, Jack Carter, Norm Crosby, Shecky Green, Buddy Hackett, and Don Rickles. There were two former presidents and their first ladies, Gerald and Betty Ford and Ronald and Nancy Reagan.

There were people (those lucky enough—like Hope himself—still to be among the living) from every important step in his entertainment career: Eddie Rio from vaudeville; Fred De Cordova from Broadway; Honey Chile Wilder, now Princess Hohenlohe, and the gag writer Sherwood Schwartz from his radio days; Dorothy Lamour and Jane Russell from his movies; Frances Langford and Patti Thomas and one of his pilots, Bob Gates, from his World War II GI entertaining; and of course the producer-writer Mort Lachman and the long list of fellow stand-up comics who had appeared with him so many times on television.

The writer Hal Kanter had written scripts for some of Hope's movies and some of his Oscar monologues. Both General William "Westy" Westmoreland and a fellow USO trouper, Johnny Grant, testified to Hope's loyalty to the GI throughout the gritty Vietnam years. And Les Brown, with the band members Stumpy Brown and Butch Stone, were fond of reminding everyone that they had "seen more of Hope's ass in the last forty years than any of Hope's immediate family."

Here were celebrities from many walks of life who considered themselves blessed to be invited to this party because for the seven hours that the party lasted, Bob was in the midst of it. There were very few people who didn't manage to have a private moment or two with him. And Hope found himself spending even more time with people like Jimmy and Gloria Stewart, the astronaut Alan Shepard, Donald O'Connor, Gene Autry, Buddy Rogers, and the blind golfer Charlie Boswell.

Bing's widow, Kathryn Crosby, sent her regrets, but present were widows of some of Hope's close friends—Flo Colonna for Jerry, June Haver MacMurray for Fred, Frances Bergen for Edgar and Charlie, Josie Wayne for John, and Mousie Powell for Bill.

Dolores arranged a kind of Major Bowes Amateur Hour, which turned out to be an endless entertainment loosely emceed by the announcer, Dennis James, who let the show "happen" in a rather high-schoolish manner, considering the wattage of the performers. She had hired some amusing variety acts, including a clever dog act called "A Mess of Mutts," and many of the party guests—Betty White was one of them—lined up to deliver birthday tributes to Hope. Almost all the comedians did a routine. Ann Blyth sang, as did Dolores Hope, and there was even a serenade by the Los Angeles Master Chorale led by the chorale's director, Paul Salamunovich, a neighbor of the Hopes'. Finally, a huge birthday cake was brought out as 14 Hope family members—children and grandchildren—gathered around to sing to this "godfather" of comedy.

Looking back over the evening, it was probably Red Buttons who had Hope laughing the loudest. He was the most subtle in making the point that everyone else sitting under the canvas tent wanted to make about this man. He had done it all and he was still here, and would be remembered in the history of entertainment as being the country's most honored because he had perhaps been the most peripatetic of performers. "I'm here for one specific reason," Buttons stated. "Bob has always, ALWAYS been there for us. It doesn't matter where. He was *there*. The man was *there*, joking, clowning, singing, dancing, giving—he was *there*. The man was *there*. It didn't matter where. You called him—he went. He was *there*."

Buttons had touched a nerve. The tent full of celebrants applauded loudly.

"On my way here I put down a few things on these cards, some of the places Bob has been to, joking and clowning, singing and giving—in Rome, when Jill St. John, Susan St. James, and Eva Marie Saint were all canonized at a three-for-one sale—Bob was there—he was there—and Dolores was with him.

"In Berlin, at a protest rally of handball players who want the Wall rebuilt, the man was there—he was there—and that's why I am here.

"In Barcelona, in a sitzbath where herniated flamenco dancers soak their castanets, he was there. God bless him—he was there.

"In Lourdes—he was there—when a William Morris agent said that Mary would return—but not for the same money—he was there.

"And that's why I am, Bob—here. We love you. God bless you."

Bob was feeling very mellow as the guests were departing. Even though it was well past 2 A.M., he had decided to take his usual late-night walk and asked his good friend and golf buddy, Alex Spanos (the owner the San Diego Chargers), to

walk with him. Hope's pace had slowed some. Spanos said, "Bob, this was a fabulous night—as a child did you ever dream about being anything like what you've
become?"

"Sure. When I went to the movies. I even wrote a poem as a kid about a dream
I had about the circus."

"Do you remember it?"

"No. But it turned up a few years ago in Cleveland when Ringling Brothers
asked for circus memorabilia to be put into a time capsule that would be opened
in 2075. I must have written it when I was at Fairmount Junior School."

"Can you at least paraphrase it?"

Hope's famous memory began to kick in. "Well, it goes something like this.

I dreamed I was a circus clown
I wore a funny suit.
My shoes were blue, my nose was red
I had a horn to toot.
But when I tried to take a step
My feet refused to move.
I looked down to see the cause
A lion held me in his paws.
I asked him please to let me go.
He growled and moved away.
'I'll let you free to do a show
And come again another day.

Jolly Follies: 1903 to 1928

1

The Road to Cleveland

"I was born in 1903 at Eltham in England. Eltham is about ten miles from Charing Cross Station. It's pronounced without the h. *When I was about two years old, my father and mother moved to Bristol. My mother was the daughter of a Welsh sea captain. Her name was Avis Towns. My dad's name was William Henry Hope."*

In the winter of 1890–91, James Hope, a contractor and master stonemason, decided to take his son William Henry (called Harry by family and friends) with him to join a work crew building the new stone docks at Barry, across the Bristol Channel on the southeast coast of Wales. Harry, one of seven brothers and two sisters in a family of artisans, was a stonemason like his dad, but he wanted more from life. He dreamed of being an architect. So whenever he, his brothers, and father traveled away from their home at Weston-Supra-Mare to a construction site, Harry spent his free hours reading, mostly books about building and design, but he also liked history. And he had an eye for the girls.

Harry had just turned twenty-one. He was lithe, muscular, and handsome. His appearance easily caught the interest of the Barry town girls who came to watch the seawalls going up. One of those girls was the fragile-looking Avis Towns, who was coming home from her music lesson when she stopped to watch and admire Harry.

Avis was a sensitive and romantic teenager who lived with her foster family, Abraham Lloyd, a retired sea captain, his wife, Mary, and their son, Basil. She knew very little about her real mother and father. Her memories from her childhood were only vague fragments: handsome parents who traveled most of the time; days spent with a governess; a house in Cardiganshire on the west coast of Wales; a small lake in which a black swan paddled lazily. She remembered being told of a shipwreck in which her parents drowned, and then she was taken to a new home in Barry.

Avis thrived under the Lloyds' loving care. Gifted with a lovely singing voice, she also learned to play the spinet, the dulcimer, and the Welsh harp. Still, she was lonely and eager for an intimate relationship when she spotted the handsome and sinewy Harry Hope. She came back every day; they talked, flirted, and fell in love. James Hope disapproved and moved Harry to another location.

Separation for both was painful. Finally James decided to send Harry home to Weston-Supra-Mare. On a rainy afternoon just before he was to depart, Harry went to collect his tools from the cutting shed near the docks. As always, his eyes searched every passing couple, every solitary figure, hoping he would see Avis. Leaving the shed he saw her, and she him, and as their eyes met, Avis crumpled to the ground. Harry ran to her, and James, who had followed his son, joined them. As James looked down at Avis, Harry lifted her up and placed her in his father's arms.

"Now, what do I do, Dad?" asked Harry.

"You take her home where she belongs!"

"But I love her. I want to marry her."

"This is just a baby," said James.

Suddenly the fifteen-year-old Avis, with her Dresden-doll features, recovered from her faint and in a sturdy voice said, "I am a woman, sir!"

At that, James lifted her higher, set her on her feet, and turned to Harry. "Marry her and be done with it. We've got work to do."

Their vows were said in nearby Cardiff on April 25, 1891, and the couple went to live in the Stow Hill district of Newport, Monmouthshire, in Wales. One year later Ivor was born. In July the following year Avis gave birth to James Francis II, and Emily followed in July of 1895.

Soon after, Harry took Avis and the three children back to live in Barry where they had first met. There, in 1897, their third son, Frederick Charles, was born. He was a fretful baby, so much so that Ivor and James begged Avis to send him back. When Harry's stonecutting at Barry ended, the family moved again, this time to Lewisham in Middlesex, England. After Avis said good-bye to the Lloyds, she never saw them or heard from them again.

For the Hope family, life in Lewisham was the sweetest it would ever be on either side of the Atlantic. Harry worked steadily in good jobs, providing Avis and the children with a big stone house that had sheds, stables, and a workshop. There was space for Harry to raise prize chickens, and chrysanthemums "as big as footballs," and he kept a pony for the boys.

But Lewisham was also a time when Avis began to worry about Harry—money slipped through his fingers and he began drinking excessively. In one of those expansive states, Harry was induced by a chum to invest his savings in a stable of horses, but the chum disappeared with the money.

The Hopes moved to more modest quarters in Kent. Filled with remorse, Harry worked hard to recoup their losses, but it was difficult. Avis was pregnant again, but before the next child was born, beautiful little Emily, whom Harry idolized, contracted diphtheria and died. The birth of her fourth son, William John, helped Avis through this dark period, but Harry was now drinking even more heavily. He neglected his prize hens and, more important, he stopped reading. He went off on his bicycle and would be gone for days, cutting stone in other towns and only coming home for weekends.

Avis realized her husband was dealing with his broken dreams of becoming more than a stonemason. Work was becoming more infrequent for Harry and his skills were less in demand. Cinching their belts tighter, the Hopes moved again, this time to 44 Craigton Road, Eltham, one of the row houses Harry's father, James, had built. Harry's visits to the pub, the "local," were frequent and he justified them with the stonemason's excuse for drinking, which was that the dust from the stone is constantly inhaled and ale is best to wash it out of the throat.

It was not just Harry's drinking that frightened Avis, but his wandering eye. She had found a lady's photo crumpled in Harry's pocket, inscribed "To Harry with love." When Avis confronted him, Harry said it was a poor lovesick barmaid, and Avis broke her hairbrush hitting him.

In spite of his drinking, Harry was easy to like. He had attractive manners, and despite his salesman-like self-assertiveness, underneath he was gentle and Avis loved him deeply. She would wait up for him while he closed the pub. He might come home on foot, or in a horse-cab, but often he would be carrying a bouquet of flowers for her or some candy, like a young lover.

Harry was working on May 29, 1903, the day Leslie Towns Hope was born. Avis did not think she was due yet, but she didn't feel well. Jim was concerned and sent for the doctor. "Mahm only has the flu, dear," she said reassuringly. "Nothing to fret about." After examining Avis, the doctor came downstairs and asked Jim for some boiling water and told him to get a neighbor. Leslie was coming into the world ahead of schedule.

Avis thought Leslie was probably the last addition to her growing brood. Soon after his birth the Hopes moved again, this time back to Weston-Supra-Mare, the resort town where Harry had grown up. Avis was glad about the move; it tore Harry away from the temptation of the lady in the photograph.

The Boer War had just ended and times were tough. Jobs for stonecutters were scarce. The country's quarries were all but shut down, and there were soup lines in Weston-Supra-Mare. To save money the family moved once again, this time to Moorland Road, the last street in town, and any Hope child who could speak a complete sentence or count to ten was shoved out to find a job. Avis worked as cashier in a tea shop, taking Leslie with her, and supplemented that income by doing housework for others.

Avis tried to keep family spirits high. She played her spinet and sang songs and Welsh hymns, teaching her boys to sing along with her. She took them to watch the boardwalk buskers, the puppet shows, magicians, sword-swallowers, and often she took them on picnics.

In the summer of 1905, Harry severely fractured his ankle and couldn't work. With little money coming in for several months, Ivor found a full-time job at a dairy and then got Jim a job there too. Both boys kept their previous spots on the street selling newspapers in the morning and early evening. Even when Harry's ankle healed he failed to find work in Weston and the family moved yet again, this time to the city of Bristol, which was to be their last home in England.

It was here that new family roles developed, roles that would reshape the pattern of their lives. Ivor, partly because of Harry's drinking and his inability to find work, would become the dependable provider. Jim, on the other hand, was Mahm's protector. He was her confidant, her Lochinvar; whatever money he could earn was meant to make her life easier.

Fred idolized and imitated Ivor, which annoyed the oldest brother, especially when Fred would hang around him, finding any excuse to spin his top at Ivor's feet when he was talking to a pretty girl. Jack (William John) was the loner; he would wander off in the woods on long adventurous hikes or get himself lost in Bristol, only to be searched for by his brothers. Then there was a new one, Sydney, who replaced Leslie as the baby of the family.

Leslie's personality, at age four, was also beginning to take shape. Jack remembers that even then Leslie was a mimic. When the Hope children were taken to visit their great-great-aunt Polly who lived nearby, Leslie could always make her laugh. She was 102 and lived alone in a tiny cottage ever since her husband, a whaling sailor, had died at 97. Leslie, short-legged and tubby, would imitate some really fat person he had observed by shoving his hands into the pockets of his abbreviated pants and then pushing them out beyond his stomach. His reward was a cookie, and according to Jack, Aunt Polly would say, "That's right, laddy, I hope you always leave them laughing."

In the spring of 1906, Harry's thoughts turned to America. His older brother Frank, a master plumber, and his younger brother Fred, a steamfitter, had emigrated to Cleveland several years before. The idea of joining them looked increasingly attractive. Although stonecutting work was scarce in England, apparently that trade was still practiced in America for the construction of churches, schools, and public buildings. After much debate with Avis, Harry decided to go over alone and establish himself.

Following his departure, Avis found herself feeling lonely and depressed. She walked through the house in a daze, sometimes putting on a piece of Harry's clothing to feel his presence. Her husband's first letter convinced the Bristol Hopes that America was the most wonderful place to be. Harry said that the buildings in New York were so tall they had to be lowered to let the moon pass by. Nobody worked hard and everybody was in a hurry. Everything was abundant and there were lots of labor-saving devices. "Believe me, Avis," he wrote, "when you get here, all you'll have to do is sit on the front porch and chew gum."

In a subsequent letter Harry told Avis to begin preparations for coming to Cleveland. It was bitter cold in Bristol, but Avis managed to cut fuel costs in order to afford the $75 steerage passage for herself and her six sons. Sadly, she consigned her precious spinet and a grandfather's clock from Scotland for sale. What Avis refused to part with was carefully packed and sent ahead to Uncle Frank's in Cleveland.

After tearful good-byes to Aunt Polly and other Hope relations, Avis led her luggage-laden brood to the train bound for Southampton and then to their ship. They occupied two steerage cabins directly above the main drive shaft. It was hot and noisy and difficult for sleeping. At night, Avis brought all the boys into one cabin; she had become fearful since the first day out when she returned to her cabin from lunch to find her suitcases rifled and her beloved breast watch and its gold chain gone.

Once in New York Harbor, their ship was delayed because of thick fog. When they were finally disembarked at Ellis Island, in March 1908, they were quickly put on an immigrant train bound for Cleveland. The train was filthy and most of the time the restrooms were kept locked, which meant that everyone scrambled to use station facilities during stopovers. Food was scarce and what they found they could barely afford.

Nevertheless, the family's anticipation was boundless, their spirits indomitable, and clearly it was the thought of seeing their father at the end of the trip that made cattle-car conditions bearable. Encouraged and sometimes led by Avis, the Hopes sang—until she nearly choked from embarrassment when the boys passed the hat for coins. The boys, for their part, were embarrassed when Avis washed their underclothes and held them out the window to dry. And all the while she dreamed about the gold-lined streets of Cleveland.

2

Doan's Corners

"My first day in school in Cleveland the other kids asked me, 'What's your name?' When I said 'Les Hope,' they switched it to Hopeless. It got to be quite a rib and caused some scuffling and a few bloody ski-snoots for me."

Harry Hope—mustache waxed, pinstripe suite pressed, heart thumping like a compressor—waited nervously with his brothers Frank and Fred at Erie Station. He knew Avis and the boys would be eager to know about America and Ohio and Cleveland. What would he say? The biggest news was Henry Ford's Model T, and the new Nickelodeon on lower Euclid. And wouldn't the boys' eyes bug out when he told them the *Cleveland Press* was promising its readers air travel in the very near future! He would tell them how beautiful the lake and parks would be now that spring was coming. He would *not* tell Avis right away how little he had worked, or that he had joined a labor union for stonecutters.

America in 1908 was not the promised land Harry's brothers had described to him or the haven he had written about to Avis. There was ample evidence of achievement: the nation's ability to produce goods on a magnificent scale was reported the world over. But for people like the Hopes there was disillusionment. Life for immigrants was a 70-hour work week for $10 pay. For skilled artisans like Harry things were a bit better; a shorter week and a pay range from $13 to $19 a week. A barroom pal of Harry's just back from a job in Pittsburgh had told about conditions there that made him sick—about the surplus of immigrant workers in those steel towns stretching along the Monongahela River all the way to McKeesport. People there were clawing for available jobs, jobs that were nothing less than slavery. What could he tell his family?

When the train finally halted, Harry stalked each exit stair until he finally found Avis. The boys hung on his body until he recognized each one. The uncles were hugged as well. Somehow the luggage and travelers arrived at Uncle Frank's plumbing shop at 2227 East 105th Street. He and Aunt Louisa lived upstairs. She had prepared a meal that the boys practically inhaled, though they were disconcerted by being served kernel corn (reserved for the chickens back in England) and something called olives.

Since Frank's apartment only had three bedrooms, the older boys went to stay with Uncle Fred and Aunt Alice nearby. After a few days of doubling up, Avis found a one-family house with three bedrooms and a bathroom at Stanisforth Court on Euclid near 105th. She rented it for $18.50 a month. As for finding a church for them—there was no contest. Harry showed them the Church of the Covenant, on Euclid Avenue, where he had been doing stonework and they looked at the beautiful edifice. "When we arrived," Bob says, "we were Anglican. Then we saw the church! We liked it so much we turned Presbyterian." The minister was a friendly Scotsman, the Reverend McGaffin, who remained Avis's friend until she died.

Avis was not surprised by Harry's drinking or lack of regular employment; the important thing was that her family was together again. Actually, she understood that the age of machinery and bricklaying was making her artisan husband redundant, but Harry was either too stubborn or too proud to attempt other work. Instead, he encouraged Ivor and Jim to find jobs to support the family.

Unable to meet the second month's rent, Avis asked her in-laws for a loan. Fred's wife, Alice, was cool to the idea. She was not overly fond of Avis, her brats, or Harry's drinking. Uncle Frank demurred, asking Avis why she allowed her husband to avoid finding some other kind of work. Incensed by these attitudes, Jim earned the $10 needed. Next day, he and Ivor went out and got jobs at the Van Dorn Ironworks.

One of Harry's stonecutting chums identified the key to how the Hope family weathered the severe cold and financial panic of 1908: "I met Mrs. Hope and I could not imagine a more gentle or ladylike woman. No matter how Harry neglected his responsibilities, she was always forgiving and held to the belief that someday he would be different. There was a strong bond of affection between them and I'm sure he idolized her."

The winter was as cold as any the Hopes had known. Harry haunted the employment lists and could be heard to say, "America's a fine place for women and dogs! It's a poor place for horses and men." He did manage to form a partnership with another cutter to bid on a Cleveland high school contract. Their bid was low and they won the contract, but they failed to compute the cost of two of the building's towers and they lost money on the job.

Undaunted, Avis moved her family to a bigger house at 1925 East 105th, where she could take in boarders. The winter of 1909 in that new house was as bitter as the previous one, but George Percy Hope, the seventh son and the first U.S. citizen, was born to Avis and Harry Hope that winter. George's arrival intensified family spirits in two ways. Harry and the boys celebrated by going out in a blizzard and buying a used heating stove and dragging it home in the snow. Also, that year Harry became eligible for naturalization, and with his citizenship the whole family became Americans.

Avis's ability to make ends meet was nothing short of miraculous. She took a streetcar miles downtown to the public market and shopped from stall to stall. She made over clothes for the younger boys and devised home medicines to cut doctor bills; she kept a spotless kitchen and always had snacks for her sons whenever they appeared home at all hours from a variety of jobs. She saved pennies and finally was able to buy a secondhand upright piano so there could be music in the home. "My mother was always singing," Hope says. "In fact, that's where we all inherited our voices because all we did was sing around the house."

Also rather miraculous was the respect the family maintained toward Harry, despite his mercurial behavior. In rare working periods, Harry could be sober for months and then he was like a young lover, courting Avis with sweets and taking her for rides in the park. Or he could entertain his sons for hours with jokes and amusing stories. "He was quite a funny guy," recalls Bob. Yet he was understandably inconsistent in his interactions with his bread-winning sons.

Ivor and Jim had full-time jobs. The younger brothers, Fred, Jack, Leslie, and Sid, sold newspapers at Doan's Corners, at the intersection of Euclid and 105th. Each hawked his papers on a different corner. Leslie liked his southwest corner with a grocery store because it was an uptown-traffic side with a trolley stop and because the grocery stayed open long enough for him to duck inside and warm his hands on wintry afternoons.

Sooner or later each boy had the experience of selling a paper to "that man" in the big black Peerless limousine. Les caught him in the early evening when his hand reached out from the back seat window and handed over his two cents for the *Press*. His face was wrinkled, Leslie thought, like an old leather coin purse, and he seldom said a word when he took his paper.

One night he handed Les a dime. Les told him he didn't have any change, but the man stared until Les said he would get some. The youngster disappeared into the grocery and waited his turn for ten pennies. When he ran back to the side of the big automobile, the man leaned out slightly and said, "Young man, I'm going to give you some advice. If you want to be a success in business, trust nobody— never give credit and always keep change in hand. That way you won't miss any customers going for it." All Les could think about was the customers he had already lost because the man was so stingy. When the chauffeur drove the car away, the trolley conductor said to Leslie, "Know who that man was?" Les shook his head. "John D. Rockefeller, that's who."

The Americanization of the young Hopes happened, as one might expect, in school. Leslie's early reputation as a scrapper stemmed from his need to strike out at those who teased him about his clothes and his name. Those who didn't jeer at his Eton jacket and stiff collar were able to roast him for the way he responded to roll calls. When his last name was called and he responded with "Leslie," there was laughter, and when he shortened the name to Les there was even more laughter. "Hopelessly" and "Hopeless" echoed through the school hallways and out onto the playing field. But he was quick with his fists and could win his own battles.

His favorite class was music. His voice had developed into a strong soprano and he loved to sing in school and in his church group, the Sambo Minstrels. But his favorite activities involved footraces. He was very fast on his feet in spite of having thin, spindly legs, and his best pal, Whitey Jennings, was also fast on his feet. Les and Whitey, and sometimes Jack and Sidney, would compete for prizes (money was the prize they liked best) at various parks and picnic grounds in the Cleveland area.

They studied the neighborhood newspapers to learn about planned outings where 50- and 100-yard dashes were being held and would figure out how to compete in as many as possible. They were not above using unsportsmanlike behaviors such as giving an opponent a damaging shove at the start or a hard bump at the turn to get ahead. One of them always won first or second prize. They actually liked second prizes because they were cash and first prizes were either a cup or a merchandise certificate. The Hope boys always turned over their earnings, however ill-gained, to Mahm.

Fifty years later, at a Boys Club benefit in 1967, Hope would do a monologue about his youth that was, in fact, infused with truth:

> I came from a pretty tough neighborhood. We'd have been called juvenile delinquents, only our neighborhood couldn't afford a sociologist. I guess it's not secret, but I have a record in Cleveland. They nabbed me for swiping a bike. It's a lie. I was walking down a hill when the damn thing rolled under me and we coasted downhill right into a cop's arms. . . . Fortunately, he knew me and my brothers. . . so he arrested me. I pleaded for mercy, but the judge was an ugly, cruel, vindictive man. He turned me over to my parents.

What worried the older generation of Hopes about young Les was the way he flitted from part-time job to part-time job. Except for his feeling that he ought to be earning money for Mahm, he really had no stomach for work. He told Fred that when he grew up he had no intention of holding down a conventional job. When Fred asked him how he intended to live, Les said he just might be a movie star like Douglas Fairbanks.

True, he had scored a neighborhood success with his imitation of Charlie Chaplin. In the summer of 1915, Chaplin contests had become a nationwide rage and every kid with an urge to act blackened his upper lip, found a derby, and twirled a cane. The Hope brothers rounded up all their pals and took Les out to Lone Park, Cleveland's top amusement spot, for a Chaplin contest. When the judge put his hand over young Hope's head, the neighborhood claque took the day with their cheering, winning enough prize money to buy Avis a new stove.

Les had graduated from Fairmount Junior School to East High and also to a variety of after-school jobs like delivering packages for Heisey's Bakery. Overacting lost him that job. When he took packages to well-heeled residential neighborhoods, he would say to the lady of the house, "Boy, did I have a tough time finding this place. I spent all my carfare looking for it." Touched, the lady would say, "How will you get back?" Hope would say with a shrug, "Oh, I'll walk." Of course, Les would get a handout for carfare. The scam was lucrative until he pulled it twice on the same lady.

Whatever part-time job he held after school, Les couldn't wait until it was done so he could get to the Alhambra Billiards Parlor. He and Whitey had become quite skillful at pool—Les's specialty was three-cushion billiards. Avis's sister-in-law, Louisa, said she didn't like to see Les hanging out in a pool hall, but Avis refused to make it off-limits because she knew who his pals were and said, "He's just trying to find himself. He'll be all right, you'll see."

Hope's pals were Whitey Jennings, of course, and two fellows who not only were pool sharks but also were talented tap and specialty dancers, Johnny Gibbons and Charlie Cooley. Jennings could sing and dance, too, but he dreamed of becoming a professional boxer. Gibbons was a highly proficient tap and ballroom dancer who had big-time aspirations, but Cooley was clearly not an amateur at anything. He was already semipro as an acrobatic hoofer who had done enough work locally as a performer to be a glamorous figure in Hope's eyes. Les loved the "acting" assignments he received from his pals when it came time to shill. When a sucker came to the Alhambra, Les would pretend that he didn't know an eight-ball from a corner pocket. The sucker, baited by Les's buddies, would soon challenge him to a game and Les would usually win.

At 16, Les said good-bye to East High. He never really liked school and he was now thinking of becoming a performer. Johnny Gibbons had taught him some dance steps, and he had begun to frequent Zimmerman's dance hall both to dance and to meet girls. He still loved to sing, anytime, anywhere. When he and Whitey were younger, they had harmonized as a duo, and also with pals in a quartet on a neighborhood street corner. They like to sing outside Pete Schmidt's Beer Garden because the drunks got sentimental, and even Pete would encourage them with a quarter. That was just enough for two tickets to the Doan's Corner movie house (including candy) to watch a swashbuckler named Fairbanks.

The boys were older now, and although they were still smitten with the idea of being entertainers, both young men had thought about being prizefighters. As they advanced into their teenager years the two devotees of Fairbanks's physique and athletic prowess hung around Charlie Marotta's Athletic Club on Seventy-ninth Street working out and practicing their punches before going to "work" at the Alhambra. One afternoon over the pool table, Whitey confessed that he had decided to enter the featherweight division of the Ohio state amateur matches.

"You're kidding!" Hope exclaimed.

"I'm not either. Here's my entry form."

"Packy West?" Hope said derisively, but he had to admit that Packy was a strong name to adopt because it evoked the charisma of the legendary boxer Packy McFarland.

Envy gnawed at Les for a full day, and then he, too, went downtown. But he registered in the lightweight division. When they asked him his fighting name he said, "Packy East." He now says, "I weighed 128 and the featherweight class had a top limit of 126. I just missed getting into it. If I'd taken the apples out of my pockets, I could have qualified as a featherweight. If I had, I'd have made out better. As it was I creamed my first opponent. He was constantly looking over his shoulder for instructions. . . I finally tagged him while his head was turned."

Winning the preliminary bout at Marotta's meant that he could go on to fight in another elimination bout and then in the semifinals. But in Hope's, or rather Packy East's, case, they couldn't pair him up, so he went right to the semifinals at Moose Hall.

All of Hope's pals from 105th and Euclid came to see him fight: Johnny Gibbons, Charlie Shafer, Perry Caulking, and Kenny Fox. They were astonished to discover that Hope's opponent was to be Happy Walsh, a slug-happy "smiling muscle" who later became a local champion. Packy was more than astonished: "At the bell I crept from my corner. Nothing happened to me at first, so I threw a terrific left to his jaw and crossed my right to his button. Walsh's hands dropped to his sides. He looked at me in amazement. Then he grinned. I found out later that he always did that when he was hit. We came out for the second. Because Happy slipped a couple of times in the first I decided to make the best of it. My footwork got fancier. I pranced around on my toes. Then I wound up and threw my right. I never got it back. And that's all I remember."

3

___

Backroad Follies

"I planned to take Mildred with me when I left Cleveland to become Mr. Marvelous of the Footlights. But Mildred's mother was small-minded about it. Another way of putting it is to say that Mildred's mother got

the notion that I wasn't a divinity-student type and she refused to trust her daughter on theatrical tours with me."

Nineteen-twenty was a year of decisions for Les Hope. Uninterested in high school, he had quit in his sophomore year. As a boxer he was clearly too lightweight for the fight game. As a dancer he was good, but not good enough. He decided to divert some of his earnings and Alhambra winnings to dancing lessons from a seasoned black entertainer named King Rastus Brown over on Central Avenue.

That year he spent a lot of time riding streetcars to and from downtown Cleveland. He and Johnny Gibbons were butcher's helpers for Fred Hope, who leased a meat stand at the central market. Instead of working, the two teenagers would feint and spar like Golden Gloves contenders, tap-dance on a platform built above Fred's stall, or harmonize tunes and mug for market employees and customers. Fred, who would later marry Johnny's sister, LaRue, was more exasperated than amused.

Les had an even better reason for riding the streetcar that year. Just before lunchtime, he'd ride downtown to meet his new sweetheart, Mildred Rosequist, a salesclerk and later a fashion model at Halle's Department Store. Mildred was a pretty, willowy blonde who (Hope thought) danced better than Irene Castle, then one of America's favorite stage performers.

They had met on a group outing and she was a new face. "Les was tall and skinny and I thought 'Oh brother,'" Mildred says. "We went to a party that first night and Les got bored, I guess, and took the fellows out to the kitchen to shoot craps. I got snippy and went home." But Mildred had made an impression on Hope.

Whenever Les came to Halle's to wait for Mildred, he would stand near her cosmetics counter and stare at her. He flirted and tried to make her laugh.

"He'd come in and lean over the counter and say, 'Let's get married on your lunch hour,'" Mildred recalls. "I would say 'No'. . . because my mother told me that if I married him I'd have to go and live with his family and. . . well. . . we were better off than they were. But he would follow me home from work some nights—I mean, he would get on the same streetcar and I wouldn't even know it. It was one of those dinky trolleys and I never looked around to see who else was on it. When I got off at Cedar he'd be walking right behind me. Then I'd walk in the front door and my mother'd ask if *he* was with me and I'd say 'No,' and then he'd stick his head around the hallway door and say, 'Oh, yes I am.'"

Mildred cannot recall Les ever having a "steady" job during the time they were dating except for the summer he worked for the Cleveland Illuminating Company as a lineman. He told her he had to earn money for an engagement ring, which he presented to her in front of his second-favorite hangout at Doan's Corners, Hoffman's Ice Cream Parlor.

Mildred looked at the ring and wisecracked, "Does a magnifying glass come with it?" Les was hurt and went inside Hoffman's. Mildred followed him in and apologized. Then Les slipped down the street to the Alhambra to hustle some money to take Mildred dancing at Zimmerman's.

Some nights after work Les would steal liver or sweetbreads from Fred's stall and go up to Mildred's house, where she would fry him a late supper. When everyone was in bed and with all the doors and windows closed, they would wheel the boxy phonograph into the kitchen and practice their steps, rehearsing sometimes for hours. They wore out the linoleum, Mildred says.

Not satisfied any longer with King Rastus Brown, Hope sought out an old vaudevillian named Johnny Root, who taught at Sojack's Dance Academy, behind Zimmerman's. Mildred added some of her earnings to what Les could scare up and they took enough lessons to put together a dance act that included, not so surprisingly, an imitation of the brother-and-sister team Vernon and Irene Castle.

Their first paid engagement was a three-night stint for the social club in the Brotherhood of Locomotive Engineers Building.

"Our act was in between the other acts," Mildred remembers. "I guess we were on during intermission. . . but anyway this was the last night, and when we came to all the hard stuff, the buck and wings which were so fast. . . I just quit, and I said I was tired and I walked off the stage. Bob. . . I mean, Les looked at me with kill in his eyes—he was furious, but he ad-libbed. Maybe [because] it was his first [time] before a paying audience. . . he picked out a little old lady in the first row and said, 'See, Ma, you should never have made her do the dishes tonight.'"

There were other engagements after that. They danced during intermission at the Superior Motion Picture House and at a place on Broadway where there were vaudeville acts along with the movie. Mildred says that Hope in later years loved to tell people they were paid seven or eight dollars a performance and they split it, but the truth is Mildred never got a cent. He told her they were all benefits or something. "I think he still has a cup we won in a dance contest. I'm told it's on his desk in Toluca Lake and he keeps paper clips in it." (It is, and he does.)

Elated over their show-business success, the Cleveland Castles began to plan their future together. Les wanted to take their act on the road; he was certain some small-time vaudeville circuit would take a chance on them. Mildred's mother had a poor opinion of Leslie Towns Hope's prospects of supporting her daughter; and as far as taking her out of town without a chaperone, that was out of the question. Furthermore, she didn't think much of their act.

When Johnny Root retired from Sojack's, Les took over his dancing classes and immediately had cards printed that said:

LES HOPE WILL TEACH YOU HOW TO DANCE—
CLOG, SOFT-SHOE, WALTZ-CLOG,
BUCK AND WING, AND ECCENTRIC.

But try as he might, teaching dancing did not lead to financial success. Consequently, Les was receptive to his brother Jack's suggestion that he take a night job at Chandler Motor Car Company. His days were still free for hunting down dance engagements, rehearsing, and pool hustling at the Alhambra. At Chandler he met several other would-be entertainers and got together with three of them to form a vocal quartet, in which he sang high baritone. Working at night, the boys would take extra liberties like recording their voices on Dictaphone cylinders and playing them back to improve their tone and blend. One day they forgot to erase the cylinder. An unsympathetic executive heard their efforts and recognized the voices and Les found himself out of a job.

It seemed clear to Les that he and Mildred would continue to be sweethearts but would not go on the road. He would need a new partner. This didn't upset Mildred, who never really wanted to perform; she just liked Les and liked to dance. So Les picked a fellow he had known slightly around the neighborhood, Lloyd "Lefty" Durbin. Durbin was a good dancer, had been in Sojack's classes, and had "been around," not professionally but enough to create an act. He was light, like Les, and had a slightly unhealthy pallor, but he was energetic and clever and had style. The act they created was eclectic, working from tap through soft-shoe into some eccentric routines that allowed for humor.

Their first appearance was in August 1924 at a Luna Park amateur contest, where they were well received. They continued to break in the act as fillers on vaudeville bills in small houses in and around Cleveland for a few bucks, and one night they even danced in an amateur contest at their own neighborhood's top-drawer vaudeville house, Keith's 105th Street. (B. F. Keith was the owner of one of the country's premier vaudeville theater chains across the nation, as well as a booking agency in New York City.)

Les begged his brothers to round up as many of their pals as they could to fill the front rows of the theater. He also worked out a deal with a cute Keith usherette that allowed him to play host to a dozen or so of his Alhambra cohorts. "Zick" Zicarelli, one of that crowd, recalled, "Somehow he'd arranged to have the side door left open and we sneaked in and cheered and applauded the act. We figured if he won the five-dollar prize we'd all eat."

Durbin and Hope forced themselves on an agent named Norman Kendall, who booked local talent for a small vaudeville showcase called the Bandbox.

Roscoe "Fatty" Arbuckle was booked there; the once phenomenally popular silent film star was trying to resume a career destroyed in 1921 by scandal involving the supposed sadistic rape of a film starlet with a soda bottle. Kendall's job was to book a cheap act to flesh out the bill. He decided to take a chance on Lefty and Les, who quickly dreamed up a new act. They tapped, soft-shoed, and sang "Sweet Georgia Brown," and their finale was a comic Egyptian dance routine. In dark suits and brown derbies, they pantomimed broadly against a desert backdrop of pyramids and the Sphinx as they pretended to dip their derbies into the Nile.

Later, after several tricky dance routines, they managed to pour real water from their hats. The audience loved it. So did Arbuckle. His show didn't last long, but long enough for him to make good his promise to introduce the pair to Fred Hurley, of Alliance, Ohio, who produced tabloid shows.

"Tabs" were a peculiar genre of entertainment that was rapidly becoming the rage of lower-level vaudeville; they were miniature musical comedy revues ideal for the audiences along the Gus Sun Circuit, towns where shows were booked by the Gus Sun Booking Exchange of Chicago. To play "Sun Time" meant you toured the tank towns of Ohio, Indiana, Pennsylvania, the Virginias, the Carolinas; the likes of Will Rogers, Eddie Cantor, and Al Jolson had all taken their turns on the Gus Sun Circuit at one time or another.

Hurley was not terribly impressed with Les and Lefty—all they could do was dance, and the members of a tab unit had to be versatile, since everyone had to be able to play double and triple parts. But Hurley trusted Arbuckle's taste, and Frank Maley, who managed Hurley's 1924 tab blockbuster *Jolly Follies*, thought the boys were trainable and he needed bodies. The pay was $40 a week. Les decided to send Mahm half of his pay and trusted he could house and feed himself with the remainder.

There would be little rehearsal time. The boys would have to pick up their cues by watching performances and get help from other cast members. As musical comedy, tabs could be of two kinds—either an abbreviated fully scripted "book" show or a series of independent sketches with blackouts following each punch line. Distributed here and there throughout the show were specialty dancing and vocal and instrumental offerings. Tabs were marvelously flexible; the bill might include a silent film, or the performance could be a self-contained vaudeville presentation.

Les and Lefty joined the show in East Palestine, Ohio, and were assigned chorus parts at first. Hazel Chamberlain, lead vocalist in the company, notes that Hope's voice was heard publicly for the first time in scripted gags around Thanksgiving of 1924 at Bloomington, Indiana. She says he substituted as emcee of "Country Store Night," a rube segment of the *Follies*, and "killed" the audience by the way he read his lines. "Frankly we had all thought Lefty Durbin was the more likely of the two to be a comic," said Chamberlain, "but that night Les Hope was as much surprised as the rest of us."

Hurley was unmistakably small-time show business, but even if Hope recognized it that way, he was still thrilled to be in it. In later years he would say, "That's a lost art today. . . a tab show was a great school. . . a great place to pick up experience in doing different things. And it did more for me, as far as stage presence and confidence on the stage is concerned, than anything else."

He was discovering how much he liked traveling. Whenever the show played close enough to Cleveland, he liked to saunter along 105th Street or Euclid to the Alhambra, believing himself a big-time vaudevillian and playing it that way for his pals. But the first stop was always at Mildred's, even if his train or bus arrived at dawn. Mildred would wake up and find Les sitting at the breakfast table with her mother, needling her gently about the Hurley magic and the wicked stage. Mrs. Rosequist liked him in spite of herself, and was gradually becoming convinced of his prospects for success.

At home, his family was not impressed. They believed that this was another phase he was passing through and that when he fell on his face he would settle down to a sensible job and marry Mildred. But to prove that his lifestyle had legitimacy, Les produced a newspaper clipping from the *Springfield Daily Sun* written by the paper's drama editor, William J. Murty, who said:

> The theater is ranked, as an essential to community life, second only to the church, with which it works in harmony to bring peace, happiness and contentment to its people. . . . The Gus Sun Booking Exchange is educating the people of the cities in which it furnishes same, to an appreciation of good music, the charm of graceful dancing, the worth of keen wit, the artistry of the drama, and the originality of novelties.

Here was tangible support for his passion. Even if *Jolly Follies* was not top-drawer entertainment, it was in tune with the popular taste just as vaudeville had been for 20 years before it.

These touring shows were ideal for the backwater towns of America. Sure, you couldn't expect to find Al Jolson, Ken Murray, Mae West, Burns and Allen, or Will Rogers playing Uniontown, Pennsylvania, or Morgantown, West Virginia. These towns couldn't afford to pay the big-time salaries of $2,000 a week. Hurley paid Frank Maley $500 and Hazel Chamberlain got $300. The others got between $100 and $200, depending on their specialty. Hurley brought his *Jolly Follies* to Lima, Ohio, for a tenth of what it would take to bring the Marx Brothers to the Cleveland Palace.

Conditions on the road were frequently dreadful. The quarters that served the performers as dressing rooms were cramped, in addition to being cold and, frequently, smelling foul. Theirs was a small troupe, 13 in all, and there was the usual doubling up in cheap boarding houses and theatrical hotels. For six dollars apiece double occupancy for the week, there was a bowl and pitcher, the same linen and facecloth and bath towel for the entire stay. "By the end of the week the towels would be so dirty you would usually bypass them and fan yourself dry," recalled Hope.

Most of the theaters were small. Their backdrops were ancient, and the street scene where most of their bits were performed had buildings painted so tiny they only came up to the actors' knees. There had to be room for commercial messages. But Les and Lefty thrived in this soil.

Late in that first Hurley season Hope's love life quickened. Not that his feelings for Mildred had changed, but she had decided to date other men. Their engagement was "conditional." And Hope was beginning to think that Kathleen O'Shea, who did a piano specialty with the troupe, was nearly the most beautiful girl in the world.

In Bedford, Indiana, at a small theatrical hotel, Les decided to put passion for Kathleen before reason. He knew, as every vaudevillian knew, that hotel managers were a law unto themselves when it came to show folk and morality. Nevertheless, armed with the excuse that he had a bad chest cold, and encouraged by Kathleen's willingness to rub his chest with hot salve, he went to her room and they closed the door.

Then came a loud knock and the manager demanded an explanation of Les's bared upper body, Kathleen's hands sticky with grease. The manager terrified them both by producing a gun and pointing it at Hope saying, "Get downstairs!"

"You got me wrong, pal," stammered Les, fumbling for his shirt.

"Get downstairs!"

Several Bible Belt hotels and rooming houses shunned show folk. The impression that entertainers were loose and "fallen" was a condition assigned by curious "others" more often than it was earned by the players. In the main, vaudeville bookers, agents, theater managers, and company managers were puritanical and became like Prussian military officers if they sensed infractions. The theater owner B. F. Keith had notices placed backstage in his theaters (known as the Keith Circuit) that warned: DON'T SAY "SLOB" OR "SON OF A GUN" OR "HOLY GEE" ON THE STAGE UNLESS YOU WANT TO BE CANCELED PEREMPTORILY. Most theater managers censored their own shows, although small-town managers were less careful about the presence of blue material than big-time managers. Hurley's material was clean; Maley saw to that. Besides, *Jolly Follies* had three married men in the troupe whose wives were along, including Maley himself.

The only other problem in touring was finding decent food at the odd hours when actors either wanted or needed to eat their meals. There was the inevitable graffiti on their dressing room walls informing them which places should be avoided, along with the inevitable scrawled message "Terrible food at the Savoy, flies in the soup." This didn't help because the Savoy was the only place open after the show and *it* closed at eleven.

Tainted food was blamed for a tragedy that threatened to put Les Hope out of show business. One night in Huntington, West Virginia, Lefty Durbin collapsed onstage and by the time he was carried to a dressing room there was blood oozing from his mouth. Earlier, Lefty had complained or stomach pain and had blamed his discomfort on the coconut cream pie he had eaten earlier that day.

Durbin, in great pain, remained in bed the following day, and by evening Hope decided to take him home to Cleveland. Les rode the whole distance in the baggage car with Durbin. It was clear to the Cleveland doctor who examined Lefty that tainted or poisoned food was not the only trouble. The young dancer had what they once called consumption—tuberculosis. He had contracted it months before, and neither man had recognized the symptoms—the cough, occasional fever, loss of weight.

Durbin had lost more blood than anyone had suspected and he died three days later. Les was devastated by the loss. Also, he worried that this trip to Cleveland had cost him his *Jolly Follies* job. As Hope was leaving Huntington, Maley had said, "Don't worry, we'll fill your spot."

4

Sidewalks of New York

"Then we got a job dancing with Daisy and Violet Hilton, the Siamese Twins. At first it was a funny sensation to dance with a Siamese twin. They danced back to back, but they were wonderful girls and it got to be very enjoyable in an unusual sort of way."

When Les stepped off the train at Parkersburg, West Virginia, he learned that Maley had hired a new partner for him, George Byrne, from Columbus, Ohio. "George was pink-cheeked and naïve," Hope would later say. "He looked like a choirboy. He was real quiet. Real Ohio. He was a smooth dancer and had a likable personality. We became good friends. And later on, his sister married my brother George."

Byrne and Hope, as the alphabetical listing might have read (but Hope and Byrne was soon established as the billing), worked hard to become a unit, and in a matter of weeks were overall a smoother dance team than Hope and Durbin had ever been. They got a featured part in the 1925 version of *Jolly Follies* and later that same year in a revue called *Smiling Eyes*, subtitled "a real production of youth and class—luxuriously staged." Occasionally, if Les begged hard enough, Maley would work him into comedy bits, but generally the manager was not bowled over by the results.

As "dancers supreme," however, Hope and Byrne were noticed. They loved what the entertainment reporter for the Newport News, Virginia, *Times-Herald,* wrote: "But for the premier honors of the entire bill, Hope and Byrne came through with flying colors in the eccentric dance. Friends, it was a regular knock-out. There has never been anything better in this house of this kind. They easily take first place without contest. They tore the house down, came back for more and got it."

With every good review the team itched to be heard as well as seen. Once they decided to surprise Maley by adding a comic song to their dance spot. When the orchestra picked up their introduction music they charged on, waving their straw hats (the way Bob and Bing did much later in the *Road* pictures) and then, as their patter song music was being vamped by the orchestra, they leaned on their canes and weaved back and forth. Someone in the audience shouted, "Ye gods, are they going to jump?" Hope swears it wasn't that bad. But the next day the Uniontown reviewer wrote: "Hope and Byrne had better stick to dancing."

Or how about singing? Maley thought he was suitable for doubling in an act that in one town was know as "The Four Horsemen—A Real Harmony Quartet" and in another as "The Frisco Four—Four Horsemen of Harmony." As Lester Hope—Lester "sounded more masculine"—he joined Maley, Gail Hood, and a guy named June Hoff. Hood was a bit deaf and never knew when the quartet went off-key. The other three would look at each other accusingly and get a laugh. But Hood would go right on singing. This struck Hope as so funny that each time it happened he would laugh out loud on stage.

Offstage, Maley was critical. "So it's funny, but don't ruin the number with *your* laughter." Hope agreed. And yet it happened again. This time after the show Maley barked, "If you don't stop that guffawing, Hope, you're out of the show." Hard as it was, Hope stopped.

Despite occasional chances to do comedy, it seemed to Hope and Byrne that they were fated to be just dancers. They continued that way into 1926, appearing in two scripted tabs, *The Moonlight Cabaret*, in which they were given fourth billing, and later in *The Mix-Up*, in which they got their first top billing.

Between tabs, for a week or two at the most, the team would roost in Cleveland, where they hung out at the Hopes' and where Mahm would try fattening them up on her lemon meringue pie. They would rehearse in the living room, using the upright piano and big mirror that hung over the fireplace. As soon as he could, Les would find Mildred.

"How's Kathleen?" she asked once.

"Kathleen who?" Hope said feigning ignorance.

"The one in Morgantown," she said in a tone that cooled his ardor. It didn't take long for Les to catch on. During his long absences, Mildred would spend time at the Hopes' visiting with Mahm. George, his youngest brother, was a big blabber; he would report to Mildred all that he could remember from Les's letters about his beautiful Irish doll. But Mildred could be pacified on the dance floor, and afterward they would do some "front-porch lovemaking." When he went away again Mildred was just as undecided, and so was Les.

Early in 1926 Kathleen left the show. She had always wanted to open a dress shop in Morgantown, and with money she had saved and some money from Les, she swung the deal. In later years, whenever Les got to New York he would swing down to Seventh Avenue showrooms and sample shops to pick up stylish things cheap for Kathleen's boutique.

Day and night Hope and Byrne plotted ways to improve their act, mostly by injecting comedy. Hope stooged for Byrne's gag lines. When Byrne crossed the stage holding a hanger with a woman's dress on it, Hope asked, "Where are you going?"

"Down to get this filled," said Byrne, to audience laughter. When George came back onstage he was carrying a long plank under one arm, and Hope would ask, "Now where are you going?"

"To find a room. I've already got my board." Loud laughter.

But the reality was that if they had aspirations to go beyond specialty dancing in a tab show (and it was no secret that they did), they had to escape from *Jolly Follies*. So in the spring of 1926 they quit. Of his experiences in the tabs Hope later said, "There's no possible way to measure the value of those Hurley years. I remember when I landed the part of Huck Haines in *Roberta* and played it without falling apart on the first night, the producers didn't know how many opening nights I'd been through."

They had an introduction from one of the Hurley gang to a Detroit agent named Ted Snow. Armed with a fistful of reviews from the *Parkersburg Sentinel* and the *Norfolk Ledger* that used adjectives like "novel" and "clever" and "wonderful" and "nifty" and "phenom," and bolstered by Hope's brashly naïve version of sophistication, they got themselves booked into Detroit's State Theater. Snow got them $175 a week, which was $75 more than they made with Hurley, and two days later he was able to book them into a nightclub spot at the Oriole Terrace for another $75. They were elated.

They opened on April 25 at the State and played four shows, then jumped on a streetcar and went out to the Oriole Terrace for their late-night spot, and then back downtown to do a little gambling at Reilly's, a place they had heard about from one of the State stagehands. It would have been better for Les if it had been three-pocket billiards. As it was, they gambled away their first week's salaries that first night and as anyone who knows vaudeville can tell you, you don't get paid until the end of the engagement.

But they clicked with audiences and therefore with Snow. The emcee at the State was Fred Stitt, and Hope found himself drawn to watch and listen to this performer more for his material than for his style. Though Stitt sang a lot in his act, his comedy was patter based on "the latest happenings in the daily news." That intrigued Hope.

After the second week, the *Detroit Free Press* review of May 10, 1926, praised "the very clever soft-shoe dancers" and said "Hope and Byrne, two young men in grotesque costume with their eccentric dancing, won the big applause Sunday." Snow managed to book them at several smaller theaters around Detroit and then "by demand" returned them to the State. That second time around their names moved up in the newspaper ads and were set in larger type: HOPE AND BYRNE— DANCING DEMONS.

Ted Snow asked Ed Fishman, an agent in Harrisburg, Pennsylvania, to book the boys into the Stanley Theater in Pittsburgh. But before going to Pittsburgh, they hopped over to Chicago because Hope insisted they get some publicity photos taken by Maurice Seymour, the "Tiffany" of photographers. Les was beginning to understand the importance of smart packaging, the power of advertising, promotion, and publicity. They bought new costumes: Eton jackets and big white collars and high-waisted pants and white spats. They wore high hats and carried black canes with white tips. They posed and mugged for the camera. Then they went out and bought a new theatrical trunk—their old one was being held together by a hank of rope. They went for the top of the line put out by the company H.M., which only the class acts could afford.

The Pittsburgh date was a good one, but was merely a stop "along the way," a rehearsal for the big time, which was, of course, New York. Hope knew they couldn't hit Broadway without a fresh act, so they worked out a new routine.

"Our act opened with a soft-shoe dance," Hope said. "We wore high hats and spats and carried a cane for this. Then we made quick changes to firemen's outfits and danced real fast to 'If You Knew Susie,' and a rapid ta-da-da-da-dah tempo, while the drummer rang a fire bell. At the end of the routine I squirted water from a concealed bulb at the brass section of the orchestra in the pit. It not only made an attractive finish but it had the advantage of drowning a few musicians."

Understandably, that pair of beanpole-thin vaudevillians who came out of Pennsylvania Station on that autumn morning in 1926 and stood staring at the streets of Manhattan for the first time believed themselves to be two of the freshest, most original entertainers of the decade. They found a room at the Hotel Lincoln and went to find the B. F. Keith office, in the theater district, where they flashed their photos and asked for bookings. What they got were several audition bookings, which were tryouts in second-, third-, and fourth-line vaudeville houses, where the salary was nominal, which gave agents a chance to look you over.

Meanwhile, Abe Lastfogel of the William Morris Agency called them back solely on the strength of the photographs they had left with the agency and booked them as the "deuce" spot—second billing—in a Morris package for the Keith Vaudeville Exchange. The featured act was one of vaudeville's current successful attractions, eighteen-year-old Siamese twins named Daisy and Violet Hilton. These British-born oddities, orphaned just after birth, had been raised in San Antonio, Texas, by foster parents who encouraged their music and dance training and then exploited them as a freak-show attraction.

In their act they talked about their unusual life, sang, played saxophone and clarinet solos and duets, and danced. Then Hope and Byrne would join them for a more elaborate routine where they danced back to back. They were a well-produced curiosity that packed people in for sometimes as many as four strenuous shows a day, each requiring Hope and Byrne to do their own act in the second spot, and then a vigorous finale with the Hiltons. For six months the show played Keith houses in Washington, D.C., Baltimore, Philadelphia, Reading, Youngstown, York, Pittsburgh, and Providence.

While they were in Reading, in May 1927, Hope and Byrne had themselves billed as "Dancemedians," and once again began to feel restless as they savored local press notices like this one: "Hope and Byrne have untamed feet. They just behave as if they have no control whatsoever, but of course their control is perfect. The boys are versatile dancers with humor crowded into every step."

When the boys got to Providence they faced the producers with an ultimatum. For the hours they were putting in they wanted more money. They were told "no deal," so they packed their trunk after the last show and waved the Hilton troupe off to Boston.

Back in New York early in the summer of 1927, Hope and Byrne put up at the Somerset, a theatrical hotel just off Broadway on Forty-seventh Street. The hotel was right next to the stage door of the Palace, that legendary showcase theater (built by the Orpheum chain mogul Martin Beck in 1913), whose stage, spotlights, and audiences were sought by every artist in every vaudeville circuit across the nation. As for the Somerset, it was especially popular with vaudevillians because besides having such a favorable location, the management would carry you if you found yourself out of work between engagements. But the pair still had money from the Keith tour, thanks to the modicum of wisdom gained from their Detroit fleecing at Reilly's. Word of mouth provided them some nightclub dates, but by day they made the rounds and auditioned for every musical production and revue that was casting. In August they unexpectedly hit—and hit high.

They received a call from the choreographer Earl Lindsey to audition for the musical *Sidewalks of New York*. They were signed for specialty dancing and small speaking parts. It was a Charles Dillingham production of a show with words and music by Eddie Dowling and Jimmy Hanley. The show starred Dowling's wife, Ray Dooley, fresh from triumphing in *Ziegfeld Follies* the year before. The plot centered on the vicissitudes of an obstreperous young convent-raised child (played by Dooley) trying to find love and happiness on the streets of New York. In the cast as a tap dancer, and bringing the rehearsals of the show much publicity because of her romance with Al Jolson, was Ruby Keeler.

At the first reading at the Knickerbocker, Hope and Byrne found that their parts were small indeed—brief specialty dance bits in the show's opening scene— and they shared that assignment with another pair of young vaudeville hoofers (Charles) Gale and (Alan) Calm. It was disappointing but at least the four became good friends. In later years Alan Calm became Hope's stand-in and dialogue coach for movies and television.

The experience wasn't all bad. Rehearsals were endlessly fascinating to Hope, who loved to watch big-timers work. Being a Broadway chorus boy had its benefits, too, such as being able to charm an aspiring young actress named Barbara Sykes, who lived at the Princeton, another theatrical hotel.

Sidewalks opened at the Garrick Theater in Philadelphia on September 5. Hope, Byrne, and Calm found rooms at the Maidstone Apartments near Walnut and Tenth; Gale and his wife were nearby. The show got good notices, but as the unavoidable doctoring and tightening took place, the director, Edgar McGregor, decided the show needed an uplifting dance number. He asked Hanley to write a new scene utilizing his tune "We've Been Thrown Out of Better Places Before," featuring Keeler and putting Hope and Byrne and Calm and Gale to better use. Hanley went to work. Meanwhile the boys did their tiny bit and watched from the wings.

Hope was lonely for Barbara during the Philly tryout. His roommates suggested he invite her to come and keep house for them and comfort Lester. Hope wired her and she wired back: WILL BE ON THE SIX O'CLOCK. Les was ecstatic. He would have time to meet her, take her to the apartment, and get to the Garrick by seven-thirty. When he walked into the dressing room that night his face was serious. No Barbara. He wired again and got the same response: WILL BE ON THE SIX O'CLOCK. But still no Barbara. This went on for several days, until finally she *did* arrive on Friday's six o'clock.

In her honor Byrne and Calm planned a party at the Maidstone. They invited the entire *Sidewalks* cast of 110 and figured half would come. Half did and brought with them their fair share of bathtub gin and rotgut whiskey. The party was going fine when Billy O'Rourke, one of the chorus boys, knocked on the door. Dressed in drag, he asked if he could bring some of his friends to join the party. With the new outrageous arrivals, the noise level went up and in no time the manager came to calm things down. When he spotted the chorus boys in drag he called the police. In the meantime the O'Rourke party decided to leave, and as they headed for the third-floor stairway, the manager caught up with them. A comedy worthy of Mack Sennett followed: a massive chase along corridors, up to the next floor, downstairs, up again and down again, with the police joining in, replete with screams and pratfalls.

Hope and Barbara, Calm and Byrne laughed until they were weak and then fell into bed—Les and Barbara in the double bed behind the sliding French doors off the sitting room. The lovers talked for hours. In the morning Barbara came out, all dressed, with suitcase in hand and Les crestfallen behind her. They went to the railway station. It seems that after Les left New York Barbara had fallen in love with a piano player who lived at the Princeton, which explained why she kept missing the six o'clock.

After four weeks in Philadelphia and a week in Atlantic City, *Sidewalks* opened in New York at the Knickerbocker Theater on Monday, October 3, 1927. That was a magnificent Broadway season: 53 musicals and 217 plays. Besides *Good News*, *Rosalie*, and a *Connecticut Yankee*, there was Eddie Cantor in the *Follies*, George M. Cohan in *The Merry Malones*, and the artistic and commercial success of the 1927 season, *Show Boat*. Katherine Cornell was playing in *The Letter*, Max Reinhardt was unveiling his *Midsummer Night's Dream*, and Alfred Lunt and Lynn Fontanne were starring in *The Doctor's Dilemma*.

Sidewalks was a hit, which was probably why the new Hanley production number never materialized. Keeler's specialty dance, "The Goldfish Glide," was tremendously popular with audiences. McGregor decided the show had enough dancing; and since all Hope and Byrne were doing for their featured-performer pay was the short opening bit, he gave them two weeks' notice. They managed to stretch that to a month, and then they were back on the street.

The duo was introduced to an agent named Milt Lewis, who found them a second-billing spot on an eight-act vaudeville bill at the B. S. Moss Franklin, a big showcase theater. Cockier than ever, just coming out of a Broadway show, they decided to add more spoken comedy and deemphasize their singing and dancing. "And we knew our material had to be more sophisticated than the slapstick stuff that headliners Dooley and Sales were milking the audience with," admitted Hope. Unfortunately, what they came up with was chestnuts like this one:

HOPE: Where do bugs go in the wintertime?
BRYNE: Search me.

After their first show at the Franklin, they knew they fell short of second-spot material. At the Morris office Hope talked to Al Lloyd, who was interested enough to try to fix their act and look for bookings elsewhere. Lloyd even tried to strong-arm the senior agent, Johnny Hyde, into looking at the boys. Hyde refused.

"Why not?" begged Hope.

"Because I heard about it," Hyde said.

"You did?" Hope said, his stomach sliding.

"You ought to go west, change your act, start over," advised Hyde.

The team had hit bottom: They'd been tossed out of *Sidewalks*, were a flop with their comedy material, were almost broke, and were psychologically damaged. Hope argued loudly and strongly with Byrne that their answer was Chicago, the second-biggest vaudeville town. "That's where the money is."

They were broke enough to realize they could use some bookings on the way back to Ohio, so they called Mike Shea in Cleveland and he put them on the bill in New Castle, Pennsylvania. It was a job, but they were third on a three-act bill. It was hard to swallow and so was the pay, $50 each for three days.

The manager asked Hope, as a favor, to come out after the last act and do a solo billboard spot announcing the coming attraction, Marshall Walker. So Hope obliged; he came out and said, "Ladies and gentlemen, there's going to be a *good* show here next week." Some laughter. "Marshall Walker will be here with his Whiz Bang Revue." Hope knew the act. It was a Gus Sun attraction. Walker was a rube comic who traded on barnyard and tight-fisted–farmer jokes. "Marshall's a Scotsman. I know him. He got married in the backyard so the chickens could get the rice."

The audience roared. The orchestra in the pit below loved it, too. At the next show Hope added another Scotch joke, about the Scot who sat up all night and watched his wife's vanishing cream. That also got a roar. At the next show he added two more of the same kind and got twice as much laughter. There was so much laughter that it was clear something unusual was happening.

One of the pit musicians took Les aside. "You had that audience right where you wanted it. That's what you should be doing. Emcees are hard to find. Good ones can take over and make the place hot. Your double act with that dancing and those corny jokes, that's nothing. Listen to me."

Hope walked away and started to think hard. He didn't agree that his and Byrne's dancing and joking were that bad. Yet he had for a long time secretly toyed with the idea of going it alone. He could see himself out there on the stage like Frank Fay, vaudeville's top monologist, who pulled down a salary of $2,000 to $2,500 a week. But one of the toughest things to do is break up an act, especially when two people have shared so many hard and good times together. Whatever George's flaws, Hope *liked* him.

Byrne noticed that Les was troubled, and suspected the reason. "I think I know what you're going through, Les. You want to try a single. After what happened here I don't blame you. I'll go back to Columbus and take it easy for a while, maybe start a dancing school."

"Let me try it alone for a couple of weeks—if it works we'll break up the trunk," Hope said.

Next day they rode the same bus to Columbus and then Les took the train on to Cleveland. He tried calling Mildred and she was out of town. He went home and Mahm opened the door.

"What's happened?" she asked.

"It's Christmas," Les said.

"That's weeks away," she said, pouring him coffee. "Where's George? Something's wrong, isn't it?"

"I'm going to try it on my own. George likes the idea." Les looked at his mother and watched her face relax.

"Now, then—" she said, and Les sat there listening while his mother filled him in on all the family doings. Ivor (married 12 years) was having his troubles with Gertrude but his business was doing well. Jim was away working in Pittsburgh. Fred's marriage to LaRue Gibbons was a big success and so was his provisions business. Jack was still at Chandler and married again. Sid was in auto mechanics. Young brother George was in his last year of high school and taking dancing lessons, hoping that one day Les would put him in his act.

"Where's Dad?" asked Les.

"He keeps busy. He's out back right now—I think he's carving me a birdbath. Les, why don't you talk to him about your decision?" Avis always insisted that Harry was head of the family.

"I will," Les said. "But Mahm, what do you think?"

"I think you're every bit as good as that Frank Fay any day."

5

In the Wings

"One of the things I learned at the Stratford Theater was to have enough courage to wait. I'd stand there waiting for them to get it for a long time. Longer than any other comedian had the guts to wait. My idea was to let them know who was running things."

The morning of Cleveland's first snowfall of 1927, Les took the streetcar downtown to the Erie Building to call on Mike Shea. Shea listened to Hope's fast talk, refused the offer to read through his newspaper clips, and asked him what he wanted.

Hope said fearlessly that he could do a single act. "You know, singing, dancing, talking—working in blackface." It was desperation, and luck, that forced him to mention blackface. Shea booked a rotary unit—a different theater each night—in and around Cleveland, and he had a spot for Hope.

Grateful and cocksure, Hope danced out of Shea's tiny office and down to the street level. "I went out, bought a big red bow tie, white cotton gloves like Jolson's, a cigar and a small bowler which jiggled up and down when I bounced onstage," he recalls. "I'd picked up some new material here and there, plus a few things I'd thought up. For an encore I did a song and dance. I scored well even if I was scoring in a Lilliputian world."

He lived at home, ate well, and could take the streetcar to whatever theater the unit was playing. The fourth night, however, Hope missed his trolley. By the time he got to the theater it was nearly time to go on, so he didn't try to apply his burned cork. He just grabbed his bowler, stuck a cigar in the corner of his mouth, and sailed out through the wings. Somehow he scored even larger than he had in blackface. "Leave the cork off," Shea told him. "Your face is funny the way it is."

Funny would not have been Hope's self-appraisal. He thought himself handsome, even sexy. All the next day he stared at himself in his wardrobe mirror, and discovered that the way he tilted his chin or darted his eyes back and forth could be amusing. But it was the audience's reaction to his corkless face that convinced him.

After the New Year, Hope regained his confidence and decided to go to Chicago for a fresh start. With his engagement to Mildred now officially off and his family's blessing in hand, he dropped a note to George Byrne and told him what he planned, packed his trunk, and hopped a train for Chicago. He began haunting agents' offices, but he couldn't make a dent. He had no contacts, and it didn't seem

27

to matter that he had worked a lot, even on Broadway. Luckily he found a coffee shop that had a waitress who thought he was cute and so he ate on credit.

Chicago, like the rest of the nation, was booming in the spring of 1928. It was the biggest entertainment center west of the Hudson and like New York was riding the crest of a motion picture wave. Most of the theaters in town had converted to a combination of feature films and vaudeville. The bill included a screen feature accompanied by rotating acts booked by RKO (Radio-Keith-Orpheum, the organization that ruled the vaudeville booking business), a house orchestra, and frequently a house master of ceremonies who stayed for weeks, sometimes months. It was a busy town; it was a tough town.

It was late May when Hope decided he was ready to admit failure. He owed money for food, for clothes, for musical arrangements; he was starving and he couldn't pay his rent.

He was leaning his skinny frame against a newspaper hutch on the sidewalk in front of Woods Theater Building. He was working up his nerve to show the Clara Bow–ish receptionist at the Marcus Loew Agency his sexiest grin, when he spotted his old Cleveland tap-dancing pal, Charlie Cooley, now a successful vaudevillian, going in. Hope admitted to Cooley how badly things were going. It touched Cooley to see the self-confident hustler this far down.

"Come with me," Cooley said. They went into the Woods Theater Building and upstairs to a small office whose glass-paneled door had on it CHARLES HOGAN–NATIONAL PLAYHOUSES INC. in gold leaf. Behind the door was a five-foot-four Irishman with sandy hair and green eyes peering through silver-rimmed glasses. He talked tough but had a soft heart. Cooley knew Hogan well, well enough so that if he said, "Can you give this guy a job?" nothing else needed to be said.

It happened that Hogan had to fill a master-of-ceremonies spot at the West Englewood Theater for three shows on Decoration Day (now Memorial Day). "It pays—" But Hope didn't even hear. He almost wept. The pay was $25.

After the second show the manager at West Englewood said to Les, "You're going to play the Stratford next Sunday."

"How do you know?" asked Hope.

"Hogan called to find out how you were doing and I told him. Now he's putting you in for three days out there as emcee."

The Stratford was a well-attended neighborhood vaudeville theater, actually converted from a silent-movie house. They had built an apron out from the regular small stage so that the house could accommodate both a band and dance acts. The Stratford audience consisted mainly of loyal neighborhood people, so their likes and dislikes were unitary. If a performer clicked, "they let him live" and their noisy reception meant that a particular acrobatic dance team, singer, or baggy-pants comic had found a home. It was the same—perhaps even more so—with the emcee. The Stratford had had the same emcee, Ted Emery, for two years and he would still probably own that stage except that he had become "difficult" to work with and had had to be replaced. The theater had tried a succession of comedians after Emery but no one clicked, and Hope was just another tryout.

On the same bill with him was a likable little fellow named Barney Dean doing a rather tired single act. Although he wasn't much onstage, Dean was endowed with an unusual sense of humor. He had an uncanny ability to gauge the "rightness" of a piece of material and could transform a faltering bit of comedy.

Hogan was a sucker for Dean's act and booked him when and where he could. Charlie called up the Stratford manager to check on Hope and liked what he heard. Then he asked to talk to Barney Dean. He asked Dean how things were going. "We're doing fine," Dean said.

Hogan said, "I know how *you* did. You laid an egg. How is Hope doing?"

"Hope did real good. You'll be hearing about him," Barney said. Hogan trusted Dean's judgment. He struck a deal with the Stratford to extend Hope's stay to two weeks. Whenever Hogan went out there to watch the show, he realized more and more that he had a find in this master of ceremonies whose rapid patter of introduction was often better than the acts themselves. At the end of two weeks the contract was stretched to four weeks at a salary of $200.

In these initial days of his new career track Hope decided to change his name from Lester to Bob because he figured Bob sounded "chummier" and looked better on the marquee. Hogan and Dean approved. Hope found himself leaning on these two new friends for support, and they and Cooley formed the nucleus of a group that would remain intimate with Hope for the next forty years.

Hope now recognized that comic patter was his real meal ticket, and singing was sometimes a good way of getting closer to his audience but solo dancing was not needed right now. It was a folksy, family audience at the Stratford, composed of people who would return maybe twice a week. They expected to hear some of the same jokes, but they liked a change of material. Hope had to scramble to stay alive and he got jokes however and wherever he could.

He poured through James Madison's *Budget*, an annual paperbound assortment of gags, sketches, and parodies that cost a dollar. Sometimes he cribbed from *College Humor*, or begged the other acts that played the Stratford to give him jokes. Buying material from good comedy writers (if you could find them) was much too expensive for Hope.

He was a gag scribbler. His pockets were crammed with bits of paper with joke cues scrawled in the margins of the letters.

He also dreamed up gag situations. One of his most successful began with an offstage crash "that sounded like someone dropping a trunk full of glass." Hope would walk onstage dusting off his hands and adjusting his tie as if he had just taken part in a terrific fight. Then he would look back at the wings and say, "Lie there and bleed."

What the Stratford provided for Hope was the loamy soil for producing the hallmarks of a personal style. He needed the experience of handling jokes of different types, and he got it here. "I'd lead off with a subtle joke, and after telling it,

I'd say to the audience, 'Go ahead, figure it out.' Then I'd wait until they got it. One of the things I learned at the Stratford was to have enough courage to wait. I'd stand there waiting for them to get it for a long time. Longer than any other comedian had the guts to wait. My idea was to let them know who was running things."

The four-week extension eventually became a six-month stay at the Stratford, so Hope had to come up with a fresh series of jokes. And that is where speed and timing became important. If he told a bad joke fast enough it didn't matter much—it was all in the timing.

Hope was experiencing the heady sensation of being in control, of manipulating his audience. He learned the discipline of always being "up" for an audience, whether it was 2 or 20 or 200 people, and just keeping up a nonstop pace whatever the audience's response.

He also had the freedom to experiment, and although he was attracted to subtle material, he knew that the audiences he played to were not capable of a great deal of subtlety. "There's a line between smart and too smart. They liked a simple kind of humor but also I could get them to work on a gag they thought was more subtle than it really was. But it made them feel good they'd won a contest."

Stratford's regular paychecks were doing wonders for Hope's total persona. The kind of act he adopted—bowler and cigar and more than a touch of brash—was helping to build his reputation as a new boy in town. He stood six feet tall and had a lithe, athletic body. He had sandy hair and sexy eyes that could flicker with interest when he listened or conversed, and could quickly change to a sensual stare. Eating regularly had filled out his frame just enough. Employment gave a boost to his romantic endeavors, too. He had a small, cozy apartment, and he had Louise Troxell.

Louise was a local product, daughter of hardworking Roman Catholic parents. She had some office skills and planned to be a secretary. But she also had one eye on the stage. With her doll-like face, stylishly marcelled hair, and fashion-model body, Louise was as classy as anyone Hope had encountered the day she sauntered into one of his hangouts near the Stratford. They met and soon fell in love. In October of 1928, when Hogan offered Hope a change of pace from the Stratford, suggesting he hit the road for a while, the comedian decided to take Louise along and put her in the act as a foil, his Gracie Allen.

He would be working onstage and in the middle of his patter, she would appear. "All she had to do was walk on and stand there looking beautiful while I told a story, then feed me lines," Hope explained. "She'd come out holding a little bag in her hand and say, 'How do you do?' and I'd say, 'What have you got in your little bag?' and then she'd say, 'Mustard.' And I'd say, 'What's the idea?' And she'd say, 'You can never tell when you're going to meet a ham.'"

The punch line got a laugh because it put Hope down, and when Hope grimaced with pain from being derailed by such a cute dumbbell, it engaged audience sympathy.

They played a few dates on Keith's Western Circuit, including South Bend, where Hope learned the importance of topicality and of awareness of context. "I was still wearing the brown derby," Hope recalls, "and I had a big cigar stuck in my kisser. When I walked out onstage in South Bend, there was a roar of applause. When I told my first joke they screamed. I couldn't figure it out. Then finally I got it. I had a Notre Dame audience. Al Smith, who was a Catholic, was running for President. A brown derby and cigar were his trademarks."

Just before 1928 became 1929, Hope went to Chicago and signed a contract on New Year's Eve with Charlie Hogan to appear for four weeks, with an option for six months, back "home" at the Stratford. By the end of the run, Hope was making $300 a week.

This time at the Stratford, Hope was confident of his technique, but he was really desperate for material. Whatever he found he was using up too fast, and he always needed more. He lifted routines from other comics and adapted them as he saw fit. Not that this was such a rare practice. W. C. Fields was notorious for lifting lines, and Fred Allen was irked for years by an episode arising from Al Jolson's theft of material from him. Bert Lahr accused Joe E. Brown of stealing his comedy character, and Hope, himself, when accused of adopting J. C. Flippen's brown derby and his cigar-twirling mannerisms, said "That's not true. You notice how Flippen rotates that cigar from right to left—well, I do it from left to right."

Hope was always prowling for walk-on gags, especially necessary for an emcee who must make frequent appearances and disappearances.

He dipped into his stockpile of material and put together an act he called "Keep Smiling," with Louise, of course. They played dates for the small-time Western Vaudeville Managers Association in Sioux City, Iowa; Peoria, Illinois; and Bloomington, Indiana; and then he got a wire from Hogan telling them to go immediately to Oklahoma City. "Keep Smiling" was booked as the featured comedy in a four-act vaudeville bill touring the Interstate Vaudeville Circuit—another midwestern booking agency known as Interstate Time.

For the first time in his life Hope had the star spot on the bill. His pay began at $300 and soon moved to $325 a week. He could afford to give Louise some spending money and send Mahm $50 or so, and after Hogan had taken his, there was still a bit for tucking into a shoe.

The other acts were average small-time vaudeville. Third billing went to a mediocre dancing act performed by the Cirillo Brothers, four zesty Italians from Springfield, Massachusetts. Hope thought they were wonderful. In fact, 25 years later they showed up with regularity doing bits on his televisions shows of the 1950s and '60s. All about five feet six, they were hot-tempered and lusty bachelors. They traveled in their own Ford touring car with its superchrome fittings, running boards, and a rumble seat that saw its share of sexual conquest in country lanes just outside town.

After Oklahoma City, where audiences were fairly responsive, the troupe moved to Fort Worth for a two-week stay. At the first show, as soon as the Cirillos came offstage, Hope swung out through the wings and launched into his snappy opening material, but there wasn't much reaction. The Louise spot worked, and after that he had to work even harder—played even cockier, faster, more flippant to get a response. It wasn't working. "I had killed them with this stuff at the Stratford," Hope said, "and I hadn't done that bad in Oklahoma City, and it was the same act. Here I was laying the biggest egg in my life so far. I really died! I didn't know what to make of it."

When Hope came offstage, there was no loud applause dragging him back for a bow or an encore. In a foul temper, he threw his derby on the floor and said furiously that he was quitting the show. "Get me a ticket back to *my* country!" Hope, known to the troupe as mild-mannered and friendly—a bit conceited, perhaps fresh, yes, audacious and flirty, sometimes—had never been known to be mean or loud or foul-mouthed. The unit manager quietly told someone to go and find Bob O'Donnell.

Angry and disappointed as he was, Hope was persuaded by Louise to go back out for the afterpiece, the final segment of a vaudeville bill where the acts return for the closing production number.

Afterpiece over, Hope went grim-faced to his dressing room and slammed the door. There was a short silence, and then a person Hope had never seen before opened his door and stepped inside. Hope faced his dressing table, still wearing his white flannel trousers and dark serge coat.

"What's *with* you, fancy pants?" O'Donnell asked.

"Who are you?" Hope asked, turning away from his mirror, ready to order the intruder out. No reply. Hope turned back and looked at himself in the mirror and then looked up at the stranger's mirror image. Then he removed his coat and started to take off his makeup. "I'll tell you something, I don't get this audience," Hope said, turning around. "I'm not for these people. That's the matter."

"Why don't you relax?" O'Donnell said, still standing. "You've got plenty of time. Why not slow down and give the audience a chance? These people are Texans and they like things a little slower, but they're nice people. They came inside to be happy. It's summer and it's hot. This is Texas. Let them understand you. Why make it a contest to keep up with your material?" He moved toward the door and said, "Relax and I guarantee, you'll be all right."

"Thanks so much," Hope said sarcastically. O'Donnell walked out and the unit manager stepped in. Hope demanded to know who that man was. When he learned O'Donnell was the manager of the Interstate Vaudeville Circuit, Hope said, "I don't care who he is—how much nerve can one man have?"

But Hope gradually cooled down and decided the advice might be worth taking. O'Donnell was out there for the next show and then came backstage. Hope had worked less abrasively and admits, "That was a turning point for me." O'Donnell worked with the comedian for the remainder of his Fort Worth engagement. "He changed my tempo and made me wait for laughs from *all* my material," said Hope, "and I had no trouble getting through to the audience after that."

From Fort Worth the troupe moved to Dallas. Hope had learned an important lesson—the need to be sensitive to geographical and cultural differences in audiences. The troupe pushed on through August of 1929, and in Charleston, Hope received a telegram from a Lee Stewart in the B. F. Keith office in New York. This somewhat disconcerted Hope, because for months he had been corresponding with a pair of New York agents named Morris (not William) and Feil, and he assumed that if anyone should be contacting him it would be one of them. With the kind of encouraging and flattering mail they had been sending him, he figured them for a clinch deal at the Palace—or perhaps an audition for the Shuberts.

What Hope could not have known was that his new mentor, Bob O'Donnell, had been so impressed with his talent and headliner potential that he had wired the Keith office urging them to sign Hope for the Orpheum Circuit—the big time. In his wire to Hope, Lee Stewart suggested that he leave the company and come back to New York immediately. Bob and Louise drove triumphantly northward in the secondhand Packard that Hope was forced to describe as "a shiny monster that ate gas and oil like a dragon eats people."

In New York they checked into the Hotel Lincoln and as early as he dared the next morning, Hope went to see the agents from whom he had received so much flattering mail, Morris and Feil. He breezed into their office, what there was of it.

"Here I am," he said confidently.

"Who *are* you?" asked Feil.

"Bob Hope. I'm the fellow you've been writing to."

"What do you do?" asked Morris.

Hope looked disdainfully at Morris. "You mean after all our correspondence you don't even know what I do? Okay, just give me my photos."

He called Lee Stewart and went to meet him at the B. F. Keith office. Stewart seemed intelligent and straight. He said to Bob, "Keith wants you to show us your act. O'Donnell says you're good."

"Where does Keith want me to show?" Hope asked shrewdly. He had some experience with New York houses and the ones he hadn't played he knew about from the vaudeville grapevine—the ones to play, those to avoid if you could. "At the Jefferson," Stewart said. The Jefferson, on Fourteenth Street, was known for being a tough place to show, for rowdy audiences.

"I can't show there," Hope said flatly. "I'll show uptown at the Hamilton, or Riverside or the Coliseum." Then something perverse forced him to add, "If you want me you'd better hurry. Don't fool around."

"You're sure you won't play the Jefferson?" Lee pressed.

"NO JEFFERSON!" Hope snapped and he was downstairs and out on Broadway walking under the Palace marquee with his nose and chin high. Back at the Lincoln, he called the William Morris office and tried to get some interest going based on his Interstate Time. Then he phoned a spotter, a freelance talent scout he had learned about at the Publix Circuit, yet another booking service, and took some photos over there.

It was several agonizing days of waiting before Lee Stewart called to tell Hope he had an uptown theater for him to show in. It was Proctor's Eighty-sixth Street, a local uptown showplace. The date was four days the next week.

"Who's ahead of me?" Hope asked.

"Leatrice Joy from the movies," Lee said.

"Okay," agreed Hope.

"It's not much money," said Stewart.

"I don't care about the money," Hope announced.

"Are you nuts?"

"I just want Keith to see the act. Publix is after me," Hope said cockily, "but I'm willing to let Keith see the act, too. Then if you don't like me, okay. But I don't need the money."

Hope was bluffing and probably Stewart knew it. "Okay, okay, but a word to the wise, kid," Lee warned, "Publix is no Keith and William Morris isn't going to put you on the Orpheum Time and they sure as hell aren't going to put you in the Palace." It was Stewart's way of reminding Hope of the subtleties and politics of the booking business and, particularly, that it was Keith, not Morris, who booked the Palace.

Hope called Charlie Yates, an agent who had once bailed out Hope and Byrne when they were starving, to see if he could find a little neighborhood spot where Hope could try out some new ideas. Yates found a little theater in Brooklyn, the Dyker, which would put Hope on for $75. Hope's material was too subtle for a raucous crowd who liked physical stuff and the band members would be the only ones who thought him funny. But Lee Stewart came out to Brooklyn to catch Hope's last show and on the way back to Manhattan on the IRT, the two men engaged in some plain talk while Louise napped with her head on Hope's shoulder.

"Look, Bob, I'm sure you've guessed that Proctor's Eighty-sixth is nothing like the Dyker. It's a big barn. Do you think you can hit the back of the top balcony?" Lee asked.

But Hope wasn't worried about projecting. If there was one thing he had it was a big strong voice that carried and could be heard in the last row.

Hope finally turned to Stewart. "Listen, Lee, I open there tomorrow, and if I bomb, we don't talk to each other again. Okay?"

Hope rose earlier than usual. Backstage before the midafternoon show, he asked the doorman what the audience was like. "Tough," he said. "Toughest in New York."

"Tougher than the Palace?" Hope asked incredulously.

"Who ever told you the Palace is tough? Critical is the word. That's an audience at the Palace of pros, and if you're good enough to be booked there, the audience knows that, respects that, and they're on your side. Here is different. Here they dare you to be good. This is a show house—but I don't have to tell you that. Who are you showing for, Keith?"

Hope nodded. Not normally given to jitters or nerves, he was suddenly terrified. He went outside into the alley and walked back and forth. He walked over to Madison and then around the block, twice. Back in the theater he stood in the wings watching the other acts, chewing his prop cigar. Louise stood a few feet away, watching him, leaving him alone, aware that this showing for Hope was his passage to the Palace.

Leatrice Joy went onstage to big applause. Hope was aware that the newspapers were carrying stories and items about her stormy marriage to the matinée idol John Gilbert. Hope had never forgotten how that audience in South Bend had reacted because they thought he had linked up with the morning's headlines. What if—? But by the time he was fingering that thought Leatrice Joy was making her exit. She took her bow and the music changed to an up-tempo entrance for Hope.

He tilted his derby, wobbled his cigar, and strode out to the center of the stage. When the music faded and the audience settled for a bit, Hope looked out into the faces and picked out one a few rows back on the aisle. "No, lady, this is *not* John Gilbert." It turned out to be the right thing to say. The audience roared. For the next 17 minutes he used every good gag he knew, including a few modified Frank Tinney bits that were surefire. He would hear and feel the audience's warmth. After he and Louise did their routine, he wound up with a song and dance—and then off. The gags had been fresh enough; his timing impeccable. The audience asked for more.

"I came back for two bows," Hope said, "then dropped my left hand as a signal to the electricians and the orchestra leader. I'd arranged that signal in advance. It meant that the orchestra would stop playing my bow music while the applause was at its peak, then the spotlight would go black leaving the audience with nothing. It worked the way I hoped. The audience couldn't switch off their applause that quickly, so they kept on clamoring. I stood there in the wings for a full forty seconds and let them applaud."

When the stage manager nervously prodded him to take his final bow, Hope said, "Relax, brother, I'm the one who's showing." He waited a few more seconds, then signaled for the spot. He strutted back out to stand in the light, did an encore dance, and walked off.

Lee Stewart wasted no time getting backstage to congratulate him. "I knew you had it. How about that audience?"

"How about the way I bombed at the Dyker?" Hope mocked, recalling Stewart's fear expressed the night before on the IRT.

"That's no theater," Lee said, smirking.

A few minutes later Johnny Hyde came in to Hope's dressing room and told him how much he liked the act. He asked Bob if he would accompany him down to the Morris office after the next show.

Hope refused, insisting the interval was too short between shows.

"Then how about after the last show tonight?" Hyde asked.

"At *midnight* you'll be there?" Hope said smiling.

"We'll be there. We're in the Bond Building," he prompted.

"I know where you are," said Hope.

But after the next show, Stewart had a contract in his hand offering Hope the Orpheum Circuit—the big time—at $400 a week. Hope turned away from Stewart and said, "Not enough." Lee said Keith wouldn't go above $450 and Hope said, "Fine." He signed for three years with a vision of PALACE stamped on his eyeballs.

Brash and Impudent:
1929 to 1937

6

Hollywood, Take One

"I sat there waiting for me to appear on the screen and leave me speechless with my talent. Then the screening began. I'd never seen anything so awful. I looked like a cross between a mongoose and a turtle."

The panic that swept through offices in the financial district the morning of October 24, 1929, was only the herald of a terrible wipeout. It was several days before *Variety's* editor, Sime Silverman, would print his sardonic WALL STREET LAYS AN EGG headline on the front page of the flagship entertainment industry organ, and weeks before the bewildering truth registered generally.

Brokers and investors were said to be jumping from the windows of upper stories of Wall Street buildings, but along Broadway B. F. Keith agents were so busy worrying about threats to their 300 vaudeville theaters having nothing to do with the financial crisis that they hardly noticed. Their panic stemmed from a wave of newness in the entertainment industry. It was not only the sudden success of Warner Bros. talking pictures, but the creeping delirium of radio and all that free entertainment. The Keith task was to convince the American public that quality entertainment was still a stage full of girls, comics, and acrobats; that vaudeville—the richest single vein in the mother lode of American humor—was an American institution too essential to fade.

There is no evidence to suggest that when Bob Hope selected the job of comic monologuist over any other specialty in entertainment, he was aware of following in the rich tradition of oral humor in America—or, for that matter, that he was consciously patterning himself after Artemus Ward, Petroleum Nasby, Mr. Dooley, or his fellow vaudevillian Will Rogers. The phrase "cracker-barrel" applied to comedians who talked to audiences in a way that resembles folk wisdom; this surely didn't enter into Hope's thinking—although some 12 years later Alva Johnson, writing in *Life* magazine, would connect him with this seam of American humor. True, Hope admired some of the monologuists who "thought funny," like Frank Tinney and Frank Fay. But Hope chose his comic style because it evolved rather naturally, and he could make a good living at it. And, besides his trigger joke sense, he had a smooth singing voice and was very agile on his feet.

If Hope felt deep inside that America was holding a death watch for vaudeville he certainly didn't express it openly, nor was he likely to, now that he was an exclusive Keith property. It was something like being stamped USDA CHOICE. And because of this new status he knew he had to bring something fresh and special to his premier Orpheum tour across some legendary stages, including that of his hometown Cleveland Palace, the old Chicago Palace, and the St. Paul Orpheum.

Hope was deeply concerned about the quality of his material, and he felt compelled to find professional help. He had heard about a gag writer named Al Boasberg who had turned out some funny lines for Jack Benny and Eddie Cantor and had written the popular "Lamb Chops" routine for George Burns and Gracie Allen. Hope said later, "Al was a great joke mechanic. He had a fabulous memory for classic jokes; he could fix jokes, he could switch them around, he could improvise. He could even originate jokes." Hope bit the bullet and hired his first gag writer. They would meet at a restaurant and sit until closing constructing a few gags or a routine. Boasberg was especially adept at "Dumb Dora" situations, and Bob encouraged this because he felt the bond between him and his audience strengthened during his bit with Louise and wanted this to continue to stay strong and perhaps build. Boasberg invented this kind of exchange:

LOUISE: I passed your house last night.
BOB: You did? And you didn't come in?
LOUISE: There was too much noise. Bob—what *was* all that noise?
BOB: Oh, that was my father. He was dragging my pants around.
LOUISE: A lot of noise for a pair of pants.
BOB: I know, but I was *in* them. (Pause for laugh) But Lou, you look great!
LOUISE: You look pretty great yourself, Bob.
BOB: Yes, I come from a pretty strong and brave family. Do you know that
   my brother once slapped a gangster in the face?
LOUISE: *Your brother slapped a gangster in the face?!*
BOB: That's right.
LOUISE: I'd like to shake his hand.
BOB: We're not going to dig him up for that.

For his first appearance under the new contract, and prior to the national tour, Hope was booked into the Brooklyn Albee for one week. The feel of that first weekly $450 paycheck was delicious. He immediately set aside $50 for Mahm, and Louise demanded that he raise her salary to $100. But he still had $300.

After the Albee engagement, Keith moved Hope to Proctor's Eighty-sixth. On November 5, 1929, *Variety* reported:

Hope, assisted by an unbilled girl appearing only in the middle of the act for a gag cross-fire, has an act satisfactory for the time it is playing. If some material, especially where old gags are found, could be changed, chances are this would double strength of turn. . . . Strongest is interlude in which Hope feeds for unbilled girl, latter of sap type and clever at handling comedy lines.

Although his intuition about building the Louise material was right, her hat size seemed to increase as she realized her value to the act. In fact, she threatened to quit if she didn't get billing.

Hope bristled at the blackmail and immediately wired Mildred Rosequist to join him for his national Orpheum Circuit tour (the chain stretched from coast to coast), set to begin the following week in Cleveland. Hope went a step further. He asked Mildred to marry him.

Mildred wired back that she was engaged to marry someone else and she was sorry. Hope crumpled up the telegram and decided it was smart to make up with Louise—who was just waiting for him to propose. He did and she dropped her demands.

Showing in Cleveland would obviously be a very special event for a lot of Hopes. For Bob himself it was more than local boy makes good. It was coming home for the first time since he had heard from Jim that Mahm might require treatments for a tumor that could be cancer of the cervix. But Avis would not allow a doctor to examine her. Nor would she discuss it. Mahm was just so thrilled to think that Les—no, now he called himself Bob—would soon be standing on the stage of Keith's 105th Street Theater, built in a sandlot where all her boys had played in 1910.

The more she thought about it, the more apprehensive she became about his appearance. Harry couldn't go to the opening because he was in one of his sober periods and was doing the ornamental stonework on a courthouse out of town. Avis thought it out carefully and decided she would not add to Les's nervousness by his having *her* out front being nervous, too.

That first matinée, Bob searched the audience for Avis. He couldn't believe she wouldn't be there. Earlier he had brought her a hat from New York with lilies of the valley on the brim and he would have spotted her at once. The family was well represented, but no Mahm.

The next day, after the *Cleveland Press* raved about the performance, Avis told Jim she would go with him to the matinée. They arrived during Harry Webb's zany comedy orchestra act. Jim Hope describes the event.

From the moment Mahm took her seat, she trembled from head to toe. Tears ran down her cheeks and her fingernails were cutting my hand. I was afraid she would faint.

And when Les made his appearance, her entire body stiffened. When she heard the reception by the audience, acknowledging him as a neighborhood boy, she relaxed. She listened to every syllable, nodding her head as if approving every word.

Toward the end of the act, I handed her my handkerchief thinking she'd use it to wipe the other hand. Instead she patted her forehead. Whether it was the fluttering of the handkerchief that caught Les' eye or what, but just as he was taking his last bow, he spotted us and proudly said, "There she is, folks! That's Mahm! The one with the lilies of the valley on her hat. There she is. Way back there. Stand up and let these folks see you, Mahm!"

She really didn't need to. The expression on her face was enough.

The party later that night at 2029 Euclid was festive. There was a decidedly new note of respect for Les in the air. They all agreed he had arrived. And they got to meet Louise, but there were nine different opinions of her.

The older brothers impressed Bob with their business skills—Ivor doing well in metal products, Fred doing even better in provisions, and Jim cock of the road as a traveling supervisor for the power company. Jack and Sid were still plugging away at their jobs, and George, now out of school, was sampling part-time work and dreaming of show business. Talk inevitably centered on the market's crash a few weeks before, and the unbelievable awareness that billions of dollars in corporate profits, both on and off paper, had vanished.

Bob listened to their talk, feeling instinctively that the vaudeville theaters and movie houses would not go dark. And of course, he was dead right. In the depression that engulfed the nation from 1929 to 1933, folks managed to scrape up the pocket change for tickets to movies or stage shows or to buy a radio for entertainment that afforded at least a temporary escape from the torpor of poverty and deprivation.

Bob also thought, as he tuned in and out of his brothers' lamentations, that he, strange as it sounded, just might have to bail everybody out.

As his eyes surveyed the so-familiar house with its now shabby furniture and decoration, he looked at Mahm and then at Harry, who had come home for the party. He suddenly was convinced that during the remainder of his stay in Cleveland, he and his brothers should put their parents in a new home.

Real estate values were dropping all over the city, including in exclusive Cleveland Heights, and this is where Bob decided to look. After a day or two he found a house at 3323 Yorkshire Road but kept the fact from his parents. Then, just before he left town, he announced to Avis that he was throwing out all her old furniture.

"Why ever for?" she said defensively. "It's old but it's seen us through. We don't need new furniture."

"It goes—and so do you."

"You're talking nonsense, Les."

"Seriously, Mahm." Bob picked Avis up and whirled her around. "Let's take a ride, Fred."

Bob carried her outside and put her down in the passenger side of the front seat and got in the back. Fred was behind the wheel and they drove toward Cleveland Heights. Fred stopped the car. Bob got out and opened the door for Avis. They walked up to the front door and Fred and Bob told her she was home. She cried. She told them they were crazy. She cried some more but she moved. And the only old things her sons allowed her to take to the new home were her sewing machine and her piano.

Bob and Louise went on to play the Chicago Palace. This time as they finished their comedy bit together, Hope altered the final joke:

BOB: My brother really slapped Al Capone once.
LOUISE: (*Really surprised*) He *did*? Why—he's the bravest man I ever heard of. I'd like to shake his hand.
BOB: We're not going to dig him up for that.

The joke got a huge laugh. After the show, Frank Smith, the Palace manager, told Hope that the Capone joke was in doubtful, perhaps dangerous, taste. He went further: "I think you ought to drop it."

"I can't, Frank," said Hope, "not with that size laugh."

"Laugh or no laugh, if you're smart you'll dump it. The boys from Cicero, sometimes even big Al, come down here on Saturday nights. I wouldn't care to be you if they don't like it."

"I'm going to keep it in," said Hope, and he did. On Sunday morning his telephone at the Bismarck Hotel rang. The caller asked for Ben Hoke.

"Who's this?"

"Never mind who. You the comedian doing the Al Capone joke?"

"Who *are* you?" repeated Hope.

"Do yourself a favor. Take the joke out of your act. We'll be around to show our appreciation."

The call persuaded Hope to drop the gag from the remaining Chicago performances. He fully expected to encounter some sinister characters whenever he and Louise emerged to walk along the dark theater alley, but no one ever showed up.

After playing some smaller houses in Illinois and Michigan, they moved on to the Twin Cities for a split week at the St. Paul Orpheum, and then on to the Orpheum in Winnipeg. Up to this point they had been traveling in winter wind and snow, but by the time they reached Calgary the weather was springlike. Hope was restless for some physical activity, and he began talking about learning to play golf. Actually it was a matter of renewed interest.

"I had tried to play in Cleveland during the early 1920s," Hope has since said, "but I just had no feel for the game. I had never taken lessons and I was terrible. But during the spring of 1930 on the Orpheum circuit, I'd be waiting around the hotel lobby in the late morning when the Diamond Brothers, another act, would come down with their golf clubs. They played every day. One day I said, 'Oh, hell, I'll go out there with you.' I hit a bag of practice balls and played a few holes. It was fun." Before that 1930 tour was over, Hope had played a number of full rounds and started a lifelong love affair with golf.

Vancouver was next and then Seattle. Hope was receiving regular communications from Al Boasberg: wires, letters, or phone calls with gag ideas. During one of the Portland calls, Boasberg offered to set up a screen test for Hope in Hollywood. One of Al's friends, Bill Perlberg, was a successful agent and had some strong studio contacts. Hope liked the idea.

After their week in San Francisco, Bob and Louise hit Los Angeles and checked into the Hollywood Hotel. Perlberg called Hope at the hotel and Hope played coy.

"My friend Al Boasberg thinks you're worth taking a look at for pictures," said Perlberg. "He thinks you've got style."

"Boasberg drinks," said Hope, expecting a laugh. No laugh.

"How would you like to make a test?"

"I think I can squeeze it in before we go to San Diego."

"Thursday you get yourself out to the Pathé lot in Culver City."

"What will I be doing? I mean, isn't there a script?"

"You'll do your regular act," Perlberg said. "I hear you have a dame with you. Bring her along."

"How big an audience?"

"No audience."

On Thursday morning Bob and Louise took a cab out to Culver City. When the technicians were ready to roll, Hope launched into his act and a few people on the set—stagehands and assorted bystanders—laughed loudly here and there. The act didn't work quite the same without a real audience, yet Hope felt cocky about the test. He said, "I was so sure I clicked that even though I dropped a bundle in a gambling joint in Agua Caliente that first weekend in San Diego, I was oblivious—I could see movie offers pouring in."

Hope left his whereabouts in San Diego with Perlberg's office and all weekend expected a phone call. But none came. Puzzled and offended he called Perlberg on Monday morning when they got back to Los Angeles.

"How about the test?" Hope asked.

"Yeah?" said Perlberg.

"Well—when do I see it?"

"You want to?"

"Sure I do."

"Pathé will be happy to show it to you."

"Okay. But how do you like it?"

"Go out and see it," replied Perlberg.

Hope went out to Culver City alone. He was directed to Projection Room 3-H but no one offered to take him in. He sat in the darkened cubicle alone. He later told the biographer Pete Martin, "I thought it was strange that nobody else was there until I looked around and saw that even the projectionists were wearing gas masks. My nose hit the screen ten minutes before the rest of me. I always knew my body had angles but didn't realize how much they stuck out.

"It was awful. I felt I was watching a stranger I didn't want to know. Of course there was no audience and no laughter, but even so I couldn't believe how bad I was. When the lights came up I wanted to get out fast."

Hope was hurt by the rejection, so he immediately adopted the attitude that he was too good for Hollywood. Louise agreed with him. As they made their way through the Midwest it was encouraging to hear the laughter of the audiences repeated again and again on afternoons and nights in Denver, Omaha, Kansas City, and St. Louis. But it was the New York Palace that really mattered and pulled them east like a magnet.

"Who needs Hollywood, anyway?" Hope asked arrogantly. They actually convinced themselves they had just had a very close call.

7

Swimming the Palace Moat

"Isn't this some theater!. . . I was just standing out in front watching the other acts when a lady rushed up to me and said, 'Pardon me, young man, can you help me find the rest room?'. . . and I said, 'Yes, ma'am, it's just around the corner'. . . and she said, 'Don't give me any of that Hoover talk.'"

Hope's inaugural Orpheum tour ended in 1930 and Lee Stewart applauded the results. Despite a worsening economy, box-office receipts stayed healthy for vaudeville. Stewart assured Hope that he would be going out for a second national tour in a couple of months. In the meantime, Hope decided to "slide in" to Cleveland to see Mahm, while Louise went to Chicago to see her father.

Actually, there was more to the Cleveland visit. Bob had received a letter from Avis while on the road. It was all about George, her last and, in many ways, her most worrisome son. Since his graduation from high school he had flitted from job to job. However, he had shown signs in school of being interested in "theatrical things," wrote Avis. She thought that maybe Les could counsel him.

"Can't he help you somehow, Les?" asked Avis. "Maybe he could watch and listen and learn for a time. It would do him good to get away from here."

"Let's see you dance, George," Bob said. "Go ahead, Mahm—play a little 'Tea For Two.' George—try a soft-shoe."

"I can't, Les. Not well enough. I've tried. But I'll get it—I really will. I promise. I'll do anything you ask me to do. I want to go with you."

"Okay." Bob noticed Avis was smiling. "Okay, I've been thinking of putting together my own little unit. I've got a lot of ideas for doing some crazy—very different kinds of things. I could use you as a stooge."

"A what?" George asked.

"I'll put you in the audience. When I'm up there doing my monologue, or whatever's going on, you'll start heckling me. I've been thinking of asking Toots Burdock—a pal from Toledo—to do that also. The two of you arguing and making smart comments from the audience would be all part of the act."

George was barely 20, but he was eager and Bob was willing to take a chance with him. Besides, he could save a little money on George, in view of the payroll he was contemplating. He envisioned having his own touring company.

Meanwhile, back on Broadway, Lee Stewart kept pushing his favorite client during celebrated Wednesday afternoon executive sessions in the conference room of the imposing Palace Theater Building. In today's vernacular, those were real power meetings; attended by two dozen Keith managers and bookers, those meetings determined the fate of the country's vaudeville performers. So great was Keith's control of the business that two words from the mouth of one of these managers, "No interest," could ruin a career. Hope hungered for a chance to qualify for a shot at the New York Palace, and Stewart was persistent on his behalf, working him as much as possible in New York showcase houses.

Booked at the cavernous RKO Coliseum, on West 181st Street, Hope found himself sharing the bill with the most talked about picture of the year, the Academy Award–winning *All Quiet on the Western Front*. An uncompromising antiwar film, directed by Lewis Milestone, it starred Lew Ayres as a sensitive young German soldier. Ayres generates exceptional audience sympathy throughout the film.

In a powerful closing scene, Ayres's character is killed by a single sniper bullet while reaching for a butterfly that has landed on a barbed-wire fence. As comedy emcee for a split-week engagement (three days at the Coliseum, three at Fifty-eighth), Hope was to bounce onstage immediately following the film. The pit orchestra leader, Sid Fabello, arranged a special musical bridge between the movie fadeout and the vaudeville portions.

At the first matinée, when the screen rumbled upward to clear the stage for Hope's act and the spotlight caught Hope entering stage left, hat moving, eyes sparkling, firing off his first line of paradiddle, he was as welcome as the plague. Weeping eyes had not yet dried and some people were moving up the aisles toward the lobby. "I should have known it couldn't possibly have worked," Hope said. "The audience was still in shock. The mistake was putting that film with vaudeville. And if I had been smart I would have leveled with the audience. You know, go out there and lay it on the line. I would have said, 'Hey, my part of the show has to go on sometime. They say I'm funny—at least that's what they're paying me for.' But what I *did* do was get mad."

Hope came offstage and indulged in one of his infrequent tantrums. He demanded to know how the management expected him to get laughs after such an emotionally draining film. Somehow he endured three more agonizing days, sighing with relief when he was able to move over to Proctor's Fifty-eighth Street for the second half of the week. Proctor's Fifty-eighth was known for taking vaudeville seriously and would never fall into the same trap as the Coliseum. But when Hope opened the *Herald Tribune* Wednesday morning he saw *All Quiet on the Western Front* playing at Proctor's Fifty-eighth Street.

He grabbed the phone and dialed the Keith office. Lee Stewart was sympathetic to a point.

"Fun's fun," said Hope, "but this is ridiculous. I quit."

"What about the contract?"

"The hell with it."

"Bob?"

"What?"

"Do it!"

Hope did it. He had to comply because Keith held the keys to the dressing room doors at *the* Palace. *And needing to play the Palace was eating Hope alive,* despite his awareness of the inescapable fact that this consummate showcase of vaudeville was losing its luster.

Two years earlier, in 1927, Sime Silverman, the editor of *Variety,* had moved the vaudeville section from the front pages further back to expand the motion picture news and advertising. In 1929, *Variety* announced solemnly that "the fate of vaudeville as a business" would certainly be decided that year or the next. In panic, the New York Palace changed its show schedule of two a day in favor of the poisonous (for the performers) five a day, and despite that change the theater was losing an average of $4,000 a week.

Yet Hope still viewed the Palace as the mark of achievement, and trusted Stewart's promise that he would get a showing there soon.

Meanwhile, in the fall of 1930, he had to hit the Orpheum circuit again, and he refused to go without a new concept. His obsession was to build an act strong enough to match the talkies. Hope and Boasberg constructed a kind of minirevue that allowed the comic to work alone both as emcee and monologuist, to banter with Louise, also to do bits with stooges, followed by a substantial afterpiece. Called *Antics of 1930,* the whole thing had a flavor of what the famous (Ole) Olsen and (Chic) Johnson team produced in their zany 1938 review *Hellzapoppin'.*

This was a time to incorporate ideas Bob had been waiting to try, like using George and Toots as hecklers. Hope and Boasberg primed and pruned *Antics* right up to the day Boasberg had to leave for Hollywood to work for Eddie Cantor and also to write a movie script.

As the Orpheum tour began, the act did have a certain freshness. It opened with an actor named Johnny Peters, who looked amazingly like Rudy Vallee, seated alone onstage playing a saxophone. Hope walked out and introduced Peters, who stood up and began singing "My time is your time" into a megaphone. Hope picked up a baton and started conducting Peters. Then from one of the side boxes of the theater came some commentary:

TOOTS: Pssssst! George! How do you like it?

GEORGE: Sounds just as bad over here.

HOPE: Now, just a minute! Don't you know you can be arrested for annoy-
ing an audience.

TOOTS/GEORGE: You ought to know!

Following the monologue Hope would introduce other acts and eventually
Louise would wander onstage and they would do several routines, including this
new one by Boasberg:

BOB: What are you crying for?

LOUISE: Mother just threw father out of the house.

BOB: What for?

LOUISE: Something about saying Grace.

BOB: Ah—you mean saying Grace before meals?

LOUISE: No, saying Grace in his sleep. My mother's name is Mary.

Some of Hope's material for *Antics,* including new gags by Boasberg, was in
clear violation of vaudeville's classic taboos regarding blatant allusions to political
issues and sex. Although Keith's hard-line policies had been softening somewhat,
there were still certain theater managers who were old-fashioned. Hope's new gags
were borderline, the best of them mixing politics and bathroom humor:

"Isn't this some theater!. . . I was just standing out in front watching the other
acts when a lady rushed up to me and said, 'Pardon me, young man, can you help
me find the rest room?'. . . and I said, 'Yes, ma'am, it's just around the corner'. . . and she said, 'Don't give me any of that Hoover talk.'"

As President Herbert Hoover's attempts to reassure Americans that business
and industry would recover became futile, and his oft quoted "Prosperity is just
around the corner" sounded more and more like a national joke, that particular
gag became increasingly successful for Hope.

During the late winter of 1931, with the Depression haunting towns and villages that could hardly believe their own breadlines and soup kitchens, Hope and
his *Antics* company were luckier than many of their jobless colleagues.
Unemployment had more than doubled from 1930 figures. Some 2,800 businesses had closed and 2,300 banks had failed. The businesses that survived
announced 10 percent wage reductions, and some reductions would become even
harsher.

It was logical that radio should now become the most popular entertainment,
because it was so accessible and affordable. Movie houses enticed patrons with
cheap seats, bank nights (a drawing to attract audiences), free dishes, food baskets,
and double bills. Luckily for Hope, Keith bookings were dependable. *Antics of
1931* went all the way to Vancouver, Oakland, and Los Angeles, then came back
to the East Coast by way of St. Louis, Chicago, Milwaukee, Grand Rapids,

Decatur, Detroit, and Hope's home town, Cleveland. It was a raw, cold early February.

Bob was anxious to see Mahm. This time she seemed smaller and thinner and more fragile than he had remembered. But she and Harry seemed settled in their new "mansion."

Bob did not see Mildred, who was still engaged and not yet married, but George did. George stubbornly clung to a childhood hope that his older brother would one day realize his love for Mildred. George confided in Mildred how much he hated Louise. He said Louise went around acting as if she was already Mrs. Bob Hope. But Mildred really couldn't help George with that problem.

This Cleveland booking had further significance. Tuesday afternoon Hope's dressing-room door opened, and in walked Lee Stewart. Hope was applying makeup. He looked up.

"Bob, have I got a—"

"PALACE!" Hope yelped, jumping up and turning to grab Lee.

"You got it!"

"When?" Hope's eyes glistened.

"Monday," Lee said, thinking this was the most emotional he had ever seen Hope. Reflecting on that day and time, Stewart later revealed:

> He almost kissed me. I never saw such a happy and excited guy in my life. And it's natural. Every actor looked forward to the time when he would play the New York Palace. And thousands went through their whole careers dreaming of that and never realizing it. It gave nine out of ten players the heebie-jeebies. I've seen old-timers nervous at the thought. And Bob—he was excited, enthused, nervous—and plain scared. Before the close of his Cleveland week he was on the edge of a nervous breakdown. Yet, in spite of his nervousness his brain was clicking. He knew he was going into fast company—that he was following the best in the business.

Between shows Hope agonized. "I gotta get a gag," Hope said, looking at himself in the mirror.

"What do you mean?" Lee asked.

"I've got to get something special to carry me. I've got to find something good."

"Toward the end of the week, after Lee had returned to New York, Hope turned to Louise and said, "Listen to this. I'll get Milt Lewis to find me five or six guys to carry signs in front of the Palace, yeah, they'll carry signs that say I'm unfair to my stooges. That ought to get attention."

This would be, of course, in addition to a large full-figure cutout of Hope that he had agreed to underwrite for the Palace outer lobby with the banner: BOB HOPE—THE COMIC FIND OF THE WEST.

As Hope had predicted, the stooge stunt attracted crowds on the morning of Monday, February 11, the day the show would open. Six men in sandwich signs walked back and forth, their signs proclaiming BOB HOPE IS UNFAIR TO STOOGES—LOCAL 711 and BOB HOPE IS UNFAIR TO DISORGANIZED STOOGES, and still another, REFUSES TO PAY FOR THEIR LUMPS, BUMPS, DOCTORS, AND HOSPITAL BILLS. The gag was working just as Hope wished, but not as the Palace manager, Elmer Rogers, wished.

"For God's sake, Hope, get those sandwich men out of there! The crowd is taking that picketing seriously and won't come inside."

Fortunately, the Palace's advertising and publicity man, Arnold Van Leer, loved what he saw. Bob Hope was clearly *his* kind of entertainer, someone who understood publicity and promotion. Van Leer got on the telephone to all the New York papers to make sure they appreciated Hope's gag. Most of the press printed something about the gag and it fanned business.

Bea Lillie was the headliner and Hope was billed in the second spot, the deuce. Also on the bill were Vivienne Segal (who later would make a big splash in *Pal Joey*), Harry Hershfield, a humorist and very offbeat vaudevillian, Noble Sissle, and Harry Delmar's Revue. It was actually a second holdover week for Lillie and consequently the critics didn't pay much attention to the new acts that joined the lineup. There were a few lukewarm phrases in the newspapers, but it was Jerry Wald's assessment in the *Graphic* that sizzled Hope. Wald wrote: "They say that Bob Hope is the sensation of the Midwest. If that's so, why doesn't he go back there?"

Hope was bitterly disappointed. Hershfield, however, recognized Hope's talent and sympathetically tried to bolster his wounded feelings. It helped, but Hope was still nervous and anxious about the big Sunday-night show.

Sunday nights were celebrity nights at the Palace. Headliners like Sophie Tucker or Eddie Cantor helped to draw customers to average bills and guaranteed sellouts.

Elmer Rogers had asked Hope to emcee the coming Sunday's show and the prospect made him jittery. He would be expected to introduce celebrities in the audience (if there were any) and urge them to come up on the stage and entertain. Al Jolson, it is said, made his only Palace appearance as a Sunday night celebrity guest.

Sunday night arrived, and Hope went onstage. He was doing a rather poor job and he knew it. Luckily, though, Ted Healy ("Is evvv-rybody happy?")—who after seeing Hope on the Albee stage one time had said, "Brother, you've got it"—was seated in the front row. A few rows back was another of the day's more popular entertainers, Ken Murray. Hope thought these two could save his night.

He introduced Murray first. Murray stood in place and waved his arms to audience applause. Then he sat down while the crowd still applauded. Hope watched and waited. Then Murray stood up and made his way to the aisle and then down to the orchestra pit, jumped inside and using a trombonist's knee and shoulder climbed up onto the stage. There was continuous laughter and applause.

Murray bowed to the audience and said, "I'm going to tell a joke!" At this moment Ted Healy stood up in the front row and hollered, "I've heard it." The audience howled, and as more and more people recognized Healy the applause grew. Whatever awkwardness had existed was disappearing and the three comedians bantered through a lively exchange.

Theater and vaudeville histories could hardly record that Hope's arrival at the Palace was notable. His debut occurred at a time when the theater's management was struggling to maintain its preeminence as the country's premier vaudeville showcase. Vaudeville was dying, revived briefly early in 1932 by the record-breaking nine-week marathon run of Eddie Cantor and George Jessel—and still later that year with the return of Sophie Tucker. Those were final shining moments for the Palace, sadly in its last year, and for vaudeville in general. On November 16, 1932, when a bill featuring Nick Lucas and Hal LeRoy closed, the Palace ceased as a strictly vaudeville theater. It continued as a presentation house showing feature films four times a day and with headline entertainers live onstage (backed by a pit orchestra) between movie showings. The Palace was succumbing, like every other vaudeville house in the nation, to the allure of the silver screen.

8

Ballyhoo and Benefits, Too!

"It all seemed so strange, talking into a microphone in a studio instead of playing in front of a real audience. I was nervous on the first radio shows and the engineers couldn't figure out why they heard a thumping noise when I did my routines until they found out I was kicking the mike after each joke."

In 1932, "the cruelest year" of the Great Depression, 15 million men and women were out hunting for jobs that didn't exist. Both white- and blue-collar workers lucky enough to get a paycheck took home $50 a week or maybe $75 in two weeks.

Bob Hope had just played the Palace and because of that, RKO could merchandise him more effectively. Hope was not only regularly employed, he was now taking home close to $1,000 a week. But this was not making him complacent. On the contrary. Those who knew him during the period after his Palace opening agree that he had fresh zeal, was striving for a refinement of style. Some saw in him a new "drive," some saw a new "sense of professionalism," and others a desire "to be the best." An excerpt from a review in the *Chicago Sun* on September 4, 1931, suggests an emerging stage presence: "Equipped with the sort of engaging personality that will put over any material, Hope has the practiced trouper's idea of timing his humorous sallies, emphasizing them with mugging and pauses so they never miss."

It was clear to those around him that if anything could come close to defeating him, it would be that recurring specter: poor material. Hope had been fortunate in his association with Al Boasberg, but Boasberg had moved permanently to the West Coast to write for Cantor. Luckily, in 1931 Hope met Richy Craig, Jr., a young vaudevillian who had, Bob and many others thought, "an original turn of wit." How Craig was helping him can be sensed from review of his show that appeared in *Variety* on March 5, 1932, whose writer noted that Hope's "great comedy material" and his ad-libs not only scored with the audience but pleased his fellow performers and the pit musicians as well.

Craig's gags along with Hope's ability to make a scripted piece of comedy seem spontaneous and his "go to hell" kind of emceeing convinced Lew Gensler that the comedian was right for a revue called *Ballyhoo of 1932* that he and Norman Anthony were producing. The musical, with songs written by Gensler and the lyricist E. Y. Harburg, would be virtually an "in the flesh" version of Anthony's recently launched and already popular risqué and barbed-humor magazine called *Ballyhoo*. It was due to open in September and rehearsals were to start in July.

Hope liked the idea, and Keith was delighted to give their rising star leave from his three-year contract because his marquee value would only increase with a Broadway stage success. Hope joined an impressive cast that included Willie and Eugene Howard, Jeanne Aubert, Lulu McConnell, Vera Marsh, and Paul and Grace Hartman.

The sketches, directed by the producers, were irreverent spoofs of Greta Garbo's mannerisms, of Columbus Circle revolutionaries (Hope and Willie Howard ran around singing "Rewolt! Rewolt!"), nudists (also featuring Hope with Vera Marsh), and Southern evangelists, among others. The evening's high point came when the Howards were joined by two buxom female singers for a burlesque of the famous quartet "Bella figlia dell'amore" in the last act of Giuseppe Verdi's *Rigoletto*.

Hope enjoyed the summer rehearsals because his pal Richy Craig was featured in a Broadway revue called *Hey Nonny Nonny*, starring Frank Morgan, which Craig had helped create together with E. B. White and Ogden Nash. The revue closed early, leaving Craig saddened. Then worse news followed. Richy was told that he had an advanced case of tuberculosis. Hope was devastated; the painful memory of Lloyd Durbin's death still lingered with him. Despondent but feigning high spirits, Hope put Richy on a train for the TB clinic at Saranac Lake, New York, in July. He wished him godspeed and a quick recovery.

Ballyhoo was a shambles when it opened at the Nixon Theater, on the Atlantic City pier. "There were so many scenes," recalled Lee Stewart, "that the lights fouled up—actually it was rather frightening. There was a blazing short circuit and the theater went dark. The management feared that the audience was ready to panic and rush the doors." Lee Shubert, one of the backers, was standing backstage and asked if someone would go out front and calm the audience.

"I will," said Hope, his hands shaking. "At least, I'll try. How long before the lights—"

"Go!" said Shubert.

Hope stepped out onto an almost pitch-black stage and began telling jokes. Part of the audience thought this was the way *Ballyhoo* was supposed to open and the rest settled back, reassured by Hope's gags. As soon as he heard laughter he relaxed and kept working until the lights went on in the pit.

The same kind of scene was repeated two weeks later when the show moved to Newark. But on this night the delay in the curtain was caused by confusion over eleventh-hour changes and a new opening dance production. Shubert again ordered Hope to go out and pacify the restless customers. Hope protested that what worked in Atlantic City to quiet a frightened audience wasn't going to work for a savvy show business crowd, but Shubert kept insisting.

Hope glared at him and then strolled out as nonchalantly as he could, saying, "Ladies and gentlemen, this is the first time I've ever been on before the acrobats." Laughter. He was right—this crowd knew all about vaudeville.

"But we're doing a new number for you tonight, and we had a little late rehearsal, and things aren't quite set up back there yet. . . and. . . this is a new show. . . and—hello, Sam!" Hope looked up toward the balcony, shading his eyes to see better, and looked back at the audience, "That's one of our backers up there." Laughter. "He says he's not nervous, but I notice he's buckled his safety belt."

By then the audience was with him. Hope continued until he got the signal to get off. Backstage, Shubert, Gensler, and Anthony congratulated him, and somebody said, "God, we ought to leave that bit in the show. It's a different way to open."

Hope chalked that up to gratitude, but the next day he was approached by Gensler. Hope replied, "I like it, Lew—but to repeat what happened last night is a phony premise. Let me find something like that but more honest and flexible I'll tell ya—I'll open up a complaint department."

And that night, just before curtain time, Hope slipped into one of the side boxes (they were always slow sellers) and instead of a spotlight on the conductor for the overture, the spot focused on Hope.

"Good evening, ladies and gentlemen. Tonight we're introducing something rather novel. It's called the Complaint Department. That's me." Laughter.

"No. I'm serious. If there's anything about our show you don't like just come to me. Maybe you've got some funny ideas of your own. We can use 'em."

Hope continued in that vein for awhile longer. "Well, the management just wanted you to know how much it cares about your opinions. Now for the show! Okay, Mr. Conductor, the overture. Max? That's Max Meth, folks, our conductor!" Max didn't move. Hope clapped his hands together twice. Nothing.

From the orchestra pit came the sounds of snoring. "Hey, fellas? Wake up! Let's go! It's time to make music! Boys??? FELLAS???"

Hope took out a pistol and fired in the air. The snores became louder.

Hope turned and lifted a small cash register from below, set it on the box railing, pushed a lever, and made the bell ring. The orchestra men jumped to their positions. Max raised his baton and the overture began. Hoped picked up his cash register, bowed, and vanished. The audience roared and clapped.

Critics were more enthusiastic about the Gensler-Harburg songs than they were about the Anthony sketches or the antics of the Howards or Hope. On September 7, 1932, *The New York Times* identified Hope as "a self-confident comedian from vaudeville" and closed the review with "The chief things that *Ballyhoo* lacks are charm, distinction and any kind of theatrical allure."

During the show's 16-week run on Broadway, however, there were some interesting portents of things to come in Hope's career. For example, Willie Howard, Lulu McConnell, and Hope were asked to perform in one of the experimental television galas on CBS station W2XAB, which had gone on the air locally in 1931. They worked in front of a single camera, totally bleached out by megawatt-strength lights. The signals transmitted were fuzzy, flickering, hard-to-distinguish images. When Howard and Hope left the studio in the early afternoon, Willie said, "Television's a turkey." And Hope agreed.

Another novelty for Hope during this period was radio. This medium was no turkey. The most popular entertainers of the day, most of them émigrés from vaudeville, were being approached for some kind of radio involvement. Hope's initiation came by way of a brief spot on Keith's *RKO Theater*, but more notable were several guest appearances on *The Fleischman Hour*, a variety program that had about 24 million listeners every week, rated third in the nation.

Hosted by Rudy Vallee, the program was eclectic, ranging from Olsen and Johnson to John Barrymore, and despite its obvious showcase allure, Hope did not feel especially comfortable. There was no live studio audience, hence no feedback. "It all seemed so strange, talking into a microphone in a studio instead of playing in front of a real audience," Hope says. "I was nervous on those first radio shows and the Vallee engineers couldn't figure why they heard a thumping noise when I did my routines until they found out I was kicking the mike after each joke."

One of Hope's happiest times during the run came when Richy Craig returned from Saranac Lake. He seemed healthier but complained of being not quite recovered and he lacked his old confidence; he was apprehensive because he had been out of circulation for nearly five months. As it happened, Hope was scheduled to do a benefit in Poughkeepsie on Thanksgiving Eve and asked Richy to join him.

Hope opened the show, and after Vera Marsh sang, Richy came on. Watching and listening from the wings, Hope thought the young comedian was really back in stride. Then he heard a heckler trying to ruin Richy's act and was worried that his pal's physical and mental rehabilitation might not withstand the attack. But without faltering, Richy said, "They took a fellow to the hospital in Poughkeepsie just last week. . . He had to have a brain operation. . . so they took out his brain and examined it. . . and while his brain was out, he got up off the operating table. . . and jumped out the window. . . but they found him. . . He was sitting in a theater heckling the actors."

When Richy finished to generous applause no one was applauding harder than Hope. Then he went out onstage and together they sang a parody about Milton Berle stealing other comedians' jokes. That worked well with the audience, too.

Hoped liked doing benefits for several reasons. They gave him the opportunity to try out new material and provided valuable audience exposure; and sometimes they were very well publicized. Generally the listing was alphabetical rather than according to a performer's "star power," so you never could feel second or third rate (even if you were). Doing benefits afforded him incomparable chances to meet and show-off with other name performers and to mingle with the affluent. Important, too, of course, was that by doing benefits you were perceived as being generous and caring. And, he knew Mahm would like that.

9

Bing, Berle, and Broadway

"Tamara led into it by saying, 'There's an old Russian proverb: "When your heart's on fire, smoke gets in your eyes."' And I wanted to say, 'We have a proverb in America, too: "Love is like hash. You have to have confidence in it to enjoy it."'"

Even before the *Ballyhoo of 1932* cast could adjust to the chilling fact that the show would be closed down on November 30, Hope got Lee Stewart to find another booking. He landed at the Capitol Theater on Broadway at Times Square for two weeks beginning December 2. His name would be paired on the theater marquee with that of Bing Crosby, who was making his first personal appearance in New York since his splashy 1932 motion picture success in Paramount's *The Big Broadcast.*

The two men had met casually just weeks earlier near the Friars Club on Forty-eighth Street. Bob was in *Ballyhoo;* Bing had hit town to star in the Cremo cigars radio show; neither of them had any notion they would be headlining a bill together in a few weeks.

From the start they liked each other. More significant, they watched each other work. As Crosby watched Hope, he envisioned the possibility of some banter between them. So the next Sunday Bing came to the theater earlier than usual.

"How do you feel about working in a couple of jokes?"

"What kind?" asked Hope.

"Well—something along the 'Who was that lady?' line, I suppose. What do you think?"

"Why not let me come out and say, 'Hey, Bing. Do you think we ought to do some of our impressions for this crowd?' And then you say, 'Do you think it's the right crowd?' And I say, 'I don't know. Maybe we should risk it.' That kind of thing. Then we'd do some of those really old solid routines—like the two farmers meeting on the street."

Crosby liked it. Instead of farmers, however, they did two businessmen meeting on the street and reaching into each other's pockets. Then each would walk back to his own side and come back as two orchestra leaders meeting on the street. When they met midstage each pulled out a baton and conducted the other as they conversed. Then they would walk back to their own sides of the stage and return to do another silly routine.

"The gags weren't very funny, I guess," admits Hope, "but the audience laughed because Bing and I were having such a good time—and I guess it was clear that we liked each other. We would laugh insanely at what we dreamed up."

Hope cannot recall whether "ski-nose" and "butter-belly" were born during this engagement or not, but the camaraderie that later spawned such sobriquets *was* formed at the Capitol. They broke each other up with their improvisations during their "impressions" onstage, and almost every show presented a challenge to them to maintain poker faces.

Toward the end of this pleasant Capitol engagement, Hope faced several unpleasant situations. First, there was the sad news that his mother's cancer was incurable, that it was a question of time—months, a year perhaps. She was now confined to her bedroom. Bob paid to have a new telephone line installed by her bed so they could talk frequently. He also wrote letters filled with anecdotes and cheerful news about his on- and offstage activities, sometimes including a joke. Avis kept them all within reach for reading and rereading. As for Harry—he shuffled aimlessly around the rooms and grounds of their new Cleveland Heights house, somewhat lost and helpless.

Another serious problem was Louise. She had been a valuable part of his stage act for five years, and for whatever she had contributed to his success he was grateful. But now she wanted more—she wanted to be Mrs. Bob Hope. When he was in *Ballyhoo* and she was idle, they would fight and she would go home to Chicago to cool off. He had never said he would not marry her. She wanted to know when. He said soon. She said *now*. It was a standoff.

His baby brother George, who had joined his traveling company as a stooge, had turned out not to be very dependable. George hankered for show business, but when Bob tried to help him improve his stage presence and his performing, especially his efforts at dancing, George would argue and resist and finally stomp back to Cleveland, angry. Mahm would tell George that Bob needed him, and it would be a back-and-forth situation.

Hope's perennial professional problem was his hunger for new comedy material. One stinging line from the *Herald-Tribune* review of his just ended Capitol appearance haunted him: "Bob Hope. . . acted as master of ceremonies using material that was not new but effective." To change that, he obviously needed jokes written exclusively for him, in the most up-to-date comedy tone. Richy

Craig had provided some material, but apparently not enough, and Hope's reliance on old material was dangerous. And sometimes his judgment about jokes utterly failed him.

When the Capitol called Hope back in late 1932, he demonstrated a peculiar lapse of sensitivity, judgment, and taste. In spite of his awareness that this theater typically appealed to an older, family type audience, Hope introduced into his act a questionable satire on motherhood. In his routine he sang a serious, sentimental song entitled "My Mom" in a heartfelt way, and while he was singing, a character actress he had hired would walk out from the wings posing as his mother, and interrupt his song asking for food and to have her teeth fixed. Hope would rebuff her questions with insults, and finally the actress would be led offstage by attendants. Hope ended his song with "She's my Madonna, my mom." Capitol management asked him to withdraw that part of his act, but he refused.

"You're upsetting people," said the Capitol's manager, Louis Sidney. "You should know this audience. They're complaining about the way you treat that lady. Please take it out."

Hope refused. Then he got a call from Major Bowes, host of the *Capitol Hour* radio show. "Bob, you're going to take that Mom bit out of your act, aren't you?"

"What is this? Major, it's a funny bit. I have a mother, too, you know——." Hope stopped. Was that Avis trudging out to center stage? "Yeah, you're right. Thanks."

This lapse was an anomaly in view of his feeling for Avis and what she was now going through. He later explained that what blinded him was the concept of the gag, its sharp poke at traditional values.

Traditional values led Hope to another error in judgment. On January 25, 1933, Louise finally pressured him into making an honest woman of her. They stopped in Erie, Pennsylvania, on their way from Cleveland to New York. The couple, nervous but not exactly naïve, made their way to the town's registrar's office, applied for a marriage license, and went through with the ceremony. Curiously, Grace Louise Troxell listed herself as a "secretary" on the marriage papers, while Hope appears as a "salesman."

For the next several months they continued touring and performing together, but it was not a happy union or one that would last. Hope felt he owed Louise something after all the years she had put in with him. But paying that debt with a wedding ring was not the answer. Within a year they would agree to go their separate ways and the marriage would be quietly dissolved.

Later that year, Hope got another crack at the Palace. But it was a sad and shabby time for a house once known as "Heaven on Forty-seventh Street." It was no longer able to attract the biggest names, no longer able to compete financially with the Capitol or the Paramount. By September 1935 its economic disease would prove fatal.

Before the bitter end, however, in 1933, during the Palace's last stand as a showcase for vaudevillians, Max Gordon saw Hope perform there and decided to sign him for a leading role in his production of the Jerome Kern–Otto Harbach musical comedy *Gowns by Roberta*. The show was about an American college full-back who inherits his aging aunt's fashionable dress salon in Paris. When he takes over the business he falls in love with the head designer, who, in true musical comedy style, turns out to be a Russian princess. The fullback's best pal is a fast-talking orchestra leader named Huckleberry Haines. The show's conflict, mild as it is, centers on the question: Will the fullback end up with the Russian princess or his college sweetheart?

Gordon went to Kern and told him he believed their search for a Huckleberry Haines had ended. "What are you trying to do, Max—palm off one of your old vaudevillians on me?" Kern asked tartly.

"Okay, okay," countered Gordon, "we don't have anyone for the part. Let's go over there this afternoon and you decide."

Gordon and Kern sat in the back of the Palace watching Hope work, and then went around backstage. Gordon let Kern ask Hope if he would accept the part, and Hope didn't hesitate.

Hope enjoyed the elegant company. The legendary British star Fay Templeton had been coaxed out of retirement to play Madame Roberta. The singer Tamara, highly publicized after being discovered entertaining in a tiny Russian café on Fourteenth Street, was hired to play the dress designer. She was given the show-stopping song "Smoke Gets in Your Eyes." George Murphy, who had scored in Heywood Broun's *Shoot the Works*, was hired to play the fullback, but early in rehearsals was replaced by the juvenile actor Ray Middleton, who had a better physique. Murphy took the smaller part of Haines's manager. In other small parts were the suave Sydney Greenstreet, handsome Fred MacMurray, and rubber-faced Imogene Coca. And in the pit orchestra, well hidden from view, was the drummer Gene Krupa, who was receiving nightly lessons in reading music from a trombonist named Glenn Miller.

From the earliest rehearsals Hope thought the book too melodramatic for musical comedy. Because it lacked any true humorous moments, and laughs must emanate from carefully placed comedy lines, Hope tried wherever he could to hone a ragged line into a sharper edge, clearing every change through Otto Harbach.

"There was one line I really wanted to insert that everybody thought was too much,. . . " says Hope. "In fact, so much so we shouldn't even discuss it with Otto. You see, the big moment in the show was when Tamara sings 'Smoke Gets in Your Eyes' to me. I'm sitting there. . . . I light a cigarette and watch her. . . . I'm listening to her tell me she's in love with Ray Middleton, but it's not going anywhere. She leads up to the song by saying, 'There's an old Russian proverb: 'When you're heart's on fire smoke gets in your eyes.' And I wanted to say, 'We have a proverb in America, too: Love is like hash. You have to have confidence in it to enjoy it.'"

Harbach didn't like the line, feeling it would disrupt the beautiful ballad coming up. So Hope reluctantly dropped the idea.

The musical was expensive, with costs running around $115,000. Though it was decorative, Gordon felt it was not impressive enough, but Kern was overall supervisor of the show and he was calling the shots. It offered many lavish numbers, yet when the show tried out in Philadelphia it looked patchy. Opening-night reviews were sufficiently bad to convince Kern their show needed an overhaul.

Max called the writer and director Hassard Short in New York, and Short agreed to do the necessary rewriting and redirecting, under the condition that both Kern and Harbach stay out of his way.

Short arrived in Philadelphia the next morning with a mink-lined coat thrown over his shoulder and said he was ready. Almost at once he redesigned the sets and ordered new costumes. He speeded up the action and advised Hope to "do whatever you can think of to get laughs. It's deadly."

Hope, encouraged by that, found a place in the show for the gag "Long dresses don't bother me—I've got a good memory," and still wanted to use the hash gag in his scene with Tamara. One night in Philadelphia, Hope talked about the joke to Kern and said he would like to try it. Harbach was not around and Kern said, "Why not?"

"So I put it in," says Hope, "and I was right, because it pulled one of the biggest—no, the biggest laugh in the show. It served as a release in a dramatic scene. And pretty soon Otto heard about it and was nice enough to say the joke was successful and that he had been wrong."

In all, Short's reconstruction work was miraculous. Gerald Boardman, a historian of Broadway, writes, "[Short] created a mounting of such visual beauty that many of the libretto's languors were handsomely glossed over."

By this time Hope knew that his mother was dying. He managed to telephone her several times a week, and every third week he would make a trip to her bedside. He drove his shiny Pierce-Arrow all night to arrive in Cleveland Sunday morning before noon and spend a few hours talking to her and his dad and brothers. Then he would drive back Sunday night, rehearsing lines, singing songs, whatever it took to keep himself awake.

Roberta, the new title for the show, opened at Manhattan's Amsterdam Theater on Saturday, November 18, 1933. It was definitely not a smash hit. Most reviews were divided between "nice" and "forget it!" Brooks Atkinson of *The New York Times* wrote, "The humors of *Roberta* are no great shakes and are smugly declaimed by Bob Hope, who insists on being the life of the party and who would be more amusing if he were Fred Allen." But Percy Hammond of the *Herald-Tribune*, describing Hope as an "airy sort of a chap" and "a quizzical cut-up," approved his comedy style. The influential Robert Benchley, writing in *The New Yorker*, didn't help box-office receipts when he quipped, "Its bad points are so distracting that it turns out to be one of those praiseworthy musicals during which one is constantly looking at one's program to see how much more of it there is going to be." But despite the reviews the show had a cumulative growth and finally became the second-longest-running production of the year. *Roberta* would be turned into a successful Hollywood film, not once but twice: in 1935 with the same title, starring Fred Astaire and Ginger Rogers, and in 1952 with the title *Lovely to Look At*, starring Kathryn Grayson and Howard Keel. Hope himself would stage the show twice for television.

One night during the run of *Roberta*, Richy Craig appeared backstage, ashen-faced and a bit shaky.

"Are you okay, Richy?" Hope asked.

"I'm fine. Really I'm fine. I need your help."

"Anything. What is it?"

"It's our pal, Miltie."

"Berle?"

"Yes, Berle. You know how I feel about his stealing gags. Well, I think I've found a way to cure him. Next Sunday night, there are four benefits—big ones—here in town and I want you to do them with me."

"Four? Come on, Richy, even I—Bobby the benefit nut—try to draw the line at three."

"I've seen you do five! Now, listen—don't ask how I did it, but I have in my possession just about all of Berle's current act. Berle is scheduled to do these same benefits Sunday night and I know the order in which he plans to do them. I want us to get on the bill early enough at each one and 'do' Berle's act before he gets there and when he follows us, he'll die."

Hope fell down laughing at the idea and agreed, although the more he observed Richy's pallor the more he worried.

That Sunday night Hope and Craig got an early spot on the Level Club benefit, did Berle's jokes, and grabbed a cab for the Waldorf-Astoria to do the second benefit. Berle arrived at the Level Club, got his cue to go on, did his jokes and bombed. Berle was stunned.

At the Waldorf-Astoria, Berle came in and stood around for a few minutes and then the stage manager gave him the signal to go on. The same thing happened. When he came offstage, he said to the stage manager, "I don't get this at all. Something stinks and I don't think it's me." One of Berle's pals came up to him. "Hope and Craig were here ahead of you doing your stuff and then said to the audience, 'Don't tell Berle we were here. Let him bomb!' and they ran out."

Berle then switched his schedule for the next two benefits. He took a fast cab uptown to the Nordacs Club for the retarded children's benefit and did his act plus all he could remember from both Hope's and Craig's material. Then he tipped off the audience to what they had going.

When Hope and Craig arrived at the Nordacs, they did their act and bombed. They were still pitching when Berle walked out onstage and said, "I finally caught you—you sons of bitches." Before they left the stage, the comic Jack Osterman came up from the audience and added a few more jokes, one of which was a put-down of Craig. He cracked, "What did you do before you died?" It brought a big laugh.

A few weeks later, Richy could no longer hide the fact that his tuberculosis had returned. But this time he wouldn't give in. One night after his fourth show at the Palace, he sat in his dressing room coughing blood. Berle came in and found him. While Richy was rushed to the hospital, Berle went out on the Palace stage and did Richy's act in the fifth spot. Craig died three days later.

Hope and Berle organized a benefit in Craig's memory for his widow, Hope, who was deeply touched when she handed him her husband's old joke books. "That was some night," he later said. "We got everybody in town to appear. It was really something—Eddie Cantor, Ted Lewis, Pat Rooney, the Ritz Brothers, Martha Raye—forty acts. Richy would have loved it!"

10

Inspiration Point

"From then on I was at the Vogue every night, waiting to take Dolores home. I must have given the doorman at her apartment hundreds of dollars in tips to let me park in front of the joint and sit there with her. . . . It was our Inspiration Point, our Flirtation Walk. . . there in front of the Delmonico on Ninth Avenue."

No period in Hope's life was probably more packed with emotional highs and lows than the last months of 1933 and first months of 1934. For openers, he had *Roberta*. He was working with giants in a show that was tuneful and attractive if not the dazzling hit the critics had expected of Jerome Kern. And even though the show's first weeks in New York were shaky (Max Gordon had twice asked the cast to take salary cuts), Bob was making more money than ever before.

He could even afford to hire a chauffeur for his Pierce-Arrow. He bought a Scotch terrier and named him Huck. He reveled in the fact that he was occupying the legendary Marilyn Miller's old dressing room at the New Amsterdam. Now that Louise had gone back to Chicago for good, he reveled even more in the number of showgirls that Huck, his Pierce-Arrow, and his unfailing seductive approaches could deliver to his Central Park West apartment.

Still, there was an undeniable feeling of sadness that he wasn't fully able to comprehend. With his marriage to Louise over, he felt lonesome when he watched happy couples like George and Julie Murphy. He was feeling that way the night George, Julie, and their friend Bobby Maxwell invited him to join them for an after-show drink at the Vogue Club on Fifty-seventh Street. The Vogue had been put on the map by Bea Lillie, and on this particular night, December 21, a singer named Dolores Reade was appearing there.

Dolores Reade had a Libby Holman–Marian Harris type of voice, low and husky. When they walked into the club she was singing "It's Only a Paper Moon." Hope liked what he saw and heard immediately. She was tall and graceful with the studied poise of a fashion model. He learned that she had been dating Bobby Maxwell on and off. She ended the set with "Did You Ever See a Dream Walking?" and came over to their table.

Up close she was both livelier and more beautiful than she had been in stage light, and Bob was intrigued. They all agreed to go dancing at the Ha Ha Club. When they got there, George and Julie danced. Bobby Maxwell disappeared completely. Dolores and Bob made small talk. "I hadn't caught his name and wasn't the least interested," she would later say, "but to make conversation I asked him if he wanted to dance. 'No,' he said, 'I don't like to dance.' I thought that was odd—especially because I figured he was a pal of Murph's and was in his show, and maybe even a chorus boy."

"But when he said he didn't want to dance that was all right with me, too. But then George and his wife came back to the table and George asked me to dance. We danced around the room just once when Bob cut in, saying, 'I've changed my mind.' I was so astonished that for the first time I took a good look at him. I saw a very young and, at that moment, a very serious fellow—but then and there, I knew I liked him."

They ended up at Reuben's for a sandwich at about two in the morning. By this time Bob was aware that Dolores was something different. He knew he wanted to see her again and he asked her to come to *Roberta*. She picked a Wednesday matinée, two days after Christmas. Bob left tickets for her at the New Amsterdam box office.

Bob went to Cleveland for Christmas. The Hopes felt it might be the last Christmas for Avis, whose condition had deteriorated in the past few months. Bob knew that Dolores had made an impression on him when he found himself describing her in response to questions about his marital status. These kinds of questions coming from his brothers were natural, since Ivor, Jim, and Jack were already working on second or third marriages.

When Bob rushed back to New York the day after Christmas, he was thinking about seeing Dolores backstage after the matinée. He had failed to describe his leading role in *Roberta* on purpose because he wanted her to be surprised. Dolores said later, "When I got home that morning after spending those first few hours with Bob, I told my mother that I had met my future husband. Being accustomed to my crazy outbursts, she casually asked me who he was. I turned to her and confessed I didn't really know—probably just a chorus boy."

Dolores came to *Roberta* with a friend, and when it was over she declined to go backstage. Bob was mystified. Two days later he couldn't bear not knowing why, so he went back to the Vogue.

"What happened?"

"I didn't come back because I wasn't aware you had such a big part in the show—I mean, I ought to have known. I thought you were in the chorus," she said sheepishly. "I'm embarrassed."

Bob waited until she finished her show and they went out for a drink. "What are you doing New Year's Eve?"

"Working," she replied. "You?"

"Same. How about after?"

She nodded and smiled. They sat outside the Delmonico on Ninth Avenue, where Dolores lived with her mother in an apartment short on privacy. Besides, Dolores's mother, Theresa Kelly DeFina, had vowed she would raise her two daughters in a careful Irish Catholic fashion and live to see them married to good Irish Catholic men. The men whom Dolores and her sister, Mildred, brought home seldom were good enough. To Theresa this "chorus boy" was no exception.

Dolores felt that she needed to put some time and distance between herself and Hope. Her hesitancy about their deepening relationship was supported by her mother, who insisted on accompanying her to Florida on January 14 for a singing engagement at Miami's Embassy Club.

Dolores and Bob talked to each other for hours by long-distance telephone, and during one of these calls confessed their love for each other. During another call Bob mentioned marriage, and Dolores offered to break her Embassy Club contract.

But before that could be decided, on Sunday, January 22, 1934, Avis died, and Bob went to Cleveland. His mother's death was both a blow and a relief. He had watched her waste away, and near the end he knew it could only be a continuous series of injections and pills to deaden the pain. She had shrunk to 75 pounds. In her helplessness she no longer represented the indomitable Mahm he knew, his best girl, his biggest booster.

It was Avis who had stood up for him against his dad or his brothers when he quit well-paying jobs because they interfered with his plans for a show business career. It was Avis who wrote letters of encouragement when he was starving in Chicago. He was glad she would not be in pain any longer.

As for Harry, he was devastated. Bob had to return quickly to New York after the funeral, and he had to trust that his brothers would look after their dad.

Lonely and drained of energy, Bob called Dolores in Miami and proposed to her. She reassured him of their love by canceling the second-month option at the Embassy to come home, and she arrived back in Manhattan February 14.

In Hope's 1954 autobiography *Have Tux, Will Travel,* the comedian and his cowriter, Pete Martin, tell their readers that Bob and Dolores went to Erie, Pennsylvania, to be married on February 19, and since 1935, the Hopes have celebrated their wedding anniversary on that date. Fact and myth about the wedding date and location seem to intermingle when it comes to circumstances that are both reported and recollected by family and friends. When the Hopes are asked about the discrepancies, Bob says, "Ask Dolores," and to the same questions Dolores responds, "Ask Bob."

But common sense leads one to suspect that the following scenario played out: During the next six months, from March until August, Theresa waged an unrelenting campaign against the idea of Dolores and Bob's marriage. The gossip columnists were busy too. One item pointed out that Bob's heart belonged to "someone else" (presumably Louise) and that he was not available. Dolores raised this issue of "someone else" and Bob insisted it was nonsense. Dolores was mollified but Hope made a trip to Erie to make certain his marriage to Louise had been annulled.

During the spring and early summer of 1934 Hope continued in *Roberta*, continued to sit in front of the Delmonico with Dolores, continued making wedding plans despite Theresa's resolute objections, and watched his professional life take a couple of important turns. For one, he acquired (or was acquired by) a top-flight agent, Louis Shurr, who had been watching him at the Capitol, the Palace, and onstage as Huck Haines and saw big dollar signs in this young comedian's future.

Shurr handled clients like Bert Lahr, Victor Moore, Lou Holtz, William Gaxton, Ken Murray, and a variety of newcomers, including the actor and dancer George Murphy. Shurr was one of New York's more colorful figures, a shortish (five-foot-five) beak-nosed go-getter who drove around in a chauffeured limousine accompanied by one or another leggy showgirl who would be wearing a mink coat that Louis lent to all his dates.

Shurr was dubbed Doc by his Times Square clients and friends because he had been successful in "saving" a few troubled Broadway shows during their out-of-town tryouts. Currently Shurr was vigorously touting George Murphy for a film contract and he had the personal conviction that Hope, too, would ultimately make it in the movies.

Hope, however, besides sharing the general Broadway snobbery toward Hollywood, still tasted bitter gall over his 1930 screen test for Pathé. And he didn't need Hollywood's money. Between his *Roberta* salary and his radio guest spots he was able to save $500 a week. So he was lukewarm when Doc Shurr said he was trying to land him the part of Huckleberry Haines in the already announced film version of *Roberta*. Although Bob was rejected for that part, which went to Fred Astaire, Shurr did manage to get him an offer from RKO for a featured role in a picture starring the comedian Jack Oakie. The producers demanded a screen test and Bob reluctantly agreed because it could be made in New York. When Dolores came out of the screening room after viewing the test, she said she thought Bob looked like a turtle.

In March Hope did agree to an offer from Educational Pictures in Astoria, Long Island, to make a musical short with big band vocalists Leah Ray called *Jumping Beans*. The deal would be extended to five more shorts if the first one clicked.

Hope was stricken when he saw himself in *Jumping Beans* at the Rialto on Broadway. He was embarrassed at the way he and Leah cavorted about the set after consuming Mexican jumping beans. Slinking out of the theater, Hope bumped into Walter Winchell, who asked how he liked his film debut. Hope cracked, "When they catch Dillinger, they're going to make him sit through it twice."

Winchell, whose daily column was a rat-a-tat-tat firing line of gags and one-liners, used Hope's wisecrack the next day. Jack Skirball of Educational Pictures phoned Doc Shurr and screamed, "We're having enough trouble selling that guy without him knocking the picture. He's fired!" Shurr phoned Hope and scolded him. Hope in turn called Winchell and begged for a retraction but Winchell refused.

A week or so later, Shurr had another screen offer for Hope, this time from Warner Bros., who wanted Hope to appear with Dorothy Stone in an abridged version of Cole Porter's 1929 Broadway musical, *Fifty Million Frenchmen*. It was to be called *Paree, Paree* and would be shot entirely at Warner Bros.'s Eastern Studios on Avenue M in Brooklyn, using the new Vitaphone sound technology Warners had used to make its 1927 hit *The Jazz Singer*. Hope managed to keep his mouth shut when the studio screened it, and Warners was pleased enough with his performance to pick up his option for five more short comedies to be made at Eastern during the next two years.

Hope was beginning to appreciate the power of film. He had a new taste of the medium and it was not so bitter. Besides, he watched enviously as two of his fellow players in *Roberta* packed off to the West Coast with movie contracts. The first was the amiable Fred MacMurray, who had borrowed Hope's black silk topper to go with his rented tuxedo for a Paramount screen test in New York. Weeks later, MacMurray was in Hollywood costarring with Claudette Colbert in *The Gilded Lily*.

Hope was trading stories with some actors in Doc Shurr's Times Square office the day Shurr told George Murphy to start packing so he could pick up a Columbia Pictures contract in Hollywood. Hope looked at Murphy and rather pleadingly at Shurr as he said, "Murph, if it can happen to you and Fred, maybe it can happen to me."

11

Say When!

*"I stroked her arm . . . I nibbled it gently . . . Then I hugged her
. . . She did another half-chorus and I lay down on my back and looked
at her adoringly. If it hadn't been so obvious to the onlookers that we
were really in love, the act would have fallen flat."*

Hope's *Roberta* contract expired in June, and to avoid going on the road with the
show he decided not to sign another agreement. As it turned out, the show lasted
only another two months and closed in New York. But it proved a milestone in
Hope's career. He was now a genuine Broadway headliner—without an immediate offer, to be sure, but with talents that Louis Shurr believed to be highly marketable.

Assured by Doc Shurr that by late summer 1934 there could be another
Broadway show in the offing, Bob asked the Loew's booking office (Loew's Inc.
had purchased B. F. Keith) to set up an eastern cities vaudeville tour for himself
and Dolores for the summer. Her mother sent up a howling objection: "Not without a chaperone, you don't." But Dolores countered with an assurance that she
was a lady and went on planning to go.

Hope set out to create an entirely new comedy act. His old one had been given
to a young, struggling comic named Lew Parker, and Parker was doing well with
it. In gratitude, Parker introduced Hope to a pair of young gagsters, Lester White
and Fred Molina, who were fresh from writing variety shows at New York
University. Hope liked their bright, contemporary college humor and asked them
to write him a touring vehicle. (White would still be writing for him 40 years
later.)

Hope created his fiancée's material himself. After finishing the monologue, he
would introduce Dolores and she would come onstage and sing one song. During
the applause for her number, Hope would wander back on, letting her begin her
second song. Then he moved closer and looked her over appreciatively. He would
look at the audience and let them feel his lovesick pleasure. When Dolores continued, still relatively unshaken, Bob would stroke her arm and examine it lust-
fully. He would even bite her playfully, inviting audience giggles. Then he would
hug her and that would break her up. Hope would say, resting his head on her
shoulder, "Don't let me bother you. Just keep right on."

Dolores would restore her dignity and begin again, but this time Hope would
lie down on the stage in front of her, relishing every movement she made. By then

the audience was enjoying it as much as Hope but, as he points out, only because the clowning was done in the spirit of two people in love. "That was an exciting and challenging experience," recalls Dolores. "What he expected was perfection. He never let down for a moment onstage and heaven help me if I did!

"I simply had to go out there every show and pitch. Hard. We did six and seven shows a day. Sometimes my mind would wander and that was fatal. Bob would get very angry and right there in the middle of the act, he'd crack, 'What's the matter with you, tired?'"

That particular Loew's tour lasted about ten weeks and went as far south as Washington, then hit Baltimore, Wilmington, and Philadelphia before going into New Jersey, Connecticut, and finally Boston. The freshness and satiric bite of the material White and Molina had turned out for him was not lost on critics and audiences—or other comedians, for that matter. Doc Shurr telephoned Hope in Hartford to tell him the successful actor-singer Harry Richman wanted him for his new Broadway musical, *Say When*.

In early August Dolores and Bob came into Manhattan to do their show at the Capitol Theater and also to officially announce their engagement. This item appeared in the August 4, 1934, *New York Herald Tribune*:

BOB HOPE TO WED MISS READE

Bob Hope, who played a comedy lead in *Roberta* last season, and Miss Dolores Reade, a nightclub singer, announced their engagement yesterday. They will be married about Thanksgiving. Both are appearing in the stage show at the Capitol Theater. Mr. Hope has also appeared in *Ballyhoo of 1932* and in vaudeville.

Dolores went apartment hunting and Hope began his huddles with the librettist Jack McGowan and the composer Ray Henderson, who were producing the new Harry Richman musical, *Say When*.

It was about two radio entertainers (Richman and Hope) who meet a wealthy banker's two daughters (Betty Dell and Linda Hopkins) on a transatlantic liner and fall in love. The rich banker objects to having show business sons-in-law until the entertainers find that there is a stray blonde in the banker's life.

Richman, a true superstar of the 1930s, was the one who had picked Hope as his costar and he had put $50,000 of his own money into the show on the condition that Hope appear in it. Richman's regard for Hope never faltered, even when he realized that Hope had most of the best lines. It was the songs that troubled him. "The book was very good but the music only mediocre," lamented Richman. "When I tried to get it changed, I discovered to my surprise that I couldn't change a note without the author's [McGowan's] consent, and he wouldn't give it."

Actually, Richman seemed to be the only one suffering. Henderson and McGowan were enthusiastic and confident of their star's performance. They even had a notorious backer who attended rehearsals faithfully and seemed content with the progress of his investment. His omnipresence intrigued Hope, until one day he asked Richman who the man was. "That's Lucky Luciano," said Richman. Hope didn't ask any more questions but wasn't sure he liked working for a gangster.

With tryouts set for Boston, the Loew booking office asked Dolores whether she'd like to do a single (one-person performance) at Boston's Loew's State during the *Say When* run. She hesitated. A nightclub single was one thing, but doing a proscenium-stage act without Bob scared her. But she put together a few songs, packed what she hoped were the right clothes, and prayed.

Bob spent most of his first days in Boston ironing out wrinkles in his part and sleeping-in mornings. In fact, he was still asleep when his bedside phone rang. It was Dolores. "Come over here," she said, half crying. "This is a mess. It didn't work. They didn't like me. The band was too loud and the lights were awful. It was *all* wrong."

Hope dressed and raced to Loew's State in time for her second show. She was right. The best part was her voice, and that was partially drowned out by a loud band. Hope played tough manager, demanding a magenta spot for her dress, a pin spot for her face, and a mute for the orchestra and suggested some simple staging. Dolores took notes. This mustn't happen again.

Things at *Say When* were also smoothing out except in Richman's head. He knew he was supposed to be the show's strongest element and was afraid it wasn't working out that way. When the show left Boston on Sunday, November 7, for the New York opening at the Imperial the next night, Richman was still scrapping with Henderson and McGowan about writing him a hit song. On the train that Sunday afternoon, Richman asked Hope to share a bottle of champagne in his drawing room. Hope believed Richman intended to suggest a switch that would beef up his part and weaken Hope's. But instead the veteran showman praised Hope's singing voice and timing, apologizing for his own inability to generate excitement. "I'm the star of this thing, Bob, but if I'm weak, it won't help any of us."

Yet opening-night reviews were the sort box-office managers fall on their knees for. Brooks Atkinson of *The New York Times* said the offering at the Imperial was a "lively show made to order for the itinerant trade of the Great White Way." John Anderson in the *Evening Journal* called it a "daffy and hilarious show"; Robert Benchley of *The New Yorker* called it "a real musical comedy"; and Walter Winchell, writing in the *Mirror,* put the cherry on top with "merriest laugh, song and girl show in town."

Was there a better time than this to get married? reasoned Bob and Dolores. This had to be the best time—they were deeply in love, they envisioned an autumn wedding, and besides, some of their closest friends just happened to be in town. Bob and Dolores have always been private about the details of their nuptials. But Milton Berle, who is quoted as having been an invited guest, says he recalls that it took place on a November afternoon in a small Catholic chapel in midtown Manhattan and that Fred MacMurray and George and Julie Murphy attended. Berle added that it was a very happy day.

But it was not happy days for Harry Richman. Despite rave reviews, he still wanted to improve his part. By now, Henderson and McGowan had become convinced that the show needed only a more cooperative star, not new material. The show was a critical hit, so from the producers' point of view there was no reason to make changes; even the least savant of theater touts would bet that *Say When* would be in black figures within three months.

Finally Richman gave up trying to doctor the show's book and score. But he told Hope, "If I can't be happy this show is doomed." The producers were in a squeeze. Richman had the controlling share of money behind the show, so they had to try to please him. Another factor in the show's future was that on November 21 a musical opened down the street at the Alvin that boasted a tuneful score by Cole Porter and a talent-heavy marquee that included Ethel Merman and the two popular stars William Gaxton and Victor Moore. Audience excitement and glowing reviews touted it not only as the hit of the season but as the fourth biggest show of the decade. The show was *Anything Goes*, written by Russel Crouse and Howard Lindsay and directed by Lindsay. Not that there wasn't room for more than one smash musical on the boards. But *Say When*'s star fire had gone out and the cast knew it. Richman pulled rank and after eight weeks gave two weeks' notice.

Hope was not caught off-guard by this move, as Richman had kept his costar informed of his every intention. So Hope urged Shurr to find him a big Christmas present to make him forget the demise of *Say When*. Shurr responded almost immediately with an audition for a spot as emcee of Bromo-Seltzer's radio show *Intimate Revue*, which starred Jane Froman and James Melton and featured Al Goodman's orchestra.

Hope panicked because he needed a fresh monologue for the audition. Once again it was Richman who stepped in. He invited Hope to his famous Beech Hurst, Long Island, estate, opened the elegant bookcase coverings on his extensive joke files, including innumerable radio scripts, and told him to take his pick of the material. Hope took about a dozen or so scripts and was quoted for years afterward as saying, "Harry Richman was the guy responsible for my success in radio." As for Richman, he decided to go to Florida to try something else. He did return to Broadway a decade later in *New Priorities of 1943*, a vaudeville melange that closed after 54 shows.

Bob and Dolores finally got a kind of honeymoon when Hope was asked if they would like an all-expenses-paid cruise to Bermuda in exchange for his entertaining the passengers one evening aboard the ship. Hope agreed but stipulated that he was not to be introduced as a working guest. "I don't want the people on the boat to think I'm singing for my trip." When he was introduced he stood up and said, "I'd like to do a little something to entertain you but I have a sore throat." It was supposed to be a gag but nobody laughed. Hope could see from the captain's dark demeanor that he might consider throwing Hope overboard—so he quickly did a 20-minute show.

Hope's audition for the Bromo-Seltzer show was December 21, and it was clear to the sponsors that the live audience liked him. The laugh arrow kept kicking to the right side of the meter. He was signed and his first regular show was January 4; *Variety* reviewed the show on January 15, 1935:

> Hope is intermittently very funny. At other times either his material falters or his delivery is a bit too lackadaisical. In general Hope should avoid too much nonchalance. It's a luxury not allowed by radio. He must work to put himself and his stuff over, as the poker face mugging that means something on the rostrum doesn't percolate through the cosmos. Hope is easy to take but hard to remember. His problem then is one of emphasis. A good central idea rather than reliance on kidding the announcer and the patter of bright persiflage would hold more weight.

Hope himself was not entirely comfortable about what he was doing in the early Bromo-Seltzer shows. But there was an idea growing in his mind that he hoped would add variety to his radio personality. He decided he needed another foil, a Louise for radio. Dolores was not suited for the role, and besides, she didn't want to do it. At Doc Shurr's office one day Hope met a winsome young Southern girl named Patricia Wilder, a runaway from Macon, Georgia. She was a perky honey blonde with a quick, natural wit, and Hope thought she would be a perfect partner.

She was nicknamed Honey Chile, largely because of her accent, which Hope described as "thick spoonbread," and possibly because of her hair color. Shurr had set up a Capitol Theater engagement for Hope early in the new year, and this proved an ideal time to give Honey Chile a trial run before a theater audience. "I took her on for a couple of tryout shows," Bob said. "I was worried about the possibility of her having stage fright—until she walked out in front of her first Capitol audience and said, 'Pahdon me, Mistah Hope. Does the Greyhound bus stop heah?' and instead of looking at me, she looked at the audience knowingly and smiled. I knew then that Honey Chile was born unembarrassed."

12

The Fabulous Follies

"When I began to warble this ditty to Eve, she walked away from me and I followed her, sang another eight bars, leaned over her shoulder and breathed deeply with unrequited passion. When I looked into Eve's eyes and sang, 'I can't get started,' the people couldn't believe it. The first four rows could hear my motor running."

Hope had known from his early days in vaudeville that his comedy could benefit from having a female foil appear onstage as part of his act. She acted in a sense as a jester, pulling the rug from under his feet. He was impressed with the huge success George Burns enjoyed when he added what vaudeville called the "dumb Dora" antics of his wife, Gracie, to his act. Ultimately, all the successful radio comedians had female partners for getting laughs—Jack Benny had his wife, Mary; Fred Allen had Portland; Fibber McGee had Molly.

What made the sixteen-year-old Patricia Wilder different from Louise Troxell or even Gracie Allen was clearly her thick Georgia accent and the deft way she handled her innocence and her sweet look. The Honey Chile character was such a hit that she was written into the *Intimate Revue* scripts. The routines were simple, but Hope discovered that it wasn't what she said; it was much more *how* she said it:

HOPE: You know, Honey Chile, there's a lot of comedians on the air. Why did you pick me as your partner?

HONEY: 'Cause I had a fight with my folks and I wanted to do something to disgrace 'em.

HOPE: Uh-huh, you probably picked the right party. . .

HONEY: You know, Mr. Hope, I've got two brothers at home that I'm sure would be a big hit on radio—

HOPE: What can they do?

HONEY: The same as you, they just act crazy.

HOPE: Aha. . . What's their names?

HONEY: The oldest is Ed.

HOPE: What's the young 'un's name?

HONEY: Ed. . .

HOPE: Two boys in one family by the name of Ed?

HONEY: Yes. Father always said that two Eds was better than one.

HOPE: Your father said that? What's keeping him off the air?

In spite of publicity, positive critical response, and fan mail, the Hope–Honey Chile exchanges came too late in the series to boost the ratings of a doomed show, and it was broadcast for the last time on April 5, 1935.

During the month that followed, Hope took Dolores and Honey Chile on the road to play a few of the big Loew's movie houses. During that era of entertainment history when vaudeville was scratching and clawing for survival, the act was held over in Chicago!

Their return to New York was Hope's first opportunity to respond to Warners' urgent reminder that he owed them the second Vitaphone comedy short. But when Hope checked in at Eastern Studios on Brooklyn's Avenue M in the early hours of May 10, he was gritting his teeth. By 1935 Hope had established a pattern difficult to break: he was a night owl. He liked staying up until two and three in the morning and then being able to sleep until noon. Unfortunately, film companies traditionally rolled their cameras by the light of day and they started at dawn.

Working for Sam Sax, the studio boss, also wasn't easy. Sax paid his players high salaries but worked them unmercifully so that he could complete a two-reeler in three days. The first of three films that Hope made for Warner Bros. in the middle months of 1935 was called the *Old Grey Mayor*, a farce about the undoing of an eloping couple. The other two were *Watch the Birdie*, in which he played a wise-cracking, practical-joking lover, and *Double Exposure*, in which he played a wise-cracking, practical-joking photographer.

In between and after the Vitaphone shorts, Hope continued to work the Loew's chain with Dolores and Honey Chile. In late summer, Louis Shurr struck a rich vein of gold. He was able to negotiate with Jake Shubert for Hope and another of his clients, Ken Murray, to have leading comedy spots in a new edition of *Ziegfeld Follies*, which was being coproduced by the Shuberts and Lorenz Ziegfeld's widow, Billie Burke.

The undisputed draw for this edition would be Fanny Brice, with John Murray Anderson directing. Anderson hoped to have the show ready for Broadway by mid- or late fall, but casting difficulties, illnesses, and production snags for a show touted as "the most fabulous *Follies* of them all" delayed the schedule by two months. Rehearsals got under way in October, with out-of-town tryouts set for November. However, not until Christmas night, 1935, did the highly publicized show opened at Boston's Opera House.

The rest of the cast was strong: Gertrude Niesen, Josephine Baker, Eve Arden, Judy Canova, Edgar Bergen and Charlie McCarthy, Cherry and June Preisser, Hugh O'Connell, the tap-dancing Nicholas Brothers, and Stan Kavanaugh.

The show was designed by Vincente Minnelli, and he had created what was universally regarded as a tastefully sumptuous production. George Balanchine was making an auspicious debut as choreographer. The show had Ira Gershwin lyrics with added special material by Ogden Nash, Dave Freedman, and Billy Rose, set to music by Vernon Duke. The brothers Shubert, Lee and Jake, beamed with pride and wielded their power throughout the entire affair.

As the show unfolded in Boston, it became clear that it needed pruning. Anderson saw that it was too long on male comedy and too short on good material for his "Funny Lady," Fanny Brice. One of the males would be eliminated. Hope's comedy was thoroughly integrated throughout the evening as he shared the stage first with Brice, then with Niesen, and later with Arden. And he had the show's hit tune, "I Can't Get Started with You." Murray, on the other hand, had just two solo monologues, and the unofficial odds were that Murray would be eliminated.

Lee Shubert drove to Boston for the tryout, and when the curtain fell he went backstage to see Murray. He told him that his act was "dirty" and asked him to change it. Murray was offended. He eventually walked out of the show, but not for that reason. From the start he had been angry about his billing, claiming to have been hired by Lee Shubert to be the lead comic. His agent, Louis Shurr, had set the deal. Interestingly enough, though, Hope also had been hired as the lead comic and his agent also was Louis Shurr. Shurr's explanation to each of his clients must have been classic.

Now the *Follies* began to shape up beautifully. Hope could not have been more content with the month in Boston. He had two important scenes with Fanny Brice, one, "Fawncy, Fawncy," in which they parodied wealthy Britons, and another where he played the director of her enfant-terrible "Baby Snooks" sketch. But Hope's standout scene came with the tall, statuesque, redhead beauty Eve Arden (veteran of an earlier *Follies*) to whom he fervently sang "I Can't Get Started."

In this scene, set on a street corner, Arden was in a stunning evening gown and Hope in evening clothes. He was trying to seduce her, but without success. As he tried to persuade her, she was hailing a cab. Undaunted he sang about his accomplishments as a hero in the Spanish Civil War, as a globe-trotting pilot, as a North Pole explorer, as a consultant to Roosevelt, even as God in *Green Pastures*. Arden remained unmoved. Then Hope desperately grabbed her, embraced her passionately, and slowly she melted. At this, Hope straightened up, adjusted his cuffs, exulting in a conquest, and said, "That's all I wanted to know. Well, good night!"

Hope had other reasons to be jubilant at this time. During rehearsals for *Follies* he had signed on to provide the comedy for a radio series known as the *Atlantic White Flash Program* (Atlantic White Flash was a gasoline brand) with the singing star Frank Parker and Red Nichols and his Five Pennies. Part of Hope's charm for the sponsors was that he was a *Follies* star, and another part of his attraction lay in the prospect of having an additional draw from Hope's much talked about foil, Honey Chile. The sponsors were so enthusiastic that they arranged to send Honey Chile to Boston so that Hope's comedy segments could be inserted into the show from a radio station there during the *Follies* tryout month.

However, Hope's Yuletide gift from Honey Chile was bittersweet. She told him she had just been signed to an exclusive RKO contract and would be leaving for Hollywood in February. Hope was bitterly disappointed. They worked well together and he really liked her. Some Hope insiders have suggested that she was more than a stage foil, but Honey Chile, now in her eighties, denies their relationship was anything more than genuine and mutual affection. "Rumors get started," she says. "How, I don't know. We just did cute things together. He loved me. . . he still loves me. And I love him. And I love his wife, maybe better than I do him."

Hope wired Louis Shurr and asked him to search for a new Honey Chile. Meanwhile, Hope, whose memory has always been unusually accurate about names, places, and faces—especially where attractive women are concerned—remembered a young blonde who had auditioned for the role a year before. She was pretty green-eyed Margaret Johnson, a well-educated Dallas girl whose aspirations included teaching after she earned her master's degree from Baylor University. She was also photogenic and, as it turned out, ambitious.

She was no Patricia Wilder, but she was suitably fey in her reading of the part. Her drawl was genuine, and when the switch took place in late January the transition was smooth.

The saddest part of the Boston tryout was seeing Edgar Bergen and Charlie McCarthy leave the show. Hope and Bergen had become pals and Hope respected Bergen's extraordinary presence with his gagster dummy. But Anderson had to cut a vaudeville act and Bergen was getting less applause than Stan Kavanaugh's juggling.

The *Ziegfeld Follies* 1936 edition opened January 30 at New York's Winter Garden. It was a lavish, elegant, and funny show, and the critics, not surprisingly, cheered Fanny Brice, Gertrude Niesen, Bob Hope, and Eve Arden. They were less enthusiastic about Josephine Baker, whom New Yorkers found too chic and too French. Reviewers raved that this *Follies* was better than the previous Shubert revival. Minnelli, Balanchine, and Anderson had given the *Follies* back its grandeur.

Arden wanted very much to be Fanny Brice's understudy, but the Shuberts claimed it was impossible to understudy a unique performer, one who never missed a show. But Eve had gone ahead and learned the Brice sketches anyway and was a capable comedian. One night, Fanny was too ill to go on and the Shuberts wanted to close down, but Eve argued her case and won.

Then she developed stage fright. She said to Bob, "The only place where I'll panic is the 'Baby Snooks' sketch. What if I blow it?"

"You won't. We'll do what Fanny and I do. When she has any line trouble I just grab her and tussle for a few moments, just long enough to feed her a cue and she's fine. You'll be, too."

Hope's assessment of the legendary Fanny was predictable. He found her magical as an entertainer and troubled as a woman. Despite a reportedly happy marriage to Billy Rose, this forty-something woman seemed lonely, and sadness crept into her joking whenever Bob and Dolores shared a late supper with her.

Brice was plagued by painful arthritis; she also had severe toothaches. Her doctor had prescribed analgesics, but one night before curtain time she had apparently mistaken her sleeping pills for her painkillers. Hope remembers sadly that in the last act of the show she couldn't remember where she was and would start the number over again. "We were all in the wings watching her," he said, "and dying for her because she was such a marvelous woman and such a great star.

"I'm sure each of us was trying to figure out how we could miraculously save her from this. John McManus conducting in the pit tried to get her out of it musically but she was dazed. Fred De Cordova, our stage manager (many years later producer of NBC's *Tonight Show Starring Johnny Carson*) finally had to bring down the curtain. He brought her off quietly and she didn't come back for the finale. I'll never forget seeing her—*her*, floundering and confused."

Brice, like Hope, kept up a killing schedule, and it was increasingly evident that her health was a problem. She was, however, in rare form on a May night in 1936 when New York's richest and most celebrated turned out for a gala marking the thirty-fifth anniversary of the Shubert family's theatrical life. Al Jolson, Sophie Tucker, Jack Benny, Bert Lahr, Ethel Barrymore, Helen Hayes, Katherine Cornell—so many others—performed. Hope was an emcee. Yet scarcely a week later, on May 20, the Shuberts announced that the *Ziegfeld Follies* would close for a vacation, and promised that it would reopen in September, when its star attraction had regained her health.

But Hope didn't mind. His radio status was improving, mostly because he took seriously his job of producing weekly comedy for the *Atlantic Family* (the new name of his show). One reporter marveled at his modus operandi:

Bob has three writers [Lester White, Fred Molina, and Bud Pearson] who work for him. Early on Monday mornings they bring the prepared script to his apartment and the four go over it together. Sometimes it's swell and sometimes it isn't, and when it isn't they often stay up all night Monday and Tuesday trying to rewrite it. They dig into Hope's collection of 80,000 jokes for ideas, they try to rehash old material, to think up new stuff. By Wednesday morning the sponsor must have a copy of the script. By Wednesday night he OK's it or he doesn't OK it. If he doesn't, Bob and his writers work all day and night Thursday rewriting it again. Friday it's rehearsed and changed and shaped up. Saturday it's rehearsed some more. Saturday night it goes on the air, and Monday the whole procedure starts over again.

But meticulous concern over the script wasn't the whole reason for the show's success. Hope's wisdom in featuring the Honey Chile character so prominently, plus a barrage of promotion by the ad agency N. W. Ayer, and an outside press agent were equally important. By the end of April, what had originally been thought of in the trade as the Frank Parker Show was slowly becoming known as the Frank Parker–Bob Hope Saturday Night Show, and some columnists reversed the billing, and some even omitted Parker's name altogether.

When Louis Shurr asked Hope whether he wanted to exercise his option to rejoin the *Follies* when Fanny returned in mid-September, he said no. He did exercise his option to make two more Vitaphone comedy shorts for Warners in Brooklyn, *Calling All Tars* and *Shop Talk*, arguably the best of his two-reelers.

As if working that hard for pay wasn't enough, Hope managed to fill some of his late weeknights and almost all of his Sunday nights with benefits. It didn't matter how many—if he was needed he went. In the May 30, 1936, *Billboard*, Alan Corelli, spokesman for the New York Theater Authority, an association of theater owners and producers, was quoted as saying, "In looking over the 200 benefits of the past season, Willie and Eugene Howard, Howard Hershfield, Rudy Vallee, Bob Hope and Pat Rooney appeared in the greatest number."

During the first week of June it was announced that Frank Parker would desert *Atlantic Family* for Paul Whiteman's radio program, leaving Hope virtually in charge of the store. When the sponsor asked if he would continue through the summer—the time most radio personalities took off for a Hollywood film commitment or to do the state fair route or just to rest—Hope eagerly said yes.

Even with new visibility as the absolute star of the show, Hope was still being plagued by barbs from critics about the quality of his material. The large number of comedians working in radio at the time, all of them depending on a limited number of gag writers and using them at high speed, meant that mediocre material and gag larceny were not uncommon. The *Atlantic Family* had a lower-than-most rating, but Hope was gaining valuable experience for what lay ahead.

13

Red Hot. . . or Not

*"I'm afraid I used to go a little too far clowning. . . in the show. I used
a lot of ad-libs and tomfoolery not in the script. Every three or four days
the stage manager came to me and said: 'Mr. Hope, I wish you'd use
more discretion.'"*

It is probably safe to say that in many minds in 1936 Bob Hope was like the American economy—coming right along. The fact that he was being evaluated so carefully and critically by the media was promising. Although his radio ratings were not threatening to topple Jack Benny or Fred Allen or Burns and Allen, they were higher than those of Fibber McGee and Jimmy Durante. Because he had scored so well in *Say When* and the *Follies*, he was an obvious contender for Broadway roles.

On the home front, things were blissful. Bob and Dolores were still very much in love, and they enjoyed Manhattan living in a spacious Central Park West apartment—with an enormously long green and white living room and a spectacular view of the park and the buildings lining Fifth Avenue beyond— and their Scottie dogs.

Both Bob and Dolores seemed to crave activity. Bob's day was broken up into hours for writing and editing jokes and comedy, playing golf in the summer, and working out at Harold Reilly's gym in the winter. On weekends the couple played 72 holes of golf in Westchester County or Connecticut, and Bob, especially, was becoming remarkably skilled in the sport. He could never get enough of it. Since he first sampled the game in Cleveland back in the 1920s and then got the fever playing with the Diamond Brothers on the Orpheum tour in 1930, he had played on more than a hundred courses around the United States, not to mention Bermuda.

Dolores had been playing since she was a teenager and it was one of the things that sweetened their early romance. She enjoyed golf with or without Bob, and loved playing bridge and entertaining at home. On March 6, 1936, the *New York Journal* said of Dolores:

> She's becoming one of the most popular hostesses among the air crowd; if you're invited to one of the famous Saturday night parties she gives for her bridge-fiend hubby, you've received as coveted an invitation as there is to be had in radio.

She supervised their domestic and social lives as much as Bob allowed, did some charitable work in her Catholic parish, and as often as she was invited to do so, sat in on Bob's writing and rehearsal sessions. Bob would ask her to read aloud sometimes. Although he would frown when she offered suggestions, after she left the room more often than not he would follow her advice.

Late in the spring of 1936, even before *Follies* shut down because of Fanny Brice's illness, Louis Shurr was busily trying to sell to Vinton Freedley, the *Anything Goes* producer, the idea of using Hope in a new musical comedy that bore the title *But Millions!* Already set to star was Ethel Merman. This show was generally expected to be a reunion of the talents responsible for the enormously successful *Anything Goes* (420 performances): Merman, William Gaxton, and Victor Moore, the songwriter Cole Porter, and the writers Howard Lindsay and Russel Crouse. Of course, Lindsay would direct.

Broadway soothsayers and oracles worked overtime trying to predict who actually would be signed for the show. Despite rumors that Gaxton and Moore would star, there were also hints that Jack Haley and Jack Benny were being considered for the two suave comic roles. Merman recalled that Lindsay, Crouse, and Freedley wooed Gaxton by promising him the fattest part, but did not anticipate his arrival at a meeting between them and herself when they were telling her how big *her* part would be. Gaxton listened while Lindsay and Crouse double-talked, then walked out and never came back. As it happened, he had already received a better offer for a bigger part in the musical, *White Horse Inn*.

Early in June, Freedley and Shurr arrived at terms that gave Hope star billing in what would have been the Gaxton role. But the producers were still searching for a low-comedy star. Victor Moore was not being sought, but Jimmy Durante *was*. However, Durante was vacationing on the island of Capri. Freedley attempted several unsatisfactory transatlantic telephone conversations with Jimmy, sent telegrams, and received cryptic replies. Finally, another comedian, Lou Clayton, signed for Durante. Now the only remaining stumbling block was an unsatisfactory book, which carried the new title *Wait for Baby*.

Lindsay and Crouse were credited with rewriting *Anything Goes*, but this would be their first original script together. They did a lot of staring at each other and then some staring away from each other. Finally, Frank Sullivan, a fellow writer, begged them to get away from steamy, sticky Manhattan and take up residence at Saratoga Springs. There they wrote the first act. Inspired, they booked passage on a steamer for Ireland, and in the clear air of shipboard life, they trashed what they had written. Back in New York City they started again, and came up with an incredible script called *Red, Hot, and Blue!* The plot almost defies description, but one observer attempted to characterize it this way:

> Former manicurist, now a millionairess, "Nails" O'Reilley Duquesne (Merman) hires happy ex-con "Policy" Pinkle (Durante) to help her conduct a lottery for charity which she decides to "throw" in favor of her boyfriend, Bob Hale (Hope), who is in love with the memory of a lost childhood sweetheart who branded herself by sitting on a hot waffle iron. (Not your simple little boy-meets-girl plot this!) In the end, "Nails" and her lawyer find true love but not before plenty of burlesque situations and jokes.

Despite the delays in what was a cumbersome book, Cole Porter completed his score and began publicly to extol its virtues. He was particularly pleased with one number called "It's De-lovely," which originally had been written for an MGM film, *Born to Dance*, but had never been used. Porter said the song was inspired during a 1935 trip around the world when at the sight of the Rio de Janeiro harbor at dawn he was impelled to say, "It's delightful." Porter told one reporter that his wife, Linda, was with him and she responded with "It's delicious!" He told another that it was his dear friend Moss Hart who responded with "It's delicious!" In both versions of the story Porter said it was Monty Woolley, standing nearby on deck, who offered "It's de-lovely!"

Delightful to Hope was the fact he would sing the number with Merman and also would be working on the same stage as the incomparable Durante and a few other friends such as Lew Parker, Grace and Paul Hartman, and the very funny Vivian Vance.

Rehearsals were hilarious, according to Hope. And he could only be an amused bystander to the nearly disastrous billing battle that concerned the positioning of star names above the title. Merman had been promised the left-hand position, but then so had Durante. Hope hadn't been promised anything other than star billing, so the standoff was between the steel-throated Ethel and the whisky-voiced Jimmy—or, rather, their agents. Finally, it was Cole Porter who suggested a criss-cross arrangement whereby the billing alternated every other week.

What unnerved Hope during rehearsals was the way the book kept changing. When the show opened in Boston, the notices were barely kind, the chief complaint being that there was too much dialogue. The show lasted three and a half hours, two and a half of which were the first act.

Freedley pressed for a tighter show and asked Porter to write a new Merman song to substitute for one that wasn't working. Cole obliged with the sardonic, bluesy "Down in the Depths on the Ninetieth Floor." But when the music director, Robert Russell Bennett, urged Cole to improve one of the composer's favorite numbers, "Ridin' High," Porter not only resisted haughtily but walked out. He took the train to New York, having bid farewell only to Merman.

Freedley was livid. He implored Porter to return. The cast, struggling with daily book changes and seeing Porter's defection, sniffed disaster. But when the show reached New Haven for an additional tryout week, the critics blamed the score for some of the show's unevenness and Porter relented and returned to work.

Whatever the wrinkles, Hope was unashamedly awed by the outstanding talent he worked with in *Red, Hot, and Blue!* Especially in Durante he recognized a highly skilled artist who took very seriously the business of being an "irresistible vulgarian." Hope recalls one time when Durante missed a cue in Boston: "He walked to the edge of the pit and said, 'Ha-cha-cha' to the orchestra—and then he came back to me, gave me a frustrated look, and slapped his hips. Next he walked over to the wings and said in a loud voice, 'Trow me da book.' No one can blow lines louder and funnier than Jimmy and it broke up the audience. Later I realized that this forgetfulness on Jimmy's part was framed. He's worked it out down to the last frustrated motion."

If Lindsay and Crouse and Freedley were alert to Jimmy's cutting up and word torturing, they were also wary of Hope's ad-libbing. They admired the way he could work in a topical reference, and the way he would punch up a flabby line. But they suspected he might damage the show if he was given a free rein.

Merman had some of those same fears. "Hope would almost rather kid me and break me up and get the chorus girls—or anyone else on the stage—to laughing than. . . make the audience laugh." Hope is quick to admit that where Merman was concerned he may have gone too far. "I probably kidded around with her too much. I was using ad-libs and tomfoolery not in the script."

Merman has been quoted as saying she specifically objected to the way Hope lounged at her feet during their second duet in that show, a love ballad called "You've Got Something." Hope says, "I read that [Merman's opinion] and it simply isn't true. Merman was a great audience—the greatest audience. It was the number—a bad song—it needed some help. It wasn't Merman who got upset, it was Porter. He told the stage manager to tell me to quit clowning and sing it straight."

Red, Hot, and Blue! opened at the Alvin Theater on October 29, 1936, and it was a gala occasion. Everything about it added up to success—its stars, producers, writer, the music. The advance sales alone guaranteed it would be a hit. Cole Porter arrived for the opening with Mary Pickford on one arm and Merle Oberon on the other, and as was his custom at all first nights of his musicals, he laughed heartily at each bright spot as if he were hearing and seeing it for the first time.

Howard Lindsay remained at home in New Jersey taking telephone reports from his wife, Dorothy Stickney, at the Alvin. Russel Crouse paced the lobby. The critics were generous, agreeing it was no reprise of *Anything Goes* but simply a nonsense vehicle for its clowns. So the book was dismissed, and even Porter's music, except for "It's De-lovely," was judged second-rate. Merman and Durante were seen as the show's energy and several critics boldly called it Durante's triumph. Hope was not ignored. Walter Winchell wrote: "Hope is a clever comedian when the material is better than it is at the Alvin," but John Mason Brown wrote, "Hope as a comedian is a cultivated taste that I must admit I have never been able to cultivate." The *Evening Journal's* John Anderson wrote: "Mr. Hope is, as usual, urbane, sleek and nimble of accent. He knows a poor joke when he hides it and he can out-stare more of them."

Raves or pans, what mattered most was that Hope was back on Broadway in an important showcase. He was back in New York where motion picture and showcase deals were set by Hollywood "scouts" and advertising agency executives, and where visibility was the key. By now Hope had all but dropped the pretense of total contempt for Hollywood. He was more than ready. And he also knew that there was hardly a home in the nation without a radio set, and he longed to be invited into every living room in America.

The period when he was performing in *Red, Hot, and Blue!* was to be a crucial regrouping period for his career. He felt constant pressure to locate the right radio format, something different and a packaging that would deliver big-star prominence. He had a fair name already, but he was best known on the radio for dizzy dialogues with Honey Chile and on the screen for "selected short subjects." His best work to date had been his stand-up comedy for Keith and Loew's audiences, and his suave comic portrayals on the Broadway stages.

As 1936 faded into 1937, *Red, Hot, and Blue!* was still doing brisk business. Hope was drawing a four-figure weekly salary, but for the first time in several years his name was less visible on the entertainment pages than it had been. He certainly hadn't slowed his pace, especially when it came to benefits. Of the 125 major benefits that the New York Theater Authority reported for the 1936–37 theatrical season, Hope contributed to over half either as the emcee or as a performer.

Being associated with Durante meant that there was abundant opportunity for benefits. Jimmy was a pushover for any touch. One night some "boys" in Hackensack asked Durante to come across the river and do a few jokes for them at their annual banquet, and Jimmy asked Hope if he'd like to go along. Hope agreed, although Jimmy was not clear—which was characteristically Durante—about who would benefit from their performance.

In front of a nondescript hotel, they piled out and went upstairs and down a long carpeted hallway to a banquet room. The roar of "Jimmmee" and a few calls of "Schnozz" and "Schnozzola" went up, then Durante went to the platform, which held a three-piece band, and launched into his trademark routine, "Who Will Be with You When You're Far Away." Then he sang "Inka Dinka Do," got a big hand, and paused to address his fans.

"Hey," he said, "I want you to meet a guy who's in the show with me—Bob Hope. He's a good friend and I know you're going to like him. Bob—"

Hope jumped up at his name. In the short time he had been waiting for Jimmy to finish he had found out that these tough-faced men were beer salesmen. And he soon found out that they were not laughing at his sophisticated stand-up material with its double meanings. Hope said later, "I went over with a hush and I thought *I've done my part.* So I looked around and said, 'Hey, let's bring Jimmy back.' Everybody applauded but Jimmy wasn't there. I looked toward the door. The doorman shrugged and said, 'He went that way.' I said, 'Well, get him, will you?' and to kill time plunged into a golf routine for four or five minutes. 'Now, here's Durante!' Those hard-faced citizens out front applauded again. I looked at the door and the guy standing there says, 'I told you he went down the hall,' and I said 'Fellas, it's been wonderful.'"

Hope waved and went for the door. Out in the hall he looked for Durante, thinking he might have had an emergency call to the men's room. Then he went to the hotel desk and there was told that Jimmy had left some time ago.

On the street Hope found Durante and his pal Harry Donnelly sitting in their big car. They were laughing. "How'd it go up there?"

"I thought this was *your* night. What kind of thing was that, leaving me hanging out like that?"

Durante was nearly choking with laughter. "I didn't figure you'd talk all night." Jimmy enjoyed his joke. It may have been his way of letting Hope know who was the star, or of dulling some of Hope's brass.

Hope didn't appreciate the gag at the time. But when *Red, Hot, and Blue!* had ceased to play to capacity crowds at the Alvin, Paramount persuaded Freedley to close on Broadway and move to Chicago. Except for an opening-night snafu over scenery, the musical was acclaimed by the critics and settled down for what appeared to be a long run.

One night during the first week, once again Durante asked Hope to do a benefit with him, at the Lake Shore Athletic Club. After the curtain calls, at about midnight, they changed and drove over to the club. Everyone in the room sounded
drunk. There were shouts of "Hey Jimmy!" and "Hey Schnozz" and Durante sat
down at the piano and did his showstopper in *Red, Hot, and Blue!* and a joke or
two, and then called for his costar Bob Hope. Bob came out, sized up the crowd,
which was fast nearing a boisterous state, did some snappy lines, and got a good
reception. But suddenly it was déjà vu. At one point he looked over and saw Jimmy
heading for the door, so in a loud voice he said, "Thanks, folks, I've enjoyed this.
But I've been on long enough. Let's bring back Jimmy Durante."

The audience reacted raucously. They applauded and cheered. Durante turned
around just as he was signing an autograph and someone told him he'd just been
reintroduced. He stood there, bowing and blowing kisses.

Hope was still praising him, however. "We can't let him get away without your
favorite number." Now the crowd was on its feet. "How about it, Jimmy?"

Jimmy started back toward the stage. "Jimmy Durante, right here, ladies and
gentlemen!" Jimmy came toward him and Hope was applauding as he said in an
undertone, "Hackensack, you son of a bitch!"

Hope went outside and took a cab back to his hotel. The next day Durante
scrawled YOU ARE A LOUSE on Hope's dressing-room mirror and scattered face
powder around.

This episode notwithstanding, the two men had tremendous respect for each
other, and for roughly forty years they enjoyed any opportunity to work together
that came their way.

14

Laughter in the Air

*"I was doing a Broadway show and vaudeville in between. I saw radio
as promotion—as pure publicity to build an audience for my stage work.
But then the more I got into it I saw the way it was going and it's the
hot thing of the future—and—I really liked the money."*

The closing of *Red, Hot, and Blue!* at Chicago's Civic Opera House on May 3,
1937, only two weeks after its warm critical reception, dismayed its producer but
not its stars. Merman, Durante, and Hope had other fish to fry.

Ethel went off to Hollywood to make the film *Happy Landing* with Sonja
Henie and Don Ameche. Jimmy stayed in Chicago to fulfill a nightclub engagement before doing some radio guest shots. And Hope, having gotten a call from

his agent, Louis Shurr, hurried back to New York to write a comedy script for his audition with the Lennen & Mitchell ad agency to be master of ceremonies and resident comic for the Jergens-Woodbury–sponsored *Rippling Rhythm Revue*. In the golden age of radio broadcasting, the ad agencies exerted major control over both the content and the finances of broadcast production. The show had originally been conceived as purely musical variety, to air over NBC at nine on Sunday nights, but the sponsors had noted that Sunday was fast becoming the comedy circle and they were throwing Hope's hat into the ring.

Hope kept up with developments in radio comedy and he was well aware of what other comedians were doing. The question was: How different could he be? After Louis Shurr's call to him in Chicago, Hope had only five days to create a fresh format. Feeling that his vaudeville background was his strongest asset, he decided to borrow some components from his current stage act.

At the top of the show he wanted to use the heckling stooge idea, so he wrote the following opening. A newsboy calls "Extra! Extra! Read all about it! Hope goes on the Woodbury program—Extra! Extra!" Next, the announcer, Ben Grauer, was to say: "It's the talk of the town! Bob Hope joins Woodbury's *Rippling Rhythm* tonight. Everyone—everywhere—is talking about it—on the streets!"

(*Sounds of traffic*)
FIRST MAN: Hey, Sam—what's your hurry?
SECOND MAN: (*Breathless*) Didn't you hear? Bob Hope's going on the
    Woodbury program tonight. See ya!
FIRST MAN: Where you goin'—rushing home to your radio?
SECOND MAN: No—I'm going to the movies.
(*Drum and cymbal*)
GRAUER: In the homes!
WOMAN: John, what on earth are you doing?
MAN: Haven't you heard? Bob Hope goes on the Woodbury program
    tonight.
(*Crash*)
WOMAN: Why, John, you broke the radio!
MAN: You're telling me!
(*Drum and cymbal*)

After a suitable straight program opening and soap commercial message, Grauer would introduce Hope as that "young comedy star" who will keep the audience "lathered with laughs" with "his new brand of humor." Then Hope would say, "Ben, that 'lathered with laughs'—you've got me washed up already." The new brand of humor was essentially the cluster of jokes Hope used to introduce variety acts—just as he had done so many times in vaudeville. But he was different from the other Sunday night comedy turns. Jack Benny, Fred Allen, Fibber McGee and Molly, Amos and Andy—they had the advantage, or disadvantage, of already having well-entrenched personae or being locked into an ongoing comic situation in which they played their lines. A large measure of Hope's newness to a huge radio audience was the impudence of his manner.

Later in the show he worked with a brand-new Honey Chile, a perky young actress named Clare Hazel from Bennettsville, South Carolina. The sponsor offered two reasons for the disappearance of Margaret Johnson. Her voice was too similar to that of Judy Canova, the star of an NBC radio program immediately preceding *Rippling Rhythm Revue*, and—really more pertinent—Johnson had had an offer from Columbia Pictures.

Some reviewers found Hope labored. But *Variety*, the source most actors believe—and sponsors too—said on May 12, 1937:

> Bob Hope's addition to *Rippling Rhythm* as M.C. and funster appears just what the doctor ordered. Certainly his presence patches those lulls which have been bobbing up of late. Fashion in which Hope maneuvers the program, glibly filling in gaps and introducing numbers, definitely sets him up. Result was one of the swiftest moving *Rippling* stanzas in many weeks. Hope added enough fresh chatter and gags to give entire broadcast a lift.

When it was announced a few weeks later that the Woodbury program had been picked up for another 13 weeks, Hope's spirits soared. Radio, he now believed, was his route to popular success and was exactly where he wanted to be. But he realized he needed an expert to guide him through the fast-growing complexities of this big-business medium. Louis "Doc" Shurr, who had set up his Broadway show and short film deals, was only peripherally involved with the Woodbury contract, and he clearly did not possess sufficient experience and clout with advertising agencies for making radio deals.

"I met a young agent named Jimmy Saphier. I not only got to know him, I liked him. I found him a shrewd boy who knew the business, my kind of guy." Hope sensed Saphier to be both creative and courageous. And he was right.

It was a good match. "I had watched Hope at the Capitol and had seen him in a Broadway musical before I heard him on radio," said Saphier, "and I felt it was a shame the home listeners weren't getting the best of him. Radio simply wasn't using his talents properly. I knew this, and I sensed Bob knew it but didn't yet know how to overcome it. His work with the foil was funny, but his strength seemed to me and also to him—eventually—to be centered in what he did best: the monologue." In fact, Hope predicted, "The monologue shows promise of being a major radio trend."

Hope and Saphier signed an agreement for a one-year period. They never signed another, and their highly profitable association lasted nearly 40 years, until Saphier's sudden death from a brain tumor in 1974. Of course, Hope continued to retain "Doc" Shurr for movie deals, through 51 feature films, until pancreatic cancer killed Shurr in November 1968.

The other area Hope felt deficient in was his public relations. He had noticed how network-radio publicity could result in phenomenal national exposure with a single news item. And one experience in particular suggested strongly to him the value of a press agent in softening a negative story. The incident revolved around Hope's role as first baseman on a softball team that was made up of radio actors and musicians (and press agents) who played exhibition games for charity in Central Park on Sunday afternoons. The games attracted attention, but it was the team effort and the charity—not the individual celebrities—that got the publicity.

One Sunday in June, two days after Hope had signed a contract with Paramount Pictures for his first Hollywood feature, *The Big Broadcast of 1938* (an event that received far less publicity than it deserved), he was feeling pretty cocky and was "cutting up." According to an Associated Press wire story on June 23, 1937:

> Those baseball games are still going on in Central Park. Frank Parker, who started them, hasn't turned up in the last few Sundays, but he has sent his substitute, Bob Hope, to play first base. The guy is always clowning. Last Sunday there was quite a turnout of spectators. Honey Chile, Bob's stooge, was on the sidelines heckling as Hope let the ball go by him. She brought three very charming ladies along, and Bob put on a show for them.
>
> Radio celebrity or not, it didn't make much difference to the rest of the gang who take their baseball seriously. A press agent playing shortstop almost took a poke at Hope for missing a beautiful throw to his position. "Keep your mind off the girls, you lug," he yelled at Bob. "This is a ball game." Hope quieted down.

It was painfully evident that Hope saw the occasion as a perfect opportunity for a spotlight on himself, Honey Chile, and *Rippling Rhythm*. The stunt showed bad judgment. After that story hit news columns and some radio newscasts, Hope became increasingly convinced that he needed an experienced press agent who had some clout, who could minimize any damage to his reputation, who could maximize the attention he felt his Paramount movie deal and his new Honey Chile deserved.

The publicist Hope admired most was Mack Millar, who was handling press for the bandleader Shep Fields, among others. Mack was acquainted with most of the East Coast reporters and columnists who mattered (and, as it turned out, much of the Hollywood press clan, too) and he was especially chummy with the Hearst newspaper chain writers as well as several Hearst executives. He was a tough-talking, softhearted guy who gave as good as he got from the likes of Walter Winchell, Ed Sullivan, and the influential columnist Damon Runyon. Hope knew it would be difficult to entice Mack away from New York to the West Coast, where he needed him, but approached him anyway.

"Shep has been signed for *The Big Broadcast*, Bob," said Mack. "So I'll be out there for a few weeks and if there's anything I can do, I will. In fact, if there's anything I can do for you while you're still in town, let me know."

Not long after that, Hope asked Mack if he could help him publicize his prediction concerning the monologue. A few days later Mack called to say he had set up an interview between Hope and Sam Kaufman of the *New York Sun*. Kaufman was a crack entertainment columnist whose policy was well known among publicists: Sam Kaufman does his interviews *without* press agents in attendance. Hope's interview with Kaufman, which appeared on August 5, 1937, in the *New York Sun*, was a remarkably self-fulfilling prophecy:

"I'm curious about your monologue prediction, Bob—er, do you mind people calling you Bob right away?" Kaufman said, peering through thick steel-rim glasses.

"No—no, that's fine. Well, it won't be totally new because Will Rogers certainly clicked with it on air some years ago. But the monologue is now showing definite signs of being a main comedy trend. The stunt is a takeoff on the old vaudeville days and that, perhaps, is why former stars of variety shows—like myself—can spot early signs of its big radio future."

"Tell me more about a monologue."

"Well, my solo bits are patterned after my stage style. True to vaudeville formula, I attempt to make my topics newsy and seasonal. But I also find that the microphone has certain limitations that are absent from the stage, and I can't, for example, make humorous references to certain events like child marriages and coronations."

"Why not?" Kaufman said as he smiled a broad, gold-toothed smile. "Too timely—too touchy? Sponsors nervous?"

"Frankly—yes."

"Okay. Do you want to say more on that?"

"Frankly—no."

"Oh. . . well. . . uh. . . What else can't you do in radio?"

"See, I've always approached it like I would do the stage. And you can't."

"Didn't Winchell tag you for your mannerisms?"

"Yeah—Winchell said that he would tell me to 'stop that God-awful *hmmmm-ha-ha-hmmmm* noise' I made at the end of each joke. He said, 'It may be funny on the stage but on the air it sounds as if he'd eaten too many green apples.' Do you believe that? So, I've cut out the moans, coughs, and grunt and all the ways that I was trying to convey grimaces—and then the press and audiences seemed to love it."

"What's this controversy about live studio audiences?"

"Well, I've had some doubts. You know *Radio Daily* quoted my question about whether the people at home were getting as much kick out of the program as the people in the studio. It's not difficult to get laughs from your studio audience because you can influence them by your physical personality—but I'm not at all sure the listener is having the same hilarious time, and, after all, it's the listener who pays for the performance."

"Do you need an audience?"

"I do. But I worry about the listener. I work best before an audience. I can feel out a response. Now, maybe an audience wouldn't be right or necessary for some of the situation comedies. But I have to say that comedy and laughs go together."

"He who laughs alone laughs least?" Kaufman suggested, smiling.

"Exactly. Studio laughter can be just as important to the faraway listener as it is to the comedian."

"Then it's good for everybody?" Sam asked.

"Not really. The critics object—they say we clown around for the studio audience and try to break them up and the home audience misses the gag."

"Don't you think that's a fair criticism?"

"Probably—but let me tell you from an entertainer's point of view, it's important to get the feel of audience response while on the air. This is especially true of monologues. The only way you can time a piece of material right is with an audience. Counting their laughs and observing their expressions are both vital to a successful comedy program. I've counted twenty laughs in an average monologue bit. This is important from a production standpoint because it allows us to accurately time the show. I know where to pause to let a joke strike home. If I fail to hesitate at just the right moment, the point of the joke might slip by."

"Do all comedians analyze their style and their comedy production this carefully?"

"I don't know about the rest, but I would bet a guy like Benny—in fact, I *know*—he simply has to consciously make these judgments. He has such fabulous timing. His whole act is timing. And *he* needs a studio audience as well. He gives 'em that look. It's all a matter of eye appeal."

"Explain that."

"Eye appeal may sound silly for a radio show but not really. Take Honey Chile. I've had three of them since the *Intimate Revue*—Patricia Wilder, who got a movie contract out of it; Margaret Johnson, who is also headed for Hollywood; and now Clare Hazel, who does legit stage work all week. She's touring in *Brother Rat* and then flies in here to do our program on Sundays. Each one was picked for looks as well as voice."

"You find looks that important?"

"Yeah, and for two reasons. First, a beautiful girl adds a decorative touch to the studio setting and as I already said I believe in catering to studio audiences. Second, when it comes to publicity and photographs—everyone wants to know what we look like—the program gets a much better break with a pretty girl as a subject."

"One more question. What got you into radio in the first place?"

"Well, as you know I was doing a Broadway show with vaudeville in between. I saw radio as promotion—pure publicity to build audiences for my stage work. But then the more I got into it, and saw the way it was going and it's the hot thing of the future—and. . . I really liked the money."

"One more?"

"Sure. We've got a few more minutes."

"You're going to Hollywood?"

"Yeah. I'm doing it. All my friends tell me it's not going to be as bad as I think."

The door opened and Dolores stepped in. "Is it okay? Are you finished?"

"Not quite. Dolores, this is Sam Kaufman of the *Sun*. My wife Dolores, Sam. She knows how I feel about moving to the Coast. We've always hated the idea of leaving New York. And this may not be permanent—probably won't be. I've only signed up for the one picture—with options if that one works. Sounds good, though—Shirley Ross, Dorothy Lamour, W. C. Fields, and Shep Fields, with our radio band, too. Remember Lamour when she used to sing at Number One Fifth [a New York restaurant-club]? Beautiful girl."

"And Jack Benny."

"No. Benny's out—that's how I got the part."

"Oh," said Kaufman. He peered at Hope. "But what about your radio show? Your thirteen-week contract with Woodbury?"

"My boy Jimmy Saphier has been talking to them. They're thinking about switching the show to Hollywood anyway. And even if they don't, we feel we can work it out so I can continue to do my part long distance—from the NBC studios in Hollywood. It's been done before."

Kaufman stood up to leave. He smiled. "Still playing first base in Central Park?"

"You heard about that, huh?"

"I heard you nearly decked some press agent."

"No, it was the other way around. But, I could have flattened him. It was a celebrity charity game. What do you want? People come out there expecting some high jinks. We're not baseball players, for God's sake—we're entertainers. What's wrong with getting a few laughs?"

Hooray for Hollywood:
1938 to 1941

15

Hollywood, Take Two

"When I stepped off the train in Pasadena, there was no block-long limousine waiting to whisk Dolores and me to a mansion in Bel Air. No dancing starlets with baskets of grapefruit. Not even a redcap with wilted gladiolus."

For many years Hope has joked about what didn't happen when he, Dolores, Doc Shurr, and their two Scottie dogs got off the Super Chief that Thursday, September 9, 1937, in Pasadena. To hear him tell it, their arrival went unnoticed.

Not quite. A Paramount publicist and a photographer from the *Los Angeles Morning News* were there. Dolores picked up the Scottie named Suds to strike a pose with Bob, and the photographer snapped a standard publicity shot of two stylish visitors from the East.

On page 13 of Friday's *Morning News*, a small photo was headlined A COMEDI- AN AND HIS WIFE. The caption indicated that Hope had "never appeared in a major screen feature."

Hope admits that he was still nursing a "log-sized chip" on his shoulder from the 1930 screen-test rebuff. He tartly reminded Shurr that their "seven-year Paramount contract with options" worked both ways. And Shurr was just as quick to give Hope a reality check: What they really had was a one-picture deal with no promises after that either way.

The Hopes checked into the Beverly Wilshire Hotel and although the film was not scheduled to roll until the following Monday, Bob went to the studio that same day to meet the producer, Harlan Thompson, and some others on his staff. Assistant producer Billy Selwyn wanted Hope to hear the duet he and Shirley Ross would be singing in the picture. As they walked over to the music department, Selwyn praised the bouncy tune and the lyric that Leo Robin and Ralph Rainger had written and described the urbane setting. Hope nodded. He had read the script.

The plot of *The Big Broadcast of 1938* was standard silly, involving a transatlantic race between two ultramodern ocean liners, the S.S. *Gigantic* and the S.S. *Colossal*. The drawling W. C. Fields would play the skipper of the S.S. *Gigantic*, with Hope cast as a radio announcer who is emcee for the musical variety shows that take place in the ship's lounge. Hope's character was a stereotype of the ego-ridden entertainer on the make. He has three failed marriages, one of them to Shirley Ross. In their bittersweet duet, "Thanks for the Memory," Shirley and Bob engage in a sophisticated exchange about their past life together.

Hope liked the song instantly and asked if he could borrow a transcription so Dolores could hear it. When he got back to the hotel, Dolores was already upset.

"I don't think I like this town," she said.

"Why? You'll get used to it."

"I went to the beauty parlor today—it was one where everybody goes. The manicurist asked me what I was doing in town and I told her you were in show business and that you were here for *The Big Broadcast*. Then she asked me my name. I told her and she didn't even look up. I repeated 'I'm Mrs. Bob Hope' and she said she never heard of you. I said you were one of Broadway's biggest stars and a radio name as well. I told her to listen Sunday night— "

"That reminds me," interrupted Bob, "did Wilkie Mahoney call?" Mahoney was a gag writer who had been hired to write monologues for Hope's Hollywood inserts to the Woodbury program, which still originated from NBC's Manhattan studios.

"Bob, don't you care?"

"Sure I care, Dolores, but wait until you hear the song they've given me in the picture. I brought it home for you to hear."

From the massive Capehart phonograph in their suite tinkled an up-tempo melody rendered by the studio pianist. "What do you think?"

"This is your solo?" she asked.

"No, I only have a duet with Shirley Ross. It's called 'Thanks for the Memory' and there's a whole scene built around it."

"I don't think it's much."

"I think it's terrific myself," Bob said defensively.

"You know what I'd like?" Dolores said.

"What?"

"To have a good cry."

"Go ahead," Bob said.

Bob spent Sunday rewriting and timing the *Rippling Rhythm Revue* monologue and other comedy bits with Wilkie Mahoney. Hope would be delivering them beginning shortly after six Sunday evening from NBC's Sunset Boulevard and Vine Street studios in Hollywood for inclusion in the nine o'clock New York show.

The next afternoon, he and Dolores went to NBC so that Bob could work with the engineer in timing his comedy to fit the appropriate spots in the show. When the NBC executive who had been assigned to assist him with the inserts finally showed up, Hope asked him what time the audience would be ushered into his studio. He got a blank look from the NBC staffer.

"What audience?" he finally asked.

"For my monologue."

"There isn't going to be any audience."

"*What?* I have to have an audience to bounce my comedy off of or I'm dead. What shows are here today?"

"Bergen's next door."

"What time?"

"Five-thirty to six."

"Perfect!"

Hope went next door where Edgar Bergen with his dummy, Charlie McCarthy, was rehearsing, and at the first break Hope asked if he could steal Bergen's audience. The ventriloquist, once bounced from the *Ziegfeld Follies*, now had *the* top-rated show on Sunday night. He liked Hope and agreed to help. Together they instructed the NBC ushers to set up the velvet rope so that the audience filing out of the Bergen studio would be led blindly like cattle into Hope's adjacent studio.

Once there, the audience was bewildered. Some refused to stay. A few recognized Hope but most were uneasy. Hope stood on the stage saying, "Come on in, folks, and sit down. I'm Bob Hope and I'm going to do a show for New York in a minute or two. It's a very funny show and I think you'll enjoy it." The audience ended up loving it, and for the following two weeks, until the Woodbury series ended, NBC printed tickets and Hope had his own laughers.

Early Monday morning, September 15, Hope reported to Paramount for makeup. After introductions, the makeup expert Wally Westmore invited Hope to sit in the chair and then, like a portrait artist or photographer, studied his nose from every possible angle.

"I can shadow this for you now but if you're smart you ought to think about some surgery."

"What?" Hope flared up. "I've been doing pretty well with this nose up to now."

"All I can tell you is that the camera is going to get a lot closer to you than any audience has so far."

"You never played vaudeville," cracked Hope.

Later that night Dolores reacted violently. "No! They're not going to talk you into it. I love your face the way it is."

"But it might make a difference when it comes time to offer me a better contract."

"Bob, your whole personality is in your face. They want to turn you into just another leading man. No—please don't."

Nevertheless the idea of Bob's bob was kept alive at Paramount by executives who couldn't make up their minds and by Westmore when he saw Hope in the makeup chair each morning.

Another problem was Hope's vaudeville-style line delivery. After each comedy line he would pause for a laugh. "I was merely observing the tried and true theatrical impulse to wait for laughs," Hope observed. "I felt I could shake the habit but it might take time." After a few days, Hope's remarkable self-discipline took over and the pauses disappeared.

Quite understandably, Hope had yet to grasp fully what it would take to transfer his stage personality to the movie screen. Even more critical than his line delivery was his failure to sense the important role of the eyes in creating a credible film performance. Mitchell Leisen, the director, finally decided he should counsel the newcomer.

"You know that Harlan and I saw you in *Follies* and in *Red, Hot, and Blue!* and we liked the way you work. When Benny dropped out on us we both thought you were the only one," Leisen said.

"Thanks, Mitch, I appreciate that. But I must be doing something wrong."

"Not wrong. I want to give you some advice and I hope you remember it. Try to think through your eyes. When you are thinking about what you are going to say, you will alter the muscles of your eyes. All the great movie actors deliver the line with their eyes before they say it with their mouths. Remember that—think the emotion and it will register in your eyes."

Those wise words preceded the filming session in which Hope and Shirley Ross were to sing "Thanks for the Memory." Leisen wanted to try something unusual. Normally, Bob and Shirley would have prerecorded the song and then synchronized their lips to the soundtrack. This time, Leisen ordered the Paramount orchestra moved on to the set, and against the wishes of the composers, Robin and Rainger, he slowed the tempo.

When Hope and Ross finished the scene, both the composers were in tears. One of them said, "We didn't know the song was that good." The crew applauded.

Hope later learned that Dorothy Lamour had been offered the song. She had realized it could result in Hope's making an impression and had generously insisted that he and Shirley do it together.

Hope was grateful that he got on so well with his director—unlike W. C. Fields, who refused to take direction from anyone. He would rewrite his lines and then proceed to do the scene in his own style, which infuriated Leisen.

Fields, who was particular about the company he kept, seemed to like Hope and sometimes invited him to share a dressing-room drink.

"He didn't like too many people," Hope explained, "and he didn't want people around. But he liked me, and I got to know him. He was marvelous. All he ever really wanted to do in the movies was to rework his vaudeville material and make it fit in whatever picture he was making. He'd read a script and tell the producer he could fix it up for $50,000. What he would do was put in business from his vaudeville act, like the golf game he put into *The Big Broadcast.*"

At that time Paramount was a powerhouse of comedy talent, and for Hope to be in the company was both unnerving and challenging. Besides Fields, under contract were very funny entertainers such as George Burns and Gracie Allen, Jack Benny, Ben Blue, Bob Burns, Charles Butterworth, Bea Lillie, Harold Lloyd, Martha Raye, Charlie Ruggles, and Mae West. On the dramatic side were box-office winners Edward Arnold, Lew Ayres, Gary Cooper, Bing Crosby, Robert Cummings, Marlene Dietrich, Dorothy Lamour, Carole Lombard, Ida Lupino,

Fred MacMurray, Ray Milland, Anthony Quinn, George Raft, Shirley Ross, and Randolph Scott.

Being part of an important film factory and only a beginner, so to speak—pending contract renewal—compelled Hope to step up his publicity operation. One day on the *Broadcast* set, Hope spotted Mack Millar, out from New York, talking with his client Shep Fields.

Hope waited until they were finished before asking, "What's your opinion of Paramount's publicity setup, Mack?"

"Tops."

"They'll treat me right?"

"That depends. No studio publicity department, no matter how big and how good, can do what they should do for all its stars. They do their best job on stills. They shoot up a storm, they'll send out as much as you're willing to pose for. The news and feature side is tougher."

"I'd like to hire you, but you're too far away. I can't afford you."

Mack took a long, long look at Hope. "Yes, you can," he said. "My wife, Rita—lovely gal—wants to move to California. If you'll be my first client, I think I can swing it. I'll need $200 a week." Millar looked at Hope searchingly.

"One fifty—with promises," countered Hope.

"Deal."

There was no formal contract, no terms, no guarantees, but their relationship lasted until Millar's death in 1962.

Mack's immediate strategy was to augment every news story or puff item the studio publicity office issued, and to make up a few of his own. In early November there were two news items in particular that Millar could exploit. One, Paramount liked the rushes of *The Big Broadcast* well enough to pick up Hope's option. Two, Hope had been handed an important role in a major film production called *College Swing*, a part originally announced for Jack Oakie, on loan from RKO.

Hope's landing an "A" picture like *College Swing* was a career break. According to Oakie's publicity, the reason for his exiting the picture was "interfering schedules" at RKO, but *Daily Variety*'s version of the story suggested that Oakie felt he might get lost amid the likes of talents such as Burns and Allen, Martha Raye, Edward Everett Horton, Betty Grable, Jackie Coogan, Charlie Butterworth, and John Payne.

Oakie's defection caused Hope to ask questions. After reading the script, he was inclined to feel there was little "stand-out" potential in the role. Hope discovered the producer was Lew Gensler, his old friend from *Ballyhoo of 1932*. Figuring Gensler owed him something from that 16-week run of *Ballyhoo* (if only a little unpaid salary), he persuaded Lew to fatten the part.

The plot of *College Swing* was even sillier than that of his first movie, but he was lucky in having zany comedy scenes with the loud-mouthed Martha Raye.

Mack Millar predicted that their novelty duet "How'dja Like to Love Me?" by Frank Loesser and Burton Lane would be as big a hit as "Thanks for the Memory." It wasn't.

During the shooting, Hope was his usual gregarious self and was especially fortunate in two of the friendships he made among the unusually large featured cast: the mustachioed trombonist Jerry Colonna and the singer (and golf nut) Skinnay Ennis. Both would become close friends and were professionally linked to Hope's entertainment career throughout the next 25 years.

However, the Paramount relationship that Mack Millar and the studio public relations staff pushed for publicity mileage was that of Hollywood newcomer Hope and established star Bing Crosby. A golf match sparked the reunion between the two men, who had shared the Capitol Theater stage in New York five years earlier. A publicity stunt for charity, the first of many, many to come—this one at Lakeside Country Club in Toluca Lake—brought this United Press International wire item on October 15, 1937:

> On Sunday, Crosby and Bob Hope, who just arrived from Broadway to work in pictures, will play for the dubious title of "Golf Champion of the Entertainment World." The loser will work for one day in the other's current picture.

It was a smart public relations move, one that ensured national publicity, to put syndicated columnist Ed Sullivan in the match as Bing's partner. Hope, who shot an 84, lost to Crosby's 72, and there were suitably chagrined looks on Hope's face in press photographs over the prospect of his working as an extra in Crosby's film *Doctor Rhythm*.

But publicity stunts, column items, a yet unreleased movie, and a sluggish schedule on *College Swing* (a project that Hope privately felt would be a dog) were the extent of Hope's credentials in a tough and snobbish town where an entertainer was chiefly recognized for his box-office charisma. Also, Hope was concerned about his stalled radio career and badgered Jimmy Saphier incessantly to find him a series. Unfortunately, no sponsor thought Hope was quite ready to compete with radio's superstars—the likes of Jack Benny and Burns and Allen.

Meanwhile, all Hope could do was to keep himself visible through studio publicity appearances, fan magazine interviews, and any golf-related events with or without Crosby. One of his favorite things was to go down to the racetrack at Del Mar that Crosby owned and hand out trophies in the winner's circle—and, of course, to clown with Bing. But activity didn't calm Hope's impatience. Both he and Dolores were discouraged and Dolores was especially not happy living in a rented house (they leased it from Clark Gable's second wife, Rhea). She thought maybe they ought to go back to New York.

The Hopes' most cheering gift that first Christmas in California came from Jimmy Saphier, whose negotiations with Albert Lasker, the owner of the Lord &

Thomas ad agency, netted Hope a promising guest-star arrangement on the Lucky Strike–sponsored *Your Hollywood Parade*. What appealed to Hope most was Lasker's guarantee of a permanent spot on the show if Hope clicked in one or two guest appearances.

Dick Powell was the show's headliner, Rosemary Lane was the girl singer, and the music was by Al Goodman's orchestra. The theme of the hour-long program was Hollywood—its films, its people, its music, and its glamour. Movie personalities were interviewed by Powell or performed in scenes from current Hollywood films or in original short radio dramas by the playwright and writer Arch Oboler.

Hope's initial guest appearance was scheduled for December 29, and because *College Swing* was still shooting, he and Wilkie Mahoney would sit up evenings until after midnight—sometimes they'd work the night through—preparing two five-minute monologue segments. The first segment featured gags about Christmas and self-effacing remarks about his own tentative movie career, followed by a dialogue with Powell that further publicized the recent golf match with Bing Crosby.

In his second monologue segment the subject was Santa Anita and horses and more about Hollywood stars:

My grandfather, Colonel Hospitality Julep Hope, A.B.—Always Broke—was interested in horses ever since he was old enough to steal them. . . Granddad's racing colors were beautiful. . . black and white stripes. . . He had his winter quarters at San Quentin. . . He would have enjoyed Santa Anita, especially on opening day. . . with all the movie stars and the fashion show. . . What a day for the stars to dress. . . Paulette Goddard came in with a silver-fox cape around her neck, which later turned out to be Charlie Chaplin. . . Barbara Stanwyck took no chances. . . She had her tailor with her.

Hope's material was not hilarious, yet his timing must have worked especially well because the trade press and the daily radio columnists praised his debut.

Lasker, too, was enthusiastic when he telephoned Jimmy Saphier to say that the owner of Lucky Strike, George Washington Hill, thought Hope gave his show a new sound. Hill was, as radio sponsors go, an omnipresent force in all three of his radio programs. He liked Powell's singing but thought him dull as an emcee and would prefer to have Hope headlining *Your Hollywood Parade*. But Powell's contract was ironclad and the best Lasker could offer Hope was a regular featured comedy spot on the show for the remainder of its run—which, sadly, was short. Its last broadcast was on March 23, 1938.

Before that date, however, Bob Hope was "discovered" by Hollywood's—and many of the nation's—most influential columnists and motion picture critics. On March 8, *The Big Broadcast of 1938* was previewed by most of the major news outlets, accompanied by the usual Paramount barrage of publicity. Mack Millar worked tirelessly touting his client's feature-film debut to editor pals and syndicated columnists across the nation. Abetted by—perhaps even despite—the press-agent hype, the scene between Hope and Shirley Ross singing "Thanks for the Memory" was widely noticed and applauded.

This standout scene in an otherwise mediocre film caused both powerful Hollywood columnists, Hedda Hopper and Louella Parsons, to predict film stardom for Hope, and on the East Coast the likes of Walter Winchell, Nick Kenny, Ed Sullivan, and Damon Runyon echoed that general thought in varying degrees. Runyon was so impressed that he wrote the first half of his syndicated column celebrating the emotional impact of the Hope-Ross scene; this line of Runyon's was music to Hope's ear: "What a delivery, what a song, what an audience reception!"

Hope was also beginning to reap personal affection and respect because of his emcee chores at several important industry events, including the Film Welfare League, a glittering Temple Israel benefit, and an all-star tribute to the memory of a famed vaudevillian, Ted Healy. At the Ted Healy affair, Dolores took the stage to sing three ballads, and during the third song Bob repeated his vaudeville trick of lounging at his wife's feet. The lingering, noisy applause they received was helpful in making Dolores feel she just might begin to belong in her new surroundings.

As Hope was handed his third film assignment at Paramount, *Give Me a Sailor*, a second-rate potboiler with Martha Raye, other demands on his time were increasing, especially for studio promotions, publicity, and benefits. Capable as he was, he didn't have time to do it all and needed a buffer, a road manager, someone he could trust who would help him to keep things straight and, importantly, to say no—a hard thing for him to do.

Bob instinctively thought of his brother Jack, the older brother, an aspiring songwriter who was keeping himself alive by supervising two meat markets in Akron, Ohio. He was sensitive and intelligent and was a fan of Bob's. He was also between marriages. So Bob picked up the phone one day.

"How's it going, Jack?"

"Lovely. Say, Les, I've got a song that would be just the thing—"

"Forget the song, Jack. How would you like to drop what you're doing and come out and help me? I need someone to take care of my business."

Jack was stunned, then shouted, "Of course I will. I'll leave right away."

Jack quit his job, packed his bag, got into his 1937 Pontiac, and drove nonstop to Los Angeles. Having no idea where to find the house that Bob and Dolores had leased, he drove straight to the Paramount lot. Exhausted and grubby, he pulled up to the DeMille Gate in his dusty roadster and asked if he could talk to Bob Hope.

"Who shall I say is calling?" asked the stone-faced guard.

"His brother!" With blond hair, blue eyes, and a thin face, Jack in no way resembled Bob. "I'm his brother." His eyes searched the guard's face. "*I really am!*"

The stand-off between the gate man and Jack Hope lasted until Bob was finally reached by phone. Jack had arrived at a time when Paramount guards would have heightened reason to be protective of a new studio property. Louella Parsons, the Hearst soothsayer, whose words were gospel to some and a scourge to others, had noted in her October 10, 1938, column: "Bob Hope, scoring both on radio and in *Big Broadcast*, has been given a star dressing room at Paramount."

16

This Is Bob (Pepsodent) Hope

"I believe I was the first of the comedians to hire several writers at a time. I think I was also the first to admit openly that I employed writers. In the early days of radio, comedians fostered the illusion that all of those funny sayings came right out of their own skulls."

Three "B" movies at Paramount following *The Big Broadcast of 1938* and two hit songs with Shirley Ross, "Thanks for the Memory" and "Two Sleepy People," had given Hope some name value, but no new "A" script came his way. Though the studio gave him a dressing room with his name on the door, he still had reason to think he had a stalled movie career. Little did he realize that it was toothpaste that was going to make him a star.

Even before *Your Hollywood Parade* was canceled, talks between Albert Lasker in Chicago and Jimmy Saphier in New York had begun, and the transcontinental conversations between Saphier's office and Hope's new dressing room at the studio became longer and more frequent. The subject of all these negotiations was a very big prize—a long-term radio contract. Lord & Thomas had reached the decision that after nine years the *Amos and Andy* sales pitch for Pepsodent toothpaste was losing its power. Now the agency boys were searching for a new comedy sound to sell their product, and they liked the breezy, topical monologues they heard from Hope on their own *Your Hollywood Parade*, hosted by Dick Powell.

Hope, of course, wanted top money, but even more than that, he wanted creative control. Saphier wrote Bob a letter outlining the details of a proposed six-year contract, to begin September 1938 at $3,000 a show, which in 1944 would increase to $5,000 per program. It guaranteed Hope full production control. But Saphier red-flagged the fact that Pepsodent's head man, Edwin Lasker, Albert's brother, had not signed on the dotted line because of Hope's tendency toward risqué material, and because Hope was considered by some industry people to be too brash. Saphier wrote:

If ever there is the slightest question raised about the good taste of any joke, he [Lasker] thinks that the mere fact that anyone questioned it should be sufficient reason to take that joke out. I quite agree with him in this respect. . . . One off-color gag in an otherwise socko routine can easily nullify all the good efforts of your work.

The other point is also one we have discussed before, and that is the case we should take to prevent your being a smart aleck. . . . On this show let's try to build a lot of sympathy for your character, and have the rest of the cast bounce their jokes off you. This, too, is very important, as only sympathetic comedians have a chance for long life on the air.

Saphier's perceptions were sharp, and Hope agreed to it all. At last he was to have his very own radio show and he was grateful.

However, as to that other medium, film, Hope was troubled about his future on the big screen. It was option time again, and Paramount was being cagey. *Give Me a Sailor* was finished but not ready for release. *College Swing* was playing in theaters but Hope's performance hadn't thrilled the critics. And although *The Big Broadcast of 1938* was no longer before the public, the hit tune "Thanks for the Memory" *was*. Mack Millar made certain that the polished oak desk of the studio boss, Y. Frank Freeman, and the polished desks of all the other Paramount executives had multiple copies of Damon Runyon's glowing review of Hope's performance in that film, and any other Hope clippings he could find. But still no contract.

Hope, however, was not idle. He grabbed the offer of the producer Eddie Lester to recreate his role of Huckleberry Haines in the Los Angeles Light Opera's West Coast premiere of *Roberta*. Hope was delighted to be back onstage and showing Los Angeles what he could do with an audience. The show opened June 6 and ran through June 21 at the Philharmonic Auditorium downtown. Tamara and Ray Middleton returned to their original roles, and a young screen actress named Carole Landis played Sophie. The opening was a glittering event. Jerome Kern was on hand to take a bow for the new songs he had written for this revival. Hollywood loved *Roberta*.

The day the show opened amid a flurry of high-strung publicity, Frank Freeman called Shurr to say the studio was picking up Hope's contract. Further, they planned to rematch Hope and Shirley Ross immediately in a film tailored especially for them entitled *Thanks for the Memory* (actually, it was a dusted-off shelf property formerly called *Up Pops the Devil*).

Shurr reminded Paramount that there would have to be a slight delay in plans because while the studio had been vacillating, Hope had signed himself to a summer vaudeville tour on the Loew's circuit. Dolores would be his vocalist and Jackie Coogan, his clowning partner; the day after *Roberta* closed, Hope, Dolores, and Coogan flew to New York. They opened June 23 at Loew's State and Bob was happy to be back on Broadway. Once in New York, he found himself describing, and defending, life in Hollywood.

"What's the essential difference between your work in films and your work on the stage?" a *New York World-Telegram* reporter asked.

"This!" Hope said as he jutted out his chin, raised one eyebrow, and fixed his eyes in a silly stare. "That's right for the screen. That—and a close-up—and you've got what the camera needs." Then he reassembled his features and made a different kind of body movement. He hunched forward and raised his neck like a giraffe. "Now, this is what you have to do here so they can see you all the way to the back row."

"Do you like it out there?"

"Why not? They're giving me better parts. And I can play golf with Dad— Crosby, that is—all year round, and go to quiet parties."

"Quiet parties?" the reporter asked incredulously.

"Most of the movie fellows don't drink. You can't drink and get up at five o'clock. So you can go to a party and when the waiter asks 'What would you like?'—you can say 'a glass of water' and nobody notices."

On July 17, Bob and Dolores went back to Los Angeles. And this time their arrival was marked by a move toward permanence, a leased house with their own furniture on Navajo Street in the Toluca Lake section of North Hollywood. They were just a short walk from Hope's favorite golf course, Lakeside.

For that matter, it was just a short walk to Warner Bros., to Universal, and to Columbia's location ranch. Crosby was a neighbor, and so were W. C. Fields, Mary Astor, George Brent, Ruby Keeler, Jimmy Cagney, Humphrey Bogart, Ozzie and Harriet Nelson, Slim Summerville, Broderick Crawford, and a number of directors, writers, and producers. It was convenient to almost any place in the city and yet it had the privacy film stars claimed they craved. There was a modest, man-made lake around which were several waterfront estates and hideaway homes with views of the golf course.

Their Navajo Street house did not have a view of the lake but it was comfortable and they were soon settled into a social life revolving chiefly around playing golf, attending events at the Lakeside clubhouse, and mingling with their Toluca Lake neighbors. Of these, Dolores was especially grateful for the early and close relationship they developed with Charles and Mildred MacArthur, who lived nearby. He was one of the film colony's best talent agents, and she was a Yorba, a sixth-generation Californian who knew the territory and was both a Lakeside and Pebble Beach golf champion.

For the first time since moving to California, Dolores felt her home-making instincts ripen. She was 28 and wanted children before she got any older. She and Bob had tried strenuously to conceive while they lived in New York, but no luck. Now it had become evident that if they wanted children they would have to consider adopting them. Dolores was ready, and she got Bob to promise that when the time was right they would look into adoption. She anxiously wanted this to be the right time.

Eddie Lasker finally signed the pending contract, and the press announcements of Bob Hope's new radio series for Pepsodent appeared in mid-August, but still nothing changed at Paramount. The studio seemed to have low-budget pictures in mind for him, so Hope returned to work to make *Thanks for the Memory* with a resigned attitude. He told Hedda Hopper, who had a featured role in the film and who also was a *Los Angeles Times* gossip columnist, that he refused to get into a battle with Paramount for putting him in "B" pictures. "I'd rather make a good 'B' [movie] than an epic that people take instead of sleeping pills."

Besides, he had plenty on his mind. He was now a radio producer, when he wasn't acting on a soundstage. His dressing room, which had always been a turmoil of wardrobe and dialogue conferences and an endless chain of meetings with talent agents and publicity people, was now the scene of interviews with gag writers and meetings with NBC officials and advertising agency executives about format and procedures.

Shirley Ross was impressed with Hope's editorial skills, his ability to improve a line or fix a comedy scene. She told a writer, "He's shrewd. I don't think there's anyone in Hollywood his equal at weighing the possibilities of a joke. And I don't know anyone with such a terrific capacity for work and play at the same time. No matter how hard he's working, nothing interferes with his love of fun."

Hope's addiction to working a live audience led him to use his stage crew for testing jokes both behind and before the camera. He gagged his way through rehearsals and frequently the director, George Archinbaud, was not amused. A case in point was the chewing-gum episode.

Both Hope and Ross chewed gum for relaxation and to keep their breath fresh. They chewed through rehearsals, which irritated Archinbaud, who could not get his camera focused "as long as those two wagged their jaws." There was a standoff, and word spread that there was trouble on stage 8.

The showdown came the day Bob and Shirley were scheduled to sing the film's love ballad, "Two Sleepy People." Rumors—deftly choreographed by Hope and Millar—spread through Paramount that they were planning to sing and chew gum at the same time. The day of filming, office workers and assorted technicians from other film units sneaked onto the Archinbaud set to watch Ross and Hope work—or, more precisely, to watch them chew. Archinbaud's temper rose, and the more he fumed the more obstinately the stars chewed. Then Archinbaud's attitude shifted. He remained patient while his stars sang in rehearsal, "Here we are—out of cigarettes—holding hands at midnight 'ad-libbing'—chewing wads of gum. . . ." Archinbaud announced a take and just as he asked the camera to roll, Hope and Ross on cue removed their gum and stuck it under the arms of their chairs. A ripple of giggles ran across the set behind the crew, and Archinbaud hollered "Quiet!" As the prerecorded music started, Hope said sotto voce, "I thought we'd draw a better house than this—most of these are in on passes."

It was fortunate for everyone at Paramount that vaudeville had trained Hope to a grueling schedule and also that he was fiercely ambitious, but probably it was most fortunate for Hope himself. Otherwise he never would have been able to make movies and put together his radio show simultaneously. But put together a show he did.

His biggest dilemma was format. How innovative could he afford to be? As Hope looked over the radio winners—Benny, a fall guy whose show revolved around a clearly defined stingy character, and Bergen, a self-effacing ventriloquist at the mercy of an impudent brat—he was building confidence that what he contemplated was different enough to catch on. He believed that what his sponsors liked about him was his snappy traveling salesman-like monologue.

Most half-hour comedy formats were in two parts: first came a spot with the star and the cast, and after the middle commercial time came the main sketch or development of the running situation. Hope saw his show in three or four distinct segments. First would come the monologue, and after that would be the spot where the personalities and quirks of the cast could be developed, then came a guest-star exchange with Hope, and finally a song sketch that might include everyone. The song sketch had worked well on the Woodbury show, and he felt it was worth repeating. Hope was depending on his fast-paced rhythm to sustain the twenty-nine-minute show.

He needed the best new writers he could find, and soon ferreted out a group of young gag specialists that before long were known as Hope's army: Al and Sherwood Schwartz, Milt Josefsberg, Jack Douglas, René Duplessis, Norman Sullivan, Norman Panama, Melvin Frank, and Dr. Sam Kurtzman. It was going to take an army of funny minds to think up a first-class monologue plus sketch material every week, and Hope liked the idea of hiring a lot of young, ambitious guys all on the make and all in competition with each other. He wasn't paying them very much, so he could afford a lot of them. He planned to order from each writer a full show and he would take the best from each for a final script.

Instead of his usual beautiful-girl foil, Hope hit upon the idea of using Jerry Colonna. Colonna had impressed Hope during the filming of *College Swing*, but it wasn't until Hope had worked several of Bing Crosby's Del Mar Turf Club parties that he realized that Jerry, with his bulging round eyes, walrus mustache, and piercing voice, was a versatile, zany entertainer.

All the successful radio half-hours had entertaining announcers to welcome the guest stars, and Hope selected Bill Goodwin for this role because he was especially clever with comedy lines. For the customary funny orchestra leader, Hope chose his golfing pal Skinnay Ennis, who had put together his own band a few months earlier. If anyone on the show could act the foil, it would be the lean Ennis, whom Hope would call "spaghetti in search of a meatball." Rounding out the weekly musical chores, including commercial spots, would be a group called Six Hits and a Miss: Marvin Bailey, Vin Degan, Howard Hudson, Mack McLean, Jerry Preshaw, Bill Seckler, and the Miss, Pauline Byrnes.

Ten days before the September 27 debut of the show, Hope called the "Navajo Street gang" to his house for a story conference. He told them the guest star would be the sophisticated screen actress Constance Bennett.

At first Hope selected Gershwin's rollicking tune "Wintergreen for President" from the Broadway musical *Of Thee I Sing* as the show's musical theme—the new words were "Here's Bob Hope for Pepsodent"—but then found that it would cost the program $250 for each weekly use. Hope balked at this; furthermore he had already begun to use "Thanks for the Memory" as his walk-on music for personal appearances and benefits. Lord & Thomas agreed to drop the Gershwin tune in favor of an up-tempo opening and a closing sentimental version of "Thanks."

On that first Tuesday, Hope spent the day as usual at Paramount, and then drove the few blocks from Melrose to the Vine Street parking lot. At six o'clock, Hope went onstage and after a brief introduction, Bill Goodwin broke in on cue to announce the show's guests: "Connie Bennett, Jerry Colonna, Skinnay Ennis and his orchestra and Six Hits and a Miss." Then Hope continued.

> Thank you, Bill. That's our announcer, ladies and gentlemen, known to his intimates as Bill "Teeth" Goodwin. Show them your teeth, Bill. . . . That's enough. Two more payments and they're his. My uncle just left town. . . . He was here with the American Legion Convention. . . . It was a nice, quiet convention. The second night the boys at the hotel gave the house detective twenty-four hours to get out of town. But I want to thank the American Legion for getting me a half day off last week at Paramount. They came over to the set I was working on and took the camera with them as a souvenir. Paramount didn't mind that so much, but they'd be very thankful if the fellow from Texas would please bring back Dorothy Lamour.

The monologue, which lasted seven minutes and contained 23 tightly compressed jokes delivered at top speed, is a model of some four hundred such radio monologues Hope was to present between 1938 and 1952. His character is alternately self-confident, self-effacing, impertinent, and ingratiating. The careful balance between subtle jokes and buffoonery and the wide range of joke types would become integral parts of Hope's versatile style.

The entire program moved swiftly and the show was evenly paced between comedy and music. Hope closed with the song that became his lifelong signature, "Thanks for the Memory." *Variety's* review on October 5, 1938, warmed Hope's heart:

> That small speck going over the center field fence is the four-bagger Bob Hope whammed out his first time at bat for Pepsodent. If he can keep up the pace

he'll get as much word of mouth for 1938–39 as Edgar Bergen got for 1937–38. He sounded like success all the way.

Hope must be trying because the script showed plenty of thought. But it's his particular gift not to seem to be trying. And that's a great psychological aid. It suggests wearing qualities.

Or, maybe, we're neglecting the writers. However he or they is/are, house rules allow an extra bow.

Pleased as he was at the show's initial reception, Hope was still not satisfied. He thought the show too disconnected and too reliant on jokes rather than character. In the weeks that followed—which saw a variety of guest stars, including Madeleine Carroll, Shirley Ross, Groucho Marx, Joan Bennett, Pat O'Brien, Rosalind Russell, Paulette Goddard, and Judy Garland—Hope tried to establish himself as more of a type. He carefully selected gags that accentuated either the dumb wise guy or the bragging-coward character.

Besides leaning heavily on his comic sidekicks Colonna and Goodwin, Hope began giving more funny lines to Skinnay Ennis. Then he added other characters, some played by Mel Blanc, others by Elvia Allman and Blanche Stewart. Hope invited Patricia Wilder, his first Honey Chile, to do a few shows, and after she left he hired the comedienne Patsy Kelly as a full-time regular.

Besides its flexible format, the key to the show's success was its tight, unhackneyed writing and Hope's skillful editing. The comedian's rat-tat-tat delivery, his infectious traveling-salesman manner, which seemed so right for that era in American social life, his average good looks, which his films and still photographs established for the public—all this was building an audience.

Jerry Colonna had become one of the show's most popular attractions because of his nonsensical phrases like "Greetings, Gates, let's operate" and "Who's Yuhudi?"—which were fast becoming street parlance.

By the end of December, it was clear to Lord & Thomas, to rating services like C. E. Hooper, Inc. (which called their product "Hoopratings"), to radio critics and columnists, and to the general public that Hope's show was a hit. The annual Radio Day poll of newspaper critics showed Hope in fourth place behind Jack Benny, Fred Allen, and Edgar Bergen.

With his ever-growing success, Bob stayed true to his word to Dolores and told her to proceed with plans to adopt a child. They decided on a boy, and took the advice of George and Gracie Burns, also unable to have their own child, to apply at what was perhaps the country's most distinguished foundling home, The Cradle in Evanston, Illinois. In opening negotiations with The Cradle's director, Florence Walrath, they discovered, to their disappointment, that there would be a long waiting period.

With the Pepsodent show grooving into a workable routine, Hope turned to his limping film career. He agreed to do a Preston Sturges script, yet another "B" effort called *Never Say Die* that Paramount had sent him in which he would again costar with Martha Raye. Hope and Raye made it a romp and its dismissal by critics as a failure is somewhat unfair.

When Paramount analyzed the reviews of their new film *Thanks for the Memory*, they realized that the song "Two Sleepy People" would probably become a hit parade item. Quickly they hired Lew Foster and Wilkie Mahoney to rewrite for Hope and Ross a Ben Hecht–Gene Fowler play called *The Green Magoo*, renamed *Some Like It Hot*. Despite some potential, including another hit parade song titled "The Lady's in Love with You," the picture never really sparkled.

In February 1939 Hope was asked by the studio to be a presenter at the Academy Awards ceremonies at the Biltmore Hotel in downtown Los Angeles. Hope's growing reputation as *the* master of ceremonies in town was probably the reason for the choice. It was the beginning of a long association.

In March two noteworthy events occurred. The first was an awakening by Paramount executives to Hope's talents. They had noticed his audience appeal at the Academy Awards and also were extremely impressed by his accelerating radio career and general public appeal. They decided to cast him in a picture called *The Cat and the Canary*, costarring one of Hollywood's most publicized actresses, Paulette Goddard. After reading the script, Hope sensed the opportunity this picture represented.

The second event was an opportunity of a different sort. Bob had accidentally opened a letter postmarked England that lay in a pile on his desk. After reading it he was tempted to call Dolores immediately but decided to wait until dinner to speak about it.

"How would you like to take a trip?" he asked.

"You heard from The Cradle?" Dolores asked eagerly.

"No. Where would you most like to go?"

"Evanston."

"I know how much having a son means to you, Dolores," Bob said, looking at her across the table, "but I'm talking vacation."

"You're what? You—a vacation?" Dolores couldn't believe her ears. "Bob, you're kidding!"

"No. Now where have you always wanted to go?"

"Paris."

"Okay, you got it."

"When? I don't believe it."

"I got a letter today from my Aunt Lucy in England asking for an autographed picture. She said she'd been getting mail recently from relatives all over Britain asking if I was Harry's boy who'd made good. She lives in Hitchin, Hertfordshire, with my grandpop and she asked if I'd like to come over and visit and stay with them. Grandpop is ninety-six and still rides his bicycle every day."

"What has that got to do with Paris?"

"We'll do both. I finish the *Cat and the Canary* in the middle of May and our last Pepsodent show is June 20. We can play a couple of vaudeville dates they want me for on the way to New York."

"Will we play Chicago?"

"We can."

"Bob, will you—?"

"I'll call Florence Walrath tomorrow."

17

Reunion Abroad

"Of course, my steward told me when I got on board, 'If anything happens, it's women and children first, but the captain said 'in your case you can have first choice.'"

It really was like old times, being back at the Orpheum in Minneapolis and taking in that special backstage smell. Bob thought the familiar odor especially heady that steamy afternoon of June 26, 1939, when he, Dolores, Jerry Colonna, his brother Jack, and Jack's new wife, an actress named Marion Bailey, began their first week on the road.

Next week they would play Chicago, and after a stopover in Cleveland to pick up Uncle Frank, they would slide into Atlantic City for a two-day appearance on the pier, and then into New York for ten days at the Paramount. After that it would be an honest-to-goodness vacation—sailing on the *Normandie*, a Hope family reunion in England, and a European holiday.

The 65-minute show they unveiled at the Orpheum was the product of Hope's new radio writers and his own voluminous gag files. *Variety* of June 28, 1939, found it to be "loaded with good material," and Hope was tagged as "flip and fresh, yet friendly and intimate." This engagement was special because it marked the start of a lifelong stage association between Hope and Colonna, one that went beyond the weekly radio stints to include turns in countless American cities and military bases the world over. Their signal shtick was kicked off by Colonna's hollering from the wings, "Hey, Hope! Your laundry's back!" Bob would holler back amiably, "Thanks, Jer!" Then Colonna got an audience scream with "They refused it!"

In Minneapolis Dolores was on edge. Before leaving Los Angeles they had scheduled their screening interview at The Cradle for their last day in Chicago. Florence Walrath had told Dolores that The Cradle had "passed" the prospective parents in a "preliminary examination stage." She explained, however, that a microscopic investigation of the Hopes was still in progress.

The interview went well. Mrs. Walrath dealt directly with what she termed the sensitive problem of children brought up in the glare of publicity in celebrity households. She had numerous examples in her files of entertainment children whose role models were less than exemplary. But she added that she was encouraged by respected character witnesses in Los Angeles that the Hopes were "conservative," "sober," and "loving." As Bob and Dolores were leaving, Mrs. Walrath invited them to stop at The Cradle on their return from Europe because she believed she "just might have the right child for you."

"A boy," stated Bob emphatically.

"We'll have to wait and see, Mr. Hope," she said.

That evening, Bob and Dolores were invited to a dinner party aboard the yacht of Pepsodent's boss, Ray Smith, at anchor out on Lake Michigan. At seven-thirty Albert Lasker stopped at the Drake Hotel to pick up the Hopes and drive them to a Lake Michigan pier where a launch was waiting. As the tender plowed through choppy water, Lasker raised his arm and pointed off toward the impressive silhouette of the boat they were approaching. He put his other hand on Bob's shoulder and said, "I want you to remember one thing: Amos and Andy built that boat."

Hope's usually mobile face froze. Dolores saw an expression she had rarely seen but she knew it meant that Bob was capable of saying just about anything. She held her breath.

"When I finish with Pepsodent—our Mr. Smith will be using that yacht for a dinghy," Bob said with only his eyes smiling.

The rest of the evening was pleasant. Smith toasted Bob's first successful season. Then, as they walked slowly to the gangway, Smith reached into his inside jacket pocket and produced a fat legal-sized envelope. "I hear that you are taking a vacation in Europe. Here's something that may come in handy on the trip." Bob thanked him and slipped the envelope into his pocket. They said goodnight.

Back in the hotel room, as he was removing his dinner jacket, he ripped open the envelope. Inside were round-trip tickets (deluxe suites both ways) for outbound travel on the *Normandie* in July and return travel on the *Queen Mary* in September. There was also a $2,500 letter of credit on a London bank.

"Dolores," Bob said, waving the tickets and the letter of credit, "start brushing four times a day."

The following week, the Hope clan—Fred and LaRue, Sid and Dorothy, Ivor and Gertrude, and Bob and Dolores—held an informal reunion around a large table in the dining room of the Hotel Cleveland. Sid, a mechanic and a farmer, was living quietly at Ridgefield Corners, Ohio, about 40 miles southwest of Toledo, and so his presence there was a special treat. Ivor and Bob discussed arrangements for opening their jointly held company, Hope Metal Products. Everyone was relieved that Bob had gotten his kid brother George a writing job in Hollywood. Jim was missing from this group, but no one was surprised. He had gone to the West Coast even before Bob and had tried to break into show business. He had failed and had let it be no secret that he was envious of Bob's success.

The remainder of the tour went by swiftly. After Atlantic City Bob and the troupe opened in New York and during their twelve days at the Paramount they managed to see the World's Fair, in Queens. Mack Millar had succeeded in convincing fair organizers to declare a "Bob Hope Day at the Fair," and Bob and Dolores rode in an open car through the fairgrounds with New York's colorful mayor, Fiorello La Guardia.

Before transatlantic air travel became routine, a passage on an ocean liner like the *Normandie* and the *Queen Mary*, which took about a week, was the accepted mode of traveling between North America and Europe, whether one was emigrating or going on holiday. The passenger lists represented a cross-section of society, and departures were a festive, quasi-public event. Bob and Dolores had an inkling of the celebrity-filled passenger list for their European summer crossing, but they were not at all prepared for the dockside confusion of what the press described as "an army of 500 autograph seekers staging wild scenes." Screaming fans encircled Norma Shearer, Madeleine Carroll, George Raft, Roland Young, Ben and Bebe Lyon, Edward G. Robinson and his son Eddie, Jr., and Charles Boyer and his wife, Pat. It was a media feast. Besides the film stars, the press was pursuing the best-selling author Marjorie Hillis, Prime Minister John Cudahy of Ireland, and the former president of the Dominican Republic, Rafael Trujillo. As Dolores and Bob headed for their gangway, they were trailed by newsmen asking for details of their family reunion in England and their first European holiday. They were asked whether they feared the war clouds hanging over the Continent and Hitler's threats. "There won't be a war," said Hope confidently.

Before Hope could expound further, the newsmen thronged to an official limousine that had just pulled up. Eleanor Roosevelt stepped out, surrounded by Secret Service men. She had come to say both official and personal good-byes to her uncle, David Gray, who was accompanying Treasury Secretary Henry Morgenthau on what was mostly a vacation in Scandinavia.

Looking at this carefree throng in such a holiday mood, it was unthinkable that there could be a world conflict coming. Not one of Hope's monologues for Pepsodent during the past season had suggested world or national upset. In fact, the nation's recovery from a deep recession to a mood of prosperity seemed complete.

With all the friends and celebrities on board, the voyage was much more of a social whirlwind than Dolores and Bob had anticipated. Everyone, including Uncle Frank, had a wonderful time. When the *Normandie* docked at Southampton on August 7, Uncle Frank went straight to Hitchin in Hertfordshire. The other Hopes took the train to London.

During their first week there the Hopes began to unwind. They hardly missed a day of playing golf, and each night they saw a play or a musical. One day they drove out to see Bob's birthplace at 44 Craigton Road, Eltham.

The second week they went up to Hitchin to spend a day or two with the Hope patriarch, Grandfather James, who at ninety-six still ruled the family. Bob and Dolores took a room at the Hitchin Inn and threw a big family party at one of the local pubs. Uncle Frank had already had his own homecoming party, so this one was really for the purpose of letting some forty British Hopes gather to bask in the pride of having a famous film-star relative in their midst. Hardly any of them had seen one of Bob's movies, but they knew he was a celebrity in the States.

After dinner, the guests awaited living proof of their American cousin's fame. Bob got up and told a few jokes, which got a rather cool reception. His grandfather, unsmiling, just stared at Bob, who finally said, "Hey, let's bring Uncle Jack up here. I understand he's a pretty good whistler."

Then the patriarch stood up. "You're doing this thing all wrong," he said. "You don't know these people. You're a tourist. Let me do the introducing." For the next 20 minutes Grandpop introduced the entire Hope clan and even danced a little dance step to prove what a ninety-six-year-old could still do.

Paramount's London office had a photographer sent up to Hitchin, and Bob and Dolores posed for pictures with the aunts and uncles, and with the remarkable James Hope. Then, after a round of farewells, Bob and Dolores returned to London. A few days later they headed for Dover and the boat train to Paris.

Sadly, they were never really able to explore the enchantment of Paris. Americans were beginning to sense what seemed so clear to international observers after the German invasion of Czechoslovakia in March—including so unlikely a person as the gossipy Louella Parsons in Hollywood—that Hitler's troops were poised to march into Poland. At their hotel, the George V, Bob spent most of one night on the transatlantic telephone with Paramount executives and NBC radio brass who wanted the Hopes to return to Los Angeles as quickly as possible. The lead item of Parsons's Friday, August 25, 1939, column revealed:

With the war imminent, Hollywood yesterday realized how many of its important stars are still in Europe. Tyrone Power and Annabella. . . Charles Boyer. . . Robert Montgomery. . . Maureen O'Sullivan. . . Bob Hope, who planned a European holiday, is cutting his visit short to hurry home.

Bob and Dolores were booked for deluxe-suite accommodations for the mid-September sailing of the *Queen Mary* from Southampton. Now it was rumored that the August 30 sailing might be her final civilian crossing. First-class space was finally located for the Hopes on what later would be described as a "woefully overcrowded ship." Even for seasoned vaudevillians, the frantic dash over the English Channel to make Southampton in time for the *Queen Mary's* sailing was a chilling experience. Hundreds of frightened Americans and Europeans were hell-bent on making that crossing.

On September 1, German troops marched into Poland. In spite of so much evidence, Hope refused to believe war was that close. How he could have misread Hitler's invasion of Poland as anything but an invitation to massive conflict is puzzling.

On Saturday, September 3, both England and France declared war on Germany. The passengers got the news early the next morning. Dolores was coming back to the cabin from Mass and woke Bob.

"You were wrong," she said, holding the bulletin in her hand.

"What happened?" he asked sleepily.

"'German troops in "blitzkrieg" action have reduced Polish towns and villages to rubble,'" Dolores read to him. "It says here that Russian troops have entered Poland from the East and that the Poles are trying to save themselves. It's awful. The British Dominions have called emergency parliament sessions for the purposes of declaring war. If Canada goes—surely we will, too."

"Now, Dolores—"

"Bob, you ought to see what's going on up in the salon. People are sobbing. One woman stopped me and said that there are German submarines waiting for orders to sink this boat. They've issued blackout instructions and people are crying—and scared—"

"There's nothing to be frightened about."

"I'm thinking that if the Nazis blow up this ship we'll never see our baby boy."

"Stop that. I've got to get up and see the captain. We're supposed to do a ship's concert tonight but I don't know if we should."

As it turned out, the captain thought comedy was exactly what the *Queen Mary* passengers needed at this time, so Hope spent the rest of the afternoon putting together a routine and writing special lyrics for his theme song.

When he went onstage that night and looked around the room, he decided to begin by telling the truth. He admitted that he had told the captain he didn't think doing a ship's concert was appropriate. He said he still wasn't sure, but that the captain and a few others had prevailed. "Maybe—just maybe they're right. It might help if all of us here try for a few minutes to forget the tragedy that faces the world and have some fun."

Hope's comedy character of the brave coward was probably never more gratefully received than it was that night when he cracked, "Of course, my steward told me when I got on board, 'If anything happens, it's women and children first, but the captain said in your case you can have your choice.'" He did his regular vaudeville act for an hour and finally sang the parody he had written that afternoon:

Thanks for the memory
Of this great ocean trip
On England's finest ship.
Tho' they packed them in the rafters
They never made a slip.
Ah! Thank you so much.
Thanks for the memory
Some folks slept on the floor,

Some in the corridor;
But I was more exclusive,
My room had GENTLEMEN above the door,
Ah! Thank you so much.

The crowded-to-capacity salon roared when Hope finished his song. The captain asked him for a copy of the parody for the ship's log, and sent a copy to the ship's printing shop. When the ship finally docked in New York at the Cunard Line pier, each departing passenger received a copy. Bob reminded Mack Millar to run a copy of it over to *Variety*, where it was used as a boxed item in Wednesday's roundup of returning show business figures from abroad.

From New York the Hopes rushed to Mrs. Walrath's office in Evanston. She told them they had passed final inspection, and that they could have a baby girl about eight weeks old. Dolores melted when they went to the showing room. She didn't want to leave the baby when Mrs. Walrath asked if they might go back to her office to talk. She asked the Hopes how they felt.

"She's beautiful," said Dolores.

"She's all right," said Bob.

"Perhaps you ought to wait—" Mrs. Walrath said.

"No, we want her," said Dolores.

But Mrs. Walrath had the feeling Bob was uncertain about adoption. Dolores assured her that Bob was only disappointed because he had had his heart set on a boy, and that her husband often used flippant remarks to mask his emotion.

Nevertheless, Mrs. Walrath made them wait. Bob and Dolores went on to California while some legal papers filed with the State of Illinois cleared. Finally, one morning the following week, Dolores answered the telephone to hear the news that she could come back to The Cradle for their new daughter. Dolores went alone and brought home "that little puzzlehead," as Bob had called her. They named her Linda Theresa.

18

Three for the Road

CROSBY: As I live—Ski-snoot!
HOPE: Mattress-hip!
CROSBY: Shovel-head!
HOPE: Blubber!
CROSBY: Scoop-nose!
HOPE: Lard!
CROSBY: Yes, Dad!

NBC ordered star treatment for Hope when he began his second season of broadcasts. They even tossed a party to launch the freshly decorated Bob Hope Radio Studio in their block-long pale-green building at the corner of Sunset and Vine. But the other cause for rejoicing, as Hope returned to the air, was that Judy Garland had joined his cast as a regular who would be singing and doing comedy with Bob. Garland had guest-starred the season before, and the chemistry created between Hope and her had generated enough audience response to convince Pepsodent that Judy's price—recently boosted by her recognition as a major talent stemming from her performance in *The Wizard of Oz*—was worth paying. Judy's initial dialogue with Hope went this way:

> HOPE: Ladies and gentlemen, one of my most pleasant duties in returning to the air this week is to present a new addition to our cast, Metro-Goldwyn-Mayer's young singing star of *The Wizard of Oz* whom you will soon see with Mickey Rooney in *Babes in Toyland*. . . Miss Judy Garland!
>
> JUDY: Thank you very much. Hello, Mr. Hope.
>
> HOPE: Hello, Judy. You know, the last time you were here you were just a guest. Now that you're a permanent member of our cast, how do you feel about it?
>
> JUDY: Oh, I'm really happy to be here, Mr. Hope. You know, my school-teacher's happy I'm on the program, too. She says I ought to be glad to take anything to get started.
>
> HOPE: But, Judy. . . are you sure you'll feel at home on this program?
>
> JUDY: Oh, yes, Mr. Hope. . . . You should have seen the strange creatures I worked with on *The Wizard of Oz*.
>
> HOPE: Judy Garland, is that the way to talk to me. . . after I've been so nice to you?. . . Why only yesterday I bought you an ice cream soda—with two balls of ice cream, too!
>
> JUDY: Yeah. . . and with two straws, too!
>
> HOPE: Well, I gave you a head start, didn't I?

Hope's writers traded on Judy's "little-girl-next-door" image at the start, but by the close of the radio season they had brought her up to her actual age—eighteen—and there was more sting in her voice when she deflated Hope's ego and dampened his fumbling romantic attentions.

Another innovation of the 1939–40 Pepsodent season was in the already familiar character voices of Elvia Allman and Blanche Stewart. In a sketch on October 24, the ladies were cast as a couple of ugly coeds the bandleader, Skinnay Ennis, had "dug up" as dates for Hope and Goodwin. The idea caught fire.

> BLANCHE: Say, we'd better finish dressing right away, Cobina. . . . What are you going to wear, your organdy creep de shiney. . . or your *liver-pill schlemiel*?

ELVIA: Oh, I dunno . . . I wanna look good . . . but I wanna be ready to defend myself at the same time. . . . Say, Brenda, have you seen my bottle of bay rum?

BLANCHE: Don't you remember? We used it last night . . . in the Martinis! Well, whaddya know, Cobina! I can't find my false eyelashes!

ELVIA: I got them. . . . I'm brushing off my coat!

BLANCHE: I wonder if they're too long? Should I cut them down to three inches?

ELVIA: I don't know . . . but every time you wink your eye, you flag down the Super Chief. . . .

Audience reaction at both previews and regular shows proved so enthusiastic for these new characters (who were, essentially, satiric jabs at two society debutantes, Brenda Frazier and Cobina Wright, Jr.) that Hope made the shrill, frustrated old maids a continuing feature.

All in all, Hope's show was better than before. Tightly written, sometimes outrageous, always topical, the *Pepsodent Show* had risen in popularity to become the third most-listened-to radio program in the nation, just behind Jack Benny's and Edgar Bergen's shows.

One of its dominant themes, sometimes as much as 50 percent of the program's total content, was Hope's exaggerated view of life in Hollywood. For example, "I'm happy. . . My sponsor is a really nice fellow. . . We get along swell. . . All afternoon here at rehearsal we were playing piggyback—*he* was riding *me*!" In the satire, the comedian managed to fit more and more comfortably into his role as quavering braggart and lovable fall guy.

This characterization was also working well for Hope on the screen. His newest film, *The Cat and the Canary*, opened in November to spectacular critical notices. The respected critic Howard Barnes wrote in the *New York Herald Tribune* on November 23, 1939, "Mr. Hope is a pillar of strength in holding the film to its particular mood of satirical melodrama." Hope's own favorite among the reviews appeared in the *Motion Picture Herald:* "Paramount here has solved neatly for itself, exhibitors and customers, the heretofore perplexing problem of what to do with Bob Hope, admittedly one of the funniest comedians who ever faced a camera, yet never until now the surefire laugh-getter on the screen that his following knew him to be in fact."

In addition to developing the character Wally Hampton, on which so many of his future film assignments would be based, *The Cat and the Canary* gave him the first opportunity to wisecrack in a manner that seemed entirely spontaneous and was as unexpected by the movie audience as the stage ad-lib.

Credit for the success of Hope's rendition of Wally Hampton must go to the producer, Arthur Hornblow, Jr., who lectured Hope sternly on the importance of taking direction, and to the stage-wise Elliott Nugent for his patient and intelligent handling of the comedian both in front of and behind the camera. It was a happy marriage of stars, script, and production. Hope called his leading lady, Paulette Goddard, "beautiful and talented." And it didn't hurt the picture that Paulette was both protégée and wife of the world's most famous clown, Charlie Chaplin.

At one of the celebrity events at Santa Anita racetrack one Saturday during the filming, Hope spotted Paulette on Chaplin's arm and went over to say hello.

"You know Charles, don't you?" she said.

Hope had always admired Chaplin—he had even won a prize or two in Chaplin look-alike contests at Luna Park. A few years before, Hope had waited on the sidewalk outside a New York City restaurant for an hour and a half because a friend had told him that Chaplin was inside. He would have liked to tell him all that, but such blatant idolatry wasn't good form. Instead he told him how much he had admired *Modern Times* and what a treat it was working with Paulette.

"Young man," Chaplin said, "I've been watching the rushes of *The Cat and the Canary* every night. I want you to know that you are one of the best timers of comedy I have ever seen."

Normally Hope's reaction to such a flattering remark would have been to wise-crack—but this was one of the very few times in his life when he could not crack wise.

Nugent understood Hope's absolute dependence on the wisecrack as the supreme comic technical device. He had the sensitivity to recognize that in the role of Wally Hampton the comedian's screen persona was coming into bloom and insisted that the topical gag be fired off in the most spine-tingling moments of the picture.

Some of the most quotable jokes from the film come in moments when Wally is feeling terror. Once when he is forced to sleep in a spooky mansion, Nydia Westman asks, "Don't big empty houses scare you?" "Not me," says Wally, "I used to be in vaudeville." And, "Even my goose pimples have goose pimples." There is even a foretaste of Hope's lecherous lines: "My mother brought me up never to be caught twice in the same lady's bedroom."

The only classic Hope gag not used in this film was his Crosby put-down. It was *comme-il-faut* for the "boys" to publicly insult each other (much the way Jack Benny and Fred Allen tore each other down), at least as far as golf tournaments and each other's radio programs were concerned. Bing, on the air for Kraft Foods since 1935, had started using Hope-assassination jokes in the spring of 1938 during a Hope guest shot.

Hope retaliated by telling jokes about Crosby's reluctant racehorses. "Let me tell you about those streamlined trains. They go right by Crosby's stables, and every morning Bing goes out and lines up the horses. 'See,' he tells them as the trains whiz by, 'that's what I mean.'"

Before long they had worked out a series of epithets for each other that if and when they were strung together sounded like this:

BING: As I live—ski-snoot!
BOB: Mattress-hip!
BING: Shovel-head!
BOB: Blubber!
BING: Scoop-nose!
BOB: Lard!
BING: Yes, Dad!

That kind of word-slinging plus their Saturday night clowning at Bing's Del Mar Turf Club were noted by Paramount's production chief, Bill LeBaron. The studio owned a property called *The Road to Mandalay* that scriptwriters Frank Butler and Don Hartman had adapted from a South Sea tale entitled *Beach of Dreams*. LeBaron had first thought of casting Fred MacMurray and Jack Oakie as a couple of vagabond entertainers on the lam in the tropics. Both stars turned him down. LeBaron's thoughts then turned to the combination of Burns and Allen with Crosby, but George and Gracie couldn't fit it in.

What about Lamour in a sarong with Crosby and Bob Hope? The idea, first suggested lightly, became a hot business proposition and Butler and Harman went to work retailoring their script. Bing said, "I was intrigued with the idea of working with Bob and Dottie because it seemed to me it would be a winning combination. A foreign land, natives, music, Dottie in a sarong, Bob being a clown, me singing the ballads."

Paramount put Victor Schertzinger in to direct the script, which now had the title *The Road to Singapore*. Schertzinger's background was in musicals, and he was used to directing his pictures in a leisurely and dignified fashion. "His awakening was rude," Crosby recalled. "For a couple of days when Hope and I tore freewheeling into a scene, ad-libbing and violating all of the acceptable rules of moviemaking, Schertzinger stole bewildered looks at his script, then leafed rapidly through it, searching for the lines we were saying."

Lamour, who prided herself on the accuracy of her lines, was also bewildered because she failed to recognize her cues.

Enter two angry writers, Butler and Hartman. They resented all the tampering with their words. To rub even more salt into their wounds, Hope called out, "Hey, Don, if you recognize any of yours, yell 'Bingo!'" At which point, an enraged Hartman left the stage to complain to LeBaron.

Schertzinger told someone, "You know, I really shouldn't take any money for this job. All I do is say 'Stop' and 'Go.'" But the director soon realized that the movie emerging each day was fresh and spontaneous; besides, the front office was delighted.

Bob and Bing were reassured as well. One day they slipped unnoticed into back seats of the darkened projection room during the eleven o'clock rushes and heard one or another of the production staff and studio brass howling with laughter.

The plot line for *The Road to Singapore* was simple and accidental. Josh Mallon, played by Crosby, and Ace Lannigan, played by Hope, run off to the South Seas to avoid unwanted weddings. They land on the island of Kaigood, where romance beckons in the form of sexy Mima, played by Lamour, and danger threatens from Mima's dancing partner, Caesar, played by a menacing Anthony Quinn. The one-line plot for this *Road*, as well as for the sequels, was always this: The boys are in a jam, or as many jams as possible, and they have to clown their way out.

"The jams are plotted in the script," Crosby said, "and although they're bogus situations and on the incredible side, they are important because they hold the story together and provide a framework for our monkeyshines. Gags can't be played against gags; they have to be played against something serious, even though the serious stuff is melodramatic. Hope and I invent many of these gags from predicaments as we go along."

There were times during the filming that Hope and Crosby got so carried away with their ad-libs that they forgot about Lamour and she would yell, "Please, fellas, when can I get my line in?" Bob has said, "We used to rib her mercilessly. It used to get so crazy that it was like a tennis game with Dottie in the middle watching. Fortunately, she had a great sense of humor. Most dames would have walked off the set in a huff. Bing would say, 'If you find an opening, Dottie, just throw something in.'"

"After the first few days," Lamour said, "I decided it was ridiculous to waste time learning the script. I would read over the next day's work to get an idea of what was happening. What I really needed was a good night's sleep to be in shape for the next morning's ad-libs. This method provided some very interesting results on the screen."

Singapore did much to foster the Hope-Crosby friendship. It was a symbiosis that suited each admirably and apparently was a response to a need in both men. Bing, for example, frequently appeared to associates as cold and unresponsive. He was puzzled about his own success and once called himself a freak in the business; he had actually considered retirement in 1937. Many people, including Crosby's biographer Barry Ulanov, believe Hope gave Bing a "shot of adrenaline; he made Bing's work a pleasure; he helped squash Bing's tentative plans to retire to his ranch, or sail around the world, or breed horses for a living."

And the move toward intimacy was significant for Hope as well. He had been close to Whitey Jennings as a youth, and Richy Craig on Broadway, and there would be a handful of reasonably close men friends during his career, friendships fostered largely on the golf course. But his closest male attachments were to his brothers, and those relationships were the result of his closely held view of family ties.

Ulanov, in his portrait of Bing, observed: "They played games with each other, and for each other, like little boys, never ceasing to find delight in each other's company, wondering constantly that this sort of game could and would continue to be a job."

Perhaps symbolic of that childlike approach to their work was the pat-a-cake sequence they performed in each *Road* picture. The "boys" would get themselves trapped, usually menaced by burly thugs, and to get themselves out they would face each other, raise their palms, and play pat-a-cake for a few moments and then, in a surprising switch, smash their opponents in the jaws. It was to their credit that their taste dictated the limits of their insouciant behavior. For example, there is just the right amount of abandon in the scene in *Singapore* where Hope and Crosby don sarongs and cavort to their own ocarina accompaniment.

True, they may have gone over the top with the epic noon-time soapsuds fight that left a foamy trail from stage 5 to the Paramount commissary. Bob, Dottie, and Bing began spraying each other with cans of special effects soapsuds on the soundstage and chased each other down studio streets and around lunch tables. A mostly amused audience of film workers applauded, but Paramount brass bemoaned the delays in repairing hair, makeup, and costumes. Yet it was the unexpected, the circus atmosphere, that prompted hairdressers, cameramen, and grips to literally fight for an assignment to a *Road* picture.

Needless to add, a pall fell on the lot when *Singapore* was wrapped up. But Paramount brass rejoiced. All those Hope-Crosby high jinks were expensive. Besides, Arthur Hornblow was biting his nails waiting to reteam Hope and Paulette Goddard in *The Ghost Breakers*, a follow-up to the box-office winner *The Cat and the Canary*, in which Hope, as Larry Lawrence, is innocently embroiled in a murder and Goddard conceals him in her steamer trunk as they head for her haunted castle on an eerie island off the coast of Cuba.

During the filming, Hope was tapped to be the single master of ceremonies of the twelfth Oscar awards dinner, to be held February 29 in the Ambassador Hotel's Cocoanut Grove. The year 1939 had been an especially auspicious one for Hollywood. The film capital's combined skills had turned out more critically acclaimed motion pictures than any previous year in the colony's history, including Selznick's monumental four-hour *Gone With the Wind*, MGM's beguiling *The Wizard of Oz*, John Ford's stark and classic *Stagecoach*, MGM's touching *Good-bye, Mr. Chips*, Goldwyn's romantic *Wuthering Heights*, Warners' emotional *Dark Victory*, as well as the tough *Of Mice and Men* and the politically disturbing *Mr. Smith Goes to Washington*.

Those ceremonies marked the last time that the winners' names were given to the press in advance of the actual presentation. The *Los Angeles Times* released the names in its early-bird edition and destroyed the suspense. The following year, the Academy brought in the firm of Price Waterhouse to control the results.

The night belonged to *Gone With the Wind*, and Hope cracked: "What a wonderful thing, this benefit for David O. Selznick." Eight Oscars were given out for the Civil War spectacular, including the prestigious Thalberg prize, to Selznick personally. Hope was particularly proud that his Pepsodent songbird Judy Garland won a special statuette "for her outstanding performance as a screen juvenile during the past year."

When *Singapore* was sneak-previewed in Hollywood in late February, Hope devoted a segment of his Pepsodent show to a sketch based on the film, and when it was released in March, he did another sketch about it, and still another in April. Fortunately, the movie received glowing reviews and proved a box-office winner. Paramount quickly sent Hartman and Butler to the attic to dust off another unused script. Hartman said once, "You take a piece of used chewing gum and flip it at a map. Wherever it lands you can lay a *Road* picture so long as there are jokers who cook and eat strangers. If they're nasty and menacing, it'll be a good picture. The key is menace offsetting the humor." They found a Cy Bartlett script called *Find Colonel Fawcett,* a quasi-serious Stanley-in-search-of-Livingstone theme, and Butler and Hartman turned it into *The Road to Zanzibar.* Paramount invited Hope, Crosby, and Lamour to travel again.

Hope, however, had already arranged to take his radio show on the road for the last five weeks of the Pepsodent season and at the same time to do personal appearances in Joliet, Chicago, Detroit, Cleveland, and New York. It was vaudeville time again, and to Hope there was nothing more exciting. Moreover, now he had two sizable film successes behind him and was still working for the same money; maybe they'd appreciate him more when they knew he was building a bigger radio audience.

Even Hope did not know how big that audience had become. When the Pepsodent gang (plus Dolores) opened in Joliet they were asked to add an extra show because of the crowds trying to get in. The Chicago crowds were the same—only more so. Hope had contracted for five shows a day at the Chicago Theater, but the lines circling the entire city block were such that the management realized that even the five shows could not accommodate everyone.

"Let's cut the movie entirely," suggested Hope.

"Can't do it," said the manager, although his face showed he was thinking about it.

The financial agreement for this tour was that Hope and his troupe would have a $12,500 weekly guarantee and 50 percent of everything over a $50,000 gate. The house attendance record was being broken daily. The theater was taking in $73,000 a week, and Hope saw his personal share reach $20,000.

Hope looked outside again and saw those lines. "Well, at least why don't we cut out the news and previews at all performances and see if we can squeeze in one more show."

They did better than that. They shaved enough to do seven stage shows. The crowd didn't stop even for rain. Hope called Louis Shurr.

"Doc, I want you to fly to Chicago."

"Why?"

"I want you to see something."

"I really can't leave town right now."

"What's more important than me?"

"Well—"

"You don't happen to have Abe Lastfogel's number handy do you?" Abe Lastfogel worked for the William Morris Agency and was by then near the top of the hierarchy. Morris had always wanted to get Hope to move to his agency and tie him up for all media. Shurr found the fastest way to get to Chicago and made his way backstage.

"Come here," Hope said, and walked the little man over to a peephole in the Lake Street door of the theater. "That's important. How often do you see the crowds that big? That is a $50,000-a-picture crowd and I want you to go and see the boys at Paramount and tell 'em that's what my price is going to be."

But Doc had another plan. He had already talked to Paramount's boss, Y. Frank Freeman, who insisted that Hope fulfill his current option price. But Shurr also knew that Sam Goldwyn wanted Hope for a picture. Goldwyn had just lent Gary Cooper to Paramount and felt he deserved to have the favor returned.

Shurr went to Freeman and asked if Hope could be lent out to Goldwyn. Freeman agreed, providing that Hope completed his current schedule of four films. Then Doc and his partner, a tough bargainer named Al Melnick, went to see Goldwyn.

"I knew you would work it out for me, Louis," Goldwyn said. "I'm going to make a very funny picture with this Hope."

"For what kind of money, Sam?" asked Doc.

"What does he want?"

"A hundred thousand," said Melnick bluntly.

Goldwyn sputtered and told them to forget it. Meanwhile, Mack Millar had made certain that Hope's public appearance tour, with its record-breaking crowds, was a topic of all the syndicated columnists. Offers and counteroffers continued. Hope was willing to stake everything on the figure Melnick proposed to Goldwyn. Unless he could establish his worth away from Paramount, he would be another victim of the big studio practice of working actors at originally-agreed-upon contracts long after the actor had begun to reap big profits for the studio.

Goldwyn, on the other hand, figured Hope would capitulate sooner or later. Then, in a fortuitous turn of events, Paramount asked Hope to emcee the premiere of *The Westerner*, the film the studio had made with Cooper as a loan-out from Goldwyn. The premiere was to be staged simultaneously—or nearly so—in Dallas and Fort Worth, and eight stage appearances for Hope were scheduled in a single day. Hope was anxious to do it because he wanted Goldwyn to be grateful to him, and he knew that Goldwyn would be there as one of the celebrities from Hollywood. He let it be known how inconvenient this act of goodwill was for him, since his Pepsodent radio series was having its seasonal premiere the same week.

The last show of the day in Fort Worth was held at the Will Rogers Coliseum. Just before going onstage Hope said to Goldwyn that he certainly hoped they would be able to get the deal set for their picture together.

"Later, Bob," said Sam, "we'll talk later." He was smiling.

Hope was smiling, too. He had an idea. Part of the prearranged stage business for the film premiere was to have all of the Hollywood celebrities—Cooper, Edward Arnold, Charlie Ruggles, Lillian Bond, Bruce Cabot, and Goldwyn—troupe across the stage single-file behind him, unannounced and without even a glance toward Hope and the audience. Hope would look fleetingly over his shoulder and turn back to the audience to say, "Oh, that's the new unit breaking in for next week." Sam loved being part of the shtick like that.

They did the shtick as planned, until Hope said, "And now may I present one of the really great men in our business, Mr. Sam Goldwyn."

Goldwyn came out beaming to big applause. He bowed and when it was quiet looked at Hope. "I haven't made a comedy since Eddie Cantor left me. I never found a comedian who I thought could do as well—until now. I finally found one in Bob Hope."

Applause. Hope took the mike firmly in his grip. "That's awful nice, Sam. Now let's talk about money."

"Later," Sam whispered. "We'll talk later."

"No, let's talk about it here. These people won't mind. Let's get really comfortable. Why don't we just lie down and talk things over."

Hope got down on the stage floor and brought the mike along with him. The audience roared. Hope waited and finally Goldwyn, caught up in the spirit, got down on the floor with Hope. "Now, Sam, about my salary." Goldwyn reached for the mike but Bob pulled it away. "What did you say, Sam?" Then Bob whispered something in Goldwyn's ear and they both got up. "It's going to be a pleasure to make a picture with Mr. Goldwyn." The audience was howling and the media people all took notes.

Hope returned to Paramount to make *The Road to Zanzibar* with Crosby and Lamour as well as Una Merkel and Eric Blore. Victor Schertzinger was directing once again, and he had learned some things about the Hope-Crosby chemistry since *Singapore*. He saw more comedy in Crosby as the schemer and Hope the victim, and likewise it worked better when Crosby was the lover who wins and Hope plays "junior" who is all false confidence and nervous laughs and loses the girl.

Clowning on the set was standard procedure even though the frequent comic disruptions and the flow of traffic caused by casual visitors and invited guests frustrated producer Paul Jones's efforts to bring *Zanzibar* in on budget. But not all the gags were laid on Crosby and Hope by each other. One day during a rehearsal Hope and Crosby were exchanging one of their rapid-fire routines designed to upset Dorothy. When they finished they turned to her and said, "How about it, Dottie?" Lamour smiled demurely, and as her smile widened she exposed to the camera and the crew—and her costars—a row of blacked-out front teeth. Bob and Bing fell down laughing.

Meanwhile the Pepsodent season was prospering, despite the loss of Judy Garland, who after winning an Oscar was forced to leave the Pepsodent show because of the increasing demands of her MGM contract. The show returned to a guest-star policy, while it continued with strong cast spots featuring Brenda and Cobina and the antics of Colonna and Ennis. Ben Gage had replaced Bill Goodwin as the personality introducer. The show had gained so much popularity that not far into the season the most reliable radio rating service, Hooper, was 28.2, just a few points behind Edgar Bergen's show. Jack Benny still held the commanding lead at 36.2, but *Radio Daily* named Hope the "top comedian of the nation" on the basis of a poll of radio critics.

At home, Dolores was trying to adjust to the shrinking slice of Bob's time allotted to her and baby Linda. With a five-day shooting schedule at the studio and a weekend schedule of rehearsals and the show's preview, it was catch as catch can. She was thrilled when a call came from Florence Walrath, in Evanston, to tell her that the baby boy they had asked for was finally available, and Bob asked if he could do the honors of going to pick up the baby alone at The Cradle. Later he reported to his friends, "The attendants stuffed me into one of these rear-entrance zoot suits and a surgical Santa Claus beard. Then they marched me into a glass cage and exhibited me to a series of little characters who went wild about me. At least they clawed the air and screamed."

Humor aside, what took place when Hope stood at the nursery viewing window and a tiny male baby was held up for his inspection was unexpected. The infant turned his face and showed a profile that caused a nurse to say, "He looks just *like* you." Bob thought so, too. When they walked away from the window he said, "That little character with the ski-slide nose—that's for me."

Bob called Dolores and she went to Chicago to pick up Anthony—little Tony—and fly back home with him.

Now that their family was expanding, the Navajo Street house was too crowded. So Bob and Dolores looked around in the Toluca Lake neighborhood and found a white-brick, 18-room English Tudor-style mansion for $28,000 on nearby Moorpark Street. It was not far from Crosby's estate and still very close to Lakeside. The Hopes fell in love with the place, even though it had a leaking roof. In the months and years that followed this move, the Hopes bought all the property around their home that they could acquire, added a separate office building, and built spacious guest quarters over their four-car garage, a swimming pool, and tennis courts—and still had room for a three-hole golf course. Over the years the house would undergo many expansions and several reconfigurations to accommodate Bob's mother-in-law, Theresa DeFina, and two more adopted children, Nora and Kelly.

19

Covering the Bases

"I'm happy to be here again, ladies and gentlemen, for my annual insult. (He pats Oscar on the head)... Remember me, shorty?... Snob!... I don't mind not winning, but the Oscars look at me as if I was an agent... The only thing I ever got from the Academy is saddle blisters..."

The strong, aristocratic timbre of Franklin Roosevelt's voice broke the tension of 1,400 filmmakers meeting at the Los Angeles Biltmore for the thirteenth annual Academy Awards banquet on February 21, 1941. Roosevelt, just reelected for a third term, had asked the Academy for six minutes of time in the ceremony's agenda to praise the movie industry for its contribution to national defense and for boosting American patriotism and morale. The President's aides could hardly ignore the statistic that in the year 1940 motion picture admissions exceeded $735 million, and industry predictions indicated that the figure would rise to a billion in 1941.

Hope was the emcee for this Oscar ceremony and was in his usual playful vein. Looking longingly at the long row of gleaming golden statuettes, he said, "I see David Selznick brought them back!" referring to the unprecedented *Gone With the Wind* sweep the year before.

He glanced accusingly at his own studio's banquet table. "They've just loaned me to Samuel Goldwyn for one picture—a sort of lend-louse bill." The audience roared. "I see Paramount has a table, Metro-Goldwyn-Mayer has a table, Warners has a table and Twentieth Century–Fox has a table. Monogram has a stool."

It was the Academy's first awards using sealed envelopes, and Hope had just cracked that the banquet was "six courses of nervous indigestion," when Walter Wanger stepped to the microphone:

Ladies and gentlemen, I would like to pay tribute tonight to a man who has devoted his time and energy to many causes. His unselfishness in playing countless benefits has earned him a unique position in a hectic community where his untiring efforts are deeply, profoundly appreciated. Ladies and gentlemen, the Academy this year presents a special award for "Achievements in Humanities"—for his unselfish services to the motion picture industry—this silver plaque to—Bob Hope!

Hope was stunned. "I don't feel a bit funny," he said, holding up the plaque and kissing it. "How am I going to get this thing in my scrapbook? I'll have to build a whole new room for it."

When Hope sauntered into his Paramount soundstage the next day he was applauded by his coworkers. The movie was *Caught in the Draft*, probably Hollywood's first comedy about the rather serious subject of conscription. Hope was cast as Don Bolton, a movie star who resists the draft but then enlists in the Army to win the Colonel's daughter, played by Dorothy Lamour. It was produced by Paramount's new production chief, Buddy DeSylva, and directed by David Butler.

The film then ran into weather problems and attempts to shoot some essential scenes on location were repeatedly thwarted. Finally the weather cleared, and because they were already way over budget, Butler was trying to get his last two important location setups in a single day. He had two locations, both about twenty miles away from Paramount and six miles from each other.

Butler completed the first setup in early afternoon and asked Hope to meet him for the second at Paramount's ranch in Malibu Canyon, which happened to be an area Hope knew had some especially good real estate opportunities. He piled his makeup man, Harry Ray, into his car and they drove off to look at the property. Hope lingered too long and the daylight began to fade. Realizing this, he raced to the ranch just as Butler was exploding. The studio quickly brought in a truckload of extra lights to augment the fading sunlight. Paramount was angry with Hope, but Hope bought the land that today is worth millions.

The thoughtlessness and self-indulgence revealed in this episode came to the surface a number of times during Hope's first flush-of-success period in Hollywood. His platoon of writers, who spent more time with him than his family, saw a man the public didn't. It was they who daily fed the showman's ego and did what they could to feed his hunger for approval (though only an audience could really satisfy that appetite). They saw that beyond the normal drives of an entertainer, Hope craved the material rewards of success to make up for all he hadn't had as a child, for those years of struggle as a hoofer.

When his writers called him Scrooge, it was less for his penuriousness than for his running roughshod over the sensibilities of others. They tell how Hope on one payday stood up on a chair and made airplanes of their checks, floating them down to waiting hands. It was a gag, of course, but it was also a clear message conveying his status—and theirs.

They sometimes called him Piggy because at writing conferences there evolved a ritual of Hope sending out for his prime passion, ice cream. It was the youngest or newest writer who must go for it, and invariably Hope would order less than his writers could eat. Bob would take his share, and the others scraped up what was left.

The writers worked on holidays and were summoned from a dinner table or whisked out of town on a moment's notice at Hope's whim. And frequently their caviling was only an excuse for a gag at Hope's expense. One of the best examples of this comes from senior gagsmith Norman Sullivan, who says that Hope hired some young "relief writers" for the summer months and that one of these part-timers asked him, "What does Bob do about summer?" Sullivan replied tartly, "He lets it come."

Actually, those same writers expected to be awakened in the middle of the night by Hope, they sweated for him, they got ulcers for him, they waited for Christmas presents from him, they idolized him. In those days there was always about an even dozen gag writers but not always the same dozen. They were replaced when they lost their freshness. Mort Lachman said, "There were nine thousand guys waiting to write for Hope." There was excitement writing for him. He was on his way up. He was hot and getting hotter.

In March 1941 his movie career was blooming. One New York critic said, "*Road to Zanzibar* is mostly nonsense but it is nonsense of the most delightful sort." Hope had started filming the spy spoof *Nothing but the Truth* with Paulette Goddard and there was success written all over that picture.

Hope was pleased with this radio season, too. One Saturday afternoon after Hope had finished a script session at NBC in Hollywood and was leaving the parking lot, producer Al Capstaff hailed his car to a stop. "How would you like to do the show for the Air Corps at Riverside—one of our Sunday night previews, or maybe the real thing—out at March Field?"

"Why not invite the fellas to the studio?" Hope countered. His routine, a grind to any other performer, was demanding but comfortable; it was nicely geared to his golf game and he didn't have to drive more than fifteen minutes to either studio.

"Too many guys."

"How many?"

"A thousand—maybe two."

Hope's eyes blinked. He turned his head away and thought about that-size crowd fanned out in front of him. He could hear the sound that two thousand joke-hungry servicemen could make, all laughing and applauding.

"Get more details. I like it." He drove away.

The arguments in favor of originating a show from a military base were hard to beat. It would be an innovative radio idea. It would provide Hope with responsive, enthusiastic audiences. It would offer him a body of engaging, topical subject matter that was tailor-made for his persona. Last but certainly not least, it would be a humdinger of a promotion for his soon-to-be-released *Caught in the Draft*.

Hope's first GI broadcast, from March Field, in Riverside, California, was on May 6, 1941. The program was produced in his established radio format, with opening monologue, cast-member comedy, music, a guest-star sketch, and the usual commercials. The important difference was the total adaptation of the comedy to a military context. These excerpts from the initial monologue are indicative:

How do you do ladies and gentlemen, this is Bob March Field Hope. . . telling all soldiers they may have to shoot in the swamp or march in the brush, but if they use Pepsodent no one will ever have to drill in their mush. . . Well, here we are, ladies and gentlemen, at March Field, one of the Army's great flying fields, located near Riverside, California. . . and I want to tell you that I'm thrilled being here. . . and what a wonderful welcome they gave me. . . As soon as I got in the camp I received a ten-gun salute. . . They told me on the operating table. . . but all these fellows were glad to see me. . . One rookie came running up to me, very excited, and said: "Are you really Bob Hope?" I said: "Yes" . . . but they grabbed his rifle away just in time. . .

The opening "This is Bob [wherever he was] Hope" not only bracketed the context within the personality, but also telegraphed the significance of the context. Furthermore, his use of "Well, here we are at . . ." immediately fixed a geographic location, establishing Hope as a traveler, a fast mover. "I'm thrilled being here," for all of its surface enthusiasm and ingratiation, implied the incongruity of Hope being "thrilled" to be entertaining at some remote military installation under the circumstances of national mobilization. Hope and his writers elicited both soldier and civilian laughter from instances of simple, hare-brained foolishness, reluctant heroism, and even blatant cowardice set against a high seriousness, a stern military regime where ordinary men were being prepared for war. Hope's exploitation of the soldier's resentments, hardships, and habits permitted the soldier to laugh at his environment and at himself as a victim of that environment while arousing sympathy in the general audience.

It took several days to assess the impact of the March Field experiment and consequently the following week's show originated from Paramount's studio on Melrose Avenue. But on May 20 Hope took guest star Priscilla Lane and his regular cast to the San Diego Naval Station. The show's third GI trip, the next week, was for Marines at Camp Roberts, in San Luis Obispo, and on June 10 Hope took Mary Martin and director David Butler to the Army's Camp Callan, in Torrey Pines, just north of San Diego, where he also previewed, to a wildly enthusiastic crowd, his latest film effort, *Caught in the Draft.*

From the moment of its release the new movie was a runaway box-office success; it became the biggest moneymaker Paramount had that year. On July 7, 1941, *Time* magazine reviewed the film favorably, and then followed with ten paragraphs of personality profile concentrating on Hope's business acumen:

Bob Hope has made twelve pictures to date (three of them this year), has five more lined up and waiting. He is on the NBC air every week for Pepsodent. If people grow weary of Hope's stylized impudence, it will be largely due to the star's appealing avarice. Physically, Bob Hope's biggest asset is his chin, a granitic abutment fit to warm the heart of any quarry-bound sculptor. However, he rarely leads with it. Around the Paramount lot he is known as a "hard man with a dollar."

Bing Crosby fired off a letter to *Time* that said, "My friend Bob Hope is anything but cheap. He does an average of two benefits a week. His price for a personal appearance would be about $10,000, so he gives away $20,000 every week of his life. Is that cheap?"

The magazine rebutted, "*Time* agrees with Bing; however, Bob from time to time has been known to put undue pressure on a nickel."

The one incontrovertible statement by *Time* was that Hope had a sharp business sense. His instinct for marketing and promotion was acute, and Pepsodent was anxious to involve him in a national promotion stunt that could put their toothpaste into the top sales bracket. They were searching for something that gave them a closer identification with Hope. Along the way Hope had an idea.

As soon as his last Pepsodent show of the season was aired and the final scenes for *Nothing but the Truth* were dubbed, Hope took a plane for New York. Pepsodent's marketing genius, Vic Hunter, and Lord & Thomas's John McPherrin sat down with Hope in the comedian's St. Regis suite. Hope suggested, "Instead of running a contest or giving away a lifelong dental policy or whatever, how would you like to give away a book that I would write, a comic autobiography— you know, one where I could really rib myself like I do on the air. I've got a dozen clever elves on the Coast to help me. Do you have any idea how much fan mail we've been getting, and how much of it asks for pictures and biographical stuff? There's another angle to this. I've got a picture that will be released in the fall, just the time you're ready to drop this stunt. It's called *Nothing but the Truth*. I think we can tie the two together in some way—maybe use that as the title. Why don't you talk to the boys at Paramount?"

Lord & Thomas was thrilled to have so much of its creative work already done, and Paramount saw the potential of a national promotion for one of its stars. Pepsodent agreed to pay for the book's printing; Paramount agreed to help promote it. Their plan was to photograph every major Hollywood star reading a copy of the book. Lord & Thomas planned a mock "literary tea" at the Stork Club, a premier dining spot for the rich and famous, for press and celebrities. All this for a book that would cost ten cents and a box top from a tube of Pepsodent. Hope retained the copyright.

Elated by the prospects of adding "author" to his accomplishments, Hope left New York for Cleveland to talk with Ivor about the possibility of Hope Metal Products, their jointly held company, picking up some defense contracts, and to see the rest of his family there. He shared with them his most recent letter from Granddad in Hitchin, who, nearly ninety-eight, was "busy dousing incendiary bombs" and serving as a self-styled air-raid warden.

Hope then went back to Hollywood to begin *Louisiana Purchase*, the screen version of Irving Berlin's long-running Broadway original. Paramount's script was a toothless satire of fiery Louisiana politics and the corruption surrounding the Huey Long family.

It was fortunate that the Hope writers weren't overtaxed trying to punch up the *Louisiana Purchase* script that summer, because their backs were bent over their typewriters pecking out pages of one-liners suitable for inclusion in the comic reconstruction of the comedian's thirty-seven-year life. In late-night hours and in scattered periods on weekends, Hope dictated bits and pieces of ideas he wanted included in the book and gags that he thought should be developed. Neither he nor the writers cared about biographical accuracy. The thrust of the humor was to deflate the Hope success story, meanwhile satirizing elements of the American Dream.

Taken as a whole, *They Got Me Covered* (as the volume was finally called) was a 95-page paperback giveaway distributed in the hundreds of thousands as a souvenir program for Tuesday night's broadcast. The first half, focusing on struggles for fame, was Horatio Alger peppered with folk wit; the second half, with its put-downs of the glamour life in Hollywood, was almost a predecessor of *Mad* magazine. The principal running gag, as expected, was Hope's adolescent-style lechery for the likes of Hedy Lamarr and Madeleine Carroll. Not surprisingly, one quarter of the book was devoted to a smart-alecky behind-the-scenes look at his own Pepsodent show, including a burlesque scene showing a dozen gag writers at work.

The pages seemed to be meant for reading aloud. It was a long monologue without the dots and dashes of Hope's delivery. Alva Johnson, commenting on the book in *Life* magazine, was the first critical observer to apply the word "humorist" to Bob Hope, and also the first to suggest his resemblance to others allied with the popular oracle tradition in American humor, such as Josh Billings, Bill Nye, and Petroleum V. Nasby.

The strength of the book rests in a simple, graceful quality that Woody Allen, among others, has cited as the epitome of Hope's style. Much of the book is still funny today, particularly the sequence that covered his ill-fated boxing career:

> I was very popular because I had a peculiar weaving, bobbing style the crowd loved to watch. I used to weave and bob around the ring for ten minutes after the other guy had won and gone home. I'll never forget my first fight. When the bell rang I danced to the center of the ring—then they carried me to the corner. Then the bell rang again and I danced to the center of the ring—then they carried me to my corner.

While *They Got Me Covered* was rolling off the presses and waiting to be ordered by Pepsodent users, Hope took his radio gang to Chicago for the program's 1941–42 seasonal premiere on September 23. Hope proudly introduced Frances Langford as his newest cast regular, aware that her popularity as a movie and recording personality would be an immediate asset to the show's ratings. And to fire up the book promotion, Hope's longest comedy sketch that night was all about the publishing business.

Several of the comedy sketches during the fall season were derived from Hope's tongue-in-cheek autobiography. These constant reminders to the 23 million weekly listeners speeded up the mail-in orders for the 2 million copies Pepsodent had had printed as a first edition.

That same fall of 1941, Hope was finally to make a movie with Paramount's beautiful English-born star, Madeleine Carroll. For the two previous radio seasons Hope had been praising her looks and joking about making a film with her. Hope learned that it was Carroll herself who had suggested they be teamed for a film. Bob asked his two young writers Norman Panama and Melvin Frank to write a screenplay for him. They called it *My Favorite Blonde* and it involved a second-rate vaudevillian with a penguin act who becomes unwittingly involved with a beautiful British secret agent who is trying to keep Nazi spies from stealing the plans of a new fighter plane. Really?

Hope had agreed to ride a horse on December 6 in the annual Santa Claus Lane parade along Hollywood Boulevard, sponsored by the Hollywood Chamber of Commerce. Hope said he would ride providing they gave him a worn-out delivery-wagon plug, and as he plodded along, he would be preceded by a huge placard reading BING CROSBY'S FASTEST RACEHORSE. Hope was warmly applauded by the huge turnout of fans and Christmas shoppers who lined both sides of Hollywood Boulevard that Saturday afternoon.

Hope slept late on Sunday morning. It was eleven when Dolores came in with his coffee and the newspapers. As she walked toward her dressing room, she told him about the photos of the Santa Claus Lane parade in the rotogravure section of the *Daily News*, and about a rather extensive feature piece on *Louisiana Purchase* in the *This Week* magazine supplement of the *Los Angeles Times* of December 7, 1941. When his eyes began to focus Bob scanned the *Los Angeles Times* article.

One paragraph in the story disturbed him, because it revealed fairly accurately his income. There were all kinds of nuts running around, and he had two little children who could be kidnapped. The story said:

The comedian's gross income during 1940, from radio, movies and personal appearances, totaled $464,161.78. Even after business deductions, Bob paid, for 1940, federal and state income taxes totaling $142,047.66. His 1941 gross income will probably rise to $575,000, but considering the defense rates Congress has approved, he may remind himself of his favorite joke about Crosby: "Bing doesn't pay a regular income tax. He just calls up Secretary Morgenthau each year and asks, 'How much do you boys need?'"

It was eleven-twenty. He was listening with one ear to the pro football game coming from New York's Polo Grounds and musing about the article. Dolores had gone downstairs to supervise the children's lunch and had come back up to her sitting room next to their bedroom. She had snapped on her radio to listen to the New York Philharmonic concert because Artur Rubinstein, whom she had recently met, was going to play a Brahms concerto.

Then Bob heard words he couldn't quite believe, and yet he knew he had heard them. He sat up straight, yelling, "Dolores!"

She came quickly to the door. "What happened?"

"The Japs bombed Pearl Harbor," he said savagely.

"Are you sure? There's nothing on CBS but music." She went back to her own radio. "Oh, my God," she said, returning with the front page of the *Los Angeles Times* in her hand. "Bob, do you realize that Japanese envoys were meeting with Secretary of State Hull today—"

"Those bastards. They've stabbed us," he said, getting out of bed. "Dolores, why don't you drive with Jack and me to Long Beach tonight? We're doing a preview of our show for the Navy. It ought to be some kind of show."

On Tuesday evening Pepsodent relinquished its airtime to President Roosevelt, who had asked for the most-listened-to time slot on radio for his second declaration-of-war speech to the American people.

Bob's public and private reaction to the nation's crisis was reflected by his opening speech on the December 16 broadcast. There was no signature theme song. He began:

Good evening ladies and gentlemen. . . This is Bob Hope, and I just want to take a moment to say that last Tuesday night at this time I was sitting out there with you listening to our President as he asked all Americans to stand together in this emergency. We feel that in times like these—more than ever before, we need a moment of relaxation. All of us on the Pepsodent show will do our best to bring it to you. We think this is not a question of keeping up morale. . . To most Americans, morale is taken for granted. There is no need to tell a nation to keep smiling when it's never stopped. It's that ability to laugh that makes us the great people that we are. . . Americans! All of us in this studio feel that if we can bring into your homes a little of this laughter each Tuesday night we ar helping to do our part.

Clown Hero: 1942 to 1945

20

Victory Caravan

"I don't know if you've ever been kissed by a camel, but I've got to tell you it's not like being kissed by Raquel Welch. This particular camel may have been listening to my radio show because after he kissed me he spat right in my face!"

It was New Year's Day, 1942, and Hope was lying in bed listening to the Rose Bowl game. Ordinarily he would be in Pasadena watching the game. But this year, for precautionary reasons—what had been described as "sensitive wartime restrictions"—the game had been moved to Durham, North Carolina, where Oregon State had gone to play, and, as it turned out, to win.

As had been the custom for the past three years, the Hopes would hold an open house in Toluca Lake. Their guests included the Crosbys, the Colonnas, the Malatestas (Dolores's sister and brother-in-law), the MacArthurs, maybe Jack Hope and his new wife, Lee, and George Hope, as well as David Butler, Louis Shurr, and the Jimmy Saphiers.

Instead of the trip to the Rose Bowl, there would be a punch bowl, a buffet, and perhaps a screening of *Louisiana Purchase* or Bing's latest, *Holiday Inn*. Hope was stretched out on his oversized bed and, while he listened to the game, was scribbling down some parodied lyrics to his theme song, which he might sing, if asked, later in the day.

This had been an extraordinary year for him with some very thankful memories. Both the press and his film colleagues had boosted his stock.

Hope had received many awards besides his special Oscar. In a Radio Daily poll of the nation's radio critics Hope was voted not only the "Leading Entertainer" and the "Leading Comedian" in America, but also their "Champion of Champions"—their most prestigious commendation. The Hollywood Press Photographers Association also had given him its highest award. Perhaps closest to his heart, on December 26 *Motion Picture Herald* had announced that with the enormous box-office returns from *Caught in the Draft* Hope had joined the inner circle of top moneymaking film stars.

From abroad, Granddad's most recent letter described the long queues outside London's Odeon Theatre, where *Caught in the Draft* was playing. James Hope wrote that the film was playing continuously night and day, and asked Bob to come to Britain as soon as possible to entertain his "countrymen" and to make them forget their troubles. Hope said he was going to do just that.

In fact, 1942 was a cyclonic year, despite Hope's getting several warnings from his doctor, Tom Hearn, to slow down. There was an exhibition golf tour with Bing Crosby for the Red Cross and other war relief causes in February. There was the filming of *Road to Morocco* (probably the funniest *Road* picture); after that came the Hollywood Victory Caravan of twenty-one major film stars touring the country for the Army and Navy Relief Fund; then back to Hollywood to film Goldwyn's *They Got Me Covered*; then off to Alaska for his first overseas USO (United Services Organization) tour, interlaced with at least fifty benefit appearances, and of course his regular schedule of weekly radio shows, most of which originated from military bases. And since it was Hope's custom to preview a radio show at one base and do it live from another, he ended up with two GI entertainments a week.

After Bing and Bob did the Red Cross benefit golf match in Sacramento (which made extra headlines because Bob, with all his pranks and banter, won), and after each had performed his weekly radio chore, the two met at Paramount to prepare for the *Road to Morocco*. For some, this film typifies what is meant by a Hope-Crosby collaboration. Director David Butler, a serious, meticulous craftsman, had learned to capitalize on his stars' improvisations. His early schooling in the rough-and-tumble Mack Sennett silents enabled him to anticipate and deal with the unexpected.

The one thing all three men knew with certainty was that a *Road* picture meant spontaneity, and that too many rehearsals deadened the fun. "If anything happened that was out of the ordinary," Butler said, "I'd always let the camera run—and we got some of our funniest stuff after the scene was over. I'd even let the camera roll until they got off the set, or walked out, or whatever happened."

The *Morocco* script, once again a product of the imagination of Frank Butler and Don Hartman, was ideal wartime escapism. Crosby as Jeff Peters and Hope as Turkey Jackson are shipwrecked and washed up onto the Moroccan shore. Crosby sells Hope into slavery to pay their dinner check, and Hope becomes the captive of the beautiful Princess Shalimar, played by Dorothy Lamour. Eventually Crosby arrives to save Hope from the vengeance of the sheik, played by Anthony Quinn, and Crosby wins Lamour—naturally.

One of the film's funniest sequences typifies the Butler approach. At the opening of the movie, Bob and Bing do a scene with a trained camel whose assignment was to sneak up behind them and lick first Bob and then Bing on the cheek. The gag in the film was that each man thought the other was doing the kissing. Hope said some years later, "Don't know if you've ever been kissed by a camel, but I've got to tell you that it's not like being kissed by Raquel Welch. This particular camel may have been listening to my radio show because after he kissed me he spat right in my face."

Hope staggered backward, shocked by the unexpectedness of the spit and repulsed by the vile stench of the spittle. Crosby doubled up with laughter as did most of the crew. Butler kept the camera rolling.

"Great scene," Butler said finally. And when someone remarked what a lucky break they got with the camel, Butler said, "Lucky my foot. I worked with that beast for weeks!"

Morocco had its perilous moments as well. Butler took the cast over to the Twentieth Century–Fox backlot to shoot a scene in which Bob and Bing were being chased down a narrow alley by a band of wild horses. Hope and Crosby took their places and on signal began to walk down the alley. They were supposed to reach the halfway point when the horses were cued to move. But when Butler yelled for a camera roll, the assistant director had already cued the horses and they were soon bearing down on Bob and Bing. The two turned and saw they could be trampled to death before they reached the other end. Bing saw a hole in the pavement and dropped, while Bob flattened himself against a shallow doorway until the horses got past.

They angrily made their way back to Butler. A former stuntman himself, Butler had not seen any danger in asking Hope and Crosby to work with the horses.

"What in hell was that?" screamed Hope.

"You nearly lost your stars, Dave," said Crosby, nursing bruises from his tumble.

Butler's hulking frame was shaking and between laughs he said, "Yeah—how about that? We got a great shot."

Just as the filming of *Morocco* ended, Paramount released *My Favorite Blonde*, and Hope arranged to premiere the picture at military bases in connection with his Pepsodent show originations. At his radio show on April 7 he played host to hundreds of young air cadets in Hollywood. The next week he introduced Rita Hayworth to airmen at Santa Ana and to sailors at San Pedro, and in both halls the noisy welcome almost lifted the roof.

On April 29, Hope, Frances Langford, and Jerry Colonna flew to Washington, D.C., to catch up with the Hollywood Victory Caravan. This was a very special train that had just crossed the country carrying some of the nation's most popular entertainers, who had been enlisted by the War Activities Committee to bolster the Army and Navy relief funds. They had agreed to spend two weeks on a whistle-stop tour of 12 American cities. Right from the train they were whisked off to a reception on the White House lawn.

First Lady Eleanor Roosevelt personally thanked each of the stars, including Desi Arnaz, Joan Bennett, Joan Blondell, Charles Boyer, James Cagney, Claudette Colbert, Bing Crosby, Olivia de Havilland, Cary Grant, Charlotte Greenwood, Bert Lahr, Laurel and Hardy, Groucho Marx, Frank McHugh, Ray Middleton, Merle Oberon, Pat O'Brien, Eleanor Powell, Rise Stevens, and Spencer Tracy—and now, of course, Bob, Frances, and Jerry.

A three-hour variety package of popular songs, dances, comedy sketches, dramatic scenes and readings, and even operatic arias had been created by producer-director Mark Sandrich and musical director Alfred Newman. The special material had been written by such heavyweights as Lindsay and Crouse, Moss Hart, George S. Kaufman, and Jerome Chodorov with original music by Jerome Kern,

Johnny Mercer, Frank Loesser, and Arthur Schwartz. Hope, the master of ceremonies, was faced with the responsibility of keeping the show moving, holding it
together by introducing acts, joking between acts, as well as acting in scenes with
Claudette Colbert, Spencer Tracy, Bing Crosby, and Jerry Colonna.

After the lawn party they all converged on Constitution Hall for a rehearsal
that lasted all night. From the start of the tour Hope was the subject of admiration for his high energy level and his unerring ability to thread the ragged
parts of the show together. He was also the target of some playful barbs because
he was trying, as usual, to sandwich in his radio show, golf exhibition matches
with Crosby, and whatever other business he could accomplish in cities they
were visiting.

Before they stepped out onto the Constitution Hall stage for their opening
show, on April 30, Groucho Marx dropped an acerbic comment as he fretted
about his own role in the show. "It's all right for guys like Hope. He has seventeen
guys writing his jokes for him. But I've got to do the worrying about my own
materials." Sandrich told Groucho that Hope had only six writers along and their
job was to write his radio show for the next two weeks. Groucho snapped, "Only
six? For Hope that's practically ad-libbing."

At the Caravan's next stop, in Boston, there were thousands of people waiting
at South Station when the train pulled in, and thousands more lining the streets
leading to the Statler Hotel. Hope had made prior arrangements to meet Fred
Corcoran, head of the Professional Golf Association, for dinner at the Union
Oyster House and confessed to Sandrich and other Victory Caravan officials that
he would not be riding in the motorcade from the station to Boston Garden. The
news irritated both the Boston and the Caravan officials, but Sandrich said,
"What the hell! Who's going to know?"

With difficulty, Hope and Corcoran managed to push their way through
huge street mobs to the Union Oyster House, where they sat in an obscure corner and ate shrimp and soft-shell crabs. Corcoran was describing to Hope the
exhibition matches that would be sandwiched between the Caravan shows and
Hope's radio show the following week when a man from a nearby table interrupted. "I want you to know that your appearance here has been a life-saver for
me, Mr. Hope. My wife has been giving me holy hell because I forgot her opera
glasses, and she was saying the evening would be ruined unless she could get a
close-up view of Bob Hope—just as you walked by our table. Thanks. It saves
me a lot of grief."

Hope smiled. "Nice I could help." Then he stood. "Hey, what time is it?" As
usual he was without a timepiece. "We've got to get to that parade."

Corcoran threw a wad of bills at the waiter and they ran for the door. The
streets outside were jammed. Haymarket Square was impossible to penetrate.
They started to walk toward North Station. People were facing the street and
cheering. Bob muscled his way through the line and tried to see the motorcade.

"Isn't this silly," he said. "All these people standing on the street trying to get a peek at a homely guy like Hope. What's he got I haven't got?"

"Ahhhh—shut up!" the man beside him said.

Corcoran stifled a laugh and suggested to Bob that what the other stars had, and what he didn't have, was a ride to Boston Garden. A few minutes later they managed to find a taxi and the driver ingeniously carried them to about five hundred yards from their destination. Hope jumped out, pushed through a line of spectators, leaped over a sawhorse barrier, and ran up to and climbed on the running board of one of the moving convertibles. Once in, Hope started waving at the crowd. A scream went up, "There's Bob Hope!" He was told later that there were many such screams all along the parade route—all mistaken identifications—because in twilight the stars were not easy to distinguish, flanked as they were by military escorts.

The Boston show went better than Washington's had, and Philadelphia's the next day was better than Boston. The train pushed on toward Cleveland, Detroit, Chicago, St. Louis, St. Paul, Minneapolis, Des Moines, Houston, and Dallas. Hope's chores were so well grooved that he could actually enjoy his departures from the tour to do his radio show and golf benefits.

Even though he seemed to be looping in and out of the Caravan life, Bob's value to the tour was unquestioned. His nightly high spirits and his good-natured wisecracks about a band of Hollywood gypsies kept the stars laughing both on- and offstage. One of Hope's most engaging routines onstage each night was his sly revelation to each audience of the secrets of backstage life—what was really going on between whistle stops. Sadly, Hope was missing most of that camaraderie himself.

But Hope was always a part of the marvelous before-show dressing-room tableau. John Lahr described a nightly ritual of that tour presided over by the beloved Stan Laurel and "Babe" Hardy, who always managed to be first to arrive backstage at any theater: "Their make-up would be set out neatly in front of them with a clean towel folded carefully over it. Between them each day was an opened bottle of whiskey. Laurel and Hardy waited quietly as the actors came in. Gradually everyone moved down toward their corner, sharing a drink and theater talk."

Groucho, at first reluctant to enjoy the Caravan, later confessed how much he enjoyed taking part in quartet contests from midnight till daybreak. He admitted he was amused by a "million-dollar crooner straining his voice to top the sound of the train and trying hard to outdo an obscure baritone who insisted he was Bob Hope." Marx caught himself before he became maudlin about the tour, adding, "It isn't safe for a comic to get too sentimental." Bert Lahr had no compunction about sentimentality. He called the wartime fund-raiser a "caravan of love."

Perhaps the best reflection of the stars' attitude was witnessed the final night, in Houston. A capacity crowd of 12,000 in the Houston Coliseum cheered and stomped, unaware that there were actually two shows going on simultaneously that night. Because it was Tuesday night, Hope's Pepsodent show was being broadcast from an adjacent theater filled with hundreds of airmen from Ellington Field. Hope, Langford, and Colonna dashed back and forth between theaters doing their Caravan solos and sketches in addition to their thirty-minute broadcast. Cary Grant shared the emcee chores with Hope that night for the Caravan show. When the broadcast was finished, travel-weary stars from the Caravan began showing up at the second theater to perform for the spellbound GIs. The show for the airmen lasted two hours and it was one o'clock before the applause ended.

After the Houston show, the Caravan stars dispersed. They were all very, very tired. But Hope, to everyone's disbelief, was starting out with Langford and Colonna for four more weeks of entertaining GIs. They were scheduled to do 65 shows at a variety of military bases and hospitals, including Pepsodent radio shows at New Orleans; Atlanta; Quantico, Virginia; and Mitchell Field, Long Island.

The Victory Caravan was merely the vanguard of the movie industry's war effort. Through the War Activities Committee, Hollywood raised nearly a million dollars for the USO, over a million for the war bond drive, and more than two million for Army and Navy relief societies. It distributed films to camps and bases and set and met a long-range goal to raise a billion dollars in war bonds by sending seven troupes of film stars to appearances in five thousand theaters located in three hundred cities across the nation.

Although many stars were doing camp shows and selling bonds, Hope's GI entertaining would become legendary. This 65-show tour was merely a foretaste of what was in store for him during the next three years, during which he would become remarkably adept in becoming a part of his audience, in speaking the GI language, in ribbing their gripes. His many walks through hospital wards to cheer the sick and dying were never easy experiences, but he knew instinctively that the only way he could get through an intensive-care or burn ward was with gags. One of his earliest incursions into this sensitive area made a deep impression on him. He shared some of these feelings with Al Sharp, a reporter from an Atlanta newspaper, when he arrived at that city's Biltmore Terrace hotel on May 26.

"Come on in here," said Hope in a tired voice. He drew the reporter away from the crowd in his suite to another room, closed the door, and dropped down to a couch. Hope had a day's stubble of beard. "Phew. Boy, am I tired—I mean really tired. We did three shows last night down in Louisiana and then flew in here a little while ago in an Army transport." Hope yawned. But he wanted to talk.

"We've been on the road for two weeks. And what do you know? Our baggage is lost. Just like vaudeville. They tell me it'll be here tomorrow morning. I hope so because I've got a few more weeks of this to go. But I'm kidding. I love it. And I get a kick out of flying in those planes. We do quite a bit of it—going to and from Army camps and Navy bases. You see a lot—and it's interesting—and it's tough.

"The other day in New Orleans," Hope continued, "the merchant marine hospital staff heard we were in town and asked us to come out and cheer up some survivors from a tanker torpedoed near there a few days before. I was a bit upset about trying to cheer the boys up. We knew some of them were burned so badly they would die. But they wanted the gags, so we went."

Hope stood up. "After seeing those fellows all burned, I thought as I came out of the hospital, that's what Lew Ayres meant when he refused to kill folks." (Ayres had made national headlines with his announcement that he was a conscientious objector.) "Of course we've got to kill people—because we've got an aggressor creeping up on us to stab us in the back. But I admire Ayres for his stand. It took courage to do that. It's against his religion to kill folks. He's volunteered for the Medical Corps—and it takes courage to go into the front lines and care for people." Then, finally winding down, Hope was silent.

21

Frozen Follies

"We were trying to get back to Anchorage from Cordova when the sleet and hail hit us. It got worse and worse and then over Anchorage our radio went out. Dubowsky, the crew chief, handed us Mae Wests and gave us instructions: 'If we have to abandon ship, pull this! If you land in water, pull this!'"

Hope spent the summer of 1942 working for Sam Goldwyn—that is, during the week he worked for Goldwyn and on weekends he worked for Uncle Sam, doing shows at military bases and PGA-arranged war-relief golf benefits with Crosby.

He settled into Goldwyn's Santa Monica Boulevard studios in mid-July with his costar, Dorothy Lamour, and the director David Butler to do the picture he had wrestled from the legendary producer on that Dallas stage. Doc Shurr's partner, Al Melnick, had carved an extraordinary money deal that guaranteed Hope $100,000 and a percentage of the box office for his work, a deal particularly remarkable at a time when studios had agreed to curb salary increases for the war effort.

Hope used to say laughingly that he shamed Goldwyn into his salary demand. Goldwyn may have been eccentric, but he was a good businessman. Even without his glasses he could read box-office figures, and he was impressed, as most producers would be, that the New York Paramount in January had taken in the unheard-of figure of $24,000 for a single day's admissions to *Louisiana Purchase*, grossing a mammoth $92,000 for the week. Since then, *My Favorite Blonde* had smashed all the previous attendance records at the Paramount for its four-week run in May. Hope was clearly one of the hottest properties in films and was worth Sam's investment.

When Sam learned that Hope's comic autobiography, *They Got Me Covered*, had sold 3 million copies, he changed the movie script's title to match it and thus reap the publicity rewards of the book's success. Hope was cast as a clumsy foreign correspondent recalled by his Washington office for having missed the story of the Nazi invasion of Russia. He and his fiancée, played by Lamour, expose Axis saboteurs and he gets his job back.

One day Hope's former stand-in, Lyle Morain, visited the set in his sergeant's uniform. He asked Bob to consider making an entertainment tour of some desolate bases far north in Alaska, remote but crucial to American defense, where some of his buddies were stationed.

Al Jolson had recently returned from doing shows in Alaska, arranged by the War Department. The comedian Joe E. Brown had taken a load of athletic equipment up there and traveled for 33 days from base to base by plane and dogsled. Hope picked up the phone and spoke to his pal Edgar Bergen, who admitted he "relished thirteen shows a day, done in gun emplacements, on the sides of hills, the backs of trucks, on barges and landing wharves." Hope asked brother Jack to find out if an Alaskan tour could be arranged.

Hope called newlywed Frances Langford, who was interested in going, but said she doubted that her husband, Jon Hall, would let her go. Hope called Hall and convinced him that Frances would be in safe hands. Next, Hope called Colonna, who was ready to go but had a practical concern: "How can we get to Alaska in September and still do our first Pepsodent show?"

Hope had an answer, though he was talking off the top of his head. "I'm nearly finished with this picture for Samuel the Golden, and barring trouble we should be doing the final shots on Saturday, September 5. If we could fly out on Tuesday the eighth, we'd be up in the north country for a good ten days. We could get back to Seattle on the twenty-second for the radio show, fly around Washington and Oregon to camps and bases there, then back to Seattle for our second radio show on the twenty-ninth. Easy. We'll need a musician. Any ideas?"

"Get Tony Romano. Best guitar in the business."

Early on the morning of September 5, Jack Hope came into his brother's dressing room.

"Bad news, Bob," Jack said into the mirror. "General Buckner, the commander up in Alaska, can't guarantee you'd be able to get back to Seattle in time for the radio show; weather's too variable. They've got unflyable conditions everywhere—thick fog-heavy rain—"

"Is that final?"

"It's fair warning, I guess."

"Send him a wire. Say—"

Jack interrupted, "His message came by way of the Victory Committee in Washington—"

"I don't care where it came from. Send Buckner this wire direct from me—from us—right now. Say 'Four disappointed thespians with songs and witty sayings are anxious to tour your territory. Please give us your consent and let us take our chances with the weather.' Sign it Bob Hope, Frances Langford, Jerry Colonna, and Tony Romano. Do it now."

Bob and Dolores went up to Pebble Beach to play some golf and to wait for Buckner's response. On Sunday, Jack reached them with a terse message from Alaska: YOU LEAVE TUESDAY. It was signed Major General Simon Buckner.

The troupe flew to Seattle and then north along the Canadian and lower Alaskan coastline, over the almost unspeakable beauty of white-crusted mountains, endless forests, and wild waterways, past Juneau and Whitehorse to Fairbanks. When they stepped off the plane they were disappointed to see that the airport looked pretty much like Lockheed's in Burbank.

Almost immediately they met Special Services Captain Don Adler and their pilots, Captains Marvin Setzer and Bob Gates. Over dinner at the local officers club that night they learned they would be hopping from outpost to outpost in the Army's stripped-down version of the DC–3. They were advised to enjoy these few comfortable hours in "the country club of Alaska," because everything beyond Fairbanks was rugged.

On their way back to the VIP billets, Hope bought a hundred postcards, which he planned to write as they flew around the country. They headed for Nome in the morning and stopped once, at Galena, for refueling. While they waited, GIs seemed to materialize from nowhere, and when a crowd had gathered it seemed a good time to break into their act and so they joked a bit and sang some songs from the back of a truck. Then they flew on to Nome and the Bering Strait, an area the GIs had tagged Devil's Island. Hope later wrote:

We went right to work doing shows for small groups in one Quonset hut after another. They were a tough audience, those guys in Nome. They'd been there so long they didn't want to thaw out. It wasn't their kind of country in the first place. Most of them were from Alabama. . . but when those kids did finally warm up, it was terrific. We came out of one hut and there were about six hundred standing in the rain. We tried to do a show but if Tony had gotten out his guitar it would have shrunk. . . so we packed the whole six hundred guys in one Quonset hut that normally holds three hundred. Now I really know how it feels to play a packed house. We were working on the stove.

After an entire day of hut shows, the local commander collected the overflow of servicemen, including some Russians, into a big hall in downtown Nome and that show lasted all evening.

The little band of entertainers, military escorts, and pilots were fast becoming Hope's "family." They shared the same goals and the same hardships. Langford was called Mother, Captain Setzer was Junior because he was the youngest, and Hope was their Dad.

At Fort Richardson in Anchorage, Buckner and his aides welcomed them. Over a Ping-Pong game the general told them what good things he had heard about their tour so far. "What we're suffering most up here, Bob, is cabin fever. Some of these boys have been stuck out in a godforsaken outpost for more than a year—with old books, old newspapers, old movies and stale relationships. I don't think you have any idea what you're doing for them."

After a big show at Fort Richardson, they hopped over to Annette, Canada, to do a show for the Royal Canadian Air Force. In that audience were about thirteen hundred U.S. Army construction engineers and workers building the new Alcan Highway. They had come to the show in bulldozers, jeeps, trucks, anything that moved. They were a highly vocal audience of rough, tough, but friendly men.

One joke that everyone loved was one that Hope had been telling since Nome:

You heard about the airman who was making his first parachute drop? Well, his first lieutenant told him which cord to pull, and told him that when he hit the ground there would be a station wagon waiting to drive him back to the base. So the airman jumped out of the plane and when he pulled the cord nothing happened, and he said, "And I bet the station wagon won't be there either."

They got as far as Cordova on their way back to Anchorage when their pilots decided to set the plane down and spend the night.

"Ahhh, come on, Junior," coaxed Frances. "The general's invited us to a big block dance in Anchorage tonight. Let's go on."

"Can't risk it, Mother," said Setzer. "We got strict orders not to fly you at night. It's our ass if we do."

"If the weather's good, I'll take the responsibility," said Bob. "You can blame me."

They took off and were barely into the air when they began to get some sleet and hail. The pilots plowed on, and though it is not a long ride from Cordova to Anchorage, it seemed endless in weather that got even worse.

It became clear to the passengers in the main cabin that there was trouble. They could hear Setzer and Gates shouting at each other just before Corporal Dubowsky, the cabin steward, closed the cockpit door. Hope looked at Colonna, who was slowly stroking his mustache and looking at Hope with those huge brown eyes.

The call light flashed in the cabin and Dubowsky went into the cockpit. When he came out he sat down next to Langford. He reached under her seat and took out a parachute and a Mae West lifejacket.

"You'd better put these on. We may have to ditch. If we should have to abandon ship, pull this. If you should land in water, pull this one."

"Water?" Frances asked.

"I think we're lost," said Dubowsky and moved over to show Hope, Colonna, and Romano how the parachute worked and how to activate the Mae West in the water.

"How bad is it?" Hope asked. "I mean, really."

"They're having trouble with the radio."

Just then the plane felt like it had been smacked by something hard. "What was that?"

"Felt like prop wash from another plane—and, man, that was close."

"This kind of thing isn't very good for my guitar," said Romano, who had turned chalk white.

"Remind me to tell you something when we're all landed safe and sound," said Langford, smiling.

Hope stared at her incredulously.

"I bet the station wagon won't be there either," said Colonna expressionlessly.

After an eternity of circling and waiting to see if things would clear, they saw a jab of light and the plane dipped and started downward. The plane came out of the soup in a blaze of searchlights. The prop wash they had felt was from a United Airlines ferry-service plane that had radioed the report of a backwash. Buckner had ordered every available searchlight trained on the sky. When Setzer and Gates saw a finger of light pierce the fog, they took a chance that it might be the field.

Hope, with his steel-trap memory, asked Langford what she was going to tell them later.

"I have always wanted to make a parachute jump. I was really half hoping we'd have to."

The weather didn't clear for two days. Hope learned that Bill Lawrence, the producer of the Pepsodent show, had arranged for Edgar Bergen and Kay Kyser to substitute in the opening show. But on Monday the weather broke and they flew down to Seattle in time to rehearse and do the show. The next morning Hope said to the other three, "Let's go back."

So instead of playing for Army and Navy personnel in Washington and Oregon, they flew back to Alaska and spent the next five days in the Aleutians, landing first in Anchorage to meet Setzer and Gates and a new plane.

Their first stop was Maknek, on Kichak Bay, near the Katmai Volcano at the headlands of the Alaskan Peninsula. Then they went farther out, to Unimak Island, where their audience was fanned out in front of them, sitting on the cold, wet ground. Told that there was a lot of guard duty there, Hope asked a kid sitting at his feet if he had to walk much. There was a sprinkling of laughter at the question, but when the kid replied, "I don't know—but when I enlisted I had feet!" Hope roared, and so did the rest of the audience. The comedian was learning what the GIs wanted most, liked best—needed—was humor turned on themselves, a chance to ventilate their hardships, their fear, their loneliness.

After their last show, at Kodiak, Bob, Frances, Jerry, and Tony flew back to Seattle to do the season's second Pepsodent show. Next day they were back in Hollywood.

For a time, Alaska was foremost on Hope's mind. He talked about the trip to everyone who would listen; he was clearly affected by the condition of the men. He had never imagined that one of the horrors of military and defense duty could be an unbearable loneliness and boredom. He urged other performers to go there. He said publicly that he had asked Paramount to delay *Let's Face It*, his next major film role for his home studio, until he could do another tour of Alaska. But he was also talking about wanting to entertain GIs in England, North Africa, and the Pacific.

The delay in starting *Let's Face It* had other components, however.

Let's Face It was a Herbert and Dorothy Fields–Cole Porter musical that had run for a year on Broadway starring Danny Kaye and Eve Arden. Shurr and Melnick were trying to convince Paramount executives that Hope should now be paid the same kind of money Sam Goldwyn had thought he was worth.

In the meantime, Hope continued to originate his radio show from Army camps and Navy bases that Pepsodent and the War Department thought had especially needy audiences. *Road to Morocco* was now in release, and *The New York Times* applauded the film for its lampooning of exotic romance pictures. Also on the edge of release was *Star Spangled Rhythm*, a prime example of the film genre of the picture designed to utilize all of the studio's stars in a single, patriotic variety format—exemplified also by *Stagedoor Canteen*, *Hollywood Canteen*, and *Thank Your Lucky Stars*—that flourished during the war. *Star Spangled Rhythm* was an extravaganza built around a GI storyline. It featured Bing Crosby, Ray Milland, Vera Zorina, Victor Moore, Mary Martin, Veronica Lake, Fred MacMurray, Dorothy Lamour, Dick Powell, Alan Ladd, Franchot Tone, and Paulette Goddard—all doing songs and sketches that were at odds with their screen images. Hope played master of ceremonies and acted in several sketches.

In November and December Hope took advantage of the delay in starting *Let's Face It* to take his radio show east of the Rockies to originate his radio shows for GIs in Colorado, Oklahoma, Missouri, Iowa, Ohio, and Indiana. When he returned, the *Let's Face It* deal was set; Hope would again receive his $100,000. Harry Tugend wrote the screenplay and although some of the good Porter music was retained, the film was retailored to fit Hope. There was no attempt to use Danny Kaye's tongue-twisting patter songs or to duplicate his acting style. It was, rather, a surefire formula for success, casting Hope as another GI in a musical farce loaded with topical gags—rationing and shortages, Veronica Lake's peekaboo hair, Wendell Willkie's defeat in his 1940 run for president, and Hitler. Hope's costars were Eve Arden, Betty Hutton, and Zasu Pitts.

In February, during the filming, Hope and Lamour were invited to make impressions of their hands and feet in wet cement on the forecourt of Hollywood's

Grauman's Chinese Theatre. A large crowd watched Bob and Dottie hug and clown a bit, then Hope dipped his nose in the cement. "This isn't quicksand, is it?" Laughter from the crowd. "If this hardens I won't be able to blow for months."

On March 4, 1943, at the Ambassador Hotel's Cocoanut Grove, Hope appeared once again as master of ceremonies for the annual Academy Award ceremonies. Plaster statuettes (replaced by gold ones after the war) were handed to Greer Garson for her portrayal of a courageous British housewife during the Battle of Britain in *Mrs. Miniver* and to Jimmy Cagney for his energetic *Yankee Doodle Dandy.* "White Christmas" was the best song and the entire evening had a warm sentimental feeling about it. It was also characterized by military ceremony and uniforms sprinkled throughout the audience. Marine Private Tyrone Power and Air Corps Private Alan Ladd unfurled a huge industry flag that carried the names of 27,677 film workers who were in uniform.

The subject of who was and who was not in uniform ultimately became a sensitive topic in Hollywood. Specifically, the subject of whether or not actors should be drafted was being aired by syndicated columnists, fan magazine writers, and editorial pundits. Hope once discussed this question with Ed Sullivan, then a columnist for the *New York Daily News.*

"Some night I'll be out there telling my jokes," said Hope, "and some big guy will stand up in the front row and he'll give me a Bronx cheer and yelp, 'Why-in-hell aren't you in service, Hope?' And that is the $64 question I won't be able to answer."

Sullivan reasoned with Hope that in or out of uniform he would undoubtedly be doing the same kind of job: boosting morale. So why not continue to do camp shows as a civilian? Yet obviously Hope was troubled.

Sullivan took the issue to his readers, and a week or so later he wrote in his *New York Daily News* column, "Here's something interesting—and it indicates how smart is John Q. Public: Nearly everyone says that Bob Hope, married and father of two adopted children, should be deferred."

Another of Hope's journalist friends, a McNaught Syndicate columnist named Henry McLemore, was in London as a correspondent. He wrote an open letter to Hope on April 24, 1943, urging the comedian to go to Britain to entertain. Hope asked his brother Jack to begin working with the Camp Show Division of the newly created United Services Organization (USO) to see how long a tour he could make and whether or not he could broadcast his radio show from overseas. Pepsodent was enthusiastic but Paramount was not. Hope owed them movies. Hope learned that the USO preferred a summer tour, which meant the radio season would be finished before he left.

Hope astonished everyone with his decision to hit the road in April as soon as *Let's Face It* was completed, to do a ten-week camp-show tour through Arizona, Texas, Louisiana, Florida, Georgia, South Carolina, Virginia, and Ohio. If the USO European tour began in June, Hope would be on the move continuously for five months.

From his friends and associates came concern for his health. Dolores had never stopped worrying about Bob's health nor his workload nor the constant traveling, but she had grown less edgy since she had begun her own job, with the American Women's Voluntary Services. She wished that Linda and Tony saw more of Bob, but she had made a kind of peace with herself about his absences. "He's done this all his life," she would say, "and he's always traveled. I think he really loves that life. He's a rover by nature. The first year we were married I saw so little of Bob that I wasn't sure we'd make a go of it. Now, of course, I've gotten accustomed to his being away and I couldn't imagine life being any different."

Being on the road for so many years had, as Dolores points out, become the habit, and the hypodermic of making a live audience roar with laughter was the fix. Some of his associates have suggested that the Hope libido might also have been an important motivator. And being on the road would easily provide opportunities for brief extramarital encounters, either prearranged or inspired on the spur of the moment at the venue where he was entertaining.

Just being Bob Hope ensured him instant allure, and being away for extended tours created almost certain vulnerability. His ego and its sexual drive and now a clear patriotic call seemed to be setting the pace.

Bob's brother Jack tried to dispel fears that Bob couldn't stand the pace. "Our grandfather's still riding his bicycle to the pub at ninety-nine. Aunt Polly lived to be a hundred and three. We're sturdy stock."

Bob took Barney Dean along with him on the camp tour as part valet, stooge, companion, and jester. Dean's pixie appearance and wild sense of humor lightened the load during that grueling grind through the Southern camps. Barney told Crosby, "I don't mind telling you it was a great experience and a mad one. In the first place, there were never less than three telephones in our rooms, and all of them rang at the same time every second of the day and night. And people, people, people. It was maddening. But Bob didn't seem to mind. In the second place, he thinks he's Superman. He does practically all the work himself. He's so healthy he never gets tired. He made me weak just watching him."

Barney was never able to forget what happened the night they arrived in Atlanta, grimy and exhausted and ready for a rest before the next day's Pepsodent show. Frances and Jerry collapsed in their rooms. Everyone else was looking forward to a bath and relaxation and a change of pace. When the telephone rang in their hotel suite Barney grabbed for it. Bob was stretched out on his bed. The voice belonged to one of Paramount's wardrobe boys who had been drafted and was now stationed near Savannah.

Bob reached over to his bed table and grabbed his extension. "Mike!—Hey— How about that?—You like it, huh? Where?—Albany? Where's Albany?— Barney?—Hundred miles? That's nothing—Sure we can—We'll be there—What do *you* think?—Why shouldn't I come?—You get the guys lined up—We'll be there—we're leaving now—" Hope called some of the others—understandably, they begged off. But Hope went. He took Barney with him and he did a show for the stunned wardrobe boy and his Army buddies. Just like those vaudeville days. Hope would do anything, go anywhere to get onstage.

22

Tonic in the Foxhole

"Well, I'm very happy to be here . . . (Boos from the audience) *. . . of course, I'm leaving as soon as I finish this show . . . but this is a great country, Africa. . . . This is Texas with Arabs . . . I was on the 'Road to Morocco' once, but this time I'm doin' it the hard way."*

When Bob and Dolores arrived in New York on June 16, 1943, and checked into the Waldorf-Astoria to await his flying orders for his European tour, the comedian felt ill. The day before he had received his first typhoid and typhus shots and now all he wanted was to crawl into bed.

When he was on his feet again, he was told that the USO wanted him to be photographed and briefed and given a special passport. He was also told that there would likely be a delay in their departure. The USO did not want news of the departure of the Pan Am Clipper leaked. There was a "gentleman's agreement" at the start of the war that no unarmed clippers would be attacked, but, as Hope commented to Dolores, "everyone knows the agreement isn't worth the gentleman it was written by."

Finally they were told to be at Pan Am's Marine Terminal at La Guardia Airport at one o'clock in the morning on June 25. After customs and ticket processing, they waited in their small family groups for the famous Clipper bell to ring. When it clanged, Bob and Dolores still lingered by the gate.

Bob kissed her. "Well—" he said.

"Well—" Dolores looked at him. In this half-light he still seemed too tired to be starting out on such a trip. "Take care of yourself."

"You know I will."

Dolores hugged him close. "Please be careful."

"I told you I would."

"Well, do," she emphasized.

"I will." When the "all aboard" was yelled, Hope looked once again at his wife and started toward the plane. He said, "I wish you were going," but he wasn't sure she heard that.

One of Hope's major disappointments in those final weeks before embarking on his USO European tour was that Colonna could not go. Jerry's commitments for films and personal appearances were too binding and too important to his income.

In his place Hope decided to try Jack Pepper, a song-and-dance man he had known in vaudeville and had met unexpectedly during his Southern camp tour. At Loew Field in Texas, Private Pepper had broken through a crowd barrier and run to shake Hope's hand. Hope called Pepper's commanding officer and asked to borrow the chubby performer for a few weeks. As for the others, Langford had gotten reluctant permission from her actor-husband, Jon Hall, to be missing for another two months, and Tony Romano, luckily, was available to be their "orchestra."

Finally, after delays for bad weather and refueling, the Hope entourage arrived at Foynes, Ireland, where they transferred to another plane for a ride to Bristol, where they would board a train for London. In London they had reservations at Claridge's, and were surprised to find that the hotel, despite shortages and depleted staff, managed to be proud and poised. Londoners in general accepted their city's disfigurement by bombs, tight rations, and their daily fear of attack with almost incredible good nature.

The troupe was taken in tow by Bill Dover, USO chief in England, who found them a bar of soap, which they shared and nursed for weeks. Next day they endured still more shots and fingerprinting. They were assigned APO (Army Post Office) numbers so they could receive mail. They met Captain Eddie Dowling, whom Hope had not seen since *Sidewalks of New York*. Eddie, a Special Services officer, arranged for newsreel coverage "to let the men know you're in the neighborhood." They also met Hal Block. He was the radio gag writer the Office of War Information had sent to Britain to help entertainers like Hope slant their comedy material properly for British audiences and the American troops stationed in England.

That afternoon Dover found Hope a driver and a Signal Corps photographer and they drove to Hitchin to see his granddad. He spent about three hours with the old man talking family. James Hope said bluntly that his grandson wasn't spending enough time with his family and understood only too well Hope's poignant story about how four-year-old Linda had said "Good-bye, Bob Hope" instead of "Good-bye, Daddy" when he left California.

Next morning they were introduced to their drivers, all from the English Women's Corps—Zena Groves, Eve Luff, and Marie Stewart—and their transportation, two 1938 Hudsons and a 1938 Ford painted countryside brown. That morning they began a remarkable five-week odyssey through thousands of miles of unmarked lanes and roads (intentionally unmarked to confuse potential invaders), entertaining at three and sometimes four installations a day. Venues included huge bomber aerodromes, smaller fighter bases, supply depots, and many hospitals, where they did jokes and sang songs, free-wheeling their performances as the situation required.

Their first full show was at a bomber base called Eye Aerodrome, near Honnington, and they arrived just before a mission was to fly out. Onstage a few minutes later, Hope said:

> I've just arrived from the States. You know. . . That's where Churchill lives. . . He doesn't exactly live there. . . he just goes back to deliver Mrs. Roosevelt's laundry. . . You know, they're drafting all the leading men in Hollywood. But Crosby is still there. If they keep it up, most of the romantic heroes will be on the adrenaline side. . . Can you imagine Lana Turner waiting to be kissed by Lewis Stone while he looks for a place to plug in his heating pad. . . ?

The Hope troupe quickly caught the spirit of their mission and after that there was no limit to their energies. "We soon discovered you had to be pretty lousy to flop in front of these guys—they yelled and screamed and whistled at everything," Hope later said. Their third show was at a supply depot, and their fourth and final show of that first day was performed at a large hospital—actually, it was a series of eight-to-ten-minute shows in a number of different wards. During the walk-through, Hope would go to each bed and say something like "Did you see our show—or were you sick before?" or his celebrated "All right, fellas, don't get up." At one point he decided to give them a little soft-shoe dance between two beds and the floor happened to be highly polished. Hope slipped and fell on his left wrist. They took him to X-ray and there was no serious damage, but it bothered him now and again during the next five weeks.

However, no injury, discomfort, weariness, or personal inconvenience seemed to slow Hope and company in their energetic crisscrossing of Britain, at least according to this account of their marathon by the actor Burgess Meredith in a letter to Paulette Goddard:

> The most wonderful thing about England right now is Bob Hope. The boys in camp stand in rain, they crowd into halls so close you can't breathe, just to see him. He is tireless and funny, and full of responsibility, too, although he carries it lightly and gaily. There isn't a hospital ward that he hasn't dropped into and given a show; there isn't a small unit anywhere that isn't either talking about his jokes or anticipating them. What a gift laughter is! Hope proves it.

Hope and his troupe moved to the west of England, to Wales and then back to London. When they went north to Colchester in Hertfordshire, not far from Hitchin, Bob arranged for his granddad to see the show. In fact, Hope went to his cousin Frank Symons's house, where James was living, and found he had gotten out of a sickbed and was dressed in morning attire, wing collar and all. Bob brought his grandfather up onstage and joked with him and they posed for many pictures. Later, Hope had reason to worry that he had done the wrong thing. The following week, on July 22, when Hope was playing Yorkshire bases, he got word that James was dying. By the time Hope got to Hitchin the old man was gone, but Bob was there to see the streets lined with many townspeople paying their respects.

From Hitchin Hope flew over to Belfast in a Flying Fortress for three days of shows in Northern Ireland. The Army gave the Hope Gypsies several forms to fill out, one of which asked for the person to notify in case of death. Ever mindful of publicity, Hope scribbled: "Louella Parsons, *Los Angeles Examiner*." The gag writer Hal Block, sitting next to Hope, howled. Hope said, "I promised Lolly first crack. I hate to do it because if we go down, Hedda will never speak to me again."

Two events marked the final days of the five-week invasion by Hope. The first was a big farewell variety show at the Odeon Theatre exclusively for servicemen, produced by Eddie Dowling and featuring, besides the Hope troupe, Adolph Menjou, Hal LeRoy, Hank Ladd, Stubby Kaye, Brucetta, Grace Drysdale, the Blossom Sisters, and several other performers from USO units. King George and Queen Elizabeth were reported to have come in after the show began and sat quietly in a darkened box without fanfare.

Vogue's London correspondent, Lesley Branch, asked Dowling if she could watch Hope prepare for the show because her magazine wanted a picture of him at work and "rehearsals show you both actor and man." What impressed her was the man in motion, his unflagging pace. As she watched what could only be described as the pandemonium of a big complex variety show in rehearsal, she discovered the other facet of his effectiveness—his concentration. In her September 1943 feature for *Vogue* she wrote: "He was there, in the middle of it all, keeping right on rehearsing various acts impervious to the uproar, as concentrated as a Yogi."

The second event began at a cocktail party the day of the Odeon show, given at the swank Dorchester Hotel in honor of a group of "inspecting" U.S. senators. Attending the party were Averell Harriman, Anthony Drexel Biddle, Ambassador John Winant, and a host of generals and admirals. The only reason Hope went was that he believed Winston Churchill would be there, but the prime minister couldn't attend. Hope revealed his disappointment to one senator he knew, Happy Chandler, and the Texas politician said he could fix that.

The following day, Chandler called Claridge's and asked Hope to accompany him to the House of Commons. Hope was picked up in Chandler's Rolls-Royce and in a few minutes the car stopped in front of 10 Downing Street. Hope looked wonderingly at the senator and asked, "Here?" Chandler nodded.

A group of senators were standing in Churchill's study waiting for him to come in when Chandler and Hope joined them. Almost simultaneously Churchill walked in from another door. The receiving line moved quickly and suddenly Hope was standing in front of Churchill. The prime minister looked—and looked again—and smiled. Hope shook Churchill's hand and told him what a pleasure this was. Hope had been told Churchill laughed heartily over *They Got Me Covered*. But before words could be exchanged, Churchill and the senators stepped out to a small garden for a conference. Ambassador Winant moved quickly to Hope's side and suggested he wait for Chandler in Churchill's study. Hope said he would leave as soon as he got Churchill to autograph a five-pound note that the pilots of his Pan Am clipper had presented to him as a "short-snorter," a member of an informal club of pilots, crew, and passengers who have made a transoceanic flight. A dollar bill or a five-pound note signed by at least two club members signified a certificate of membership. While Hope waited, Winant obliged, taking the bill to Churchill out in the garden, and when he returned Hope left, but not before being asked to sign the official guest book.

That same day, July 31, a remarkable newspaper column, "There Is a Man," by John Steinbeck, appeared in London's *Daily Express*. Steinbeck had filed it July 20, 1943, with the *New York Herald Tribune* and it had been picked up by countless papers around the world. Steinbeck saw Hope as a clown-hero to the GI:

> When the time for recognition of service to the nation in wartime comes to be considered, Bob Hope should be high on the list. . . .
>
> He has caught the soldier's imagination. He gets laughter wherever he goes from men who need laughter. . .
>
> It is hard to overestimate the importance of this thing and the responsibility involved. The battalion of men who are moving half-tracks from one place to another doing a job that gets no headlines, no public notice and yet must be done if there is to be a victory, are forgotten, and they feel forgotten. But Hope is in the country. Will he come to them or won't he? And then one day they get the notice that he is coming. Then they feel remembered.
>
> This man in some way has become that kind of a bridge. It goes beyond how funny he can be or how well Frances Langford sings. It is interesting to see how he has become a symbol.

Bob Hope could not help but be moved by the implications of Steinbeck's commentary, coming as it did from one of America's most sensitive and careful observers.

The next day Hope and his eager band were flown to Prestwick, Scotland, to await their transfer to North Africa. While they waited, Hope was asked to perform in a staging area for newly arrived GIs. Not unexpectedly, Hope led a rousing chorus of "We're Off on the Road to Morocco" as their plane took off from Prestwick and headed south for Marrakech. The troupe's arrival in Morocco, however, had been set for two days earlier by the USO, and so their military escorts had flown back to Tunis. Fortunately, General Jimmy Doolittle had insisted that a B–17 stand by in Marrakech just in case. So after a quick look around the town, they took off for Algiers, where they were met by Captain Mike Cullen of Special Services and three other officers who would be their hosts for the next month. One of those officers, Colonel Bill David, insisted that Hope accept a green linen suit of his to replace the wool clothes Hope had worn throughout Britain. That green suit was all Hope wore for the next four weeks through North Africa and Sicily.

When it was safe to fly, they took off for Tunis, where they were warmly welcomed by Jimmy Doolittle. They immediately went to work, first at the Red Cross Club for two shows back to back, and then alternating between bomber and fighter groups for three days. Hope's opening phrase itself always met with an unfailing roar from the troops:

Hiya, fellow tourists. . . [*Cheers*] Well, I'm very happy to be here. . . [*Boos*]. . . Of course, I'm leaving as soon as I finish this show. . . But isn't this a great country, Africa. . . This is Texas with Arabs. . . I was on the *Road to Morocco* once. . . This time, I'm doing it the hard way. . . and I tried to find a few Lamours over here, but they all wear their sarongs a little higher. . . under their eyes.

As the Hope troupe worked its way through these audiences of combat-hardened desert troops and fighter pilots, media people were becoming more and more curious about the comic's extraordinary rapport with his GI audiences. Whether in those godforsaken outposts of Alaska in 1942, the staging areas and air bases of England, or here in blazing Africa with whipping gritty sand making life unbearable, he approached GI, or "foxhole," humor as if he were standing on a small piece of America. "My jokes were no different than ones I told at Camp Callan," he has said, "except that they're localized." The essential element of foxhole humor, in Hope's view, is that the GI laughed hardest when the joke was on him. "He can take it. The more the joke's on him the better he likes it. He's laughing off the icy cold, the searing heat, the bugs and the scorpions, his fears and his frustrations."

It was, essentially, the same kind of humor Bill Mauldin gave World War II grunts in his "Willie and Joe" cartoons, the approach that characterized the unsentimental, moving, amusing, and always insightful dispatches of the correspondent Ernie Pyle.

Sometimes it was the GI himself who provided the big laugh. "Just as I stepped up to the microphone to start the show," Hope said, "a light tank came shoving through the crowd like a fat woman making for a seat in a crowded subway car. People gave way in all directions. A tank commands plenty of respect. I thought it was out of control. It looked like it was ready to mow us down and I was ready to jump off the platform, when suddenly right in front of me it stopped."

The tank's top flew open and a soldier climbed out wearing a tanker's crash helmet and "enough grease on his face to sing 'Mammy.'" He lifted out a folding stool, which he set up on top of the tank. He sat down, crossed his legs, smiled, waved at me, and said, 'You can start now.'"

Before and after the laughs and sometimes during was the reality of war. The troupe endured several terrifying air raids, with tracer bullets as well as bombs dangerously close to them. Ernie Pyle, in one dispatch titled "Bob Hope Visit Is Tonic to Troops," which appeared in the *New York World Telegram* on September 16, 1943, described something of what the Hope troupe must have felt under enemy attack: "I was in two different cities with them during these raids and I will testify they were horrifying raids. It isn't often that a bomb falls so close that you can hear it whistle. But when you can hear a whole stack of them whistle at once, then it's time to get weak all over and start sweating. The Hope troupe can now describe that ghastly sound."

The invasion of Sicily on August 18 paved the way for the Army's reluctant decision to let the Hope group fly to Palermo three days later. It was the closest to ground fighting they would get; the smell of battle was still in the air.

The events of Sunday night at the Excelsior Hotel in Palermo would stay with Hope for a lifetime. He had gone to bed at eleven-thirty after a tiring day of entertaining, only to sit up with a start a few minutes later. "All of a sudden there was a distant *VOOM!* and I saw a tracer bullet go scooting across the sky. Then I heard the dreaded drone of bombers. They had to be Krauts and I knew we were in for it."

The docks of Palermo, which were certainly the target for the raid, were only two blocks from the Excelsior. "They say when you're drowning your whole life flashes before your eyes. I don't know about you but with me it's the same way with bombing. Did I think of my first professional tour in vaudeville—no, I thought of what I didn't say to Dolores when we stood by the Clipper dock. . . I thought of doing everything in the world but going to the bomb shelter in the basement. I began to stutter to myself."

Right about then, a huge hunk of red-hot flak flew past his hotel window and he heard the unmistakable whine of a plane dive-bombing. "One Nazi, obviously aiming for my room, also let go with all his machine guns on his way down. Between the strafing and the screeching of the Stukas as they dived, you've got a noise that I'd trade any day for a record of you-know-who.

"And the Germans weren't making it all themselves. We were throwing plenty of stuff at them, too. I joined in. I threw up my dinner. After you've listened to a raid like that for a little while you begin to be afraid that just the noise will kill you, and then after you've listened to it a while longer you begin to be afraid it won't. You want to curl up in a ball. . . You want the ball to be batted out of the park. . . You want. . . it was the most frightening experience of my life."

Military observers agreed that the Germans had thrown a hundred Junkers (single-engine dive bombers) with fighter escort into that raid. Hope was still in bed shaking when Captain Cullen came into his room to tell him Frances was safe, although there was plaster all over her bed and floor. Tony had been with the chef in the kitchen and Pepper had been in the shelter.

Next day they crossed Sicily to do several shows, including one for the 9th Division and another for the 1st Infantry, both between Palma and Licata. From Licata they were flown back to Bone, Tunisia, where they appeared before a big audience of soldiers, sailors, Wacs (Women's Army Auxiliary Corps), WRENS (Women's Royal Navy Service), and Red Cross personnel in a staging area for the continuing Italian invasion.

Hope, nearly numb with fatigue, limped out onstage still in his rumpled, soiled green linen suit. He hollered "Hiya fellow tourists!" It was during this show that someone way back in the crowd called out, "Draft dodger! Why aren't you in uniform?" Hope figured that whoever said that was either too blind to see the caked mud on his suit or too embittered to care or it was his version of foxhole humor. Hope yelled back, "Don't you know there's a war on? A guy could get hurt."

From Bone they flew to Kairouan to do two shows for the troops of the 82nd Airborne Division. They remained overnight to have breakfast with them and then headed for Algiers, where they were treated to fresh laundry and Hope finally peeled off the green linen suit. Following an afternoon show, Hope huddled with writer Hal Block over a script for a radio show they would be recording for a delayed broadcast from Algiers to the States.

In the midst of rehearsals, Captain Cullen interrupted them to say that General Eisenhower would like them to visit his headquarters. For Hope this was a supremely rewarding experience. "Meeting General Eisenhower in the midst of that deadly muddle was like a breath of fresh air in a lethal chamber. It quieted us all, brought us all back to our senses, and in every way paid us off for the whole trip."

Eisenhower told them how much they were appreciated and autographed pictures for them. Before they left he said: "I understand you've had some excitement on your trip. Well, you're perfectly safe here in Algiers. We haven't had a raid in three months. We're too strong for 'em. They can't get in."

That night after the broadcast, Hope went back to the Aletti Hotel. He sat in the lounge with a few foreign correspondents who were anxious to hear about his tour. At about three in the morning he went to bed and an hour later was roused by a loud door-rapped instruction to go to the bomb shelter at once. For the next hour and a half occurred one of the worst air raids Algiers had suffered. Wave after wave of Junkers hit the Allied flak and some bulldozed through. Even the unflappable Langford trembled and cried through this one. It was a nerve-racking finish to their tour. They missed their eight o'clock plane for Scotland, but their escorts pulled some strings in high places and that same evening they were on their way back to Britain.

From London they got as far as Iceland, where they had to refuel, and as soon as they landed were told that foul weather over the Atlantic would delay them. So they agreed to do two shows but actually performed three because this was Alaska all over again—as lonely and forsaken an outpost as they had ever encountered. Finally, they left for California.

By any standard the 20,000-mile trip was dazzling. *Time* was impressed enough to put Hope's likeness on its September 20, 1943, cover (his first of several). Inside the magazine in an article titled "Hope for Humanity," the comedian was elevated above the dozen or so major entertainers who were then trouping the war zones. He was labeled a "legend," one that had sprung up "swiftly, telepathically, . . . traveling faster than Hope himself." *Time* said that throughout this "tearing trip" of 250 shows in 11 weeks, Hope represented "measurable qualities in a mystical blend" that rendered him "funny, friendly, indefatigable and figurative." In the eyes of the magazine's editors, Hope seemed to be developing into an American folk figure—to the delight of millions of people and especially to hundreds of thousands of American GIs.

> Thanks to his vibrant averageness, Hope is any healthy, cocky, capering American. He is the guy who livens up the summer hotel, makes things hum at the corset salesman's convention, keeps a coachful of passengers laughing for an hour when the train is stalled. With his ski-slide nose and matching chin, he looks a little funny but he also looks normal, even personable, seems part of the landscape rather than the limelight.
>
> And while he hugs the limelight with a showman's depthless ego, in Hope himself is a hunger, or perhaps a final vanity, to reach people as a human being. For a performer who scarcely takes time out to live, perhaps it is the only way of being one.

He was being hugged home as a hero—at the breakfast table, at Lakeside Country Club, at NBC studios, at Paramount, even at the driving range he owned across from the Warner Bros. lot.

Dog-tired, he answered the many queries by telling anecdotes and would end with "but wait till you read the book!" There was growing opinion, derived from those who traveled with him, friends and acquaintances around Los Angeles—Dolores especially—that he was a somewhat altered, perhaps sobered, Bob Hope.

The sportswriter Braven Dyer heard him telling some locker-room buddies at Lakeside that it was "the most wonderful experience of my life—I wouldn't trade it for my entire career. Until you've actually seen them in action, you have no conception of their courage. And that noise—that terrifying noise of battle—is awful. I don't know how those kids stand it day after day, but they do." Dyer said the sincerity, coming from the normally flippant and unsentimental Hope, moistened several pairs of eyes.

Dolores felt that Bob was experiencing a deeper love and respect for people as he dealt with the indelible images and personal encounters of the grueling tour. She would hear Bob on the telephone for weeks after his return talking both long and short distance to parents, sweethearts, and sometimes children of the servicemen and -women he had met on the trip. Hope had come home with his pockets literally stuffed with scrawled names and addresses and wisps of paper with messages to be delivered. What *Time* had metaphorically called "the straight link with home" was being lived out in fact.

23

Presidential Pundit

"I think I should apologize to our President for some of the things I've said on radio. . . especially about Mrs. Roosevelt. Like when Churchill and Roosevelt were discussing campaign strategy, they talked about when to attack the enemy and how to keep Eleanor out of the crossfire. . . "

When Hope returned to the States, he discovered folks on the home front were hungry for any news about GI Joe as well as for first-person accounts of being under fire. He felt that the war correspondents who had covered his foxhole tour—Ernie Pyle, Bob Considine, John Steinbeck, Quentin Reynolds, Mos Miller, and Bill Lang—had written vividly but had only scratched the surface. Actually, an idea for writing some kind of eye-witness account, presumably humorous, had been germinating in Hope's mind for much of that 11-week tour.

Now that Hope was home, the national magazines and Sunday supplements were calling Mack Millar demanding byline stories or routines of his gags and anecdotes about the trip. For several nights Hope worked very late at his desk reconstructing events and sorting out faces, places, and conversations. Fortunately, his photographic memory restored to him details of geography, the sound and texture of audiences, and the physical settings in Britain, North Africa, and Sicily. But after a few nights, it became clear to him that he was envisioning something more than a mere article or two. Millar had had a call from Simon & Schuster, who were very interested in getting a book out by Hope. Bob had an idea.

He had known for some time a writer named Carroll Carroll, one of the J. Walter Thompson agency's best men. Originally from New York, Carroll had come to Hollywood to work with Bing on his *Kraft Music Hall* show, and had also made some valuable contributions of gag ideas for several Crosby films and the *Road* pictures. More important Carroll was doing some work for the Office of War Information (OWI) and understood military lingo and what was going on in Europe and in the Pacific. Bob asked him to come to the house.

Over mixed grill in the family room, Hope told Carroll that Simon & Schuster wanted a manuscript immediately and that he needed someone to help him.

"I've never written a book," said Carroll. "What's wrong with your own writers?"

"I don't want them. Have you ever tried?" Hope took some sheets from a big brown envelope and handed them across the table. "This is what I've been working on but the publisher says it isn't a book—yet. Fool around with it and do a beginning. If we like it and Jack Goodman of Simon likes it, we'll go. You ought to know *this*, though, all *your* money is up-front. The royalties go to the National War Fund."

Carroll took the brown envelope and tipped it over. Out fell numerous scraps of paper, including several matchbook covers, three scribbled-on Claridge's envelopes, dog-eared pages of monologue with both names and memory joggers, some business cards and part of a menu from the Aletti Hotel in Algiers. "What do you want to call this book?"

"*I Never Left Home.*"

"Why?" Carroll asked.

"Because everywhere I went I was meeting people from places I knew or had played in vaudeville or had lived. I kept running into people I knew."

"And they knew you. I understand what you mean. It's a great title. I'll work out something from this material and let you see it soon."

Carroll went back to his office and tried to work on current assignments, but he kept returning to Hope's material. He read it through. It was the week of the *Time* cover story. He leafed through Hope's copy. It was soon clear to him that the compassion Hope displayed overseas was missing in what he had written. Carroll decided that if Hope was to be perceived as "the straight link with home," those same home folks must see through Hope's eyes the sacrifice of everyone in uniform, and each GI reading this book must sense the nation's gratitude. Carroll grabbed a sheet of typing paper and stuck in the machine. He wrote what he believed to be a moving preface and he also arranged some of the early material into a scenario that was both lively and suspenseful. He sent it to Bob.

Hope read it immediately. Four days later, he called Carroll and told him he had read the preface to his editor and they both loved the concept. After tinkering with the opening words they let the preface stand and it became the most compelling and motivating writing in the entire memoir:

I saw your sons and your husbands, your brothers and your sweethearts. I saw how they worked, fought and lived. I saw some of them die. I saw more courage, more good humor in the face of discomfort, more love in an era of hate, and more devotion to duty than could exist under tyranny.

I saw American minds, American skill, and American strength breaking the backbone of evil. . . . And I came back to find people exulting over the thousand-plane raids over Germany. . . and saying how wonderful they are! Those people never watched the face of a pilot as he read a bulletin board and saw his buddy marked up missing. . . . I didn't see very much. And God knows I didn't do any fighting. But I had a worm's eye view of what war is.

Dying is sometimes easier than living through it. . . .

But this is not a book about the serious side of the war. That isn't my field. All I want you to know is that I did see your sons and daughters in the uniforms of the United States of America. . . fighting for the United States of America.

I could ask for no more.

Hope and Carroll met every Wednesday evening with a secretary named Jane Brown in the Hope's living room on Moorpark Street.

"It was a hard grind," Carroll recalls. "I was still doing my regular job at J. Walter, and writing for the OWI. Hope edited each chapter as it was finished, made notes for me and gave copies to his team of gagmen to punch up with fresh material. Then I went over the whole thing again, took the best of the new stuff from his gagmen and dovetailed it into the appropriate places."

They worked that way for ten weeks and by December it was ready for the publisher. Simon & Schuster sent it to artist Carl Rose, who drew a series of witty illustrations. It was slotted for spring publication.

Meanwhile, Hope's sixth season for Pepsodent had begun, and predictably the Hope show became the most listened-to radio program in the nation. The Pepsodent show was originating from a different camp or base each week, and the guest stars were entertainers such as Marlene Dietrich and Jimmy Durante. His cast regulars were Frances Langford, Jerry Colonna, and Vera Vague; Skinnay Ennis had joined the Army, and now his bandleader was Stan Kenton.

At Paramount there was consternation over the making of the much-anticipated next *Road* picture, *Road to Utopia*. Getting Bob, Bing, and Dottie together was difficult. While the effort went on, Bob kept busy doing two or three benefit appearances a week. He appeared on numerous transcribed Armed Forces Radio *Command Performance* shows for servicemen and -women, kicked off the Motion Picture War Chest Campaign, and found time to head up a fund-raising drive to help the YMCA keep the children of war-working parents off the city streets.

When *Road to Utopia* finally rolled in November, there was some discord among the famous threesome who had traveled those other successful roads together. This was the first *Road* script not written by Hartman and Butler. Two of Hope's newest writers, Norman Panama and Melvin Frank, had dreamed up a Klondike gold rush cliffhanger about two vaudevillian con artists who find a stolen map that rightfully belongs to the beautiful Sal, played by Lamour. The film contained some of the wildest stunts of all the *Road* pictures, and ended with a sequence that raised some eyebrows.

Mel Frank recalls that after he and Panama finished their script came the idea of selling the idea to each principal individually. "In those days," says Mel, "they were *enormous* stars. It's impossible to imagine the prestige of those three people. You really had to have their okay on the script, even though they were under contract and could be forced to do what you wanted. So we would sit down with Crosby and explain our ideas and we would make it sound like it was going to be *his* picture. Then we'd tell Hope the story and make it attractive from his point of view. Then we'd tell it to Lamour, though she knew we had already run it by the other two."

It was particularly tricky to convince actors—even the zany Hope and Crosby—to do complicated or potentially dangerous stage business, like a scene in *Utopia* that involves a trained bear. In that scene Bing and Bob crawl under a rug in a mountain cabin to hide when a grizzly bear comes in looking for them. The bear was supposed to walk over the lump in the rug.

The trainer warned the two actors not to move when the scene was over until he had reclaimed the bear and chained him securely off-camera. It all worked well in rehearsal, but for the actual take, when the boys scrambled for the rug and the bear came in growling, he stood on top of them and menaced them dangerously. Hope and Crosby were terrified while the trainer struggled to take control of his animal. After some sharp words to the director, Bob and Bing went to their dressing rooms and refused to continue to work with the bear. The following day the same bear tore the arm off his trainer.

Aside from such near misses, the two men of this now-famous trio were beginning to adopt an approach to movie making even more casual than before, one that was occasionally accompanied by thoughtlessness. "We had a ball," said Bing. "We had directors who let us suit our own schedules. If we had a golf game or wanted to hit the track for a big race at Santa Anita, I'd say 'Can't you do something with Hope or Lamour today?' and we'd work it out."

On one of those "work it out" days, both Bob and Bing wanted to play in a charity match and were oblivious, or pretended to be, that they were supposed to shoot a musical scene with Lamour. As a matter of fact, it was a scene that was being rescheduled from a previous Hope-Crosby truancy.

That day Lamour got into her costume, a tight corset and long black evening gown, after her 6 A.M. makeup session and arrived on the soundstage at about nine o'clock. No Hope. No Crosby. She and the rest of the players, the extras, and the crew waited. Most of that time she had to lean on a slant board provided for actresses with wardrobe too tight for sitting.

At the lunch break she got out of the gown, and though she objected loudly, she agreed to get back into it for the presumed afternoon shooting. At about four o'clock, Gary Cooper wandered onto the soundstage and heard a furious Lamour sputtering about two inconsiderate actors. "Dottie," Cooper said, "if I were you I wouldn't take it. Go back to your dressing room, get out of your dress, and get the hell out."

Lamour left in a rage. No sooner had she gotten into her street clothes than the boys arrived. The Paramount production chief's office called to find out why she wasn't on the set. She told the Paramount brass how she felt, and although both Hope and Crosby guiltily teased her about being temperamental and in their own ways both apologized, Dottie later said, "For once somebody got through to them and they never pulled another stunt like that on me."

Utopia provided Bob and Bing with their most-repeated duet, "Put It There, Pal," and it also provided Hope with his most quoted gag line from any of his collaborations with Crosby. In the picture, the boys courageously saunter into a rough Yukon bar, and when Hope is gruffly asked what he wants to drink, he says, "Lemonade." But when he sees the incredulous look by both Crosby and the bartender, he adds quickly, "In a dirty glass."

The film also provided the censors with a dilemma. In previous *Road* films, Bing had always gotten Lamour at the finish, but in this one a crack in the ice pack separates Bing on one side from Bob and Dottie on the other. Many years later, an aging Crosby pays a call on the long-married Hope and Lamour and when the couple's son is introduced he is the image of Crosby. It was a racy touch for its day but the censors let it pass.

When *Utopia* finally finished shooting, Hope was left with a bad head and chest cold, presumably caused by fluctuating temperatures on the soundstage. The cold had also settled in Hope's left ear and was exceedingly painful. His doctor, Tom Hearn, advised him to stay in bed. Although refusing that advice, Hope did listen to Dolores's protests when he wanted to leave with the Pepsodent cast for a month-long camp tour of the South. So they flew without him to Brookley Field, Alabama, and that next Tuesday night Hope did the monologue from his Hollywood studio.

A few days later, somewhat recovered, Hope flew to Florida in time to rehearse for the March 7 show at an officer's training school. Almost nothing in this world could have kept him from getting back on his feet because he knew he had to be up to speed for a singular honor to be accorded him the following Saturday, March 11. This year it was NBC's turn to provide entertainment for the Gridiron Dinner in Washington, D.C.—the annual roast of capital politics and politicians by the press corps. President Roosevelt was to be their honored guest, and Hope, who had been waiting for such an opportunity to do an in-person show for the President, cabinet members, and assorted D.C. elite, was truly excited.

On Saturday, Hope flew to Brookley Field to play golf with General Mollison, but the weather turned so stormy that their game was rained out. There were fears that no planes would be flying and NBC was pulling all its top-level strings to get Hope to D.C. Mollison got a teletype from General "Hap" Arnold that read: HAVE PLANE COMING NORTH TONIGHT STOP MAKE SURE HOPE IS ON IT HAP.

The storm had hit Washington but it hadn't stopped a glittering crowd from showing up. Hope was an hour late arriving at the dinner and the actor Ed Gardner had replaced him as emcee. Fritz Kreisler had already played, Gracie Fields had sung, and Elsie Janis had entertained, followed by a trained seal. When Hope arrived Fred Waring and his Pennsylvanians were in full swing. Hope was the tag end and he knew, after this long show, that he had to be fresh. The head table, the President's, would be to his left, and the audience had turned their chairs away from the banquet tables to face a small stage. Hope bounced out, and his first political wisecrack, jabbing at Roosevelt's problems with Congress, was an instant hit. The audience looked sideways at the head table to see the President's reaction. Hope pressed on:

> Trying to find a room in Washington is like trying to find "My Day" in the *Chicago Tribune*. . . [*Loud roar of laughter*]. . . and did you know. . . [*Continued laughter*]. . . and did you know, speaking of the *Chicago Tribune*. . . that Fala is the only dog ever housebroken on that paper? [*More loud laughter*]

Hope looked to his left and Roosevelt's head was tilted back and he was laughing. The references to Eleanor's daily newspaper column, "My Day," and mainly to the President's feud with Robert McCormick, who owned the *Chicago Tribune*, were front-page items everywhere in the United States. Hope probably couldn't have scored in front of a more receptive audience, or one that would send more glowing accounts to the corners of the nation and around the world. Several members of the Fourth Estate suggested the comparison made by the syndicated columnist Richard Wilson in the next morning's *Des Moines Register*: "The gap left by the death of Will Rogers, as a comedian whose barbs at politics and politicians were generally appreciated in Washington, has been filled. Bob Hope has stepped into the shoes of Will Rogers in this respect, and from now on he will be sought in Washington to provide that extra touch at the capital's lavish functions."

For the next few weeks, Hope and his radio cast performed at camp shows, and after a brief rest in Palm Springs, Bob checked into the Goldwyn studios for his second feature for Sam. The script, *Sylvester the Great*, was a period piece, a comedy swashbuckler about a hapless actor protecting a princess from pirates. Hope's leading lady was Virginia Mayo; his costars in the film, Walter Brennan, Victor McLaglen, and Walter Slezak, were particularly effective, with Crosby appearing in a cameo. *The Princess and the Pirate* (the release title of the film) turned out to be the last film Hope would make for a full year.

The reason for this year-long hiatus in movie-making was an impasse that developed between the star and Paramount. Hope said, "I asked my lawyer, Martin Gang, how I could hang on to some of the money I was earning instead of seeing it all going to finance those B–17s and battleships. He told me the only way was to form my own production company and make movies in partnership with Paramount." The notion was, of course, not popular—at least at that time. Hope braced himself for a fight, possibly a long and bloody one.

Hope and Paramount chief Frank Freeman went to lunch at Perino's, and after a few amenities, Hope dropped his bomb. "Frank, I'm going to form my own production company."

Freeman looked stunned. "Why do you want to do that?"

"Money—so I can hang on to more of it."

"It won't work, Bob. We couldn't allow it. I want to talk to you about the movie we want you to do called *Duffy's Tavern*. Now, what's bothering you about it?"

"Frank, I'm telling you I'm going to make pictures for my own company. I'd like to have more say in what I make and how I make them."

"I don't see how we can let you do that, Bob. If you insist we'll have to suspend you."

"Okay, I guess you'll have to suspend me."

In early May 1944, about a month before the Goldwyn film finished shooting, the USO announced and Hope confirmed that he would take Frances Langford, Jerry Colonna, and Tony Romano to the South Pacific war zones during July and August. At the same time, the *New York Herald Tribune*'s nationally syndicated supplement published a Hope-authored piece called "Sure Fire Gags for the Foxhole." Both the announcement and the feature story fit into a larger publicity and advertising campaign to promote the forthcoming publication of *I Never Left Home*. Simon & Schuster launched a barrage of newspaper copy, taking full-page ads that made optimum use of the clever Carl Rose illustrations as well as special-ly posed comic photographs. Hope offered several promotional suggestions, which were adopted, including cartoon ads with gag lines from his writers that poked fun at him and the book.

The first edition of 100,000 copies appeared in an eight-ounce paperbound format suitable for mailing to servicemen and women overseas. It sold for one dol-lar. Almost immediately a hard-cover edition of another 100,000 copies appeared in the bookstores to sell for two dollars. By September a half million copies had been sold, and by the following year a million and a half copies would be sold.

Influential columnists like Walter Winchell, Leonard Lyons, Erskine Johnson, and Hedda Hopper gave it their rapturous blessing, as did critics like Bennett Cerf in the *Saturday Review of Literature* and Tom O'Reilly of *The New York Times*.

A highly dramatic testimonial of Hope's identification with the GI came on Tuesday, June 6, which was Hope's final broadcast of the season but, much more momentously, was D-Day on the shores of Normandy. That night Hope aban-doned his prepared jokes. He sat for several hours with his writers creating a patri-otic and sometimes very moving monologue that included this passage:

You sat there and dawn began to sneak in, and you thought of the hundreds of thousands of kids you'd seen in camps the past two or three years. . . kids who scream and whistle when they hear a gag and a song. . . And now you could see all of them again, in four thousand ships on the English Channel, tumbling out of thousands of planes over Normandy and the occupied coast, in countless landing barges crashing the Nazi gate and going on through to do a job that's the job of all of us. The sun came up and you sat there looking at that huge black headline, that one great bright word with the exclamation point, "INVA-SION!" The one word that the whole world has waited for, that all of us have worked for. We knew we'd wake up one morning and have to meet it face to face, the word in which America has invested everything these thirty long months. . . the efforts of millions of Americans building planes and weapons. . . the shipyards and the men who took the stuff across. . . little kids buying War Stamps. . . and housewives straining bacon grease. . . farmers working round the clock, millions of young men sitting it out in camps and fighting the battles that paved the way for this morning. Now the investment must pay—for this generation and all generations to come. . .

Hope's words were heard by an audience estimated at 35 million people, many more than would listen to one of the President's fireside chats. The text was widely reprinted.

On June 22, Bob, Frances, Jerry, Tony, a vivacious young dancer named Patty Thomas, and the durable gag writer Barney Dean took off in a C-Litter, a military medical air-lifter, which was en route to an American base on the Pacific island of Saipan to pick up wounded soldiers. More than a few people in Washington and in Hollywood (Dolores had her say) thought that the Japanese-infested southwest Pacific was no safe place for entertainers. The first stopover was safe enough, Hickham Field near Honolulu.

From Hawaii they flew in General MacArthur's personal plane, a big Liberator called *Seventh Heaven* and piloted by Captain Frank Orme, to the desolate atoll named Christmas Island. "The only entertainment they'd had there till we arrived," Hope said later, "was the Gary Cooper troupe the year before. This is a place with flying cockroaches, blister bugs, land crabs and other crawly things, enough to make you cringe. And no fresh water." The GIs were extremely grateful. The next day the entertainers were glad to be headed for Canton Island, which had fresh water but otherwise wasn't much different. Again they were badly needed. Their next shows were at Tarawa and then on to Kwajalein, in the Marshall Islands. Hope commented on the makeshift windmills that operated the island's laundry, and he told his audience that he heard a voice with an Alabama accent holler out, "We'll sure enough be clean with Hope on the island. He'll keep those windmills goin'."

From Kwajalein they hopped back to Saipan, to Majuro in the South Marshalls, and then to Bougainville. Signs of exhaustion were beginning to show on everyone. They were doing five and six shows a day. By the time they had played Munda and Tulagi, they agreed to take an offered Australian rest cure.

They hitched a ride over to Brisbane with Lieutenant Frank Ferguson, who incidentally lived in North Hollywood near the Hopes and who was to fly them in a big PBY, a Catalina Flying Boat, to Sydney. The prospect of clean laundry and sleep made the all-day plane ride bearable and they were in high spirits.

Ferguson let Hope take over the controls and fly the Catalina when they were a few hundred miles from Brisbane. He was standing behind Hope when the right motor conked out and the plane started to dip. Ferguson shoved Hope from the seat and hollered orders for everyone on board to help jettison everything that was loose. They obeyed, throwing their luggage, souvenirs, cases of Scotch, and the plane's tools overboard.

Ferguson was trying to find water for his ship's pontoons because they were now flying over land. His finger found the Camden Haven River on the navigational map and he lowered the plane toward it. There wasn't much water in the river, but he believed he saw enough to make a landing. They braced themselves for impact and when the aircraft hit the water, it bounced, landed, bounced again, and came to a stop on a sandspit. While it was bouncing, Ferguson yelled for them to jump out as soon as they were able because fumes from the fuel might blow the plane sky-high.

Shortly after, local residents who had watched the troubled plane coming down appeared at the riverbank, some with small boats to bring the crew and entertainers ashore. Then the locals found some vehicles to drive them to the nearest little village of Laurieton, where almost the entire population of six hundred turned out in the streets to register disbelief, then joy, at having Bob Hope in their midst.

Hope & Company decided to show their appreciation by performing for their rescuers, and the postmistress declared it "the greatest day in the history of Laurieton." By noon, nine Australian and American military staff cars arrived to pick them up for the 100-mile drive to Newcastle, where they boarded a plane for Sydney. Newspaper headlines in the Sydney *Daily Telegraph* on August 15, 1944, announced: BOB HOPE'S PLANE IN FORCED LANDING STOP STARS DOWN ON NORTH COAST; it stirred the citizens of Sydney into a frenzied airport welcome. Thousands of cheering people filled the streets to watch them arrive at the Australia Hotel. Three squealing young women threw themselves on the ground in front of Hope as he stepped from his car, and one woman, in the excitement of the moment, threw her handbag at his head; Hope chewed gum rapidly and looked apprehensively around until he was rescued by military police.

Dolores finally got a call through to Bob's hotel room and told him the earliest reports of the Laurieton ditch were that the plane was missing. She told him to get plenty of rest. But it turned out not to be much of an R and R for them. The Hope troupe entertained at two hospitals and a benefit for dependents of service personnel, and performed their show for movie cameras in a local studio for distribution to remote areas of Australia and New Zealand.

Hope also turned journalist when King Features Syndicate wired him that the interest in his South Pacific tour was so intense that they would print a daily column if he could manage to write one.

He was willing, but there would be problems—the least of which being Hope's ability to get what he wrote transmitted to New York from places they were playing or stopping for the night. Their route was purposely random island hopping to entertain in jungle areas and on available stretches of beach. Communications were carefully monitored. Also, the military did not want the whereabouts of the troupe known until after they had departed the combat zone. Because it was hit-and-run entertaining, Hope decided he should write his impressions out of sequence. His first column described the dramatic ditching of the Catalina at

Laurieton, and the second one was about their layover in the Christmas Islands. He used USO directors and information officers, anyone who had access to precious air waves, to get his stories to New York. A few days into this exercise, Hope panicked and hollered for help. Suddenly Frank Robertson, an International News Service war correspondent, appeared one morning and said he would be tracking the Hope troupe and helping out with the columns. The pieces began appearing in American newspapers as "Bob Hope's Communiqué" on August 28, 1944.

That four-day Australian respite over, the troupe returned to the shooting war. They resumed their backbreaking schedule, this time starting with New Guinea. First stop was Hollandia, then Noemfoor, where the U.S. Army Air Force "black widow" night fighters were based. Hope said, "We just finished our show there when we heard they shot a Jap about a thousand yards from the stage while we were on. And I *had* to ask, 'Was he coming or going?'"

They flew in tiny planes not much bigger than Piper Cubs to places like Wakde and Owi and Aitpe—places they couldn't find on a map and couldn't pronounce. They had to take PT boats to do shows in the islands of Woendi (which the Navy referred to as "Wendy") with names like Endila, Lumbrum, Los Negros, Manus, Ponam, and Pitylu. Some 18 years later Hope was presented with the Congressional Medal of Honor in the White House Rose Garden. After handing him the medal, President Kennedy (who had spent much of his World War II duty in a PT boat) said, "Bob, I was one of those lucky guys who sat in the rain on a 'Wendy' island watching you and your troupe perform."

When the tiny travel-weary troupe stepped out of their military transport at Burbank's Lockheed airstrip on September 10, Hope told reporters that they had covered a total of 30,000 miles and had performed 150 times. He said their homeward Pacific crossing from New Guinea to California took 50 hours including one stop at Wake Island, where they did their final show.

In an Associated Press interview, Hope—the man Steinbeck had called "driven"—said: "Funny thing how these trips have changed us. Everyone claims I'm a little more serious than I was. I suppose they mean a little more hammy. Those men—those soldiers—they're not just a bunch of crap shooting, wolfing guys we like to joke about. These men are men, with the deepest emotions and the keenest feelings that men can have about everything life holds dear."

In another interview he paraphrased what he had written in one of his daily columns: "A soldier's the most sentimental guy in the world, the most religious and the kindest. I guess the nearer you get to death, the better you become. It's getting good the hard way—but that's the only way you ever really make it."

Nothing could please Dolores more than to read those words and to verify her surmise that Bob had experienced some kind of spiritual awakening. At home in front of the children he was a hero and he showed off his souvenirs. He was particularly proud of the Japanese pistol a GI had thrust on him after one of the shows and he delivered a lecture on the use of firearms. "You've got to be very sure they're empty before you pull the trigger," he said. As he demonstrated the gun discharged and a bullet ripped through the door of his wardrobe closet. Dolores screamed. Bob apologized.

Two days later Hope was doing his radio show at the Marine Air Station in Mojave, California. And he would continue to do his show from camps and bases across the nation throughout the autumn of 1944 and well into the spring of 1945.

Hope did not show up at Paramount for the shooting of the studio's star-filled movie *Duffy's Tavern*, as he had warned Frank Freeman months before, and in fact he did not drive through the studio's DeMille Gate again until mid-September 1945.

The media were quick to respond when the studio announced his suspension. But Hope had this to say: "We've both said our little sarcastic things. But I really suspended the studio. I'm not on salary. My contract calls for straight picture deals. The time out will be added on to my contract. And if someone will suspend the war I'll be happy to start another picture. As it is, I'm booked with GI Joe, and besides, it'll give the country a nice rest. How often can people stand to look at my kisser?"

24

It's Not Over Till It's Over

"When I walked into USO headquarters in Chatou, it looked as if Central Casting had opened an overseas branch. I ran into Alfred Lunt and Lynn Fontanne, Bea Lillie, Reginald Gardiner. . . Really, a lot of stars like Cagney, Cooper, Annie Sheridan and Paulette Goddard made off-shore trips and never said a word about it. So different from YOU-KNOW-WHO. . . "

Nineteen forty-five was a year when everything came together for Hope. Not that there was ever much doubt about his continuing appeal or the value of his accomplishments. But the events of this year were of the sort that sealed his destiny.

In January his radio program became, for the first time, the undisputed national pastime, having finally outdistanced its closest rival, *Fibber McGee*, by six points in the Hooper ratings. Consequently, Pepsodent and Hope negotiated a new ten-year contract and although neither Lever Brothers (makers of Pepsodent) nor Hope would reveal the exact figures, Jack Hope said there was a million dollars in the contract for every year it ran.

And, like Will Rogers years earlier and Eleanor Roosevelt more recently, Hope had joined the Fourth Estate. His daily humor column, now called "It Says Here," was a staple item in all the Hearst newspapers and a fairly well publicized feature in other large and small dailies nationwide. Hope supervised its production; that is, he generally chose the topic and edited what the writers submitted.

As a satiric commentary on selected phenomena of the 1940s, the column allowed Hope to risk more colorful language than NBC censors would allow in his radio monologues. Furthermore, in print he discovered other things besides Hollywood to joke about. As his worldview broadened and his interest in the humor of politics gradually increased, so did the frequency of observations that he was something of a latter-day Will Rogers.

It was a year of much travel: after two strenuous national camp-show tours, the comedian surprised no one by taking yet one more USO troupe to Europe, the last of his four wartime entertainment marathons overseas. He trouped tirelessly for two and a half months in England, France, Germany, Austria, and Czechoslovakia.

And 1945 was the year that Harry Truman invited him to entertain the first family at the White House. It was also the year that Hope, once again in charge of the Oscar ceremonies, gritted his teeth when his pal Crosby stepped up on the stage of Grauman's Chinese Theatre to accept a coveted gold statuette for his role as a priest in *Going My Way*. But the Oscarless Hope, not to be outdone, could point with pride to his own unique 1945 statue honor, a bust sculpted by Max Kalish to be placed in the Smithsonian Institute's gallery of noted Americans.

More significant in 1945 to businessman Hope was his victory over Paramount in his fight to become an independent producer. He formed Hope Enterprises and won the right to a voice in his own film projects.

But it wouldn't have been much of a year without an award or two. As it turned out, Hope was making a national camp-show tour in January, when his brother Jack arranged to have his radio show performed for the Signal Corps installation at Fort Mammoth, New Jersey. Then he could slip into Philadelphia to be honored at what many over-the-street banners proclaimed as BOB HOPE DAY, complete with a ticker-tape parade. Philadelphia's Poor Richard Club, proper and prestigious, had voted him their gold medal for his "outstanding contribution to the nation," the second entertainer in their forty-year history to be so honored. The first was Will Rogers.

Hope made it back to Hollywood just in time for his role in the most ambitious *Command Performance* radio program attempted by Armed Forces Radio during World War II. *Life* magazine gave it a major photostory on March 12, 1945. It was a musical comedy based on Chester Gould's popular comic strip *Dick Tracy*. The show was called "Dick Tracy in B Flat or For Goodness Sake Isn't He Ever Going to Marry Tess Truehart?"

And what a glittering assemblage of stars it had: Bing Crosby, Frank Sinatra, Jimmy Durante, Judy Garland, Dinah Shore, the Andrews Sisters, Jerry Colonna,

Cass Daley, and Harry Von Zell. No commercial radio program could have afforded to put such a cast together. Free admission tickets were fiercely fought over by its mixed-branch servicemen and -women. They cheered Durante as The Mole in his version of "The Music Goes Round and Round," and whistled salaciously when Garland as Snowflake said to Flattop, "I appeal to you on bended knee," and Hope leeringly quipped, "Kid, you appeal to me in any position."

After that broadcast, Hope retreated to Palm Springs for a rest. His doctor, Tom Hearn, warned him about a slight rise in his blood pressure. He was advised to rest between radio broadcasts. One of the gossip columns suggested he was ill; another report from the Midwest had him dead. Mack Millar says that about once a week his office would receive an inquiry concerning Hope's death. And such inquiries and reports of his demise have continued from that time until the present. The most recent and probably the most notable was in June 1998, when an updated obituary (all the wire services and major newspapers maintain updated obits in preparation of the inevitable) was inadvertently circulated on the Internet. A copy was handed to a Congressman who was speaking on the House floor. He interrupted his speech to announce the comedian's death to an aghast, emotionally aroused floor and gallery. A short time later a correction was announced, and the *Congressional Record* was set straight. Hope's laconic quip was "Last time I felt, I'm still here."

Hope was quite alive that evening in April 1945 when he presided over the Motion Picture Academy's seventeenth annual Academy Awards ceremony. Hope took over the emcee job when the show went live on network radio that night, and before he had a chance to begin his monologue, Walter Wanger walked out on the stage to award him a lifetime membership in the Academy. Hope cracked, "Every year they give me a consolation prize. A life pass. . . Hmmmmm. . . now I know how Roosevelt feels."

When Gary Cooper announced that Bing Crosby had won an Oscar for his role in *Going My Way*, Bing came up to the stage, bald-headed and somewhat shy. When Cooper handed him the statuette, he looked as if he might not say anything, and Hope snapped, "You'd *better* say something."

Crosby said, "It just goes to show you what a great and democratic world we live in, when a broken-down crooner like myself can win this Academy crockery. If [director] Leo McCarey can lead me through a picture like this one—now he can find me a horse to win the Kentucky Derby."

And Hope leaned into the microphone, "Now I know how Dewey felt! . . . No, I think it's just great! Really!"

Ingrid Bergman won for her performance in *Gaslight*. During a mix-up in the presentation of the gold figurines, Hope said, "Wouldn't it be wonderful if there was one left over?"

Less than a month later, on April 12, 1945, the world was jolted by the death of Franklin Roosevelt from a cerebral hemorrhage. FDR had gone to Warm

Springs, Georgia, to prepare for the inauguration of the United Nations at San Francisco at the end of April.

When the President died, Hope wanted to reflect his and the nation's grief in his daily column but chose a rather oblique approach. On April 21, 1945, he wrote an open letter to Roosevelt's dog:

Dear Fala,

You probably don't remember me. But I knew you back in our kennel days when we were a couple of young pups—in fact we chewed our first bone together, remember? In writing you this letter, I'm speaking for dogs throughout the world. For we are all deeply grieved to hear of the death of your master. Your personal loss is felt by all of us. You know as well as I do that leading a dog's life is no bed of roses. But a dog's life is for dogs. Human beings shouldn't horn in on our territory. But lately a lot of men and women and kids have been leading a dog's life, and your master was one of the humans who didn't like to see that sort of thing happening. That's why we respected him—he wanted to keep human beings in their right place. And he did something about it. He made plans, and people had confidence in his plans because his integrity and sincerity were felt the world over. In other words, he made a lot of people see the light, or as we'd put it, he put them on the right scent. Let's hope they can keep their noses to the ground and work it out for themselves, even though his personal guidance has been taken away from them.

With deepest sympathy,
Fido

Hope devoted eight of his daily columns to the United Nations Conference at San Francisco, so it is surprising that there is no mention in any of his May columns of the cessation of war in Europe. On the other hand, it is not surprising that Hope was saying nothing in print about his sticky contract squabble with Paramount. He didn't have to, really, because the syndicated columnists—some fed information by Mack Millar—were doing the job for him. One of the most widely read, Florabel Muir, summed up the situation as a "Mexican stand-off" and laid the problem at the feet of Paramount's new ruling executive, Henry Ginsberg, who had jockeyed the corporation through its recent $16 million winning streak. In the *New York Daily Mirror* on April 22, 1945, Florabel wrote: "Henry would like to give Bob Hope what he wants but he feels that if he does he will establish a dangerous precedent... When a star of Hope's stature announces he doesn't want to work for nothing, who can blame him? Which is why we are going to see more and more top stars going as independent as they can."

Muir's column preceded by only a short time the succinct announcement by Paramount on May 6, 1945, that Henry Ginsberg had signed a new seven-year exclusive contract with Hope that allowed the comedian to make one film a year for himself and to work in partnership with Paramount on other projects. The battle was won and its outcome was a benchmark for Hollywood filmmakers. It opened the floodgate for independent movie deals and tolled the death knell of big-studio autonomy.

On May 12, Hope took his Pepsodent cast to Washington, D.C., for a three-hour show, which included his radio broadcast, to kick off the Seventh War Loan Drive. Sixty-five hundred people pledged $2.5 million in bonds to see the show, and one of the rewards for Hope was an invitation by Harry Truman to perform in the Gold Room of the White House. He took Frances, Jerry, Vera, Tony, and Skinnay Ennis (just back from the war) to entertain the Truman family, whose members had gathered from near and far. There were about 35 or 40 people in the audience. As they walked in, Hope cracked, "Man, this looks like Missouri already." The President laughed.

Truman asked to see the same show Hope had been performing at U.S. camps and overseas. Afterward there was lemonade and cookies and a tour of the White House personally conducted by Harry, Bess, and Margaret. When the house tour was finished, they stood in the portico where two months earlier the vice president had become President, and from somewhere nearby a cannon fired two shells. Margaret said excitedly, "What was that, Dad?" And before Harry could respond, Hope quipped, "Nothing, my dear. Just my hotel's auditing machine figuring up my bill."

With praise from the nation's new President still ringing in his ears, Hope moved from the White House to the Smithsonian for the unveiling of his statue in the "living hall of fame." It was announced that 8 million GIs had voted him this honor in a survey of U.S. and overseas troops.

Hope and his radio cast went to Chicago and continued to promote the Seventh War Loan Drive there. The comedian was joined by his pal Crosby, and together they raised hundreds of thousands for the war-loan cause, exchanging verbal barbs as they drove, pitched, and putted balls over 18 holes at the Tam O'Shanter course. In the days that followed Hope juggled benefit golf matches with Crosby and war-loan Pepsodent cast shows to finish out his radio season. One of the largest of his fund-raising broadcasts was in front of 50,000 war-loan bond buyers who jammed Notre Dame Stadium at nearby South Bend on May 28 to watch the "Pepsodent Players" romp through their specialties.

After the final shows in Sedalia, Missouri, and Salt Lake City, Hope realized how seriously he needed a few days' rest. But then, refreshed, he and Dolores flew to New York so she could wave him off on the *Queen Mary* for his two-and-a-half-month journey to entertain American occupation forces in Europe. The USO had sent out an impassioned bulletin to ask entertainers *not* to abandon the GIs now that the shooting war had ended. Hope was among the first to say yes, and although he could not take Langford (she had signed a contract to do a summer radio program), he collared Colonna, Patty Thomas, singer Gale Robbins, pianist June Bruner, accordionist Ruth Denas, and comedians Roger Price and Jack Pepper.

The Hope troupe opened at London's Albert Hall on the fourteenth of July for 10,000 airmen and the next day moved across the Channel to France. Their first stop was at the USO's French headquarters, at Chatou. Hope later said, "It looks as if Central Casting had opened an overseas branch. I ran into Alfred Lunt and Lynne Fontanne, Bea Lillie, and Reginald Gardiner. . . . Really, a lot of stars like Cagney, Cooper, Annie Sheridan, and Paulette Goddard made off-shore trips and never said a word about it. So different from YOU-KNOW-WHO. . . "

In fact, there were quite a few other big names in Europe entertaining the occupation forces that summer. In Paris to prepare for their next show, Hope learned that he had just missed seeing his pal Crosby as well as Ingrid Bergman, Jack Benny, Al Jolson, and Fred Astaire, all of whom were just headed for or returning from troop locations in France and Germany.

From Paris they were driven to Amiens to entertain assault troops who had been first ashore at Normandy, and from there south to Marseilles, where they performed for 150,000 weary GIs reassigned from the South Pacific who were waiting around in dusty, barren staging areas. There Hope was delighted to run into more USO stars—Sonja Henie, Mickey Rooney, Bobby Breen, and opera's glamorous Grace Moore.

A lighted platform at the end of a soccer field in Nice was where Hope did one of his last shows in France. During the evening he learned that Maurice Chevalier was sitting out front. Chevalier, accused of collaboration with the Nazis, had become a controversial figure during the war. Hope had known him at Paramount and respected him. When Hope asked to have Chevalier brought backstage, one American officer objected strenuously.

"Don't introduce him. He's suspected of being a traitor."

"Hope glared at the officer. "I don't know anything about that. I'm not a judge and jury. I'm just an emcee and that guy is a hell of an entertainer. Bring him back here."

Chevalier came behind the platform smiling, but looking a bit uncertain. He was wearing a white turtleneck sweater and red trousers and it was clear he had hoped to make an appearance. He went out and sang "Louise" and several other Chevalier standards and the audience gave him a standing ovation. Later, sipping brandy in the chateau where the Hope troupe was housed, Chevalier said to him, "I will always remember this thing you did for me tonight on a football field."

After leaving Nice they landed in Germany for nearly a month of shows in 13 troop locations from Bremen to Munich. They played for the 29th Infantry Division at Bremen, Airborne Division troops in Berlin, the Air Force at Bad Kissingen, the Army at Heidelberg, more Air Force men at Fürstenfeldbruck, and an armored personnel division at Fritzlar. The Navy called him back to Monte Carlo to play for the crew of the destroyer USS *Gridley* and then right back to Kassel, Munich, and Nuremberg for the GI Olympics. Hope was sitting in the old Nuremberg Stadium (now called Soldiers Field) when the announcement came over the sound system that Japan was offering surrender. It had begun to rain, but even so, the crowd went wild and the hugging and cheering lasted for 30 minutes. "Even C. B. DeMille couldn't have improved on the noise those Yanks made," said Hope.

At Mannheim Hope picked up prizefighter Billy Conn as a replacement for Patty Thomas, who had become ill and was hospitalized for a few days. They finished the tour in Austria and Czechoslovakia. The talk everywhere was: When would V-J Day happen?

And there was other talk, too. Wire-service reporters were on Hope's trail. One asked what would happen to Bob Hope after V-J Day? How would he reconvert from war to peace? At one point he said, "In common with the GIs, I kept thinking of a nice long rest. The only difference was that the GIs really wanted one and I was afraid I'd be given one."

The gossip and entertainment columnists began speculating about Hope's transition back to civilian radio. The sponsor, Pepsodent, was getting letters, too. Apparently, after five years of war the home listeners felt deprived of having humor directed at them.

NBC radio got mail from people asking, "Why isn't Hope doing shows for *us* now?"

Hope believed that his answer to reporter Jack Holland ought to suffice: "As long as there are fellows—and girls—still in the service, they get the first call. They need entertainment now as much as ever—if not more. The days they spend waiting to get home or the hours they lie in hospital beds are plenty tough—and a laugh won't hurt them."

But his critics didn't stop. After all, the war was over.

Comic Drummer: 1946 to 1951

25

So This Is Peace?

"On the second anniversary of D-Day, we established a small beachhead at Spokane, Washington, and started crisscrossing the country. . . double-crossing the audiences. . . The guys showed up just the way they did when they were in the Army. Only this time they had to pay."

Shortly after World War II had ended, the worldview of the average American, civilian or ex-GI suddenly shrank. The forced altruism of the past five years switched to self-centered survival. "Reconversion" was the newfound word for how to beat the shortages and unemployment.

While diplomats and politicians were busy trying to find out how much validity there was in Wendell Willkie's "One World" dream, the guy with the lunch pail was trying to figure out how long before his wife could have her new washing machine. Peace had promised a payoff and people were anxious to collect.

In much the same frame of mind (although with the sound of laughing GIs still ringing in his ears), Bob Hope came home to Hollywood from five years of giving away much of his time, energy, and talent, and decided he needed to play catch-up. He had to refire the burners under his flagging movie career. His last film, *Road to Utopia*, had been both a critical success and a gold mine, but that was months ago and the money was long spent. Normally Paramount would have at least one Hope film in reserve waiting to be released, but now the cupboard was bare.

To make matters worse, Hope came home to studio squabbling. While he was still in Europe, Paramount hustled to find a suitable vehicle for his triumphant return to the lot, finally settling on a comic version of Booth Tarkington's novel *Monsieur Beaucaire,* which Rudolph Valentino had swashbuckled through in 1924. Everyone agreed that Hope's reluctant hero persona in powdered wig and satin breeches was funny, not to mention light-centuries removed from khaki and parade drills.

Norman Panama and Melvin Frank labored over the script and had completed most of it when Henry Ginsberg assigned Paul Jones as producer. Jones was dissatisfied with the script and hired a new writer. Angrily, Panama and Frank complained to the Writers Guild, which supported their claim of having been unfairly dismissed. So the project was hung up. But Hope pressured Ginsberg to back down, and forced Jones to accept the Panama-Frank script, which Hope and director George Marshall found hilarious.

The movie had a strong cast. The women—Joan Caulfield, Marjorie Reynolds, and Hillary Brooke—were attractive, and the character parts, played by Joseph Schildkraut, Constance Collier, Douglas Dumbrille, Patric Knowles, Cecil Kellaway, and Reginald Owen, were exceptionally effective. Yet making the picture was a taxing experience, even for the energetic Hope. Each day he was faced with elaborate sight gags and gimmicks, pratfalls or water dunkings, as well as tricky dueling scenes with Schildkraut, a skilled fencer. And although Hope could always hold his own in close-ups, in this case he was grateful for a fencing double. Jack Hope noted that Hope was uncharacteristically impatient more than usual.

After all, he had a new stake in the outcome. When the picture was previewed in nearby Alhambra, the audiences laughed, but Paramount executives, along with their new partner, Hope, felt it looked "too straight," perhaps even too subtle. So comedy writer Frank Tashlin was hired to heighten the slapstick, and after some reshooting the film was previewed again. Bingo! Audiences loved it. *Monsieur Beaucaire* was to firmly take its place among Hope's best.

Almost at once Hope began another film, *Where There's Life*, in which he plays a bumbling disc jockey who discovers he is heir to the throne of a mythical kingdom. The script was based on a story idea by one of his gag writers, Mel Shavelson.

The film was nothing exceptional. It simply provided Hope with a fairly predictable lifestyle for a few months. In fact, between this film and the one before it Hope was reasonably sedentary for almost a year, which was unique in his career. It gave him more time to be with Dolores, Linda, and Tony. Forced to rise early (something he abhorred) during filming, now he could have breakfast with them. If he had a late studio call, he could play games with them. He would grab his movie camera and follow them as they romped with Suds (the Scottie) or Red Sun (the great Dane), splashed at the shallow end of the huge swimming pool, or waved their rackets at him on the tennis court. His Toluca Lake property now comprised ten acres of backyard, and also included an abbreviated pitch-and-put golf course.

During this period Bob got closer to another member of his family, his mother-in-law Theresa DeFina. She sold furs at the Franklin Simon department store in New York, but she liked California and loved being with her grandchildren, so she would come for a month or so in the spring. Considering her hostile reaction to Bob when he married Dolores, the unexpected had occurred. Over the years, Bob and Theresa developed a joking relationship based on genuine respect. There was a toughness in Theresa that reminded Hope of Mahm.

Theresa recognized Bob's need for family love and support; she considered him shrewd, clever, and protective of things he and she valued, and frequently found herself at odds with Dolores over decisions he made or intended to make. Theresa encouraged Bob and Dolores to adopt more children; she volunteered to go to The Cradle with them, or for them, if need be, if Florence Walrath could find another baby. She knew that although Dolores had for a long time hoped to adopt children, the six years since Tony had joined the family had been hectic and disrupted by the war and by Bob's long absences. But now she and Dolores could increase their pressure; they enjoyed success the day they heard Bob say, "Dolores, let's try for another girl."

Another family member Hope got to know better, but unfortunately lost in 1946, was Uncle Frank, his dad's older brother. Uncle Frank had moved from Cleveland to El Segundo, California, in the 1920s and was a frequent visitor at Moorpark Street. Still a clear-thinking 81, Frank, a hard-working tradesman all his life, brought Bob and Dolores his commonsense philosophy, his attitudes about human dignity and thrift. "Such a beautiful man, in looks, in thoughts," Bob said. "Dolores and I were completely in love with him. He was a great stabilizer. He taught me moderation."

Hope's deeply embedded family instincts—belonging, being loyal, even protective—were genuinely strong. But for a man continually on the run and driven by his kind of ambition, these feelings for his "nest" family—Dolores, Linda, Tony, and Theresa—were often compulsively shared with a much larger "family"— his listeners seated around their radios, his legion of movie fans, and the GIs who still treasured his wartime devotion. Their overt affection, coming from all parts of the nation, was very embracing and satisfying to him, and the sound of their applause frequently drowned out the cries for help and affection coming from his own home.

Then, too, he never let go of that enduring closeness to his brothers; despite differences and disappointments, his loyalty never faltered. In addition, he had become a "big daddy" to many of his relatives, in-laws, and friends from his vaudeville days—some in Ohio and others nearer Toluca Lake. These relationships often involved financial assistance. Hope considered them investments. But however he viewed his role as provider and benefactor, he had to be increasingly concerned and increasingly in charge of his financial future and the empire he was building.

In an article entitled "Hope Springs Financial," *Newsweek* reported on May 6, 1946, that Hope's current annual earnings were impressive. He would gross around $1.25 million from movies and radio shows that year and would receive another $30,000 from his newspaper column. Trusted advisers like insurance man Al Lloyd and accountant Arthur Nadel had steered him into annuities, blue-chip stocks, and government bonds. His investment in (part ownership of) Hope Metal Products, under his brother Ivor's direction, was netting about $100,000 a year.

Legal wizard Martin Gang responded to Hope's need to protect his income by creating a new corporation just to handle personal appearances; Bob had decided it was time to stop doing them *all* for charity. Gang further suggested that Hope create another corporation to cover activities that fell into categories other than films or personal appearances. Hope planned to write another book with Carroll

Carroll, this one humorously documenting his USO experiences in the South Pacific and more recently in Europe. Also, he had been approached by Capitol Records to record and release a dramatized version of *I Never Left Home*.

In spite of all his holdings, Hope had a rude awakening. After the war he found himself cash-poor. When he opened his income-tax bill and saw the figure $62,000, he almost fainted.

Fortunately, he and Nadel persuaded the Treasury Department to grant him an extension based on two things: one, his promise to pay as soon as he started his next movie, and two, a not-so-gentle reminder of the number of successful war-bond and war-loan drives he had kicked off and continued to support during the past five years.

Peacetime brought Hope yet a second rude awakening. For the first time in several years his radio program had slipped to a decimal point behind *Fibber McGee*. The advertising agency and network boys offered this explanation: He had neglected to alter his format; he had insisted on continuing to play for military audiences, which had alienated his civilian home listener; and that listener, they said, was more tuned to situation comedy and wanted to put the war behind them.

Hope was so accustomed to receiving praise from critics for his wartime shows that he was baffled by their current "picking" on him. He discussed this with the *Milwaukee Journal* entertainment writer J. D. Spiro on the set of *Where There's Life*. "They're undoubtedly right when they say that my radio show hasn't been all it could be. I know it needs some reconversion, but it takes time to reconvert, and we haven't had it. After four years of playing to thousands of GIs all over the globe, you can't just come down instantly to playing to three hundred people out in front."

"Will you change your show, Bob?"

"Yeah—somewhat—for the fall. We'll probably go more toward situation, but you know my style is topical stuff. Anyway, we'll have Vera Vague back—and Colonna. Langford's gone, but we'll have some big guest singers."

Despite his assurances to his media critics and his sponsor that he would make changes in his show, there were no perceptible differences during that season. Nevertheless, when both the Hooper ratings and Crossley Surveys, Inc., came out in late spring, Hope was the leader. This intensified his feeling that it didn't matter so much what he was doing because the people out there liked him.

Knowing they liked him and feeling that a top-ticket personal appearance tour was a sure way of getting enough money to pay his taxes, Hope asked Louis Shurr to book a national tour of 29 cities in 31 days. Whew! On such short notice he couldn't book his resident touring company, but he booked a young Paramount newcomer, Olga San Juan, as his sexy singer, a chorus line of starlets, and some backup variety acts. Hope asked Mack Millar to line up several publicists who could begin tub thumping through Seattle, Spokane, Denver, St. Louis, Oklahoma City, Chicago, Houston, New Orleans, Birmingham, Atlanta, and Norfolk. Ultimately it was Jack Hope, Rufus Blair of Paramount publicity, Louis

Weiner, who was Crosby's press agent, and Mack himself who hit the road to pressure newspaper city rooms with press releases, to circulate posters and broadsides, to set up street banners. Hope had said to them, "The big thing to promote is Hope in person with a big Hollywood show. Do whatever it takes to get a crowd—skywriting, door to door. Just do it!" After all, there was nothing new in show business promotion since P. T. Barnum.

After breaking-in performances in Glendale, San Diego, and Fresno, the troupe boarded two chartered Transair DC–3s and took off for Spokane. Not only would there be a two-hour stage show in the Gonzaga Stadium, but there would also be an exhibition golf match with the city's most famous native son, Bing Crosby.

Rain threatened to cancel the Hope-Crosby match, but it took place anyway in foul weather, and Seattle's *Post-Intelligencer* sent one of its reporters to do a story. The article that resulted may well be the first major newspaper piece whose theme was an attempt to put the mythic and symbolic elements of Hope's image in perspective. To the reporter, Douglas Welch, the *Newsweek* account of the recent formation of Hope's corporations, coming as it did on the heels of his stunning wartime philanthropy, seemed like the seed of a good feature story. Welch approached Hope's agent, Doc Shurr, to help him get to the entertainer. "Bob Hope is big business and we want to write him up as we would any successful corporation."

Welch pressed Shurr for information about Hope's finances and income taxes and about Hope Enterprises. Shurr refused to answer, snapping, "There are too many people already thinking about Hope's income and his taxes and we don't want any more. No! Forget it!" Shurr turned to leave, then countered with "Now, why don't you write something people will want to read—like, for instance that we have 40 people in the troupe, that we have some very beautiful girls, that the show is really colossal and straight from Hollywood." Then Shurr did walk away, muttering loudly, "What kind of questions are these?"

Welch never got to interview Hope, but his story, which appeared in the *Post-Intelligencer* on June 6, 1946, could have been worse. It could have included a verbatim report of the journalist's encounter with Doc Shurr, and *that* would have really angered the comedian. First of all, Shurr, Hope's agent, was not supposed to be doing press agent Mack Millar's job; more important, Hope was quite adept at media relations and if Welch had talked to him he probably would have been able to change the tenor of Welch's story, which labeled Hope as a "Corporation":

Wherever he goes, the whole board of directors ambles right along with him. They not only do all the things that the directors of any company normally do, but in addition they have been trained to laugh in the right places. "Oh, that Hope! He kills us," the directors say in chorus, laughing fit to kill and slapping their thighs. "That's our boy over there making funnies. Yes, it is! That's our boy!" In public, Hope looks like a parade. Even when he goes to the gentlemen's retiring room he looks like a platoon. He is constantly surrounded with busy, worried and preoccupied people, with briefcases, papers and knitted brows.

Spokane was also the setting for a curious nonencounter and revealing look at the relationship between Bob and his older brother, Jim. Jim was probably the only family member who was not able to accept Bob's phenomenal success gracefully, and Bob sensed this.

Jim had come to California in the mid thirties, even before Bob, to try his hand at selling real estate and had also found some work as an extra in movies. His first marriage had been a disaster but in California he met and married pretty Wyn Swanson, young and talented with an ambition to be in show business. She looked good onstage and had an appealing singing style; she could write in a variety of forms, including comedy, and she composed songs. Together, Wyn and Jim created a vaudeville act and were booked by the Levey office, primarily on the strength of the Hope name. They were shipped out to the sticks and were currently playing a series of towns and cities in the Northwest, where stage shows paired with movies could still attract a fair crowd.

Unknown to Jim and Wyn, but certainly not unknown to the Levey office, they were booked into the Post Street Theater in Spokane to collide with the week that Bob and his extravaganza would be playing in Gonzaga Stadium. On Bob's first morning in the city, Don Halladay of the *Daily Chronicle* was ushered into Hope's suite at the Davenport Hotel for an interview. "How are you feeling?" asked Halladay.

"Look at these blisters," Hope said, pointing to his feet. "We just finished a picture by working half the nights, and on Memorial Day, too, so we could make this date." He yawned. "And I didn't get to bed until nearly three. Felt like I was directing traffic all night. I thought the cabs were coming in the window but I was having such a nice carbon monoxide snooze."

"How does it feel with two Hope shows playing the same town?"

"What?" Hope asked, looking at Mack Millar. "What does he mean?"

"Your brother Jim," said Mack. "Jim and Wyn are playing a vaudeville date around the corner at the Post Street Theater."

"You got to be kidding," Hope said laughing. Then, not laughing: "How come nobody told me?"

"Nobody knew until this morning."

Halladay's eyes were traveling back and forth from Hope to Millar. Then Mack said quickly, "But they ought to do pretty fair business considering everything—"

"That," Hope broke in, "is unfair competition." Then he turned to Halladay and said brightly, "You know, I've got six brothers and each of them is playing a town."

Later that afternoon, an unidentified reporter from the *Daily Chronicle* called Jim Hope at his hotel, asking if he and Wyn would be available for a news photo with his brother. Jim was told he would be alerted to the exact time and place after the details had been cleared with Bob. Wyn was thrilled. She and Jim rifled through their wardrobe trunk for the best of their street clothes and became more excited when another reporter called from the city newsroom telling them to stand by.

They stood by as long as they could and then dashed for the theater. There had been no further call. Jim was too proud to telephone Bob or the newspaper. They were later told that Bob had turned down the suggestion of a press photo or a joint news interview. In fact, a *Chronicle* reporter told Jim that his brother was emphatic in refusing to see him. "It was a silly thing, silly and thoughtless," Hope said much later. "As I look back, I remember thinking something secret was going on. But I was wrong." Jim also found out that Bob asked Louis Shurr to "slip over to the Post and catch Jim's act."

Later that same night, Jim and Wyn had a late after-show supper at the Davenport and heard people excitedly saying that the Hope troupe had come back from Gonzaga Stadium and were upstairs getting ready to go to the airport. The couple stood unobserved in the lobby crowd as Bob left the hotel. Nor did anyone recognize them as they walked arm in arm back to their hotel. Wyn Hope has since said, "Somehow I feel that if Bob had read a review of our act before he was asked to meet with Jim, it would have worked out. Believe me, Jim Hope and Wyn Swanson were no threat to Bob's career and fame. In fact, we were helping to bury vaudeville."

Hope & Company flew out of Spokane, moved from city to city until they had pretty much covered the nation, and started back toward California. Their last shows were in Kansas City, and during the very last performance, Fred Hope called the theater to tell Bob that their younger brother Sid's cancer, which had been in remission for a time, was spreading.

Sid Hope knew he was dying, which was why he needed to see Bob. For the past seventeen years he had lived quietly as a machinist and farmer in the little village of Ridgeville Corners, Ohio. Sid never craved the business or entertainment worlds that attracted his brothers; he preferred the country life with Dorothy, his wife, and their five children. Sid was too young to die. He was only 41, two years younger than Bob.

When Bob first got the call from Fred, one of his backstage guests happened to be Secretary of War Harry Goodring, who immediately arranged to have a Navy plane fly Bob from Kansas City to Columbus, pick up Fred, and then continue on to Toledo. The brothers would then drive the rest of the way from Toledo. After the Toledo visit, the Navy plane was instructed to go to the airport at Defiance, Ohio, near Ridgeville Corners, wait for Hope, and take him back to Kansas City, where a connecting Transair DC–3 would be waiting to take him back to California.

In Ridgeville Corners, a sleepy landscape of scattered farms, very few people would ever know that Bob Hope, the famous comedian, had driven part of the night with his older brothers Jim and Fred to be with Sid, Dorothy, and the kids. They were the look-alike brothers, Bob and Sid. That's what Dorothy was saying as they sat outdoors on lawn chairs in the shade. Sid was amused when the smallest of his kids tried to climb up into Bob's lap. Fred came out to join them and Bob pointed to Fred's crop of wavy hair. "If Paramount saw that they'd cancel my contract." Bob amused everyone by telling them about filming the bear scene in *Road to Utopia*.

Sid, reluctant to have his brother leave him, told Bob that the nearby Archbold Airport had a 2,800-foot runway that the Civilian Aviation Authority supervised 24 hours a day. Bob asked Fred to call Defiance and find out if the Navy pilots could pick him up in Archbold. They could and they did.

Before Bob left he said, "Sid, you're going to get well."

"Don't need to lie, Les. I know I'm dying. I have cancer. I just wanted to ask one favor—please take care of my kids." And Bob did that as long as it was needed.

In August, when Bob was not quite through the shooting of *My Favorite Brunette*, Sid died, and Bob chartered a plane to take the California Hopes to Ohio. Every living offspring of Harry and Avis Hope gathered at Ridgeville Corners' St. Peter's Lutheran Church.

After the funeral, Hope stepped back into his life of making movies and preparing for his fall radio season in his usual driven fashion. *Brunette* was a frenetic, fast-paced spy comedy in the tradition of the successful *My Favorite Blonde*, but this time it was Hope and Lamour being chased by Peter Lorre, Lon Chaney, Jr., Charles Dingle, and John Hoyt. It was Hope's first independent film production and he did not spare the cost. He paid Bing Crosby $25,000 for a cameo appearance in the movie's surprise ending.

If he was being meticulously careful to make an appealing film comedy, he was just as neglectful of the changes he had vowed to make in his radio program. So the morning after the September 26 Pepsodent premiere, Hope should have been prepared for the critical response. From the *Chicago Daily News*, the headline read: TOOTHPASTE BUT NO NEW TEETH IN BOB HOPE'S OPENING SHOW. The dean of radio critics, Jack Gould, writing in the Sunday, October 1, 1946, *New York Times*, put it in harsher terms:

> Bob Hope opened his ninth season on the air last Tuesday evening in the noble tradition of Jake Shubert's "The Student Prince."
>
> You could enjoy it if you had not heard it the first, second, third, fourth, fifth, sixth, seventh and eighth times.
>
> It was all there in this order: (1) Irium (a new ingredient in Pepsodent) (2) Pallid Patter (3) Irium (4) Joke about Bing Crosby (5) Jerry Colonna Arrives (6) Hope Insults Colonna (7) Colonna Screams (8) Irium (9) Vera Vague Arrives (10) Hope Insults Vera (11) Vera Shrieks (12) Irium.

On the other hand Hope's ratings were good enough news to Lever Brothers' head Charles Luckman for him to agree to raise Hope's weekly take by $2,500.

And Hope had to believe that it was his tireless "machine-gun sputtering" of gags—at least to GIs—that earned him the American Legion's highest award, its Distinguished Service Medal, in San Francisco on October 1. He stood on the stage with Secretary of State Cordell Hull and FBI Director J. Edgar Hoover to receive the honor. Hope had the audience on its feet when he said, "Until every hospitalized kid is on his feet again, this job isn't finished."

Two weeks later he was able to top himself. He was summoned to Washington, D.C., where before 40 top military men, the chiefs of staff, congressional leaders, and his personal hero, General Dwight Eisenhower, he was honored for his wartime entertaining with the nation's highest civilian award, the Medal of Merit. As the press photographers and newsreel cameras clicked and turned, Hope said to the group, chewing gum vigorously, "A little more respect, please, fellas." After the ceremony he sat with Eisenhower in his Pentagon office, where they reminisced about their meeting in North Africa and Hope reminded him of that blitzing air raid in Algiers. Hope polished the medal with his sleeve and Ike laughed when he heard "Boy, wait till Bing hears about this!"

All Bing had to do to hear about the medal was turn on his radio or look in the afternoon paper because the story blanketed the nation's front pages.

Hope went from the Pentagon to the White House for a meeting with Harry Truman. It was a short meeting and a private one. Hope later said, "I had to thank him—after all, he had to put his okay on it." Hope told his friends afterward that he was shocked by Truman's drawn, tense face, so different from two years before.

Just before he was to fly back to California, Dolores called to say they had to meet in Chicago. Florence Walrath had their baby girl waiting for them at The Cradle.

They went to Evanston to pick up a two-month-old that they already knew would be of either Italian or Irish parentage—because Dolores had made it a condition—and when Bob took his first look he said, "What a doll!" Dolores smiled and didn't seem to hear all of what Mrs. Walrath was saying. She only heard something about the baby being Italian, and then it dawned on her that there was more, which was "And I have a surprise for you. We also have a little boy and he's Irish."

"You mean—" Dolores watched while the nurse came with another baby, this one three months old. "Oh, I don't think—"

Bob left her in the viewing room and walked back to Mrs. Walrath's office to sort out the legal details with a lawyer. Dolores joined them and wanted to draw Bob away so she could discuss with him the idea of taking two babies.

"Dolores—I've already signed—for both."

"Whatever made you do that?" Dolores asked when they were leaving.

"I couldn't bear to think of leaving him behind," Bob said.

A few days later there was a double baptism for their two-month-old, Honorah, which would soon be shortened to Nora, and their three-month-old,

Kelly, at St. Charles Borromeo in North Hollywood. When it was over, Bob stayed behind for a moment talking to a priest in the vestry. Suddenly he turned and found a man standing next to him with a baby in his arms.

"Take him out to the car," Hope ordered.

"Oh no you don't," said the stranger. "This one happens to be mine."

26

King's Clown

"The King watched us leafing through the book of autographed pictures and then slipped me the royal needle. 'Look at him,' he said, 'he's hurrying to get to his own picture.' 'Why not?' I asked. 'It's the prettiest.'"

As 1946 came to a close, Americans were reading novels by John Marquand and Erskine Caldwell; nonfiction works like *Peace of Mind* by Joshua Liebman, *The Egg and I* by Betty MacDonald; and Hope's third book, *So This Is Peace*, which had jumped in a few weeks from sixteenth to fifth place on the best-seller lists.

Hope had once again asked Carroll Carroll to organize his personal notes, his newspaper columns, monologues, and press clippings and create a pastiche covering his South Pacific and European entertainments, as well as his most recent month-long tour of one-night stands through postwar America. Carroll attempted to make something meaningful out of the ironies in the word "peace," and the opening lines were deft:

We're at peace. We're not enjoying it, but we're at it. And it's sensational what can happen in just one year of it.

We have famine in the midst of plenty and plenty in the midst of famine. The United Nations held meetings. But the meeting nations were never united. Great Britain's Lion turned on Russia. The Russian Bear tried everything but Unguentine on [U.S. Secretary of State] Byrnes. And the whole UN setup got a cut out of Connecticut.

But we're doing all right. As soon as the war ended, we located the one spot on earth that hadn't been touched and blew it to hell.

This book was intended to be a sequel to the enormously successful *I Never Left Home*, so it had its share of monologue-like gags delivered in the style that one of his writers, Les White, called "the Commando technique—you strike hard and fast and then move on." But there were also passages of rich sentiment and more insights into the phenomenon that was Hope's inimitable brand of foxhole humor. All in all, the book was uneven; but the promotional campaign was stunning, making use again of irreverent full-page ads that insulted Hope:

> We are forced by a contract to announce that, over the protests of his tax man, his public, and ourselves, this man has written another book. Piqued by the small sale of *I Never Left Home* (1,620,000 copies, mostly to relatives), Mr. Hope has gritted his tooth and sat down to (some perspective advance readers say "sat down on") his typewriter to produce this minim opus. It dealt off the bottom of the deck, with reconversion. It is no funnier than *I Never Left Home*, Hope says. It couldn't be.

Just before Christmas the book passed the quarter-million sales mark. On New Year's Day, 1947, 1.5 million people lined Colorado Boulevard in Pasadena to watch Dolores and Grand Marshal Bob Hope waving from a rose-covered float in the fifty-eighth Annual Tournament of Roses parade. Hope hated the four-thirty wake-up call and the five-thirty limousine, but loved the screams of recognition as the float turned the corner at Orange Grove and headed down the boulevard. He would be grand marshal twice more in his lifetime, but never with quite so much exuberance.

Early the next morning, Hope reported to a Paramount Pictures soundstage to begin work on his fifth collaboration with Crosby and Lamour, this one called *The Road to Rio.* The big difference was that on this trip Bob and Bing each owned a third of the picture. Crosby had formed Rainbow Productions about the same time Hope Enterprises was born, and Bing's deal with the studio was similar to Hope's. Lamour had no such production company and said later, "It was one of the biggest mistakes of my life not to make a producing deal with Ginsberg." After all, Lamour had been the bigger name than either Hope or Crosby when they first came to Paramount.

Lamour also said that *Rio* was a better experience for her because Bob and Bing seemed to have developed new attitudes about the business of picture making. As part owners they were suddenly concerned about time and cost. Hope said, "Bing and I hardly left the set, except to go to the men's room."

Rio's plot was familiar. Scat Sweeney (Crosby) and Hot Lips Barton (Hope) are on the lam and stow away on a liner bound for Rio de Janeiro. They meet beautiful Lucia Maria de Andrade (Lamour) and naturally become embroiled in a sinister plot. It was all very predictable and it was predictably well received by *Road* picture fans—which was a large number of fans indeed. Adding to its popularity was the fact that one song, "But Beautiful," had climbed to the top of sheet-music sales charts and also was scaling the summit of the hit parade.

During the filming of *Rio*, Paramount Pictures launched the first commercial television station west of Chicago. The studio had been experimenting with the new medium since 1939 (television was introduced to the nation at the New York

World's Fair), and was trial-broadcasting (or rather narrow-casting) to a few home receivers from their tiny station called W6XYZ, headquartered on the studio lot at Melrose and Bronson. On January 22, 1947, that pioneering station became KTLA and inaugurated service with a special telecast to probably no more than 350 sets.

Bob Hope was emcee and he introduced producer Cecil B. DeMille, Dottie Lamour, Jerry Colonna, William Bendix, Ann Rutherford, William Demarest, Peter Lind Hayes, the Rhythmaires, and the DeCastro Sisters. Hope recalls that he and his cohorts were not happy about the intensely hot lights that made them all wringing wet after just a few minutes on the set. As he watched them one by one slipping out of the studio, he said, "I don't know where you're going to find performers who will undergo this kind of heat."

Of course, it was still a year or two before many performers would have to care. Radio was still the chief free entertainment in the nation, and Bob Hope was still the undisputed comedy king. As long as this was true, complaints from the sponsor could be largely ignored.

However, in April the "king" was censored by NBC and a barrage of criticism arose from the Fourth Estate about the network's foolishness or lapse of judgment. It all started with Fred Allen, who on his Sunday night program told a joke about a "mythical" (but recognizable) NBC vice president, and was cut off the air for about ten seconds. Hope was incensed about NBC's thin skin and arrogance. "If Allen's gag had been in poor taste or blue, I could see it." Hope started to refer to Allen's trouble with NBC on his following Tuesday night show and was blanked out for six seconds. Hope was saying: "You know Las Vegas. . . that's the place where you can get tanned and faded at the same time. . . Of course, Fred Allen can get faded any time . . ." That same evening Red Skelton joked about Allen's being censored and he, too, was cut off.

Two weeks later, NBC cut Hope off the air because he said to his guest star, Frank Sinatra, "I'll be seeing you tomorrow night on your show." At rehearsals he had said "on CBS" but had decided to cut it from the script. Nevertheless, the engineers, warned by the NBC censors that Hope might say "CBS," had cut him off. Hope was livid and was tempted to get into a blistering fight with the network. But the situation was quickly diffused by NBC President Niles Trammell, who issued a statement saying that Allen should never have been faded. Furthermore, he suggested that Allen, Hope, and Skelton be made honorary vice presidents of NBC. The whole trivial brouhaha was a publicist's dream and Hope ended his season with his all-time highest listening audience.

As that season ended, Hope gave in to Dolores's insistence on a vacation. They chose South America and took Linda and Tony along. Bob also took his masseur from Lakeside Country Club, Frederico Miron, known as "Doctor" Freddy Miron. He was legendary among Hollywood movie stars and moguls for his expert hands. Freddy was a native of Cuba and so he could interpret for the Hopes as well as baby-sit with Linda and Tony when needed. This was the first of many, many trips that Freddy would take with Hope from that time until his death in the 1970s.

On their arrival in Rio, it was hard for them to ignore the splendor of Guanabara Bay and the Coreovada peak where stood the statue of Christ with his arms outstretched. Hope stopped in the tobacco shop of their hotel and bought as many postcards of that famous statue as they had, and mailed them to his writers and his buddies at Lakeside and at NBC. All the cards had the same message: "Look who was there to greet us and was Dolores tickled! Bob."

At the Montevideo airport, the Paramount field man met them and whisked them off to the elegant summer home of a wealthy Argentinian, Albert Cernadas, in Uruguay. Cernadas was the most recent husband of Hope's former radio stooge, Patricia (Honey Chile) Wilder, and the Hopes had the estate all to themselves. It was winter in South America and Cernadas had taken Honey Chile to Europe for the summer sun.

The rest of the vacation was spent in Buenos Aires, Santiago, Lima, and finally Cartagena, where the Hopes boarded the Grace Line's newest luxury ship, *Santa Rosa*, for the cruise back to New York. Bob acquired a badly sunburned face, which delayed for a week the start of his new movie *The Paleface* (how ironic!) with Jane Russell.

His role as Painless Potter, a correspondence-school dentist, was a vintage role and the genre that film critics seem to love most: the cowardly braggart, the unwilling hero. And the comedy was certainly heightened because he was viewed as the unlikely husband of the curvaceous Jane Russell, playing Calamity Jane. Part of the film's huge success has to be attributed to the song, "Buttons and Bows," written for Bob by the team of Jay Livingston and Ray Evans, whose first collaboration for Hope had been *Monsieur Beaucaire*.

"Buttons and Bows" was a superb saddle-jogging song that everyone knew would be a hit. When the time came to record it commercially, the industry was facing a strike. The very day the musicians were to walk out, Dinah Shore recorded the song with eight impatient musicians who seemed to be in a crouch position, ready to run out the door. Fortunately, her version of the tune sold in the millions and "Buttons and Bows" went on to win the Oscar for best movie song the following year.

While all this was happening at Paramount, there was trouble brewing in Hope's radio paradise. Pepsodent, which had dumped *Amos and Andy* at its height, was now losing its enthusiasm for Hope's show. It was costing them more money than a radio show ought to, partly because it traveled and traveling shows were expensive to produce, and partly because of Hope's $10,000-a-week salary. But there were other complaints: Hope's reluctance to reconvert more swiftly to peacetime radio (there was a definite trend toward *situation* comedy) and his occasional lapses in taste (perhaps the most notorious was his gag about the woman's skirt so short that she had two more cheeks to powder), and his fast-paced life, which allowed him to dole out only a fraction of the time necessary to produce an effective comedy product.

Insiders were not surprised to see the fight brought out into the open. Hope announced that after the season premiere, now originating from Hollywood's El Capitan Theater, he would take the radio show on the road. On October 1, 1947, *Variety* blasted his first show:

> Here's the epitome of radio's "sad saga of sameness." Apparently it's just too much to expect that Hope would ever veer an inch from his time-tested routine. His answer, it goes without saying, is: Why get out of a rut as long as there's pay dirt in it? And top pay dirt at that! By Hooper's count, too, Hope seems to be justified. His routine is apparently one of the things we fought the war for, like Ma's apple pie. Question simply is: Who's going to outlive the other, Hope or the listening public?

Hope had no time to heed this warning because he was, as usual, moving too fast. Professionally, he could smile at it when he landed on top of the ratings in late October. Personally he was on cloud nine because five of the greatest entertainers in all of show business—Jack Benny, George Jessel, Al Jolson, Eddie Cantor, and George Burns—keynoted a Friars Club roast on November 2 where they paid tribute to him in their usual outrageous manner.

Two days later, Hope took his radio show to Claremore, Oklahoma, to observe what would have been Will Rogers's sixty-eighth birthday. Hope's broadcast was remarkable. His closing, much to the amazement of his writing staff and the ad agency people, was a sermonette on Hollywood politics. Hope's weekly policy was to close his broadcast with a fervent plea to his listeners to support some charity. During the war he had pitched war bonds and patriotism, and in peacetime he favored a variety of philanthropies. But this night he chose to close his show with a comment about the Hollywood Communist investigation going on in Washington:

> The only sad thing about coming to Claremore is that Will Rogers isn't here to say a few words about our troubled times with the tolerance and humor that made him an all-time great. "I see by the papers," he might have said, "they've uncovered a few Reds out in Hollywood. Personally I've never preferred my politics in Technicolor, and when boy meets girl in the movies, I like to have them riding on the Freedom Train."

This is the most subtle public mention of the growing "red-baiting" that Hope ever made, and there is reason to suspect that he would not have done this on the air without the illusion of Rogers's style. When asked why he normally avoided hot-buttons issues, he said, "I'm usually selling a product everybody buys and I can't afford to alienate my audience. It's tough to do a comedy show and stay in the middle and please everybody when you're kicking current subjects around all the time. Will Rogers used to get away with it. But he was supposed to be a cracker-barrel type. I've got a lot of crackers in my barrel but there was only one Will Rogers."

What brought the fight with his sponsor, Pepsodent, to media attention, however, was not this speech but Hope's decision to accept an invitation from Buckingham Palace to attend the wedding of Princess Elizabeth to Philip Mountbatten and to headline a giant command performance gala at London's Odeon Theatre. He found out that he would be able to prerecord parts of his program in advance (Bing Crosby was prerecording his *Kraft Music Hall* show every week) and broadcast the monologue portion of the program live from London. Pepsodent bellowed its objections, asking Hope to cancel his London plans. Hope refused. Pepsodent issued an ultimatum stating that unless he did so, the firm would "deprive him of his regular Tuesday night facilities on the National Broadcasting Company."

The real issue here was that Hope wanted to continue to crisscross the nation with his radio cast because he loved doing personal appearances, he loved doing his radio show in front of big crowds rather than being limited to a Hollywood studio, and Lever Brothers thought he was costing them too much.

Jimmy Saphier hastily flew to New York and the rumor mill began churning. The most persistent version had Hope leaving Pepsodent and NBC, joining the American Broadcasting Company, and, under Kraft Foods' sponsorship, being slotted in a time period back to back with Bing Crosby. It was an ad man's dream and apparently it worried Lever Brothers.

Meanwhile Bob and Dolores went off to their royal wedding and command performance. They threw a large sailing party in their *Queen Mary* suite the day they left New York. At one point Hope turned to Saphier and said, "Forget Luckman, Pepsodent, Lever Brothers. Make the best deal you can with anyone." Then he turned back to the party.

This London invitation was a high point in Hope's life in comedy, partly because there was still something inside him that was British, but mostly because his ad-libs with the British King made world headlines. Hope's personal staff for the trip included Norman Siegel of Paramount publicity and three of his writers, Larry Klein, Jay Burton, and Fred Williams. To the surprise of many people—including Hope's other writers—Williams was to be one of his all-time favorite gagsters. Williams, an easy and frequent drunk, had been writing on and off for Hope since World War II. When Williams was in the Army, he had told the commanding officer of his remote camp in Texas that he could deliver the Bob Hope show to entertain the soldiers. He had not consulted or informed Hope and when the commanding officer phoned Hope to confirm, Hope had been willing to save Fred's neck.

At the command performance following the royal wedding, Hope charmed the audience, which included, of course, the British monarchs, George and Elizabeth, and their daughter Princess Margaret Rose, as well as Denmark's Queen Ingrid and Romania's King Michael. Princess Elizabeth and her Philip were honeymooning at Romsey in southern England. This evening's gala performance was not in honor of the royal nuptials, but rather was a benefit for the Cinematograph Relief Fund (akin to the Hollywood Motion Picture Relief Fund). Hope had brought with him, as a gift to the newlyweds from Hollywood's film colony, a richly embossed album whose pages contained stamps bearing likenesses of past and present movie stars, and the stars' autographs.

The Associated Press reported that the royal box shook with laughter over Hope's routine about how difficult it was for him to get tickets for the wedding and how far away he had to stand to watch "four white mice pulling a gold-colored snuff box."

All afternoon at rehearsal Hope and Sir Laurence Olivier were joking about their nervousness connected with the protocol required for introductions to the King and Queen.

What Hope did not need was a drunken Fred Williams wandering around backstage and being loud and offensive. Hope had to scold him, "Simmer down, Fred, the King and Queen are out front." Williams was reported to have said, "Who gives a fuck? We broke from the British Empire in 1776 and I'm glad as hell of it."

That night, as the King and Queen and Princess Margaret walked down a double line of stars and were approaching the Hopes, Bob looked impishly across at Olivier and Olivier's eyes darted frantically down toward Hope's crotch. Clearly Olivier was trying to alert Hope that something was amiss below his waist and possibly that Hope's fly was open. Bob, half suspecting a trick but still not entirely certain, broke his formal receiving-line smile and looked down at his fly. At which point Olivier stifled a triumphant smirk.

After the receiving line, Hope was scheduled to present the stamp album to Margaret Rose in behalf of the newlyweds. Jay Burton, carrying the heavy album, handed it to Bob, who opened it for the princess to see. As he was thumbing through the pages, the King looked over Margaret's shoulder and said, "Look at him, he's hurrying to get to his own picture."

"Why not? It's the prettiest," Hope replied.

"Is Bing's autograph there, too?" the King asked.

"Yes," said Hope. "But he doesn't write—he just makes three X's."

"Why three?" the King asked.

"He has a middle name, of course," reminded Hope.

The King laughed and handed the album to the Queen, who said, "Elizabeth would never forgive me if we left this behind."

The following day newspapers in London, New York, and the world over carried front-page items with headlines like KING MAKES 'STRAIGHT MAN' OUT OF BOB HOPE. Even the stern-voiced Edward R. Murrow couldn't resist including the story in his communiqué from London. So many news people wanted to interview Hope that Norman Siegel thought it best to call a news conference at the Dorchester the following afternoon. And during his exchanges with the media, Hope announced to the assembled press corps that he was flying to Germany to entertain American occupation forces.

Dolores was astonished. Laudable as Hope's gesture was, she felt her husband was pushing too hard. How close to actual physical collapse he was cannot now be judged, but those around him saw a man who should have been in bed. However, it seems that earlier that day Hope had met with Secretary of State George Marshall, whose remarks about the "forgotten" occupation forces in Europe affected him.

In spite of his exhaustion, Hope insisted on doing whirlwind shows in Frankfurt and Bremerhaven. He didn't hold back with a voice that was tired and a throat that was irritated and slightly infected. Near the end of the Bremerhaven show his voice literally gave out and he couldn't talk. His audience recognized a much-too-tired trouper who simply could not go on and they stood up and cheered him.

Hope had planned two more shows, at Munich and Garmisch-Partenkirchen, but they were not to be. He flew back to London and got ready for his Tuesday night radio broadcast with the British comedian Sid Fields. The next day Hope decided not to return on the steamship *America* with Dolores, but to fly back to New York that same day for talks with Lever Brothers' Charles Luckman.

The two men met over lunch at the Waldorf-Astoria and temporarily settled the matter. Hope would not leave Lever Brothers, but as to his association with Pepsodent, that was another matter. Hope could travel with his radio show to a few college campuses, balanced with other shows from the El Capitan Theater in Hollywood. And Hope would probably have a new Lever Brothers product to flog in the coming year, and he promised to overhaul the show.

Two days later, Hope surprised Dolores by meeting her ship's early-morning arrival. They stayed in New York long enough to see the highly touted Joe Louis–Joe Walcott prizefight at Madison Square Garden and then returned to the Coast.

Before going to Palm Springs for a rest, Hope went to see his friend and doctor, Tom Hearn, for a full physical examination. Hearn told him it was imperative that he restrict his activity to his radio program.

Paramount publicity told him that there were at least a dozen press interviews on hold pending his return from Europe. He liked the sound of a news conference; and 25 top local and wire-service journalists as well as entertainment columnists showed up at Paramount to hear him answer questions about his recent trip to England and Germany, to hear his opinions about America's posture in a postwar world, and to get a scoop about his next film. His serious tone—on the heels of jokes about King George joining him for the next *Road* picture—surprised almost everyone.

"The most important thing for us in America today is to maintain our friendship with the people of Europe. We have to support the Marshall Plan. This is a wonderful Shangri-la we're living in over here and we should share it with the Europeans before other forces move in and make them our enemies."

"What's next for you, Bob?" asked a reporter from the back row.

"Rest," Hope said.

"What about the benefits you're supposed to do—the scholarship fund for Occidental College, the Shriners' charity show, the boys home in Pomona—Mack was telling us—"

"Well, you know how it is—you can't let the kids down."

"If you're booked through Christmas and touring hospitals in January, when will you rest?"

"I sneak a nap between three and six."

"Weren't we supposed to talk about your next picture?"

"Yeah. It's called *Sorrowful Jones* and it's a remake of *Little Miss Marker* that starred Shirley Temple a few years back. Damon Runyon wrote it and Bob Welch is going to produce it. We've got Lucille Ball and are still looking for a little girl to play Martha Jane."

"We hear you're going serious in this one."

"Who snitched? Mack tell you? Well—why not? It's about time I did something a little different. It's still a comedy but I get to do some straight scenes for a change. Listen—if Dad can do it—"

If any doubt existed about Hope's value as a news source, it was dispelled at that news conference. Journalists covering the Hollywood beat were not used to hearing a comedian deal with issues. It must have been his tone of voice when he recalled his conversation with George Marshall and his own understanding of what needed to be done to bolster the European economy. Those reporters who filed deadline stories after they talked with Hope were more interested in his worldview than his newest movie.

What had led to Bob Hope's becoming an authority on foreign policy? If there was any interest in his opinion of how America was viewed abroad or behaved abroad, it would undoubtedly stem from the media and public awareness that he had entertained strenuously for the military around the world and had come into frequent contact with high-ranking officials. His sponsorship by the USO was also, in effect, a sponsorship by the Department of Defense (traveling as he did in war zones) and also had been given the blessings of the State Department. All in all, Hope was an asset to the U.S. Government with his willingness to entertain whenever they needed him.

So what was happening was not such a sudden phenomenon, but rather a gradual awareness on the part of the media that Hope was becoming a jester in high places. Increasingly he had access to important politicians, businessmen, and the military. And although it cannot be said that in 1948 Hope was in any sense an adviser to such important people, he was often in their company and sometimes was a sounding board for their philosophic views. Furthermore, no one—no newsmaker nor member of the news media—could overlook the power of a topical comedian who reached more than 30 million people every week.

27

Christmas in Berlin

"This certainly has been an unusual experience, flying into Berlin. It's the first time I was ever in a corridor and didn't have to worry about house detectives. . . "

As the forties began to fade, television was like an underworld mobster trying to muscle in on show business. Movie moguls, radio producers, and ad agency executives helplessly watched the little round picture tube gathering strength, not at all certain where it was headed. But radio as the core of family entertainment was beginning to decay. The *New York Times* critic Jack Gould wasn't concerned that television would kill radio; he believed radio would kill itself. On September 19, 1948, he wrote:

> Can it overcome its repetition? Can it meet the incessant cries of its professional critics that it must develop "something new" and "something different" or, like vaudeville, slowly perish from familiarity?
>
> Mr. Hope, this season, has dispensed with the talents of Vera Vague and Jerry Colonna and is trying a less brash and more humble routine. . .

To quicken audience interest, Hope hired Doris Day, whose recordings and Warner Bros. movies had swiftly lifted this former vocalist with the Les Brown band to stardom. Bob had come close to hiring her the year before when he was auditioning bands. His brother Jack had brought him a recording of Les Brown's group playing "Sentimental Journey" with a vocal by Day. He ended up hiring Les but not Doris. As Brown explains it, "It wasn't that he didn't like Doris's singing. It was really a matter of Hope's loyalty to Langford, who had a drinking problem, and Hope, who is one of the truly compassionate people in our business, didn't want to compound Langford's problems by firing her after all they'd been through."

Hope also hired the comedienne Irene Ryan and a fresh young male singer, Billy Farrell. Les, of course, became musical director and Hy Averback was Hope's comedy announcer. There was also a new product, Swan Soap, to push.

What Jack Gould termed Hope's "less brash and more humble routine" was a revamped monologue format billed as "Bob Hope's Swan's Eye View of the News," a sort of comedy Walter Winchell spot. The season premiere show of September 14 went like this:

> HY: Denver, Colorado. . . The Western phase of the election campaigns will begin in Denver next week. President Truman will speak one night and will be followed two nights later by Governor Dewey.
>
> HOPE: Well, the campaign promises to be a hot battle. . . Truman announced he's not going to leave the White House, and Dewey says he's moving in. . . I can just see the towels in the White House bathroom. . . marked "His" and "His". . .
>
> HY: Berlin, Germany. . . Big four talks over removal of Soviet fuel and food blockade were on the verge of collapse as President Truman announced today that the American Airlift will continue to bring supplies into Berlin at all costs. . .
>
> HOPE: From what I hear, everybody over there blames the situation on the way the Russians have policed the city. . . You see, Berlin is divided into three zones, British, American, and "Wait until it gets dark, Fritz, and we'll make a dash for it.". . . And when the Americans do something they do it thoroughly. . . Yesterday a B–39 flew in a hundred tons of chewing gum. . . and right behind it was a plane with a load of theater seats to stick it under. . .

This new format traded more heavily on Hope's increasing dependence on political humor, but by no means did politics dominate his monologues or sketches. An analysis of his radio monologues of this particular period reveals that most strongly represented among his gags was the self-deflating joke, pulling the rug out from under himself, just as most other comics of the day were doing—Jack Benny, Ed Wynn, Eddie Cantor, Fibber McGee, all the way down the line. Running second was the joke centered on the entertainment world—his rivalry with Crosby, or his current film's leading lady such as Dorothy Lamour or Jane Russell, more often than not tinged with sex. Politics ran third.

But that was an all-important third in the fall if 1948. When Truman defeated the Republican candidate, Thomas E. Dewey, to widespread amazement (every major newspaper and pollster in the nation had predicted a Republican landslide), Hope sent a one-word telegram to the White House that said "UNPACK." White House publicists and press corps alike seized on this one-word take on a surprising turn of events, and the joke blanketed the nation's newsprint. Hope was highly flattered when he heard that Harry placed the telegram under the glass top of his Oval Office desk, where it was very visible.

Truman continued to be ideal humor material for Hope. In contrast to the patrician Roosevelt, Harry's "hellcat" image made him human and somewhat unpredictable. Hope's capital cronies informed him that Harry chuckled over the comedian's mild attacks on Truman's fights with his Republican Congress, or his White House piano playing, or his squabbles with Washington media over daughter Margaret's unfulfilled musical aspirations.

All these political gags pleased the radio critics, who liked the new "feel" of Hope's radio show. Hope's rating was a respectable 23.3, a notch or two behind Jack Benny and *Fibber McGee.*

Interestingly enough, on the night of Hope's seasonal premiere, Tuesday, September 14, Milton Berle sashayed out to center stage of a New York television studio as master of ceremonies of the first *Texaco Star Theater.* And although there were only 47 television stations in the nation, and scarcely one million sets in use, mostly in the East, "Uncle Miltie," as he characterized himself, captured considerable media attention.

The fact that Berle chose Tuesday night, which to years of radio listeners was "comedy night" and to many of these listeners was "Hope night," to lead off the program with a bullet-like monologue with one-line topical gags so close to the Hope style fascinated many observers. One of those curious observers was the Associated Press reporter Bob Thomas, who visited Hope at Toluca Lake. "What about television, Bob?" he asked.

"As a matter of fact," Hope said almost confidentially, "Hope Enterprises is already working on some video ideas, along novelty lines, including a show for me."

"A weekly show?"

"Nah, that's too much. People could get tired of you that often. I'd like to do occasional shows, full-hour shows. Imagine—imagine what you can do on television!

"Radio—people complain if you try to milk an audience with sight stuff. But with video everything is sight. You know how I sometimes throw the script during my radio show? Well, I could throw it at the audience and they could throw it right back."

"You seem to be cagey about television, Bob," Thomas said smiling.

"I guess I'm still waiting to see how it goes."

"How about Berle?"

"I think my material sounded pretty good in video," Hope cracked. "Seriously, I don't think I would work that hard. He's doing both his radio show and this Tuesday night television show for Texaco. And I understand he took a sizable cut in pay to do television. He must be nuts. If we could do a radio and television version of our show at the same time—maybe, what do you think? They tell me Berle's entire budget for the Texaco show is $15,000. Is he working free?"

"I hear General Motors wants to get you into television." Thomas probed.

Hope looked steadily and seriously at Thomas and did not answer. Finally he said, "That's right."

"So—?"

"I don't have any time," Hope said hurriedly.

"Are you being hassled by Paramount, or NBC, or Lever Brothers?"

"Uhhhh—" said Hope, "not at all. I'm free to do anything I want. Listen, when they can pay me. . . "

A few weeks later, Hope decided to take Dolores and the kids to Lake Tahoe for Christmas. But a call from Washington changed all that. Stuart Symington, secretary of the Air Force and one of Hope's golfing partners at Burning Tree, suggested strongly that President Truman would be grateful if Bob would headline a troupe of entertainers who would give up their holidays at home to go over to Germany and cheer up the GIs involved in Operation Vittles, as the Berlin Airlift was called. Symington graphically described the cadre of Air Force pilots who were flying these mercy missions. Literally without sleep, they would fly back and forth every few minutes between Wiesbaden and Berlin's Tempelhof Airport, ferrying bags of coal, sacks of flour, and cans of food through a narrow, perilous air corridor.

"We'll do it, Stu. Dolores wants to come, too. But I'd like to do my radio show from Berlin. What do you think?"

The next day doors began to open. Both NBC and Lever Brothers blessed the venture. The White House gave Hope a starter set for the guest star line-up: Vice President Alben Barkley and the Air Force hero General Jimmy Doolittle. On his own, Hope enlisted Irving Berlin, newsman Elmer Davis, the beautiful Jinx Falkenburg with her husband, Tex McCrary, a dozen of the Radio City Music Hall Rockettes, and, of course, his own Swan Soap radio gang, minus Doris Day, who had a film commitment. In her place Hope invited the popular radio singer Jane Harvey and took Tony Romano to play intimate guitar accompaniments for her and for Dolores to sing "Silent Night." The Hopes' children, heartbroken about their lost holiday, had to stay in North Hollywood.

They traveled in Symington's Constellation and the spirit generated among the troupe en route to Berlin was extraordinary. Symington had not only given Hope much logistical support, but was along on the trip himself, as were Hope's omnipresent confidant Charlie Cooley, his agent, Jimmy Saphier, the radio producer Al Capstaff, and three writers, Mort Lachman, Si Rose, and a newcomer, Larry Gelbart.

Gelbart (of *M*A*S*H* fame) later talked about how he felt in his new job: "With Hope you literally didn't know from one day to the next which corner of the planet you were going to be hurled to. Telephoning you at home, at almost any hour of the day or night, was a favorite pastime of his. Conducting what seemed like a routine conversation, Hope would suddenly inform you that you were about to join him on a month-long tour across the country or that you'd better check to see if your passport was valid because he was expecting you to accompany him on a trip to entertain the military personnel on duty with the Berlin airlift."

Their first stop, for refueling only, was Burtonwood, a British air base where the airlift shuttle planes and crews returned for rehabilitation, repair, and rest after their schedule of nonstop runs over West Germany and on into Berlin. It didn't take Hope more than a few minutes to discover how serious the morale problem was here. These GIs were the heroes behind the scenes of these internationally applauded and publicized humanitarian flights. But they were bearing the brunt of intense resentment from Britons living in local towns and villages who were suffering the roar of so many loud-motored freight planes.

Several officers asked Hope to do an impromptu show. Hope couldn't refuse them and, besides, the rehearsal time was useful.

At Wiesbaden the GIs had been waiting in a big drafty hall for several hours, and let out an ear-splitting war hoop when the Rockettes tap-tapped out onto the stage in their abbreviated tights.

After shows at Nuremberg and Frankfurt, there was a Christmas Eve party hosted by General Lucius Clay, who during the festivities informed Hope, sadly, that decreasing visibility and heavy snows might prevent the entire troupe from reaching Berlin in time for the radio show the next day if they waited any longer. So Bob hugged Dolores good-bye and got into an airlift plane with Al Capstaff, Hy Averback, and Larry Gelbart, who was banging out monologue material amid the crates of canned milk and corn, as they flew the two-hour ground-hugging, wing-scraping corridor route to Tempelhof in the heart of West Berlin.

Early Christmas morning, Dolores and the rest of the cast managed to hitch-hike their way into Berlin on a series of freight planes, and that afternoon, on one of the cruelest days of that winter, they entertained at the Tatania Palast Theater, an old music hall, in close to freezing temperatures with only their own and the GIs' body heat for warmth. Hope opened with a gag that referred to the local black market and it produced an almost deafening roar:

How do you do everybody. This is Bob (here in Berlin to entertain the men in the airlift) Hope saying I'm here with Swan in lots. . . Meet me tonight in Potsdamer Platz. . .

As we arrived over Berlin several Soviet planes started to buzz us, but the first Russian pilot took one look at me and said, "They're okay—look at the hammer head and sickle". . .

And the people here really seem to know me. Whenever I walk down the streets of Berlin, everybody follows me yelling and cheering. Any of you fellas know what *Schweinehund* means? . . .

Before the show ended, Staff Sergeant Robert Kelso of Armed Forces Radio came up to Hope as he stood in the wings and begged him to come to his radio station after the show to talk to all the GIs who couldn't see him in person. Hope, preoccupied, brushed Kelso aside with "Yeah, yeah, sure—I'll try to do that."

There was an after-show party given by the Clays in their West Berlin quarters for the Hopes, the Irving Berlins, Symington, Secretary of War Kenneth Royall, and U.S. Ambassador to the Soviet Union Walter Bedell Smith and his wife. That party broke up after midnight, and heading back to their hotel in an assigned vehicle, Bob reached into his pocket and produced the business card that Sergeant Kelso had thrust at him earlier in the wings of the Tatania Palast. "Where is this?" Hope asked their GI driver.

"Not too far, sir."

"Wanna try it?"

"At *this* hour, Bob?" asked Dolores.

"Go," he said, and they drove off. Twenty minutes later, on an unlighted street, the staff car chugged to a stop, out of fuel. They trudged the last few blocks on foot, through snow-covered passageways, some still littered with rubble, helped along by the driver's flashlight. Finally they arrived at the address. Inside Kelso sat hunched over a control panel and turntable playing records and talking. He turned around and nearly fell out of his chair. "Oh, no—nooooo . . ." he said. He turned back to the mike and faded out the recording he was talking over as he said, "You're not going to believe this one." Still talking, he slipped out of his chair and said, "Hey guys, have I got news for you. Here's Bob Hope. I'm turning the mike over to him."

Hope started talking. Kelso poured Dolores some coffee and slipped away. The driver slipped away, also, to find some fuel, or another vehicle. The Hopes were absolutely alone. Bob kept his monologue going, all the while gesturing to Dolores to find out what was happening, but she couldn't find anyone anywhere. In relating this later Hope said that at least 20 minutes went by before Kelso returned. "Nice of you to come back," cracked Hope. Kelso had run off to wake up the other disc jockeys at Armed Forces Radio because "Who would have believed me when I told them that Bob Hope dropped in on me at two-thirty in the morning the day after Christmas?"

28

The Funniest Laughmaker

"I used to call [Doris Day] 'Jut-Butt.' I'd say, 'You know, J.B., we could play a nice game of bridge on your ass.' A truly great body and she was wonderful about taking my kidding."

Four thousand miles west of Berlin, people were standing in triple lines, stretching way back from the marquee of the Paramount Theater in New York's Times

Square, waiting in the damp cold air, anxious to get inside to see Bob Hope's latest movie, *The Paleface.*

It had opened a few days before Christmas, and Howard Barnes in the *Herald Tribune* had written: "Rarely has he been so funny." Bosley Crowther, writing in *The New York Times,* was less enchanted, calling the picture "just another amusing run through of well-worn slapstick routines by a boy who has bunions on his bunions from the number of times he's run the course."

The film, however, would become Hope's biggest moneymaker, grossing about $7 million and entrenching his popularity as one of the nation's most watched and listened-to entertainers.

In addition to its hit parade ballad, "Buttons and Bows," this Technicolor film also offered Hope at the peak of his form as a visual comic. It was probably Hope's most accomplished "reluctant hero" characterization. As a traveling salesman caught up in classic Western gunfights, with screaming Indians, hair-raising chases, and tough-talking outlaws—and with Jane Russell, one of America's sexiest women, as his love interest—his prissy braggadocio was exactly right for the public at this time. Lucky for Hope, too, because what he was currently giving his radio audience was becoming less and less appealing and they were becoming less and less loyal. His Hooper and Crossley ratings at midseason showed he was trailing *Fibber McGee,* Bergen, Benny, and Allen.

That rating gap was one reason Bob was anxious to take his radio cast out to the American people in yet another whirlwind cross-country tour. Hardly taking time to catch his breath from the Berlin Airlift junket, he started out again.

He nearly lost the tour's important "added attraction," Doris Day, whose movies were making her a hot property. She didn't like the money she was offered, not to mention some phobias she had developed as a live performer. Only when Hope agreed to pay her $2,500 above her regular radio salary did she agree to join Irene Ryan, Bill Farrell, Hy Averback, and Les Brown for the tour.

The 36-city marathon began in Texas, made a big southern-city sweep, traveled as far north as Boston, then turned back across the country, to end in Oakland, California. True, Hope wanted to get closer to the people, but he also needed cash. He had to cover his taxes and to put up his share of the next movie project, *Where Men Are Men* (the fourth remake of Harry Leon Wilson's novel, *Ruggles of Red Gap*).

Surprising no one, the tour was an enormous success. In terms of revenue, it netted Hope $700,000 (top money for a live show tour in 1949), which meant that his personal daily share was about $11,000. He was enjoying himself immensely. His deeply ingrained vaudeville gypsy persona was in full swing. His appreciation of Doris was growing steadily, but as he later confided, he was not able to talk her into his bed. Though he did admit, "I used to call her 'Jut-Butt.' I'd say, 'You know, J.B., we could play a nice game of bridge on your ass.' A truly great body and she was wonderful about taking my kidding. I always called her 'J.B.' on the radio show, but only the band knew what those initials stood for."

Hope said that Doris, like Judy Garland, had "natural talent." He lauded her comedy timing, the way she handled a ballad, and especially her smile. "She has that rare quality of making people feel good by just walking on—whatever she radiates lifts them." Hope was shocked when Les Brown's musicians told him Doris was a nervous wreck most of the time. Stumpy Brown said he had noticed problems when she traveled with them as their band vocalist but now the weekly broadcasts from the El Capitan Theater were causing Doris serious stage fright.

She herself would say, "My overriding memory of these shows was how much time I spent in the toilet. I had by then developed a real aversion to live radio, and before every performance one end of me or the other would erupt. Bob would be out front warming up the audience and I would be flat out in my dressing room moaning to either my agent or the producer that I simply couldn't go on, that I had to be taken off the show—that I just couldn't do it—I couldn't go out there and face all those people—and sing!"

Doris had plenty of adjectives for the Hope whistle-stop shows as well, calling them "frightening, educational, exhausting, enjoyable, depressing" experiences. During that six-week swing, they hit a different city every day and on some days, when a matinée was included, they might manage two cities. It was winter and as Doris later wrote in her autobiography, "We often flew through storms and turbulence that had me praying more than once. I developed a chronic fear of flying that haunts me to this day."

However, she confesses having learned a great deal from Hope about timing and delivery. Hope was, to her, "a joyous man to be with. There's something quite pixie about him, his mischievous face, the way his teeth take over his face when he smiles. And the way he swaggers across the stage, kind of sideways, beaming at the audience."

Doris found him naturally funny, "in fact, funnier than when he's restricted to his writers' material."

When that tour ended in early February, the script for *Where Men Are Men*, now retitled *Fancy Pants*, was still not ready. Hope played a lot of golf (naturally), did some radio guest appearances, and made an important decision about his career. Saphier reported to Bob that CBS wanted him to quit his 10-year association with NBC and join a few other defectors to CBS—Benny, *Amos and Andy*, Bergen, even Crosby. CBS was expanding, offering better money deals, long-term contracts, better time slots, and promises of television shows. But Hope, though concerned about his lag in the ratings and certainly interested in more money, decided not to budge. What neither he nor NBC announced publicly was that in his new exclusive contract NBC would be bankrolling some future projects of Hope Enterprises, and they had contractually agreed to promote all of his efforts for the network more intensely. And, lest anyone think he was not worth more money, NBC was talking seven figures in their plan to retain his services for television.

Time and *Newsweek* had both recently labeled Hope a newly arrived millionaire on the basis of his income from radio and movies alone. Actually his investment portfolio included some bonds and stocks, but mostly he had acquired real estate and its value was steadily increasing, yet he was cash-poor. When he learned *Fancy Pants* cameras wouldn't roll until late spring, Hope told Louis Shurr to book him another series of one-nighters with Doris, Les, and the rest of his radio cast. For 16 grueling days in April, they did a lightning tour of 21 cities in 15 states, doing straight personal appearance shows, several benefits, a couple of golf exhibitions, and two Swan radio broadcasts. All because Uncle Sam had to have his money on April 15.

Fancy Pants finally came before the cameras in June, directed by the inventive George Marshall. Bob and his costar, the multitalented and convivial Lucille Ball, were the toast of Paramount in those days because *Sorrowful Jones* was garnering better-than-average critical notices nationwide for both stars. Unexpectedly, there was critical praise for Hope's sentimental scenes with little Mary Jane Saunders, the appealing moppet in the film. Paramount publicists were voicing the possibility of an Oscar for Hope.

Paramount front-office boys approached Hope with the idea that he should recite the Gettysburg Address in *Fancy Pants* just the way Charles Laughton had delivered the speech in his version of *Ruggles of Red Gap*. Hope said to Hedda Hopper, "When I suggested that same idea a few months ago they laughed at me. You know what changed their minds? They've been reading the *Sorrowful Jones* reviews that say Hope can really act. Do you know how tough it is for me to try being serious? People look at me and they automatically start to laugh. Working with that kid gave me a chance to do something serious without being too obvious."

During this time, Bob and Bing got involved in an oil venture. At a Fort Worth benefit, Hope had met an oilman, Will Moncrief, who invited him to put up $50,000 to tie up a few thousand acres of oil-speculation property near North Snyder in Scurry County, West Texas. Hope asked Bing to go along. Their first drop ended in failure; the drilling brought up salty water. Hope wanted out, but Bing said he would sink another $50,000 if Hope would. On August 9, it became for both of them "the road to oil." Six miles northeast of their first site, at Huckabee, they hit a gusher capable of producing 100 barrels an hour that in the months ahead paid the two partners close to $3.5 million apiece.

Hope's oil euphoria lasted a few days, until he took a fall. The *Fancy Pants* script called for his character, Humphrey, an English actor-turned-butler in the Old West, to ride a horse. Lucille Ball offered to teach Bob how to ride, not on a real horse, but on a wooden barrel contraption rigged to buck and roll. Hope nervously agreed when he watched a stunt extra test it. He was helped up onto the wooden horse, but when it began to buck, he was not fully prepared, slipped, pitched sideward, and fell. He lay on his back with his eyes closed, unable to move.

He was carefully raised on a stretcher and rushed to nearby Presbyterian Hospital, where the emergency-room doctors at first believed he might be paralyzed. By the time Tom Hearn arrived, the shock and spasm had lessened. There were no broken bones, just badly bruised muscles. And headlines!

And what headlines they were. A steady procession of publicists, agents, writers, more publicists, celebrities (a record number and all being photographed and interviewed, much to the consternation of an overworked hospital public relations office), and lawyers, all trouping to Hope's bedside during his week-long stay. The most persistent gossip column rumors were that the comedian would sue Paramount for some astronomical amount. Wrong. Hope was too shrewd a businessman for that, but also too shrewd a publicist to resist teasing studio boss Henry Ginsberg in a way that brought Hope, the studio, and *Fancy Pants* untold thousands of dollars in free media attention. All the entertainment trade papers and five major dailies plus suburban papers printed Hope's open letter to Ginsberg, which said in part:

> If your economy-minded production heads had used a real horse instead of putting me over a broken-down barrel I would not have landed on my back on stage 17 with an injury which you will see from the bill, was not cheap. . .
>
> When I woke up in the hospital, four nurses were standing over me, a doctor was feeling my pulse, and another doctor was on the phone checking with the Bank of America to see how much we could go for. . .
>
> X-rays and more X-rays. . . It seems they couldn't find much wrong with me. . . I could see I had *them* over a barrel at this point—if the word is not too sensitive for you—and with one longing look at my gall-bladder, they let me go home.
>
> The remainder of the bill will be self-explanatory, although I imagine the occupational therapy—$1,400—may be a little out of line. You see, Henry, the occupation I picked was horse playing and we both know it's not a poor man's pastime. Please understand this puts me in deep debt to you, almost as deep as you are to the doctors.
>
> Yours in our great work
> Bob Hope

There was little doubt around Paramount that Hope was a master of the media event and there was less doubt that this accident would boost the box-office for *Fancy Pants*.

Hope opened his 1949–50 radio season on September 21 (his twelfth year on the air for Lever Brothers and also his last for that company) in El Segundo, California. His monologue for this suburban audience addressed the subject of America's fastest growing preoccupation:

But I'm glad to be back on radio. It seems to have so much more to offer than television. . . things like money. . . but I like television. . . I have one of those sets with a screen so small you have to sit right up next to it. Last night during dinner Hopalong Cassidy lasso'd three of my boiled potatoes. . . and all during dinner I had to keep Milton Berle's hand out of my soup. . .

More and more Americans were hoisting TV antennae up onto their rooftops, or crowding around store windows on Saturday nights to laugh at Sid Caesar and Imogene Coca in Admiral's *Broadway Revue.* This was a smart mixture of sophisticated and slapstick comedy mounted with taste and elegance and for the first time Hope believed this medium might prove to be his "room," too.

He was sufficiently interested to tell Saphier to reopen discussions with General Motors. His timing, as usual, was impeccable. Dr. George Gallup, the highly respected head of Princeton University's American Institute of Public Opinion, had just released results of a poll taken to find out who and what made the American people laugh. Three thousand personal interviews were conducted with a cross-section of men and women over 21; rich, poor, young, and old were asked this question: "Of all the comedians you have heard or seen perform on the stage, on the radio or television, or in the movies—which one do you think is the funniest?" The following story was printed coast to coast:

Princeton, N.J., Sept. 18—All America loves a laugh, and almost every American has his or her own idea as to who is the funniest laughmaker ever in the business.

But the reigning comedian, in the public's mind, is Bob Hope. He outdistances his closest rivals in the American Institute of Public Opinion's first "comedy star derby"—with stage, screen, radio or television stars all included—by a commanding ratio of almost 2¹/₂ to 1. Next come Milton Berle, Jack Benny, Red Skelton, and Fibber McGee and Molly—all close on the heels of each other.

Milton Berle's sudden rise in popularity was continuing into his second season on the air, for which the critics had dubbed him "Mr. Television." Add to this Hope's less-than-commanding supremacy in those parts of the nation where television viewing was densest—the Northeast and Middle Atlantic states—and the message was becoming clearer and clearer to him about the power of the video image.

Hope could not help be impressed with the dramatic leap in the number of TV stations—127—now beaming signals, or the fact that now there were network TV shows beaming coast to coast.

Saphier told him that the latest Commerce Department figures showed over 2 million sets in use.

But Hope felt he had reason to worry about his movie career. It was clear to him and to motion picture executives throughout the industry that some movie houses—in spite of having tried double- and even triple-bill offerings, Screeno (bingo on the big screen), dinnerware and silverware giveaways—would be going dark. The television, like radio when it came along, was novel. It was a new family activity and it was cheaper than movies and other box-office entertainment.

It was clear that studio feature-film schedules could change, that the big investments would be for epics and super-ballyhooed spectaculars with special effects in an effort to draw people away from the tube. Hope feared that his December release, *The Great Lover*, a nice little comedy with a beautiful newcomer, Rhonda Fleming, might suffer from this spreading apathy.

His fears subsided when *Motion Picture Daily* announced he was reigning king of the box office. He needed the assurance of being the number one guy in pictures, and even enjoyed the wild audience whoop when he and Dolores stepped out of their limousine in front of Hollywood's Pantages Theater on December 20, the night of the premiere of *Twelve O'Clock High*.

Hope generally avoided premieres. He told Louis Shurr one time, "For all the fuss and trouble involved, there wasn't much of a publicity payoff." But this night was special. It was the dramatization of Brigadier General Frank Armstrong's real-life efforts to shape heroes out of the airmen in his 8th Air Force Wing during World War II in England. Hope had become an Armstrong fan when they met in England in 1943 and knew he would be at the premiere along with General Curtis LeMay and Hope's pal Stuart Symington, who was accompanying Armstrong to Alaska for a Christmas visit.

At the post-premiere supper party at Romanoff's, Hope sat next to Armstrong. Armstrong was talking about his Alaskan Command when he said impulsively, "Bob, why don't you fly up there with me tomorrow and say Merry Christmas to the boys?"

"Not this year, Frank. I left my kids last year for the airlift and I can't do it again."

The next day Symington telephoned Hope. "Stu, my man," said Hope, "I thought you'd be on your way up north by now."

"I had some last-minute things here in Los Angeles." There was a pause. "Bob, how about saying yes to that invitation from Frank."

"I don't want to leave the kids. You grabbed me last year, remember?"

"Why not take the kids?"

From a distant part of the house, Hope could hear a voice screaming, "Yes, Daddy, yes!" and he knew Linda had been listening in on the line again.

He yelled, "Dolores!" and she suddenly appeared in the doorway of his room with both Linda and Tony jumping up and down. "Tell him it'll be thrilling," she said.

Hope told Symington he would bring Linda and Tony but that the two toddlers, Nora and Kelly, were not ready for that yet. Symington then slyly told Hope that Armstrong had not left for Alaska either and was prepared to fly them in his own B–17. A few moments later Armstrong himself called and said, "I'll meet you at four o'clock at the Hughes Aircraft runway."

It was then noon and Hope realized he had no more than three hours to put together an entertainment unit. Cowboy singer Jimmy Wakely agreed to go. So did Patty Thomas and Les Brown's piano player, Geoff Clarkson (who lived nearby in Toluca Lake and always seemed to have his bag packed). Bob asked Dolores if she would sing for her trip. She said yes, but what would she wear?

Next, he called his senior writer for his radio show, Norman Sullivan, and said, "Norm, you're going to have to put next Tuesday's show together without me. I'm going to Alaska."

There was a pause, and then Sullivan said, "Very well, we'll move your pin on the map."

Hope roared and said, "I'll call you tonight from somewhere for some deep-freeze jokes."

At three-fifteen Hope was packed and standing in the downstairs entryway waiting for Dolores. Linda and Tony were in the car. Mildred MacArthur had come by to help get everyone organized and packed.

"Dolores!" Bob yelled, "we're leaving!"

Mildred came to the top of the curving stairway and looked helpless. Bob knew from that look that Dolores was not nearly ready.

"Dolores! Get down here—now! There's a B–17 parked on a runway about an hour from here in holiday traffic—waiting for us and we're going to be on it. I mean right now."

Mildred MacArthur said that in all the years she had known the Hopes, Bob was never angrier or more resolute than he was at that moment. He would have left without her. As he headed for the driver's seat, Dolores dashed out, threw her bags onto the laps of her children in the back seat, and jumped in the front, and the car sped away.

Armstrong's B–17 dropped the Hopes off in Seattle, Bob called his writers, and Symington's Constellation picked them up early the next morning for the trip to Anchorage. It was 20 degrees below zero and they had to make an instrument landing in dense fog. After their planeside welcome the Hope children were whisked off to the Armstrongs', and the entertainers went to the base hospital for their first show. All in all, they did 12 shows in three days and had to eat five or six Christmas dinners.

Hope never failed to convulse his appreciative audience of "crease-faced, red-eyed, purple-nosed" GIs when he grabbed the mike and jutted out his chin to say, "Be happy, you guys, be proud, brace up—you know who you are, don't you? God's Frozen People!"

At one of the last stops, Eilson Air Base, the little troupe sat down for their third Christmas turkey dinner of the day when Bob noticed quite a few uniformed men standing against the mess-hall walls staring at them.

"What's with these guys?" Hope asked an officer. "Don't they get to eat?"

"They've already eaten, Bob. The men up here drew lots to get into the recreation hall to see your show and these guys lost—so they get to see you eat."

"Hell, that's no good," Hope said. "Have you got a good electrician on the base?" When the electrician arrived, Hope showed him how to rig up the phone to the public address system. In a short time he was doing a monologue.

Between that impromptu show and their final appearance for the Navy on Kodiak Island, Hope developed a bad cold and lost his voice. Even with a whisper mike he could hardly be heard. That night, when he climbed aboard the Symington plane to go home, he said to the steward, "Just find me some soup and some sleeping pills."

29

TV—That Dreadful Thing

"I want to thank the thousands who wrote letters about the first show. . . Also the three who mailed them. . . No. . . I did get about five thousand letters. . . The FBI is going over them now. . . "

The second half of the twentieth century was barely three days old when subfreezing temperatures gripped Southern California. Some cultists said it was the wrath of God.

A highly respected scientist was interviewed about the possibility of a new ice age. Hope felt like he was still in Alaska, and was trying desperately to shake the cold he had caught there. So, after meeting with his writers to set material for his Tuesday show, he headed for Palm Springs to recuperate in the sun and play a little golf. He was confident that in 72 hours he would be at the top of his form, but perhaps even more important, in shape for the Crosby Pebble Beach tournament the following week.

But it wasn't any warmer in the desert. In fact, fruit growers were smudging their groves day and night hoping to salvage something of their crops.

Elsewhere in the nation, and in the world, places that were usually freezing at this time were even icier, but for a different reason. A cold fear was spreading across Western Europe and indeed around the globe because of a confirmed report that the Soviets had tested a second A-bomb in Siberia.

On a more personal front, Lever Brothers was starting to act cool—let's call it cold—toward Hope and his show, partly because of his recent plunge in the ratings to a dismal 13.9, which was half of what the Benny show was getting. More distressing, *Fibber McGee* (who followed Hope on Tuesdays) had a higher rating.

Also, Lever Brothers was openly rankled and fussing over Hope's originations from colleges and military bases that they felt were unnecessary and for them too costly.

Saphier had seen the end coming for some time and had already begun casting his net for new sponsors. But to him a more pressing matter was television. So while Hope was ridding his body of a cold, touching up his swing in the backyard, and cursing the chilly rain that kept him off the golf course, Saphier called to say he was bringing a mutual friend, Hugh Davis, down to the Springs for a talk.

Davis, executive VP of the advertising firm Foote, Cone & Belding in Chicago, brought a fresh offer from the Frigidaire Division of General Motors. When Davis thought Hope was in a mellow mood he said, "What about television, Bob?"

"Naw, I don't think so," answered Bob. "I'm busy enough. Besides I don't know much about that medium."

"What would it take to change your mind?"

"You can't pay me enough."

"What do you want?"

"Fifty thousand," Hope said coolly, knowing the figure was beyond any being contemplated, let alone paid to any performer in TV. Davis brought his hands together in a praying position, smiled at both of them and said, "Ball's in my court."

The next day the perennial "bad boy" of the Hope gag writers, Fred Williams, came from L.A. to do some script rewrites with Bob, and made it a foursome for a round of golf before it rained. After Saphier and Davis left, Bob and Fred worked on dialogue for the retakes of *Fancy Pants*—they would have worked later but Hope made the mistake of suggesting "a little drink." Fred managed to drain the bottle. At about eight-fifteen, Hope decided the best way to handle a drunken Williams was to get him back to Los Angeles. They got into the Cadillac with Hope at the wheel humming "Buttons and Bows."

At Beaumont, Hope turned onto Highway 60 toward Riverside and as usual pushed the gas pedal to the floor. The big car raced ahead at 75 miles an hour, all alone on an asphalt pavement slick from rain, and greasy in patches where growers were smudging the orange trees.

Hope is hazy about whether or not he jerked the wheel, but the car swerved suddenly, slid sideways, hit a ditch, and rolled over like a stunt car before slamming into a tree. Both doors opened on impact and the men were hurled out in opposite directions into ankle-deep mud. "I remember seeing little sparks," Hope said later. "I remember how my neck jerked and how I thought, 'This is it. I'm going to die.' I remember everything that happened until I got hit on the head and blanked out."

Fred never lost consciousness; he sobered up fast. He felt a sharp pain in his left leg but realized he had to get Bob and put distance between them and the Cadillac in case it caught fire or blew up. As he limped toward Bob he could see that the comedian, now somewhat conscious, was trying to stand up—so he headed for the road and flagged down an approaching car.

Tires screeched and the car stopped. At the wheel, Sam Crother murmured, "Holy shit!" when he sighted the muddied Williams, and almost laughed when he saw the equally muddy Bob Hope testing to see if his arms were still able to swing a golf club.

Crother drove them to Riverside Community Hospital. Fred's injury was only a bad bruise and he stood ghoulishly over Hope while he was being examined.

When the doctor came back with the developed X-rays, he said, "You're a lucky man. By rights you should be dead. Anyway you have a fractured clavicle and you won't be playing golf for a while."

A *Riverside Press and Enterprise* reporter stuck his head around the corner. "It really *is* you. What happened?"

Hope described the accident, concluding with, "It's all right though. The thing I hate is that I'll have to miss the Crosby. That's what I went down to the Springs for," he said wistfully. "I went to practice up on my golf. I was just in my prime, too."

The accident altered more than Hope's golf plans. Since he would have to be in a cast for several weeks and strapped up for a month after that, he could not make a movie.

But he could stand on a stage and tell jokes. He asked Shurr to book him on an eastern cities public appearance tour with his radio gang, and Lever Brothers reluctantly went along with it, vowing that this was the last time they would pick up such a tab.

A few days after the accident, Hope got a call from Hugh Davis in Chicago. "Would you consider doing one television show for forty thousand?" asked Davis.

"For myself?" Hope queried.

"Yes."

"You mean they'll supply the guest stars and the rest of the production?"

"Yes."

"You're on. I'll have Jimmy call you right back." Saphier worked out a package deal of four additional shows for a total of $150,000. Frigidaire had an existing agreement with CBS, which could have been a problem because of Hope's long-standing network affiliation, but that got smoothed out and Hope's TV debut was set for an NBC broadcast on Easter Sunday.

Meanwhile, sandwiched in between his usual heavy personal-appearances schedule and his regular radio show schedule came an extraordinary—some skeptics termed it risky—return to vaudeville. He signed a contract for $50,000 a week to appear at the Paramount Theater on New York's busy Times Square as the stage attraction with an Alan Ladd film called *Captain China*. Worried about the nosedive movies were taking, Hope was determined this engagement would not be ordinary. To help ensure this, he hired Jane Russell and the Les Brown band.

And to superhype the event, Hope summoned the full phalanx of press agents and publicity support. He customarily relied on publicity people the same way he did on gag writers, hiring as many as he needed for the job, and he knew them by their strengths. Some comedy writers excelled at one-liners and monologue material, others wrote clever sketches; some wrote smart subtle gags, others were better at pie-in-the-face stuff.

It was the same with publicists. Mack Millar was the mainstay, a crusty, unrelenting old-time press agent who knew how to deal with the green-eyeshade editors in the Hearst city rooms. He blustered his way from coast to coast, extracting pro-Hope stories and items from reporters who respected him because he always could deliver his client and because he knew the territory. Then there was Frank Liberman, a former Warner Bros. staffer, who though young, was experienced, intelligent, tasteful, witty, and discreet. His specialties were working with the wire services and entertainment trade papers and the tricky job of planting hot exclusive items and whispering juicy secrets to be used by gossip queens Hedda Hopper, Louella Parsons, and a string of others around the nation. Both Rufus Blair and Norm Siegel of Paramount's publicity office were superb writers, and Hope trusted NBC's highly regarded publicity chief, Syd Eiges, to cover him with his top writers and photographers. Then, too, Hope retained special people all over the country, such as Arnold Van Leer in Boston or Bob Bixler in Dallas, who might be asked to saturate any or all of New England or Texas for a day, a week, or a month.

But Hope himself was the master publicist. He never refused a request for an interview, developed phone friendships with reporters and columnists nationwide, and had almost daily contact with people like *Variety*'s Army Archerd and the *Chicago Sun*'s Irv Kupcinet, and it paid off.

En route to New York, Hope sidetracked to do two things in Washington, D.C. One was to drop by the office of his pal Stuart Symington, who thanked him officially for his Berlin Airlift and Alaskan entertaining by giving him the Air Force's highest civilian commendation.

The second was to emcee and perform at his favorite capital dinner, the annual White House Correspondents' Association banquet for toasting and roasting the President. That performance of Hope's got better-than-average press coverage partly because of what he said to and about Truman. Of a chief executive who once was a haberdasher he joked, "He can shake your hand and measure you for a suit at the same time. . . Never trust a politician who knows how to measure your inseam,. . . " and Harry joined in the loud laughter. Hope had an opportunity to get something else off his chest. One of the guests at the banquet was Charles Luckman, whose sudden demise as chief executive of Lever Brothers had caused some speculation in high business places. Hope had felt that Luckman displayed disloyalty (the one quality Hope feared and loathed the most in people around him) for backing away from his radio show after Hope had placed big bucks in that company's pockets for years. Hope rarely let personal animosity get into his comedy, but this time he grinned and cracked to the black-tie audience, "I hear Lever Brothers are behind a Broadway show called *Where's Charley?*" Luckman didn't laugh. After dinner, Hope told those around him, "I was only kidding." But he wasn't.

In New York, Paramount's theater manager, Bob Weitman, told Hope that business in Times Square was rotten, so Bob shouldn't think any less of himself for not being able to pack the cavernous Paramount Theater as he had so many times before. This was a gauntlet dropped at the comedian's feet. He *had* to show Lever Brothers, Paramount, NBC—and General Motors—that he was still the undisputed "star of stars."

What no one could understand was why Bob Hope would be willing to subject himself to six 45-minute shows a day for two weeks. One person who sought the answer was Otis Guernsey, Jr., the *New York Herald Tribune* critic. When Guernsey was escorted backstage at four-thirty the first day, Hope had already done three shows. He was sprawled on a cot in his dressing room "like a king at a levee, in the attitude of self-satisfied exhaustion." George Raft, a drop-in pal who had just executed a soft-shoe routine with Hope onstage, and Jack LaRue, a one-time screen idol who now owned a restaurant near Hope's house in Toluca Lake, were sitting nearby relaxing with the comedian. There were six or seven other hangers-on. It was hard to distinguish who was talking.

"There was a line outside at four A.M., I hear."

"I don't believe that, but the house was jammed shortly after eight when we opened the doors," said Weitman. "We're already two thousand ahead of *Samson and Delilah*."

"We keep this up and we may knock the building over," said Hope, his eyes closed.

Guernsey waited, anxious to ask Hope some questions. Finally he saw an opening, "Bob, Otis Guernsey of the *Trib*."

"Yeah, hello." He sat up and stuck out his hand.

"I've been figuring out," said the critic, "that you'll be on stage here at the Paramount fifty-six times in two weeks—that's more hours than you do for radio in a year. Why? It can't be for mere cash."

"You're right. Matter of fact, I'll work harder in one day on this stage than a whole week of one-night stands when I leave here. And I'll make a lot more money on the road."

"Then why?"

"First of all, I love it. Or I wouldn't do it. You have to understand the full benefit of these two weeks won't be apparent until it's over. See, I started in show business with this sort of racket, and I feel that you've always gotta go back to where you came from, every so often, to sharpen up."

"You? Need to sharpen up?"

"Why not?" Hope grinned. "I haven't done a regular stretch before a paying audience in eleven years. This audience—it varies from show to show—there's a lot of ribbing at the first ones, but it begins to soften up as the day goes on. At the end of my run I should have improved my comedy timing and everything else about the act under all kinds of conditions. You know, Otis, there is nothing quite as stimulating as the atmosphere of a stage job."

Another Broadway critic, Alton Cook of the *Post*, covered the Paramount opening: "Bob has mellowed considerably in the decade he has been away from Broadway stages. He no longer is so strenuously eager to please. His charm has increased with his new casual air. The test is that he stays on stage without much assistance for 40 whole minutes, a very long time for anyone to remain the life of the party and get away with it."

What was most significant to Hope was that he broke the theater's box-office record with receipts of $141,000 the first week.

By the second week Hope was really flying high. His genial mood prompted Leonard Goldenson, then head of United Paramount Theaters, and Bob Weitman to approach him with a request that he spearhead the national fund-raising drive for Cerebral Palsy.

"There are a half million kids and adults afflicted with this thing, Bob," said Weitman, trailing Hope as he headed for his bathroom.

"I don't see how I can give it the time it deserves," said Hope.

"If you could see those kids," pleaded Goldenson. "They need us—need you—need hope, if you'll pardon the pun, and we'll collect the money in theater lobbies or wherever we can. Your drive and exposure would give us a boost."

"Okay. What do you want me to do?"

"You can start by going with me to P.S. 135 over on Fifty-first Street tomorrow for some publicity. They've got special classes for palsied kids there. Bob, to say I'm grateful—no, to say I'm blessed is more like it."

Hope had resented the bulldozer approach at first. But the next day, when he went to the school for publicity pictures and four-year-old Alice White dragged her heavy braces over to his side and five-year-old Terry Wetzelberg climbed up on his lap, he was hooked. So much so that he ordered Mack Millar to include cerebral palsy appearances throughout the remainder of his spring tour. He did CP interviews and photo shoots at Rochester, New York; Cincinnati, Ohio; Owensboro, Kentucky; and in three different cities in Kansas. For these final shows of the tour, he replaced Jane Russell (who had film commitments) with a former big band singer turned actress named Marilyn Maxwell. Max, as he called her, was 17 when she toured with Buddy Rogers's band in 1938; MGM had signed her in 1942 and put her in a few unexceptional pictures. She knew the ropes but as yet hadn't gotten a big break. She lacked the Russell charisma but she was a sexy blonde and Hope seemed to be drawn to her type. She managed to match his wit onstage, as well as off, and probably at that time neither of them knew what was ahead for their relationship. Hope also hired a young singer named Antonio Benedetti, whom he had heard singing in a nightclub, and that was the beginning of Tony Bennett's career.

After resting at home for a few days following the tour, Hope flew back to New York to rehearse for his long-awaited television debut. The cast, assembled at NBC's refurbished-for-television studio, New Amsterdam Roof, included Bea Lillie, Douglas Fairbanks, Jr., Dinah Shore, the dancer Hal LeRoy, a novelty pianist named Maurice Rocco, the singer Bill Hayes, and the Mexico City Boys Choir. Max Liebman, who had created the successful Sid Caesar–Imogene Coca TV series, was producing, and Hal Keith would direct what was being called a *Star Spangled Revue.*

It would be a 90-minute program, telecast live to 27 stations of the NBC network and kinescoped (capturing the screen image on film) for rebroadcast a week later to 18 other NBC-affiliated stations west of the Rockies and along the Pacific Coast. As had been urged by Saphier in the deal they cut, Frigidaire had arranged with its dealerships in 18 top markets to take two and three newspaper ads in the Easter Sunday papers. NBC alone (and this was specified in a clause inserted in the contract Saphier revised for this special) spent a whopping $25,000 on publicity and promotion, and network officials confidently expected to draw the largest viewing audience for a single show in TV history.

Of the many "opening nights" in Hope's varied career to date, this was the roughest one. "I couldn't believe how nervous and jumpy I was. You'd have thought I was some green kid the way I reacted. I worried about my material and especially the pacing of it. I knew this was a quite different medium from either radio or film but I hadn't figured it out yet." He was jittery enough to believe he could use an extra bit of luck, so he phoned his secretary, Marjorie Hughes, at his Toluca Lake office and asked her to send him by the next airplane the black silk topper he had worn in *Roberta.* In the opening sequence of the telecast he decided on a classy image; he would appear in white tie and tails.

Hope's opening monologue, if not the snappy stuff that had tickled both the critics and the Paramount Theater audiences a few weeks before, did provide a foretaste of the heavy commercial drumbeat that would permeate his broadcast comedy through the next decade:

What a fine-looking audience... (*Looks the audience over and counts on his fingers*)... Oh, excuse me... I thought I was still over at the Paramount Theater working on a percentage... Now ladies and gentlemen, doing this big special Easter show on television is a high point for me... For years I've been on radio—you remember radio? ... Blind television? ... But I want to tell you that Frigidaire has been a brick about the whole thing... especially where the money is concerned... Ah, the money... Are you listening, Washington?... Yes, Frigidaire has been very generous with me... They told me I could have my money any way I wanted it... big or little cubes...

Hope's new top-hat image, the presence of high-profile show business names in an expensive, classy format, and the choice of Easter Sunday for broadcasting— all had a cumulative effect on Hope's debut. It wasn't the material as much as the personality of the star, the publicity buildup, a glamorous showcase, and a general realization on the part of everyone involved that television had broken out of its shell. This NBC special had cost the sponsor and the network four times the amount for the entire season's production budget for Milton Berle's top-rated weekly show.

When the 90-minute telecast ended and the critics hit their typewriters, opin- ions were divided. Without exception, Hope's $40,000 salary and production costs were not overlooked in those judgments.

The reigning television critic, John Crosby of the *New York Herald Tribune*, writing on Monday, April 11, 1950, called Hope's "invasion" of television "his- toric," because most stars, he said, were avoiding "the dreadful thing." He wrote that in light of the unprecedented production costs, the "debut fell rather seriously short of expectations," but conceded it was a "pretty good show." Crosby's major criticism was that "Hope appeared to be trying to find some middle ground between movie technique and radio, to discover, in short, what television consisted of exactly. He never quite succeeded."

The *New York Journal-American*'s John Lester found Hope "petrified with fear," while Ben Gross in the widely read *Daily News* called Hope "telegenic, easy-going and graceful. His personality, somewhat subdued yesterday, is much better suited to TV than to radio."

Variety was generally disappointed both in the comedy and in Frigidaire's com- mercials. Harriet Van Horne in the *New York World-Telegram and the Sun* praised Hope's "showmanship" and felt the success of the show rested in his personality.

A week later in the Sunday edition of *The New York Times*, Jack Gould wrote a rhapsodic review, which NBC immediately used in full-page ads in media in their major markets. Everyone came off looking good, said Gould, especially Hope:

> What the viewer saw was the true Hope of the old "Roberta" and Palace days, the master of ceremonies who was relaxed, and leisurely, and never in a hurry. Here was the polished clown in the tradition. His impishness had the light touch, and his gags were sent across the footlights with the deftness of deliver- ies. To the audience at home he communicated that priceless feeling that they, too, were conspirators in the make-believe while to his supporting company he conveyed that esprit and cohesion which is the trademark of a born showman.

Hope himself considered his debut and the show something of a disaster. He had been nervous and jumpy before the cameras, and when he looked at the kine- scope of the telecast, it showed. He returned to the West Coast knowing that he had to improve the sketch ideas his writers had submitted for his second TV special, and to work out some other problems that had arisen in connection with his next film project, *The Lemon Drop Kid.*

When Saphier was casting about for guest stars to headline the second Frigidaire telecast, he discovered some attitudes that really irked Hope. They came from major entertainers and their agents who felt that Hope's inflated TV salary made it difficult for "less reckless sponsors" to put the talents of Bing Crosby, Al Jolson, Frank Sinatra, or Danny Kaye into the new medium. To prove how wrong this was, Hope hired Sinatra to make his TV debut on his Mother's Day Frigidaire show. Then he hired Peggy Lee and ballet stars Michael Kidd and Janet Reed and comedian Arnold Stang. He also brought back Bea Lillie and Bill Hayes.

Hope and Sinatra arrived in New York with plenty of rehearsal time. Hope was determined that this second outing would win over all the critics as well as the home viewers.

In his opening monologue he poked fun at his spotty debut:

How do you do, ladies and gentlemen. I'm very happy to be here again on television. This is my second show for the Frigidaire people. . . *I'm* surprised, too. . . I saw the kinescope of my first show on the Coast. It's convenient. . . I can lay 'em here and hatch 'em a week later. . . And I want to thank the thousands who wrote letters about the first show. . . Also the three who mailed them. . . No. I did get about five thousand letters. . . The FBI is going over them now. . .

This show went far more smoothly than its predecessor and was warmly received by the critics. Hope confessed to Dolores that part of his nervousness had been adjusting to the moving cameras and gesturing technicians. "It was like trying to do a nightclub act with three waiters with trays walking in front of you every time you reached the punchline." He decided to take control of the situation. "I tied down the cameras, and gave orders that no one moves while the show is on—the one way not to get killed on television is to set it up the way *you* want it, not the way *they* want it."

Hope was back in California after his second TV special when the stalemate between him and Lever Brothers became a parting of the ways. After 12 years of being consistently in the golden circle of radio giants (in first place for several seasons), Hope was being dropped because of irreconcilable differences.

Those differences had by now gone beyond the objections to his traveling the radio show, or even to his slump in the ratings—though that was serious. It now centered on Hope's demand that he be allowed to prerecord his radio show on tape, as Crosby was already doing. His contract with Lever Brothers specifically limited his services to "live broadcasts." Hope had his lawyers take the matter as high as Superior Court, which ruled against the comedian. Defiant, Hope announced he would pretape his show anyway, and Lever Brothers pulled the plug.

In the meantime, Saphier had been busy working on a deal with NBC. So, almost simultaneously with the Lever decision, the network could announce it was signing Hope to an exclusive long-term agreement for both radio and television which, Hope confided (publicly), would net him annually close to a million dollars. This contract—let the record show—lasted with modifications and some notable increases—until 1995.

His final Lever contract had been raised to $22,500 for each broadcast, which netted him something like $875,000 for the season. Now, with an exclusive NBC contract and with what he might make from a new sponsorship deal, he would be doubling his income for the same effort. At the moment, however, he had no sponsor, though Saphier was talking to the agencies representing Chesterfield Cigarettes and Buick Motors. Luckily, his new contract guaranteed him airtime even without a sponsor.

Meanwhile, Hope checked into Paramount to begin work on his second Damon Runyon characterization, *The Lemon Drop Kid.* From the start it had been plagued with script and casting snags. Originally Hope had wanted as his costar Jan Sterling, a striking blonde who had made a stir on Broadway in Noel Coward's *Present Laughter.* She wanted to do it but she could not wait out the picture's delays.

So Hope decided to cast—in her first costarring role—the blonde he had just finished touring with, Marilyn Maxwell. She was not bound by a studio contract so Paramount could use her. He already admired the smart way she handled a comedy line, and was sure she would learn more from association with him; he liked her not-so-dumb-blonde sexiness and he hoped her career might take off the same way that Marilyn Monroe's had. Equally pertinent here, to be sure, was the fact that he had recently begun an intimate relationship with her.

The Lemon Drop Kid was a blatant attempt to recapture the blend of cynicism and sentiment that had made *Sorrowful Jones* so appealing. Both the studio bosses and Hope believed there was big money in this one if properly done. Same producer, same director, but somehow this film was expected to succeed on standard sight gimmicks. The day they filmed Hope as a little old lady furiously peddling a bicycle down a busy city street, Bing Crosby was on the sidelines watching and called out, "What's the matter, kid? Did the front office preview your last picture?" Hope nearly ruined the very expensive shot laughing, but that would have been the least of the problems facing this picture before it wrapped up.

30

Taking the Beach

"I really didn't intend to perform so far north, but the First Cavalry went through and the suction pulled me with them. . . And some of these towns are changing hands so fast, one soldier bought a lamp for three thousand wan and got his change in rubles. . . "

A few days before Hope started *The Lemon Drop Kid*, North Korean troops burst across the 38th parallel, swept south, and surrounded Seoul. On June 25, 1950— the first day of shooting the picture—Douglas MacArthur assumed command of United Nations Forces for an unconventional police action that would become known as the Korean War.

The initial counteroffensive of that conflict began in mid-September, but even before that, a plan was building in Hope's mind for taking a USO unit to the fighting front. He shrewdly calculated that at the same time he could make several personal appearances in Japan; *The Paleface* was already doing good business there but it could run much longer if Hope showed up.

Hope got things moving by calling one of his golfing buddies, the World War II flying ace Emmett "Rosy" O'Donnell, now the general in charge of all Far East bomber squadrons. Several days later, new Air Secretary Thomas K. Finletter offered Hope the use of two C–54s, which would allow him room for a troupe of 50 entertainers. That meant he could take the entire Les Brown Band along, as well as his radio technicians. It could be the largest GI overseas entertainment ever attempted. Hope grabbed at the opportunity and agreed to an early October departure, just as soon as *The Lemon Drop Kid* could be dubbed for sound and music and he could step before the television cameras in the third *Star Spangled Revue* by Frigidaire from NBC in New York.

Happily, Hope's new radio sponsor, Liggett & Meyer, got enthusiastic about his idea of prerecording his 30-minute show from various locations during the four-week Pacific Rim tour. They also liked his choice of glamour girl, Jane Russell. He then signed country singer Jimmy Wakely, dancer Judy Kelly, the singing Taylor Maids, a specialty dance group called the High Hatters, and, of course, Les and the boys.

He also planned to take his brother Jack; his boyhood sidekick and ever-present handyman, Charlie Cooley; his masseur, Fred Miron; his announcer, Hy Averback; producer Al Capstaff; and his NBC soundman extraordinaire, Johnny

Pawlek (who would figure prominently as advance man and general trou-
bleshooter for Hope throughout the remainder of his professional life).

Hope would take a couple of writers, and certainly he would ask Larry Gelbart,
who as a newcomer to his writing staff in 1948 had added so much to his Berlin
Airlift tour. Hope felt that Larry was particularly skillful with GI humor, and most
of America would agree with that—if not then, certainly in later years, when
Gelbart was the celebrated creative force and producer of the long-running award-
winning *M*A*S*H* TV series, based on the Korean War.

Gelbart would say, "The most exciting thing about working for him was his
unfailing ability to provide everyone in his orbit with the element of surprise. . . like spending Christmas in the midst of the war in Korea by way of
Alaska and Okinawa. . . Traveling with Hope almost nonstop for four years provided me with the invaluable experience of being able to turn out pages in all sorts
of places: on planes, sometimes commercial, sometimes cargo, quite often military; in train compartments or on ships' deck chairs; in bouncing jeeps and
kamikaze taxis, in elevators and dressing rooms, in Quonset huts and rest rooms."

When he viewed the rough-cut of *The Lemon Drop Kid*, Hope was disappointed,
feeling that it lacked the Runyonesque sentiment he had gotten out of *Sorrowful
Jones*. Paramount studio boss Barney Balaban disagreed, and wanted it readied for
a final cut. "Let's get it out for the holiday trade," he argued. "No, it's not ready,"
said Hope, reminding Balaban of his partnership interest and pointing out weaknesses in what was potentially the film's most heart-warming scene. It was a
Christmas sequence for which Livingston and Evans had written a marvelously lilt-
ing tune, "Silver Bells," and Hope saw "hit parade" flashing before his eyes. Hope
suggested the studio hire Frank Tashlin to do some rewriting. Tashlin agreed but
only if he could direct the retakes. Paramount howled, but finally relented.

Unfortunately, by the time the differences were resolved, retakes could not be
scheduled until November, when Hope would be back from Korea and Maxwell
returned from an eastern cities tour with Dean Martin and Jerry Lewis.

In late September, Hope flew back to New York for his third and final
Frigidaire special, this time costarring Lucille Ball, Dinah Shore, and Bing's brother,
Bob Crosby, with help from the Jack Cole Dancers and the Al Goodman
Orchestra. Hope was beginning to get the feel of what he should be doing in this
medium, as Terence O'Flaherty's review in the *San Francisco Chronicle* of
September 26, 1950, affirms:

> I love you, Bob Hope. Last night the cinema kid with the ski-shoot nose gave a
> little peek of what television is going to be like when the big entertainers move
> in and take over. For the first time, "The Star Spangled Revue" turned out to be
> something approximating the grandiose title of the show. Hope himself had
> good material to work with and he looked happy about it. . . All in all, it was

"one fine, fat show," as my neighbor, Mrs. Pellachotti, expressed it, and she is a very particular woman.

Hope came home from New York a bit wrung-out and had hardly enough time for a restful turnaround before preparing to leave again, this time to Hawaii, where the Far East tour would begin. At the last moment Jane Russell canceled because her film *Macao* was not quite finished. Hope tracked down Marilyn Maxwell, on tour, in Pittsburgh, where she excitedly agreed to sign on, but she said she would have to catch up with them after her tour ended in a few days. So Bob booked the blonde singing actress Gloria DeHaven—who had joined him for a show in Cleveland on his 1949 cross-country tour—to be his GI whistle bait for the first few days of the Pacific tour and the first radio broadcast. The writing team would consist of Gelbart, Fred Williams, Charlie Lee, and Chet Casteloff.

That initial chunk of the Asian tour was a series of Hawaiian puddle jumps from Hickham Field to Pearl Harbor and to hospitals like Tripler on Oahu. Then they moved on to Johnson Island, Kwajalein, Guam, and eventually Okinawa. By this time Maxwell had caught up with them and DeHaven had gone home. The unit was well broken in, spirits were soaring, and the Les Brown musicians were trying to live up to Hope's humorous line about them: "The band loves flying— sometimes they even come inside the plane."

Hope was lucky to have that band. Les provided a high-quality sound, a consistent source of comedy, and, above all, that quality Hope craved, loyalty. His band was one of the hottest moneymakers in the nation at a time when big bands were going out of style. Yet Les would invariably juggle or cancel dates to arrange his schedule around Hope's.

On their arrival at Haneda Air Base, outside Tokyo, Hope received a formal invitation from General MacArthur to lunch with him at the American embassy the following Tuesday. The message included an invitation for Hope to bring 20 members of his troupe. Hope's problem was how to choose the 20. The stars were automatically included, as was Jack Hope and the producer, Al Capstaff. Hope decided to fill the remaining eight spots by a lottery open to everyone except the musicians. Of the four writers who were on that trip only two, Gelbart and Williams, won the lottery. Typically, Charlie Lee, with his British reserve and general air of ennui, would never admit to caring, but Castelhoff was another matter. He behaved as if being excluded was something unthinkable and he literally begged to be included.

"Would you like to take my place?" Hope asked sarcastically.

"Hey—would you?" Chet said. "No, I suppose not. But there must be a way—"

"Chet—they only have room for twenty of us. We can't embarrass them. Besides you lost fair and square."

Late Tuesday morning staff cars picked up the 20 card-carrying invitees and took them to the embassy. The other guests at the lunch were members of the general's staff and U.S. and U.N. diplomats. When MacArthur himself arrived, they

The classic Bob Hope profile at a personal appearance in the late 1960s
(NBC Photo, Burbank)

Harry and Avis Hope just after their marriage at Cardiff, Wales, April 25, 1891

(Bob Hope family photo album)

(inset) Five-year-old Leslie in Bristol, England, in 1908 before coming to America

(Bob Hope family photo album)

(above) A Harry Hope Family Portrait: Jack, George, Harry, Ivor, Jim, Sid, Avis, Bob, and Fred in front of their Cleveland home in 1926

(Bob Hope family photo album)

(right) Hope was still answering to Leslie when he danced with his sweetheart Mildred Rosequist at local spots around Cleveland in 1924.

(Bob Hope personal file)

Hope and dance partner George Byrne, Cleveland, 1925
(Bob Hope personal file)

In 1926, Leslie became Lester Hope when he and George Byrne toured the Sun Gus Vaudeville Circuit in *Smiling Eyes.* The cast is shown here in Lima, Ohio.
(Bob Hope personal file)

In 1934 when he was appearing in Jerome Kern's *Roberta* on Broadway,
Hope met and married fashion model and nightclub singer Dolores DeFina.

(Photo: Maurice Seymour)

(above) In 1936, Bob hit it big on Broadway. Here in a scene with Jimmy Durante and Ethel Merman in Cole Porter's *Red, Hot, and Blue*

(Bob Hope personal file)

(right) Bob Hope, Dorothy Lamour, and Bing Crosby in *Road to Singapore* in 1939

(Copyright 1940 Paramount Pictures, courtesy Universal Pictures)

Hope and his 96-year-old grandfather, James Hope, during the comedian's first visit to England in 1939

(Bob Hope personal file)

Bob with radio show cast: Frances Langford, Bob Chester, Vera Vague, and Jerry Colonna, 1943

(NBC Photo, Burbank)

(above) In the rain on a summer day in 1944 on a remote South Pacific island, Hope entertains battle weary troops near the close of World War II.
(Bob Hope personal file)

(left) Bob Hope as Eddie Foy in the 1955 film biography *The Seven Little Foys*
(Bob Hope personal file)

The Bob Hope Family: Kelly, Nora, Tony, Bob, Dolores, and Linda, 1965

(NBC Photo, Burbank)

1965 USO Christmas tour. Among Hope's gifts to the troops were (left to right) Carroll Baker, Dianna Lynn Batts (Miss World), Anita Bryant, Hope, Kay Stevens, and Joey Heatherton.

(NBC Photo, Burbank)

Both Hope and Cardinal Francis Spellman toured South Vietnam during Christmas 1965. Spellman quipped to Hope, "I follow you around to give absolution."

(NBC Photo, Burbank)

In a 1966 television special, Hope brought together some of his motion picture leading ladies. Left to right: Vera Miles, Signe Hasso, Lucille Ball, Joan Fontaine, Dorothy Lamour, Hedy Lamarr, Virginia Mayo, Hope, and Joan Collins

(NBC Photo, Gerald Smith)

In May 1951, Hope receives the highest USO honor from Harry Truman in the Oval Office, honoring a decade of entertaining the military.

(White House Photo)

In September 1962 in the White House Rose Garden, John F. Kennedy presents the Congressional Gold Medal to Hope for outstanding service to his country. In between is Senator Stuart Symington.
(White House Photo)

Hope with Lyndon Johnson on April 1, 1966, just outside the Oval Office after receiving the USO Silver Medal for twenty-five years of GI entertaining
(White House Photo)

Hope and Richard Nixon compare noses on a Palm Springs golf course in 1971.
(NBC Photo, Burbank)

Jimmy Carter wishes Hope "many happy returns" at a birthday reception in the White House in late May 1978.

(White House Photo)

Hope, Ronald Reagan, Gerald Ford, and George H. W. Bush all seem to like what they see at a 1980 Republican rally.

(Photo, Tom Carter, Peoria Journal Star*)*

Hope and Dwight D. Eisenhower salute the winners of the Bob Hope Desert Classic golf tournament at the Eldorado Country Club, January 1966.

(NBC Photo, Burbank)

A thrilled entertainer at the unveiling of the USAF C–17 aircraft named
The Spirit of Bob Hope at Long Beach, April 1997

(Courtesy McDonnell Douglas Corp.)

were ushered into a big dining room. A white-gloved Marine seated each guest at the long formal dining table according to name card.

Hope noticed out of the corner of his eye that one guest still stood, looking bewildered, and Hope suspected the worst. He looked around and spotted Casteloff sitting immediately to the right of the General. Hope was flabbergasted, embarrassed. But before he could try to correct the situation, Mrs. MacArthur had already called for another chair and place setting and everyone squeezed together to make room. No one at the luncheon had a better time than Chet, applauding the general's welcoming remarks and feeding him jokes.

Later that day Hope did his monologue and a comedy sketch with Maxwell for the Chesterfield radio show in front of 3,000 GIs in the Ernie Pyle Theater. And that night, a longer version of the show was presented to 10,000 GIs at one of Tokyo's cavernous municipal halls. Hope came out grinning and launched into a monologue that was designed for American consumption. Here was a 1950s version of foxhole humor, in which Hope was still the "straight link with home," and his gags glorified the sacrifices of the occupation troops and perpetuated a lingering American bitterness toward a people who had caused so many young American deaths.

Yet it was something different when Hope was not facing GI audiences but was face to face with his movie fans. Marilyn Maxwell told friends later, "In Tokyo, when people recognized him they yelled, 'Ooooooo, Bobba Hopa!' and one time when we were going some place in a convoy, a really old American-built sedan absolutely crammed with Japanese just barged into our procession and serenaded him with 'Buttons and Bows.' Bob stopped our car and got out and shook every hand that was stretched out of the car windows."

Inevitably the most grueling yet exciting moments of the tour took place in Korea. Their destination was Seoul, but their landing was diverted from nearby Kimpo Air Base because it had been sneak-bombed a few hours before their scheduled arrival. The troupe landed at an auxiliary base and, bundled in GI winter uniforms, huddled in the backs of trucks that took them over shell-cratered backroads to a stadium in the capital city.

Thousands of GIs had been sitting there for more than an hour in bitter cold and biting wind, some in icy mud and most carrying sidearms, many with rifles resting on their knees. Hope, his face reddened with cold, delivered a particularly pointed monologue about the mercurial nature of the war where battle lines were almost impossible to follow and where there was the smell of the Soviet presence:

I really didn't plan to perform so far north, but the First Cavalry went through and the suction pulled me with them. . . . And some of these towns are changing hands so fast one soldier bought a lamp with three thousand wan and got his change in rubles. . . Seoul has changed hands so many times the towels in the hotel are marked "His," "Hers," and "Who's Sorry Now?". . . . But the way the war's going now doesn't bother the Russians. They just run the newsreels backward and it looks like the North Koreans are advancing. . .

From Seoul the troupe moved on to Taegu, then Taejon, where Hope remarked to his pilot, Colonel Leyden, "You know, I promised to do a show for the First Marines. Do you know where they are?"

"Sure," said Leyden, "they're at Wonsan."

"Can we go there?"

"Why not? We just took it—no sweat."

Their planes flew eastward, circled the Sea of Japan, and made a long, sweeping approach to the Wonsan airstrip. "When we looked out of our plane windows, we saw a most startling thing," Maxwell later said. "Below us was what looked like the entire Seventh Fleet forcing a huge beachhead landing. We even thought we saw one ship hit a mine."

When the two C–54s came to a halt on the airstrip at Wonsan, there was no sign of humankind anywhere, no ground crew, no one. The buildings seemed deserted; there was an eerie feeling of sudden abandonment about the scene.

Crew members of both planes advanced with weapons drawn to a nearby hangar, which was empty. Finally everyone stepped out of the planes—a bit cautiously—and were wondering what to do next when they heard motor sounds and saw several jeeps come speeding across the runway. Out of one stepped General Edward Almond, and out of another emerged Vice Admiral Arthur Struble, both looking stunned. "How long have you been here?" Almond asked, bewildered.

"Twenty minutes or so," said Hope. "Where *is* everybody?"

"Twenty minutes?" said Struble incredulously. "You beat us to the beach."

"Come on," snickered Hope. "How could *we* beat you to the beach. We heard you had already taken this port."

"We just landed. When you flew over, couldn't you see us?"

"Yes, but—we thought it was our audience coming to see the show," Hope cracked.

Almond and Struble had been six days late taking Wonsan because, as official dispatches described, "bad weather and one of the densest mine fields in history delayed the landing." Meanwhile, South Korean troops had done their part in flushing out the enemy and driving them north toward the Chosin reservoir. A headline in the next day's *Los Angeles Times* told it all: BOB HOPE AND MARILYN MAXWELL IN WONSAN BEFORE LEATHERNECKS.

After the two-hour show, Struble invited Hope (alone) to spend the night on his ship, the *Missouri*. Hope, exhausted, agreed gratefully. When Struble and Hope stepped out of the Navy chopper onto the flight deck, hundreds of sailors were standing at attention in two long lines. The two men walked in a kind of review between those lines and Hope heard muffled greetings here and there like "Hey Bob," and "Ski Snoot" and way off in the distance someone shouted, "Old Niblick Nose." After a stiff drink and a good dinner Hope wandered out toward the fantail and soon found himself doing a short performance for some of the crew.

Next day, the remainder of the troupe was choppered out to the *Missouri* for a two-hour show and that afternoon the whole troupe was transferred over to the *Valley Forge* for a similar event on its flight deck.

Their final show in Korea was to be performed in the yard of the former Communist headquarters at Pyongyang for what remained of the divisions that had just fought to defend the battle line drawn at the Yalu River. Troupe members were driven from airstrip to show site in armored personnel carriers, and as they bumped along they could not avoid seeing the body of a 12-year-old boy who had just been shot, and several more bodies hastily covered with straw.

Conversations with Admiral Struble and General Almond had given Bob the feeling that this strange, confusing war was not the simple matter several officers at the MacArthur luncheon in Tokyo had guaranteed it would be.

As he waved good-bye to the GIs, who swarmed about the troupe's planes just before takeoff, Hope caught the eye of one soldier who hollered to him, "How about your parka?" Hope took his warm garment off and threw it to the young man. Les Brown was standing next to Hope and another GI begged for his. Les threw it to the kid. In minutes the rest of the troupe had shed the thick jackets and thrown them to guys who needed them.

After leaving Korea, they stopped in Tokyo so that Bob could record a tribute to Al Jolson, who had just died. Jolson, in failing health, had come to Korea in September and had tirelessly sung songs and talked with combat troops wherever they could land a helicopter. And it was believed that the strenuousness of that trip hastened his death.

The final leg of the tour took place in what the GIs called the "Icebox Circuit"—the Aleutians and mainland Alaska. Hope and the group landed at Shemya, where four hundred entertainment-starved men were waiting, and found the same kind of needy troops at Adak and Amchitka. They went on to Anchorage and then to Fairbanks, where Hope did his fourth radio show of the tour. As it came to a close, Hope, in a voice resonant with emotion, paid tribute to the many people who had helped make the Korean tour possible, to the GIs, and to the United Nations forces he had entertained. Once again, Hope was most eloquent when defending the courage and the mission of the military:

It's a long way from the conference rooms of Lake Success to the marshaling yards outside Pusan, Korea, but when we saw the grouping of French, Turks, Filipino, Australian, British and South Koreans in one composite army while a Swedish group was setting up a field hospital for the wounded, we knew, and we're sure Joe knows by now, that the United Nations is far past the blueprint stage. It's in the bazooka, bomber and battleship stage, and the men fighting alongside each other may not understand each other's language, but they understand each other's ideals. . .

Besides the four NBC network radio broadcasts that originated from staging areas and actual battlefield locations, Hope decided that he wanted to re-create for the American television audience (now growing by the thousands daily) exactly what the war-zone shows had been like. He had picked a lot of newsreel film, and had plenty of NBC photographs and four writers to supply continuity and colorful narrative.

So for his fourth Frigidaire special, Hope decided to re-stage his recent entertainment package for the troops. He had always seemed to be unerring in his perception of American taste in entertainment and American public sentiment, which at this moment in time was focused on the fathers, brothers, sons, and some daughters serving and dying in Korea. Thanks to modern technology, he could dramatize for TV his 1950s adventures at the fighting front and at last offer to his public realization and reinforcement of the figurative image of himself as a clown hero. It was an image that heretofore had been available only in the stories that journalists reported in newspapers and magazines and on radio, or that Hope himself humorously recorded in his two wartime memoirs. It was a precursor of the television specials based on his overseas entertainments for American GIs that would be so eagerly watched in the years to come.

A typical review of this show was Bill Irvin's in the *Chicago Sun-Times* of November 27, 1950: "It is little wonder that Hope and company wowed 'em in Wonsan and toppled them in Tokyo. . . Hope's Sunday night show didn't measure up to some of his previous TV appearances but it packed the quota of laughs needed by GIs in Korea, and that's the important thing."

Almost immediately after returning from Korea, Hope went to Paramount for the retakes of *The Lemon Drop Kid*. He liked Tashlin's new script pages, and especially the re-staging of "Silver Bells," where he and Marilyn are strolling and singing in the falling snow. The whole picture came together and "Silver Bells," destined to be a Christmas standard, sold over a million and a half copies of the sheet music and close to 32 million recordings. When their schedules permitted, Bob and Marilyn got together to record the song, but Bing had beat them to it, and in December his version sold the most copies and filled the airwaves.

As the year 1950 ended—a year in which the comedian had a brush with death, made his television debut, closed an era with the radio sponsor that launched him, set the Paramount Theater box-office record, took the most ambitious show ever attempted to an overseas GI audience, and was risking the stability of his life with Dolores with an extramarital love affair—Hope drove himself at a murderous pace.

Inevitably someone had to ask the question "Is Bob Hope killing himself?" There was a certain déjà vu in the rash of newspaper and magazine stories and gossip column items that had this common theme, such as this one from the highly read *Modern Screen* for July 1950: "Practically everyone who has worked with Hope during the past two years had made a similar observation. It is impossible to watch the unrelenting way he drives himself without nervously wondering when the breaking point will come."

Jack Hope suggested his brother might never have lost his adolescent fear that "this might be his last week's work, and that if he isn't good, people might not ask him back." Hope's drive to take all the marbles is very natural, very basic, very American, and to achieve it takes guts and practice and a "depthless ego." To be *the* preeminent American entertainer, he had to excel in all media to bigger audiences than anyone before him had ever known.

There were observations by longtime studio associates that his driven behavior as a kind of show business traveling salesman was not only necessary to continually confirm his comedic preeminence, but also to confirm his virility or masculinity by acting out what traveling salesman jokes were all about. And during this time, according to those same studio associates, there were assertions that Hope had more than once disregarded the rules of proper marital behavior.

The Hollywood gossip columnists' tongues were wagging. Louella Parsons, never idle when a back-street rumor was circulating, suggested that something might be amiss in the Hope household. She ran this item: "In an exclusive interview with Dolores Hope, I have learned that there is absolutely no truth to the current rumors that Bob Hope and his leading lady, Marilyn Maxwell, are serious about each other just because they have been seen together so much."

Dolores continued to act as if Bob was hers alone and on his recent return from the Far East she created a five-foot-square greeting card and an NBC photographer shot Hope with Nora and Kelly standing next to him. Here is their message, partly written by the children but also showing Dolores's fine hand:

We are so happy you are home
Now promise us you won't roam
Away before we've kissed your cheek
At least until some time next week
For daddys come and daddys go
But you're a special kind you know
Now promise us that you won't roam
We are so happy you are home
(Until at least some time next week)

It is much easier to understand Hope's vagabond obsession in terms of his consistent striving for more money. Hope cites a night in Oakland, California, when he came offstage dripping with perspiration and he held up a check for $19,000 for one night's work. "Gee, look at that, Charlie. Remember when we used to get five dollars a day for hoofing in Cleveland?"

As for his depthless ego and the insatiable need for applause, he says, "There's nothing in the world like hearing people laugh. It's the greatest noise there is. . . without live audiences to play to, I'd be cutting doilies in no time."

As to rumors about Hope's roving eye, his longtime agent and personal tour manager, Mark Anthony, would say, "The boss knew a number of people, including newsmen, who were wise to his playing around on the side, but he counted on their loyalty to keep it quiet. When I told him he was pushing his luck he would say 'Don't worry about it' and I figured if he didn't, I wouldn't."

It's fairly certain that it was the laughs rather than the $25,000 weekly salary that motivated him to travel his Chesterfield radio show from one military base to another during the Korean conflict. Liggett & Meyer, a tobacco company, were perfectly content with this because so many GIs smoked and the show's military flavor suited the "Sound Off! One! Two!" theme of their advertising campaign.

Hope picked West Coast camps and bases to broadcast from in those early months of 1951 so he could make a comic intrigue film, *My Favorite Spy*, with the beautiful Hedy Lamarr at Paramount during the week. This time he played a burlesque headliner who is a perfect double for a notorious undercover agent.

During the final days of shooting, in early April, Hope was becoming increasingly restless and ready to leave for his spring tour. He had asked his British agent, Lew Grade, to book him on a two-week swing through the music halls of England and Scotland. He also was arranging to prerecord a Chesterfield radio show from a few military bases before settling down for a full week at London's famed Palladium, probably the last bastion of continuous week-to-week vaudeville in the world. (New York's Palace rarely opened its doors these days, except, perhaps, for something like Judy Garland's latest "comeback.") In addition, Hope had agreed to be a guest celebrity competing in Britain's Amateur Golf Championship, to be held at Porthcawl, Glamorgan, in Wales.

Hope publicly announced he was asking Jane Russell to come on this tour, but she was otherwise engaged and he happily chose Marilyn Maxwell. Hope's final domestic show was taped in Durham, North Carolina, on April 13, and the next day Bob and Marilyn were aboard the *Queen Mary*. Rumors about the relationship had become so open that they couldn't escape Dolores. According to one of Hope's secretaries at the time, a tearful Dolores reached her husband on the *Queen Mary*. He told her not to worry.

Along with the other arrangements Hope had made for this British tour was one decidedly unique commitment resulting from an impromptu promise. It all started on the set of *The Lemon Drop Kid* the year before. One day during shooting, Hope was introduced to an open-faced, round little man with a stiff white collar, an Anglican priest from England named James Butterfield who was touring the United States drumming up contributions for his version in London's East End of Father Flanagan's Boys Town. Butterworth's rehabilitation center was called Clubland and it now faced extinction because it required major financial help to repair extensive bomb damage during the blitz.

Hope listened to the kind-faced vicar and said, "Listen, I may be in London next spring, and if I am I'll do a benefit for you."

Butterworth beamed but he was also cautious; he had heard promises before. When Hope went back into a shot, Butterworth asked Charlie Cooley, "Does he mean it?" Both Cooley and Monty Brice chorused, "When Hope says he'll do something, he'll do it!"

Just before leaving for England, Hope heard from Lew Grade that the Palladium had booked Judy Garland for the time period Hope had specified, and the alternate dates the Palladium offered did not fit the comedian's schedule. Grade countered, however, with a two-week booking at the Prince of Wales Theatre and Hope agreed. Then he thought of Clubland. He made sure that the money he was getting for his British tour was sufficient to allow him to give some of it away, and told Grade, "Lew, have your office make the contract between the Prince of Wales and Reverend James Butterworth. I'll play the two weeks for $25,000 a week, but only if the club gets the dough."

Butterworth was summoned to Grade's office and when he was told of Hope's generosity, he cried. When Hope and Maxwell walked down the gangplank at Southampton, Butterworth was waiting on the dock.

In every English and Scottish appearance, Hope was a sellout. In London he was literally mobbed by fans and autograph seekers when he tried to get through the alley to the Prince of Wales stage door and had to have help getting to his dressing room. For the first show he stayed onstage for 80 minutes, the longest single stage show he could remember giving. He spotted the vicar's face beaming up from the first row. When he got offstage, elated, he said, "Where's Jimmy? Where's Jimmy Butterworth?"

"He's just leaving. He said he didn't want to be in the way."

"Bring him back," said Hope. "I want him to come to the party."

The after-show party was held at Ciro's. The little priest went and kept saying to anyone who would listen, "I can't believe all this money is ours." Every night for two weeks Hope had the same kind of enthusiastic crowd and each night he could look down and see the adoring face of "the little Rev." Afterward Butterworth would come backstage and try coaxing Hope to visit Clubland. Finally on Friday of the second week, Hope went to the rehabilitation center with a check for 20,000 pounds sterling. The priest took him on a tour through the carpentry shop, the gymnasium, the table tennis alcove, the works. Finally, Father Butterworth shoved a little boy named Michael forward to accept the check from Hope while news photographers clicked away.

Many years later, at a film festival in Acapulco, Mexico, Michael Caine came up to Hope at one of the receptions and said, "Bob, I've waited years for the opportunity to tell you in person that I was that shy urchin that took the check from you at Clubland."

Sandwiched in among the other events of that tour were some GI shows that were taped, one at Burtonwood, England, and several in Germany, including one in West Berlin. And Hope did get to play the Palladium after all. At a Sunday night charity gala to benefit Britain's equivalent of Actors Equity, Hope and Maxwell filled the headliner spot and were joined by comedienne Beryl Reid, harmonica virtuoso Larry Adler, actor Peter Sellers, and singer Petula Clark.

Hope and Maxwell had a few days of relaxation in Ireland and then went to Porthcawl for the British Amateur tourney. In the two rounds of the golf tournament, Hope lost to a spectacled, pipe-smoking Yorkshireman named Chris Fox. As one newsman reported: "Munching a slice of homemade cake given him by a woman spectator, and with his free hand around his stage partner, Marilyn Maxwell, Bob Hope walked down the 17th fairway here, beaten but happy."

Back in California a few days later, he wrapped up the Chesterfield series for the season and went to Washington, where Harry Truman presented him with the USO's highest honor on the tenth anniversary of his first GI show at March Field in 1941. The plaque read simply: TO THE GI'S GUY.

~Court Jester: 1952 to 1963 ~

31

Liking Ike

"I'm really on the spot when I do political jokes . . . I'm usually sell-ing a product everybody buys and I don't want to alienate part of my audience . . . "

The politicization of Bob Hope was a gradual, somewhat random matter. If he appeared to bend with the wind, it was because on Tuesday nights he was a door-to-door salesman and he couldn't afford to offend his customers. His interest in politics followed his fame and financial security.

In 1951, current public opinion blamed Truman for "handing" China to the Communists, for "losing" the Korean War, for "harboring Reds" in the govern-ment. Considering Hope's Horatio Alger views of the American system and his intimacy with the GI and with high-ranking military brass, it is likely he applauded Truman's policies of economic reconstruction, his Berlin Airlift, his tough stand on Korea, and his consistent support of the United Nations.

But it is more certain that Hope, along with so many Americans, welcomed Republican promises of prosperity and a pledge to rout the Reds from high places and maintain a posture of world supremacy.

Hope and the American people both encouraged a somewhat reluctant Republican candidate for the presidency who was approaching slowly on a white charger, whose courage had won his nation a stunning victory in 1945, and whose charisma had landed him the presidency of Columbia University. Hope and the nation—and most of the world—liked Ike.

In one of Hope's Chesterfield monologues of that period, delivered just after Britain's Princess Elizabeth and Prince Philip visited Washington, D.C., there is a rather backhanded reference to Truman's uphill struggle to gain popular appeal:

Then Elizabeth asked Margaret [Truman] what a Republican was. . . and Margaret said, "I don't know, every time the subject comes up, they make me leave the room". . . But they had a nice visit and when the princess left the White House, she said, "I hope to be back next year, Mr. President". . . and President Truman said, "Me, too!"

It became increasingly clear that Dwight Eisenhower was more than just a national hero to Hope. He was someone the comedian felt drawn to because of their wartime meeting in North Africa, and more recently, in 1946, Ike had pinned the Medal of Merit on Hope's chest.

In the spring of 1952, Truman declared he was not a presidential candidate. Despite election-year accusations of "scandalous administration" aimed at the President, Hope did not join the media attack. "I'm really on the spot when I do political jokes. I would never do a joke to hurt a campaign or any party. I can't afford to go out and start knocking Democrats and knocking Republicans. I'm usually selling a product everyone buys and I don't want to alienate part of my audience."

In Hope's radio monologue of May 15, with the presidential campaign in full swing and a feeling in the air that the Truman administration was almost history, he dismissed the first family, but in a rather benign way. The only real bite among the gags was Hope's pointed reference to Senator William Fulbright's current Senate investigation of steel industry fraud, which haunted Truman's final Washington days:

> They finally finished remodeling the White House and it's open to tourists. . . President Truman isn't too happy about it. He's annoyed at the Republican visitors. They keep bringing their suitcases. . . I don't know whether the Democrats expect to win the election or not but the whole second floor is done in coonskin. . . They had to build the whole White House out of wood. . . the President is allergic to steel. . .

The way Hope approached this particular election year is indicative of his growing interest in public affairs generally during a uniquely expansionist decade of his life. For example, in June 1952 he enthusiastically endorsed the National Broadcasting Company's shrewd suggestion that he serve as one of the radio and television news commentators at both the Republican and Democratic conventions in Chicago. This had resonance with the satiric way the humorist Will Rogers had covered political conventions. Rogers's daily news column—generally featured on the front page of major newspapers across the nation—delivered sharp jibes at the sleeping delegates and "windy speeches." Hope was to deliver a short monologue at the start of each evening of NBC's news coverage.

Before going to Chicago, Hope elected to take on a really big assignment and a much-applauded chore. He agreed to produce and co-host with Bing Crosby and Dorothy Lamour a ground-breaking entertainment event, a 14½-hour fund-raising television special (now called a telethon) to raise a million dollars to send the 333-member Olympic team on the "Road to Helsinki."

Inspiration for this high-endurance TV fund-raiser came from Hearst syndicated sports writer Vince Flaherty, a two-fisted drinking and golfing buddy of Hope's and Crosby's. Flaherty, with the blessing of Avery Brundage, the president of the International Olympic Committee, got promises of financial backing and all-important publicity coverage from Hearst's domestic and foreign operations to help sponsor the telecast.

Nothing like this had ever been attempted. In addition, it would mark Bing Crosby's television debut and promised such attractions as Frank Sinatra, Burns and Allen, Uncle Miltie, Dean Martin and Jerry Lewis, Frankie Laine, Donald O'Connor, Peggy Lee, Eddie Cantor, George Jessel, the Ritz Brothers, Abbott and Costello, Fred MacMurray, an array of famous sports figures, a host of kiddy-show favorites, and a steady succession of jazz musicians and big bands. Who was not going to tune in for this event!

Most of it would take place on Hope's home stage, the El Capitan in Hollywood, although there would be feed-ins from CBS studios in New York, where most of the athletes would appear. Most historic of all, *both* NBC and CBS would carry the show to their hundreds of stations.

During the long day of preparation leading up to the telecast, a steady stream of writers, technicians, cue-card printers, musicians, agents, publicists, and messengers fast-tracked between the Tudor-style Hope office in Toluca Lake, where an augmented clerical staff was coordinating the telethon, and the main house. Those who had reason to deal with Hope personally could approach his bedroom by a special spiral staircase leading up from the main hallway. As one or another staffer knocked and came into the bedroom, they were often surprised to see Hope still in his pajamas, peering at them above his half-glasses, surrounded by a seemingly disorganized array of paper.

At the office end, the unflappable Marjorie Hughes supervised construction of the long, long script. She and Hope had culled through thousands of gags in his now-famous joke vault, arranged in categories such as sports, sports figures, Crosby, Lamour, *Road* pictures, leading ladies, elections, conventions, and, of course, Olympics. They came up empty on Finland and Helsinki.

Hope's writers had been working almost nonstop for days and were ordered to stand by all through the telethon as well. Hope attended to each set of details meticulously, personally making sure that both networks were providing fresh studio audiences for each hour of the long broadcast to keep enthusiasm high for the rotating performers.

By midafternoon he had gotten out of bed, finished his favorite lunch, lamb chops, and was now sitting behind his massive oak desk. Using three telephone lines he talked to stars, agents, producers, press agents, musical arrangers, and conductors in a fascinating display of show business communication that alternated between flattering, commiserating, cajoling, encouraging, promising, and pressuring.

Inside the main house, Dolores and Mildred MacArthur helped the cook and two maids prepare dinner for the immediate family and a few of the children's friends.

When dinner was announced, Hope came to the table with a sheaf of monologue jokes hoping to try out some of his material on his captive audience (as he often did). But these captives—Dolores and Mildred, 13-year-old Linda, 11-year-old Tony, and the 7-year-old Nora and Kelly—were more interested in the food:

roast beef with Yorkshire pudding, five vegetables, two salads, and strawberry shortcake—and no one was listening. Hope finally gave an exasperated shout: "Dolores! How do you expect me to compete with this kind of food?" He dropped his napkin, jumped up hurriedly, and passed his newly hired personal appearance agent, Mark Anthony, in the pantry.

"Come on, Mark, drive with me to the show." He got behind the wheel with Mark beside him and the car moved down the driveway until the big gates opened electrically. Then Hope sped away toward Hollywood.

Less than an hour later, Dolores, Mildred, the children, and some close friends in the neighborhood gathered around the oval picture tube in the family room. The household help came in from the kitchen and stood watching and laughing at Hope's monologue before they served mixed drinks and coffee. As the hours went by, the children nodded and dozed, a few were taken home, and the Hope kids went up to bed. Soon the only ones left were Dolores and Mildred, who went upstairs to Bob's room (adjoining Dolores's) because the picture tube in that TV was bigger than the one in her room.

At 6:30 A.M. little Nora, in pajamas and barefoot, leaped up on the bed, waking Mildred. She leaned on her mother and beckoned to a second little girl, shy and tentative, the three-year-old daughter of one of the maids.

Linda, also in pajamas, came in whispering, "Is Daddy still on?" She sat on her father's short divan with her arms locked around her knees. Kelly came in next and crawled up next to Nora. Finally Tony and his pal, Patrick Wayne (John Wayne's 11-year-old son) came into the room in pajamas with their six-guns strapped around their waists, trying to seem nonchalant. They dropped into sitting positions at the end of the bed.

"Did he get the million?" asked Tony.

"Not yet, dear," said Mildred, "but he will."

Two and a half hours later the million-dollar figure did pop up on the tote board and everyone at the El Capitan screamed and hollered. (Of course, a month later the Olympic Committee was still trying to collect on some of the pledges.)

At about eleven o'clock Hope and Doc Shurr walked into the family room for a small breakfast. Then Hope crawled into bed.

A few days later, Hope took part of his family to Chicago for the Republican National Convention. Dolores suggested they take Linda and Tony, because they could use the experience for their civics classes at school.

Hope's writers had given him some ammunition to use for cracking jokes about the two competing presidential candidates, Robert Taft and Dwight Eisenhower. Although he was no longer writing his daily column (after William Randolph Hearst died, the editors decided to forgo Hope's writers' contribution), King Features syndicate asked Hope to resume the chore for one week in Chicago. Some of his jokes had a Will Rogers twang, "This town was known as the Windy City even before the politicians arrived," and "The hotels are jammed. . . hot and cold running rumors on every floor."

By the time the Democratic National Convention met, a few weeks later, the excitement over political conventions was waning. NBC complained about its loss of listeners and viewers. The biggest media rattle was all about Republican vice presidential candidate Richard Nixon's criticism of Democratic presidential candidate Adlai Stevenson's humor.

Since this was turning into a political year for Hope, he decided that it would be good for publicity and for his ego to run for office in the show business arena. Bob had Mack Millar leak the story to Chicago columnist Nate Gross, who wrote in the *Chicago Herald-American* on June 20, 1952:

BOB HOPE SEEKING AGVA PRESIDENCY

Town Tattler: Bob Hope is running for president, but this is no mock campaign like that being conducted by my tongue-in-cheek pal, Jimmy Durante, or my perennial presidential favorite, Sophie Tucker. . . Bob's candidacy is for president of the American Guild of Variety Artists. . . To Bob it would mean the attainment of a boyhood dream. At long last everyone would address him as "Mr. President."

Needless to say, Hope won by a landslide and went off quite content on a summer holiday with Dolores and the kids to Vermont.

But relaxation for Hope always had its limits. When he had learned from Lew Grade that his postponed London Palladium engagement could be rescheduled from July to September, he decided to yield to Paramount's suggestion for him to do a European promotion tour for his film *Son of Paleface*. His first stop was Stockholm, and the media and public response to his interviews and walk-ons between film showings was sometimes near riotous. Then he dropped off in London long enough to do a *Paleface* promotion on his way to the South of France at the invitation of Prince Alex and Princess Honey Chile Hohenlohe (Patricia Wilder had a new husband), who were hosting social evenings in Cannes and Monte Carlo. From the Nice airport he flew up to Helsinki for the Olympic Games and stayed two days before leaving for London.

He was enervated by his long-awaited, and to him long-overdue, commercial debut at one of the world's most famous music halls. After the offstage announcement and the "Thanks for the Memory" walk-on, he waited for the thunderous applause to die down before telling the Palladium crowd how good it felt to be back home. "I came over on the *United States*. . . It's a wonderful ship. It costs us ninety million. . . that's money we had left over after Churchill's last visit. . . You have to hand it to Churchill. . . if you don't he comes and gets it from us anyway. . . "

The Palladium monologue was partly written by a London-based comedian, Denis Goodwin, who had been referred to Hope by Charlie Lee. The topicality of the humor was deft and tasteful. One of London's more respected critics, Peter Forster, had this to say:

A brilliant Palladium bill is headed by Bob Hope, surely the most endearing of the American comedians. His very entrance is a joy as he ambles on, jaw jutting, eyes roving, abounding in that old, indefinable, heart-warming quality of your true star comedian.

Mr. Hope is funny to look at, funny to hear, funny without effort and without flagging. What matter how many joke writers assist? Today's comic with radio, film and TV markets, must use material in a month that would have lasted an old-timer a decade. Nobody could provide Mr. Hope's impeccable timing or the charm that robs personal comment of any offense.

Hope's shadow during these two weeks at the Palladium was the lovable Anglican priest, Reverend Butterworth, who finally convinced Hope he should come to visit the refurbished boys' hospice to see what had been done with his money. Butterworth posed for photos with Bob in the main vestibule next to a stone marker that proclaimed Hope's beneficence. Hope's plaque was adjacent to one placed there in honor of the dowager Queen Mary, who was the school's patroness. Hope was so touched by Butterworth's devotion to rebuilding these boys' lives that he volunteered to do another benefit.

He telephoned Lew Grade to help him book the Stoll Theatre and to find some supporting acts. Hope wasn't anxious to book a big show because he had an ace up his sleeve, a somewhat chancy card, but one well worth playing if he could. He had heard from one of his writers that Crosby would be in London for a day or two en route to a movie location near Paris. Bing had never appeared on a London stage and if he were to show for this benefit it would cause a sensation.

Bing was staying at the Savoy, and his reaction to Bob's telephone invitation was negative and rather cold. He said that an appearance was out of the question. He didn't have his charts, he didn't know the musicians, no, he preferred to pass. Bob thanked him and hoped he would change his mind. Crosby's occasional bouts with booze, his uncordial, even nasty behavior around those he worked with or knew intimately, were factors Hope had grown accustomed to over the years with Bing.

Meanwhile, Hope dropped hints with some media contacts that Crosby might, just might, decide to make his London debut at the Clubland benefit, and then left the decision up to Bing. He had considered having the jovial little reverend call Bing, but he was worried about what Crosby might say to him.

At show time there was no Crosby. Yet Hope still clung to the vain belief that Crosby would try to surprise him. Jack Buchanan, a leading British entertainer, had agreed to introduce the first half of the show and he was now onstage. Bob was going over material for his second-half monologue with Denis Goodwin when a stagehand sidled over to Hope and told him confidentially that Crosby had been spotted at a pub "over the road."

Hope told Denis to stand by while he and the stagehand took off to locate Bing. When they walked into the pub, Bing was obviously relishing his drink and conversation with some of the locals. He invited Bob to join him and had no apparent intention of getting made up or putting on his toupee, or singing, or joking, or anything but drinking.

"Come on, Hope—join in," he said in a manner that suggested he had already enjoyed several drinks, "or. . . don't. . . as the case may be. . . "

"Thanks, Dad, but you see there are a lot of folks sitting there over the road, and it's for a good cause." Hope often called Bing Dad.

Bing gave Hope a look that for all the world said "I don't give a damn," then took another puff on his pipe, swallowed his drink slowly, set it down, and turned: "What are we waiting for?"

Hope took Crosby up to a rehearsal hall where a pianist, Pat Dodd, had been standing by in case Crosby showed and wanted to rehearse. But some overzealous agent had gotten wind of Hope's good fortune and steered about two dozen journalists and photographers to the rehearsal hall. There was no time for a run-through.

Hope dashed down to open the second half and in his act he did his usual gags about "Dad." Then someone near the front of the theater hollered "Where is he?"

Hope shaded his eyes as he looked down toward the front rows and said confidentially: "Well, you know it's pretty late for that old gentleman to be out. He's probably in bed sipping his hot milk." The audience moaned. Then the spotlight moved across the stage, and there was Bing, with his pipe, his hat tilted up from his forehead, leaning against the proscenium arch. The British comedian Donald Peers, who was also on the bill, recalls, "The applause was like something you never heard. It was just fantastic. And went on. He did some signature tunes and there were lots of titles shouted at him from the audience. He would start one or two, but not having rehearsed them he would get so far and say, 'Well, that's enough' or 'I can't remember the rest of the words.'"

Bob and Bing did some of the crossover exchanges that they had used at their first Capitol Theater date in New York and then Crosby threw Hope a "you owe me a big one" look, waved at the audience, and said good-bye. Hope was, however, content.

By the time Hope got back to Hollywood, it was time for his first television appearance of the new 1952–53 season. The Frigidaire contract was finished, and Saphier had negotiated a new deal for Hope to headline a group of comedy specials on NBC, sponsored by Colgate. As the years unfolded, regardless of sponsorship the show would always remain *The Bob Hope Show* and would always be familiar because the format hardly ever changed from that 1952 season to Hope's final TV show 40 years later. What had worked on radio was transferred to television: an opening monologue (always the highlight of the program) followed by skits and musical performances with his guest stars.

But his style was different now. In his 1950 debut he felt his audience expected him to be up-tempo and visual, even in his monologue, but later his own sense of timing, the TV critics, and his wife convinced him that if the urbanity and subtlety of his humor was to really hit home, he had to temper that super-salesman style of delivery. What Dolores wanted to see dominate his stage image was her husband's "incomparable ease." Hope himself saw the need to go from fast to a more relaxed, casual, and easy manner.

When he walked out to center stage in front of a drawn curtain on October 12, 1952, he did so with a new confidence, one that suggested he was now totally in charge. It was less than a month to Election Day, and Hope, quite uncharacteristically, devoted his full monologue to politics:

Thank you. . . I'm happy to be here on the *Colgate Comedy Hour*, and by the way, I want to thank all the candidates for giving up this time to make room for *another* comedian. . . I'm so confused I don't know whether to join the Democrats who are voting for Eisenhower, or the Republicans who are voting for Stevenson. . . or Crosby, who's still voting for John Quincy Adams. . . This election will really make history. It'll be the first time the General waits while the troops make the decision. . . And both parties are after the farm votes. They've made so many speeches, the farmers expect the biggest crops of their lives. . . Eisenhower paid us a visit this week and tied up traffic. Naturally, everybody was excited. The Republicans out here think he can walk on orange juice. . . One Democrat walked into the Republican rally by mistake. I saw him this morning. It's a beautiful embalming job. . .

The monologue's total concern with things political makes it a rarity among the hundreds of radio and television monologues in Hope's career. But the humor is essentially harmless, though expertly crafted. Hope writer Charlie Lee, in a *New York Times Magazine* article, said: "His stuff seems braver than it is. When you examine one of his jokes it's never lethal. We never do anything about a politician that really hurts—it's always their golf shots or their noses or their money—never their policies, never what they're doing."

Hope's valedictory to Truman's administration came at the close of the comedian's November 1952 television monologue. He talked of other matters and commented on the Republican jubilation over Eisenhower's election plurality. In the style of the cracker-barrel humorists, he delivered a mock farewell note, suitably folksy, from one leader to his successor:

Dear Ike. . . Have found it necessary to leave town. Sorry I can't be here to meet you. You'll find sandwiches in the icebox, cigars in the humidor, and Landon in the deep-freeze. However, I don't suppose you'll be eating the sandwiches inasmuch as you just cooked Stevenson's goose. . . In the Blue Room you'll find a large picture of Taft, send it back to him. . . Please erase the mustache first. My future plans are indefinite. I'm thinking of writing a book, but I'm having trouble getting a typewriter from General MacArthur. . . I've even thought of staying on in town here. . . but Bess wants me to get into something with a future. . . I must say it's pretty dull here in Washington these days. I'd like to play a little poker. . . but where can you find three other Democrats now? . . . There's a rumor going round that you have an important job for me in your Cabinet. Do you really think we need an ambassador to Abyssinia? . . . Signed, Anxious

One of Hope's really difficult decisions in 1952 was whether or not to lampoon one of the most controversial and volatile, if not the most odious, subjects of the still-young decade—Senator Joseph McCarthy and his hunt for American Communists.

Mort Lachman says that Hope's hesitancy about ridiculing McCarthy and the "red scare" was founded on the fear of misreading public sentiment. Yet many in the Hollywood community were pro-McCarthy—Ronald Reagan, for example. Still, a full 18 months before the senator was finally and fully discredited, Hope decided it was a joking topic. On his heavily watched December 1952 telecast, the comedian told his Christmas show audience that he'd had a letter from Santa Claus:

Dear Robert. . . Thank you for your nice letter. . . and the beautiful new brown suit you sent me. . . but tell Senator McCarthy I'm going to wear my old red one anyway. . . I had it first. . .

In May 1953, referring to a golf game in Washington with Eisenhower and some of his cabinet, Hope cracked:

I had to be cleared by the FBI. . . the Secret Service. . . the Army and the Navy. . . and *they* all had to be cleared by Senator McCarthy. . .

Hope began receiving hate mail from upset Americans who branded him a Communist. This shook him but he continued using jokes involving the color red throughout 1953. By early 1954 he was using jokes that suggested the senator's creeping paranoia:

Senator McCarthy was out here for a visit, but he rushed back to the nation's capital. He's been gone almost a week and he doesn't even trust the Republicans with Washington that long. . . He almost missed speaking here. . . He got off the train and spent two days at Union Station investigating red caps. . .

When the Senate investigation hearings began, Hope's humor reached its sharpest edge:

Senator McCarthy is on a new type of television show. It's sort of a soap opera where everyone comes out tattle-tale gray. . . but I have it on good authority that McCarthy is going to disclose the names of two million Communists. . . He's just got his hands on the Moscow telephone directory. . . Even President Eisenhower is careful what he says on the air these days because McCarthy may demand equal time in the White House. . .

Those words hardly constitute a stinging denouncement, but considering Hope's 15-year avoidance of such controversial material, it was significant. Hope knew he was solidly in step with Eisenhower's contempt for McCarthy, and that even Republican congressmen were ready to smash the Wisconsin lawmaker. Still, for once Hope found himself ahead of public sentiment. It would take months and a bizarre display of the senator's arrogance and recklessness through protracted televised hearings to convince the broad electorate of McCarthy's demagoguery.

Hope's reaction to McCarthy only strengthened both his joking relationship and his growing personal closeness with Ike. Of all the Presidents Hope joked with or about, from Roosevelt to Clinton, some of whom he joined on the golf course or chatted with in the Oval Office or even on his bedside telephone, only one—Eisenhower—was to him a true hero, and it was nice that Ike liked him, too.

Even when Ike was campaigning for the presidency as a politician and peacemaker and wearing civilian clothes—and after his election—Hope saw Eisenhower's military prowess as his most captivating aspect:

This election has created a new slogan. It's now "Join the Army and see the White House". . . Now that he's President, Ike is Commander-in-Chief of all the armed forces. The poor guy—he just can't get his discharge papers. . . Having a general for President is going to be something. . . I can't wait until he puts Congress on KP. . .

But it was ultimately the golf course that cemented their closeness. It began in April 1953 when Hope reacted to media coverage of the President's golfing jaunt to Augusta, Georgia. The comedian displayed unrestrained enthusiasm with his television audience:

Did you see him arrive in Georgia with his golf shoes under his arm? I think he's working too hard. . . I always wear mine on my feet. . . But no matter what jokes we make about our President's golf, we feel as the rest of the people in this country do. . . and this is what I mean:

(Sings)
You're free to go where you go,
Do what you do,

Just follow through,
And we'll be happy.
As long as you've got that drive,
We'll all survive,
Just follow through,
And we'll be happy.

Hope appears to have assumed the role of presidential apologist and new golf partner. Within a week of that telecast, he received a phone call from his old pal Stuart Symington, now a senator from Missouri and a staunch Democrat, inviting him to play a round at the Burning Tree Country Club near Washington. Besides Symington, the foursome would include General Omar Bradley and the President. Hope recalls: "Ike and I were partners, and on the first tee, I asked him how he wanted to bet on the round. Ike said with an infectious smile that he'd just loaned Bolivia two million but he'd go a dollar. And he won. But the next day we played again and we weren't partners. I beat Ike for four dollars. I'll never forget the sour look on his face when he paid off. 'Why didn't you play this well yesterday?' and he wasn't laughing, either."

The following night was the White House Correspondents' Association annual roast and emcee Hope took full advantage:

I knew the President when he was still a general and really had power. . . I played golf with him yesterday. . . It's hard to beat a guy who rattles his medals while you're putting. . . Ike uses a short Democrat for a tee. . . He was hitting the ball much farther than I. . . he had Senator McCarthy's picture painted on the ball. . .

Not surprisingly, Hope did not deal directly with the subject of Eisenhower's serious heart attack of 1955, but during Ike's recovery in the first term and well into the second, the comedian excused the President's frequent absences from the White House by ribbing his artistic side:

Of course he paints a lot now instead of playing golf. It's fewer strokes. . . As a painter he's way ahead of his time. . . We won't have apples that shape for a hundred years, at least. . .

Besides his ridicule of McCarthyism, the only other substantive issue in the Eisenhower administration that Hope joked about was the growing criticism that America was lagging behind the Soviets in the missile race. Hope said:

Ike visited Cape Canaveral the other day. He felt right at home there with those big divots. . . One rocket's been in Florida so long, it has a tan. . .

Hope's affectionate good-bye to Ike when he stepped down as chief executive provided a succinct summation of the comedian's benign joking relationship with a President and a friend:

> You remember Ike. . . He was the pro in the White House. . . He'll have a lot of time to play golf. . . The unemployment office doesn't have many jobs in his category. . . but I hope he enjoys himself. . .

Hope remained loyal to Ike to the end of the President's life. He raised millions of dollars to build the Eisenhower Medical Center in Palm Springs, many thousands more for the building of Eisenhower College in Seneca Falls, NY, and more untold thousands for the Eisenhower Wing of the American Hospital in Paris. Toward the end of Ike's life, when he was at Walter Reed Hospital in Washington, Hope dropped by with a few golf jokes. Later, while he was talking with Mamie in the hallway outside the President's room, she said, "Maybe you'd better say good-bye to him now." Hope looked at her and then went back into the room, where he shared one final golf story with Ike.

32

Have Tux, Will Travel

"It's starting out to be a busy year for me. With my television show, my daytime and nighttime radio shows, pictures, personal appearances. . . I'm also working on a plan where when you close your eyes, I appear on the insides of your eyeballs. . . "

Probably the most persistent cliché in the media's coverage of Hope, particularly in the early fifties, was that of his unrelenting lifestyle. It was one thing for him to demonstrate during World War II that he could drive himself to exhaustion making GIs laugh, but in the ten years that followed, he stayed on the merry-go-round, loving every turn. But for him could there ever be enough brass rings?

Astonishment bordered on disbelief in 1952 when Jimmy Saphier completed negotiations with General Foods for an unprecedented $2 million radio deal that would deliver Hope to American homes—mostly their kitchens—each morning, five times a week beginning in November. General Foods—specifically, its brand Jell-O—also agreed to pick up the tab for his nighttime radio show beginning the following January. This omnipresence was a gamble for Hope's seventeenth consecutive season on NBC, but he pointed out that CBS was airing Arthur Godfrey on both radio and television almost around the clock and that hadn't affected *his* popularity.

This experiment was, as several tagged it, "Hope for the housewives." It amounted to 15 minutes of comedy patter, bits of music, casual chat with guest stars, and ad-libs with the studio audience at 11:45 in the late morning, when lunch was being prepared. On his very first broadcast, November 10, Hope's voice was heard for about 10 seconds because the remainder of the show was devoted to taped messages of insult and sarcastic good wishes from cronies like Benny and Crosby, who, as *Variety* put it, were "kidding on the square" about the whopping salary Hope commanded for his daily grind.

Next day, however, Hope ribbed himself and his new assignment:

This season I'll be broadcasting Monday through Friday. Mmmmmmm . . . Hope will be on the air five days a week. Isn't that wonderful? This new arrangement should make me very popular. When I did my show just once a week people used to say, "Wasn't Hope lousy last Tuesday?" Now they can say, "If you think he was lousy on Tuesday you should have heard him on Wednesday. I hear he was almost as bad Wednesday as he was on Friday when I turned him on because he made me sick Thursday."

The critical consensus was that the highlight of his show was the unscripted exchanges with his studio audience. It was never questioned that Hope's absolute forte as an entertainer was his live stage presence and his rapport with an audience. "Most people asked how old I was and stuff like that, which is fun because I have stock lines for a lot of it," Hope said. But one day this guy got up and waved his hand and said, 'Which way does a pig's tail turn, clockwise or counterclockwise?' It was such a wild question that the audience laughed like hell, and when they stopped I said, 'We'll find out when you leave.' The theater rocked, it just rocked. It was so good that after that I put a plant in the audience for some of those shows just to hear that laugh again."

Although the new Hope format didn't exactly steal the market, his A. C. Nielson rating of between 3 million and 4 million listeners a day was considered an achievement. General Foods felt easier about their big investment, which also included a new edition of the comedian's radio program.

After 16 years of being heard on Tuesday—it used to be called "Bob Hope night"—the new show would be aired on Wednesday. Sponsored by Jell-O, it was produced by Jack Hope and announced by Bill Goodwin, with music by Les Brown's band and with comedy written by the likes of Larry Marks and Norm Sullivan. On the kick-off show Hope's guest was someone who had been a supreme Jell-O salesman for many years:

(*Sound of door opening*)
BENNY: Hello, Bob!

HOPE: JACK BENNY!

(*Applause, applause, applause!*)

HOPE: Gee, this is great, Jack!

BENNY: Don't mention it, Bob. I figure the least a person can do to honor an old friend is to drop in and pay his respects.

HOPE: I'm still warm, Jack. Feel. . . (*Extends wrist*). . . You sound like the advance man for Forest Lawn. . .

BENNY: I'm sorry, Bob. . . I didn't mean it the way it sounded.

HOPE: Forget it. I really appreciate your coming over here, as busy as you are with radio. . . television. . . *counting*. . .

BENNY: (*Ad-libbing*) I'm a guest here and haven't had a joke yet. (*Laughter*). . . Oh, it's nothing.

HOPE: You can kid about it if you like but this is a very generous thing you're doing, Jack. . . dropping in to wish me luck on my opening show.

BENNY: Bob. . . (*long Benny pause*). . . I'm not here *just* to wish you luck. There's a slight misunderstanding here.

HOPE: Misunderstanding?

BENNY: Yes. . . you see, I'm not here entirely on my own. . . Mr. Cleaves, the head of the Jell-O Company, sent me over here to supervise your opening show.

HOPE: (*Indignant*) You? Supervise *my opening show?*

BENNY: Now, Bob, don't get all worked up! Look at it this way. I've had a long and very pleasant relationship with the Jell-O Company and you've just joined up. In a manner of speaking I was here before you.

HOPE: You were here before *anybody!*

And so it went. Right down to the closing tribute with which Hope always closed his nighttime radio or television program. This particular tribute should be noted because it sounds a very dominant and very sincere theme in the comedian's worldview:

Ladies and gentlemen, the noisemakers and paper hats have been put away, and 1953 is getting down to the business of being a New Year. . . and this promises to be a big one. . . a year in which the attainment of peace and security will be everybody's job. . . the men at the top. . . the kids at Korea. . . and we at home. The best way to start this job is with optimism and faith, faith in the things that have made us strong and free. Always remember, defeatism only leads one way, down. So let's start 1953 with the firm belief that things can be better if we work making them that way. So from all of us to all of you everywhere. . . the best of everything in 1953.

If you were nimble enough to keep up with Hope as he made his daily rounds you would be sure to hear him say at least once one or the other of these phrases,

"That sounds like a defeatist attitude to me" or "What's the matter with you? That's a negative thought!"

To a nation that had just elected Eisenhower, Hope's show-closing tribute could hardly fail to be moving. On January 14, 1953, *Variety* had a terse but accepting response to his opening show: "After many years of bigtime radio, it's virtually impossible to associate Bob Hope with any other format . . . the same fast-gagging, informal and always likeable comic."

Curious that *Variety* and other show business sages were slow to catch on to America's increasing infatuation with television as the 1952–53 season rolled on. A death rattle could be heard in the comedy and variety programming of nighttime radio that season. Only four of the major programs—Hope, Crosby, Benny, and Bergen—would survive. Sponsors were simply not interested in reaching so few listeners.

So it is significant that at a time when entertainment tastes were changing, Hope still enjoyed success in all media. Happily still holding a radio following, he had been particularly busy at Paramount during that year. He made *Off Limits*, a film that mixed military policemen and prizefighters in which he costarred with Mickey Rooney and Marilyn Maxwell. Then came another wacky excursion with Crosby and Lamour, their first in five years and their first in Technicolor, *The Road to Bali*. Finally there was a frothy thing called *Here Come the Girls*, probably the closest Hope ever came to being in a typical Hollywood film musical, with Rosemary Clooney, Arlene Dahl, and Tony Martin.

NBC couldn't have been happier about the size of Hope's viewing audience for his monthly *Colgate Comedy Hour*. General Foods was pleased enough with Hope's sales pitch to sign him to another exclusive television contract for the next three years. Then of course there were also the personal-appearance shows that his agent Mark Anthony was now booking for him at $5,000 to $10,000 a night.

Then, too, he found time to be president of the American Guild of Variety Artists and honorary chairman of nationwide fund-raising for the Cerebral Palsy Fund and of the Damon Runyon Cancer Fund and the Boy Scouts. His tolerance for work was incredible, suggesting an extraordinary range of interest and perhaps the fear of having an empty moment in his life. His marvelously efficient secretary, Marjorie Hughes, unmarried and a workaholic, almost totally devoted to serving and protecting her celebrity boss, complained only that his correspondence piled up on his desk and her completed letters went unsigned. She had to invent strategies like meeting him at two in the morning to finish a set of letters or to reset the order of a monologue.

Mildred MacArthur noted that Dolores very often seemed like a single parent and wished for the sake of the family and the marriage that Bob would spend more time with his wife and his children. But she also believed that Dolores had successfully weathered the Maxwell situation. When the Hope-Maxwell relationship was at its hottest, Marilyn was married to Andy McIntyre, a Beverly Hills restaurant owner. In 1951, when she believed for a time that she might have a chance of getting Bob away from Dolores, she divorced McIntyre. She later admitted how mistaken she was and understood too clearly the characteristics and level of Bob's infatuation with her. She saw the pattern of his gypsy life, his need for variety, and more important, she came to understand what perhaps Hope did not—the depth of his family ties.

And Marilyn knew herself. She also was addicted to variety and adventure. She had admitted to many affairs, one in particular with Frank Sinatra while he was married to Nancy, which continued until she met Hope in 1950. Later she confessed that she was seeing both men at the same time. Marilyn was quoted as saying she and Hope agreed to end their affair, and not a small part of their decision had to do with the nature of Hope's celebrity, which in 1953 had reached a pinnacle.

The Friars Club testimonial dinner for Hope on February 27, 1953, deserves special attention, not only because the major standup comedians of America were honoring one of their own—they had done that before twice on a large scale, when they applauded Joe E. Lewis in 1951 and honored Jack Benny in 1952.

This occasion deserved special attention because of the distinctly broader scope as well as the caliber of the roasters and toasters who sat at the head table and the fact that it was being broadcast by NBC. When the Friars saluted Lewis and Benny, all the big comedians showed up—George Jessel, Milton Berle, George Burns, Eddie Cantor, Fred Allen. For Hope there was Allen, Berle, and Jessel plus an eclectic group that included newspaper editor Louis Seltzer of *The Cleveland Press,* Senator Stuart Symington, and two city mayors, Cleveland's Tom Burke and New York's Vincent Impelliteri. There was also America's eldest statesman, Bernard Baruch, colorful former Vice President Alben Barkley, and Hope's military hero and pal, Rosy O'Donnell. There were also four important entertainment power brokers, movie czar Eric Johnston, RCA chief Frank Folsom, NBC's top man, Frank White, and the octogenarian chair of Paramount, Adolph Zukor.

Hope had agreed to the testimonial, providing that it could also be a fundraiser for a few of his personal charities, the USO, the Cerebral Palsy Fund, the Boy Scouts, and of course the Friars Relief Fund. He wanted a minimum of award-giving, and finally consented to receiving one Boy Scout statuette from the 12 possibilities offered. The other 11 awards were later mailed to his office, where they joined a disordered array of certificates, plaques, medals, statuettes, and memorabilia on walls and other surfaces around the room.

Fifteen hundred people were invited to see and hear Hope roasted—people like the New York celebrity restaurateur Toots Shor, columnist and TV show host Ed Sullivan, sportswriter Bob Considine, and now retired theater owner Bob O'Donnell.

Dinner chairman Jesse Block referred to Hope as "your average American who makes three million a year." Berle called him "America's second greatest comedian." The elderly Baruch, who had gotten up from his sickbed to attend the banquet, said, "May the Lord take a liking to you but not too soon," and then was escorted back to bed. And there were the expected accolades describing what Hope had meant to the GIs and to show business in general—not to overlook the money he had made for Paramount Pictures, the National Broadcasting Company, and, as several pointed out, the U.S. Treasury.

After a shiny-faced Boy Scout came up from the audience with the statuette, Hope asked Dolores to stand. She took a rather short bow and Hope said, "Is that all you're going to show of that fashion investment?" After the laugh, he added, "I suppose this is the first time Dolores really knows what I do for a living. She probably thought I was a test pilot for United Airlines." Next, the comedian asked his brothers Ivor, Fred, and George to stand and then he even introduced and thanked his press agent, Mack Millar. Hope sorely missed two of his favorite Friars that night, Benny and Crosby. Jack had been rushed to Cedars of Lebanon Hospital in L.A. suffering with an abdominal pain that turned out, happily, not to be serious. His staff sent a telegram that simply said, I LOVE YOU. Of Crosby's absence Hope said, "You know Dad goes to bed around six these days." However, Bing's attitude was clear on such matters: "I never go to those things."

It was a good night for charity. The roast netted $20,000, and Friars historian Joey Adams said, "Hope thanked everyone in the room except the men's room attendant," and seemed genuinely moved by the expressions of love that poured out to him from the four corners of the room." Before he sat down Hope said, "This could happen to a guy like me only in show business. This *has to be* one of my finer moments."

Following the roast it was business as usual. He flew to Denver for his first board meeting as part owner of a high-powered radio station, KOA. He came home to do another *Colgate Comedy Hour*, went to Washington to play golf with President Eisenhower, judged a dance contest with the Duke and Duchess of Windsor at the Greenbriar Hotel in White Sulphur Springs, West Virginia, went back to New York to emcee the Damon Runyon Cancer Fund benefit, back again to Los Angeles to do the annual Police Show, then to Chicago for a Cerebral Palsy Fund telethon, played in a charity golf match, did another *Colgate Comedy Hour* (this one in New York), and finally flew back home on May 30 to celebrate his fiftieth birthday a day late. Whew!

Shortly afterward, Hope checked into Paramount to begin his forty-ninth film since 1933, when he stepped before the cameras at the old Warner Bros. studios in Brooklyn. This latest would be called *Casanova's Big Night*, and would be his thirty-sixth starring role in Hollywood. A costume farce reminiscent of *Monsieur Beaucaire*, it also starred Joan Fontaine and Basil Rathbone, under the skillful direction of Norman McLeod.

Making *Casanova* anchored Hope in one spot long enough for him finally to spend some hours with freelance writer William Thornton Martin, professionally known as Pete Martin. Martin was a prolific author who had just collaborated with Crosby on a lighthearted autobiography titled *Call Me Lucky*. Hope decided that he needed an autobiography, too. The deal he cut with Simon & Schuster called for a prepublication series of episodes from Hope's life to run in the *Saturday Evening Post* for nine weeks under the title *This Is on Me.*

When the hardcover version of this same material appeared later in 1954, the episodes were rearranged and there were some additional chapters. The new title was *Have Tux, Will Travel: Bob Hope's Own Story, as told to Pete Martin.* Hope announced that any profits derived from sales of the book would be channeled into the Bob and Dolores Hope Foundation, created to handle the hundreds of requests his office received for handouts, and into the Cerebral Palsy Fund.

From Phillipe Halsman's rather prosaic photograph of Hope on the dust jacket to the index at the rear of the book listing names, places, events, and dates to suggest accuracy, the narrative is "This is how I got to be where I am today." And it is never very serious. In fact, it begins with a disclaimer called "Warning!" which makes patently clear that "that breezy Hope—that Hope you see on your screen or TV set—is me."

He explains that the narrative will not attempt to probe his inner self and admits he gets peeved and sometimes disillusioned with people he has liked and trusted. And he insists that in spite of the business he is in, he is "normal emotionally and mentally."

The book is not an extended monologue and in writing the "autobiography," Martin does make an effort to illuminate the Hope personality in and out of the spotlight, but the private man always seems to be pretty public. Up until the 1940s, Martin follows Hope chronologically. From the early 1940s to the early 1950s, the book deals in themes like GI entertaining, near-miss accidents, golf, his attitudes about comedy and comic performers, and his relationship with his family and his coworkers, all of which has a feeling that it was lightly sprinkled with powdered sugar. Yet running under and through the episodes is the unmistakable drive that has brought him to this success level.

Hope's boyhood is presented in a series of idealized tableaux, and the comedian's deeper relationships are not shared with the reader at all. Hope does not emerge as an unfeeling person but rather as one who has difficulty expressing emotion.

This superficial kind of autobiography was very much in vogue in the fifties. *Saturday Evening Post* readers expected a certain candor, but the chief requirement for a success story in that publication—or in *Readers Digest*, for that matter—was an uplifting message. Hope fitted the prescription admirably. His only revelation of any "wandering eye" was the terse phrase "I'm no angel" followed by "I've known very few angels. My mother and Dolores are two."

However, there were events in Hope's life that could have helped to flesh out parts of the Hope personality. Indeed, *Have Tux* is more noteworthy for what it leaves out than what it includes. But it is not surprising that Hope omitted the widely publicized 1943 court battle involving him, his brother Jim, and the woman Jim lived with, Marie Mali (before he met and married Wyn), who insisted she be known as Jim's wife. This was a chunk of the comedian's life that challenged both his cherished family loyalty and his generosity. In early 1940, when Hope was tasting his first big success in radio and films and needed more office help, Jim asked Bob to hire his girlfriend, Marie, on a part-time basis to assist Hope's then secretary, Annabelle Pickett. Marie already had a full-time job as a secretary with Texaco, but she was impressed with her "brother-in-law's success" and wanted to be part of the excitement.

Marie assisted in the cataloging and indexing of Hope's 60,000 jokes, answered photo requests, and addressed some of the 10,000 Christmas cards that went out of the Hope office every December. Her salary was about $50 a month. She only worked a few hours each evening and, at going clerical rates, was taking home about $12.50 a week. But when she and Jim found out just how much Bob was making, she felt grossly underpaid. Bob promised her a bonus. Meanwhile, Jim asked Bob for a loan, which Bob agreed to with expectation that it would be repaid.

In late 1942, against Jim's strenuous objection, Marie hired a lawyer and brought suit against Hope for two years' back pay at the rate of $50 a week, or roughly $5,000. Hope's lawyers, Struggles & Russell, filed a countersuit against Jim to recover the $1,400 loan. The case came to superior court in January 1943 on a slow news day and suddenly it was a big local as well as national story.

Marie told the court that when she tried to discuss money with Bob, "he told me to sit tight—that I'd get a big hunk of bonus. But the bonus wasn't forthcoming." Her attorney told the court that people doing similar jobs in Hollywood were paid $150 and $120 a week (for full-time work).

Hope countered through his attorneys that he "definitely did not promise her a bonus," and furthermore he objected to letters Marie had written criticizing his secretary, which "caused an uprising in my organization."

Jim and Marie were crushed when the jury failed to agree on a verdict and not surprisingly Judge Jess Stephens threw the case out of court. Through the long and raucous legal wrangle, Jack Hope, representing Bob, and Jim Hope faced each other in court daily and never spoke. Jack was saddened that such an unnecessary and unpleasant matter—and such a media event—caused the first serious rift between the Hope brothers. And it does certainly shed more light on the cold shoulder that Jim and his new wife, Wyn, received in June 1946 when both brothers were appearing on stages in the same city, Spokane, Washington, and Bob refused to acknowledge his brother's presence.

That messy business had a positive side, however. It was during this legal fracas that Marjorie Hughes arrived, fresh out of Sawyer's Business School in Los Angeles, and was hired by Annabelle Pickett. Later Marjorie said, "I found out why I was hired—there was no star-struck faltering in my voice, no celestial fire in my eyes." In time Hughes's orderly mind, her intense loyalty, and her discretion won Hope's respect and won her the job as his private secretary for 31 years.

Another event that might have added zest to Bob's autobiography was the day the police raided his home. In was spring 1946 and Hope had just finished four days of preparation for his role as producer-director-emcee of the annual Los Angeles Policeman's Benefit Show at Shrine Auditorium. That show, on a Saturday night, was a big success and the next day, Hope was rehearsing and doing the Sunday run-through preview of his Pepsodent show at the El Capitan in Hollywood.

At home, Dolores was hosting a huge open-air Roman Catholic benefit. She was extremely devout in her religious life, attending Mass daily at nearby St. Charles Borromeo, where the two children attended school. Those close to her felt that the church helped fill the void caused by Bob's frequent and often long absences, especially in wartime and afterward as well. On this occasion she had thrown open their six-acre side lawn for an old-fashioned country fair and bazaar to raise money for an order of Carmelite nuns. Perhaps it was out of naiveté, and perhaps not, that so many of the attractions at this outdoor party were games of chance, some dice games, some wheels of fortune, some raffles for baked hams and home-baked pies and cakes.

About an hour after the crowds had entered the Hope grounds, several North Hollywood police cars roared up and officers swarmed through the fair. "It's a raid," gasped Dolores, and a detective spoke into a bullhorn, "We have a complaint that there is gambling in progress here. We're going to have to ask you to leave."

The police broke up the games and closed down the party and Monday morning newspapers carried bold headlines about the gambling raid at the Hope residence. Of course Dolores was distraught, but Bob took it calmly and decided not to make a fuss, despite his associates', and his wife's, sputtering about the ungratefulness of the men in blue for whom he had been raising funds. The next spring Hope emceed the Policemen's Benefit Show just as he had for the previous 6 years and as he would continue to do for 20 more.

Although Hope was eager to talk in *Have Tux* about bad-taste gags and jokes that misfired, he failed to mention a $100,000 libel and slander suit brought against him in 1950 by the Forest Hotel on Forty-ninth Street in New York. While Hope was playing the Paramount he had cracked, "I got into town today and the mayor gave me the keys to the city, and I checked into the Forest Hotel, where they gave me a cell—the maids change the rats every day." The hotel management brought slander charges for the joke itself and libel charges because it was scripted, which would indicate premeditation.

Martin Gang, who by then had become Hope's attorney and has since remained his legal adviser, filed an affidavit denying the comedian used a script for personal appearances, and said, "Any reference to the hotel was without malice." The words of that joke, according to the lawyer's statement, "in the light of the circumstances surrounding their utterance, could not have been understood by any reasonable person to have been uttered other than in jest." There was, subsequently, a quiet settlement of court costs.

Another lawsuit Hope omitted from the autobiography was the one he instituted against Time Incorporated in late 1950, charging that in the November 6 issue of *Life*, his good name had been maligned by the critic John Crosby. In a piece titled "Seven Deadly Sins of the Air," Crosby wrote, "Writers got $2,000 a week in Hollywood for copying down Fred Allen's jokes and putting them on Bob Hope's program." Hope asked the court for damages in the amount of $2,010,000, claiming the article implied he was guilty of plagiarism, which exposed him to hatred and ridicule by the public and tended to discredit his standing in the entertainment business.

But in May 1951, Hope requested the suit be dropped, because he was satisfied, after private discussions, that the "offending paragraph had been left in the story inadvertently and there was no intention to harm him." *Life*'s publisher, Andrew Heiskell, went public to soften the media coverage, saying his magazine "had been on most friendly terms with Hope for many years and wished to continue."

The year *Have Tux* appeared, 1954, was a benchmark for Hope. A quarter of a century earlier he had been a hungry comedian in a Chicago vaudeville house, leering and gagging his way toward the top. Now he had gotten there, and could not know, of course, that there lay ahead for him another 40 years of his career or just how celebrated he was yet to become.

He was undoubtedly beloved by a large segment of the American public through the force of his personality and his jokes and because of his screen image, which cast him as the perennial juvenile—as Leo Rosten said, "The perfect symbol of the man Fate is determined to make a jerk." Rosten also describes Hope's "take-off of the adult wolf with adolescent impulses." He calls the type "a tie-fumbler and a neck-stretcher who ogles the dames and hints at midnight seductions, but you know he'll end up with candied cashew nuts and a yuke. He is Penrod playing Don Juan. The minute a babe sails into view, he breaks into a leer, but he breaks into a sweat if a girl so much as flutters her lashes. His leer, indeed, shows the triumph of innocence over intention, his type gets seasick in a boudoir."

This powerful image of Hope's screen persona is what made possible a fairly smooth ride through the publicity surrounding *Confidential* magazine's account of his alleged affair with one of Hollywood's more sexually active and publicity seeking starlets, Barbara Payton. The story was written by Horton Streete on the basis of information apparently supplied by the actress and some of her friends and presumably verified by *Confidential*'s attorneys.

The relationship was described as beginning in March 1949 in Dallas, where Hope was playing in a charity tournament. Streete wrote that the millionaire oilman Bob Neal had introduced them at a party in his hotel suite. He quotes Payton as saying, "We hadn't known each other six hours before we knew each other as well as a boy and girl can." The story never became more explicit, but continued to characterize a frantic, catch-as-catch-can affair carried out by means of meetings in New York, Washington, and other cities.

Among Payton's revelations were these: that Hope was no "Casanova," that he was "one of the closest guys with a buck she ever knew," that he was vain and "seldom passed a mirror without taking a long look at his own ski-nose," and that he liked her cooking.

For Hope to admit to his fans in his autobiography that he was "no angel" was perhaps enough, since the comedian's sly way of referring to sex both on and off the screen implied much more than it actually said. Nor, for that matter, did he need to say that his "attractiveness to other women," as Dolores referred to her husband's playing around, was big news. Dolores did say, "Every woman's husband is attractive to some other woman. I have tried to do the only thing any woman can do—keep busy, try to remain interesting, and cling to my own conceits. When doubt has troubled me, I think, 'But why shouldn't he love me before anyone else?'"

33

Beyond the Iron Curtain

"It's very exciting to be here in Moscow with you Democrats . . . You must be or you wouldn't be here. . . I hope you'll be cooperative tonight. On my passport I wrote "comedian" and I'd hate to have the Russians think I lied. . . "

On March 19, 1953, an event occurred in Hollywood that many observers believed would never happen: the motion picture business finally recognized television. Motion Picture Academy of Arts and Sciences historian Robert Osborne explains: "Close to the time for the Oscar show to take form, several major film companies—Warner Bros., Columbia, Universal-International and Republic—refused to come up with their usual share of the expenses to underwrite the ceremony. Had NBC-RCA not made a $100,000 bid for radio and television rights at that moment, there would have been no Oscar ceremony that year."

And if there had been no ceremony, Bob Hope would not have emceed the Awards show for the seventh time, nor would a nationwide audience have had the opportunity to witness his third Academy honor (still not for acting), a statuette for "his contribution to the laughter of the world, his service to the motion picture industry, and his devotion to the American premise."

It was quite a night for the movie industry, being the twenty-fifth Oscar handout. Not a bad night for television, either, since it was the first time viewers were treated to such an overflowing cup of big-time film stars on their home screens. This was the year that DeMille's *The Greatest Show on Earth* won for best picture, and Hope can always say that he acted in an Oscar-winning movie because of his cameo appearance in that film (he was in the circus tent audience eating popcorn with Crosby).

Shirley Booth almost did a pratfall coming up on stage to accept her award for *Come Back, Little Sheba.* Gary Cooper drawled a shy "Thank you" for *High Noon,* and DeMille received his statuette from the hands of the legendary Mary Pickford.

Hope's monologue that night was fittingly pungent, rapping the running battle between the entrenched film colony and the newcomer, television:

> Everyone said that television and the movies would finally get together and it finally happened. Tonight, you're watching the wedding. The only thing you couldn't see was the shotgun. . . What a marriage! Now the question is which one wears the nightgown. . . Paramount doesn't mind my doing television shows. . . In fact, they insist on it. I think it's a pretty sneaky way to cripple a new medium. . .

Paramount executives were indeed arguing that television would destroy his movie audience. Big boss Barney Balaban warned Hope that *Casanova's Big Night* could lose a million dollars because theater owners were up in arms over what they viewed as unfair business practice. They were angry that Paramount, which controlled them, would not let them pick and choose which pictures to show. To retaliate—or just out of spite—they opted not to show films that Paramount figured to make big money on.

Although *Casanova* ended up earning more than $3 million at the box office, movie making was in a troubled metamorphosis. Studios tried lavish spectaculars, three-dimensionals, concentrated on fewer film starts of higher quality—anything and everything that might bring back the departing moviegoer.

Worried by all this as a coproducer and weary of the brickbats frequently tossed at his film acting, Hope was willing to try something novel, something more challenging.

Beyond the defensive gags he tossed off at Oscar time, he was desperately hungry to earn a bonafide Oscar. It was about now that two of his former radio gagmen, Mel Shavelson and Jack Rose, approached him with a concept for a dramatic film biography of Eddie Foy.

Foy was one of America's most beloved vaudevillians who just happened to be, as a number of other performers observed, a son-of-bitch offstage. He had married a beautiful Italian dancer and was an indifferent husband and irresponsible father to seven children. When Foy's wife died suddenly, he was left with the kids, and in desperation turned them into a successful vaudeville act. The script for *The Seven Little Foys* was strong, clearly one in which Hope's personal life experience in vaudeville would be essential and in which his accustomed dumb-fall-guy persona would be out of place.

"I like it," said Hope to the two writers.

"Then you're in trouble," said Shavelson.

"Why?" asked Hope, looking over his half-glasses.

"Because I want to direct it," responded Mel.

"That's no big deal. My last three pictures were so bad I can't sink any lower."

After taking a careful look, Hope Enterprises took 44 percent, leaving the rest to Shavelson, Rose, and Paramount.

"The biggest challenge about doing *Foys*," said Hope, "was that for the first time I had to play a real-life character and one that the public knew, and having to do some pretty heavy scenes. I wanted to get inside Eddie Foy as much as I could, so I read everything I could find, and even studied some old silent films he had made. Luckily, we had help from Brian and Charley Foy—and Eddie Jr. agreed to be technical adviser on the project."

Before Hope started filming in August 1954, he went into training like an athlete. To match Foy's consummate artistry as a hoofer, Hope hired one of Hollywood's best teachers, Nick Castle, to help him freshen his footwork. Shavelson and Rose approached Jimmy Cagney to play a cameo part in the film, recreating his Oscar-winning role as the entertainer George M. Cohan. And when Hope and Cagney join forces for a challenge dance during a Friars Club banquet sequence, their performances display a virtuosity that is generally considered one of the finer moments in film history.

Hope was truly thrilled that Cagney agreed to do the cameo, and touched by Cagney's rationale when he said, "I'll do it on one condition."

"What's that?" asked Jack Rose.

"That I don't get paid."

"But why?" asked Shavelson.

"Because when I was breaking in as an actor," said Cagney, "I could always get a square meal and a place to flop at the Foys'. This is my way of paying them back."

As a serious actor, Hope was fairly successful reaching Foy's darker side—his arrogance, his hostility, his self-indulgence, his unpleasant attitude about human relationships, and his consuming self-pity over the death of his beautiful wife, Madeleine. Hope said, "The toughest scene for me was when I had to plead for custody of my children who were taken from me for child labor law violation. It was a long dramatic speech, quite different for a guy accustomed to one-liners. But on the night before I did the scene, Barney Dean died. Maybe that's how I got through it."

The total effect was a credible film biography. There was added reality in Eddie Foy Jr.'s narration. To some extent the script, and more pointedly, Hope's portrayal, was criticized for lack of warmth, suggesting that "the humor lacked the endearing qualities needed to offset the cutting edge of Foy's calculating side."

When in the following year the *New York Daily News* critic awarded *Foys* four stars and reflected a general feeling that this was a benchmark for Hope, who, he said, "doesn't have to take any more insults from Bing Crosby about his acting.

Hope can now hold up his head with Hollywood's dramatic thespians as, for the first time in his career, Hope isn't playing Hope on the screen. He's acting and doing a commendable job."

And over in the enemy camp of television, Hope opened his fall season of specials still highlighting his unique position as *the* enduringly popular monologuist on the entertainment scene, which was telling—so many funnymen had turned to situation comedy for survival. Critic Will Jones of the *Minneapolis Tribune* seemed overjoyed that Hope on TV was playing himself. "It suddenly struck me that it's been a long time since I've heard a comedian do that." He went on to criticize other comedians for performing as "imps, pixies, buffoons, clowns, sad sacks" and all "acting like mad."

World-Telegram and Sun critic Harriet Van Horne gave Hope a mixed review: "Perhaps Hope is shrewd, rather than reactionary, to cling to these machine gun solos. He does them awfully well. . . Other comedians come equipped with wittier jokes and a more satiric outlook. But they don't get the unremitting laughs Hope gets."

The critics harping on his show's "sameness" miffed Hope. In fact, when he received an invitation to emcee a royal command performance in London, he had Saphier tell NBC he intended to cancel his scheduled November television special and instead film an "international revue" in Europe with stars like Maurice Chevalier, Orson Welles, and Edith Piaf, none of whom had yet appeared on American television.

When NBC officials demanded to know how Hope could rationalize leaving them with an unfilled 60 minutes, costing them $100,000, the comedian got on the phone. He argued it was important for both him and them that he create a "first" and film a show abroad because "TV comedy shows are full of the same old faces getting older."

NBC advised Saphier that Hope simply could not treat them this way, and Saphier reasoned back that his client was trying to make TV history on their network. Hope's final response was "Let them sue me if they want" and he flew to England on October 15, 1954. In London he rehearsed the benefit show and tried to assemble an interesting cast for his first international revue.

He flew to Paris and charmed Maurice Chevalier (who said he owed Hope one) into making his U.S. television debut, saw French ballerina Laine Dayde and knew she would be perfect, and cabled his pal Bea Lillie (who was on the Riviera with Noel Coward) for a return engagement. He heard the 182-voice Cologne Male Choir at a London concert and signed them on the spot. At his command performance he was intrigued by "two noticeable blondes," Moira Lister and Shirley Eaton. He hired the suave Reginald Gardiner as a topper (announcer) to mouth the General Foods commercials in a haughty British manner.

When the filming was over, Hope flew to Paris. One day he sat in the drawing room of his Hotel George V suite and chatted with Art Buchwald, who was then writing his "Europe's Lighter Side" column for the *International Herald Tribune*.

"What did you do about commercials?" asked Buchwald, knowing the British didn't need them to support their television

"We had originally hoped to use Reggie Gardiner," Hope said, "but ended up with a wonderful BBC newsman named McDonald Hobley—veddy distinguished voice—a guy who had never done anything like talking about Jell-O or Swansdown or Minute Rice. He said to our audience, 'Now, however amusing it may sound to you, don't laugh at the commercials. So while I mention names that you have never heard before—or are likely to hear again—*do* be serious, won't you?' He killed me."

"I hear they almost didn't let you into France."

"This is such a great country. They give you the choice of going to jail or becoming a citizen of Paris. I forgot my passport. I left it in London—and the French authorities threatened to lock me up. Next thing I knew they were kissing me on both cheeks and pinning a medal on me."

Martin Ragaway, one of three writers traveling with Hope, came into the room and Buchwald asked him if he had seen much of Europe on this trip. Ragaway replied, "He locked us in our hotel room in London for three days and kept the key. Finally, on the third day, he said, 'Gee, I've been very inconsiderate of you people. You boys probably haven't seen anything of London. No, don't go away.' Then he went downstairs and bought 40 picture postcards of London and sent them up to us."

Over the many years that Hope hired gag writers to supply his material, these jokesters always had plenty to say about his behavior away from home or his being very close with a dollar. Agent Jimmy Saphier said, "I can't vouch for the extra women in Bob's life because I hardly traveled with him, but as for the money, Bob always paid top dollar for his writers and they knew it. I don't know what's wrong with Hope wanting to get his money's worth. I know he always included them in whatever he was doing whenever he could."

Hope flew back to Los Angeles in time to watch the international show on his own TV set. He thought it could have been better, and a large number of television reviewers in America agreed. The show had, predictably, a huge audience. Actually it wasn't all that bad. Unfortunately, the NBC publicity office had fired off a barrage of hyperbole, with press releases that raved, "With the simple idea of producing the first truly global television show, Hope made history." And inevitably, someone was going to vomit verbally (and it happened to be someone from the *Washington Star*): "If this is history, [British historian] Arnold Toynbee has been ploughing a long furrow in the wrong field."

Hope's next movie, *That Certain Feeling*, which he made for Paramount in late 1955, fared much better with the critics. It was based on the Jean Kerr–Eleanor Brooke comedy success on Broadway, *King of Hearts*. Benefiting from a very literate script, nicely adapted by Panama and Frank, and superbly directed by Panama, Hope was able to deliver a first-rate performance as a neurotic cartoonist named Francis X. Dingman, who has trouble juggling his work and his wife, played by

Eva Marie Saint, who had just won a supporting-role Oscar for *On the Waterfront.* This is probably Hope's most sophisticated motion picture.

About this time, Hope dropped a couple of remarks to Hollywood columnist buddies about retirement and, of course, the item needed to be verified. A long-standing media friend, Associated Press reporter Bob Thomas, came to lunch at the house and asked, "Do you mean it?"

"I was down in Palm [Springs] playing golf with Charlie Yates," said Hope, with a frightened look, "when he died right next to me in the golf cart. He just lay back—and went. I was there with him for twenty minutes before they came for him. You know he was my first agent in New York. He was a close friend. It happened so fast."

"What were you thinking?" asked Thomas.

"It didn't really affect me for three days. Then the shock set in. I was terribly upset. I began to feel all sorts of pains and things wrong in my body. I thought I was dying. About this time NBC came to me with a new contract and I said nothing doing. I was going to retire."

"Are you serious?"

"Sure I was serious. I was terribly depressed. I went to see Tom Hearn and he gave me a complete physical. He chased me out of his office. In fact, he chased me down the street. He said I was too healthy. And you know my spirits changed."

"To what?"

"I signed a five-year deal with NBC to do eight shows a year. I finished the movie with Eva Marie Saint and now I plan to do two television shows in Europe because Louis Shurr tells me the deal is set to go to London to make a film with Katie Hepburn. Taking the whole family with me."

Thomas felt that he just might have been set up for a punch line, and went off to write the story just that way.

The picture in London with Katharine Hepburn, originally titled *Not for Money,* was a story scripted by the playwright Ben Hecht about a lady Soviet pilot who lands her plane in the American zone in postwar Germany and is handed over to an American major to democratize. Hepburn's original leading man was to have been Cary Grant. But when Grant proved unavailable, Hope's name was suggested (it was for Hope an allowed outside film deal with MGM), and although there were mixed feelings, especially from Hecht, the idea looked better after they screened *The Seven Little Foys.*

From the start things went badly between Hecht and Hope. It was all about the unfinished script. When Hope arrived at London's Dorchester Hotel, where he believed everyone was staying, he called Hecht to find that he was staying at the stuffier Connaught Hotel. "Ben, this script isn't finished," Hope said.

"I'm aware of that," said Hecht, "but it's coming along."

"Maybe I can help," offered Hope, meaning he would assign a couple of his writers to punch it up. The sound of this raised the hair on the back of Hecht's neck.

About 10 minutes later, Hecht and Hepburn and an assortment of production people arrived at Hope's suite, prepared to frame out the closing scenes.

Suddenly aware that he was expected to solve the film's ending, Hope said, "Wait a minute. It's not *that* large. I just had a couple of hokey thoughts about the script."

But at that point Hope's "hokey thoughts" were more than anyone else could offer and he *was*, after all, their partner, an entertainment superstar who had a considerable track record of successful movies. So as the days went along Hope's and his writers' ideas were reluctantly accepted in the interest of completing the project. Clearly Hecht and Hepburn were not pleased, nor, for that matter, was Hope. "But we managed to get through the picture," he said, "and I must say Katie was a gem. She played the Jewish mother on the set, fussing over everyone who happened to sneeze."

Hope's writers eventually took over the final doctoring of Hecht's script and renamed the film *The Iron Petticoat*. By now Hecht was fully enraged, and he took out a full-page Hollywood trade paper ad to tell the industry how he felt

My dear partner Bob Hope:

This is to notify you that I have removed my name as author from our mutilated venture, *The Iron Petticoat*.

Unfortunately, your other partner, Katharine Hepburn, can't shy out of the fractured picture with me.

Although her magnificent comic performance has been blow-torched out of the film, there is enough left of the Hepburn footage to identify her for her sharpshooters.

I am assured by my hopeful predators that *The Iron Petticoat* will go over big with people "who can't get enough of Bob Hope."

Let us hope that this swooning contingent is not confined to yourself and your euphoric agent, Louis Shurr.

Ben Hecht

Hope replied in kind, advising Hecht that the picture had been improved immeasurably following his departure. Of course this was not the case. The film project, even with its good moments, was a mistake, and it was retired after its initial release.

But what rose rather majestically from the ashes of this sorry venture was a kind of phoenix. Because Hope truly worshipped the thought that he could be recognized as the first entertainer to do or be something no one else had yet achieved, he was now consumed with the idea of filming a show inside the Soviet Union. It was a notion that germinated while he shot *The Iron Petticoat*. He knew it was a formidable challenge—but think of the publicity that would be generated.

First attempts at getting inside Russia were in the hands of Betty Box, producer of *The Iron Petticoat*, who had tried to clear on-site locations for filming. When those negotiations collapsed, Hope thought, *Why not try to stage the world premiere of the picture in Moscow? If not that, why not try to televise an NBC comedy special from Moscow?*

He was holding that last thought, but first he was committed to two back to back film projects. Shavelson and Rose had persuaded him to attempt a second straight dramatic part based on his Foy success. They showed him Gene Fowler's biography of New York's colorful Mayor Jimmy Walker. But the cost projection was sobering. To ensure accuracy and prevent any possible grounds for a lawsuit, Shavelson and Rose had to pay $50,000 for rights, negotiating with Walker's first wife, his sister and two adopted children, and his second wife, actress Betty Compton.

Attorneys worked many weeks before production could begin to reduce the potential for litigation over the movie's interpretation of Walker's personal and political escapades. Costarring with Hope in the film, titled *Beau James*, and adding immeasurably to the credibility of the biography were Alexis Smith as his first wife, Vera Miles as Betty Compton, Paul Douglas, and Darren McGavin. George Jessel, Jack Benny, and Sammy Cahn appeared in cameo roles.

Believable as Hope is in this picture, which holds up well even today, one feels that he could have gone further in clarifying the dualities in Walker's personality. Walker was both attractive and unsympathetic, witty but naïve, moral as well as corrupt. Naturally the lighter moments worked particularly well, but Hope is also superb in several dramatic scenes. His portrayal of Walker as a broken man, conning acquaintances for enough money to afford his own exile from the city he had ruled and loved, is one of the comedian's most effective moments on film.

Critics greeted *Beau James* graciously but without the depth of analysis many felt it deserved. Most critics have considered Hope's Jimmy Walker role to be another milestone in his long movie career for another reason: it was his only tragic role, and was his final attempt to tackle anything totally dramatic.

By contrast, his next film, *Paris Holiday*, was based on a Hope idea and also was produced by him, at a staggering cost. His male costar was the celebrated French comedian Fernandel and a major problem was that neither comedian could speak the other's language. Fernandel smiled a lot, particularly over the $120,000 he was paid and because he could sleep in his own bed at night. Two beautiful female costars, Anita Ekberg and Martha Hyer, added glamour but could not repair the weak plot with its spies and long chases.

Hope's jokes about the financial whipping he took are bittersweet: "*Paris Holiday* set a new record. Three men were killed on the picture—all of them auditors. We went a million dollars over budget, but it was all United Artists' fault. Handing me the money to make a movie is like asking Dean Martin to tend your bar." Hope's critics and his friends said, "Stick to acting."

In November 1957 Hope went to London to tape a television special and to sneak-preview *Paris Holiday*. While he was there the obsession for entertaining inside Russia manifested itself again. He went to the Soviet consulate at 5 Kensington Palace Gardens and applied for 16 visas for himself, his personal staff, writers, and technicians. He also telephoned the newest member of his public relations staff, Ursula Halloran, a recent graduate of Penn State with smoldering good looks, whom he found enormously sexy and very personable. She was to be his main New York contact person and he trusted her with the important job of going down to Washington, D.C., to convince Soviet embassy officials that he would like to be involved in a cultural exchange, premiering his new movie *Paris Holiday* for Moscow moviegoers.

Then he telephoned NBC's Moscow correspondent, Irving R. Levine, to ask him for advice and any possible help in facilitating his request. Weeks went by and one day he decided to try reaching Jock Whitney, U.S. ambassador to the Court of St. James, and asking him to help speed up the process. Luckily, Whitney was in fact going to a Whitehall cocktail party where he was almost certain to meet his Soviet counterpart, Jacob Malik, Russia's ambassador to Britain. Whitney called Hope back in Los Angeles and said that Malik inquired, "What does your Mr. Hope want to do—entertain our troops in Red Square?"

More weeks passed. Ursula Halloran wasn't making much progress in Washington, despite the goodwill Hope had accumulated with so many government people. Hope impatiently called Irving Levine again and asked why he couldn't simply book himself on an Aeroflot plane and fly into Moscow. Levine diplomatically explained why that was impossible.

Then quite unexpectedly, while home in California, Hope got a call from NBC's Washington office. It was Julian Goodman, the bureau's chief, informing him that there were six visas waiting for him at the Soviet embassy. Hope had applied for 16—now, who would go? He would need writers and intended to take Mort Lachman and his writing partner, Bill Larkin. He had to have a dependable cameraman, and he chose one of Britain's most outstanding lighting and cameramen, Bill Talbot. If he was to accomplish the cultural exchange part of the plan by premiering *Paris Holiday*, he needed someone from United Artists, and they chose Arthur Jacobs. He felt that he needed to reward Ursula Halloran for all her work, and besides, she was "a smart little cookie." That was the crew.

Hope received official State Department instruction on the behavior expected of him and his associates inside the Soviet Union. He was cautioned that their visas were limited to Moscow. He was told that the film he shot there would be developed there. Hope agreed, excited that his would be the first American television show produced entirely inside Russia. A week later, Hope and the reduced television crew, flew from New York to Moscow, with a print of *Paris Holiday* in the overhead rack.

Hope was greeted at the airport by Irving Levine, and standing nearby to cover this whirlwind seven-day trip were two reporters from *Look* magazine, an International News Service correspondent and a freelance Magnum photographer.

Hope also had been assigned an Intourist representative who served ably as interpreter, guide, and suspected KGB informant.

Hope was making this trip at a time when American-Soviet relations were surrounded in mystery, suspicion, and—as always—competition. Consequently in his public statements about this adventure, Hope shrewdly played to American taste by exaggerating the cloak-and-dagger aspects: "Whenever I'd enter a room, I'd pound on the wall and yell 'TESTING! TESTING! ONE! TWO! THREE! AM I COMING IN LOUD AND CLEAR?' And whenever we were discussing anything that in any way might be misinterpreted, one of us would look up the ventilator and holler, 'ONLY KIDDING, KRU!' We were actually half joking when we did this, but it was a joke only because there was a possibility that the Big Bear *was* listening."

Arthur Jacobs failed to pull off the hoped-for coup of premiering *Paris Holiday* in Moscow, and Hope registered both displeasure and disappointment. Jacobs did manage to get Hope on a worldwide radio conference circuit with Fernandel in Paris to plug the picture. Fernandel's grasp of English was defective, there was too much static on the line, and this was decidedly not the cultural exchange "first" that Hope had counted on. Having nothing more to contribute, Jacobs flew back to New York.

With guts, ingenuity, and daring, the further-reduced team of five toured Moscow with their watchful hosts, Hope, Lachman, and Larkin selecting sites and often loading film, Halloran printing cue cards and pressing wrinkled garments, Talbot lighting and shooting scenes at carefully approved locations, as well as sneaking forbidden still and motion pictures for later insertion into the TV show. All of them depended on blind luck to prevail.

At Red Square, Talbot shot Hope against the spiky Kremlin towers, walking toward Lenin's tomb with that perennial snakelike line of Soviet citizens in the background. Then he walked across the square to complete an assignment he had been given before he left home. He told Talbot with a grin, "Jack Benny asked me to bring back a fur hat with a part in it." He walked inside the GUM department store to look for a fur hat and thought he would check out some perfume for Dolores. Here he used Talbot as a one-man audience testing reaction to some Lachman and Larkin lines: "Don't let anyone tell you that Russians aren't passionate. At the perfume counter they were showing such sexy sounding scents as 'Kremlin' and 'Our Moscow.'" I don't know how they missed 'Moonlight on the Collective Farm' or 'Volga Boatman.' Ahhhh, here's 'Essence of Tractor.' This one not only smells good, it's wonderful for lubricating a fan belt. Instead of 'My Sin,' they've got 'Where Do I Go to Confess?'" People pointed at Hope, but only Talbot was laughing.

Hope also had help from Soviet cameramen in shooting the incomparable Moscow circus and an equally incomparable (for different reasons) fashion show at GUM. He was offered and decided to use what was described as exclusive footage of the violinist David Oistrakh, the ballerina Galina Ulanova, Russia's most beloved clown, Popov, and the very controversial (always a few steps ahead of house arrest) comedian Arkadi Raikin. Hope also bought footage of the Ukrainian State Dancers from the Ministry of Culture.

Ambassador Llewellyn Thompson's office remained in constant touch with Hope and discovered that the Soviets were stalling Hope over the arrangements for a public hall where the comedian could perform his personal appearance act for the English-speaking community and foreign diplomats. Thompson hastily interceded and offered Hope his private residence, Spasso House. In a matter of two days he had managed to build a camera platform for Talbot and the Russian crew, set up stage facilities in the large reception hall, and hand-deliver the invitations.

Just prior to filming the show, Hope went back to his hotel room and found his briefcase forced open and pages of his jokes spread out all over his bed. There was no effort to hide the perusal of his material, mostly gags he was using in his monologue or had considered using. Some of them had made him so nervous he had rejected them, like: "They have a national lottery here. It's called living."

For that very select audience at Spasso House, Hope did about an hour's worth of comedy, which included many jokes about Moscow and the Russians, regrets that his audience wouldn't have the first look at *Paris Holiday*, and numerous topical references that would please his American TV audience. These gags ended up in the TV monologue:

> The State Department was glad to have me come here. I'm Cooperative. . . I'm personable. . . I'm charming. . . expendable. But it's a thrill to be in Russia. . . Oh, I know I'm in Russia. How about that vodka?. . . Now I know how they got their Sputnik up first. . . and I'm surprised the whole country isn't up there with it. . . It's pretty nervous staying in a country where the Government owns everything. If you steal a towel, it's a federal rap. I've had to unpack three times. . . But it's amazing the way people can get the wrong impression. One Russian official showed me a picture of the starving people in America. People without shoes and nothing to eat, absolutely desperate. And I couldn't argue with him. . . it was a picture of the bus station at Las Vegas. . .

Because of Russian help in photographing the monologue, the film was processed in a Soviet film laboratory, and the jokes were studied carefully. First they were examined by the Cinema Section of the Ministry of Culture, and then they were checked and double-checked by Alexander Davydov, head of Soviet Film Export and his deputies. At a cocktail party given by the Ministry of Culture on Hope's final evening in Moscow, Davydov and two of his deputies led Hope into a small antechamber.

"Mr. Hope, the monologue which we have in our lab is magnificent," said Davydov, "but there are just a few jokes which might better be left out."

"Which ones?" Hope asked nicely.

Davydov recited from prepared notes: "'The Russians are overjoyed with their Sputnik. It's kind of weird being in a country where every 92 minutes there's a national holiday. Anyone without a stiff neck is a traitor. It's a big topic of conversation everyplace but the dog show.' Traitor is a very serious charge in Russia," he said.

"We are not implying Russians are traitors," argued Hope. "What we are trying to do is state in a humorous way how proud the people are of their Sputnik. Exaggeration is one of the basic forms of comedy."

Davydov thought about this and then said, "Perhaps you could eliminate all reference to the Sputnik. It's not really a subject for comedy."

"We are anxious to cooperate but we must be reasonable," Hope said. "Satellites and missiles are a big topic in Russia just as they are in America. We both lose if we treat you any differently than any other country in the world. Listen, here are the jokes I told on my last television show: 'I guess you heard the big news from Cape Canaveral. Our government has launched another submarine. . . Actually the test firing of missiles is going very well. They hit the target every time. As a matter of fact, there's hardly anything left of Bermuda'"

The three Russians laughed. Hope beamed, figuring he had won the round. Then Davydov said that he would submit a list of jokes that he would appreciate being cut out, and Hope stopped fighting and agreed to abide by his wishes. Next, Davydov, still smiling, presented Hope with a bill for $1,200 for the use of Russian technicians and lab fees. He said he would be pleased to release the film if Hope would assure payment.

After Hope's departure the next day, Lachman and Larkin collected the film and rushed it back to Hollywood for editing. It was broadcast as Hope's Easter Show on April 5, 1958, with Hope narrating a mostly humorous commentary. Though it was not one of Hope's most widely watched programs, Nielson released audience rating figures that showed 25 million people, or more than a third of all available viewers, watched his Moscow show. NBC scheduled an encore telecast after they learned that the program had won two of the TV industry's most prestigious honors, the Peabody and the Sylvania awards for 1958.

In the closing sequence of that program, Hope is seen walking through the rather gloomy snow-bound streets of Moscow, intercut with shots of people staring at the camera curiously, just doing Russian everyday things, while in a voice-over Hope adds a final tribute; it has the resonance of prophecy:

> For five days and nights, I have stared and walked and wondered. It's a strange city. I missed the street signs, the hubbub of traffic, the colorful clothing, the billboards, and the neon gleaming in the night. Yet there is much that is the

same: people trying to make a living, people trying to keep their families together. And kids, wonderful kids with great faces. It would be wonderful if someday
their kids and our kids could grow up in a world that spoke the same language
and respected the same things. Right now the world is busy building a bomb
for every letter in the alphabet. That cannot be the answer. But there must be
one. We must find some plan for peaceful coexistence, so that human beings
don't become obsolete.

34

Dropped on His Head

*"I put in a call for Marilyn (that's Hollywood talk for I had my agent
call her agent) and as it happened Marilyn really wanted to come, but
couldn't because of studio commitments (that's Hollywood talk for we'll
never know whether she wanted to or not)."*

Of all the sex goddesses and superstars who invaded Hollywood, there was only
one that Hope wanted for his radio and television shows and couldn't have—
Marilyn Monroe. The closest he came was Christmas 1954, when Air Force
Secretary Harold Talbott asked Hope to put together an entertainment package
for GIs stuck in the remote ice-bound terrain of Thule, Greenland, a so-called
hardship base. The cold war with the Soviets was at its hottest. Thule was both an
early-warning station and a Strategic Air Command base with severe morale problems. And, very important, Hope's closet military pal, Rosy O'Donnell, was in
command there.

Talbott pitched hard for Hope to bring Marilyn. Presumably she was the Air
Force secretary's personal choice. She was certainly the hands-down favorite of the
Thule GIs.

When Hope agreed to make the trip he exacted a promise from the Air Force
to give him, beyond the usual transportation, some technical assistance so he
could film the shows for a television special. (Although no one knew it then, this
would mark the beginning of almost 20 years of annual GI Christmas shows.)
Hope wanted Marilyn but he couldn't get her, despite the fact that she had once
told him she would go with him whenever he asked. Hope was positive she was
being overmanaged and that the request never got to her.

He was fortunate in signing a major film star, William Holden, who was bringing his beautiful wife, Brenda Marshall. But Hope still wanted a marquee sex
queen, and later said, "I had just about given up when, a few nights before we left
for Greenland, I emceed a Big Ten Conference football banquet, and among the
guests was a beauty contest winner, Miss UCLA. She was wearing a rather tight

sweater with team letters and the 'U' and the 'A' were outstanding. Although she was a virtual unknown at the time, this doll was strikingly beautiful. Obeying an impulse, I invited her to come along."

The "virtual unknown" was Anita Ekberg. Besides the Holdens, Hope also had invited pop singer Margaret Whiting, comic sidekick Jerry Colonna, dancer Patty Thomas, and in other acting roles, Peter Leeds, Robert Strauss, and Charlie Cooly. Columnist and actress Hedda Hopper was booked as a special attraction. The Les Brown Band was along, too, despite the fact that the 100-member Air Force Band had been booked for Thule even before Hope had agreed to go.

There were five or six thousand men stationed there. Two hundred of them had worked steadily around the clock for two days prior to Hope's arrival to erect a temporary stage in a huge hangar, laying cables, setting up lights and chairs, connecting microphones and loudspeakers. The Hope plane landed in subzero weather. Worse, because it was so close to the North Pole, there was an eerie darkness twenty-four hours a day at this time of the year. Hope's monologue fitted the formula for foxhole humor:

I'm very happy to be here in Thule. The temperature is 36 below. . . only we don't know below what. . . the thermometer went AWOL. . . The guys get pretty lonesome up here. When a wolf howls he starts a community sing. . . It's so lonely here one guy is going steady with his tattoo. . . and his friends keep asking him if she's got a sister. . . You're not even allowed to think about girls up here. At night a sergeant walks through the barracks and wakes up anyone with a smile on his face. . .

Hope's main comedy sketch for the troops was about GIs in Greenland who write back to the States for a mail-order bride. Anita Ekberg played the bride and when she entered in a fur coat the capacity audience of 3,000 men stood up and cheered and stomped and whistled. "She took off her coat," said Peter Leeds, who was appearing in the sketch, "and she stood there in a low-cut gown that showed cleavage that made Grand Canyon look trivial. It was bedlam."

Hope's second show and final filming of that 1954 Yule trip took place at Goose Bay, Labrador, on New Year's Eve. By this time the whole cast was well grooved into their lines and the tempo of the show was exactly right. At the show's end, the cast sang "Auld Lang Syne" and Hope hollered out, "Happy New Year and God bless you" and there followed madness—people laughing and crying, blowing horns and throwing confetti.

Nine days later a documentary of this tour was presented on the *Colgate Comedy Hour*, and that showing handed Hope his largest television viewing audience to date. It was one of the biggest audiences drawn by any commercial program up to that time—60 percent share of the sets in use were tuned to it.

The following Christmas Hope was in London finishing *The Iron Petticoat* and still the USO found him. They asked him to do some holiday entertaining for GIs still stationed in Britain, but the shooting schedule couldn't be bent sufficiently, particularly since the Hecht-Hepburn difficulties prevented completion of the movie. But since he was committed to filming one television special in London with a December 27 broadcast date he decided to do the show at an American base in Keflavik, Iceland.

During the auditions for talent in London, the good looks and unusual physical attributes of a tall, shapely blonde named Joan Rhodes struck Hope. A former fashion model, she was then making her living performing a strong-woman act in European music halls. She could snap eight-inch nails, rip telephone books, bend steel bars, and invite heavy men to come up from the audience and lift them up over her head. Hope decided she would be a treat for the GIs in Iceland.

Together they worked out a funny routine. Hope would be singing "Embraceable You" alone onstage when Joan would walk out seductively and without warning lift Hope up into her arms and cuddle him while he was still singing. The sight of this appealing woman lifting Hope as if she were King Kong got so many laughs at rehearsal that the comedian decided to take the comic routine one step further.

For TV cameras in Iceland, Hope suggested that she lift him up over her head. "When the big moment came," he painfully recalls, "she hoisted me up and I stood on her hands. There I was—high over Iceland—then she began to totter. I thought she was ad-libbing that totter. Well, she wasn't. I went over her head onto the floor and the floor was cement. The audience roared when I hit. They thought it was part of the act. The TV cameras filming the show were still going, and on me, and I yelled, 'Cut!'" Hope's nose was bleeding but otherwise he didn't seem to be badly hurt. He was slightly traumatized but he managed to finish the show.

In November 1956 Air Force Secretary Talbott again asked Hope to entertain for hardship-duty GIs, this time in Alaska, which resulted in a particularly delightful Christmas TV special with a huge viewing audience, which thrilled his new commercial sponsor, Chevrolet. Hope's costars on that six-day tour, of three Air Force bases and the Alaskan Command headquarters, were Ginger Rogers and Mickey Mantle.

Ginger was her usual vivacious, glamorous major-film-star self, but most of the attention on that trip was focused on the young centerfielder who had just been named "outstanding athlete of the year" by U.S. sportswriters. In addition to leading his league in home runs during 1955 and 1956 and also being voted "most valuable player" for those years, Mantle had become a national hero and, luckily, was a natural comedian. Hope's gag writers produced one of their cleverest sketches for Mantle and Hope, a satire on the modern Army draftee, played by Mantle, who arrives at boot camp and is met by a tough first sergeant, played by Hope.

A second sketch found Hope the unsuspecting victim of a prop bottle being smashed over his head by Ginger. The gag had worked perfectly in rehearsal, but when she zapped him with it at Ladd Field in Fairbanks the bottle was frozen— it had been left outside. The blow stunned Hope into momentary unconsciousness but he recovered quickly and went on. He cursed prop man Al Borden. This was the second time in two years that Hope had sustained a blow to the head but then no one seemed to be counting.

During the summer of 1957, when Hope was winding up *Paris Holiday* with Fernandel, he had to find a European audience who could understand English enough to appreciate his comedy for a Timex Watch Co. television special he was committed to. His writers suggested he find some GIs, and they settled on Nouasser Air Base, 20 miles outside Casablanca in Morocco, of all places. Three Air Force C–54s were supplied to pick up a troupe of 70 in California—entertainers, including the Les Brown Band and technicians—plus wardrobe, scenery, and all manner of equipment, for the flight to Paris, where they were making a rehearsal stop, before going on to Morocco. Hope invited a few media people, including Art Buchwald, to come along on this "road to Morocco." The Hollywood cast included Marie "The Body" MacDonald, the actress who had recently held the nation spellbound by a charge of having been "kidnapped" that later turned out to be bogus, dancer Ann Miller, singer Eddie Fisher, and Bing Crosby's eldest son, Gary.

Hope by now had considerable experience piecing together these shows on foreign soil, but Buchwald was fascinated with "how much blood, sweat and tears, and an occasional laugh, went into the making of the production." Clearly Buchwald had not guessed the pivotal nature of Hope's leadership and kidded about it engagingly:

> Mr. Hope, who oversees every part of his production, is an exacting boss. Five times a day everyone in his troupe had to kneel down and facing the direction of NBC, chant: "There is only one Hope and Timex is his sponsor." Anyone found sleeping during the three days we were in Morocco had his option dropped. Rehearsals, which started in Paris three days before the trip and continued right through the weekend, ran until 2:30 in the morning. At dawn, while a man stood on a minaret overlooking Casablanca, calling faithful Moslems to prayer, Hope stood on the roof of the El Monsour Hotel calling his people to rehearsal.

The Christmas tour that year, 1957, was certainly the most ambitious Yule offering Hope had attempted to date, and it became the prototype for all successive overseas trips to entertain GIs during the next 15 years. There was nothing impromptu about it. Hope set aside nearly a month of his life: a week and a half for rehearsing and two full weeks, beginning December 15, for a back-breaking itinerary that included shows in Hawaii, Wake Island, Okinawa, South Korea, Guam, and Kwajalein before their plane would finally touch down in Los Angeles on December 30.

Along with his permanent musical appendage, the Les Brown Band, Hope took one of Hollywood's glossier sex symbols, Jayne Mansfield, who was incomparable in thinking up stunts to attract attention to her straw-colored hair and her ample breasts, like appearing for photos in a pink furry bikini. Mansfield's husband, the weightlifter and wrestler Mickey Hargitay, was ever at her side. Also on the trip was singer Erin O'Brien, and Hope had once more invited some favorite media people: Hedda Hopper, now almost a regular, Al Scharper of *Variety*, Mike Connolly of the *Hollywood Reporter*, Terrence O'Flaherty of the *San Francisco Chronicle*, and Irv Kupcinet of the *Chicago Sun-Times*. They were all filing daily stories about the tour and Hope had slyly and wisely enlisted them for singing and acting bits in his comedy sketches as well.

On Christmas morning in Seoul, Hope and some of his talent and staff were invited to breakfast at commanding officer Major General Thomas J. Sands's headquarters, and there met for the first time the archbishop of New York, Francis Joseph Spellman, the peripatetic Roman Catholic cardinal who had become as famous as Hope for his Christmas visits to GI bases around the world.

The comedian was clearly not prepared for the whimsical side of this remarkable man. "Cardinal," Hope said, "it's amazing how far we two have had to travel before we finally met."

"Yes," Spellman said, "and I'm glad we're not competing for audiences either—though I understand we're playing some of the same spots."

Hope laughed. "I play 'em first—and you come along and give 'em absolution."

Al Scharper of *Variety* was at that breakfast, too, and when Hope introduced him as editor of *the* show business daily, the cardinal didn't miss a beat with "I'm pleased to meet you. I work for the other Bible."

The most moving moments of that tour took place in shows at two extreme hardship-duty bases along Korea's 38th parallel. At noon the troupe performed at Bayonet Bowl for the 7th Infantry Division, whose men were "perched on a hillside, crouched in the snow." Potbellied stoves backstage kept the entertainers from freezing while they waited to go on. Musicians took turns leaving the windy stage to thaw their fingers over the stoves. Hope hollered into the wind:

Here we are in Korea. . . the Miami Beach of the Far East. . . (Big roar). . . And how about this weather. . . all day long my undies have been creeping up on me looking for a place to hide. . . and if they find one, I'm going to crawl in, too.

Hedda Hopper wore three layers of clothes to do her comedy bit with Hope, and during Erin O'Brien's "I'm Dreaming of a White Christmas," her dream really came true.

When the technicians had wrapped up that location and the troupe moved farther southwest along the Demilitarized Zone to perform for the 1st Cavalry Division at Wallenstein Bowl, daylight was beginning to fade. A big bundle of fog began rolling up one of the valleys, and it was chill and damp. It was about five below during the show and the helicopter pilots who had dropped them into the site warned Hope that he had better cut the show short.

Hope was reluctant to leave early, as he had been warned to do. He said later, "I was held back by the eyes of the men out front following the members of our cast as, one by one, they were hustled off to the waiting choppers. It was like the look on the faces of people at airports seeing other people off or on the faces of your kids when you tell them you're going out for the evening. I'd start another routine, then another. I couldn't help it."

There were no more shadows, just darkness and a few last lights on the stage. The chopper crews were told to count noses and take off. The nose they couldn't count was still onstage. "Barney McNulty, who holds my cue cards, had been ordered down off his platform and there I was still serving cold ham. Some guy came up and took a firm hold on my arm and led me away as I was probably halfway to a punch line."

It was precisely that kind of attitude that extended Hope's "soldier in greasepaint" image year after year and fixed his identification with the GI more securely than even the servicemen could imagine.

For Hope, those animated faces, so expressive in joy and sometimes near tears, and the sounds they made—the whistles and cheers when the girls appeared, the rise and fall of laughter, the truly enthusiastic applause, and that massed sound of the troupe and the audience singing "Silent Night" was intoxicating. When the results appeared on film, Hope the producer had a tough time deciding when to stop showing the different expressions on their faces, those portraits of ecstasy and of wonder and of sadness at being separated from home.

All this made the Christmas shows unique among entertainment offerings. The American television audience could see that Hope had gone to faraway places, had endured the same unpredictable weather and hardship conditions the GIs were subjected to, and had brought them a laugh and a touch of home in icy cold or blazing heat, on a wind-swept stage or in a cavernous hangar. As they watched the television show in January it was clear enough that the entertainment was frequently dispensed on the run, that Hope could not be with the troops more than an hour or two, that his hospital ward walk-throughs, poignant as they were, could not be long. But those visual images of Hope and his troupe giving up their holidays to make this trip reached deeply into the emotions of many Americans.

By the following December, the Bob Hope "Christmas Show" was an established event. The 1958 tour itinerary was picked by the USO in consultation with both the State Department and Department of Defense. They were the ones who knew where the biggest need was and they supplied the transportation. Hope Enterprises footed the bill for the talent who would appear onstage and on television (including the Les Brown Band) and the technical and production staffs as part of their agreement with NBC. Jimmy Saphier said, in response to a letter in *Parade* magazine from a "curious viewer" asking about Hope's profits from his Christmas shows, "Hope Enterprises produces all the television shows and tries to stay within the budget allotted for each one. The Christmas show is different. We never manage to stay in the black. We go way over and Bob never bats an eye. He knows what we spend over our budget comes out of *his* pocket."

In 1958 the 12-day itinerary started with a short stop in the Azores for refueling and a chance to rehearse for a runway audience, then to Port Lyautey Naval Air Station, Morocco, then to more military audiences in Spain, Germany, and Italy—and finally a refueling stop and show in Iceland on the way home. The day they left Hollywood Hope was still on the phone with Saphier trying to locate a glamour queen for the trip and left with his agent's promise that he would guarantee a Brigitte Bardot or Sophia Loren who would be with them for at least two or three shows. As for the rest of the cast, Hope chose folksinger Randy Sparks, dancer Elaine Dunn, country singer Molly Bee, his faithful, high-spirited Hedda Hopper, and the irrepressible Jerry Colonna.

But no matter how you cut it, this trip had trouble branded on it from the landing in a near hurricane on the Azores airstrip to the Les Brown saxophone player who was left behind in a Keflavik, Iceland, men's room. There were peculiar time constraints imposed by project officers and inflated expectations by commanding officers and other hosting dignitaries; the distances between shows were great and the amenities, rustic—particularly in Morocco. All these factors taken together conspired to drag Hope down. He managed to sleep for only seven of the tour's first 76 hours.

A few minutes after landing at Moron, Spain, they sloshed through the rain to the mess hall for a quick meal. The base commanding officer, Colonel Ernest Nance, was there to greet them, and as he stepped forward to grasp the comedian's hand, Hope felt something snap inside his head. He felt unsteady and sagged to a nearby bench. "I saw his welcoming smile through a haze," Hope said. "The walls of that room closed in on me. I shook my head to try and remove the mental fog but it wouldn't clear up." Frank Liberman, doing media and press relations on this tour, said, "Hope mumbled something about the thousands of airmen and their families he was supposed to do a show for, but he ended up at the base hospital stretched out on an examining table. His face had turned a ghastly white."

Hope looked up at the two young Air Force doctors examining him and told them he was feeling better, but they had already injected him with something to make him sleep. When he awoke several hours later, he was allowed to go over to the hangar show site and make a brief appearance. Next day, after Hope had a full night's sleep, the troupe flew on to Madrid for a much bigger audience at Torrejon Air Base.

Saphier had failed to snag Loren and Bardot and had cabled Gina Lollobrigida's business manager. She was, fortunately, working in Spain on a film, *David and Bathsheba*, and probably could be reasoned with—for the right money—to make a guest appearance. Jack Hope called Gina's manager and was told she would come to Torrejon for a few hours providing they could pay her $10,000 in cash in advance. Hope wanted to make sure she could handle a song as well as a comedy sketch so he had Jack cable her manager: CAN SHE SING? A few hours later a cable was returned: SHE CAN SING AS WELL AS SHE CAN ACT. A howl of approval went up in Hope's hotel suite and the writers struggled to top each other with smart-ass lines like: "Too bad she can't be with us longer." No one in the Hope troupe was carrying that much cash so Jack Hope, traveling with the entourage, had the money wired from Los Angeles to a local bank. When he picked up the cash he went to Gina's hotel room and counted out the bills on the end of her bed while she and a companion watched.

Gina sang "Non Dimenticar" and did a sketch with Bob, who had made a remarkable recovery overnight. Before she walked out on that makeshift stage of the Torrejon aircraft hangar that night, she exacted a promise from Hope, his perennial chief cameraman, Allan Stensvold, and his favorite soundman, Dave Forrest, that in their hands she would come across on film like a glamour queen. They promised and they delivered and so did she.

On Christmas Day, they arrived at Rhine-Main Air Base near Frankfurt and did a show, which followed by a big holiday bash thrown by the commanding general. During the cocktail reception that preceded the dinner, Hope was suddenly afflicted by the mysterious ailment again and taken to the base hospital. This time the local German press, the wire services, not to mention Hedda Hopper, had a story too big to leave alone. Hope's latest hospitalization suggested there was something seriously wrong. Hedda's "Collapse" story in the *Los Angeles Times* frightened Dolores, who called in a frantic state to say she was on her way. Hope told her not to come, that it was nothing, and indeed nothing showed up in medical examinations except exhaustion.

The next day he walked onstage to a tremendous ovation at Hanau, Germany, and he seemed fine. From there they flew into West Berlin for a huge combined services show at Fluegelhorst Gymnasium. Hope told anyone who asked about his health, "Those dizzy spells were just the speed of this trip and my lack of sleep." But at Keflavik, Iceland, the last stop of the tour, after his dance routine with Elaine Dunn, Hope felt dizzy again and this time he was almost certain it had something to do with his eyes. He wondered, too, if the fall he had taken on his head here at Keflavik in December 1955—or indeed the frozen prop bottle rap on his head by Ginger during the previous Yule trip—might have caused more damage than he thought.

When he arrived home in North Hollywood, Dolores had arranged a consultation with Tom Hearn for January 2. The exam showed Hope's blood pressure was up to 165. But he insisted on driving to General Laboratories, where the Christmas show footage was being processed and screened, because he felt sole responsibility for selecting each frame for the TV version. One afternoon after the screening he stopped by Lakeside for a hole or two of golf and "everything seemed out of focus for a bit" and then it cleared up.

On January 8 he drove down to Palm Springs to play golf with his pro circuit buddy Jimmy Demaret. "I found myself stumbling. I played three holes and was suddenly very tired. I turned to my caddy and he just knew I was quitting. When I got to the locker room, I looked up at the wall and the pictures hanging there started dancing around. I was really scared."

Hope let Mark Anthony drive him back to Los Angeles and he went immediately to see eye specialist Maurice Beigelman in Beverly Hills, who diagnosed a blood clot in the vein of Hope's left cornea. He warned Hope about the danger of overwork and stress of any kind lest the clot move and destroy his vision totally.

Hope tried to cut back, but felt his responsibility as overseer of his monthly television specials was too great to allow a let-up, so he pressed on. One night in February he was too dizzy to continue and Mort Lachman had to drive him home. Dolores called in two more eye specialists, and they repeated Beigelman's warning about the danger of stress. But after two days of inactivity, he was restless and went back to the studio.

Then, at a rehearsal for his March TV show, his vision fogged up so badly that he called Beigelman, who then placed a call to one of his colleagues, Algernon Reese, at New York's Columbia Presbyterian Medical Center. The following day Bob and Dolores were on a plane heading east.

Hope's New York press agent, Ursula Halloran, posted a local and national news alert and the press responded in force. One wonders what, in her zeal, she reported to the media. It could have been lack of precise information, or her lack of experience with crisis communication, which seems possible, because the logical media approach would be to wait for a medical report before inviting overwrought headlines such as BOB HOPE IN WEAK CONDITION—SUFFERS HEART AND EYE TROUBLES, and BOB HOPE SERIOUSLY ILL—FLYING HERE TO SAVE EYE. A more professional media representative would have considered the effect of Hope's condition on both his network, NBC, and his commercial sponsor, Timex.

At Columbia Presbyterian, Hope was subjected to intensive examination by Reese and his associates, and finally, after several days, one of those colleagues, Dr. Stuart Cosgriff, came into Hope's room at the hospital. "Mr. Hope," he said, "you've got to slow down. You've been moving too fast."

"I can't help it. It's those laughs."

"I know, but your blood vessels can't hear them."

"What have I got, doctor?"

"You're suffering from a circulatory problem. It's a vascular thing."

"Will you operate?"

"No."

"But isn't there some treatment," asked Dolores.

"Bob Hope controls the treatment. We can take care of it here with cortisone and tranquilizers. Nature's been kind to you, sir. It's given you a warning. Sometimes it doesn't, it just strikes. If you take care of yourself, I mean rest and proper care, you'll get the other half of your sight back."

When Bob and Dolores arrived back in North Hollywood a few days later, there were many well-wishing messages from people all over the country, including some offers of transplants. Hope told Marjorie Hughes to tear up his personal-appearance schedule and write a letter of regret to those involved with all his canceled events. He was determined to meet his television show commitments for the rest of the season.

"It was probably the most difficult thing I ever had to do," Hope confessed, "and I almost drove Dolores crazy with it. I actually had to learn how to rest. I had to learn how to conserve my strength—like sitting down during TV rehearsals and letting Alan Calm stand in for me. Dolores has been great. She screens my calls after Miss Hughes has screened my calls. She sees that I get at least eight hours of sleep and has really cut down our social engagements. Even if she just thinks I'm getting tired we go home. Last year she sent me a 'Congratulations wherever you are' birthday card. This year she may get tired of knowing exactly where I am."

35

A Jester in Camelot

"And I think President Kennedy has picked some pretty good help. . . Harvard is emptier than our Treasury. It's quite a thing. There's so many professors in the Cabinet, you can't leave the White House without raising your hand. . . "

Years before the eye problem flared—in fact, ever since 1957, when the Christmas shows on television reinforced dramatically Hope's image as "the GI's guy"—Mack Millar could be heard campaigning for the government to do much more in expressing its gratitude.

"He hasn't done so badly," offered Jimmy Saphier. "He's been honored by three Presidents in one way or another. He has a whole pile of medals and awards in his office from every branch of the military. What more does he want?"

"What Congress did for George M. Cohan and Irving Berlin," answered Millar. Cohan and Berlin had both received the Congressional Gold Medal.

"But would they do it for Hope?"

Hope apparently thought so, because he urged Millar to make a concerted effort that in fact took five years to come to fruition. Millar began by speaking with his other comedian client, Eddie Cantor, about a campaign to promote a medal, and Cantor himself began an exploratory maneuver with Senator William Knowland of California. In the spring of 1958, Cantor sent a message to Saphier: "For more than a year I have tried to have Senator Knowland get to the White House so they might have Congress strike off a medal for Bob Hope. It would be good not only for Bob, for no man deserves the honor more, but it would be good for all of show business."

Knowland's final correspondence with Cantor included a copy of a letter from Wilton Persons, deputy assistant to Eisenhower, stating that Hope had already received the highest honors available to American entertainers; he continued, "Further recognition, at least at this time, would not be advisable in view of the fact that several thousand entertainers have participated in the troop entertainment program and over-emphasis on the contribution of any one person might adversely affect the entire program."

Hope got a bit miffed and said, "If they won't go for the Congressional Medal, then let's try for the Nobel Peace Prize." Millar nodded and smiled, knowing that he could probably arouse sympathy from some of the comedian's highly placed golfing partners.

But Hope knew deep in his heart of hearts that action always speaks louder than words, that nothing could be more influential than his own behavior, and he knew there was something he could do. Despite stern warnings from his eye specialists and a blunt order from Tom Hearn to behave, a stubborn, determined Hope proceeded to make arrangements for a USO Christmas tour in 1959. Dolores opposed it, but Bob assured her that he now knew how to handle his illness—besides, he felt stronger. In honesty, he was less enthusiastic when the Defense Department suggested he entertain in the frozen wilds of Alaska. But he was soon dreaming up ways of dramatizing and glamorizing the subzero tour for maximum publicity.

The first thing he did was sign Jayne Mansfield, the buxom actress who had developed into a publicist's dream, second only to Marilyn Monroe. Hope also signed fast-rising young Western television star Steve McQueen, and invited McQueen's beautiful wife, Neile Adams, along to sing and dance.

Also, Hope decided he could cinch the appeal of this trip by reuniting his World War II cast. He coaxed Frances Langford out of comfortable retirement (she was now Mrs. Ralph Evinrude) and found both Patty Thomas and Tony Romano available, and his faithful sidekick Jerry Colonna was always ready. Les Brown was unavailable, so Hope put the final nostalgic touch on this tour by hiring the Skinnay Ennis Band. And as an added boost to the news coverage, he invited his heavy-drinking Hearst reporter friend Vince Flaherty to come along, and the Hearst people agreed that Flaherty would write a series of feature stories on the whole trip.

On that long haul from Los Angeles to Anchorage, they stopped at McChord Air Force Base, in Tacoma, Washington, to refuel. Eager airmen were trying to find Mansfield but she spent most of her time in a public telephone booth, and when the troupe deplaned at Elmendorf Air Force Base, Anchorage, there was an Alaskan animal trainer waiting for Jayne. He had a baby lion with him and when she cuddled it, a barrage of media and GI photographers went crazy. They went crazier still when she insisted on putting the baby lion in the dogsled with herself and husband Mickey Hargitay as they were driven to their quarters. The cub was tame but his teeth were razor sharp, and his playful nipping and romping with Jayne for photographers during cast rehearsals particularly disturbed Frances, Patty, and Neile.

Jayne was obsessed with being the center of attention. Bob sensed her publicity needs (and his own, at this point) and didn't interfere. Jayne told Flaherty, "I will never permit anything to stand between me and 170 million people—we were meant for each other."

But Jayne had a tendency to go overboard. Her enthusiasm for titillating both her GI audiences and the press was boundless. On Christmas Day at King Salmon, their northernmost stop and a hardship post, where you got to most places by underground tunnels and where troops were rotated often and the base psychiatrist was overworked, Jayne decided to give the boys a "special thrill." The show took place in a reverberating metal Quonset-type hangar whose stage was improvised of two flatbed trucks hauled together. Soundman Dave Forrest was having trouble with his preshow adjustments because the troops sitting on the bare cement floor waiting for Mansfield were very boisterous and sex-hungry.

For their intimate comedy spot, Bob and Jayne were to come onstage from opposite sides and meet at the microphone, with Bob going out first to bring her on. As he climbed up to the flatbed and started toward centerstage, he looked across to where Hargitay was helping Jayne up the narrow steps on her side. She was in a sheer, very low cut pink gown—so low cut that her nipples were exposed. From the GIs crowded close to the stage angling for photographs, this brought war hoops, whistles, and shouts that shattered the eardrums.

Hope turned back, leaned down toward his brother, and over the roaring noise shouted, "Jack, I don't *believe* her. She can't do *that*! We're filming."

Jack turned Bob around and headed him back toward centerstage, shouting, "You're the only one who can handle this!"

And Jack was right. When Bob reached centerstage he hollered, "We've got a gal here—I think you're going to like. It's Mr. and Mrs. Mansfield's favorite child, Jayne—right here."

Jayne came out all smiles, eyes and teeth flashing, her breasts jiggling like molds of Jell-O in pink containers. As she got closer she could not avoid the insistent bobbing of Hope's eyes downward, and by the time she got to his side, she had managed to pull her dress up.

Through the noise and the flashes, Hope said, "I think they like you, darlin'."

Before she could respond, one out-of-control GI threw himself on the floor prostrate in front of the stage and yelled, "Just let her breathe."

That night at a cast party, Hope asked her to sing "White Christmas" and she did it with considerable warmth and simplicity. He said, "Somewhere beneath that blond hair and that plastic makeup was a lovely young woman singing softly, and meaning every word of it." Hope hired Jayne for shows time and time again and in fact used her on a TV special just before her fatal auto accident. "She had joy, that girl. She had bounce. She was an upper all the way. She had fantastic style. I could never figure her out. One minute she was the most naïve little girl in the world and the next minute you had the feeling she was putting the whole world on. She had a pool that was pink and heart-shaped—and that was Jayne—pink and heart-shaped. I really miss her."

During that Alaska USO trip, Hope had a brief flare-up of his eye trouble but was careful to deny it. He was convinced that although the nation could be sympathetic with his misfortune, nobody really likes a sick person. Most of all, no entertainment corporation wants to put their money on a poor risk. He became irritated that this author, who had been hired by NBC to publicize the Hope TV series (and later was hired by Hope as his personal publicist), had reported some moments of dizziness at the Fairbanks show to an Associated Press stringer. Alarmed, Dolores telephoned from Toluca Lake, but Bob dismissed the story as the work of an overzealous press agent.

During the months that followed that Christmas trip, Eisenhower was easing himself out of public life and a new young President for Hope to joke about was coming forward. Hope's approach to Jack Kennedy was extremely interesting because of all of Hope's joking relationships with Presidents, this one came closer than any other to the classic role of court jester. Hope's Kennedy humor sprang initially from superficial aspects of the Massachusetts politician's life, but gradually became more concerned with presidential decision-making and issues arising from the new regime that many in time would refer to as Camelot. Hope came to see the Kennedys as an American royal family:

> Here was a man with all the trappings of a King Arthur, a beautiful wife of great breeding and taste, two adorable children, an extended family of wealth, influence and some mystery. But most of all this young man had charisma and a wonderful sense of humor.

Hope first noticed Kennedy humorously when his popularity was growing as a candidate in the spring of 1960: "I must say the Senator's victory in Wisconsin was a triumph for democracy. It proves that a millionaire has just as good a chance as anybody else."

In February 1961, Hope was asked to share the dais with Kennedy at a very exclusive convocation, the politically irreverent Alfalfa Club, in Washington, D.C. By this time the jabs were less superficial. In front of cabinet members, congressmen, top military men, and judges, Hope said slyly:

> And I think President Kennedy has picked some pretty good help. . . Harvard is emptier than our Treasury. . . It's quite a thing. There's so many professors in

the Cabinet, you can't leave the White House without raising your hand. . . The Secretary of Defense was 20 minutes late for a meeting this morning and he had to bring a note from his mother. . . They're doing great, but one little thing worries me—what if a war starts during recess?. . .

Hope admits that it was not his own humor that night but one of Kennedy's quips that produced the loudest laughter. The President feigned surprise that anyone could possibly object to his nominating his brother as attorney general, adding, "What's' wrong with his getting a little legal experience before he goes into business for himself?"

In mid-April, Hope made a sly reference to Kennedy's rocking chair, and then said:

And have you heard about President Kennedy's new youth peace corps to help foreign countries? It's a sort of 'Exodus' with fraternity pins. . . Did you read where President Kennedy's press conferences were being beamed to Russia? The Russians love the show. . . they've added a laugh track. . . And did you read where President Kennedy's asking for two and a half billion more for the budget? He's using it for petty cash. . . And our national sport is back on the scene this week. . . with the crack of the bat. . . the old squeeze play. . . the crowds screaming—yes, it's income tax time again. . . That's "The Price is Right" with Democrats. . .

Hope's humor here is wittier, more sarcastic, more skeptical, more probing than most of his monologues in the past. Camelot seemed to bring out the best in Hope and his writers. The monologues often played off other Kennedy family members, like this from an overseas Christmas show in 1962:

It's been a slow year back home—only one Kennedy got elected. . . The Kennedys had a nice Christmas—Jackie got a new pair of water skis, the President got a pair of hair clippers, and Ted got Massachusetts. . .

The state of Hope's comedic art during this high-quality period is probably nowhere better displayed than in the monologue for the closing show of his 1960–61 season:

There's trouble in Cuba. . . Laos. . . Vietnam. . . Along about now, Mr. Nixon must get the feeling he won. . . Things are so bad that last week Huntley tried to jump off Brinkley. . . Even Norman Vincent Peale said a discouraging word. . . Laos. . . Vietnam. . . Cuba. . . the Congo. . .

I think we're getting out of the world just in time. . . We knew something had gone wrong with our foreign policy. We sent care packages to Laos. . . and the 'Thank You' cards came back in Russian. . .

During this period it was not only Hope's humor that was maturing. He was coming up to 57 years of age but by no means seemed to act anything like a senior citizen, despite the graying in his sideburns. His body was still firm and athletic from his long, brisk evening walks and his daily golf. The eyes were very alive, which seemed to deny the trouble that lay behind the left one.

Hope knew his lifestyle had to change, saying, "I had two choices, keep up the pace of the past twenty years and find myself doing monologues from a wheelchair, or slow down and live with my illness until I had it licked."

Restricted now from his former wild schedule of whistle-stop traveling, he was forced back to the more sedentary medium of moviemaking. And the picture he chose for this slowed-down and perhaps more reflective period of his life turned out to be one of his very best. "*The Facts of Life* was a daring picture for me," he said. "It was the story of two handicapped people who fall in love. Their handicaps were his wife and her husband."

When he first read the Norman Panama–Mel Frank screenplay he thought it too straight, quite unsuitable for him. Panama pointed out that the humor was derived from the bittersweet dialogue and situation than from broader gags. Hope wavered.

When Lucille Ball read the script, she cried. She had not made a film for five years. She had just gone through the difficult divorce proceedings with Desi Arnaz, and was eager to be someone other than Lucy. And she really liked the project. She called Mel Frank and said, "It's beautiful. Who do you see playing the man?"

"Hope," said Mel.

"Okay," Lucy said, "If you can get him, I'll do it, but there's one thing—"

"What?"

"I don't want it to be *The Road to Infidelity*."

Hope and Ball agreed they must submerge their own personalities and they dug into their parts. Lucille would finish a scene and ask Mel, "Was I 'Lucy'?" She wasn't and the picture went smoothly and the rushes looked really great. Then near the end, Lucille had a freak accident involving a rowboat, falling nearly 10 feet down, bruising her face, and gashing her leg. The picture was delayed a month. Meanwhile, Hope caught his finger in a door and Mel Frank sprained his ankle. When the three returned to the set, Hope said, "Lucy needed heavy make-up to hide her injuries, my hand was in a bandage and Mel was on crutches. We looked like the original cast of *War and Peace*." Almost without exception the critics found the picture "a cut above" what either of them had been doing lately and it was a box-office winner, too.

Hope's next film, however, was a domestic comedy without much dimension. *Bachelor in Paradise* was about America's great move to suburbia and the sexual attitudes of housewives, but Hope's costar, Lana Turner, beautiful and talented as she was, just didn't seem to fit. Hope said he was forced to sit through it on a commercial flight and "the stewardess handed out programs—and barf containers—but at least nobody walked out."

Hope's third picture during the eye-recovery period was filmed on location in England. He must have rediscovered domestic life because he took all the family members who could leave Toluca Lake with him for the four months it took to film the seventh and final Hope-Crosby collaboration, *Road to Hong Kong*.

For both men, living at the Dorchester Hotel in London's Mayfair district and driving out to the Shepperton studios in the far suburbs every day was a painful nuisance. So Dolores and Kathryn Crosby started looking for houses in the country closer to the studio and to the nearest golf courses. But it was Mel Frank who found Cranbourne Court, in Surrey, and showed it to Dolores. She questioned the $1,000 a week rental but loved the butler and furnishings. She pulled Bob and Bing off the golf course to go look at it, and surprisingly, it was Bing who suggested they lease it together. Once they moved into the house, Mel Frank says, "They were like two little boys going to school every morning."

The big trouble that brewed and continued throughout the project was the choice of leading lady. Everyone's first thought, of course, was that it had to be Dorothy Lamour. But Panama and Frank thought Lamour was no longer the alluring "girl in the middle" of the two men that she had been ten years earlier; in fact, they had written her a small part, and had written a larger part for a younger love interest, for which they favored someone like Sophia Loren, Brigitte Bardot, or Gina Lollobrigida. Bing voted for Bardot and said, "Mind you, I think she might be a little on the young side for Hope."

But Bob held out for Lamour for the larger part and was not pleased that she had been offered such a small part just to keep the Hope-Crosby-Lamour tradition alive and trade on its publicity. In fact, the Panama-Frank agreement with United Artists stipulated that the picture *could not* be made without Lamour. Ultimately, when they couldn't interest Loren, Bardot, or Lollobrigida for the younger role in the script, they hired a British newcomer, Joan Collins.

Dorothy Lamour was living in semiretirement in Baltimore as the wife of Bill Howard and raising their two sons, Ridge and Tommy. When she was first contacted about the film and knew she would be included, she was thrilled. But after she was told by Louis Shurr and Panama, who would direct, that her part was a small one and that Collins would be the love interest, she was humiliated. After all, the previous *Roads* were built solidly on a triad, and besides, in actual age she was 10 years younger than Bob and Bing.

While still in Baltimore, Lamour couldn't avoid the gossip column discussions about her status on the picture. Apparently Bing didn't want her but Bob was fighting for Dorothy, then Bing was willing to have her in a small role. She thought she deserved an equal part or nothing and certainly more money or nothing, and by this time she knew they were bound contractually to use her. So the telephone calls and cables started back and forth between London and Baltimore. Time was running out and it looked bleak.

In desperation Hope picked up the phone and begged Lamour to be featured in a musical sequence and a comedy scene in which she plays herself. She liked that arrangement better, finally relented, and felt considerably better when she arrived to a very generous British press reception whose news writers were pro-Lamour in the matter of her being squeezed off the *Road*. She did her comedy scene with Hope and Crosby, sang a tune written for her, "Softer Than a Whisper," and went home to Baltimore.

When Lamour came out to Hollywood at Hope's request to help promote *Road to Hong Kong* on his television show, she heard that Bing also planned to plug the picture on his own TV special. So she called Bing and offered to appear and he told her it was too late to write her in. Dorothy says, "When Bill and I saw Bing's special we were shocked to see them using big blow-ups of me, and they kept referring to me all through the show. It's true that Bing and I were never as close as Bob and I were. But I still don't know what has happened to him. Sometimes he could be as sweet as ever and then an aloofness set in that never had been there before."

Road to Hong Kong was the weakest of the seven zany adventures. Try as they might, the old Hope-Crosby zest for on-set antics and clever ad-libs had pretty much evaporated. The film, however, did have one of their great duets, "Teamwork," and guest appearances by Frank Sinatra, Dean Martin, David Niven, Zsa Zsa Gabor, and Peter Sellers. Sellers was particularly brilliant as a doctor from India who is trying to cure Hope's illness (an eye problem, no less!). He takes out an eye chart of Hindu letters and asks Hope to read it. Hope says he can't and Sellers picks up an Indian reed instrument and starts playing, using the eye chart as music. A snake appears and Sellers charms it.

When the snake subsides, Hope asks, "What would you do if it bit you?"

"Very simple," says Sellers, "I'd cut the wound and suck out the poison."

"But what if it's in a place where you can't reach with your mouth?" asks Hope.

"That," Peter says, "is when you find out who your friends are."

Soon after that, Hope began using a variant of that joke when he returned to doing personal appearance shows. He would say that he and Bing were on a fishing trip way out in the woods and that he, Hope, was bitten by a poisonous snake on his rear end and that Bing rushed off to find the nearest doctor for help. When Bing finally got to town, the doctor said, "You'll have to suck out that poison or Hope'll die." Bob said to his audience, "So Bing *walked* back, and when he got there, I said, 'Well, where's the doctor? What did he say?' and Bing said, 'You're going to die.'"

At the tail end of both 1960 and 1961, when Dolores and his doctors felt he should seriously be honoring her and their "slow down" orders, the lure of a Defense Department request for him to take yet another USO Christmas entertainment package to needy GIs was overpowering. In December 1960, the Department of Defense asked Hope to take a Christmas entertainment troupe to the Caribbean under USO auspices. American military forces in what Hope called "the Bikini circuit" had been considerably beefed up and reinforced because of growing uneasiness over the Soviet influence on Castro's revolution in Cuba. He argued it was his duty and asked Saphier to help him find a glamour star. He set-tled for Zsa Zsa Gabor, who though she proved to be a prima donna assoluta nightmare for the other performers and the staff, held her GI audiences glued to her cleavage. Other headliners were Broadway's Janis Paige and recording stars Anita Bryant and Andy Williams. And close by Hope's side were Jerry Colonna and Les Brown with his band.

In December 1961, morale problems in the icy northeast bases of Labrador, Greenland, and Newfoundland were cited as in dire need of Christmas entertain-ment, and Hope had really begun to feel stronger by this time. He waved away all objections and told the USO that he could put together a show. He got a quick yes from Jayne Mansfield and because he was convinced that no one could top Anita Bryant singing "Silent Night," he tapped her again. He was lucky that Saphier could arrange to borrow beautiful TV actress Dorothy Provine from another network. And when Hope went to judge the Miss World Contest in November, his sore eyes became suddenly perfect, and he stuffed the ballot box for Rosemarie Frankland, whom he was allowed to crown as Miss World and who was promised favored treatment on his Christmas tour.

As Hope sailed further into 1962 it became clear to him and to his audiences that he was back in stride. Dolores was pleased that he was spending more time at home, but he was also becoming more visible in different parts of the country. In March, after receiving the Milestone Award from the Screen Producers Guild, he flew to Miami for his annual appearance at the Parkinson's Disease benefit and then drove up to Palm Beach for a Project Hope golf benefit. Back home, a few days later, he drove over to the Palladium in Hollywood because several of his writers had asked him to do some gags at their annual Screen Writers Dinner. During the evening when the emcee suggested that there just might be a few of Hope's writers in the room, 30 or 40 people stood up.

Most of Hope's early writers were still alive, and many had gone on to bigger things as writer-directors or writer-producers in Hollywood or on Broadway. But his roster of writers at that time could probably be characterized as his "Golden Age" writing staff. There was the clever and reclusive 25-year veteran Norman Sullivan, the informal dean of the group. Then there was Lester White, who had written for Hope as far back as vaudeville, and his partner, Johnny Rapp, from a distinguished comedy-writing family. Mort Lachman, Hope's head writer, was called "the owl" by his boss. Mort could double when needed as director and pro-ducer, and his partner was the brilliant satirist Bill Larkin. The one who came clos-est to receiving Hope's highest praise for subtle wit was British-born Charlie Lee; his partner, Gig Henry, was the perfect foil for Lee.

Hope was then spending $500,000 a year for gags from that group. "Our meet-ings," said Rapp, "can take place anywhere—much of the time on the telephone at *any*, I mean *any* time of day or night—in Bob's bedroom or his office, at bus depots, at an airport, sometimes in a men's room." Frequent charges have been made by his former writers that Hope treated them as menials, slaves—less than human. While it is true that they were always expected to be at his beck and call, Hope felt that for the money he was paying, he deserved that. Gig Henry said, "We always hoped for a bit more civility for our obedience." And Charlie Lee observed shrewdly, "Hope can be quite funny on his own, but we're the ones that keep him charged."

As *Life* magazine observed in mid-1962, "Any other comedian would long ago have died trying to keep up Hope's kind of humor." They went on to describe a Hope personal appearance at Oklahoma State University where his crisp, witty monologue was convincing proof that, in their words, "the champion of comedy" was still going strong:

New York has always been the melting pot but this last session of the United Nations nearly melted the pot. . . Actually it seems silly. The UN invited people like Khrushchev, Nasser, and Castro to discuss how the world can get rid of people like Khrushchev, Nasser, and Castro.

I hear President Kennedy has plans to split Massachusetts in half—High Mass and Low Mass. . . No, I like to see politicians with religion—it keeps their hands out where we can see them. . . Hollywood Catholics are different. They're the only Catholics who give up matzoh balls for Lent.

Jack Benny played golf until last year. He quit because he lost his ball. . . the string broke. . . I used to be quite an athlete myself. . . big chest, hard stomach, but that's all behind me now.

36
─────

The Rose Garden

"Thank you for this great honor, Mr. President. I feel very humble but I think I have the strength of character to fight it. . . There is one sobering thought. . . I received this medal for going out of the country . . . I think they're trying to tell me something. . . "

June 4, 1962, found Bob Hope and his eldest son, Tony, standing together at Georgetown University in Washington, D.C., for an unusual academic procession. With Dolores and Linda and a big audience looking on, Tony would be marching in to pick up his bachelor of arts degree, and Bob would step forward to have conferred on him his first honorary doctorate, in humane letters, for "unstinting generosity with his gift of laughter."

"How does that feel, Bob?" one newsman asked.

"Some educators in Cleveland are going to be surprised to see this gown," Hope said. "I went out of eleventh grade into dancing school. That's how it feels."

The Hopes injected a somewhat casual note into what was ordinarily a dignified occasion. But the playfulness had actually begun earlier, when Hope was conducted to his place in the block-long processional to the main platform. The commencement speaker, the Jesuit theologian Gustave Weigel, walked over and pinned his Phi Beta Kappa key on Hope's academic gown, to the delight of the other Jesuits.

When the Very Reverend Edward Bunn, president of the university, conferred Hope's degree, he reminded the 3,000 graduates, parents, and friends that "it is unprecedented at Georgetown for such a recipient to respond publicly," then, after a suitable pause, said "but I know you would never forgive me if I didn't ask Mr. Hope to give some kind of response."

When the enthusiastic applause faded, Hope, with his impeccable timing, said, "I wouldn't forgive you, either." Holding up the leather folder that held the parchment degree, inscribed in Latin, he said, "I can't wait to get home and have my son read this to me."

Perhaps the strongest laughs followed his closing admonishment: "My advice to young people going out into the world: don't go. I was out there last week and the stock market went down so far I came right back in. (*Big roar*) I put a dime in a telephone this morning and a voice said, 'God bless you.'"

Meanwhile, up on Capitol Hill, the House was getting ready to discuss legislation, already passed by the Senate, authorizing the Treasury to cast a $2,500 Congressional Gold Medal for Hope, the highest recognition that could ever be offered a civilian. The fact that the effort to award Hope the medal had gotten this far was testimony to the support from fellow entertainers like Eddie Cantor, genuinely devoted admirers like Senator Stuart Symington, and many others.

Probably no one had worked harder for this result than Mack Millar. But Mack in his dogged pursuit of Hope's medal was merely walking in the shadow of a man who had learned over his thirty-odd years of entertaining the importance of public relations and marketing as front-door keys to celebrity endurance. Sure, the product has to be of high quality, but that's not enough. Hope was an early believer in what today is called "relationship marketing." He felt the mere fact of his comedy was not sufficient, that no matter how clever the comic, the fickle public had to be constantly reminded of their idols. Getting recognition in high places was one way of being widely applauded. No one in modern show business was more skilled in the building and maintaining of an image than Hope.

Along with such image building went the confidence that Hope would always be a news event; furthermore, there was a tacit understanding that he could expect to get a positive spin on that news. Mack Millar had somehow been able to discourage or kill negative stories. Of course, family events that were tinged with tragedy or trouble were not as easily controlled.

In the summer of 1962, Hope accepted one of the most lucrative personal appearance bookings since his illness, the Seattle Aqua Festival in July for $100,000 and then planned a vacation with Dolores, Nora, and Kelly on a yacht in Alaskan waters. One morning early ship-to-shore radio notified Hope that his favorite brother, Jack—also his producer and the coordinator of all film and television activities—had been taken suddenly to the Leahy Clinic in Boston suffering from acute hepatitis. Jack's wife, Lee, later noted that Jack had been complaining for some time that he did not felt quite right. He was operated on near the end of July and went into a coma. Dolores flew east to be with Lee at the hospital and together they watched a silent Jack around the clock. Bob arrived at the Boston clinic on August 3, just after Jack came out of his coma, and stayed close by his dying brother to the end, on August 6.

Coincidentally, not too far from Jack's hospital room in Boston, a set of galley proofs sat on a desk in the firm of Bruce Humphries Publishers. It was a soon-to-be published book authored by his older brother Jim and it was entitled *Mother Had Hopes*.

Jim had been boasting for years that he knew more about the Hope family than anyone else and that someday he would tell all, including a generous hunk of material about Bob. Jim claimed he had kept careful notes from numerous midnight conversations with Mahm and talks with his father, his aunts and uncles, and the other brothers.

Wyn Swanson Hope had urged her husband to write the book after so many years of talking about it, and only Jim, Wyn, and Humphries knew about the manuscript. Before publication, Humphries advised Jim he wanted a foreword written by his famous brother. Jim was irate. The old antagonism returned. He said no. Humphries said, "No foreword, no book," and Jim angrily replied, "You can go to hell. This is my book and I don't want my brother to have any part of it." The galleys went into the trash. There were, however, two remaining copies of the manuscript. Wyn delivered one copy to Bob at the time of Jim's death, in 1975, and as far as Wyn could determine, Bob locked it up in his joke vault and never looked at it. Wyn gave the other copy to this author.

After Jack's death, Bob learned to depend more and more on Mort Lachman for help in his movie and television production decisions. It was Mort who got the call from producer Harry Saltzman in London (he had been involved with Betty Box on *The Iron Petticoat*) asking if there was any chance Hope would consider making a film at the Mount Kenya Safari Club in Africa. After the screenplay was punched up to resemble some of Hope's classic spy adventures of the past, the notion of an African location plus a leading lady of Anita Ekberg's description became more attractive. The picture had to be made in October and November, which meant that Hope had to tape his two fall television shows before he went (minus the monologues, of course, which were always taped at the last minute).

As Hope's luck of late would have it, internal strife in Kenya meant the location had to be canceled. But Hope had gone too far with his preparations to turn back, so with United Artists' blessing, they decided to use a man-made jungle at Pinewood Studios, in Iver Heath, a suburb north of London.

They would also have a shorter filming schedule for the upcoming picture, known as *Call Me Bwana*, and so Hope decided there was time to tackle another unfinished project, which was a further volume in his ongoing autobiography. Bob had decided the focus of this book would be his trip to Russia, with a few movie experiences and GI entertainment tours thrown in.

After discussion with his editor at Doubleday, Ferris Mack, Hope chose for his book title *I Owe Russia $1,200*, based on the bill he received from the Soviet Ministry of Culture for film clips never delivered. Hope took his golf-playing writers, Mort, Bill, Les, and Johnny away for several long weekends of work and play to develop the manuscript. They drove up to the Montecito Hotel in Santa Barbara, then down to the Kona-Ki Club in San Diego, then up to Harrah's Club in Tahoe, and finally Mort went north to Seattle with Bob while he played in a benefit tournament at The Broadmoor. Somehow the book—full of glib, monologue-type prose that was frequently funny, frequently heart-warming—got finished. It carried a special dedication: TO THE MEMORY OF JACK HOPE, MY BROTHER, MY PRODUCER, MY FRIEND.

In *Call Me Bwana* Hope played an inept explorer hired by the U.S. Government to locate, in densest Africa, an American moon-probe missile that landed there in error. Along the way he meets a beautiful enemy spy, Anita Ekberg, and, inexplicably, a champion golfer, Arnold Palmer. Everyone knew that Palmer was tucked into the screenplay so Hope would have a partner on the courses near the Pinewood Studios.

But there was to be more sadness. Monte Brice, successor to Barney Dean as the omnipresent gag writer on Hope movies, suffered a heart attack on the set November 8 and died almost immediately. That same night, when Hope got back to his Dorchester suite, there was a message waiting for him that Mack Millar had died of a heart attack in his Coldwater Canyon home in Beverly Hills. Monte was 71; Mack was only 57. At the time of his death, Mack was still aglow over his successful pursuit of the Congressional Gold Medal, and had just pulled off another *coup de maître*. He had negotiated something quite unprecedented in the history of the Hearst Publishing Company. They had agreed to devote an entire issue of their Sunday supplement, *The American Weekly*, to a 15-page photo essay on Hope, to be called "Bob Hope, Favorite Jester of the Western World." It would be published in advance of the big award.

While Hope was in London trying to finish *Bwana*, he was able to squeeze in his fourth command performance for British royalty, this one for Queen Elizabeth and Prince Philip. He also completed the monologues for his two TV specials. Transatlantic telephone lines were especially active in late November and early December as Mort and Bob discussed details concerning his upcoming USO Christmas tour of the Far East. This was scheduled to depart December 19 and take them to Japan, Korea, Okinawa, Taiwan, the Philippines, and Guam.

Hope also found himself speaking almost daily with the two men at NBC on the staff of his show who literally engineered these annual trips. Sil Caranchini supervised staging and production details at each location and Johnny Pawlek handled the difficult sound problems and other technical headaches. These two would fly to the troupe's most distant locations two weeks in advance, and work their way back to meet the troupe at its first stop.

This trip's headliners were to be movie superstar Lana Turner (in her first such live roadshow engagement) and semiregulars such as singing actress Janis Paige and pop vocalist Anita Bryant. Hope now had a deal with the Miss World contest that the young woman who won the crown would go along on the Christmas show and this year's beauty was the American contestant, Amedee Chabot. And Hope could not do without the indispensable Jerry Colonna and Les Brown.

There was a top-secret aspect of this particular trip. Quietly and "conditionally," Hope had argued the Defense Department into providing him the necessary escorts and protection needed to go into South Vietnam to entertain the Marines and "advisers" stationed there. However, not two hours out into the Pacific after their liftoff from Los Angeles International Airport, Defense Department officials radioed Hope's escort officer that the stop in Vietnam must be canceled. They feared that the escalating skirmishes there constituted an "unnecessary risk."

Hope was disappointed. He had received many letters from Marines begging him to come. But what made the cancellation especially difficult to accept was the poignant scene that unfolded in his tent–dressing room at Iwakuni Air Base in Japan on December 22. He had stepped offstage near the end of the show and went to his tent alone to fetch a tissue. In the half-light, off to the side of his make-up table, stood a tall figure wearing a maroon beret and an unusual uniform.

"Mr. Hope, may I speak with you?" he said.

"Who are you?"

"I'm from 'Nam. I hitchhiked here to see you. I won the toss. I've got a scroll here with a hell of a lot of names on it. We don't get many entertainment breaks over there, and I want you to know how much good you could do for us."

The soldier stepped aside and began to roll out the wide wrapping paper scroll, and it was long enough to stretch way beyond the edge of the tent. Hope hollered for Mort and said, "Do you believe this? Look at all those names. They're Marines from Vietnam. We gotta *do* something." Hope had to go back onstage but he asked Larry Glaab, the project officer, to call his Defense Department superiors and hold the phone for when he came back offstage.

In a few minutes they secured a priority line and were talking to the Pentagon. It was another polite but very firm turndown. All this time the young man in the red beret stood in half shadow listening, but when it came time for Hope to relay the disappointing news to his visitor, the kid was gone. He had slipped out of the tent. Janis Paige was standing at the doorway and grabbed his arm as he went by and she heard him say that he was AWOL and wanted to remain anonymous to avoid disciplinary action later.

But this trip, even without Vietnam, turned out to be extraordinarily rich and varied. Lana Turner had been a risk. She was a major film star who had precious little live stage experience. The staff and crew took bets on how much of a pain in the ass she would turn out to be. They were dead wrong. She proved to be a genuine show business trouper and even when she developed laryngitis in the bitter Korean cold, she never stopped being totally glamorous. She never missed a show and even with a raw, burning throat insisted on doing all her routines with a whisper mike. The only perk she had demanded was having her own hairdresser on the trip.

In the much-applauded TV documentary that Hope produced from this trip in January, there was the heartwarming scene of the Hope troupe in snowy Korea singing carols around the controversial Christmas tree the United Nations team had set up and decorated at Panmunjon. Hope recalls, "The Communists had demanded that this decorated 'capitalist weapon' be removed from the Demilitarized Zone." There were images of bright kimono-clad children serenading Hope at Okinawa and of Hope being carried aloft by pygmies at a Negrito village near Manila. For his monologue, the Kennedys were still one of his targets:

You know when the Russian cosmonauts landed, Khrushchev kissed them. When *our* astronauts land, President Kennedy only shakes their hands. We may be behind in the space race, but at least we know what we're whistling at. . . But there was a wonderful Christmas spirit in Washington this year. . . the Kennedys held a drive to raise money to buy toys for needy Republicans. . .

It was heartwarming to the 75 troupers who traveled the 9,000-mile trip in 12 days that the documentary Hope, Mort Lachman, and other postproduction people spent so many hours editing was nominated for a 1963 Emmy Award and won the Golden Globe Award from the Foreign Press corps of Hollywood, as well as a *TV Guide* award.

Unquestionably, that show pleased the Chrysler Corporation with whom Jimmy Saphier was currently negotiating a lucrative television deal. Hope ultimately signed a long-term multi-million-dollar package for him to become Chrysler's principal public voice. He was not only to be the corporation's celebrity car salesman but also, more important, to be producer-performer-host of the most ambitious entertainment undertaking of his career: a full-hour (occasionally 90-minute) weekly series of filmed drama, comedy-drama, and taped variety shows called *Bob Hope Presents the Chrysler Theater.*

Hope would be paid $500,000 each time he starred in a production, and $25,000 each time he filmed an introduction to the weekly series. But Hope had no artistic control over the dramas, which were to be produced by Dick Berg at Universal Studios, and this fairly quickly became the focus of much attention in the entertainment world. This was because Berg had persuaded playwright William Inge to write his first television drama, and had signed other writers such as Budd Shulberg, Don Mankiewicz, and Rod Serling, plus award-winning direc-tors and actors.

Performances by Anne Bancroft, Jason Robards, Eleanor Parker, Shelley Winters, and Piper Laurie were highly praised, and the series won several Emmy awards. But like other costly, high-quality dramatic productions on television that were critically acclaimed, it had disappointing viewing numbers, and this was not appealing to the sponsor. So Chrysler opted to dump the dramas after the third year and continue as sponsor of Hope's highly rated comedy specials. This mutu-ally satisfying Hope-Chrysler relationship, which also included an annual high-profile golf tournament, was to last 10 years, rivaling the comedian's long associ-ation with Lever Brothers on radio.

Another Saphier task at this time was to help Hope shore up his sagging pub-lic relations operation. Bob had always maintained that Mack Millar was the best press agent around. Now he was gone. Saphier, however, argued that Millar was old hat, attuned to the green-eyeshade school of newspapering (best exemplified by the Hearst papers) and uncomfortable with the new, more intellectual—even liberal—breed coming out of the journalism schools who were trained to resent hard-sell press agentry. Millar was troubled by the changing media scene, not only in Los Angeles, where seven daily newspapers had been reduced to two, but in all the major cities where dailies were amalgamating or closing down. More people were relying on television for their news, and this was a realm where Millar felt uncomfortable.

The early 1960s saw changes in public media that reflected changes in the America's public life. The emergence of a highly critical youth public soon seri-ously challenged almost every established institution—government, business, education, philanthropy, fine arts—to examine its relationships and its responsi-bility to a new society. America was beginning to discover the truth of its plurality. What had in recent years seemed to be a nation still clinging to homogeneous val-ues now found itself fragmented, required to fill the needs of groups previously underrepresented. This was the state of the nation that would shortly be engaged in a nightmare war in Southeast Asia that would not in any way resemble previ-ous wars or previous calls to service by its young people. This was a gathering storm that would confuse many people, including Bob Hope, who had always answered the call to serve his country as an entertainer.

Saphier may not have understood all of the coming complexities at that time, but what he did know was Hope's need to have his public relations brought closer to the twenty-first century. He had been disappointed in Hope's lust-driven choice of Ursula Halloran as the one to handle his television shows and other media mat-ters in New York. Since 1960 she had been racked with personal problems, some of which might have stemmed from her relationship with Hope. But generally she did not seem to be able to cope with the pressures of high-level public relations work. Reluctantly Bob agreed that she had to be fired.

Saphier convinced Hope that he needed a public relations director at Hope Enterprises who would be in charge of national media and public communications related to his USO Christmas tours, his movie deals with NBC, his personal appearances, benefits, books, recordings, and the family. In 1959 this author had been assigned by the NBC Network to cover all Hope television activities, including USO Christmas tours to Alaska, the Far East, Europe and South Vietnam. Saphier called me and said, "Bob wants you to come and work for him at Hope Enterprises. Would you like to be his new Mack Millar?" I said, "No." "Good answer," he said. "The job's yours if you want it."

Taking Halloran's place for Hope's East Coast publicity and promotion was Allan Kalmus, one of the brightest young public relations men in New York and also a veteran of NBC's media relations staff. He was clever in television promotion, had strong newspaper contacts, and, a key factor, knew his way around NBC's executive floor. Allan had what most press agents could never have or understand, the Harvard background and Madison Avenue look that distinguished Kennedy's Camelot crowd in Washington.

Kalmus was especially effective with the Associated Press and network newsrooms when the National Association of Broadcasters decided to break their tradition of only honoring industry pioneers and developers and presented their 1963 Distinguished Service Award to Hope. Then in September, Kalmus really operated at the top when it came time for the Congressional Gold Medal to be awarded.

Because there was some indecision about the actual date of the medal ceremony, Hope decided to take Linda, Nora, and Kelly with him on a short fishing trip not far from Vancouver. While they were cruising through the San Juan Islands, Stuart Symington reached them by ship-to-shore phone to announce that the medal was ready for presentation in two days. So everyone scrambled for flights—Bob and the three kids from Vancouver and Dolores and Tony from Los Angeles—to the capital.

On September 11, the Hope family was escorted into the Oval Office and then with President Kennedy went out the side door into the Rose Garden. Beyond, on the South Lawn, were seated about 100 members of Congress, including Hope's home state senators, Frank Lausche and Stephen Young, and House Majority Whip Frank Halleck of Indiana. Seated in the front row next to the Hope family was Rita Millar, who was later introduced to Kennedy as the "lady whose husband thought this up."

When Kennedy handed Hope the medal on behalf of himself and the Congress, he said it showed "the great affection all of us hold for you, and most especially, the great appreciation we have for you for so many years going so many places to entertain the sons, daughters, brothers and sisters of Americans who were so very far from home." He then beckoned to anyone in the audience who might want to come up and get a closer look at the medal saying, "This is the only bill we've gotten by lately, so we want you up here." There was laughter, but no one accepted his offer.

"Thank you for this great honor, Mr. President." Hope responded. "I feel very humble but I think I have the strength of character to fight it." He paused to let the laughter die. "This is a great thing. There is one sobering thought: I received this for going out of the country. I think they're trying to tell me something." Big laughter.

Kennedy, turning the medal over to read the back, said: "'Presented to Bob Hope by President Kennedy in recognition of his having rendered outstanding service to the cause of democracy throughout the world. By the act of Congress June 8, 1962.'" Then the family, flanked by Stuart Symington—who clearly had been a key player in bringing the medal to fruition—surrounded the President and Hope for a flurry of press photos.

Back inside the White House, a beaming Jack Kennedy took the Hopes on a personalized tour, introducing them to his staff and security officers as they went. One officer, Robert Suggs, had a sloping nose that resembled Hope's and the President called for photographers to shoot the two men in profile with his own smiling face in between. That photo landed on more front pages around the world than probably any other taken of Hope in his lifetime.

After the Hopes said good-bye to the President in the White House lobby, Kalmus invited the press corps to gather around to hear Bob's personal reactions. Hope told them what a tough competitor Kennedy was in the wisecracking department. Just then Kalmus spotted Milton Berle coming into the lobby. Berle kissed Dolores and moved into camera range with Bob.

"What are *you* doing here?" asked Hope.

"Lunch," said Miltie. "I wonder if it's free." The press corps laughed. "Where's your medal?"

Hope held it up for Berle to examine. Berle snatched it out of Hope's hand and put it into his pocket.

"Oh, you want that, too?" Hope cracked. With bulbs flashing and reporters straining to catch every nuance, Hope reached into Berle's pocket and retrieved the prize.

"My jokes you can steal—but not this. You can look at it like anyone else when it's in the shrine."

"Shrine?" several reporters asked at once.

"Oh, yes," said Bob. "There'll be a special little place with a turnstile attached." Laughter. "Don't you think we ought to make a little laundry money." More laughs.

This was the first public mention of an idea Hope had been toying with for some time, the establishment of a Bob Hope Museum, which would house the thousands of mementos, souvenirs of wars, gifts from grateful people (including British royalty), plaques, citations, trophies, scrapbooks, wardrobe and props from his films, and a viewing room for showing clips from movies and television. It was one of Hope's plans for immortality.

Another plan in the same vein was unveiled less than a month later, when Hope flew into Dallas's Love Field on Friday, October 4. As he stepped out of the plane, there were hundreds of Southern Methodist University students on hand to cheer him. The screaming co-eds—many of them in fine arts and performing arts programs—were voicing their gratitude to Hope for his beneficence. The Dallas media were fanning the publicity for his Coliseum show the next day with the happy news that he had made an outright gift of $302,000 (down payment on a $1 million pledge), the major donation for a Bob Hope Theater in the new $8 million Owen Art Center on the SMU campus.

For the month that followed the Dallas show, Hope behaved every inch the new Chrysler star-producer-commercial product salesman he had agreed to be. He rehearsed and taped his comedy special, filmed introductions to the weekly dramatic shows, filmed car commercials, and did a photo shoot for auto showrooms. He managed to squeeze in some book autographing parties, entertained at the Baseball Writers luncheon, did a personal appearance in Indianapolis, and emceed a tribute to Cecil B. DeMille.

But he paid heavily for all that indulgence. On October 25, just after saying yes to a State Department request that he take a USO troupe to Turkey and Greece in December, he was overcome by dizziness on a golf course in Palm Springs and knew the hemorrhaging had started again behind his eye. Dr. Beigelman advised complete immobility, and a frightened Hope complied for three agonizing weeks of stillness, much of it in darkened rooms.

On November 12, Allan Kalmus called from New York to tell Bob that Ursula Halloran had been found dead in her apartment from an overdose of barbiturates washed down with liquor. Hope told Kalmus he was planning to fly to New York the next day, because he needed to see Algernon Reese at Columbia Presbyterian, and would fly on to Pittsburgh for Ursula's funeral.

Reese told Hope that his eye condition could not be corrected by surgery then or ever, and that his hope for recovery might rest in a new process to repair the hemorrhaging cells, called photocoagulation. It had been developed by a Swiss surgeon, Dr. Dohrmann Pischel, who was now practicing in San Francisco. Hope flew home on November 18, after Ursula's funeral, now terrified by the prospect that his eye condition might be beyond help. He was in this depressed frame of mind the morning of November 22, when in a Dallas motorcade, John Kennedy's skull was ripped open by sniper bullets.

Hope's eye condition worsened during the next few days, while the nation mourned, and on the day of Kennedy's burial, Bob and Dolores were on a plane to San Francisco to be examined by Dr. Pischel at Children's Hospital. Pischel concluded that at this point Hope's eye could not accept the treatment. By December 1, however, Hope felt his condition to be intolerable and begged

Beigelman to persuade Pischel to treat him. On December 6, Dolores took Bob, now wearing deep dark glasses, back to Children's Hospital for the delicate treatment.

Hope was placed on an operating table, his head held rigidly in a viselike contraption, and the photocoagulation gun was positioned above his face with the pinpoint beam directed through the cornea to coagulate the hemorrhaging cells behind the left eye. The first treatment was not sufficient. On December 10 he had a second treatment and then was given special dark glasses with tiny pinholes for openings so that his eyes would focus in a straight path.

Meanwhile, the 1963 Bob Hope Christmas tour to Europe, less than a week away from take-off, had to be put on "possible cancel." Sil Caranchini and Johnny Pawlek, Hope's and NBC's intrepid emissaries to USO, were somewhere in Turkey setting up stages, having already prepared the sites in Italy, North Africa, and Greece. Mort Lachman was trying to locate them and bring them home when Hope telephoned from San Francisco that he still planned to make the trip. Lachman was stunned to hear him say, "Pischel wants me to take it easy for a couple of weeks. I'm going to slide down to Palm and lay real low. If all goes well, I'll meet you in Turkey."

Pischel thought Hope was insane, but nevertheless released him to Dolores's care, and Hope dutifully remained in his darkened bedroom at the Palm Springs house wearing those special glasses. His troupe—including Tuesday Weld, Anita Bryant (who had just discovered she was pregnant), the dancing Earl Twins, the new Miss World, Michele Metrinko, legendary vaudevillian John Bubbles, and stalwarts Jerry Colonna and the Les Brown Band—took off for Istanbul.

The troupe rehearsed at the Istanbul Hilton for two days and then did several shows at nearby air bases with Jerry Colonna as emcee. On December 22, Dolores put Bob on a TWA flight to New York, where he caught a Lufthansa flight to Frankfurt and a deliriously happy U.S. fighter pilot jetted him to Ankara.

When Caranchini and Pawlek met Hope at the airstrip and saw Hope's drawn expression and pinhole glasses, they doubted he would ever step onstage. Hope, however, knew differently. The Defense Department had assigned one of their best young medical men to this tour to watch over him, and masseur Freddy Miron was along to keep him relaxed.

After the Ankara show had been going for about 20 minutes, Hope got up from his nap and strolled out onstage to the kind of ovation that entertainers dream about. Later, commenting on this experience, he would say, "I thought that all I'd do was tell a few jokes, then get off and go back to bed. But the electric current that sparked between the crowd and me had to be the world's greatest therapy. It sure was for me, anyway, I stood there feeling stronger and stronger with every laugh."

And with each successive show Hope got braver and braver, although he sometimes felt a bit woozy onstage. By the time the troupe reached Naples, 10 days later, Hope had become irrepressible. For that last show, he decided he wanted to do the challenge dance with John Bubbles that Lachman had scrapped because he thought it too dangerous for Hope to attempt. There were audible gasps among the backstage crew when they overheard Hope say to Bubbles, "Put on your dancing shoes, John, we're going to fly tonight."

"Beautiful, baby, but what are we going to do?"

"We're going to ad-lib."

Then he and Bubbles did steps they both had forgotten they ever knew, and when they came offstage, Hope was like an excited kid.

For Hope this had been the most important "comeback" in his life.

37

Operation Big Cheer

"Hello, advisers. . . Here I am in Bien Hoa. That's Vietnamese for 'Duck!'. . . Nice to be here in Sniper Valley. . . "

When the January 15, 1964, issue of *TV Guide* hit the newsstands of America, on its cover was a Ronald Searle caricature of Hope, dressed in a dark suit, white shirt, and American flaggish tie, with his raised left hand holding the Statue of Liberty torch. The cover caption read: BOB HOPE, AN AMERICAN INSTITUTION.

The story, by Dwight Whitney, was significant because it was the first time a popular magazine (one whose circulation was reputed to be the nation's largest) had carried an article about Hope that the comedian considered "negative stuff." Why hadn't his public relations team interfered? Times had changed since the days when a press agent could get advanced editing privileges or even kill an unfavorable story.

In his story Whitney looked carefully at Hope's stature, his accomplishments, his pleasures, his worldview, and wrote what he felt:

Hope has long since ceased to be a mere jokesmith, quipster and all-around funny fellow—or even father. He is more a socio-political force. As such he belongs to no one, not even himself. It has been estimated that in the 25 years since old Ski-Nose first rose to fame on the coattails of Bing Crosby during the "me and Bing era" he has raised close to a quarter of a million dollars for worthy causes. He has traveled to almost every country of the world, often to entertain troops at Christmas, a time when any sensible father of four contrives to stay home. His stature as the world's foremost funny humanitarian has put in his pocket more brass hats, politicos, industrial wheel horses and Russian generals than any comedian since Will Rogers, and has widened his sphere of influence-without-portfolio to the point where he is sometimes called upon to facilitate matters which have baffled the State Department.

None of that was objectionable. What irritated Hope were suggestions that there was unrest or division in Hope's Camelot—particularly in regard to Dolores:

The wonder is that Mrs. Hope has managed to preserve her own individuality, and by doing so has freed him to live the sort of life he wants, a nuance by no means lost on him. She is the rock, the mother of their four adopted children, the presider over the home he needs to come back to. They are separate but equal. He fills the house with his golfing pals; she invites men of the cloth. Bob has long since become inured to arriving at his Palm Springs house late at night to find a strange priest walking the grounds. The two men introduce themselves, pass the time of day, or night, and go to bed.

Quite probably, it was essentially the unrest of the times that created both the tone of the story and Hope's reaction to it. The early 1960s were the setting for altered perceptions, just one of which involved removing the lacquered gloss over the entertainment world, ending the fairy-tale treatment of show business lives and of the end product. Especially an "institution" like Hope could now expect to have his life closely inspected by a new breed of reporters whose attitudes tended to be more liberal, whose regard for press agentry more suspicious and even hostile, than those of earlier practitioners.

Hope was by no means detached from the changing society. His youngest children, Nora and Kelly, were constantly reminding him of the "long hair" scene by their own entertainment preferences. Hope had kidded about the flower children and the new morality in television sketches and perhaps as a challenge had urged his booking agent, Mark Anthony, to increase the number of his personal appearances at colleges and universities. Since 1960 Hope had performed to enthusiastic crowds at some 20 campuses like Ohio State, Duke, Tulane, and the Universities of Indiana, Oklahoma, Maryland, and Texas.

Although he was eager to perform for young audiences and thereby extend his appeal, ironically, Hope's comic persona was undergoing a gradual change. The drug store lecher, the flip and brash smart aleck, was beginning to seem more establishment, even a bit elder statesman. Even his movie roles were changing.

Hope's only film role of 1964 was that of a widower with mixed feelings about the new sixties attitudes about sex in a weak script called *I'll Take Sweden*. Hope is cast as a worried father trying to wean his teenage daughter, Tuesday Weld, away from her motorcycle-riding boyfriend, Frankie Avalon. Hope takes Weld to Sweden, where he himself falls into a casual affair with Dina Merrill. It is basically a youth-oriented film with forced situations, and Hope seems uncomfortable in it.

If Hope's mastery of comedy seemed slightly dented by some bad decision-making in his film career, there was no question about his abiding appeal to GIs when he took a USO troupe to several embattled areas of South Vietnam during the Christmas season of 1964. In itself such a gesture was hardly novel; this was Hope's twenty-first year of going where the troops were, in war or peacetime. In this case, however, the war was a controversial and treacherous one, a war that intruded painfully and grimly into American consciousness every day on television news.

Hope learned in October that he had been cleared to go to South Vietnam but was asked by the State Department to keep it quiet for security reasons, to safeguard the lives of GIs who obviously became a better target gathered into one large audience than scattered through the jungle. Hope tried to honor his promise, but word kept slipping out. He confessed to reporters he was eager to go. Why not?

Like mainstream America, Hope trusted that with this necessary police action to fulfill commitments made by Eisenhower in 1955 and reinforced by Kennedy in 1961, we would easily push back the Commies with our expertise, our awesome war machinery, our millions of dollars. Public opinion polls of 1964 upheld the justice of a U.S. presence in Southeast Asia.

For this tour, Hope's mainstay performers were Jerry Colonna and five women: Anita Bryant, Janis Paige, rising young actress Jill St. John, singer Anna Maria Alberghetti, and Australian beauty Ann Sydney, the 1964 Miss World. Tony Hope, on Christmas vacation from his law studies at Harvard, was also invited to go along as an extra actor and jack-of-all-trades.

The tour opened with several shows that took place amidst snow flurries and bitter cold in Korea and then headed south to Thailand, with one in-between show at Okinawa. The 92-degree weather in Bangkok was a sudden shock, and their first show in up-country Thailand, at midday in Korat, was a real workout. But they returned to their rooms at the Erawan Hotel in Bangkok to bathe and put on their best party clothes to go to the palace.

The entire troupe of 75 was invited to a formal dinner at the Grand Palace (formerly the eighteenth-century walled royal city of Bangkok) with the king and queen of Thailand. After a short briefing on protocol by American embassy officials (who told them not to mention *The King and I* and never to sit with their legs crossed because that meant their toes could be pointing at someone's head), the troupe was put into a fleet of Mercedes Benz limousines and driven to the palace, the splendor of which DeMille could hardly have duplicated.

The dinner invitation had come about this way: when Hope and Lucille Ball were making *Facts of Life* at Desilu Studios in 1960, the Thai monarch, King Phumiphol, and his beautiful wife, Queen Sirikit, were guests on the set to watch the filming. As they were leaving, the king extended an invitation to Hope to visit his country and, because he had learned to play the saxophone when he was a Harvard student, he wanted Hope to bring Les Brown and his clarinet so they could "riff some jazz duets."

It was a magical evening that offered eating exotic food from golden dinnerware and watching an impromptu show performed on a specially built teakwood stage in a courtyard whose backdrop was a collection of shiny gold-leafed towers all floodlit and gleaming. It all seemed unreal. The king, thrilled to be playing with Les Brown and his band, seemed like he never wanted to stop. Though to everyone's relief he finally did.

Early the next day, December 24, with mixed emotions the troupe boarded their plane for South Vietnam. Some cast members were laughing because they wondered how their plane could take off with the added weight of all the souvenirs acquired in Bangkok. So there was applause when the C–141 Lockheed Starlifter's wheels left the runway and headed for the southern tip of Cambodia.

As the plane crossed over the Mekong Delta and finally entered the war zone, apprehension registered on many faces. But some felt more secure when they looked out through the tiny portholes and saw the fighter escorts assigned to guide them safely in. This author turned to writer Bill Larkin and asked, "What do you suppose would happen if this plane was forced down in enemy territory?" Larkin quipped, "This gang could hold out for at least a week with ashtrays alone."

Their first show in Vietnam was at Bien Hoa Air Base, a few miles from Saigon.

Because of possible enemy ground fire, the tower advised their pilots to make a steep landing, which in a plane that large alarmed the troupe. They understood the reason later when they looked at the shell-pocked airstrip and saw the few destroyed aircraft not yet hauled away.

The security measures enforced for Operation Big Cheer, the code name for the Hope USO tour, were truly remarkable. The project officer at Bien Hoa revealed to the show's director, Jack Shea, the almost unbelievable statistic that to protect the 5,000 men who had been waiting in the hot sun since 10 o'clock that morning, there were at least another 5,000 on alert somewhere beyond the perimeter guarding the show site. Almost every airman or ground soldier in view carried either a rifle or sidearm. Hope bounced out to "Thanks for the Memory," and shouted,

Hello, advisers. . . Here I am at Bien Hoa. That's Vietnamese for "Duck!". . . Nice to be here in Sniper Valley. . . You all remember Vietnam? . . . It's that place Huntley and Brinkley are always talking about. . . We're on our way to Saigon and I hope we do as well as Henry Cabot Lodge. . . He got out. . . And I understand the enemy is very close. . . but with my act they always are. . . This is terrible country for a coward. Can you imagine not knowing which way to run? . . . You've heard of the NBC peacock? . . . You're looking at the Far Eastern chicken . . .

There is much more subtlety in Hope's Vietnam foxhole humor now, in line with his expectation that he had a "hip" GI audience, one that would appreciate his satiric use of "advisers" (a euphemistic description of the young people sitting out in the audience who were shooting, being shot at, and dying). They were conscious of the media's key role in the war, understood why Lodge had been replaced by Maxwell Taylor as ambassador, and related to Hope's cowardly heroism.

Bien Hoa was never intended to be one of the major shows of this tour, but it ended up lasting two hours because the audience was so enthusiastic and so starved for entertainment. Afterward there was a fast hospital ward walk-through and a quick drink at the officer's club, and then it was on to the armed personnel carriers for the short ride to Saigon. But the plans suddenly changed. Reports of lively sniper activity on the road between Bien Hoa and Saigon suggested it was safer to fly the troupe into Saigon's Tan Son Nhut International Airport, north of the city, which was routinely secured.

Waiting in the tropical sun at Tan Son Nhut were General Ben Sternberg and his aides; the sudden switch of plans had forced them to race out from downtown Saigon and substitute for General William Westmoreland as an improvised welcoming party. The troupe was loaded into a convoy of waiting sedans driven by armed MPs. Each sedan was preceded and followed by a jeep in which there were several MPs carrying automatic rifles.

At one point on a narrow, heavily congested one-way thoroughfare, the convoy halted. An MP with a two-way radio told the driver of Hope's vehicle that there was "some kind of disturbance—a fire" at the hotel across from the Caravelle Hotel, where part of the Hope troupe was staying, but that it seemed to be under control.

A moment later the convoy moved forward, and it was easy to see why this city had been known as the Paris of the Orient as they turned into a wide sweeping boulevard lined with once-elegant French-style townhouses. On each side of the convoy, in double and sometimes triple lines, Vietnamese men and women rode on bicycles and motorbikes through the dense Christmas Eve traffic to and from downtown Saigon. The heavy smell of cheap gasoline was in the air.

When the convoy finally reached the Caravelle Hotel, where Hope and the cast would be staying, blue smoke layered with brown dust hung in the air, sirens wailed, people were running in several directions, and rubble and piles of broken glass lay everywhere. What that MP had been told was a "disturbance" was really a massive explosion with fatalities in the center of Saigon. The atmosphere was tense. This would be just the beginning.

Surrounded by MPs, the performers were escorted out of their sedans and into the lobby while the remainder of the convoy with band members and technicians were whisked off to the nearby Majestic Hotel. Both hotel lobbies were littered with fragments of glass from their shattered front windows. Bit by bit, information came through that while the Hope troupe was en route from the airport, the Brinks Hotel, an officer's billet directly across from the Caravelle, had exploded.

Earlier that afternoon, a 1956 Dodge station wagon loaded with TNT and dynamite had been driven into the courtyard of the Brinks while most of its residents were celebrating or preparing to celebrate Christmas Eve. The driver set a timing device and ran. The blast gutted the billet, killing an as yet unknown number of officers and wounding many others and causing considerable damage and terror to people in every direction from the Brinks.

Before the cast could be assigned rooms in the Caravelle, MPs went through the entire hotel with detection equipment. General Sternberg and some of the Operation Big Cheer personnel went up to Hope's suite for a serious talk. They argued that it might be too dangerous for Hope to remain in the city. But when the MPs said they could handle the security, Hope said he would stay for the two scheduled nights in Saigon.

The sole activity planned for that night was for cast members only, a reception at Ambassador Maxwell Taylor's residence. All the female entertainers were too shaken to want to leave the Caravelle, and so Hope took Les and Jerry with him. It was here with the ambassador that Hope made his formal stand about not leaving Saigon—or leaving Vietnam, for that matter—despite the demoralizing effect of the explosion and possible subsequent incidents. Taylor told Hope that the explosion had killed eight men and wounded 75 others, who had been taken to the Navy hospital. As he spoke, Garrick Utley of NBC News arrived at the ambassador's front door and he asked me to find out if Hope planned to visit the wounded.

A few minutes later Hope, Brown, and Colonna were making the rounds with doctors and nurses in the wards of the Naval Medical Corps facility. Only Hope was allowed into the burn ward, where surgeons were trying to remove shards of glass from burned bodies. Hope said, "Burn wards are the toughest of all. And when it's a combination of burn and splintered glass, well, you wonder if your stomach will let you continue. But somehow I managed. I went around grabbing all the hands that could be raised to shake and I touched those who were smiling at me." One young officer was lying on his stomach and they were taking slivers out of his rear end with tweezers, and others were waiting for that operation, with nurses dabbing them with a topical anesthetic.

One officer was bent over while a doctor and nurse worked on his head and he must have heard someone say that Bob Hope was in the ward because he jerked his head away from the doctor. Hope said, "He looked up at me, his face covered with blood, and said, 'Merry Christmas' as if he really meant it and I don't suppose I will ever forget the way he said it. It still chills me."

Back at the Caravelle, Hope noticed it was almost midnight; he had promised Dolores he would attend Mass. He called together all the troupe members that he knew to be Catholics—Colonna, Jack Shea, and Barney McNulty—and then asked the Vietnam project officer about a church they could go to. The downtown cathedral was off limits because of a recent assassination attempt, so they walked, escorted by two MPs, to the Rex Hotel, where Mass was being said in one of the public rooms.

Forty-five minutes later they were walking back toward the Caravelle through streets that were sandbagged and bunkered. The early Christmas morning had an eerie rather than a joyous feel. Suddenly, a figure stepped out from nowhere into their path and there was a brilliant flash of light. Someone screamed, someone else said, "Jesus Christ!" and Hope turned ashen. It was a GI who had been tracking the group because he wanted to get a flash photo. Hope convinced the MPs not to arrest the soldier.

Back at the Caravelle, Hope was hungry and went up to the rooftop restaurant where a private party was in progress. He convinced staff to serve him at a small table. When we located him, a United Press correspondent went up to sit with him and saw red stains on his shirtcuffs. The story of the Christmas Eve hospital visit made worldwide BLOOD ON HIS CUFFS headlines.

According to the troupe's top-secret itinerary, there were always two possible locations for each show, and the one selected would be notified two hours before show time. This meant that for the six shows Hope actually performed, 12 stages had to be built and six audiences deeply disappointed. And the irony of it all was that Hanoi Hannah, the Vietnam War's answer to World War II's Axis Sally and Tokyo Rose, who broadcast propaganda messages in English over wideband radio, always seemed to know which of the two show sites had been selected even before the Operation Big Cheer personnel did. She announced it each day on her broadcast.

Christmas morning, the nod went to Vinh Long, a small base with three hundred GIs in the Mekong Delta. Hope brought them a stripped-down version of the show, which took place on a truck bed in the most protected part of their compound. Hope's biggest laugh came from this joke: "A funny thing happened to me on the way to my hotel from the airport. I met a hotel going the other way." What amazed Hope, in this most bizarre of wars, was the lightning speed with which news traveled, allowing him to be as topical as he wished.

Later that day, Hope led his group back out to Tan Son Nhut Air Force Base, adjacent to the international terminal, for what turned out to be their biggest single audience in Vietnam, probably 10,000 or more, including General Westmoreland and his wife, Kitsie, as special guests. Afterward, Kitsie, a hardworking nurse's aide, conducted a tour for the cast through several wards of the base hospital and then invited them all to dinner at the Westmoreland's Saigon villa.

The day after Christmas, Hope's Big Cheer players flew north to a remote base called Camp Halloway at Pleiku, deep in Montagnard country and not far from the Ho Chi Minh Trail. Frequent Vietcong raids made this unquestionably the most dangerous location the Hope troupe played, although the raids occurred mostly at night.

From Pleiku they took off for Nhatrang, headquarters of the Green Berets, the carefully trained group that came first into this war. In peacetime, Nhatrang, a beautiful seaside resort and the location of the summer home of President Nhu, was this nation's Riviera. Even now it was the preferred rest and rehabilitation center; rife with Hong Kong tailors and whorehouses, it was used by the Americans, South Vietnamese, and Vietcong.

The final stop in Vietnam was Da Nang, or "Dog Patch," as the GIs preferred to call it. Because of rumored Vietcong activity nearby, armed guards were literally everywhere, including in- and outside the portable restrooms. Almost everyone in the troupe was experiencing a case of nerves. As soon as "Silent Night" had been sung and after the equipment had been packed aboard the Lockheed C–141 Starlifter, the cast, staff, and technical crew were driven in two maximum-security buses (with heavy bars over the windows) to the airstrip, where their plane was parked.

When that big plane lifted up and headed out over the China Sea, there was loud applause, partly self-congratulatory but mostly from relief. The tour's final shows at Clark Field in the Philippines and at Guam had huge audiences of mixed military units in support operations, some of them training for 'Nam, and some of them pilots and crews readying the war's inevitable air strikes. These crowds were both warm and demonstrative and Hope's troupe was totally giving and grateful. But they were also growing weary. There was a sense of "job well done" along with some aching muscles when they were homeward bound.

Hope was extraordinarily keyed up about this trip, and especially so when he viewed the dramatic film footage the camera crews had caught during this 23,000-mile adventure. And also, probably for the first time, the camera was showing Hope at age 61, without much makeup, some graying at the temples, a sunburned face, a slight paunch. He saw himself sauntering out onstage with a golf club a little less bumptiously but just as impudently, still a wisecracker. And he could see how much the GIs loved him. Loved him for the snappy and subtle jokes (how could you miss the laugh roars?), for bringing sex objects for them to fantasize about, for taking their minds off ugliness for a few hours, for squeezing a wounded GI's hand or signing his plaster cast or introducing Jill St. John to a ward of wide-eyed wounded. Except for the passing of time, those GI faces were the same, and to Hope there was no perceptible difference between the mission in Sicily and North Africa in 1943 and the one at Tan Son Nhut in 1964.

When the news stories about Hope's Christmas tour had died down, the publicity aimed at promoting his upcoming Chrysler-sponsored television special about his trip got fired up. And it was a blaze of activity. Hope spent his days either at the postproduction studio screening footage for the 90-minute telecast, or talking to local editors, wire-service reporters, and entertainment writers in distant cities. He also found time to make telephone calls to the families of GIs he had encountered at one site or another. Just as in 1943 he had pockets stuffed with scraps of paper with telephone numbers and addresses.

The program itself, part documentary, part travelogue, part pure entertainment, was unashamedly focused on the GIs. Hundreds of feet of film were devoted to shots of soldiers sitting in the mud, hanging from trees and power poles, or silhouetted as they stood on trucktops and rooftops, laughing, cheering, even crying as they watched the USO stage show. And probably the most powerful effect came from the myriad close-up faces singing "Silent Night."

According to Nielson ratings, the telecast was viewed in 24.5 million homes, or by more than half of all Americans watching television that night. And for Hope it was another milestone, the largest single audience he had ever drawn for any kind of show. In the Hope publicity office, not far away in Toluca Lake, a secretary was emptying the bulging bags of news clips sent in monthly by Burrelle's clipping service. She found herself making two big piles of clips—one containing news and entertainment stories about the Vietnam Christmas tour and TV show and the other—unexpected and almost as equally voluminous—headline stories in sports pages across the nation announcing the new Hope golf tournament.

Well, the tournament wasn't really that new, but its outgrowth was. Since 1960, during February, Hope had shown up as a celebrity amateur in a Professional Golf Association event known as the Palm Springs Classic. Invented by Milt Hicks and Ben Shearer to benefit various desert charities, the tournament was a fair success but Hicks thought it would fare better if Hope ran it. And Bob had for a long time fancied the dream of emulating the success and prestige of that famous one up north at Pebble Beach everyone called "The Crosby." However, through Crosby insiders he was familiar with the time constraints and other responsibilities that a tournament involved and had repeatedly turned down Hicks's offer.

But in early 1964, Saphier and Hope thought of involving Chrysler in the deal, and Chrysler's top man, Lynn Townsend, liked the idea. That is, he liked the idea only if Hope's name was on it. Hicks proposed that the Palm Springs Classic be renamed he Bob Hope Desert Classic and Hope reluctantly agreed to be elected its president, as long as he could be assured there was a top-drawer group of professionals running it. To distinguish it from "The Crosby," it would be the longest Pro/Am tournament in the country, with 90 holes of play instead of 72.

To cinch its drawing power and lend it immediate prestige, he felt he could lean on the professional golfers he had played with so often—Jimmy Demaret, Arnold Palmer (who had won the Desert Classic twice), fellow Ohioan Jack Nicklaus, Billy Casper, Gary Player, and Toney Penna. Saphier helped him get solid commitments from celebrities such as Desi Arnaz, Danny Thomas, Rowan and Martin, Andy Williams, Robert Stack, Lawrence Welk, and Frank Sinatra to fill the spectator gallery.

Characteristically, Hope would never be content until he knew for sure that his tournament was the glossiest Pro/Am event on the tour and could ultimately outshine Crosby's. By its second season, the Bob Hope Desert Classic had become not only the largest charity event in the Palm Springs–Palm Desert area but also the biggest golf tournament anywhere, with 128 professionals and 384 amateurs playing for a purse totaling $110,000. Chrysler sponsored two days of television coverage, and the car company's executives were delighted to be part of the major social event of the Palm Springs winter season and to be mingling with the likes of Leonard Firestone, Dwight Eisenhower, and Walter Annenberg.

Although happy with the Palm Springs festivities and publicity, some Chrysler executives, sensing a change in the country's mood toward the war, were alarmed by word from Jimmy Saphier early in February that Hope planned a sequel to his successful Christmas-in-Vietnam TV special, to be aired March 24. Hope responded, "Look at the ratings we got," and pointed to the thousands of feet of film that had never been shown. Chrysler was sympathetic, and eager for high ratings, but in their boardroom discussions it was pointed out that public attitudes about the Vietnam War were changing, as evidenced by draft-card burnings on college campuses.

Three days before the March telecast, Bob Thomas of the Associated Press drove out to Toluca Lake for a brunch chat with Hope about his reasons for pushing the Vietnam sequel. He found an unusually reflective, serious man.

"We shot thirty thousand feet of film on our trip," Hope said, "and only got to use a small part of it. See, we played eighteen different spots altogether, and really had to show all of them or we'd have been in trouble with the folks back home. There was so much of Vietnam we didn't get a chance to show. And that footage is so timely, provocative, and interesting, it'll be wasted if we don't get it out right now."

"I've been told you are using some newsreel footage, too."

"That's right, we've added some new film. We found footage of the same troops we entertained in the Philippines when they later landed in Da Nang. And we see the same helicopter we flew in reduced to ashes during a raid at Pleiku. And wait till you see the North Vietnam propaganda films NBC picked up in Japan."

One could see how Chrysler executives could be nervous about this sequel, whose tone seemed to adopt an editorial news viewpoint and was even possibly State Department–sanctioned rather than purely entertainment-oriented.

"This is important to you, isn't it?" asked Thomas.

"No, this is important to the world, Bob. Listen, if the Commies ever thought we weren't going to protect the South Vietnamese, there would be other Vietnams all over the world. That would be a lot worse than we are facing now. Like it or not, we've fallen heir to the job of Big Daddy in the free world."

Later that spring, while Hope was resting for a few days in Palm Springs, he arranged to play golf with Dwight Eisenhower at the Eldorado Country Club, where Ike and Mamie made their winter home. The two men talked about his trip to Vietnam and his television specials and the way the war was going. Hope told Ike that he had talked to a number of military leaders and they all held the view that once the U.S. military had ceased to be "advisers" and had gone on the offensive, the only course of action was to win. Hope has said that Eisenhower agreed.

In visiting Ike, Hope had yet another item on his agenda besides golf and the war. He wanted to outline an idea that he and Dolores had for honoring the former President. They had plans to begin a campaign to raise the millions of dollars required to construct the Eisenhower Medical Center—an idea first conceived by Freeman Gosden, of *Amos and Andy* fame, who had been a close friend of Ike's—for the study and treatment of respiratory and heart diseases. As a first modest but important gesture, they were donating a parcel of land they owned in Rancho Mirage for the project. Understandably, Ike was flattered and touched. Then Hope followed up by saying that he had already committed himself to be on hand in September at Seneca Falls, New York, for the groundbreaking ceremonies of the new Eisenhower College.

Between that chat with Ike and going to Seneca Falls, Hope would not be idle. In addition to his usual Chrysler TV shows, he emceed the Oscars for the thirteenth time and flew over to Dallas with the second $300,000 payment of his pledge to build the million-dollar Bob Hope Theater at SMU. He also flew out to Cincinnati to play golf with Jack Nicklaus in a fund-raiser for a delinquent boy's shelter to be named The Bob Hope House.

In June, he was so thrilled that his son Kelly was graduating from high school that he agreed with Dolores that it wouldn't be such a bad idea for him to deliver the commencement address. The brothers who ran St. John Vianney High School didn't mind either, nor did the 86 other graduates and their parents, friends, and teachers.

At the crowded Wilshire Ebell Theater, Hope said: "You can't read the morning papers without being a little worried about the current college craze of sit-ins and demonstrations. I think it's great that our young men and women are concerned about people's rights because that's the American way, that's why the world looks to us for help. Americans need the new ideas of its young people, it needs their idealism, and I only hope they aren't all hoarse when it's their time to be heard from." (The ironic truth Hope missed here was that his idealistic youth *were* being heard from.)

Two days later, Hope was flying back East to Monmouth College in New Jersey to pick up his fourth honorary degree, and from there he went right back to Los Angeles and took a short ride to Whittier College, where he received his fifth honorary degree and was shown in photos standing nose to nose with another recipient, Richard Nixon.

Almost unbelievably, he left the following day with Jerry Colonna, Tony Romano, and two attractive young performers, Tuesday Weld and Joey Heatherton, for the Dominican Republic. They had been asked to go and to entertain the Marines deployed by the Defense Department to help avert a Communist takeover of that troubled nation.

It was a quick trip, on which they did a number of short, intimate shows, and when it was over, Hope headed back home more tired than he should be knowing that in a day or two he would have to arise at dawn each morning for the shooting of his next movie, *Boy, Did I Get a Wrong Number* with Phyllis Diller and Elke Sommer. This was to be a joint Hope Enterprises and United Artists production, directed by his old friend George Marshall. Hope later admitted he had not contributed as much as he should to make it a better movie.

Of all the organizations that offered him awards that year— many of whom just wanted some good free entertainment—Hope sifted through and accepted the Splendid American Award, because it came from the even more splendid Tom Dooley Foundation, and the NBC Affiliates Award, because it was smart business to do so. The same went for the Screen Actors Guild with the added bonus that they offered him their first ever SAG Award "for outstanding achievement in fostering the finest ideals of the acting profession." But still not for *acting*. His favorite of 1965: the Eleanor Roosevelt Memorial Award from the Shell Bank

Junior High of Brooklyn, New York—"To Bob Hope, for his high ideals, self-sacrifice and good will."

During a wire-service interview for the United Press published November 30, 1965, the reporter asked Hope a rather frequently recurring question, "Any plans for retirement?" This time he snapped, "Me? Retire? If I retired I'd be surrounded by about nine psychiatrists. I'm not retiring until they carry me away—and I'll have a few routines on the way to the big divot."

38

Hope for President

"I might as well admit it, I have no politics where the boys are concerned. I only know they're over there doing a job that has to be done, and whatever is best for them is best for me."

"Hope's Hard Luck Follies" probably was the most apt subtitle anyone could have pinned on Bob's 1965 USO Christmas tour of Thailand and South Vietnam. His cast and crew were enthusiastic enough, trying hard to do a decent job—whether it was singing, dancing, and joking, or keeping costumes fresh, or cameras running smoothly or band members from sun stroke. The knowledge that a huge military audience was a tempting target for the Vietcong made the troupe a bit nervy and apprehensive. But an equally troublesome enemy was the blistering heat, an occasional torrential downpour, and always the sweltering humidity.

In Thailand their first shows were for fighter squadrons at Udorn and Takhli on stages built without adequate cover for Les Brown and his musicians, who of course hardly ever left the stage and therefore were vulnerable to sunburn, sunstroke, and sun poisoning. Les had to call up the medics for the more seriously burned players, who were forced to step down. In addition, there was real disappointment for the audiences because Joey Heatherton's appearances were shortened when she developed serious sun blisters from rehearsing and dancing a frenetic and sexy Watusi routine.

More trouble came at a huge matinée performance at Khorat in front of a mixed American GI crowd, plus a large turnout of Thai military and government officials and Peace Corps volunteers. The stage at Khorat was too small for the number of people, legitimate or not, who claimed access. Hope had just complained to Mort Lachman about being hampered in getting up and down the steps from his dressing room, when someone jostled him as he stood on a narrow lip of the stage. He lost his balance and fell five feet into the arms of a surprised security officer. Hope was shaken but able to go on with the show. Afterward, in his tent, he felt a sharp pain and allowed himself to be taken to a medical aid station near Bangkok. Doctors there told him he had pulled several ligaments in his left ankle and probably shouldn't have finished the show.

Fortunately, he could stay off his feet the next day when they flew into Saigon. There, he and Heatherton, Anita Bryant, Kaye Stevens, Diana Lynn Batts (Miss World), Jerry Colonna, Les Brown, singer Jack Jones, and actor Peter Leeds were given rooms at the Caravelle. The rest of the troupe—the musicians, Hope staff, and technicians—were taken to a newly constructed eight-story military hotel called the Myercord. It was labeled "maximum security," which meant it had a row of cement abutments protecting its approaches so a dynamite-filled vehicle could not be used as an explosive device as had occurred the year before. It also had machine gun emplacements on the roof and other armed guards on strategic external balconies. The building had a courtyard with a service bar and tables. Mary Martin's road company of *Hello Dolly!* had christened the place a month before.

Above the eighth floor was a rooftop garden area, with a splendid view of downtown Saigon and where the constant sound of distant wailing sirens was audible (some cast members thought they heard explosions, too). That night the troupe was invited by their official escorts to a Christmas party on the roof, which lasted until after midnight. At almost five o'clock in the morning, two hours before their scheduled wake-up calls, came a deafening explosion. The hotel shook, there was screaming, and doors were flung open and terrified people in various stages of undress ran along the balconies that faced the open courtyard. Everyone expected the worst, but it was quickly explained that the clean-up crew had been lowering trays of bottles and dirty dishes from the rooftop party to the courtyard below when the ropes snapped and the heavy load suddenly went crashing to the cement floor below. Only a few managed to go back to sleep.

And for some who stayed awake there were smiles on their lips at the unexpected glimpse of their quite-undressed coworkers when they ran out of their rooms in fear—especially the rotund Hope writer Charlie Lee in his underpants.

Hope's monologue for the massed audience at Tan Son Nhut Air Base resonated with a warning to any military personnel who may not yet have heard about the pockets of dissonant voices at home. He referred to demonstrations that were not always large but usually were loud and well publicized. One thing that the antiwar demonstrators had learned well was how to orchestrate their messages and manipulate them to fit the evening news:

> I just want to say that here I am. . . the longest delivery Chicken Delight ever made. . . but I'm happy to be here and I understand everything's great. . . The situation's improved. . . and things couldn't be better. . . Well? Who am I gonna believe? . . . You, or Huntley and Brinkley? . . . No, we've had all kinds of demonstrations back in the States. . . "Get out of Vietnam". . . "Don't get out of Vietnam". . . "Why don't you go back where you came from?". . . and, "I came from Vietnam, that's why!". . .

The most perilous stop of this tour was certainly their show at noon on Christmas Day at Di An, with its nearby Vietcong staging area and its underground network of tunnels that moved weapons, equipment, and nighttime raiding parties. Despite an uneasy 24-hour holiday truce, the show site that was hacked out of the jungle the day before was presumed to be an inviting target for enemy rockets. The troupe's helicopter arrival was carefully monitored and guarded, as was each subsequent movement of a performer, staff member, or technician. When Hope went to the latrine, a guard accompanied him and there was a machine-gun emplacement just outside the door. From inside came Hope's voice, "You guys afraid it will blow away?"

"No, sir, Mr. Hope. It ain't nothing to joke about. We draw a lot of sniper fire here night and day. We're not only surrounded by Charlies, there may even be some in your audience."

When he got back to the staging area, Hope listened soberly as a gruff-voiced sergeant major barked orders to an already seated audience. "Now, listen up—I want you men to keep the aisle clear on both sides of this stage in case of a mortar attack. The left side will move off to the left and the right side to the right, and you here in the center will move off to the rear. The cast of the Bob Hope Show will take cover in those cozy foxholes next to the stage."

When Sil Caranchini and Johnny Pawlek suggested that the sergeant brief the cast and crew, Hope said, "Naw, leave them alone. They're nervous enough already. They'll know what to do."

A Hope Christmas show always held a certain sense of mission and its own indelible mystique, if not the threat of imminent danger that Di An presented. Once Mort Lachman tried to articulate what he thought it was about. "Especially at a hell-hole spot like Di An," he said, "the servicemen felt so abandoned. They're so hungry, so desperate for a touch of home, a familiar face, that when they see Bob, a roar goes up, a surge of humanity moves forward, a mass of men cry out in love and friendship. There is something hysterical, religious, fanatical and overwhelming about their fervor. It happens at every outpost, every camp, every station.

"And that inspires Bob and the whole troupe to perform almost beyond endurance. The trips are hell, but every year the same crew of technicians volunteers. They come back battered and beaten, but strangely uplifted. Bob is not a religious man but there is a spiritual, missionary quality to these trips that is strangely contagious. It has infected all the members of his family, and everyone who's worked with him, which is why we have so many repeaters."

Those nine tense and traumatic Vietnam shows produced film footage more spectacular than the previous year's. It had to be painfully clear to the audience who viewed his January 19, 1966, documentary of the tour that U.S. troop strength in Southeast Asia had been dramatically raised. There were more faces to film, louder laughs to record. As in the past, Hope spent two arduous weeks of film editing, script polishing, and giving media interviews before the official screening. On the tour Hope had intercepted another USO troupe headed by Martha Raye, Johnny Grant, Eddie Fisher, and John Bubbles, and that film footage was being used along with a charming interlude with Cardinal Spellman and a confidently worded greeting by General Westmoreland. The January show attracted an impressive 55 percent of the total viewing audience for its time period.

Hope may have provided viewers with heartwarming entertainment, but he also helped raise American consciousness to the depth of their nation's commitment to Vietnam. It was one thing to see groups of 25 or 50 GIs flushing out the enemy during a jungle patrol on NBC's nightly news, but to see thousands and thousands of soldiers and sailors in Hope's audiences made the war seem much bigger.

And if Hope's efforts to lighten the grimness of war was not sufficiently applauded by newspaper editorials and TV critics, or the viewing wives, mothers, and sweethearts of the GIs, he was heartily applauded by their commander-in-chief, Lyndon Johnson, in the White House. At that time, the Senate had begun its investigation of the nation's involvement in Vietnam. Hope was invited to attend as guest of honor the USO's Silver Anniversary celebration in Washington on March 31 and accept from President Johnson that organization's highest award.

A day before the dinner, Hope was told the disappointing news that pressing matters of state would force the President to cancel his appearance. So it created a pleasurable shock of news rippling along the head table, when toastmaster John Daly stood to open the program, that Johnson's motorcade had pulled up to the side door of the Washington Hilton. Hope shuffled through his jokes to see if there were any he might want to omit or soften. When the velvet drapery at the far end of the head table was opened and the President stepped through, the orchestra struck up "Hail to the Chief," and Daly said, "Ladies and gentlemen, the President of the United States."

Johnson paused while the ballroom full of cabinet members, congressmen, judges, military leaders, business executives, actors and agents, and the media stood to applaud. When the noise finally abated and people sat down, Johnson put on his glasses and said:

> Mr. Chairman, Mr. Hope, ladies and gentlemen. . . I have come here today to honor a man with two unusual traits. He is an actor who is not, as far as I know, running for public office. . . and he is a frequent visitor to Vietnam who has never been asked to testify before the Senate Foreign Relations Committee. . . at least not yet. . .

The audience loved Johnson's allusion to Ronald Reagan, who was running for governor of California, but clearly Johnson would have been a lot happier not having to refer to the Senate's investigation of Vietnam. And as the President handed Hope a silver medal, the audience stood. Johnson took his seat at the right of the dais, and Hope waited for the room to quiet.

"Thank you very much, Mr. President." He looked to his right and ad-libbed: "Pretty crazy drop-in, isn't he?" The audience roared. Hope was off and running. "It's nice to be back in Washington—or as the Republicans call it 'Camp Runamuck'. . . No, I mean it, it's nice. . . to be back in Birdland." As the audience laughed, Johnson stared up at Hope and Hope stared back, trying to read the President's face. Then in a lowered, more confidential but still audible voice, Hope said, "I have to do it, sir—it's here on this paper." Both Johnson and the audience laughed. Suddenly the President had become a straight man and he played it to the hilt.

Hope lauded other USO entertainers in the room such as Martha Raye and Johnny Grant and acknowledged his strong supporters Stuart Symington and Rosy O'Donnell, sitting to his right past Johnson. Then he looked far to his left along the head table to where glamorous Joan Crawford was sitting. Crawford, now a Pepsi-Cola executive's widow and a board member of the USO, looked stunning in her silver lamé Balmain gown, sipping from a glass that contained pure vodka.

When the President's party cleared the room, the banquet was over and Hope had invited many of the important politicians and military brass along with movie stars and others to his suite upstairs for a late-night party. As everyone came in and mingled, Hope turned to his Cuban masseur, Freddy Miron, and said, "Where's Joan? Where's Crawford? Call her! Get her in here!" Miron, who had been Crawford's masseur long before he met Hope, went into his bedroom of the suite, consulted a scrap of paper on his bedside table, and dialed. Crawford answered.

"It's me, Joan. It's Freddy. Bob wants you to come to his party."

"Tell him I'm naked," said Joan.

"Good, Joan," said Miron, "he'll be glad you can make it."

"FREDDY!!!" screamed Crawford, "I SAID I'M NAKED!!!"

"Bob'll be glad you can make it, Joan. Hurry." Then Freddy hung up and went back into the living room to tell Hope that Crawford could join him. A few minutes later someone opened the door of Hope's suite and there framed in the doorway was Crawford, luminous in silver lamé, holding a glass of vodka in her hand. She came in, as only a glamour icon like Crawford can, through the crowd to where Hope stood talking to Symington. She said, "You know something, Bob? I haven't got a fucking thing on under this thing—and I don't give a—" She looked around. "Where's that little Cuban?"

During April, the Hopes spent much more time in Palm Springs than usual because construction was starting on the Eisenhower Medical Center. Dolores was particularly busy organizing a support group because she was to serve as president of the hospital's board. Bob could see only a hard road ahead for the center unless he could convince some of his friends in high places to dig deep into their pockets to make financial pledges to the hospital.

Later in the month, however, he flew back east to accept the Silver Lady Award—a prestigious honor from the Banshees, who are highly placed women in communications, professionals representing virtually the total media systems of the United States and Canada. They honored him for his humanity and it seemed a good sign, coming from this particular group.

The high ratings of his Vietnam television specials, approval from current and past U.S. Presidents, and perceived acceptance by much of the nation's news media gave Hope a sense of broad endorsement for continuing to fly his GI mercy missions. Opinion polls indicated most Americans still backed the nation's conduct in an undeclared war. Consequently, Hope was mystified by and was growing increasingly intolerant of the pockets of dissent. Draft-card burnings on college campuses angered him, so much so that he asked his writers to help him prepare an article for the widely circulated Hearst-owned Sunday supplement *Family Weekly*. In it he asked:

> Can you imagine returning from a combat patrol in a steaming, disease-infested jungle, tired, hungry, scared and sick, and reading that people in America are demonstrating against your being there? That people in America are burning their draft cards to show their opposition and that some of them are actually rooting for your defeat?

To Hope it was inconceivable that his arguments in behalf of American GIs who were in Southeast Asia helping to stem a Communist takeover would not be shared by every patriotic citizen. It was how the Hearst newspapers felt. But to a growing tide of fringe media voices who questioned the legitimacy of this (undeclared) war, such a position rendered Hope hawkish at worst and naïve at best.

When Hope flew to New York to promote his latest movie, *Boy, Did I Get a Wrong Number!*, he discovered that even the entertainment media seemed more concerned with his politics than his acting. Allan Kalmus brought Bruce Porter of the *New York Post* to Hope's Hampshire House suite, and although Kalmus attempted to keep the interview focused on Hope's new film, Porter kept returning to his Vietnam tours, his Washington connections, and "some voiced objections" that Hope was using his latest Christmas television special for propaganda.

"I don't think that program reflected my political views at all, "Hope said edgily, "but I'll tell you the things I said about our mission in Vietnam was what I truly believe—and I'm not ashamed to say them."

"You're not against dissent?" asked Porter.

"Listen—one group is fighting for their country and one group is fighting against their country. They're giving aid and comfort to the enemy. You'd call these same people traitors if we declared war. And I'll tell you something else—it's time for Americans to do some right thinking and some smart thinking about their country. If we left there, the propaganda value to the Communists would be devastating as far as I'm concerned. If we didn't walk out of there with honor, we'd pay for it. The whole country would pay for it."

Porter changed the subject. "What about actors in politics, Bob—Reagan and Murphy?"

"Well, Ronnie's got a great personality, and show business is not far removed from politics. Reagan has such a great appearance. I don't agree with all he says, but he sure can talk. And he *goes*. Reagan is well liked."

"What about Murphy?"

"George? He introduced me to my wife—but I still voted for him." Porter and Kalmus laughed.

After Porter said his good-byes and left, Kalmus asked, "Have you ever thought about getting into politics?"

"Why do you ask?"

"A hunch."

"Jack Warner in 1964 asked me to run for state senator on the Republican ticket. I told him it wasn't my bag. But very recently—and I don't want you to use this, at least right now—a couple of the Washington boys came out to Palm Springs to play some golf and afterwards we were sitting around. I said to—ah, one of them—'Come on, now, you didn't come all the way out here just to be whipped by me. What gives?' And after a few looks back and forth at each other, one of the biggest lawmakers in the country—"

"Who?" asked Kalmus.

"Never mind. He said to me, 'Bob, we want you to run for President. We think you could win.' And before I could reach for the barf bag or anything, he said 'We've already run a few polls and they show you'd get the popular vote.' I was speechless."

"I believe it," said Kalmus. "Weren't you tempted?"

"I'd never been asked to run for the presidency before. I told the senators that being born in England would disqualify me even though I got citizenship through my dad. They told me they planned to introduce a private members bill to nullify the native-born rule."

Coincidentally, at nearly the same time, a letter to the editor of the Louisville, Kentucky, *Courier Journal and Times* on May 10, 1966, suggested the name of Bob Hope be put in nomination for the presidency on the Democratic ticket. Part of the reasoning:

Imagine, if you can, the inimitable character of his State of the Union messages? Also, his press conferences would be both interesting and witty. . . And there is a sound historical precedent for choosing a comedian to guide our destinies in these crucial times. After all, America has been run by jokers through much of its history.

Kidding on the square? Perhaps. But in Seattle in the early summer of 1966, radio disc jockey Jack Morton of station KVI conducted a listener survey asking the question: "If Bob Hope were to run for the office of President of the United States today would you vote for him?" Men responded they would vote for Hope 63 percent yes to 37 percent no. Women said they would vote for the comedian 62 percent to 38 percent. From Hope came the emphatic, "Thanks, but no thanks."

Such admiration further suggested to Hope that people agreed with him about the nation's military commitment. And Hope, follower of public opinion, had to believe that he was thinking like the majority. That belief must have been behind his decision to share his feelings about the war in still another—but familiar— channel. He sat down for sessions with Lachman and his other writers to fashion from his monologues, production diaries, trip logs, and the personal reminiscences of about two dozen staffers a book about the 1964 and 1965 tours of Southeast Asia. He called it *Five Women I Love: Bob Hope's Vietnam Story*; though it could in no way match the gallantry or popularity of a work like *I Never Left Home,* it was often very funny and touching.

But unlike Hope's other books, this one was confined to one arena, Vietnam. It was about both the laughs and the girls Hope "packed to take along," and about the horrors of war and the courage of the GI. After talking to some of the front-line troops, he said, "Not knowing where the enemy is or who's firing at you can be unnerving. Not knowing where your friends, or the people back home, stand can be shattering." In the final pages of the book Hope published what might well serve as his manifesto for this period:

> I might as well admit it, I have no politics where the boys are concerned. I only know they're over there doing a job that has to be done, and whatever is best for them is best for me. I bow to no man in my love for my country, and if my zeal for backing these kids to the hilt means offending a few part-time citizens and thereby losing a few points in the Nielson, so be it. . . These kids seem to be a lot more optimistic about this commitment than a lot of our citizens at home. In their everyday job of fighting this treacherous war they know there's no alternative. . . They're not about to give up—because they know if they walk out of this bamboo obstacle course, it would be like saying to the Commies—"Come and get it."

Hope's compassion for the GI was sincere, and so was his belief in the Yankee tradition of fighting for freedom, and his fear and hatred of Communism, and his conviction that you fight a war to win. All this anchored him firmly on one side of the mounting worldwide controversy over America's role in Vietnam.

Also in the fall of 1966, during a five-hour plane ride between New York and Los Angeles, his seatmate in first class was a young recording producer named Dick LaPalm who presented him the opportunity of releasing a long-playing disc of his USO shows in Vietnam. Hope gave LaPalm the soundtracks of his 1964 shows in Korea, Thailand, Vietnam, the Philippines, and Guam, convinced that "there ought to be plenty of people out there interested in having this recording as a piece of history."

Hope and the other stars on the recording agreed to assign their profits to the USO, but unfortunately there weren't any profits to turn over, despite the fact that the disc was marketed in time for Christmas sales. The recording company was a small one with limited distribution; more troubling, there was something vaguely distasteful about the title, *On the Road to Vietnam*, which several critics cited as "opportunistic." Nevertheless, the recording is a worthwhile document, and offers convincing aural proof of Hope's updated foxhole humor and his glib explanation of why he did the tours: "I looked at them, they laughed at me, and it was love at first sight."

For the Christmas 1966 GI tour (again backed by the Defense Department and the USO) Hope headed back to the war zone and other nearby Southeast Asian points. For the first time in several years of Hope's asking her, Dolores agreed to come along, as did the two youngest Hopes, Nora and Kelly. Hope was pleased that his friend Rosy O'Donnell, now retired from the military and the newly elected president of the USO, would also be along. Stuart Symington, on a tour of the area, agreed to be an occasional drop-in. And in an official escort capacity was Colonel Bob Gates, the pilot who had flown Hope and his party through that harrowing Alaska flight in 1942. And he expected to meet and get some footage of Cardinal Spellman in Saigon.

There was something noticeably missing from this trip, and it saddened Hope. In October, Jerry Colonna had suffered a stroke just after driving home from the NBC studios in Burbank where he had taped a show with Bob. He had become paralyzed through most of one half of his body and his speech was impaired. But with therapy and almost daily encouragement from Hope, either by telephone or in person, Colonna was making a slow recovery at the Motion Picture Hospital in Woodland Hills. But it seemed likely he might not be able to travel again. Hope said, "And how we missed that special whimsical madness he brought to so many of our overseas shows."

Although Hope never ever produced less than a professional show overseas, his 1966 edition had particular distinction, despite the absence of Colonna and, more pointedly, the absence of a big sex star. Hope had a hunch that his choice of comedienne Phyllis Diller would be a winner and he was right. The troops gave her the kind of reception they usually saved for a Raquel Welch. Vic Damone was a tireless performer on stage and in hospital wards and the youthful and skillful Joey Heatherton and Anita Bryant never failed to bring the GIs to their feet.

The unexpected emotional high from the trip came from Dolores. In the early shows she sat in the audience and Hope asked her to "take a bow" along with Nora and Kelly. But in Vietnam, when she stood up, the audience cheered so loudly that Bob asked her to come up onstage. He said, "Why don't you sing 'White Christmas.'" She turned to Les Brown and said, "I'm not sure I remember all the lyrics," and Bob said, "Go ahead, I'll feed them to you." Hope later said, "She handled it beautifully, with a mixture of worldliness and motherliness that had a lot of people out in front and backstage crying. She was hammy, too, and got a second standing ovation. But I kept her in the show anyway."

For the record, this trip marked the first time Hope allowed himself to express publicly a position on the war. There seemed to be a demand that people—especially the in-your-face type like Hope—should take a stand on the Vietnam issue. Hope had reached a personal decision: he wanted to see this war brought to an honorable close. After his show for the 4th Infantry at Pleiku, Hope was jeeped over to a news conference in a nearby building. Midway in the proceedings a reporter from *The New York Times* asked the comedian bluntly if he considered himself a hawk or a dove. "You can call me a hawk," Hope said, "if it means that I want to see this thing brought to an early end."

Rosy O'Donnell felt that Hope got added fuel on that trip from "insider" talks with Westmoreland. O'Donnell said, "Bob and Westy would sit up talking a lot that trip. They'd talk about the war, what was happening at home, what it all meant. And that reinforced what Bob was seeing in hospitals. He was terribly torn up by those wards, trying to be glib with a guy whose guts are coming out. Hope put on a bold front but when he got into the back room with his drink, he'd ask why we subject our boys to this, to get killed, to get maimed for what—to fight and not to win?"

In spite of what sounded like saber rattling, Hope's televised documentary of his 1966 Christmas tour was restrained. This telecast, again sponsored by Chrysler, was even more popular than the previous year's, watched by nearly 56 percent of the available viewing audience.

Hope's heroic image was extended and even more sharply defined in March 1967, when it was publicly revealed that during his Christmas Eve arrival in Saigon in 1964 he had been the unmistakable target of Vietcong terrorism, and that he and his USO troupe narrowly missed assassination or serious wounding. While troops of the 2nd Field Force were flushing out sappers operating in a network of underground tunnels, they seized a number of official VC papers, including one that uncovered the plot. Hope received a note from Lieutenant General Jonathan Seaman that said, in part: "A few minutes ago I read a translation of a document we captured a few days ago in which the VC were pointing out their weaknesses in conducting successful terrorist activities in cities. This quote should interest you: 'Attack on Brinks BOQ missed Bob Hope by ten minutes due to faulty timing devices.' I'm *not* kidding."

Naturally the news moved swiftly through the Hope organization and was passed on by Hope's publicity office to Vernon Scott of UPI, who did some checking with his Saigon bureau and verified that the bombing of the Brinks Hotel was meant to kill Hope.

In the meantime, a populist movement against the American presence in Vietnam was building. On October 21, 1967, over 50,000 people paraded through Washington streets calling for peace. Yet Hope's image seemed solidly positive, at least the one of him as a "soldier in grease paint," which seemed to dominate in the late sixties and was how he was perceived by *Time* magazine. Its Christmas 1967 cover carried a characteristic likeness of Hope. Inside, a five-page intimate profile titled "The Comedian as Hero" retold for a new generation the history of Hope's three-war GI entertaining and details of his long career, calling him "the Will Rogers of the age" and commending his durability as the result of good taste. The major photograph of the article was captioned "Bob Hope wasn't born—he was woven by Betsy Ross."

Meanwhile a world away in South Vietnam, Hope was onstage telling Marines at Da Nang:

Men, I bring you great news from the land of liberty. . . It's still there . . . You may have to cross a picket line to see it, but it's still there. . . But don't worry about those riots you hear about in the States—you'll be sent to survival school before they send you back there. . . And do you get the college scores over here? You've heard the results of the big game? . . . UCLA 21, Dow Chemical 12. . . Dow Chemical just got even with the students. . . They came out with an asbestos draft card. . . Can you imagine. . . hey, can you imagine those peaceniks back home burning their draft cards? Why don't they come over here and Charlie will burn 'em for them. . .

Hope's lively cast for this show was largely dominated by the magnetism of an uninhibited Hollywood publicity product named Raquel Welch, about whom one Hope writer quipped, "Standing still she could outperform most so-called sex bombs at their shimmiest." His other guests were singer Barbara MacNair, one of Bing's twin sons, Phil Crosby, dancer Elaine Dunn, and, in a surprise comedy turn, syndicated columnist Earl Wilson. As a relief to some home viewers, this Christmas tour special had less message and more pure entertainment.

Just a week after Hope's popular January telecast aired, there came the momentous 77-day Tet Offensive in Vietnam, which managed to knock U.S. lawmakers and military alike off their feet. Shortly after that, Lyndon Johnson announced he would not seek reelection, and he announced a unilateral halt in the bombing. On May 13 the Paris peace talks began.

Also on this same day Hope was driven up along the west bank of the Hudson River to the U.S. Military Academy at West Point, New York, to accept the cadets' prestigious Sylvanus Thayer Award for outstanding service to the military, which Hope prizes as the second most distinguished honor of his life (after the Congressional Gold Medal). In his acceptance speech he appears to have settled for less than his former call for a clear military win, stating, "I'm a hawkish dove. It's nothing like a pigeon, but if I have to lay an egg for my country I'll do it."

One of Hope's jokes at West Point brought a howl of laughter. "I've had a very busy schedule entertaining the fighting men at our universities. . . I had an offer to speak at Columbia, but my insurance company canceled it." And he was applauded loudly after he said, "We may be fighting an unpopular war, but we have five or six hundred thousand of the most popular Americans I know fighting like crazy to preserve our way of life." In point of fact, several of Hope's scheduled college campus appearances had been canceled in the six months preceding this award.

Hope came back to California to the news that his longtime motion picture agent, Louis Shurr, who had been hospitalized for the past year and was in considerable pain from pancreatic cancer, was dying. Hope had been permitted by Cedars-Sinai to arrive at the hospital sometimes as late as 2 A.M. and sit by Louis's bed so they could talk together. When Shurr died in November, Hope learned from Louis's partner, Al Melnick, that the little man had spent all his money and was broke. Hope paid for all the year's worth of medical bills, both doctors and hospital stay, and Shurr's well-attended funeral.

When it came time for Hope to think about going back across the Pacific for a Christmas 1968 tour of the war zone, the Defense Department asked him to include some of the neglected areas of Korea (where Communist infiltrators had killed 90 GIs in recent months), and Okinawa (where local anti-U.S. demonstrations were an everyday event). Of course, there would be the usual shows in Thailand and South Vietnam, the Philippines, and Guam. All in all, the tour would provide enough exhilaration to keep a 65-year-old man up and ready for the 30 shows they performed in 14 days—but the end result would be total exhaustion.

His able cast, who without exception had some illness at one point in the trip, included two young, multitalented performers, Ann-Margret of Hollywood and Linda Bennett from Broadway, 12 attractive young women from Dean Martin's television show called The Golddiggers, and football superstar Rosey Grier. Of course there was Miss World, Penelope Plummer of Australia, Dick Albers, an extraordinary trampolinist, and the Les Brown Band. Hope's humor was less concerned with the antiwar movement and his tone was more breezy and assured, perhaps occasioned by the prospect of a change of administration in Washington:

Everything's fine back home. Nixon captured Washington and Jackie Kennedy got Greece. So everything's in good shape. . . Actually, I'd planned to spend Christmas in the States, but I can't stand violence. . . Besides, it was the perfect time to come to Vietnam—the war has moved to Paris. . .

Rosey Grier, who had taken a stand against the war long before he went to Vietnam with Hope, found himself the target of criticism from his friends both while he was traveling and when he returned and was seen on the January TV show. There were letters to the editors of popular news magazines and Rosey wrote this response to one:

I went with Bob because I felt he was doing something I could relate to. I wanted to show the servicemen we cared about them. That we didn't care why they were there, we cared about them. I wanted the soldiers to know where I stood. Even though I didn't approve of the war, I approved of them as human beings, doing what the government asked them because they were citizens of our country. And I approve of that.

39

Father of the Brides

"Can you imagine? . . . The Democrats charged recently that the Agnew library burned both books. . . and one of them hadn't even been colored yet. . . "

Being a newsmaker had become something of an addiction to Hope. Whether the news was self-generated, such as Hope himself picking up the telephone and calling one or more of his high-profile journalist buddies to give them an exclusive; or letting his cadre of publicists set up a schedule of interviews to promote some show or benefit; or whether it was simply his name connected to an event that provided the news value—he had reached the point in his life where he not only had to get those laughs and hear that applause but also had to know he was newsworthy. And what's more, that he commanded a positive image in American consciousness—and to some extent in the world.

That facet of his ego should have been soothed by an article that appeared in the Milwaukee *Journal* in July 1969 stating flatly that "Bob Hope had undoubtedly been the source of more news and newspaper feature stories than any other entertainer in modern history." The writer pointed out that in the paper's large clip room there were 10 bulging envelopes containing 500 news or feature stories, which to them was "solemn testimony that judicious editors and three decades of newsmen have considered him of value. A man may be fairly estimated by the number of clippings in his file. Bob Hope, no mere comic, is a man of stature and of news."

What was Hope's claim to be such a newsmaker? It stemmed from several factors: first, he was generally acknowledged as the finest exponent of topical comedy around and could be depended on to respond to any news event with a sophisticated one-liner or, as we say today, soundbite. Beyond that was the incontrovertible fact of his multimedia exposure, and his connections in high places of government, business, and entertainment. Also because he demonstrated vividly to so many people in so many different places that his heart was big and he was willing to use his performing talent to help others, whether it be his lifelong relationship with GIs or his numerous fund-raising efforts for hospitals and other charitable causes.

Add to the above his availability to the news media and his ubiquity, which often placed him in the center of breaking news. In point of fact, when the nature of Hope's image was studied in a communications experiment at the University of Southern California in 1979, all of the above characteristics were noted, as well as one that would come to trouble him in the years to follow: his reputation for being enormously rich and therefore very powerful.

That he knew how to maximize his news value was perhaps never more vividly demonstrated than in connection with certain events of 1969. It all started early in the morning of New Year's Day, when Bob and Dolores waved and blew kisses while riding down Pasadena's Colorado Boulevard (as they had done once before in 1947), as Grand Marshal and Mrs. Grand Marshal of the annual Tournament of Roses Parade.

One and a half million spectators crowded along the route and an estimated 98 million televiewers around the world watched the smiling Hopes in their specially outfitted Chrysler Imperial, complete with TV monitor and radio transmitter-receiver. The equipment allowed Bob and Dolores to chat with NBC's and CBS's (and several local station's) TV and radio announcers as they passed the reviewing stand.

All was going smoothly until Holliston Avenue, where suddenly the Imperial's motor went dead. Probably the car was overequipped. Nothing could start it again. The big Chrysler was going to be removed from the parade when five bare-foot, long-haired teenagers stepped from the sideline crowd and volunteered to push the car. Hope accepted and during the rest of the parade milked laughter from the sidelines by pretending to whip the pushers with his ever-present golf club, or sometimes getting out of the car and helping to push. At the end of the parade route he handed over to the boys his and Dolores's tickets and three more for the Rose Bowl football game.

Ten days later, both local and national news organizations showed interest in daughter Linda's spectacular wedding to Nathaniel Greenblatt Lande. Linda, the first of the Hope's four adopted children and the one who perhaps had had the closest association with her parents over the years, was 29 and felt it was time to be married.

After parochial schooling in Los Angeles, she attended the Roman Catholic University of St. Louis, where she was an English major and tried some acting ("I was not too spectacular," she admitted.) She also studied film at both the University of Southern California and UCLA. For a short time she taught English to Latino children at Queen of Angels High School. Then she seemed serious about pursuing a master's degree or even a Ph.D. in clinical psychology ("I'd always been interested in people and what made them tick.").

Now she was standing at the altar at St. Charles Borromeo Church in North Hollywood while an augmented chancel choir sang sixteenth-century motets. A monsignor was hearing the vows and a rabbi was blessing the union between her and Lande. Nat was a graduate of Duke University, the son of a prominent Augusta, Georgia, doctor whose research had been key to the development of the Pill. Nat also had done graduate work at Oxford and had been a creative project director at *Time* magazine; he was working as a producer at Universal Studios when he met Linda.

After the ceremony, on the rolling back lawns of the Hope estate, 1,000 guests were treated to an extravagantly fairy-tale reception under a billowing white silk circus tent. The glittering guest list matched and even outranked the cracked crab being washed down with Dom Perignon. Crossing the lawn one could meet Vice President-elect Spiro Agnew (standing in for President-elect Richard Nixon) with his wife, Judy, California Governor Ronald Reagan and his wife, Nancy, Ohio's Governor Jim Rhodes, former California Governor Goodwin Knight, and Senator George Murphy.

You would also meet many of the Hope relations on both sides: Dolores's sister Mildred and of course the matriarch, Theresa. Bob's brother Fred and his wife LaRue, his brother Jim, with whom he was now reconciled and whom he had recently hired to look after his landholdings, accompanied by his wife, Wyn. His eldest brother, Ivor, was recovering from a recent heart ailment, but his youngest, George, was there with wife, Mary, and their two children, Avis and Bob.

Under the big white tent strolled or sat generals such as Jimmy Doolittle and Omar Bradley, clerics such as Cardinal McIntyre, tycoons such as MCA founder Jules Stein and MCA president Lew Wasserman, and entertainment couples such as the Danny Kayes, Gregory Pecks, and Jack Bennys, as well as stars such as Irene Dunne, Loretta Young, and Danny Thomas. Hope's new around-the-corner neighbors, Dorothy (Lamour) and Bill Howard had walked over, and, in a rare tribute, Bing and Kathryn Crosby had come from Hillsborough, California. To no one's surprise, there was a whopping list of Bob's celebrity media buddies, including Bob Considine, Ed Sullivan, and Earl Wilson.

Guests were invited to inspect Linda's wedding gifts inside the house, where a string ensemble played, or to dance to one of two rotating bands on a floor built over the swimming pool under the big top. At the height of the festivities, the bride's father got the crowded tent to quiet down and made a speech: "When she was young I traveled so much she rarely saw me. When she did, she thought I was the gas meter man trying to get fresh with her mother."

If one were to have studied the expressions on the faces of both his daughters who were listening to him—one just married and the other soon to be—one could only have guessed their exact thoughts. But it was evident that they both had a great deal of affection for him, despite his often and long absences from the home. They were aware of the gossip that he had not been an entirely faithful husband to their mother and that some of Hope's absences reflected that. Both being products of careful Catholic upbringing, they realized their parents' flawed relationship was not one to emulate.

Later Linda wistfully tried to express some of what was on her mind—and perhaps Nora's, too. "I think we missed him a lot when we were growing up. The thing about him was that when he *was* there, the quality of the time was so terrific that it did make you miss him when he wasn't there. When I was very little and he was working at Paramount I remember the mornings. They were special. Then after breakfast he'd go out the glass door toward the patio doing a 'Shuffle off to Buffalo' and then he'd be gone."

When Hope finished his short monologue he turned to Nora, standing arm in arm with her fiancé, Sam McCullough, who was a young administrator at the University of San Francisco, and ad-libbed: "Why don't you two get married right away before we have to strike the set?"

Gesturing toward his friend Agnew, Hope said, "Ah, Spiro, there's the kind of golfer I go for—not a very good one."

The Hope-Agnew friendship was less than a year old. About eight months earlier the comedian had flown east to receive an honorary doctorate from Brown University and then had swung south to Baltimore to receive a humanitarian award from Variety Clubs International. Agnew, then Maryland's governor, was the banquet speaker and traded jokes with Hope. They got on especially well that night.

When Agnew was nominated for the vice presidency in Miami two months later, Hope sent him a telegram: SEE WHAT HAVING DINNER WITH ME WILL DO? Hope also offered the use of his gag writers to give Agnew's image a boost during the Republican campaign.

Over the previous Labor Day weekend, while Hope was performing in a three-day engagement at the Ohio State Fair, he set up a golf foursome for himself, Agnew, Jim Rhodes, and Pennsylvania's Governor Shafer. And from that weekend on, Bob and Spiro were buddies, communicating regularly, and Hope even added Agnew to his network of intimates who shared the latest jokes in after-midnight telephone calls.

Now, as Linda and Nat's wedding reception was drawing to a close, Bob put his suitcase in the trunk of the Agnews' limousine and got in next to Spiro and Judy and they were off to Burbank airport. They would be taking the veep's private jet to Miami, where they would all attend the Super Bowl the next day.

On January 16, NBC presented Hope's fifth Vietnam Christmas TV special, and the ratings were even slightly higher than the previous year. This is partially explained by the fact that by this time U.S. troop strength in South Vietnam exceeded 500,000. The big audience pleased Hope and he was in high spirits—though, unfortunately, not for long. The old eye problem, controlled for several years with medication and sheer luck after the last photocoagulation treatment, flared up again on the night he flew to Oakland to appear with astronaut Walt Cunningham at a "Youth for America" show.

He knew the hemorrhaging had begun again and so he called his specialists. They agreed it was best to get him to the Jules Stein Eye Clinic for observation and a possible new treatment. Dolores moved into an adjoining room at the clinic and, after three days, was able to take him home. The new treatment appeared to be successful, but nevertheless he canceled everything on his schedule except several events he did annually—the Parkinson's Foundation benefit in Miami, the Police Show benefit in Palm Springs, and the Fighter Pilots Association banquet in Houston. He cheated by doing two college shows because he was so pleased to be wanted by this age group at this particular time, one at Oklahoma State and the other at the University of New Mexico. Most of his energy had to be focused on a new film project, *How to Commit Marriage*, with Jane Wyman and Jackie Gleason, being released by Cinerama.

In midshoot, he couldn't resist the invitation from Stuart Symington to play a round of golf at Burning Tree in Bethesda, Maryland, because he sensed that his old friend had some differing views about Vietnam since the Tet Offensive. He was right and they talked. And while he was in Washington, he called Walter Reed Hospital to inquire about Ike, who was there again in another stage of his terminal illness. Mamie asked him to come and see the President because it might be the last opportunity for a visit.

And it was. On March 30, Bob and Dolores sadly flew to Washington to attend funeral services for Eisenhower. At their hotel that same day there was an urgent call from St. Joseph's Hospital in Burbank, where George Hope had been taken by his wife, Mary, after being stricken with severe stomach pains; he had immediately been operated on for a dangerous peritoneum condition.

They both flew to California, Dolores to Palm Springs and Bob to Burbank, and it was past midnight when Bob reached the hospital to find that George was out of danger. But he had a detailed discussion with Tom Hearn, who met him there, and learned more about George's general health condition—which was not good. George had lung cancer and had kept the information from everyone. Also, his drinking binges had increased and in the past week he had been found wandering around the NBC parking lot in a confused state. Bob hugged Mary, told her he would stay closely in touch, and got back into his car to drive to the Springs because Nora's formal engagement party was being held there the next day.

Bob was trying to deal with family troubles and was keeping himself on at least a half-sensible, reduced-tension kind of schedule. But there were certain contractual obligations he could not avoid such as producing his scheduled April television special. He increasingly relied on Mort Lachman to pull his shows together. But Mort was under extreme pressure himself these days because Joan Maas, his lover, who was also assistant producer of the Hope show and who had become for so many its "most valuable player," had recently been diagnosed with an inoperable, fast-spreading cancer.

This was upsetting Hope too, but he knew also that Mort was falling apart inside and needed extra support. Joan turned out to be stronger than either of them and agreed that when they finished taping on April 11, she wanted to have a farewell party and "really have a party" with no tears. They did, and Bob said in a serious moment, "It was a privilege just to have been around that gal."

The next morning he drove himself down to the desert in time for a ceremony at the Palm Springs City Hall to install Dolores as the new honorary mayor. He felt extremely tired and told Dolores he was taking a long rest. But two days later Miss Hughes called to remind him that he had promised the Motion Picture Academy he would present the Jean Hersholt Humanitarian Oscar to his lifetime pal Martha Raye for her tireless USO trouping in Vietnam.

So he gave Mort a NAFT (need a few things) call, drove back to Toluca Lake, and put on his tuxedo, and a limousine carried him off to the Dorothy Chandler Pavilion. Mort was there and they were still refining the gags when he heard "Thanks for the Memory," and he had to hustle out onstage. When the applause faded, he felt he had to do a couple of Oscar jokes. Barney McNulty popped up from nowhere and held up the cards for him to say, "Pictures have been pretty wild this year, haven't they? Oscar has been more naked than usual. . . They're doing things on the screen today I wouldn't do in bed [*applause*] even if I had the chance." More applause.

Hope then said he was there to honor "a really great gal who goes all out for the guys over there. She knows what they want—songs, laughs—as only she can do it. Such charge and excitement onstage that it would thrill even the spying Vietcong. A great gal, a great lady, a great woman, our Colonel Maggie of the Boondocks, Miss Martha Raye, right here!"

Raye thanked the Academy and the audience and looked up at Hope, "our dear beautiful legend." Applause. She had memorized her acceptance speech but forgot her lines. She giggled and said, "I'm so nervous."

Hope said, "Yes, but you're on."

"This is the happiest day of my life," she said and then added, "stateside." She was supposed to sing a song but she forgot that, too, and linked her arm in Hope's and they walked offstage to loud and sentimental applause and cheers.

Back home in Toluca Lake that night, Hope huddled with Marjorie Hughes to see what they could eliminate from his next few months' schedule. They weeded out quite a few noncontracted events, and for these Miss Hughes would write polite letters saying that film and TV schedules made it impossible for Bob Hope to appear. There was to be no hint of ill health.

"What about the Miami University honorary degree?" Miss Hughes asked.

"Where is that?"

"Oxford, Ohio, on April 27."

"I can do that." He went to Oxford and accepted the degree, but just before leaving he felt more acute dizziness than anything he had recently known. Two days later he was lying on his back on an operating table at New York's Eye Infirmary with Dr. Algernon Reese presiding over the delicate photocoagulation procedure. When it was done, and they had put the black patch with the pinhole over his eye, Reese came into his room and said, "Bob, I'm afraid this is the last time we can do this sort of treatment. There's nothing left to work with there but scar tissue." Dolores flew to New York and stayed at the hospital with him for five days before she could take him home.

This time Hope was sufficiently frightened that he decided to take a full month's hiatus. Cheered by Reese's one blessed gift, that he could play golf, he and Dolores packed a bag and they flew to Miami, then on to Aruba, then to San Juan, and then to the Bahamas.

Feeling much stronger and confident after this rest, Hope felt able to honor his commitment to the senior class at West Point to entertain at their graduation eve banquet.

And he felt well enough to appear on behalf of Nelson Rockefeller at a Madison Square Garden Republican fund-raiser on June 5. Next day he flew to Columbus, Ohio, where he was joined by Dolores and his brothers Fred and Ivor (who was not looking at all well) for a commencement eve banquet at Ohio State. Ivor had suffered a heart attack recently but Bob was assured his brother's recovery was slow but steady.

Next morning, close to nine o'clock, while Bob and Dolores were being driven to the football stadium for the ceremony, overhead rotor rasps and the chugs of Air Force helicopters heralded the arrival of Vice President Spiro Agnew and Judy Agnew. Spiro and Bob were to receive honorary doctorates before a capacity crowd of 35,000. Agnew delivered a conventional "Go get 'em Tiger" kind of speech and got a standing ovation. Hope had them on their feet, too, and the applause for him was louder and longer than Agnew's.

When the students quieted down, Hope thanked the university, greeted the students, and then looked over at Agnew: "I'm especially happy this fellow could be here today—and that you *recognized* him," he said, referring to Agnew's identity problem during the campaign. "Can you imagine—the Democrats charged recently that the Agnew library burned—both books—and one of them hadn't even been colored yet." Big roar of laughter.

Three days later Hope showed up in Portland, Oregon, for a paid personal appearance as part of the city's annual Rose Festival, and left at noon the next day for Chicago, where his latest movie, the one with Wyman and Gleason, was being premiered.

How to Commit Marriage was a solid effort on everyone's part. It was a generation-gap comedy focusing on changing perspectives about morality in general and sex in particular. Hope and Gleason often appeared at the same celebrity golf tournaments these days and had devised a well-publicized and crowd-pleasing comic rivalry.

This film traded heavily on that rivalry and was riddled with insult humor as only Gleason could fire it off. It was the next to last movie Hope attempted and it had considerable polish, largely owing to Norman Panama's rewriting and direction. The picture suffered unfairly from critics' comparisons with more modish comedies being turned out by Mel Brooks and Woody Allen. The irony, of course, is that both Brooks and Allen owed a debt to Hope's film style. Both traded on Hope's comic personae but Brooks added more sex and Allen's situations were darker.

Like everything else in the sixties, films had to be different enough to drag people out of their television-lit living rooms. There were fewer starts but each one had to be a major production because the stakes were higher—international markets, television rights, and something very new called home video sales. Movies had to meet the tastes of America's new young filmmakers and audiences, with the subject matter coming as much from off-Broadway as on, and from controversial books as well as best-sellers. Typical of the period's big successful comedies was *Bob and Carol and Ted and Alice*, about wife swapping, and *M*A*S*H*, about a surgical unit in the Korean War. Among the serious films were *Who's Afraid of Virginia Woolf*, which had the kind of profanity never before heard on the American screen, and *Midnight Cowboy*, about a male hustler in the big city. Hope's film was considered old-fashioned. But it would make its money back.

From Chicago Hope made his way to Ohio's Bowling Green University, where he picked up his thirteenth honorary degree. University officials wisely let the ceremony finish before telling him that his brother Ivor had suffered yet another heart attack and had died. As far back as Leslie Towns could remember, Ivor had been a surrogate father, the family breadwinner, and his partner for 30 years in the metal products business. Two days later, at the funeral in Gates Mills, Ohio, of the seven brothers only Bob and Fred were standing there to receive the many mourners. Neither Jim (suffering from emphysema) nor George (stable but not recovering) could make the trip.

When Bob and Dolores's plane landed at Palm Springs, they had a message from Mary Hope that George's condition was grave. At age 58, the youngest of Avis and Harry's boys was now losing his battle with lung cancer, just as he had repeatedly lost his battle with alcoholism. George had never found the fulfillment he sought in life—not as a stooge in Bob's early vaudeville act nor as a solo performer in the sad last days of vaudeville, nor as a screenwriter, nor as Bob's script reader, nor as a production coordinator of Bob's television shows. George had grown up being known as Bob Hope's younger brother, full of dreams and expectations, and they had been his nemesis and his monsters.

Hope's only paid personal appearance commitment at this time was a four-day engagement at Pike's Peak Festival in Colorado Springs, from June 21 to June 25. He had little enthusiasm for this engagement because he was reluctant to leave George, especially when he heard that the ticket sales were soft. The Air Force flew him to Colorado Springs, and he did his first show as if he were auditioning because he felt word-of-mouth would build business for the rest of the week. During that first show, George died.

Two brothers, the oldest and youngest, died in one week. Hope felt vulnerable and decided he could not continue at Pike's Peak. The promoters challenged him, but Hope had already telephoned his lawyer for legal advice, then telephoned Danny Thomas, who agreed to fill in the remaining shows. Bob spent two solitary days in the desert house before coming back to the city for George's funeral and burial at Forest Lawn Cemetery on June 24. When it was over he felt drained; he drove back to the desert and stayed there.

During the next month Hope was subdued. He rested and told Marjorie Hughes to cancel more engagements. He played golf as much as he could, and later that month he flew to Washington for two reasons. The first was to play golf with Spiro Agnew at a nearby Virginia course. The other was to meet at the request of the Defense Department with some Pentagon officials to discuss an idea they had for his 1969 Christmas USO trip.

In mid-August, Nora Hope married Sam McCullough, the young administrator at San Francisco University she had met while studying there. Their courtship and engagement had been relatively unpublicized, to the couple's great relief, and at Nora's request they were having a smaller, simpler, and gentler wedding than Linda's.

In fact, each of the Hopes' children had moved into their own lives as adults. Tony had done well at Georgetown, then had gone to Harvard to study law. There he met his future wife, Judy, also studying law. That all seemed natural and preordained. How could you worry about someone that self-assured and confident. Then there was Linda—she liked things on a grand scale and had plans for a full life. Their youngest son, Kelly, hadn't gotten anywhere near being interested in marriage.

Shortly before the wedding, just after Dolores and her mother, Kelly, Tony and Judy, and Linda and Nat had left for St. Charles Borromeo, the Hopes' parish church, Nora and the dressmaker were arranging her gown in her room. Bob was in his room waiting to be called to take her the short distance to the church. He thought he heard her call and he went down the winding front hallway staircase but there was no one there. Then he looked up and she was leaning over the banister above him. She saw him and started down the stairs slowly so that he could admire her dress. She stopped when she saw that her father's eyes were glistening.

"I've always been so proud that I had a father everybody loves," she said. "But I love you in a special way I have no words to express. The only tiny cloud on this wonderful day is that I won't be seeing you and Mother so often." She then used a name she had not for some time: "But Daddy, I can't say good-bye."

Hope was losing his "little girl" and he hadn't counted on it happening so soon. He had wanted her to have a wedding as big as Linda's, but she turned it down. She was not like the others. Nora had always been a "buddy" from her earliest days. She was the one who wanted to do songs and dances with her Dad and they all figured she had a show business future in mind. That faded away. But she was an irrepressible prankster and endeared herself forever by being such a great audience for his jokes. And he suspected and respected her vulnerability.

Now Nora had met Sam, and Hope liked him a lot, so it was with a mixture of joy and reluctance that he walked down the aisle with her that day.

Although he was supposed to have slowed his pace he didn't say no when, a few days later, a television station in Jackson, Mississippi, called him for help. On August 17, Hurricane Camille had ripped across Mississippi and Louisiana, leaving at least 200 people dead and thousands more deprived of homes and possessions. They wanted Hope to conduct a disaster relief telethon and he agreed, ending up doing an all-nighter, telling jokes and trading quips with studio guests and those who called in with contributions from all parts of the country.

In September, Bob, Dolores, and their daughter-in-law, Judy, were among the visiting notables who helped Wapakoneta, Ohio, welcome home their prized native son and world-famous moonwalker, Neil Armstrong. And still later that same month, Bob had the sad task of trying to speak some comforting words to the family, friends, and members of his own television staff who gathered to mourn the death of Joan Maas. In tribute, he said he could only guess that "someone up there must have needed her badly."

By October it seemed that Hope's energies had been greatly restored and he could direct them enthusiastically in a somewhat surprising return to "live" musical comedy. It would be another restaging of *Roberta*. But this time—30 years later—he would be playing on the stage of his very own Bob Hope Theater on the campus of Southern Methodist University in Dallas.

For his costar he picked Janis Paige and chose two equally talented newcomers, Michelle Lee and John Davidson, for the other leading roles. Tickets were being touted among the Texas rich for $500 a piece, but the cause was a good one: establishment of a Bob Hope Scholarship Fund at SMU.

Roberta became one of the more glittering events of all Texas that fall season. Added media attention came from the fact that Givenchy of Paris flew its models and fall fashion line to Dallas so they could become a segment of the musical. Hope made himself available not only for local media but for a planeload of national TV editors flown in for the occasion because NBC was videotaping each performance for editing into a two-hour holiday entertainment special for television.

On his last night of *Roberta*, during a curtain-call speech, Hope said he had faith in the youth of America. "I'm starting out next week on a series of college shows and I know I will find right-thinking young people who want this country to resolve its differences with honor."

If the political observers and pundits—and there was a growing clan of them as Vietnam became more troublesome to the nation—were astute, they would have noted that Hope showed up the very next night at a $100-a-plate dinner for Texas Republicans. He sat at the head table with Spiro Agnew, Senator John Tower, and *Dallas Times Herald* publisher Jim Chambers. Tower, as toastmaster, seemed to express the feelings of all assembled when he said he felt the Vietnam conflict would determine "whether the United States will survive as the most powerful nation in the world, and indeed the leader of the Free World. Ladies and gentlemen, no man has given more heart and more inspiration to the men who carry your flag than Bob Hope."

40

You Can't Walk Away

"I don't believe in all that sexual permissiveness you hear about today. Maybe it's because I'm at an age where my bag is my lunch. . . And all those drugs today—I'd like to see them smoke the pot I used. . . "

During 1969 U.S. and allied (Canadian and Australian) troop strength in South Vietnam had reached 600,000 and the war seemed to be escalating. Even when President Nixon announced in June that troops would be gradually withdrawn and a new program of Vietnamization would be undertaken (this was the administration's well-meaning but unrealistic plan for shoring up the war-ravaged nation's self-determination), antiwar feelings matched the summer heat.

A group of university presidents, notable clergy, literary figures and artists, and influential Democratic lawmakers had recently formed the New Mobilization Committee to End the War in Vietnam and demanded a moratorium on military actions on October 15, 1969. This orchestration of feeling was proof that vocal elements in the nation, opinion leaders, and activists from campus, church, the media, and government were gaining strength and were intensely serious when they urged, "Let's pull out of Vietnam at any price."

Richard Nixon opposed this view. So did Hope. Both argued that the price was too much to pay. We would be losing the first war in American history (somehow that argument glossed over the indecisive conclusion of the Korean conflict). Nixon was known to have said in front of his advisers, "I don't intend to be the first President to lose a war." Hope's previous meeting with Stuart Symington had led him to suspect that his good friend was among those Democratic "wise men" who favored a hasty cessation of hostilities, but this nevertheless dismayed and disappointed him.

On October 14, the eve of the moratorium demonstration, Bob and Dolores arrived in Washington for an "Eisenhower Birthday Dinner," a high-powered fund-raising event organized to memorialize the late President by dedicating and perpetuating Eisenhower College. Hope's monologue that night made clear that he did not take the moratorium too seriously.

Good evening Republicans. . . and Democrats. I like to include the help. . . Eisenhower College. . . this may be the first school to give a degree in golf. . . No, I'm delighted to be here for this fine cause. . . I think it's a great idea. . . Our future Republicans have to come from someplace. . . By the way, tomorrow is the moratorium period. A lot of kids will be out of school, and a lot of professors won't be teaching. What's new about that? . . . The President would like nothing better than a cease-fire, but the Democrats won't stop sniping. . . It isn't the philosophical protest that gets me what I resent is their moratorium against soap and water. . . I don't know what's happening to the kids in this country. When we went to school we never had a moratorium. We couldn't. . . we didn't know what one was . . . Who's kidding who? If they want to hold a moratorium, fine. But it looks pretty suspicious when it happens on the same day as the World Series. . .

Ten days later, when Hope was starting out on his fall college tour, he seemed steadfast in his refusal to believe that signs of a groundswell of dissent such as a march on Washington or flag burnings on college campuses could represent a significant voice, or that he or his writers could be guilty of selective exposure of different points of view.

When he arrived at Greenville-Spartanburg Airport for his show at Clemson University on October 25, the expected exchange with local media had a new note in it, becoming a prototype of encounters with the media to come. Predictably, interest focused on Hope's view of the recent protests.

"It didn't help a thing," he said, "to use a worn phrase, 'the moratorium gave comfort to the enemy.' But I've heard about a campus movement getting under way with plans to offset the effect of the moratorium and I can support *that.*"

"Why do you oppose immediate withdrawal, Mr. Hope?" drawled a perky blonde campus reporter.

"Because it's not the answer. Sure I want us out of there. I'd rather be playing to troops in Palm Beach, but if we don't settle things honorably, it'll start somewhere else."

This was a clear echo of President Nixon's oft-repeated phrase, "Peace with honor."

"But don't you find more and more students opposing that view?"

"I've found very little sign of unrest. It's those small minorities on campus that make the headlines. The news media are guilty of blowing this kind of disturbance way out of proportion." This was a rare instance of Hope making any disparaging remark about the news media. Yet it was the kind of remark that his friend Spiro Agnew was fond of making.

Before Hope went onstage that night he did something quite uncharacteristic. After rehearsing with the school musicians who would be playing his arrangements, he accepted an invitation from Clemson President Robert Edwards to attend a preshow reception (something he generally resolutely avoided). This time he had relented when he was told he would be meeting a group of wives and widows of fighter pilots captured or missing in action over North Vietnam, about whom very little was being said by either government.

Their frustration and their desperate appeals for any available information on the whereabouts of their husbands visibly moved Hope, and he said, "I'll try to help. I'll talk to the right people the next time I'm in Washington. I promise you I'll do whatever I can for the POWs."

On Monday evening, November 3, Richard Nixon took his plan to withdraw troops, though without a timetable for doing so, to the people in a now-celebrated television speech that included the sentence "And so, to you, the great silent majority of Americans, I ask for your support." He was asking public approval of the plan. It was a tremendous gamble on Nixon's part but he appeared to win it, gaining time to sell Vietnamization and time to negotiate a less shameful U.S. exit from Southeast Asia.

The following day, the White House announced that the President had received thousands of telegrams assuring support for his policy. The news media were skeptical, suggesting that GOP bosses nationwide had orchestrated the flurry of wires.

On November 4, under the usual glare of presidential press coverage, Bob and Dolores were guests at Richard and Pat Nixon's White House party for the Duke of Edinburgh, who was then on a multination tour on behalf of the World Wildlife Fund. In a private conversation in the Oval Office, Nixon told Hope about a grassroots movement called "National Unity Week," which was being sparked by a young orthopedic surgeon, Edmund Dembrowski, of Redlands, California.

Dembrowski had come to Washington, set up an office at the Mayflower Hotel, and enlisted the backing of top leaders in the American Legion, the Veterans of Foreign Wars, Americans for Responsible Action, and similar groups. They chose the week of November 9–15 because they hoped to counteract the impact of the already announced next major Washington antiwar demonstration, scheduled for November 15. Dembrowski had called the White House for help in locating a credible figure to be national chairman, and Nixon asked Hope if he would consider serving. The comedian agreed. Nixon also confided in Hope that there were some very high-level negotiations in progress that would surely bring the troops home quickly. Nixon said, "Bob, we've got a plan to end the war."

On November 7, Hope flew to Peoria, Illinois, for another of his college shows, this one at Bradley University. Like the Clemson show, the Bradley show was a sellout. As Hope was threading his way through a rather chaotic airport welcome that was close to being out of hand, one startled teenager shouted, "It's Bob Hope!" A brace of uniformed security policemen moved in immediately and conducted Hope into a lounge filled with reporters.

"What does National Security Week mean, Bob?"

"It's a way for people all over the country, for the silent majority to speak up."

"Then you would disagree with those critics who are suggesting that Nixon's silent majority speech was intentionally divisive."

"Divisive?" Hope asked incredulously. He seemed to be weighing the question. "Gradual troop withdrawal? Vietnamization? Certainly not. You know there's a lot of brainpower put behind this plan—not the President alone, but all the brainpower available, and that's more than these kids who are demonstrating."

Three hours later Hope was brought out to a platform in the center of the Bradley gymnasium by an honor guard of eight pompom-waving cheerleaders. A blue-gray spotlight followed him out as a band blared his theme song and the crowd rose to its feet and remained there cheering.

And so began his 50-minute solo performance, which had the audience roaring at jokes like:

I don't believe in all that sexual permissiveness you hear about today. Maybe it's because I'm at an age where my bag is my lunch. And all those drugs today. Why, when I was a kid I thought it was daring to take sen-sen. . . and sneak up to the attic to look at the lingerie ads in the Sears Roebuck catalogue. . . I'd like to see them smoke the pot I used. . .

Eventually he left the stage, pleased with the audience reception. As "Thanks for the Memories" played him back on, the audience was standing. He spoke some serious words when the audience sat and quieted down: "Thank you, thank you. . . You know—I've been—I've had the privilege of entertaining some great Americans in Vietnam. These people who say 'Get out of Vietnam' and that's all they know—that's no good. If you get out and walk away, it's like walking away from a cancer."

The next night, Hope stood in front of an audience of 15,600 students, faculty, and townspeople at the University of Illinois in Champagne-Urbana. His jokes were the same; the audience reaction strong; and his closing remarks just as fervent, although this time he used the phrase "silent majority" and spoke of the threat of a complete Communist takeover of Southeast Asia.

On Wednesday, November 12, Hope ordered his public relations staff to organize a full-scale news conference at his Toluca Lake home. He was afraid that because the media were focusing so much attention on the upcoming November 15 protest march, the purpose of National Unity Week was being forgotten.

During the news conference Hope said that much media coverage "doesn't reflect what the country is thinking." He then launched into an attack on NBC News for what he described as "rigged film clips from Vietnam," and singled out an NBC news feature about how black soldiers in Vietnam were not receiving the same treatment as whites.

Before the press conference ended one reporter asked how Hope would classify himself politically. The entertainer replied, "I'm like a California driver—right down the middle. I don't care who's in, I'm with them."

Not coincidentally, the very next night, in Des Moines, Iowa, Spiro Agnew delivered a speech criticizing the media for less-than-credible coverage of the Vietnam War. Shortly after NBC and CBS news broadcasts carried the Agnew charges, both networks received a tide of telegrams from citizens condemning broadcast journalists, and once again news directors had cause to suspect that this flood of wires was carefully choreographed.

On November 15, more than 250,000 people took part in what was probably the largest antiwar demonstration ever held in the nation's capital. That same day Hope flew to Seattle to do a show at the University of Washington. Ticket holders to the Bob Hope Show at the Hec Edmundson Pavilion on the UW campus that night had to cross a picket line to get inside.

Seven hundred war protesters holding lighted candles walked quietly outside in a vigil for peace. One faculty member who was in that peace vigil told a *Seattle Times* reporter, "Bob Hope represents one of the better-known hawks in this country and I think we're all here in response to that. But this vigil stresses peace domestically as well as on foreign fronts. So it's not so much anti-Hope as it is pro-peace."

Sitting in his suite at the Olympic Hotel talking to an old friend, reporter Bob Heilman, Hope said, "Hell, I'm for peace—but not at all costs. Why don't they march against the North Vietnamese? Why don't the dissidents march against them? Lots of our kids are being killed. And who's doing the killing? The Communists are the ones who need the demonstrations."

Despite Hope's statement to the group of reporters on November 12, that he was "right down the middle," it was becoming increasingly evident to many people that his sympathies were closely allied to current Republican thinking. His friendship with Agnew and the similarity of their views, plus his vocal support of Nixon's policies, regardless of their intent, were perceived as partisan.

He continued the practice of ending his personal appearances with serious speeches, which tended to be pleas for audience support of the administration. It was beginning to be clear to his writers and his public relations advisers that this man who had built an entire professional reputation as a performer on political neutrality was now going to face accusations of political activism, if not bias.

There was nothing new in a popular performer being partisan. America's rich entertainment history has a solid tradition of partisan humor, from its very beginnings—Ben Franklin's Silence Dogood character arguing Colonial politics in eighteenth-century Boston—all the way down to the Democrat Will Rogers humorously stumping for Franklin Roosevelt in the 1930s. But Hope's behavior was unexpected.

The performer and the partisan fused dramatically in late November, when Hope announced that for his 1969 USO Christmas tour he would entertain Americans in every part of the world and his troupe would, in fact, circle the globe. Moreover, Hope announced, their very first performance, sort of a dress rehearsal, would take place before a White House audience hosted by Pat and Richard Nixon. Then the first lady sent out formal invitations to each member of Hope's troupe—performers, production staff, technicians, musicians, and assorted others connected with the departure (75 in all)—to a formal dinner party in the Blue Room prior to the "command performance."

An unusual presidential invitation like this required extraordinary preparations. Howard Miller, West Coast director of the USO, who had skillfully arranged Hope's Christmas show send-offs for the past 10 years, was dispatched to Washington. He immediately began arranging a VIP departure ceremony at Andrews Air Force Base that would include Secretary of State William Rogers, Defense Secretary Melvin Laird, and Hope's special pals, Generals Rosy O'Donnell and "Westy" Westmoreland.

NBC's senior publicist Betty Lanigan, a seasoned newswoman who had been coordinating network publicity for Hope USO trips during recent years, had been grounded by lower-back surgery, so her boss, former UPI bureau chief Hank Rieger, stepped in. Rieger flew to Washington to work with the capital press corps and found the media quite cooperative about both Nixon and Hope. Nixon had just announced further Vietnam troop withdrawals and his popularity at the polls had climbed.

That Sunday night, December 14, the troupe had cocktails in the large foyer adjacent to the Blue Room. They went through a reception line to meet Richard and Pat Nixon (and to be photographed meeting them) and then each one took a small piece of white paper out of a silver bowl to discover their seat locations for dinner. Richard Nixon, who would sit at the far end of the room, had asked for singer Connie Stevens at his right; Pat Nixon sat at the opposite end of the room with Bob Hope at her left and this author at her right. The formality of the dinner was shattered when a member of the singing-dancing group the Golddiggers got up from her place, approached the President, and asked him to autograph her menu. Then more Golddiggers got up. Hope was alarmed when he saw a Marine guard move toward the President's table. Nixon waved the guard away and good-naturedly kept signing. Hope was about to correct the situation when Pat Nixon turned to him and said, "Bob, can I have your autograph?"

At the show that followed, the Nixons sat in the center of the front row of chairs set up in the East Room. Some of the performers were nervous because the VIP audience included cabinet members, congressmen, military leaders, and civilian notables, and because they had to make do with improvised dressing-room facilities and inadequate rehearsal time. But Hope begged indulgence from the audience and launched into his monologue. He said, "But Spiro was so great out on the golf course. . . He put his ball down on the tee and addressed it. . . Only the ball looked up and said, 'Who?'". . . and followed it with, "Martha Mitchell. . . she's the one who makes Ted Agnew look like Calvin Coolidge." Both jokes brought big laughs and applause.

The plane was scheduled to take off from Andrews Air Force Base the follow-ing noon. At eleven o'clock, as requested, Defense Secretary Melvin Laird had arrived and was preparing to make his departure remarks. The rest of the troupe was ready to go and the Lockheed Starlifter was loaded and primed for takeoff. But not Hope. He was still in his pajamas in a darkened bedroom of the Statler Hilton's presidential suite, unable to get up. Mort Lachman was trying to grasp the situation. He had sent for Hope's new senior publicist, Hank Rieger, in case things became critical.

"Do you want us to take off without you, Bob?" asked Mort.

"Yeah," Hope muttered. "I think so. You'd better. I can't make it. I can feel that old pressure behind my eyes. The thought of the next two weeks is murder."

"I'll call out to Andrews and give them the word. You know that Secretary Laird is waiting there for you."

"You're kidding," said Hope to Lachman.

Hank Rieger was now in the room and he came closer to the bed. "And Westmoreland and O'Donnell and, I believe, so is Secretary Rogers."

Quietly Hope got himself to the edge of the bed and staggered into the bath-room. Like the vaudevillian he was, he was bathed, shaved, showered, dressed, and packed within minutes. By noon he was walking into the hangar and up onto the makeshift stage. Laird, Westmoreland, and O'Donnell had been apprised of the reason for Hope's delay and were gracious in their remarks, despite their long wait. Rogers had left. Hope apologized, introduced his cast, and told some jokes and the plane finally lifted off the ground at 1:55 P.M.

The plane took them to West Berlin where they rehearsed, had a quick tour of East Berlin, and did a show for combined military commands at the huge Deutschlandhalle. From Berlin they flew south to Rome for an overnight rest before entertaining on board the aircraft carrier *Saratoga*, which was sitting off-shore at Gaeta, Italy. Then on to Adana, Turkey, for a show at Incirlik Air Force Base. By this time Hope had recovered from his eye scare in Washington and was pumped up by the adulation that flowed from his beloved GIs.

By the time the 1969 tour reached Bangkok its success was virtually guaranteed, and perhaps already cinched, by the arrival of the moonwalker Neil Armstrong. When Hope introduced him there was a four-minute ovation. Hope played straight man to a couple of Armstrong quips, but the astronaut was at his best in a question-and-answer session with GIs in the audience, which mostly involved how he felt when he stepped out on the moon's surface. But there was one question that Armstrong must have guessed would be asked sometime, somewhere. A helicopter pilot in the second row stood up and said, "I want to know why the United States is so interested in the moon instead of the conflict here in Vietnam."

Armstrong smiled and waited until the cheers and whistles stopped, then said, "Well, that's a great question—and one which—ah—which you here may feel there's a great deal of contradiction. We don't feel that's the case. The American—

the nature of the American system is that it works on many levels in many areas to try to build a peace on earth, goodwill toward men. And one of the advantages of the space activity is that it has done that, it has promoted international understanding and enabled cooperative efforts between countries on many levels and will continue to do so in the future."

At still another base a GI asked Neil if he thought humans would some day live on the moon. Armstrong said he thought they might, "but there's a more important question—we have to ask ourselves whether men will be able to live together here on earth." And the applause and cheers went on for several minutes.

Their first show in Vietnam was at Lai Khe for the 1st Infantry Division. Lai Khe was where some of the heaviest fighting of the whole Vietnam War was taking place. The morning of the show a Vietcong mortar emplacement aimed at the stage had been discovered and defused. Much of the audience was battle-weary, men who had recently been pulled off the line where friends had been killed. International media people from the wire services and newsmagazines were out in force.

Hope had been briefed about what these GIs had been through recently, but was in no way prepared for the scattered boos that greeted his parenthetical remark that President Nixon had assured him personally that he had a plan for peace. What dismayed some younger members of the Hope troupe was that when GIs in the audience raised their fingers in the peace sign, Hope insisted they were making the World War II victory sign.

Hope's own subsequent explanation of the Lai Khe reception of his Nixon comments was this: "Their boos were just a way of answering the President. They were too tired, too worn out, too disillusioned to believe that anyone had a plan to end the war and get them out of that hot, steamy, rotten jungle. They'd heard that song before."

Except for the "booing incident," evidence suggests that audiences appreciated Hope and his show as much as ever. But it was also true that this December 1969 GI was not quite the same breed Hope had met before in Vietnam. This was a young guy, probably a draftee, who could not help but be affected by the fact that 250,000 people, most of them of his same age and culture, had taken part in that "March Against Death" in Washington on November 15.

Nevertheless, Hope's commitment to the GI he knew or didn't know was total. And the idea of a dishonorable ending of America's longest and most frustrating war was unthinkable to him. Interestingly enough, on the day of the Lai Khe incident, in St. Louis, Missouri, the *Globe-Democrat* ran this editorial:

YES, VIRGINIA THERE IS A BOB HOPE

We take pleasure in answering at once and thus prominently the communication below, expressing at the same time our great gratification that its faithful author is numbered among the friends of the *Globe*.

Dear Editor:

I am 8 years old. Some of my little friends say there is no Bob Hope. Papa says, 'If you see it in the *Globe* it's so. Please tell the truth, is there a Bob Hope?

(Signed) Virginia

Virginia, your little friends are wrong. They have been affected by the skepticism of a skeptical age. They do not believe except what they see.

Yes, Virginia, there is a Bob Hope. He exists as certainly as generosity and devotion exist, and you know that they abound and give to your life its highest beauty and joy.

Alas! How dreary would be the world if there would be no Bob Hope! It would be as dreary as if there were no Virginias.

There would be no GI-like faith then, no humor, no laughs to make tolerable this existence.

Not believe in Bob Hope! You might as well not believe in Santa Claus.

No Bob Hope! Thank God he lives. A thousand GIs from now, Virginia, nay, 10 times ten thousand GIs from now, men will know his name.

Yes, Virginia, there is a Bob Hope. And he has brought hope to countless of your fellow Americans by giving up his own Christmas at home for 19 years.

As long as he lives, Virginia, there is hope he will continue to make glad the hearts of boys away from home.

The postscript on this 1969 worldwide tour comes from the American public's interest in the 90-minute television show Hope produced from the coverage of that journey. The Nielson ratings company announced that *The Bob Hope Christmas Show*, aired by NBC on January 15, 1970, had the largest audience for an entertainment program (non-motion picture or special event) in television history. It had been seen by an estimated 64 percent of all available viewers.

The Loyalist: 1971 to 1972

41

Rain on Bob's Parade

"You know I have joked about and satirized the foibles of our people and our politics. But there is one subject that doesn't lend itself to jokes, and that is the love I feel so deeply for my adopted country. . . "

If the much-quoted *Guinness Book of Records* included records set for squeezing the most money out of a charity banquet, or rounding up the biggest crowd that ever paid money to attend an indoor benefit show, or for assembling the largest audience ever for an outdoor variety show—then Hope's name would have to be placed next to each entry. What's more, he set all those records in a six-month period.

The charity banquet that raised over $2 million was a fund-raiser for the Eisenhower Medical Center, already under construction in the desert near Palm Springs. When the former president died in 1969, both Bob and Dolores seemed consumed by the same passion for a speedy completion of the hospital complex, which Ike had approved of so heartily—he had also been grateful for the Hopes' enthusiasm.

Bob and Dolores had assured the board of directors that they would take responsibility for locating a third of the $7 million needed for the first building phase—$2.3 million—before the end of 1971. Hope booked the Grand Ballroom of New York's Waldorf-Astoria Hotel for January 27, 1970, and agreed to pick up the $70,000 dinner tab so that a capacity crowd of 1,500 people, each paying $1,000, could guarantee a cool $1.5 million tax-free to the building fund. Hope would arrange the entertainment. More precisely, his current sponsor, Chrysler, agreed to bankroll a 90-minute television special documenting the event, called *Five Stars for a Five Star Man*, with Bing Crosby, Raquel Welch, Johnny Cash, Ray Bolger, and Hope as headliners.

By late November, through persistent telephoning and personal contacts (mostly on the golf course), Hope had collected nearly half of the benefit's targeted goal. Besides money pledged at fund-raising lunches choreographed by Dolores, Hope received individual pledges of $125,000 from Frank Sinatra and Irving Berlin. And his Palm Springs neighbor, *My Fair Lady* composer Frederick (Fritz) Loewe, signed a paper that willed to the hospital all his royalties from that musical after his death.

The dinner itself was the kind of highly touted, socially and politically glittering event that could attract attention from as far away as Paris. The *International Herald Tribune* story of the same date led with news that three presidents—Nixon,

Johnson, and Truman—were honorary chairmen of a dinner guaranteed to be one of the "biggest money raisers of this or any other social season."

The evening of the banquet Hope was visibly nervous, yet he managed the treacherous job of introducing political, social, and business luminaries who were seated at the three-tiered head table and launched into a monologue that included these wisecracks:

> All of the captains of industry are here. Xerox sent a copy of their president. . . And I didn't really expect Nixon to be here. He doesn't have a White House in this state. . . I see Spiro's been all over the Far East without starting a war. . . He must be losing his touch. . . And it's so cold here in New York the politicians have their hands in their own pockets. . .

Not surprisingly, Hope and Crosby in top hats and white ties and tails would weave the most magic from the evening, doing a clever song-and-dance medley from their *Road* pictures. And to Raquel Welch, whose breast-baring gown was a serious concern to NBC censors, Hope said, "My congratulations to your dress designer and I hope he gets out on bail."

The television version of this gala was aired on NBC February 16 and nearly 35 million people watched it. There was some concern, voiced by both television editors and viewers, that not a single black face could be seen either in the audience or as a performer on the show.

Hope's letter to columnist Lucius E. Lee of the Columbus, Ohio, *Call & Post* helped in some small way to put the matter in clearer perspective:

> Dear Mr. Lee:
>
> My brother, Fred Hope, who lives there in Columbus sent me your column about our Eisenhower Medical Center dinner and I wanted to write and explain a couple of things to you.
>
> As I think he told you, we tried to get Ralph Bunche on the dais that night. He wanted to come but he had his neck in a brace and didn't think it would be too comfortable for that long a time. And he was right because the show did run for almost four and a half hours. . .
>
> I also had George Foreman who had just won his fight the night before at Madison Square Garden. He hired a dinner jacket and sat at a table and enjoyed himself immensely. I didn't get a chance to get him on film because when we finally did get the show cut, the first cut was about 29 minutes over. So it was like taking blood out of your arm to get the people on that you wanted the audience to see.

Hope was always sensitive to criticism of this nature; as Mort Lachman said, "You can bet he won't find himself in that position again."

That enormously successful evening—it exceeded expectations and busted over the $2 million mark for the medical center—convinced Hope that he might press his luck and plan a similar evening for Los Angeles the following April. In fact, the second one managed to raise nearly that amount with a smaller guest list. But personal arm-twisting proved to be tougher than just entertaining at a gala benefit. "People use to walk up to me and say, 'Hey Bob, How are ya?' Now they take one look at me and quickly say, 'I gave at the office.'"

But with these donations, and what Hope had pledged from his personal appearance fees for both 1970 and 1971, it would be possible to finish the hospital portion of the Eisenhower Medical Center and dedicate it in 1971. And they did. The Palm Springs Airport hosted *Air Force One* and *Air Force Two* as both President Nixon and Vice President Agnew arrived for the ceremony. They were joined on the platform by Governor Ronald Reagan and an impressive roster of national and local government officials.

Hope hardly had time to take a deep breath when he found himself committed to yet another benefit and another big show on May 16, 1970. His confessed admiration for astronauts and the work of NASA meant that the challenge of producing a "Texas-sized" benefit in the Houston Astrodome was too tempting to turn down. A group of Houston civic boosters had a dream to build a youth center as a memorial to Ed White, one of the astronauts who perished when their capsule caught fire before the launch of Apollo I.

The prospect of filling the nation's biggest indoor sports arena (roughly 50,000) seats both intrigued and worried Hope. However, he had been pledged the full-time services of an entire Houston public relations firm to work with his own battery of publicists, plus any promotion NASA might be able to generate. For music, Hope insisted they hire the Les Brown Band. Otherwise, though, there would be no fees for performers, just expenses, so Hope had to use a lot of sweet talk. He was able to convince Gregory Peck, who had just completed five months at Cape Kennedy working on the space movie *Marooned*, to accept, and used all the charm he could muster to enlist a reluctant Cary Grant, who finally relented saying, "Only Hope could get me to do a show like this one. If it were a job I was getting paid for, I wouldn't come. I melt in front of a microphone." Other stars who reacted favorably to Hope's personal calls were David Janssen, Dorothy Lamour, Joey Heatherton, Glen Campbell, and Robert Goulet.

Also appearing that night, but not necessarily through Hope's personal intervention, were Bobby Sherman, Nancy Ames, Frankie Valli and the Four Seasons, the Friends of Distinction, Trini Lopez, John Rowles, the Step Brothers, and Heisman Trophy winner O. J. Simpson.

The show was long and it was a hit. Billed as "Bob Hope's Extra Special," it had something for every age group. But undeniably what captured the audience's full attention was Hope, Gregory Peck, David Janssen, and Cary Grant in a cleverly written song sketch called "Showmanship," and later their return at the end of the show for a funny and sentimental tribute to the astronauts, "We Love All Those Wonderful Guys." Who could avoid sensing the rarity of such an unlikely team of performers—three serious actors and Hope—singing and dancing together on a stage in the Astrodome?

Just before the close, Hope's face was flashed in lights on the Astrodome scoreboard and the comedian came out to announce that 46,857 people had paid to see the show, a record for the Astrodome and for any previous indoor variety show produced in the United States. Hope was presented with a life-size portrait of himself, which would hang in the foyer of the Ed White Memorial Center, and as he accepted it, people were up on their feet cheering and applauding as far as the eye could see in the half-light of that huge domed auditorium.

As an entertainer Hope had experienced many standing ovations in many types of venues—from big GI audiences overseas to convention halls and large college auditoriums and even stadiums, but this night was different. He told this author that something made him think of a time many, many years ago (42, to be exact) when he had invited his mother to see his vaudeville act the day he made his triumphant return to Cleveland in 1929. Now he wished she were out there tonight so he could once again look down, shade his eyes, and say: *There she is, folks. That's my Mahm. The one with lilies of the valley on her hat. Right down here. Put a spot on her. Stand up, Mahm, and let these folks see you!*

Later Hope laughed, saying, "There was a lot of Cagney in me that night. I felt like I wanted to do that final bit from *White Heat*, when Jimmy climbs up to the top of that huge gas storage tank and hollers, 'Top of the world, Mom!' as it blows sky high."

A month and a half later, working on an open-air stage that faced the Washington Monument, before an audience that one *Washington Star* news story claimed was "probably the largest outdoor audience ever assembled to watch a variety show," Hope had quite different feelings.

It all began on the first of June, when Hope responded to an invitation from *Reader's Digest* publisher Hobart Lewis, evangelist Billy Graham, and hotel tycoon Willard Marriott. These three forces shared an idea that the nation should have a grand-scale patriotic Fourth of July celebration that they would call Honor America Day. This was an attempt, like the previous National Unity Week, to rouse the silent majority and to reunite a Vietnam-polarized nation. They wanted Hope on their team.

Their plan was ambitious. They hoped to generate Honor America Day programs in cities and towns all across the United States, with a focus on the big party in the nation's capital that would include religious observances in the forenoon at the Lincoln Memorial, and a spectacular entertainment package with fireworks on the Mall facing the Washington Monument at dusk. They had already enlisted Walt Disney Productions to design and stage the two separate segments of the day.

Hope liked the concept, and at a news conference on June 4, he and Graham announced they had accepted national chairmanships. Graham's organization was to arrange the Lincoln Memorial service, and Hope would produce the Washington Monument variety show.

"It's just going to be an old-fashioned American Fourth of July," said Hope to the assembled media, "a celebration to give Americans a chance to let go—and the country's about ready to let go, believe me. We're downtrodden by the rough news from Vietnam and countless demonstrations against one aspect or another of American life, but we're trying to keep the war out of this—a celebration instead of a demonstration."

Billy Graham spoke about how much the people he had recently talked with across the nation valued their fundamental freedoms and to him nothing was more basic "than our religious beliefs." Graham made it clear that it would be an ecumenical kind of religious observance with much diversity.

When Hope was questioned about bipartisan support, he cited senators and house members from both sides of the aisle, mentioned backing from labor and the sports world and the space program, and announced that former Presidents Truman and Johnson and former First Lady Mamie Eisenhower were honorary chairs. Still, on June 9, the *Washington Post* voiced doubt that this could be an "old-fashioned Fourth."

> The suspicion, as we get it, is that any effort to make something different out of this year's Fourth of July observances is going to take on the trappings of a pro-war rally in support of President Nixon's Vietnam policy, no matter how much the sponsors wish to avoid it, just by the identity of the principal figures who have so far identified themselves with the idea—that and the electricity in the air. . . It needs a broader mix, not just of Democrats as well as Republicans. But of dissenters as well as supporters. . . They could make the point a little more explicit by trying to engage the active support of responsible leaders on the other side of the great national debate—of Hubert Humphrey, to take one example, or George McGovern.

By mid-June, the rally had, in fact, engaged Humphrey and McGovern as well as two other harsh administration critics, Senators Muskie and Mansfield, but on June 19 the *Post* persisted: "It's not enough to seek a 'broader mix' and a better balance on the letter head. The test is in the actuality."

One of the event's most vociferous critics was Rennie Davis, one of the Chicago Seven (seven men charged with disrupting the 1968 Democratic National Convention in Chicago). Davis called a news conference to publicly challenge Hope and Graham about the absence from Honor America Day participants of any representatives of the political left, which was actively protesting the administration's Vietnam policy. This in turn inspired newspaper editorials like this one on June 10 from editor Felix McNight in the *Dallas Times Herald:*

On the Fourth of July, a citizen named Bob Hope will stand alongside the Washington Monument and ask his brothers to cool their differences and act like Americans. It used to be done every Fourth of July—all over the land. Somehow, it went out of style. And we haven't been the same since. But Bob Hope, who has earned his credentials, will use the same hallowed slope that has been available to war dissenters, to rally his distressed nation around its flag. . . It's something another man 35 years ago might have done. Sadly, very few of the immediate younger generation ever heard of a man named Will Rogers. . . Will Rogers twitted presidents in homey, spontaneous humor. He could take the heaviest national issues and iron them out in plain language that all could understand. . . The closest we'll come to a Will Rogers is Bob Hope. He has the national image and respect. He has the same intense love for his country, and he has the guts to stand up to any heckling hippie.

Hope felt that all this charging and countercharging was divisive and he asked Willard Marriott, who was executive chairman of the rally, to call a news conference at the Washington Press Club on June 29. At the press conference Hope said, looking very pleased, "We've got Jack Benny, Dinah Shore, Kate Smith, Red Skelton—and there's Roberta Flack, Dottie Lamour, Pat Boone, Barbara Eden, the New Christy Minstrels, the Golddiggers, Connie Stevens, the Young Americans, Fred Waring. Not a bad list, and there's more. We may be there all night. It takes Jack Benny two hours just to say his own name."

"Some of your critics, Bob, say that young people and dissidents are being excluded," said a media voice.

"That's simply not true," answered Hope. "This is an American family affair and we hope everybody comes. You won't want to miss seeing Sugar Ray Robinson. And for those guys who say we have nobody from the talkies—how about Teresa Graves, Glen Campbell, Jeanne C. Riley, and B. J. Thomas—?"

"But what about people like the Smothers?"

"I'm glad you brought that up. I've been trying to get Dick Gregory—he's somewhere in Canada, I'm told—but we may actually have Tom and Dick. They're thinking about it. I've done them a couple of favors in the past," said Hope winking.

After the third time a reporter suggested this celebration was pro-Nixon, Marriott broke in with, "I'm telling you it will be absolutely free of politics. It's not to promote anyone's pet ideas. Everyone has been advised to stay away from politics in general and the war in particular. And that includes Bob Hope—right, Bob?"

"Willard, I can't say there won't be any political jokes—that's a matter of editing. But you know my style. As long as no one gets too serious and messes up the show. You know I gotta talk about Agnew's golf game—it's the funniest and most frightening thing happening today." Hope was referring to the fact that the Vice President's tee-shot at a recent celebrity tournament had hit a gallery spectator.

"The weather forecast is for rain, Bob," one reporter said.

"Don't worry. We'll have over 400,000 people out there—the biggest crowd that has gathered for any show."

"Bigger than Woodstock?"

"Yeah—bigger than Woodstock. And that didn't have NBC and CBS."

Hope had set up his operations base at his favorite Washington retreat, a plush, mahogany-rich suite at the slightly removed Shoreham Hotel. Early on the Fourth, Hope rehearsed with Lamour, Benny, and Shore (who had nearby suites) and resisted going over to the stage set up on the Mall because he had received eyewitness reports that a sizable crowd—variously described as protesters, demonstrators, hippies, and radicals—were wading nude in the reflecting pools, shouting obscenities during the midday services at Lincoln Memorial, smoking pot, and being rounded up by policemen on horseback. All this in a considerable amount of wind and rain.

A few hours before showtime on that Saturday afternoon, as weather seemed to be only one of the concerns, Hope remained in his suite, working with Mort Lachman on the evening's monologue and comedy material, which the writers had provided for Hope's introductions, and continuity dialogue with performers. Bob Jani, Disney's genius of outdoor spectacle and no novice when it came to dealing with troublesome weather, was both producer and stage director of the three-hour show and fireworks display. He was providing Hope, over the telephone, a running commentary about the dress rehearsal as it was progressing and simultaneously was lamenting wind damage to his stage designs.

Finally, a combination of guilt and curiosity got the better of Hope and he asked a D.C. policeman to drive him in a squad car to the show site for a conference with Jani and a short run-through with Les Brown. The rain and winds had subsided and crews were repairing damage to the red, white, and blue bunting of the Disneyesque setting.

Off to the side, eyed by security police, were a group of half-naked hippie types who were drinking Ripple and watching Hope rehearse. At one point he stopped to acknowledge their hollering, and he invited them to come see the show that night. Even as he spoke, on the backside of the stage, facing the Lincoln Memorial, a rampaging crowd of protesters somehow eluded security guards and attacked an oasis of fast-food vendors, ate all their ice cream and hot dogs, drank their soda pop, and then dragged the pushcarts into the reflecting pools.

That night, before Hope went onstage, an additional contingent of District police was called in because a rash of bottle-throwing started among the hecklers and demonstrators, who were fenced off from the main audience, which the D.C. park service was estimating at showtime to number somewhere around 350,000.

Hope, dressed nattily in a dark-blue suit, white shirt, and striped tie, stepped out onto the stage and looked toward the Washington Monument at what would seem to be an unending mass of people. "Do you believe this?" he asked. "What a crowd! Nixon took one look at this and said, 'My God, what has Agnew done now?'. . . And then Agnew looked out his window and said, 'What a great time to say something.'"

Viewers at home watching the NBC–CBS coverage got a big talent-filled show and would not have known anything was amiss on the sidelines if Hope had not ad-libbed, during one of his introductions, "Where am I? Back in Vietnam?" when some firecrackers went off at the side of the stage. Even most of that huge assemblage was totally unaware that two canisters of homemade stink bomb had been hurled by demonstrators into the audience from behind the storm-fence barriers. Quick-thinking security guards hurled them back. Only people sitting closest to the sidelines could hear the obscenities being shouted, but many gathered up their children and left.

After Fred Waring's ensemble finished a patriotic medley and Hope called everyone out onstage for a moving rendition of "Battle Hymn of the Republic," a dazzling display of fireworks burst out over the Mall area, and the massive audience began to move off to their cars and buses. Policemen conducted Hope from the stage to his Chrysler limousine, but not before some of the demonstrators had broken through the police cordon in time to beat their fists against the trunk of the automobile as it moved away.

Waiting for Hope when he got back to Los Angeles the next day was a letter from comedian Dick Gregory, which offered his explanation why he could not accept Hope's invitation to appear in Washington:

To me the Fourth of July is a time for the most serious kind of national reflection. To me it is a time to analyze the growth of the child, Independence. It is a time to "change the course of human events" and see how America measures up to its most cherished rhetoric. It is a time to apply the Declaration of Independence to our national life, rather than revere that document as a quaint expression of Americana.

So, Bob, this Fourth of July, we will be both trying to honor America in our own individual ways. You will be sacrificing your personal holiday, as you have done so many times before, giving your time and talent to bring joy to thousands of Americans. My holiday will be one of serious reflection. I currently am fasting to dramatize the tragedy and hypocrisy of the narcotics problem in America.

I long for the day when Americans can laugh and sing together, can watch Bob Hope and Dick Gregory performing together without considering our political persuasions.

42

A Partisan Voice

"Every place I go I tell what's in my heart and in my head. I don't adjust for the place. I walk in and tell it like I think it is."

By the middle of 1970, Hope's political leanings were fully apparent. He still edited his material in favor of neutrality, but even a cursory examination of his monologues throughout two decades suggest more bite to his humor leveled at Democratic administrations than at Republican ones. In addition, there were certain activities in the months before and after Honor America Day that suggested where he would put his campaign contributions and how he punched out his ballot in the voting booth.

In the spring Hope helped raise over $350,000 at a political luncheon supporting his friend the former Ohio governor Jim Rhodes for a U.S. Senate seat. (Rhodes was defeated.) He cut television and radio spots in support of his pal George Murphy's successful bid to retain his Republican Senate seat in Washington. He appeared in a short commercial film supporting Republican Lenore Romney's campaign in Michigan for a U.S. Senate seat. In addition to campaign contributions to the Ronald Reagan fund, he was also active in fundraising for the San Jose Republicans, and he and Dolores hosted a reception in their Toluca Lake home for the campaign of Barry Goldwater, Jr.

In an attempt to keep a balance, the night after the Goldwater party the Hopes flew to St. Louis, where Bob appeared at a political banquet supporting Democratic candidate Stuart Symington's bid for reelection to the Senate.

Whenever Hope was challenged about being partisan, he responded by saying that his endorsements were all isolated personal favors. The Murphy and Hope relationship dated back to 1933. Both Buckeyes, Rhodes and Hope had been golfing buddies for years. Lenore Romney and the comedian met the night she presented Dolores with an award at a USO affair. Hope called her "one of the brightest gals I've met" and, reflecting the times, added, "And I figured if we're going to have women in government, we might as well have *her.*" And his love and respect for Symington, despite Stuart's defection from his onetime hawkish Vietnam position, were well known.

Yet Hope stepped firmly into the Republican "big time" in November 1971, agreeing to entertain at a pair of expensive and deftly choreographed "Salute to the President" fund-raising affairs in New York City and in Chicago—both attended by Nixon. After Hope did his monologue at the New York banquet he slipped out with campaign director Bob Dole and they took a private jet to the Windy City ahead of *Air Force One* so Hope could begin entertaining the Republicans at the Chicago banquet and have them on their feet when Nixon walked in.

The following May, Hope headed a group of Hollywood personalities who traveled to Baltimore for a fund-raising "Salute to Ted Agnew." In September, Hope headlined a "Victory '72" dinner for the Republican National Committee in Detroit. The next day he flew back to Los Angeles to appear at a campaign dinner with Nixon. On October 6, Hope emceed a Black Republican dinner, and later that month flew to Boston to share the stage with Pat Nixon at yet another fund-raiser.

And in the intervening months, Hope made a number of appearances on talk shows hosted by Phil Donahue, Mike Douglas, Johnny Carson, and Irv Kupcinet, during which he left no doubt about his support for the administration.

This display of partisanship did not go unremarked in the national press. In fact, it raised quite a few eyebrows—and hackles. But why the fuss? Was it, after all, so important that Americans know precisely how Hope cast his ballot and made his campaign contributions? The primary issue was more probably a question of influence. As noted by the *Washington Post:* "Democratic campaign strategists groan at the thought of Mr. Hope's all-American good guy image being added to the Republican arsenal. In a recent *Reader's Digest* survey of about 250,000 high school students, Mr. Hope was named the outstanding entertainment figure of the 1960s and was second only to the Beatles world-wide."

Hope's potential for influence could not be taken lightly. His media critics were concerned that in his support of the administration he sounded simplistic, and when he said with assurance that today's young people recognize that America had not used its full capability in Vietnam ("Kids like a show of strength"), his critics said he was "out of tune."

Three major media stories—one breaking in late summer 1970, from the Associated Press; another in midfall, in *The New York Times Magazine*; and the third in the winter of 1971, in *Life*—had significant impact on Hope and on the public's perception of him.

First, there was a widely circulated Associated Press wire service story in August quoting Kenneth D. Smith, entertainment coordinator for USO Special Services in Europe, who charged that entertainers like Bob Hope and George Jessel could no longer reach today's GI.

Hope, whose eyes and ears could hardly fail to register the noisy, enthusiasm of his recent Vietnam tour, fumed at this and asked his friends in the Defense Department and in the USO organization whom this Smith was speaking for and why. Two days later, the Pentagon issued an official disclaimer and a shorter wire story said Smith had been misquoted.

However, the idea lingered in Hope's mind. Maybe Smith had a point. He talked to his writing staff and they added several wisecracks about pot smoking to his Christmas 1970 monologues overseas. And they generated unusually loud roars, whistles, and cheers, especially when delivered to Vietnam audiences. For instance: "In one barracks I passed, a group of GIs were watching *Twelve O'Clock High* and they didn't even have a TV set." But mild as this and other pot jokes in the show were, NBC refused to air them in the January telecast.

Then in August, J. Anthony Lukas, a Pulitzer Prize–winning journalist and new staff writer for *The New York Times Magazine*, arrived in Los Angeles to do a major story on Hope. The Hope West Coast public relations staff, advised by Allan Kalmus that Lukas "was not out there to do a fan magazine story," handled the writer cautiously, monitoring most of the interviews until Lukas complained that the press agents were getting in his way. He insisted thereafter on talking privately to people like Jimmy Saphier, Hope's son-in-law Nat Lande, and the writers. Even so, he was heard to say, "I have yet to meet someone who is willing to say something unflattering about the man."

But there was sufficient candor to fortify the writer's contention that lately Bob Hope had vigorously assumed new roles that to Lukas, at least, seemed unbecoming. His story title "This is Bob (Politician—Patriot—Publicist) Hope" reveals his thesis that Hope as an enormously popular voice used his undeniably sincere concern for the GI and his conservative theme of Americanism to prolong an increasingly unpopular war, and that his alliance, both silent and active, with the Nixon-Agnew team had created a potent political force.

This was the first major journalistic effort in a much respected magazine to analyze "the new Bob Hope." Some of the insights that infused this story with bite came in fact from Hope loyalists who themselves were beginning to feel the pressure and personal uneasiness of their employer's new political stance. Hope's gag writers, for instance, revealed to Lukas how frequently Hope requested one-liners from them for Agnew's use in his speeches, particularly the one that attacked the Eastern establishment press in which he said, "Newspapers perform a great service. I know at our house we couldn't do without the *Baltimore Sun*. We have two puppies and a parakeet. . . We tried *The New York Times* and it's not nearly as absorbent. . . I read *The New York Times* every day. I enjoy good fiction. . . "

One can imagine resentment bordering on anger and even revenge gorging the throat of a young *Times* journalist considering the butt of this humor.

Hope's distaste for the magazine article, which appeared October 4, 1970, was based on what he saw as gratuitous and offensive "flags" in the story. One flag had to do purely and simply with what Hope saw as disloyalty within his inner circle, for example, when Lukas wrote: "Some members of his staff feel he is growing out of touch even with the troops he visits every year in Vietnam. 'He just doesn't understand how the GI feels today,' says one of his writers. 'When he sees a V sign in his audience he thinks two guys want to go to the bathroom.'"

Lukas's view that Hope's "greatest single public relations effort has been entertainment of the military at home and abroad for the past 29 years" suggested gross opportunism on the part of Hope. The ultimate jab was contained in the suggestion that Hope and his highly motivated PR squad constituted a valuable publicity channel for the Pentagon and particularly the conservative elements within it. In a call to his lawyer, Martin Gang, to inquire about the possibility of a slander suit, Hope branded the story "irresponsible" and "inaccurate." Hope also called Allan Kalmus to obtain a complete list of every person Lukas had interviewed.

But the Lukas piece was just a prelude to events that fall that would have more far-reaching effects. In mid-November, a few days before Bob and Dolores were to fly to London (where he would entertain royalty twice and would be surprised to be the subject of *This Is Your Life*), he made a short side trip to Chicago to do a benefit as a favor to his old pal Jack Gray, and two paid ($25,000) appearances, one at Flint, Michigan, and the other at South Bend, Indiana, for Notre Dame's homecoming game.

Flying from Chicago on a chilly and overcast Friday afternoon, Hope was accompanied by a *Life* magazine reporter, Joan Barthel, who had made a name for herself with several perceptive show business profiles. Hope had agreed with Kalmus that she could be "around him" for several days to do a kind of "on the road with Hope in the seventies" piece. Barthel had pitched to her editor and to Kalmus the idea that "the private Hope is the same as the public Hope and his natural habitat is on the road."

On the plane, the noise from the jet engines forced Barthel to lean very close to the comedian. Hope was holding a paper cup of orange juice and answering her question about what he was currently saying to audiences: "Every place I go I tell what's in my heart and in my head. I don't adjust for the place. I walk in and tell it like I think it is." He sipped on his juice. "Hell, we've got to end this thing with honor.

"Look you're not going to change some people's minds," he said, looking into her face. "But they know where I've been and what I try to do over there for our guys. I just think you're going to give people confidence, people who are in doubt about our sanity."

Barthel asked if this included the college crowd.

"I wouldn't play colleges if the people didn't show up," Hope replied, "but the audiences get better all the time. I just played Athens, Georgia—eleven thousand on Friday night—and I played Auburn on Saturday—fifteen thousand more. If they turn out like that it's a sign they want to see you, they want to hear what you're saying."

Barthel tape-recorded Hope's performance at Flint in its entirety, including his final five minutes of serious talk with the audience. And the next afternoon, at Notre Dame, she observed carefully during half-time ceremonies when Notre Dame's athletic director, "Moose" Krause, conducted Hope out onto the playing field for a university-sponsored "Salute to Bob Hope." In the standing ovation that followed in that South Bend stadium where the normal noise level for any game is nearly ear-shattering, one could hear cheers and whistles, but also catcalls and even what sounded like "boos." Barthel was also close by that evening in the university sports center and tape-recorded all that Hope said in his solo performance.

After another standing ovation and Hope's serious remarks, shorter than those at Flint, Hope retired to his dressing room. Barthel stopped in to thank him for his time and to observe that she now knew the essence of the legend.

43

This Is Your Life!

"England's a great place for a comedian to work. It's an island, so the audience can't run very far."

The tip-off that writer Joan Barthel probably had an agenda for her *Life* magazine piece came clearly to Hope when he told her she could get an even better impression of a 1970s vaudevillian in action if she followed him around for the next few days and watched him perform in the land of his birth. Barthel thanked him and said she had gotten what she came for. Hope wondered about that remark but would discover all too well "what she came for" when her *Life* article appeared and with it the ensuing turmoil of 1971.

In fact, it would have been inconvenient had Barthel shown up to tag along that next Sunday, November 15, 1970, when they left New York. It had been raining in New York since early morning. It was raw and windy weather but the planes were flying at Kennedy. Dolores had flown in from L.A. the day before and now the Hopes were headed for London, where Bob was scheduled to entertain at two royal functions. As usual they were running late, and the passenger agent worked fast to hustle four hefty pieces of luggage, including Bob's theatrical wardrobe trunk, from limousine to baggage handlers.

The airline, BOAC, had already been alerted that the Hopes were en route to London. Even before their limo had glided out of the Waldorf Towers driveway, an assistant manager standing in the Towers lobby was on the phone asking a BOAC official to make sure they got on that flight. Somehow they managed to arrive at Kennedy with minutes to spare.

Hope breezed through this barely-making-flights routine with an accustomed nonchalance that could have been irritating to the airlines, except that he was a unique customer. After all, for 30 years his benign airline gags ("I knew it was an old plane when I found Lindbergh's lunch on the seat") and his omnipresence in airports and on regularly scheduled commercial flights (sometimes he racked up as many as 20,000 miles a week), rendered him a cherished unsalaried spokesman.

He was now striding a few feet ahead of Dolores toward the gate, affably smiling at people who stopped and turned in disbelief. He spotted a public telephone, and while the passenger agent escorted Dolores to the plane, Bob called "the boys" on the Coast.

It was one of his celebrated need-a-few-things calls, which could come at any hour and from any place. Usually he called Mort Lachman, who would then alert the other six. Right now Hope needed some jokes about Grace Kelly because she had, on very short notice, replaced an ailing Noel Coward as "compère" (the British term for emcee) of his Monday night London benefit. Also, he had neglected to tell Mort that he would be staying at the Savoy on this trip.

The passenger agent was hovering over Hope and was visibly relieved when the comedian finally hung up. By now his telephoning had delayed the takeoff by a few minutes. Hope walked briskly into the first-class section of the plane, humming and smiling his way to what was universally acknowledged to be "his" seats on any commercial flight—the right-side bulkhead seats. There he and Dolores could stretch out, put their feet up, be generally undisturbed. And when Hope traveled alone, which was more often than one might suspect, the airline thoughtfully left the space beside him unsold.

Soon after takeoff, Bob opened his briefcase, put on his half-glasses, and began to look over the London monologue material that Miss Hughes had put into his case. On top were the fact sheets prepared by his public relations people describing the events involving royalty, and Hope's role in each one.

Dolores glanced down and followed with interest the details of his Monday night benefit, extravagantly labeled "A Night of Nights." It was a fund-raiser for Earl Mountbatten of Burma's favorite charity, the United World College Fund, for which Bob was sharing the star billing with Frank Sinatra. Princess Grace of Monaco would also be in the show.

Two identical performances were scheduled back-to-back for Royal Festival Hall audiences, who were paying 50 pounds a ticket. BBC would videotape the first of these two shows for international distribution, and Hope was concerned that his first audience might be a tougher one to reach. He would prefer BBC to tape the second show—or both, in fact—because he had some special material he could "try out" on the first sitting.

After the second performance, he and Dolores, Sinatra, Princess Grace, and assorted other royals and members of the British elite were invited to a buffet supper at St. James's Palace, hosted by Prince Charles and Princess Anne.

Dolores had a sense of excitement at the prospect of rubbing elbows with the royals but also she was harboring a certain amount of disappointment. While she and Bob were dining with the royal family, the rest of her immediate brood—daughter Linda and husband Nat, daughter Nora and husband Sam, son Tony and wife Judy—would be lurking at the Savoy and forced to dine somewhere where they could remain anonymous and unrecognized. Yet Dolores had to appreciate the importance of these cloak-and-dagger arrangements. They were integral to Tuesday night's surprise event.

The Hope children, including son Kelly if he could be located (he was still a student, spending a semester on a Campus Afloat cruise), were being flown to London to surprise Bob in Thames Television's production of *This Is Your Life*. Hope was to be the first honoree in a British revival of America's radio-television success show of the early fifties. Dolores was pleased that this secret had been successfully kept from Bob, who generally hated surprises but mysteriously always seemed to know everything that was going on. What convinced Dolores that the secret was still intact was a conversation she and Bob had had a few days before.

"Bob, be sure and have Miss Hughes add the Annenberg dinner party to your London schedule. It's Tuesday night. They're honoring Mountbatten."

"What day is that, Dolores?"

"It's Tuesday."

"What time, Tuesday? I'm doing a talk show with Eamonn Andrews at Thames Television that night."

"It's dinner. I think seven."

"I can join you there. I should be finished by seven-thirty."

Dolores had studied his face. She was positive he didn't know. If the surprise got out, it would happen because the Thames producer had arranged, foolishly in her view, to house all of the *This Is Your Life* guests at the Savoy. Program coordinator Alan Haire confidently assured her that precautions had been taken—whatever that meant—to prevent Hope and surprise guests from meeting each other prematurely.

Actually, Dolores felt secure about most of the arrangements for this London trip. This was largely due to the numerous telephone calls she had received from Lady Carolyn Townshend, Bob's socially prominent London publicist, whose distant royal connection was useful in coordinating such high-level engagements, making wardrobe suggestions, and smoothing out questions of protocol.

By this time, Bob had removed his half-glasses and handed the fact sheets to Dolores and he was almost instantly asleep. Dolores's eyes fell on the next fact sheet. Bob's appearance Wednesday night was unquestionably the most intriguing event on their schedule. It's distinction lay in its guest list more than its performers. Under one roof, at a London nightclub called the Talk of the Town, most of Europe's royalty would assemble for a "Royal Gala Cabaret" to benefit the World Wildlife Fund, whose cosponsors were Britain's Prince Philip and the Netherlands' Prince Bernhard. And she noticed that her children and their spouses were included.

Though the invitation bore the imprint of the Duke of Edinburgh's personal stationery, it had arrived at the Hope office by way of Bob's former British booking agent, Sir Lew Grade. Hope made it clear to Grade, despite the quality of the other distinguished names on the bill—Rex Harrison, Rudolph Nureyev, Petula

Clark, Glen Campbell, Engelbert Humperdinck, and George Kirby—that he must get top billing.

But to the wealthy audience and the media the real draw of the night was going to be the royal roster. Except for the occasional royal funeral, it would be virtually impossible to find this many of Europe's past or present monarchs under one roof: King Constantine and Queen Anne Marie of Greece, Prince Don Juan Carlos of Spain, Prince Henrik and Princess Margrethe of Denmark, the Grand Duke and Duchess of Luxembourg, the Crown Prince of Norway, Prince Albert of Belgium, and possibly Queen Juliana of the Netherlands. All these would be shining alongside Queen Elizabeth, Prince Charles, Princess Anne, Princess Alexandra, and Prince Michael of Kent in an effort to raise 200,000 pounds sterling (a half a million dollars) for the cause of the world's natural flora and fauna.

Dolores's eyes were fastened on this note: "Because of possible jealousy on the part of other people, Mr. and Mrs. Hope *will not* be seated at the Queen's table at the Talk of the Town royal cabaret. Mr. Hope will be seated at Prince Charles's table at the request of Prince Charles." Then her eyes focused on one particular sentence, "Mrs. Hope will be seated at a table near the Queen." Under no circumstances did she intend being separated from Bob at this gala. She would also insist that her children not only have good seats but also be introduced to the Queen.

Bob woke up as Dolores dozed off. He rubbed his eyes and put his glasses on again. He began to paw through his briefcase for the material that "the boys" had delivered to his office. He rubbed his eyes again. Normally he would never admit it even to himself, but he felt really tired. His recent schedule had not necessarily been more grueling than usual, but the events of the past week, the shows at Flint and Notre Dame and the intrusive grilling by the *Life* magazine reporter, had probably induced some stress. Ever since he had experienced the eye hemorrhages and heard his doctors' warnings about stress, he tried hard to let things that were out of balance wash over him. But that was not always easy. He wanted things *his* way.

He had to pick gags for his Monday night shows. He had a system that worked since radio days. He looked at every writer's material three times. If he liked a joke at first reading he placed a check by the gag. Next time he would only reread the checked gags and the ones he still liked the second time got another check. When he reread the double-checked gags he would circle, and number in order, the ones he planned to use in the monologue. This time there were three he particularly liked. They got checks.

On the trip over, our BOAC jet was almost hijacked but the British are so clever. The stewardess turned out to be a man from Scotland Yard. . . Imagine that. . . just when I was beginning to care. . . All that time I'd been whistling at shoulder holsters.

When Bob and Dolores deplaned a few hours later, Lady Carolyn Townshend and Hope's London gag writer, Denis Goodwin, were waiting at Heathrow. Bob was wide awake, responding affably to their questions about his health, reciting a list of his recent activities. Dolores was sleepily cordial. She had never seen Lady Carolyn before. They had only spoken by telephone so she was not prepared to see such a pretty Swedish model–type blonde and was a bit put off by her non-stop chattering during the ride into the city.

Carolyn was saying that it now seemed that BBC planned to tape both of Monday's "Night of Nights" performances. That pleased Hope. She said that Queen Juliana of the Netherlands definitely would attend the World Wildlife Fund gala as would Neil Armstrong, Clare Boothe Luce, and Cary Grant. Grant would be there as official celebrity spokesman for Fabergé, the cosmetics and perfume company that had bought the U.S. television rights to the Royal Gala Cabaret. This news interested Hope. It meant that Jimmy Saphier would be negotiating with Lew Grade for a sizable fee for him.

Carolyn also announced there would be a news conference for Hope, Princess Grace, and Sinatra at 2 P.M. on Monday at Festival Hall, where a rehearsal would then take place at three. Hope asked her to arrange it for a later time, say more like 4 P.M. She said she would try but didn't think it possible.

It was past midnight by the time the Hopes settled into their hotel room. Bob said goodnight to Dolores and set out with Carolyn and Denis for his usual night walk. The air was cold and penetrating as they walked away from the Savoy along the Strand. Hope asked Denis to meet him the next day to go over material. He told Carolyn to make certain the British press, and particularly the wire services, knew the London performances were strictly benefits and that any fees were being assigned to the Eisenhower Medical Center. Carolyn said they could cover that and any other subjects at the news conference the next afternoon at Festival Hall.

They crossed over the Strand at Bush House and then started back toward the Savoy. Thoroughly chilled, Carolyn and Denis were relieved when Hope said good night to them in the lobby and retired upstairs.

The next day, having had only a few hours' sleep, Carolyn arrived back at the Savoy just after one o'clock in the afternoon. It was sleeting when she stepped out of the cab and she nearly lost her umbrella in a sudden gust of wind. She pulled off her rain hat and looked around the lobby. The cherubic-looking Denis came to greet her.

"He's not taking calls, according to the operator," said Denis.

"The hell," she said, with a desperate look on her face, as she headed for the house phones. The operator agreed to connect her only when she imperiously announced, "This is *Lady* Carolyn Townshend" in her well-bred voice.

Hope responded sluggishly, asking what time it was. "It's after one, Bob," she said, "and we're due at Festival Hall in forty-five minutes."

He told them to come upstairs. Dolores had gone out to shop in Lower Bond Street. He was coming out of a heavy sleep. The blackout shades were still drawn and the room was stygian.

"What time is it now?" he asked from his bed.

"One twenty-five," Denis said.

"What's the weather?" Hope asked, rising out of the bed and going into the bathroom, leaving the door slightly ajar and relieving himself noisily. Denis told him about the sleet.

Breakfast arrived with amazing speed, but Hope was on the telephone speaking in a low, rather secretive voice. He hung up the phone and sat drowsily on the edge of the bed pouring coffee. The phone rang again. This time he spoke more loudly but soothingly to Charlie Hogan's wife, Pat, in Chicago. Charlie was dying of cancer. Hogan, one of Hope's two or three most cherished friends, was the booking agent who had given him the job that saved his life in 1928 and he had remained one of Hope's agents and had been a Hope confidant ever since. Bob told Pat he would come to Chicago as quickly as he could, probably Saturday night at the latest.

"Denis, ask Carolyn if she wants some coffee."

Denis went into the sitting room and spoke to Carolyn, who was on the other phone, and then he came back. "She says no, Bob. She just wants you to hurry, please."

The phone rang. It was Lew Grade welcoming him to London. It rang again. It was Walter Annenberg welcoming him to London. Denis brought in a telegram that had just been delivered: BOB HOPE—SAVOY HOTEL WC2—BOB OF BURBANK WELCOME TO LONDON—MOUNTBATTEN OF BURMA.

At two o'clock he was still in his pajamas talking to Mort Lachman in Burbank about the monologue for his November NBC special. Then he called David Frost, asking his help with a walk-on gag at the "Night of Nights" shows. He asked Frost which glamour stars were then in London. Raquel Welch? Good, could he ask her to do the gag with him? Frost agreed to find Raquel, and to meet Hope at Festival Hall for rehearsal at three.

"What time is the news conference, Carolyn?"

"Right now. I couldn't get it changed."

"Well—let's go!" said Hope in his best Jackie Gleason–like voice. By two thirty-five they were in the chauffeur-driven car reserved for Hope and heading across Waterloo Bridge toward Festival Hall, on the South Bank.

The media people had interviewed Princess Grace and Frank and taken some photos and except for a *Daily Mail* reporter and photographer, had cleared out by two forty-five.

When Hope, trailed by Denis and Carolyn, came into the rehearsal, Frank was going over some tempi with the orchestra and Princess Grace was gone. David Frost came in and so did Raquel Welch, but only to tell Hope that she didn't think she could do the dance-on bit with Frost that night. Hope was persuasive and as they went through some steps, the *Daily Mail* got an exclusive photo story.

Hope asked Carolyn when the news conference would begin and she said they had missed it because they were late. Hope bantered a bit with Sinatra, went over the tempi of his songs with Bill Miller, the music director, and said he had to go. The ride back to the Savoy was mostly silent. Hope sailed through the lobby as if he were alone. Carolyn broke the chill by saying they would pick him up at six. Hope said, "That's fine" before the elevator doors closed.

The two performances that night went well enough. Hope was not, as several friends and critics observed, in prime form but was still sufficiently outrageous at one moment and suitably ingenious the next to satisfy an audience whose members had paid high ticket prices for a once-in-a-lifetime chance to see him, Sinatra, and a real-live storybook princess together on one stage.

Just before the first performance was to begin, Hope learned that Raquel would not appear. He suggested they find Eric Morely, the president of Mecca Ltd., the company that ran the annual Miss World Contest. (Hope was scheduled to emcee the contest later in the week.) Hope knew that Eva Reuber-Steir, the reigning Miss World, who had gone to Vietnam with him the previous Christmas, was in London. As he suspected, she was on her way to the show anyway and she agreed to do the gag with Frost. The *Manchester Guardian's* Philip Hope-Wallace, expecting to be sharply critical of a high-priced benefit marred by the intrusion of glaring lights and television cameras, was mellow in his review the next morning: "I can't say why, but Mr. Hope has charm. He clung to a microphone, ribbed the orchestra, apologized for the prompt cards during his songs, and at one moment danced with David Frost just when we thought he was cutting in to dance with David Frost's 'Miss World' partner, and referred in his immensely good-natured way to Sinatra's second wig."

Princess Anne and Prince Charles laughed and applauded from the royal box at the second performance. At about 1 A.M. they left the hall in order to precede their guests to St. James's Palace. The Hopes left the hall just after one-thirty and were among the first to arrive for supper. There was a lavish array of exquisitely served foods, and dancing to a society orchestra and polite conversation, until Dolores insisted they leave when Princess Anne retired at three.

The following morning Mildred Rosequist Brod—Mrs. John Brod—was awake at seven-thirty and dressed by eight-fifteen. Her breakfast tray arrived at eight-thirty. The Thames Television limousine was to pick her up before nine-thirty. Alan Haire had advised her that it would be a long day, mostly sitting around the studio.

She had come to London alone, which was a big mistake. But her husband was not living with her at present, and when she had agreed to appear on the program she had been told that Bob's older brother Fred and his wife LaRue from Columbus would also be in London for the telecast, so she would have company.

As Bob's first sweetheart and his first dancing partner, Mildred had known the Hope family since childhood days in Cleveland. Hope had once asked her to be his wife and they had dreamed together so many years ago of dancing their way to stardom.

Mildred had arrived in London on Sunday, was met at Heathrow Airport by a Thames Television representative, and was driven to the Savoy. At the hotel she learned that Fred and LaRue were not expected. As she was somewhat frightened of being in a foreign city, she remained alone in her room.

Now, while she waited for the telephone to ring and announce her limo, Mildred picked up the *Daily Telegraph* and worked her way back to the entertainment pages. There was a review of the "Night of Nights" benefit. She was struck by the way the story seemed to focus on Sinatra and Grace Kelly. Finally the telephone sounded, her limousine was waiting. She reached for her raincoat, umbrella, and scarf and headed for the lobby.

In spite of the late hour Dolores had finally gotten to bed the night before, she got up early, drank her hot lemon juice, got dressed, and had the remainder of her breakfast at nine. She barely glanced at the morning papers on her tray but had seen enough to be irked by the inordinate fuss being made over Frank and Princess Grace.

She had a full day ahead of her. She had remembered to tell Bob, before she retired, that she would be out shopping and running errands all day. She assured him that she would be dressed and waiting when he returned from his talk show appointment with Eamonn Andrews. Secretly she had arranged to dress for the *This Is Your Life* telecast in Nora's room, and two limousines would pick up her and the children at the Savoy between four and five o'clock. Before she went out she went to Bob's door and listened, but hearing nothing, she left quietly.

Bob opened his eyes at about noon and in the darkened room continued to doze for another thirty minutes. He fumbled for the phone, ordered breakfast, and asked to have all the national dailies delivered to his room. Then he got out of bed, padded to the door of his room, opened it, and called out, "Dolores?" No reply.

He was proud of her, the way she was carrying off her *This Is Your Life* smokescreen. She would not like knowing that he had been told. He had, in fact, known for days. One of his publicists had asked Miss Hughes what to do and she had replied, "You know how Mr. Hope hates surprises." So he was told. And he had done his best to let Dolores think she was a good actress.

Now he might well wonder about the rest of the group Thames had assembled in London. Obviously Dolores, but what about Fred and Jim? The children? His relatives from Hitchin? Crosby and Lamour? Benny? If *he* were producing his own *Life* show, would he get Arnold Palmer and Frances Langford, Colonna and Durante, Merman and Lucy Ball? Of his many writers, it couldn't be Mort because they had just talked on the phone, but what about Hal Kantor, Larry Gelbart, Charlie Lee? And he would envision people like Honey Chile and "Westy" Westmoreland. His mind then could conjure up those who could only be there in spirit—Doc Shurr, Monte Brice, Charlie Cooley, and his brothers Ivor and Jack. And now that wonderful little Charlie Hogan was slipping away.

Breakfast arrived, and with it came the newspapers and Denis Goodwin ready to work on material for his Wednesday, Thursday, and Friday appearances.

"Have you looked at the reviews yet?"

"Some," said Denis.

"Well?" asked Hope pouring himself half hot coffee and half hot milk. "Were we a smash?"

"Yes—except in the *Daily Mirror* which goes bonkers for Sinatra," Denis said holding up the tabloid and pointing to a page of mostly photos and reading, "The simple truth is that, if this really was a 'Night of Nights' at the South Bank's Festival Hall, then it was due entirely, well almost entirely, to the indestructible Francis Albert from Hoboken."

At that moment the telephone rang in Hope's bedroom and he grabbed the paper from Denis as he went to answer it. Denis could hear Bob reading excerpts from the *Mirror* article to whoever was on the other end. Hope came back to get more coffee.

"That was Mort. He's going to call back later with more stuff for the Wildlife show."

The day wore on with Hope remaining in his pajamas, nibbling fruit and drinking orange juice, working on material and talking to people by phone in various parts of Britain and America. He brightened considerably when a small, richly wrapped package was delivered to his suite. The crest on the accompanying card had "Broadlands, Romsey, Hampshire" engraved just below it. The note read:

My dear Bob,

I am writing to thank you for your splendid generosity in making the "Night of Nights" such a tremendous success, and particularly for doing two shows in one night under the duress of the Bengal Lancers!

You were magnificent and everybody loved your performance. I am looking forward to seeing you again tonight when I can express my thanks and appreciation in person.

Meanwhile will you please accept this small souvenir of the "Night of Nights." The box was designed by my son-in-law, David Hicks.

Yours ever,
Mountbatten of Burma

Hope read it aloud to Denis, and then opened the box to find a pair of exquisite cuff links in gold. He walked over to the window and looked closely at his gift.

"Who needs the *Daily Mirror?*" he purred.

Meanwhile, at the Thames Television Studio the surprise cast of immediate family, Hitchin relatives, old friends, and casual acquaintances chatted nervously in the Green Room. About 200 people sat impatient and mystified in audience seats facing a living-room stage set. An anxious Eamonn Andrews had to mollify both Green Room guests and his studio audience with assurances that Bob Hope would at any moment walk through a side entrance (they would see it on studio monitors) and then step into the set believing he was an interview subject of a talk show.

Mildred Brod had been killing time, sitting around the studios for nearly eight hours waiting for this moment, and she was not particularly thrilled. By the early afternoon the surprise guests began to trickle in one by one. First to come were the Hitchin relatives, followed by other British guests, and finally by Dolores and the children and the other American guests. When the room was full and there seemed to be a common purpose in the air, even Mildred's excitement rose to the occasion.

Hope was met outside by a page and led to a particular stage door. When he opened the door, Andrews was waiting on the other side, a camera pointing, its red light glowing.

ANDREWS: Bob, you're late. How are you? There's an audience waiting for
    you—
HOPE: Your kidding. . .

Hope sounded genuinely incredulous, and stepping toward the brightly lit stage area, he removed his coat, beaded with water from the rainy night outside. One more step into the set and then there was noisy, prolonged applause. He shaded his eyes and searched out the audience, nodded to their greeting. Having dressed formally for the Annenberg party, he cut a dignified figure as he walked to where Andrews held a chair for him. He crossed arms over his chest and looked up at Andrews, who stood waiting for the applause to stop.

ANDREWS: Bob, this is a very special week for you, and this is a very special time, and we want to make this a night you're going to remember for
    a long time—because tonight Bob Hope—this is—*your life!*
HOPE: Come on, are you serious?

Hope looked around. He grinned like a small boy. The audience was once again applauding and a lush, symphonic version of his theme song, "Thanks for the Memory," filled the studio. Andrews opened his big black book. He explained that the first guest was someone Bob would soon be seeing later that night. The figure who appeared on the studio monitors was Walter Annenberg, ambassador to the court of St. James, being picked up by remote cameras in the doorway of his Regents Park residence. Annenberg explained that his real task was to introduce yet another "surprise guest," Richard Nixon.

The President's face, on videotape, now loomed large on the monitors. He said:

America owes a great deal to Britain. . . our common law. . . our language and many of our political institutions. . . But we are particularly indebted to England for giving us Bob Hope. Not only because he is a great humorist who has given joy to millions of his fellow citizens and countless millions throughout the world. . . but because he is a fine human being who has never failed to respond in helping a good cause, any place in America or in the world. We are proud to claim him as an American citizen . . . and I am proud to know him as my friend.

Hope seemed embarrassed, touched. This did not seem the time for one of his Nixon gags. Hope sensed the moment needed a laugh, but he was at a loss. Then a slide showing the house at 44 Craigton Road flashed on the screen and Andrews said it was where Hope was born at Eltham. Hope cracked, "And we still owe some rent there."

He had found the laugh he needed and the audience responded. Then Andrews said that the baby born there was christened Leslie but the name was later changed:

Hope: "Well, I thought Leslie, you know, might be misinterpreted. Leslie's also a girl's name. I thought Bob was more chummy—and I was going to play a lot of vaudeville—and I might get up on the marquee quicker."

The audience laughed again, and Hope's name change joke led nicely into Andrews's introduction of Antonio Dominick Benedetti, better known as Tony Bennett, who walked out and hugged Hope. He explained how much he owed the comedian—for his new name and his career, launched when Bob had put him into his Paramount Theater show in New York years ago. There was enthusiastic applause.

The next surprise guests were Bob's cousins Frank and Kathleen Symons, from Hitchin. Other Hope relatives from Hitchin and Letchworth were sitting in the audience and the camera swung around on their smiles and waves. Then came a highly sentimental interlude with James Butterworth, the Anglican priest known to Hope as "the little Rev," for whom the comedian had done a series of benefits to put his war-damaged boys' refuge called Clubland back in business. The audience was effusive.

The next face that appeared was Jack Benny's, but it was on videotape because he was opening in Las Vegas that same night. Benny said it was "true love" between them.

Benny: "Now, Bob, it's your turn to say something nice about *me!* Bob? . . . Bob? . . . The whole world is waiting!"

The laughter was loud. Then a woman's voice came over the studio sound system.

Mildred: "My mother told me to forget him—he'd never amount to anything."

She walked through the rear double doors as Andrews explained who she was to the unknowing British audience. Hope waited for her to add the great line she had used when she visited him on his NBC soundstage in Burbank: "I'd like to see my mother right about now, I'd slap her right in the face!" He hugged and kissed her and as she turned to take her seat in the living-room set, Dolores came in from stage left and her entrance produced applause so enduring that it nearly covered her line.

Dolores: "Don't let them tell you wives can't keep secrets."

In quick succession came British comedians Tommy Trinder and Ted Ray, who had been added to the bill for home-viewer appeal—Trinder, particularly, because his comic style was very much like Hope's. Then came the British-born Paramount star Ray Milland, a longtime pal of Hope's who just happened to be in London.

Dorothy Lamour appeared on videotape and said, "Hi, neighbor" from Honolulu, where she was opening a nightclub act with Don Ho. General Rosy O'Donnell's sudden entrance from stage right seemed to astonish and please Hope as much as anyone's, as he heard himself praised for "tireless and courageous military entertaining." Then, to everyone's amazement, British strong lady Joan Rhodes was introduced as the woman who had dropped Hope on his head during a USO show in Iceland. Denis Goodwin came on shyly and explained the meaning of NAFT.

Then came a videotape of the very face and hand holding a pipe and a familiar voice saying in mock condescension:

Crosby: "Why, I'd be delighted to lend my stature to assist this unknown. What is it that this. . . Bob Hope. . . does? What is his talent?"

Bing's appearance was a true audience pleaser. Next came the parade of children, Linda in a dramatic white ball gown; Nora, often thought by insiders to be especially close to her father; Tony, the successful lawyer, boyishly handsome and still in awe of Bob; and an all-smiles Kelly, the show's biggest surprise because he had been flown in from Dubrovnik, Yugoslavia, where his Campus Afloat ship was docked.

The evening's final guest was Mountbatten of Burma, who said he had come partly to thank "Bob of Burbank" for his appearances at the "Night of Nights." And that was it.

When the stage manager signaled an all clear, Andrews thanked the audience and went to escort the other Hope relations seated in the audience to the stage. All the guests stood up and surrounded Hope. They moved to the Green Room for hors d'oeuvres and drinks. The party faltered, however, when Mountbatten (guest of honor at the Annenberg reception) and the Hopes (also expected to be rather special attractions at that same gathering) had to say their thank-yous and good-byes.

Most disappointed when the party limped to what seemed a premature close was Mildred Brod, whose other prospect for the evening was dining on hotel food in the solitude of her Savoy room without even a view of the Thames. Someone at the party kindly mentioned that near the Savoy was an excellent place to have a typically English meal, but there was no suggestion of companionship. Mildred tried the recommended carvery for roast beef and Yorkshire pudding and was unimpressed. Walking back to the hotel in a cold drizzle she marveled at her traveling so many miles to say, "My mother told me to forget him, he'd never amount to anything."

The following morning the Hope suite was log-jammed with activity because the children, no longer surprises, could come and go freely, sipping coffee and orange juice and munching on croissants, asking questions about the evening's Royal Cabaret Gala arrangements, and deciding on matinée theater tickets.

Mildred Brod called to say good-bye. Tony and Judy also came to say good-bye because they had to return to Washington. Bob slept through it all almost until noon, when he was awakened by Denis Goodwin reminding him that he had a date at two to tape the *If It's Saturday It Must Be* show with its host, Derek Nimmo. They had to go over material beforehand and then work on a monologue for his guest shot on a BBC Christmas special.

The Nimmo show proved to be great fun; afterward Hope and Denis drove to Leicester Square to inspect the stage setup at the Talk of the Town, where the gala was to take place. He decided he could not use cue cards, so he would forego his new song lyrics and would have to memorize his special gags about wildlife and the royals.

When he got back to the hotel he took a nap until it was time to meet the royal family. Bob and Dolores went to Buckingham Palace at about six-thirty and were introduced to their majesties at a brief cocktail reception. Then they went on to the nightclub where they joined another receiving line to meet visiting royalty.

At about a quarter to eight, the Queen's fanfare was sounded, "God Save the Queen" was played, and Queen Elizabeth II arrived with Prince Philip, Princess Anne, and Prince Charles. The ceremony and a speedy receiving line once over with, the remainder of the evening was casual. The Queen received guests at her table, and there was continuous table-hopping by royalty and commoners alike.

Lady Carolyn's table-hopping was not merely socializing. She was trying to pick up anything that might be good gag material for Hope. She didn't come up with much except that Princess Anne seemed dreamily in tune with her dinner partner, Roger Moore (who was rumored to be the leading contender in the search for a new James Bond), and also that Tom Jones had arrived at the dinner.

Halfway through the meal Hope excused himself and retired alone to the manager's office, where he could rehearse his material and not have to review it in front of Prince Charles. He brought with him the elegantly produced souvenir program, and he scribbled the first few words of each gag on the flyleaf to serve as a cue sheet. Now all he needed was good lighting.

When Rex Harrison introduced him he said:

Thank you, your highness. . . I've never seen so much royalty . . . It looks like a chess game. . . live. . . And the security here is very tight. . . They searched everyone but Tom Jones and we know he's not hiding anything. . . And I really have to mind my manners tonight. . . I'm the only one here who doesn't have his own army. . .

When he awoke late Thursday morning, Hope was in a mellow mood. Things had gone very smoothly the night before. And he was amused by the way the tabloids covered the gala: IT'S THE WEST END'S MOST FANTASTIC NIGHT EVER screamed the *Daily Mirror* on November 19 in front-page headlines showing a photograph of Bob and Dolores seated at dinner with Prince Charles. The coverage was extensive and garish and his "chess game" gag was repeated in six newspaper accounts.

As he sipped coffee, Dolores brought him two notes, both hand-delivered in late morning. The first, brought by a Buckingham Palace messenger, was encased in heavy vellum. It was addressed in longhand, but the body of the message was typewritten. It was a rather formal, form-letter thank-you from the Duke of Edinburgh, conveyed through his aide, Major Randle-Cocke. Hope smiled wryly, comparing this note from Philip to the warm, personal gratitude for the "Night of Nights" benefit expressed by his uncle, Mountbatten.

The second envelope contained a short personal message from "Sir" Lew Grade's office. Hope remembered his agent when he was simply Lew Grade and they did a "buck and wing" on the Palladium stage one night. The brief note had been dictated to a secretary but just above Grade's signature was scribbled "I am proud not only of our association but of our friendship. With affection, yours ever, Lew."

Hope liked that, even though he knew that the note from his now titled agents was also an effort to cinch his name on the Fabergé telecast. Well, if he had been *that* good, and they wanted him *that* much, the price could now go up—all going to charity, of course. He would call Saphier about that.

Denis arrived at the suite with some changes in the monologue for the BBC's telecast, for which Saphier already had a contract. Hope spent most of the afternoon on the telephone with Mort trying to clear dates for taping his November NBC television monologue and discussing plans for this year's around-the-world USO tour in December, which would include some European stops as well as the usual five or six days in Southeast Asia. They had not yet signed a female superstar and Hope was trying to sign Sophia Loren to appear on board a carrier in the Bay of Naples.

At seven he and Denis went to the BBC's Shepherd's Bush studios and when he had finished taping the monologue, he went back to the Savoy. Dolores reminded him there was a family dinner that night with Linda, Nat, Nora, Sam, and Kelly at a little Soho spot they had heard about. Hope lay back on his bed in the shade-drawn room and wished that the Miss World telecast were tonight rather than tomorrow night. It seemed like he was wasting time, though undoubtedly Dolores would have been hurt to know he thought of having dinner with them as "wasted time."

Yet as he assessed his efforts during this London stay, he had worked pretty hard, what with the two shows on Monday, the *This Is Your Life* appearance (which would be aired in two segments), the World Wildlife Fund gala, the Derek Nimmo show, the BBC Christmas monologue, and the still-to-be-done Miss World telecast—that was eight appearances in five days. It might be some kind of record.

Even if Hope's remarkable antenna system had detected trouble brewing at the Miss World contest that Friday evening, he probably still would have gone to the Albert Hall.

He had a definite stake in the proceedings since he had a guarantee from Mecca, the promoters of the contest, of exclusive rights to the services of the winner, who was always an added attraction of his Christmas USO tours and TV shows. So sticking around London for another 24 hours to crown Miss World 1971 was probably a smart move. And he remembered a number of the gorgeous Miss Worlds he had gotten to know extremely well in the past.

Yet from other perspectives he really ought to be heading back. He was scheduled to appear at a banquet for the trustees of Brandeis University in Chicago Saturday night. Even more important was Charlie Hogan, close to death from throat cancer at River Forest, a few miles from Chicago. Dolores thought Bob should cancel Miss World and go straight to Charlie. But Hope's rigid sense of obligation to be, in effect, the only name attraction in the Miss World telecast made him reluctant. His compromise was to agree to take a red-eye flight to Chicago after the show.

Tugging from still another direction was "the owl," Lachman. Mort was an exceptionally creative producer whose most aching frustration was not being allowed to put a show together without Hope's constant supervision. Hope exercised total artistic control, functioning as both executive producer and director, despite the fact that he had highly skilled and creative professionals in those positions on his payroll.

Hope spent much of Friday on the phone with Mort trying to solve the thorniest problems connected with the upcoming Christmas USO tour. Sophia Loren had tuned Hope down. So far the cast included Cincinnati Reds catcher Johnny Bench and the Golddiggers—nice but not enough to fill a two-hour stage show. Mort suggested Catherine Deneuve, and Hope approved.

When Hope arrived at the Albert Hall, just after eight-thirty, both Carolyn and Denis were there. The contest had started at eight but Hope would not be introduced and do his monologue until after nine; he would leave the stage and then go back out and crown the winner before the final curtain. As soon as he mounted the few steps to the stage and the audience spotted him there was loud and prolonged applause. Hope, with microphone in hand, waited for the applause to subside. Denis was working a few cue cards for him just below the edge of the stage. Hope looked around out front and then turned to see if there were people sitting up in the organ stalls. When it was quiet, he said, "Who are *they?* Relatives?" Laughter. It wouldn't have mattered what he said. He seemed to have them already.

I'm happy to be here tonight. . . By the way, where am I? . . . It's been such a social week for me. . . cocktails at Buckingham . . . supper at St. James'. . . and dinner at the American ambassador's—thank heaven I have a drip-dry dinner jacket. . . I'm not used to mingling with so much royalty. . . it was the first time I had to take a blood test to do a benefit. . .

What occurred next was a shocker because of its orchestration. A mannishly dressed woman leaped out of an aisle seat and activated a large noisemaker that signaled pandemonium. Other women appeared in the ground-floor aisle and some in the lower loge areas manipulating rattles and hurling stink and smoke bombs. Some of the audience ran for the exits as flour bags dropped from the balconies and ripe tomatoes were hurled across the auditorium. Several women marched down the aisles with placards printed with the message YOU ARE SELLING WOMEN'S BODIES and MISS WORLD IS A SYMPTOM OF A SICK SOCIETY.

There were probably only 15 or 20 women involved in this disruptive demonstration, but in the ensuing fracas with hall officials and police, it seemed as though there were hundreds. More people headed for the exits. The noise level was painfully high. Hope saw one woman try to reach the stage. A tomato shot past him and he left the stage in a near run.

Robbed of Hope as a victim, the women turned on the judges, shouting, "We are liberationists. Bar this disgraceful cattle market." The police moved to protect the judges, but not before a heavy noisemaker that was hurled at them landed at country singer Glen Campbell's feet. Then an ink bomb spattered two other judges, the actress Joan Collins and the prime minister of Grenada, who was standing next to Campbell. Another judge, a Danish singer known simply as Nina, screamed and a policeman led them all backstage to safety.

As the bobbies escorted women up the aisles, some others were still shouting profanities. Eric Morely went to the stage and attempted to restore order, and Hope, standing almost offstage and thus barely visible, quipped, "Is it safe?" The audience laughed in relief.

"I'm flabbergasted," said Hope. "I've never faced a *whole bunch* of mad women before. . . I'll say this—it's good conditioning for Vietnam." That brought a big roar from the crowd. And with the smell and the smoke puffs still lingering around the huge domed hall, Hope yelled brightly, "Hey! What do you say? Are we ready? Let's do it!"

Hope walked to the front of the stage next to the runway as a hand reached up to give him an envelope, *the* envelope. Hope reached down and took it, but then said, "Glen Campbell, folks. Right here!" The audience applauded while Campbell waved. Then after walking a few steps with the envelope in his hand, Hope sensed that the suspense was pulled taut. He ripped open the envelope and announced the winner was Miss Grenada, Jennifer Hosten. Evidently she was not a favorite of the crowd or in betting circles; touts had rated her chances 25 to 1.

There was applause but also some booing. Hope thought it might have some connection with the previous demonstration. Later he learned that one of the judges was the prime minister of Grenada. Joan Collins, whom he knew well from *The Road to Hong Kong*, took him aside and said, "Get yourself out of this mess, Bob. The contestants are convinced this thing is fixed."

Eric Morley then told Hope that the judges' decision was final, that he regretted the disruption but was grateful for Hope's support, and that Miss World 1971, Jennifer Hosten of Grenada, would be thrilled to go on the Christmas USO tour.

Reporters who were sent to the scene to cover the demonstration, as well as those already in the hall, now crowded around the stage door all wanting something from Hope. One reported asked, "How did you feel when this thing erupted?"

"On all the fighting fronts I've ever been to, I've never come across anything like this." Could he possibly have forgotten that wild night in 1943 at the Excelsior Hotel in Palermo?

Another reporter: "I gather you don't react well to the women's lib?"

"You'll notice about the women in the liberation movements, none of them are pretty, because pretty women don't have those problems. I don't get it. If a woman's clever, she can do just as well as—if not better than—a man."

Still another asked, "Don't you agree that there's something inherently immoral about a beauty contest ritual like this one?"

"Immoral? Is Miss America immoral? What's immoral about beauty? All it is, is a pretty girl wins a competition, travels around a lot, goes on television, makes a lot of money. There's nothing immoral about that."

"Mr. Hope, I've heard it said that your position on Vietnam is that of a right-winger."

"I'm not a right-winger. I'm middle America. I just figure that if you've got a lot to eat and there's a guy next door starving with eight kids, you've got to help him. Otherwise he's going to figure out some way to undermine you. That's why America's got to help Vietnam."

A voice from the back: "What's it like to be Bob Hope?"

"I wouldn't have it any other way."

Carolyn interrupted, saying that Bob had a plane to catch. Hope looked around and said, "Thanks, and I know you understand. With my act I have to keep moving."

44

The Road Gets Rougher

"I've seen too many wars to say that war is beautiful. I've been in burn wards and smelled burned flesh. I've walked through hospital wards where I had to grab the bed to keep my balance. If getting hooked on caring about the Americans who have laid down their lives for their country stops me from getting awards, then I'll have to live with it."

Associated Press columnist Bob Thomas previewed the Christmas show footage Hope had put together to show the American public over NBC-TV in mid-January 1971, and knew instantly he had a hot story. Hope had included pot smoking jokes that clearly indicated he knew what was going on among the troops in Vietnam, even if the Pentagon had been keeping it quiet. Thomas quotes an exchange between Hope and one of his Christmas show headliners, baseball's Johnny Bench: "It's a great sport, baseball. You can spend eight months on grass and never get busted." Hope also included the following one-liner:

But I guess you guys are too busy to be bothered by things like mosquito bites. I hear you go in for gardening. The commanding officer says you all grow your own grass.

NBC reacted by telling Hope he could not air the marijuana jokes. Hope responded that such a demand was unwarranted censorship—just as it had been for him many years ago in radio when the issue was sexually suggestive one-liners. Network brass remained unmoved. Hope took his case to the airwaves, albeit late at night, after prime time, for a discussion with *The Tonight Show* host Johnny Carson.

"I repeated a few of my pet pot jokes and argued that these guys in Vietnam are smoking marijuana because they have nothing to do and they're bored. They used to say let's have a drink—now they sit around and light up," Hope told Carson and his audience.

"But, hey. When I was young and doing *Ballyhoo* in New York in 1932, we'd go knock on a door on 57th Street, and go into a speakeasy to get a drink. Liquor was illegal then, and that was our kick."

"Does that mean you're in favor of legalizing pot?" Johnny asked.

"Hell no. I've talked to too many doctors. I know it's not good for you."

Johnny said, "Have you tried it?"

"When I was in vaudeville. I tried it and it scared me. It made me sexier and I thought I was already sexy enough." The *Tonight* crowd reacted wildly.

The following Monday morning, Marjorie Hughes sent up to Hope's bedroom a clipping from *The New York Times* Sunday edition. It was a story titled "Some Like It Pot and Some Don't" by TV columnist Jack Gould and it made him feel good. It said in part:

Hope told it like he found it during his conversation with Carson: the troops in Vietnam did respond to quips on pot, which even the Pentagon admits is heavily used there, and everyone did want peace and wanted to come home. But more by manner than word, Hope left no doubt of the war's unpopularity among the troops he encountered.

In the case of the Christmas tour, Hope is not only an entertainer and his trip not just a show in the usual sense. He also doubles as a reporter, a journalist in greasepaint, and the public would seem entitled to share in what he found out.

As a patriot and performer, Hope's credentials are impeccable. It is not unimportant, therefore, that his Christmas tours accurately reflect what he may find out, if only because he has the knack of shedding substantive light through humor rather than preachment. The country needs such a liaison man between those at home and those overseas. No one would want Hope's TV special to be stripped of its vital elements of humor, but if in his own way he can also incorporate the accompanying elements of significance, *sans* strictures by either NBC or the Pentagon, he could be even more of a national asset than he is.

Coming from such a highly respected industry voice, these sentiments somewhat reassured Hope that he was not suddenly a media target and that, in particular, he had not become a target of *The New York Times*.

A few days later he was once again jolted by what he would regard as media recklessness and probably liberal bias. Joan Barthel's abbreviated excursion with Hope in the Midwest in November had been transformed into a *Life* cover story for January 29, 1971, and it contained a land mine. There against red, white, and blue stripes was Hope's celebrated profile (this was his third *Life* cover) and the headline: BOB HOPE: ON THE ROAD WITH AN AMERICAN INSTITUTION. Inside, however, the story's headline was different: BOB HOPE: THE ROAD GETS ROUGHER, with a subhead: POLITICS IS PART OF HIS ACT NOW—SOME NEW SOUNDS ARE MIXED IN

WITH THE LAUGHTER. That subhead referred to a reference early in Barthel's story to the fact that when "Moose" Krause brought Hope out onto the football field at South Bend, some students in the upper stands booed the comedian and made thumbs-down gestures. Barthel also reported that in his Flint, Michigan, concert, Hope had called the Vietnam war "a beautiful thing—we paid in a lot of gorgeous American lives, but we're not sorry for it."

Reaction to the *Life* story was swift, both from readers and from Hope. He was especially outraged, not by the putative booing incident (which he maintained from the outset was not aimed at him), but that a journalist of Barthel's supposed reputation would think, let alone write, that Hope would find anything "beautiful" about war.

"Moose" Krause wrote a letter for *Life*'s attention, explaining that students often make loud "moo-ing" sounds whenever he appears publicly at Notre Dame. And not a single official connected with either the Flint or Notre Dame shows could remember Hope's saying that the Vietnam war was "a beautiful thing." What was universally remembered and attested to when Hope's lawyers began questioning witnesses to gain ammunition for a slander suit was that Hope referred to the men fighting there as beautiful.

In New York, Allan Kalmus contacted *Life*'s managing editor, Ralph Graves, and insisted that Hope and his lawyers be allowed to audit the Barthel tapes of both the Flint and Notre Dame performances to determine the accuracy of her quotes. But neither Barthel nor Graves would cooperate.

During the following two months a spate of anti- and pro-Hope feelings were vented in the media. Directly attributable to the *Life* story was a student protest at San Fernando Valley State College in Northridge, California, over an announcement that Hope was to receive an honorary degree. Students marched across the campus carrying signs that called Hope a "war-loving hawk."

In mid-March a group of liberal young ministers pressured the New York City Council of Churches to withdraw its earlier designation of Bob Hope as the recipient of its Family of Man Award. In February the board of directors had voted the honor to Leslie Towns "Bob" Hope; in previous years they had honored John Fitzgerald Kennedy, Dwight David Eisenhower, Lyndon Baines Johnson, and Richard Milhous Nixon.

However, Pastor Richard Neuhaus, leader of the dissident clergy, jumped to his feet at the council's assembly meeting, declaring that he and 20 other young ministers found nothing in Hope's record of public commitment to "the three pressing issues that face the council—poverty, social justice and peace. On the contrary, Mr. Hope has uncritically supported the military establishment." The dissidents successfully argued that their 1971 medal be awarded posthumously to Whitney Young, Jr., the executive director of the National Urban League, who had died in a swimming accident at Lagos, Nigeria, the week before. The vote was 34 to 22 in favor of Young.

Hope reacted to the news of Young's selection immediately by wiring Dan Potter, executive director of the council, that he was "delighted the award was going to Young. He was a great American and deserved it, and a lot more than that." But he did that before he learned the full story of the dissident pastors and their rationale, which was aired in a long story in *The New York Times*. Council director Potter responded to a request from the Associated Press for details saying his office had been "swamped with calls protesting their decision to cancel an award that Hope had already agreed to accept. Sixty long-time supporters have written to say they will never attend our dinners again."

AP's Bob Thomas called Hope and asked if he had anything to add. Hope said: "Bob, to think they could actually believe I could feel that way makes me want to vomit. I've seen too many wars to say that war is beautiful. I've been in burn wards, and smelled burned flesh. I've walked through hospital wards where I had to grab the bed to keep my balance. If getting hooked on caring about the Americans who have laid down their lives for their country stops me from getting awards, then I'll have to live with it."

Editorials in newspapers and letters to the editors were printed all across the country. Many of these were pro-Hope, like that of the Bronx resident who on March 21, 1971, wrote New York's *Daily News*, "There's no more Hope for the Council of Churches, and I think Faith and Charity are losing ground, too." The paper's television editor, Kay Gardella, called Hope to assure him her mail was predominantly pro-Hope. Kalmus did a check and found that mail was running just the opposite at the *New York Post*.

Senator Barry Goldwater, onetime Republican candidate for the presidency and a well-known conservative who had engaged in numerous battles with the "liberal media," asked for space in *The Arizona Republic* to make a statement:

> Until Hope made his long-held conservative position completely known in speeches and by backing conservative candidates, he was treated with the greatest respect and honor by the lilywhites of liberalism such as *The New York Times* and the *Washington Post*.
>
> But the moment he aligned himself with conservatism and particularly the Republican Party, he became a villain. . . What I am trying to point out is that anyone—and I don't care whether he is the President of the United States, the world's most popular entertainer, or the least known person—who dares to take a stand against the far left is immediately, viciously, libelously and scurrilously branded and it is shameful the way Bob Hope has been treated.

Later that spring, in Oklahoma City, a young television executive named Lee Allen Smith, who admitted to being "a Hope fan as long as he could recall," was growing angry about what he considered unjust criticism of his hero. As head of the Oklahoma City Association of Broadcasters, he was putting together that city's annual civic Fourth of July celebration, and Smith had received encouragement from NBC that if he could round up enough big names for the evening's variety show, the network would offer the telecast of his show to its more than 200 stations.

Smith took a chance and called Hope, and Smith's celebration was the kind of platform Hope was looking for. The sponsors of the civic celebration were so grateful they voted to erect a statue honoring Hope in the city's newly dedicated patriotic park.

The significance of this particular July Fourth celebration could not be found in either the quality of entertainment or the weight of its guest stars. It offered run-of-the-mill variety fare with performers like Anita Bryant, the Golddiggers, Les Brown and his band, celebrity athletes, and familiar-faced astronauts. Its real significance was that it was pure Oklahoma, not Honor America Day in Washington. And its centerpiece was to be an old fashioned Fourth of July address, the kind politicians used to deliver in earlier days of Americas towns and cities when folks were still innocent, the kind of speech that Americans for generations expected to hear on this day, written and spoken by Lee Allen Smith's hero—Bob Hope.

To make it happen, Hope went to his joke vault and rifled through several drawers of material—alone—and several nights in late June he worked into the early-morning hours polishing his "remarks." For two decades he had closed both his radio and television shows with brief serious comments, some about the virtues of selfless giving to charities, some about the courageous young men and women serving their country, and some about the good fortune of living in a land of liberty and free choice, as well as many other seasonal and occasional observations from a 30-year period, aimed at audiences that presumably shared in the American Dream. So he had some good old material and he created some new. Then he went to Oklahoma City.

At the top of the show he did his customary monologue and in the middle of the singing, dancing, and routines with athletes and astronauts, Hope faced the camera. With a background of music and some simple visual imagery, he spoke directly to the audience simply and eloquently. He called upon the nation to reunite. He evoked traditional values, recalled the Pilgrims and how and why the Declaration of Independence was signed, and a lot of other images that described the spirit of "can do" Americans. He was trying to induce confidence at a time when confidence in all the important American institutions was faltering or failing. Because he had written so much of it himself, this was as genuine a Bob Hope message as Americans were likely to hear. In part he said:

> These are very confusing times. Some of the people seem to be down on that dream called America today. They view Vietnam and they call it a shame—a dirty war. And it is. No one ever invented a clean one in the history of mankind. . . . Newspapers are now busy trying to prove who caused the war.

They like to give it names like "It's President A's war," or "President B's war." Well, the fact remains that it's our war. It's our kids who are fighting in it. Those bullets hurt just as much whether a Democrat or Republican started it. I don't like war—I think it stinks. . . I've smelled it in the burn wards of combat hospitals. I've seen the kids who would have loved to shake hands with me if they still had that hand. I hate war with all my guts. But I admire the guys with guts enough to fight them when they have to be fought.

But it's gone a long way, this Vietnam conflict, in disrupting our country. Perhaps somewhere along the line we could have withdrawn with grace and honor on our part. I don't know. I don't know if anyone knows. But we are committed, and bred in our very bones is the tradition or integrity that makes us keep helping the little guy. The tide seems to be turning and our troops are coming home, and in our haste to heal our wounds, to bridge the chasms, and to reunite our nation, we must remember our heritage that we always have and we always will answer a call for help.

This Fourth has been a great day to count our blessings. But do remember, the love of country, the myriad expressions of loyalty we lump into one big bag and call patriotism is not a cloak to be put on one day a year. It's a mantle for all seasons.

Probably at no other time in his life was it as essential for him to speak to "his" audience, and to speak as unambiguously as possible in order to register his strong feelings. This audience would certainly not be that huge listening, viewing body Hope had once commanded. The number who tuned in to watch Hope this July Fourth were a fraction of the adoring millions who made him their number one choice of entertainer in 1942. In those decades between the unified forties and the dissenting sixties, the nation lost its innocence.

Recognizable character types—the average American who always appeared on *Saturday Evening Post* covers—were all but gone. Take Hope, for example, who had risen to fame as one of those Norman Rockwell characters, just your average guy joking about the passing parade, your bumptious traveling salesman who despite his brash manner is really your reluctant-hero next-door neighbor. That image Hope created so indelibly throughout the forties and early fifties in his radio shows and movies was no more.

What took its place, with the same look of wise innocence, was a man who was becoming much closer to being a humorist than a mere comic. What we saw in Hope's humor of the late fifties and early sixties was a sharper edge. We saw him take a more critical approach to politics in general. His humor seemed more urbane and sophisticated. We noted in the Kennedy era that Hope utilized more sarcasm and more skepticism in his monologues. In general, there had developed in his humor such a powerful sense of neutrality and independence that it was not surprising that his writers and others close to him were distressed when his politics forced a dulling of the edge.

British pop culture scholar John Fisher, in his discerning study of a group of world-sized entertainers titled *Call Them Irreplaceable*, sums up Hope in the late Vietnam period this way:

> It would have been the ultimate irony of the Vietnam war if it had succeeded, as it threatened to do, in bringing about the downfall of the entertainer with greatest claim to be styled Mr. Sandman of the American Dream, the most decorated civilian in American history. But if Hope had proved he was not untouchable, he came through the ordeal with his optimism intact, a politically neutral quality characteristic of the American spirit which, if his television ratings are to be believed, may well have led people other than those who merely want their right-wing prejudices confirmed to forget the immediate past and identify with him still.

45

The Last Christmas Show

"I'm such a ham. Somebody said if I was in a blizzard and two Eskimo dogs walked by, I'd do ten minutes for them. But I'm not the kind of guy who's on all the time either. I don't wanna be on all the time."

If Hope had been successful in his attempt to free the Hanoi POWs in December 1971, he would undoubtedly have been on top of Gallup's annual list of America's most admired men. As it was, Hope placed ninth in the Gallup Poll, behind Richard Nixon, Billy Graham, Ted Kennedy, Lyndon Johnson, Hubert Humphrey, Spiro Agnew, Ralph Nader, and Pope Paul VI. Despite the effort's lack of success, Hope's reappearance in the top ten after an absence of a few years was probably in part a reflection of his efforts to free the prisoners.

On December 19, shortly after arriving in Bangkok during his around-the-world Christmas tour, Hope telephoned Ambassador Leonard Unger to seek his help in meeting with the North Vietnamese to discuss getting permission for the comedian to visit and possibly entertain the American prisoners in Hanoi. Unger contacted his counterpart in Laos, Ambassador G. McMurtrie Godley, and two days later word came back from Laos that the North Vietnamese diplomatic mission in Laos would consider Hope's request and would notify him within 24 hours.

Shortly after dawn the next day, a U.S. Air Force major general in civilian clothes escorted Hope and this author to the Bangkok airport and, with another civilian-clothed officer, took control of a small unmarked CIA aircraft for a 90-minute top-secret flight to Vientiane, the capital of Laos, where they hoped to meet with the North Vietnamese.

In flight, a radio message was received saying Hope's meeting with the North Vietnamese would not take place, but Hope decided to continue on to Laos anyway, to honor his promise to entertain the American embassy personnel in the Laotian capital.

Upon arrival, Hope was met by Ambassador Godley, Richard Rand (the embassy's prisoner-of-war specialist), Admiral John S. McCain (whose son was perhaps the best known of the Hanoi prisoners), and Christian Alliance Church minister Edward Roffe, who enjoyed unusually close relations with the North Vietnamese legation. Two other men suddenly appeared near the aircraft but were stopped by military police. They identified themselves as an Associated Press reporter and a photographer and they were told that this was a private meeting.

Hope and the others were ushered quickly into a nearby mobile office close to the runway, which was unbearably hot. At once, Godley and Rand informed Hope they had been successful in reversing the decision about a meeting. Reverend Roffe had been instrumental in this, and he would go with Hope as interpreter.

Roffe put Hope and this author into his '62 Buick and drove to the North Vietnamese embassy, a gracious French colonial house surrounded by a tall iron fence on a tree-covered avenue on the outskirts of Vientiane. Only Hope and Roffe were permitted to enter and Hope said his heart was pumping a bit faster when they entered a small living room and were greeted by First Secretary Nguyen Van Tranh, a young man in his early thirties.

After exchanging a few pleasantries, Hope reminded Van Tranh that he had requested a visa to visit Hanoi. Van Tranh told Hope that he himself could not make that decision until he had contacted his foreign minister.

Over tea and cookies Van Tranh said, "Our country has been at war for twenty-six years and our people are suffering, especially our children."

Hope, who confessed later that he was "winging" the entire interview, took out his wallet and turned to a photograph of his grandson Zachary (Tony and Judy's child). "Wouldn't it be great if the children of our country could help the children of your country in exchange for the release of the prisoners?"

Van Tranh said quickly, and for the first time in English, "Your President could get the prisoners of war released tomorrow if he would listen to the seven points of our peace talks in Paris."

"I don't know anything about those seven points," admitted Hope. "All I know is that the children of this war on both sides are the real victims. I would like to see the children of America contribute their nickels and dimes to help your children and get the prisoners released."

"Nixon knows well the prisoners will be released when your government agrees to a withdrawal date."

"Nevertheless," said Hope warmly but firmly, "I hope you will think about this idea of a children's relief fund, a children-to-children program to rebuild homes and hospitals and schools." He avoided using the word "prisoners" again because he knew that had altered the tone of their meeting.

While these words were being said inside the embassy, outside where this author was waiting a car pulled up and the Associated Press reporter and cameraman stepped out.

"What is Hope doing inside?"

"I can't tell you that. How did you know Hope was coming?"

"Anything you want to find out is available here for a price."

Inside, Van Tranh said he was grateful for Hope's interest in Vietnamese children.

He said he understood Hope's compassion for his countrymen who were detained. With a smile he said he remembered vividly seeing an American film with Hope and Bing Crosby called *The Road to Bali*. In conclusion he said he could not report anything definite about Hope's visa request but he hoped, one day, that the comedian would entertain in Hanoi.

Outside on the veranda, Hope and Van Tranh shook hands and a hundred yards away the Associated Press photographer snapped a picture of the handshake, which would soon be transmitted around the world. Hope declined to speak to the AP reporter, explaining that he was heading to an embassy debriefing. Later that afternoon, Hope entertained 400 people, mostly Americans but with some Laotian nationals, in the embassy compound.

Hope had planned to say nothing to the media but when he walked into the Erawan Hotel lobby in Bangkok he was met by a mob of foreign correspondents and local newspeople who had seen the brief AP newswire story. They followed him up to his suite and crowded in.

"Did you discuss this with anyone before coming to Bangkok?"

"No," said Hope. "I had been thinking of trying to visit Hanoi for some time because of my many talks with relatives of the prisoners wherever I go. They stop me at shows and airports and ask if I could do something."

"Does the President know?"

"By now he must," answered Hope. "But this is my idea."

"You talked money with the North Vietnamese?"

"I told Van Tranh that I thought my proposal could raise a lot of money."

"How much?"

"I don't know. I was thinking in the neighborhood of $10 million." Hope had never mentioned an amount to Van Tranh. "I think we could do that. We could put on shows in addition to the money the kids raised."

"Ross Perot offered ransom—"

"This is not ransom," snapped Hope. "That's a bad word. I don't think they'd buy that at all. This has to be a children-to-children agreement. Tomorrow I intend to send a formal proposal of my idea to Van Tranh."

On December 24, the AP confirmed that President Nixon did not know about Hope's intentions but welcomed the idea as a private gesture. On Christmas Day, the AP filed from Vientiane a story that quoted a North Vietnamese official (not Van Tranh) saying Hope would most likely be denied a visa and that only "courtesy" had kept Van Tranh (who was apparently not a decision maker) from saying so. But Hope was not daunted.

That year's around-the-world Christmas tour ended at Guantanamo Naval Base, Cuba, and it was there just before enplaning for Los Angeles and home that Hope heard the sad news that his old and dear friend General Emmett "Rosy" O'Donnell had died. He was to be buried at the Air Force Academy at Colorado Springs on December 29, and Hope asked his fellow troupers if they would accompany him to O'Donnell's military funeral, which they did.

Back home, Hope busied himself instantly with the details of his January documentary of the just-finished tour and fell in stride with his usual daunting schedule of personal appearances and engagements. He even found time to take Dolores, Tony and Judy, Linda and Nat, Nora and Sam, and Kelly and all the grandchildren—Linda's son Andrew, Tony and Judy's Zachary and Miranda, and Nora's Alicia—to Acapulco for a five-day "delayed Christmas" celebration. But through it all he maintained a constant vigil and never stopped hoping for a visa to visit North Vietnam.

Hope made four trips to Washington in a six-week period to talk with either President Nixon, National Security Adviser Henry Kissinger, or Secretary of State William Rogers. On his last visit Secretary Rogers had told Hope about the Nixon-Kissinger proposal to offer $2.8 billion in relief aid to the North Vietnamese. To which Hope quipped, "How did I know I was offering them a tip?" Hope backed off, assured from these Washington briefings that everything possible was being done to effect the release of POWs.

It seemed to Hope that the country was in reasonably good hands. Nixon was riding high, his trips to China and to Russia were labeled a success, the war was winding down, and there were more troop withdrawals. Hope was telling the media there might not be any reason for him to go overseas anymore. His jokes were less war-ridden. In fact, his March TV monologue was devoted to Nixon's win in the New Hampshire primary and his recent trip to China:

> President Nixon's trip was an international success. A new poll shows he had a better-than-even chance to be re-elected President in this country. . . and a forty-percent chance of being elected president of China . . . Some conservatives feared Mr. Nixon lost his shirt in China but that's not true. Kissinger found the ticket and he's going back for it. . .

Sitting in that television studio audience at NBC in Burbank, watching Hope work with Sammy Davis Jr. and Juliet Prowse, was a highly respected freelance writer, C. Robert Jennings, on assignment for *Today* magazine, a high-circulation

Sunday supplement. Jennings was trying to find his story angle, asking, "What can you say about a sixty-nine-year-old legend that refuses to die?" He thought one way might be to treat Hope as a "pukka folk hero," or perhaps to fall back on the old reliable "Old Star Interview" with plenty of jokes or, as he later wrote, "You can take the current tack, which is to misquote him ('War is beautiful'— *Life*); to denigrate him ('The funny thing about Bob Hope is that he's not very funny'—*Look*); or to make scurrilous references to his politics and sex life (*The New York Times*). But any way you go, it just won't fly."

Jennings felt he would not be able to produce a readable story out of publicist-supervised interviews, so he asked if he could go on the road, as Joan Barthel had done, to watch the moving target. The comedian sized Jennings up, preferred to believe the writer did not have an agenda, and said, "Good idea." And it turned out to be a good idea. As Jennings concluded about his assignment and the man: "So you observe, try to capture something of sinew and feeling, even indulge in a little Indian wrestling of egos—trusting that in the accretion of the details of Hope's daunting business, the flying shards of colloquial speech, the geegaws of personality at odd points of time and pressure, there might emerge some mosaic of the true man, if even a smudged one."

What Jennings saw and finally wrote about was the essence of Bob Hope—the onstage, big-as-life performer, the quintessential vaudevillian who may have whipped Broadway, radio, films, and television, but was never greater than when he was pacing the stage in front of huge GI or home-front audiences. Jennings watched him backstage, onstage, singing, doing a little dancing, some flirting with and being encouraged or put down by his girl singer—but most of all laying out with immaculate timing a series of smart one-liners and innuendoes. There were also the short funny stories that rendered him totally irresistible in the eyes of his audience and in those moments, matchless.

Jennings had the acuity to perceive what Mort Lachman and a few others close to the comedian could also perceive: that the recent suggestions that Hope might have become a different person or different entertainer during the Vietnam years was so much "twaddle." Partisan behavior notwithstanding, Hope had not changed. The world may have changed, but not Bob Hope. In his conversations with Hope, Jennings concluded that the mutual admiration between Hope and his adopted country, manifested so particularly in his relationship with the GI and more generally in his assiduous pursuit and indeed almost total realization of the American Dream, was too fixed, too pervasive for any major disruption to be possible.

"Bob, you're staring at the sunny side of seventy," said Jennings. "What about it? Isn't it time to think about quitting?"

"Hell, no. You belong to the public. You got nine people writing for you, eight people publicizing you, a large group, uh, that keeps me moving, including the Red Cross."

"But you will quit?"

"Never. Listen, I only do now the things I want to do."

And in the next few weeks—next few months—next few years—he illustrated that last remark clearly. In April, for example, he joined his favorite comedian, Jack Benny, on a platform at Jacksonville University in Florida kidding their way into twin honorary degrees. From there he flew to Palm Springs to play in the Dinah Shore Golf Tournament and then back to Los Angeles where he and Benny and cellist Gregor Piatigorsky clowned through an evening of verbal and sight gags for a Wellesley College benefit (chaired by his daughter-in-law Judy). He flew to Washington for the White House Press Photographers' Association dinner, and then right back to Toluca Lake for one of the most publicized fund-raisers of the year.

Hope allowed himself to be photographed, caricatured, cartooned, and satirized in a dozen ways as Packy East, the onetime fighter coming out of retirement to face Sugar Ray Robinson in what was billed as "The Fight of the Century." In the Hopes' spacious backyard a boxing ring was constructed and in the evening some of Hollywood's brightest and richest stars gathered to watch Hope in satin tights spar and cavort with Sugar Ray as the donations piled up. At the end, Hope was able to hand Robinson a check for $100,000 for the Sugar Ray Youth Foundation.

But sometimes Hope, shrewd as he usually was in both choosing events and sizing up promoters, could be blindsided. Such a case involved Hope's immediate enthusiastic acceptance of headlining an ambitious benefit scheme billed as "La Semaine Sportif à Paris" ("Sports Week in Paris") dreamed up by a young Georgia entrepreneur named Ramar "Bubba" Sutton. Hope got hooked because Sutton told him that all the monies raised from a series of exhibition sporting events in and around Paris would go directly to the Eisenhower Wing of the American Hospital in that city.

Sutton's credentials were not blue-ribbon, but his acceptance list with the names of NFL/AFL football players and professional golfers for exhibition matches was impressive, as was the news that Billy Casper would cohost and play with Hope in the fund-raising golf tournament. Bob and Dolores received an invitation from U.S. Ambassador to France Arthur Watson to be his guests at the official residence. Sutton had enticed several of Hope's Palm Springs and Palm Beach friends to join them in Paris as host-sponsors as long as each could come up with $10,000.

The elaborate schedule called for elegant cocktail parties and dinners, even a flight to Bordeaux for a wine-tasting luncheon with music by the Benny Goodman Quintet, all sponsored by a group of very wealthy ex-patriot Americans and Parisians on the patron list of the American Hospital.

The social events went smoothly, but financially speaking, the whole fund-raising idea was going from troublesome to perilous. Sutton's personal expenses were swallowing up funds that should have gone to the hospital. He had hired a French film crew to document the social and sports events because Hope told him he might arrange a television deal with NBC. Otherwise the American Hospital would have to sustain some of Sutton's losses.

The final two events of the week were the Friday noon celebrity golf tournament at St. Germain presided over by Hope and Billy Casper and the Friday night variety show with Hope as emcee at the Théâtre de la Musique. By this time, from what he could deduce about Sutton's lack of production experience and current mistakes, Hope figured that now everything would depend on his success in selling a TV documentary.

A few days after Hope arrived back in the States, Hurricane Agnes slammed into Florida and worked her way up through the Carolinas, Virginia, Maryland, Pennsylvania, and, finally, New York. Before she was done, Agnes would exact a devastating toll in lives—22 people known dead and another 124 missing—and property.

The Red Cross was heartened to hear that Hope had agreed to headline a gala Hurricane Agnes Telethon at Baltimore's Civic Center. With the help of Elliott Kozak of the Saphier office, Hope got to work calling the big names from a list of about a hundred celebrities to find enough entertainment for a five- or six-hour show. Hope alone was able to get commitments from Zsa Zsa Gabor, Jimmy Stewart, George Jessel, David Janssen, Steve Allen, Fess Parker, Janet Leigh, Forrest Tucker, and Joe Namath. Kozak came up with Gisele McKenzie, James Darren, Linda Bennett, Gloria Loring, George Maharis, and Tige Andrews. Looking over the list and realizing it was pure white bread, he remembered the offer he had gotten from Dick Gregory and approached him; he said he would be honored to appear with Hope for this cause.

The stage was set and the cameras were rolling, but all was not smooth. Zsa Zsa expected, after her first appearance, that she would be brought back for a second and so she went back to her dressing room for a wardrobe change. When she came back to the set ready to go on, she was told she wasn't needed. Her temper flared. She grabbed her precious Lhasa Apso, Ghenghis Khan, called for her limousine, and went back to her hotel.

Hope sent two earnest young Red Cross administrators to coax her back and she made a second appearance.

George Jessel was also miffed when he found that the acts were running so long that time might be too short for him to appear at all. However, he was not about to be overshadowed and he was more enterprising than Zsa Zsa. He went to his dressing room and, disguising his voice, made repeated calls to the telethon number demanding to know when Jessel would be on camera. And by "popular demand" Jessel was rushed on.

When Hope returned to L.A. from the East Coast he took a look at the Paris Sports Week film footage and was so appalled and disappointed that he decided to fly to Paris with Mort Lachman at the end of July to try and reconstruct the documentary and make it marketable. He hired Louis Jourdan as celebrity host for on-camera commentary and complete narration and also re-shot a number of continuity sequences.

By late summer, however, even with Hope and the Saphier office putting pressure on NBC—as well as the other networks—the Sports Week television special had lost its immediacy and its appeal for potential sponsors. Besides, the charitable cause was in France and that was pretty remote for most Americans.

Hope's irritation about all this reached a new peak when he learned that Ramar Sutton had been making some fast runs through both Palm Beach and Palm Springs, hustling Hope's friends and acquaintances for more donations—this time not for the hospital but to cover his losses and quiet his creditors. These were the same people, essentially, who had been generous when Hope pleaded for money to build the Eisenhower Medical Center.

Adding gun powder to the fire, the Martin Gang law firm told Hope that Sutton had run up hotel bills, fancy restaurant tabs, and car-leasing contracts in Florida and in California, charging the expenses to the television special and Hope Enterprises. Hope asked his staff and the Gang lawyers to find Sutton; they discovered that by then he had become a fugitive and his last known address was on a yacht, which had sailed beyond the limit of U.S. law. Ultimately, Martin Gang took depositions and went into court on Hope's behalf to face several irate creditors.

All in all, Hope was saddened because the effort was a failure and he was not accustomed to that; because a charity he had chosen to champion was stuck with many of the unpaid bills; and because an entertainment package that he had headlined and virtually produced would never be seen, at least on American TV. He had been conned.

Hope's annoyance was curtailed, however, when he had to marshal all his promotional energies, including a round of media interviews and talk-show appearances nationwide, for the release of his latest—and what proved to be his last—feature film,

Cancel My Reservation, based on a serious novel by Louis L'Amour and converted into a weak comedy script by Arthur Marx and Bob Fisher, was shot in the late summer of 1971 in intense heat near Scottsdale, Arizona. It was not a happy production, despite fine actors such as Eva Marie Saint, Ralph Bellamy, Keenan Wynn, and newcomer Anne Archer.

Young director Paul Bogart, making a transition from TV to big screen, disagreed with Hope throughout on how the picture should be shot. Too often Bogart felt he was involved in filming an anachronism.

To everyone's surprise, *Cancel My Reservation* was selected to have its initial run at New York's Radio City Music Hall, the first Hope picture ever to be screened at this famous showplace, and although it was nothing like getting an Oscar, Hope was thrilled.

Sadly, though, the film was not well received. In her review, Pauline Kael used the words "a new low." Hope must have reached a decision that this was, for him, the end of an era, or, as they say on a movie set, "a wrap." Almost immediately he huddled with AP's Bob Thomas, one of the film industry's most perceptive observers, about coauthoring a book that would chart his forty-year "love affair with the movies."

In October, amid ongoing stumping for his new movie and his personal appearances, Hope came into Washington for talks with the Defense Department. It happened to be the same day Henry Kissinger flew in from Paris between sessions of the peace talks for executive briefing. Rumors sped about the city that peace was at hand. A few nights later, when Hope was entertaining at a big Army dinner, he told his audience he would be going back to Southeast Asian military sites in December (long applause) and that he was relieved that this tour would be his "last Christmas show" (groans mixed with the applause).

In mid-November, one of the most touching moments of Hope's advancing years occurred. On a chilly morning, the 69-year-old comedian stood surrounded by giggling, screaming, adoring youngsters who had voted—not rubber-stamped an adult decision—but had actually voted to name their new school "The Bob Hope Elementary School," choosing from a list of national heroes. Hope said, "I'd get up early for this any day—though I'm not sure I can still fit in those seats." That simple ceremony swelled the list of bronze, steel, and cement monuments and memorials bearing the Hope name in various parts of America: a bronze bust in a park in Oklahoma City and another bronze in Florida's Patriot's Garden; his name on a wing of the Parkinson's Disease Hospital in Miami; a halfway house for delinquent boys in Cincinnati; a facility at Columbia University Medical Center; and the Hope Memorial Bridge in Cleveland, Ohio, which his father had had a part in building.

In addition, there's the Bob Hope Theater at Southern Methodist University; Bob Hope Drive, in the Palm Springs area, which passes the Eisenhower Medical Center; another Bob Hope Drive in Burbank; several rooms in hospitals (including the Eisenhower) across the country; and one U.S. Navy ship. In the great outdoors, you'll find the Bob Hope prize steer, the Bob Hope rose, and the Bob Hope fern.

Two days before Hope left for his "last Christmas show," legendary entertainment columnist Louella Parsons died at the age of 91. As a reigning gossip queen of Hollywood, she had been an unfailing booster of Bob and Dolores Hope since their 1938 arrival in Hollywood. Hope attended her funeral in Beverly Hills and was surprised and disappointed to see so few of the stars whom she had publicized and chided were paying their respects. Apart from Jack Benny, George Burns, Danny Thomas, Jack Warner, David Janssen, and Earl Holliman, the only other mourners were press agents who had fought to get their clients space in her daily Hearst column and her weekly radio show.

In the last two weeks of December 1972 in military sites around the Pacific and elsewhere—Japan, Korea, Thailand, South Vietnam, Diego Garcia in the Indian Ocean, on board the USS *Midway* off Singapore, in the Philippines, on Guam and Wake islands—the national spectacle of Hope's overseas Christmas shows for GIs came to an end. He took with him for this highly emotional finale comedian Redd Foxx, dancer Lola Falana, L.A. Rams quarterback Roman Gabriel, Dolores Reade Hope (who begged to be part of this one), and a group of young beauty contest winners and Hollywood hopefuls called the "American Beauties," and, of course, the Les Brown Band. He also invited two of his favorite syndicated columnists, AP's Jim Bacon and Knight Newspapers' Shirley Eder, to help chronicle this event.

Because this was a highly publicized farewell tour, the crowds were emotional and appreciative. Hope received long standing ovations and was presented with plaques, awards, trophies, citations, and honors from the Korean government, the Japanese government, and what was left of the government of South Vietnam.

A few days after Christmas, Shirley Eder wrote a syndicated column that appeared in the *Detroit Free Press* on December 28, 1972, in which she confessed to the difficulty of trying to pick the most significant from among so many intensely emotional moments on that tour. She finally settled on the moment

> when Dolores came out just before the finale. . . . Six thousand boys and men stood up when she made her entrance, then sat down again and were very still while she sang "White Christmas." I looked around at all those young men, many of them with their head lowered trying to hide their emotions. Hundreds sat with tears streaming down their faces, especially when Dolores ended the song, "And may all your Christmases be home."
>
> At this point, I looked away from them, as they tried to look away from their shipmates, because the tears were streaming down my face as well.

The accustomed 90-minute documentary of this last Christmas tour was telecast by NBC and drew the expected large viewing audience and, perhaps not expected, warm critical reaction from columnists and editors the country over. Of course, it should be noted that Hope's Christmas show followed by two days President Nixon's suspension of all bombing of North Vietnam and a deactivation of the mines in Haiphong Harbor, which relieved even the hawks.

Three days later Hope was on an American Airlines flight designated the Inauguration Special, which was full of Hollywood personalities invited to perform or just look glamorous as part of the entertainment galas scheduled in celebration of Nixon's second inaugural. Much of the buzz on that flight centered around the fact that Bob Hope was not only on board (rather than flying in his own private jet) but was walking up and down the aisles with both a script and his half-glasses in his hands. He was looking as folksy and unfamous as your Uncle Ned, stopping to talk with both known and unknown people, laughing and shaking hands, being praised for his Christmas show and being, generally, just one of the gang. This behavior, of course, could only happen on an airplane full of entertainers and technicians on their way to do a show. Of course, it was standard Hope to all those who had ever traveled with him on a USO tour; the regulars knew that one of the things he and his crew would miss the most was the quality of the Christmas show camaraderie.

Later, in the spring of 1973, with the help of Pete Martin, Mort Lachman, and NBC's Betty Lanigan, Hope began to write his fifth book, already titled *The Last Christmas Show*, which was dedicated to "the Men and Women of the Armed Forces and to those who also served by worrying and waiting." He signed over his royalties to the USO.

In its pages Hope tells how he began entertaining "a captive audience with military police guarding the gates so they can't get out" as early as 1941 (even before Pearl Harbor), and how that hook kept him coming back for more than 30 years. Near the end of the book, he comments on why time and circumstances had now dictated an end to his Christmas tours:

> "The last Christmas trip". . . You can imagine what emotions those words stir in me. I guess the strongest feeling is gratitude—gratitude that the painful war was winding down to the point where the trips were becoming less necessary, gratitude that my strength and the need for me were coming out about even. . . I felt that the last Christmas trip was almost more important than the previous ones, if only because our troops were so aware of the mixed feelings back home. They had read about the anti-war protests in the papers, and they'd heard about them in letters from home. A lot of them had started to wonder whether they were headed in the right direction, whether they were really fighting for their country, whether what they were doing was right. . . Because of this, it was clear to me that those kids needed a Christmas show more than ever.

During the Christmas seasons of 1973, 1974, and 1975, Hope visited military hospitals in various parts of the nation. Reflecting on these visits he said, "Every time we'd walk up to a bed a kid would stick his hand out and say, 'Long Binh,' or 'Da Nang.' For most of us the war is over. For many of these kids it will never end."

Legend to Icon: 1973 to 1993

46

A Night with "Pops"

"This is the grandmother I sleep with. . . She's so Catholic, she thinks Oral Roberts is a dentist, and Norman Vincent Peale is a stripper. . . "

"One of my writers, Larry Klein, looked at me one day and said, 'You know, if you had your life to live over again, you wouldn't have time to do it.' I wouldn't want to live it over again. It's been pretty exciting up to now. The encore might not be as much fun."

Hope opened his 1954 autobiography, *Have Tux, Will Travel,* with those lines. He was then 50. He was now a durable 70 and the intervening decades had seen him matching (and sometimes surpassing) the energy of his salad days. One of his favorite responses was, "I'd rather wear out than rust out." To most observers he showed little sign of wearing out, and no inclination to retire.

This is how he struck Bill Murray of *Playboy* during the hours they talked:

Hope bounces as he walks, hums little tunes to himself, seems to vibrate quietly in his chair, as if he's conscientiously, like a trained athlete, working all the time at keeping himself loose. For a man his age he's in superb condition, the jowls of his famous profile firm and his flesh tone that of a man in his early fifties. His tongue is still in great shape, too. . .

Playboy had developed a reputation for publishing incisive interviews with interesting people and had waited months to break into Hope's crowded schedule. When the comedian finally agreed to meet with Murray, he warned he didn't have much time. The subjects were predictable: his Mount Rushmore image, his conservative politics, the youth scene, Vietnam, his GI tours, and his estimated half-billion-dollar fortune. But some new notes were struck. One was Watergate. Murray wanted to know how Hope felt about the opinion polls that questioned Nixon's honesty.

"I think he has a tremendous record, I really do. What he's done with the Russians and the Chinese has taken a lot of the heat off. It was a great job. That and the fact that he had brought back 500,000 of our men from Vietnam are enough to make me like him very much."

Hope felt that the Justice Department ought to be handling the investigation rather than Congress.

"Don't you think the Watergate committee has served a valuable function?" asked Murray.

"Hell, yes, but it's dragging on and on and it's not good for the country." Of course, that conversation took place in August 1973. A full year would pass, almost to the day, before the Oval Office tapes and Bob Woodward and Carl Bernstein's investigative reporting would reveal such criminal activities in the highest office that Nixon would resign. Throughout the Watergate period, Hope did not avoid joking about John Dean, H. R. Haldeman, John Erlichman, and Gordon Liddy—even the "mysterious" tape erasures—although he never seriously impugned Nixon.

In fact, after both Agnew and Nixon had been disgraced, talk-show host Lou Gordon demanded of the comedian, "How can you remain friends with a thief and a scoundrel?" Hope faced him squarely and said, "Lou, if you were my friend in the same position, I would still be your friend." In April 1974, four months before Nixon resigned, with impeachment threatening, Hope wrote this note to Rose Mary Woods, the President's personal secretary, "Anyway 'keep a stiff upper lip' as we old English say. Give my best to the President and tell him to hit the golf course once in a while as difficult as it might be. It would be a great relaxer for him."

Those touchy subjects aside, there was something else refreshing about this *Playboy* interview. For the first time in months, Hope was being asked about his life's work. Murray said, "What is the secret of your comedy?"

"Material has a lot to do with it, but the real secret is timing," Hope replied. "Not just of comedy but of life. It starts with life. Think of sports, even sex. Timing is the essence of life and definitely of comedy. There's a chemistry of timing between a comedian and his audience. If the chemistry is great, it's developed through the handling of the material, and the timing of it—how you get into the audience's head."

"But you couldn't get along without your writers."

"Every comedian needs writers, because to stay on top you always need new material. It's like getting elected if you say the right things, but only if you say them right. The great ad-libbers are the ones with the best timing, like Don Rickles. I showed up in the audience one night at NBC where he was cutting everybody up on *The Dean Martin Show*. I walked in after the show had started and the people in the back saw me and started applauding, and then the audience in the front turned around, and they applauded, and I was taking it big. Rickles backed away to the piano and after everything quieted down, he walked back to his miked position and said, 'Well, the war must be over.' It was just magnificent timing and it hit very large. Timing shows more in ad-libs than anything else."

"Do any of the younger comics make you laugh?"

"God, yes. Mort Sahl and Woody Allen—Bob Newhart—they're great. But my favorite was Lenny Bruce. The last time I saw him was at El Patio in Florida. I'd seen everybody else on the Beach and I just saw a little ad saying 'Lenny Bruce At

El Patio' and I said, 'We've got to go.' We went out there and I sat in the back. In those days planes were falling going from New York to Miami for some reason and so he walked to the mike and said, 'A plane left New York today for Miami and made it.' That was his opening—not 'Hello' or anything. And then he told the audience I was there and he shouted, 'Hey, Bob, where are you?' and I said, 'Right here, Lenny.' And he said, 'Tonight I'm going to knock you right on your ass.' And he did. He had so much greasepaint in his blood it came out in his act. That's what I loved about him. He talked our language."

"What are your aspirations now?" Murray asked.

"To keep working," said Hope. "I want to do a film based on the life of Walter Winchell, either a movie or a two-episode television thing. I love the idea. I knew Winchell. I went through that whole era. I'll really enjoy that."

The *Playboy* interview—longer than Hope had intended—represented a turning point in Hope's media relations. Like other journalists in the early seventies who interviewed with Hope primarily to illuminate his politics, Murray found himself respecting the artist in the man. Even though the story described Hope as "proselytizingly patriotic" and "dangerously simplistic" about politics, as well as "out of touch" with both minorities and America's youth, there was also the assessment that Hope proved "time and time again—entertainingly—that he doesn't need his writers around to sound like a comedian, and a great one, too."

Naturally there were some unexplored subjects that might have given the interview and the story more dimension. One subject Murray avoided was Hope's relationship with the Vietnam POWs. Possibly Murray did not know that Hope was the national chairman of the POW-Wives bracelet campaign, but he must have known of Hope's efforts to free the prisoners and to visit them in Hanoi. Surely he must have read that Bob and Dolores were part of the entertainment at Nixon's White House homecoming celebration for the POWs. But probably only Dolores knew the depth of her husband's feelings about the length and conditions of their internment in North Vietnam. The day that the POWs came home, Hope was sitting on the end of his bed facing the television set and watching prisoners set foot on home soil. When he heard their stoic and tired voices speaking their love for America, he began to weep.

Another rather extraordinary event of 1973 that underscores the Hope concept of family, which ranged in his mind from a visionary "family America" to the more tangible "family Hope," was the way he and Dolores decided to celebrate Fourth of July that year: by assembling the largest gathering of family in Hope history. Bob invited every living, movable member of the clan (including Dolores's family) to gather in Los Angeles at his expense for a mammoth reunion. The children alone, when all were assembled in and around the Moorpark Street estate on July 3, numbered 50. Grandchildren, grandnieces, grandnephews from Ohio, Illinois, and California were everywhere, running and exploring the grounds, swimming with Uncle Bob, raiding the cookie jars that lined the counter in the formal pantry.

During the week Bob and Dolores joined the clan in a rented school bus that took them to Disneyland where the pair was hugged and tugged through half the attractions in the park. Later, without Bob, the gang went to Knotts Berry Farm, the San Diego Zoo, Universal Studios, and finally to downtown historic Olvera Street for an enchilada feast, where Dolores sang to them. All in all it was an unimaginable Hope outing. Not the least remarkable part was that Hope remembered all their names.

Another indication of Hope's deepening awareness of the importance of his family was his realization of how much he enjoyed the companionship of Dolores, and he made an effort to spend more time with her. She was still the one constant in his life. They relaxed in the desert together more often and she was making many more personal appearances with him.

But this did not mean that he had lost that old vaudevillian craving for a girl on the road, and he would still arrange meetings with this or that willing young starlet, beauty contest winner, or vocalist who could satisfy him for a night or two. But he was now 70 and though still lusty in his mind, not as active in bed.

What had finally reached Hope's consciousness was the necessity to spend enough "down" time to avoid the recurrences of the blood vessel hemorrhaging, which could certainly lead to blindness. He was also beginning to have more difficulty hearing and was consulting regularly with the renowned House Ear Clinic in Los Angeles.

Clearly, neither of these signs of an aging body meant that he would stop performing. As he said to UPI's Vernon Scott, "You can't *do that*. When you're living, you've got to live it your way. You just can't say 'I'm going to slouch it out for the next ten years.' I'm taking it easy. I only work about 200 to 250 days a year out of 365. That's not so much. I have an awful lot of free time." But it was really more a matter of scheduling; his total time on stage hadn't changed.

Whether or not Hope was slowing down, the people around him were getting older and wearing out. In the weeks and months to come some of the closest relationships he had had in his professional life would be altered. First, Jimmy Saphier, the architect of his radio and television contracts for nearly forty years, suffered a stroke in his office, triggered, it was later learned, by a brain tumor, which took his life in April. Saphier had become a very rich and very influential agent in the entertainment community and Hope was to realize how much he missed Jimmy later in the year, when many important decisions had to be made about his relationship with NBC.

Then, another difficult adjustment was forced on him when one of the two women in his life who kept him glued together decided it was time for her to quit. His personal secretary, Marjorie Hughes, had more than earned her retirement. Petite, seemingly frail, but astonishingly resilient and efficient, "Miss Hughes" had worked unstintingly for 31 years as discreet custodian and manager of his private affairs, guardian of his joke vaults, as well as sometime bookkeeper and sometime governess to the children as they grew up.

At her request, on the guest list for her retirement party, held in the gracious living room of the Hopes' home, were only those individuals (and certainly in her job she had made the acquaintance of some of the world's most famous people) that she really wanted to say good-bye to (except for a couple of newspaper people and a photographer or two). The *Los Angeles Times* reporter asked Hope if he would stand beside her and give her a farewell squeeze.

"This is not my squeezing secretary," Hope replied. "I've never even called her Marjorie—it's always been Miss Hughes and Mr. Hope—like Russia and China talking together. But seriously, no man's had a better secretary."

Three years before she left, when Richard Nixon paid his surprise visit to the Hope estate and landed *Air Force Helicopter One* on the side lawn, the comedian asked Miss Hughes to come into his office to meet the President. Nixon took her hand and said, "I bet you know more about his affairs than he does." Marjorie looked at him and then at her boss and said, "I think you're right." Then Hope added, "I know you're right."

Hope had to adjust to her absence, but his pliability, that vaudevillian ability to accept any conditions, was deeply engrained. After Miss Hughes, there was a disorderly succession of secretaries and not one of them could measure up to Marjorie's conception of how to take care of the man. One of her successors took a pile of correspondence off her desk one night and shoved it into a cabinet, where it remained for two years. When it was eventually retrieved, in that correspondence were letters from both the White House and Governor Nelson Rockefeller.

Regardless of any disorder behind the scenes, it was the out-front equilibrium that interested Neil Hickey of *TV Guide* in a mid–1970s update on the comedian. Hope was asked if he thought there was any leftover animosity by the public from the Vietnam period and whether his "consistent candor" in expressing his personal views of politics and public affairs had hurt him professionally. "I don't really know," Hope said thoughtfully. "It might. But all you can judge by is your popularity. I still play all the places I always did, and do as good or better than ever. My TV shows are still one-two-three in the ratings and I'm getting offers that are unbelievable. So I can only judge it on that."

One of these offers—to some insiders, and outsiders as well—seemed to be just that, unbelievable. It came from Texaco in the fall of 1974 and Hope accepted it gratefully. For the past several years, since the dissolution of his long-term exclusive Chrysler contract, Hope's television specials had been engineered by Saphier in what is known as a "magazine concept" with different sponsors for each telecast, and Hope missed the exclusive product identity and sponsor caressing he was used to. Saphier, of course, had been the choreographer of Hope's radio and television contracts since 1936, but since suffering a stroke earlier in the year had not been able to help make decisions.

The Texaco deal came about in an unexpected way. Hope had recently added Bill Eliscu to his payroll to negotiate the foreign rights for his last five movies. One day Eliscu called to ask if he'd like to do some commercials.

"For whom?" Hope asked tersely.

"Texaco," said Eliscu. "I met a guy from Benton & Bowles who said they want you."

"Why should I do commercials for Texaco? If they'd like to sponsor my TV specials, that's something else."

Eliscu reported back to Benton & Bowles and they asked for a meeting with Hope. Out of that meeting came a deal for Hope to produce seven hours of programming a year for three years at $3.15 million a year plus $250,000 more to do commercials as Texaco's chief spokesman.

Not long after Hope signed that contract, he was compelled to share a sad blow with many other Americans. Jack Benny died unexpectedly on December 26, 1974, of pancreatic cancer. A chapel full of Benny's friends, including some of the world's most recognized people, mourned him: Henry Fonda, Raymond Massey, Irene Dunne, Edgar and Candice Bergen, Rosalind Russell, Merle Oberon, Dinah Shore, Johnny Carson, Danny Thomas, Groucho Marx, and George Jessel were there, as were Governor Ronald Reagan, Senators George Murphy and John Tunney, and as many of Jack's old radio gang as were able to make it.

Mary Benny had asked Rabbi Magnin to conduct the service and she asked both George Burns and Bob Hope to say a few words. Burns was able to say some of what he felt and then broke down. Hope was perhaps as eloquent as he would ever again be:

> How do you say good-bye to a man who is not just a good friend, but a national treasure? It's hard to say no man is indispensable. But it is true just the same that some are irreplaceable. Jack had that rare magic—that indefinable something called genius. Picasso had it. Gershwin had it. And Jack was blessed with it. He didn't just stand on the stage—he owned it. For a man who was the undisputed master of timing, you'd have to say that this was the only time when Jack's timing was all wrong. He left us much too soon. He was stingy to the end. He only gave us eighty years and it wasn't enough.

A few weeks later Hope had reached the decision—regrettably, without Saphier's input—that his long-standing co-ownership with NBC of Hope Enterprises ought to end. There had been some differences of late about the corporation's management and especially the board's refusal to fund any further film projects. Hope and his lawyer, Martin Gang, met with Tom Sarnoff and decided to dissolve the partnership. Immediately his new independence gave him the opportunity to pretend to be listening to offers from CBS and ABC, inasmuch as his current NBC television contract was expiring soon. Hope was right. NBC was nervous that he might sign with another network and offered him $18 million for the next three years. Hope had never for a moment considered leaving NBC.

But it was not all roses. Part of Hope's agreement with both Texaco and NBC in return for this big money was that his shows would have an entirely "new look."

He would remain executive producer of very "special specials," each one the product of a different creative mind. Wonderful, said Texaco, and strongly advised Hope to clean house, by which they meant he ought to fire everyone. This, to a man whose loyalty was as unquestioned as his wealth, was unthinkable. "Now, hold on," said Hope in a meeting with Benton & Bowles and Texaco brass, "I can't do that."

But it happened anyway. Hope knew he should be the one to tell Mort Lachman (his producer and head writer for 28 years), or Les White (with Hope since his vaudeville days), or Norm Sullivan (who was part of the original Pepsodent gang) that they were victims of Texaco's housecleaning. By the time he summoned the courage to say something to each one of them, rumors had spread far beyond his reach. Hope had hired Elliott Kozak, an assistant to Saphier for many years, to manage Hope Enterprises and to book talent for his television specials. Kozak was asked to do Hope's dirty work and make the rumors official.

As expected, there were acrimonious reactions and bitterness. How could Hope break up the old gang? Vernon Scott of UPI called Hope to find out what was going on. "It had to be done," Hope said, "because I thought that, after twenty-five years, it was time to get a fresh format, some new ideas, a new style." What did Hope mean by a new style? "I mean there'll be all new productions. We'll be changing our format so that each show revolves around a total idea rather than unrelated sketches. They'll be done more in a spectacular style, with different producers for each show. About the only thing that won't change is myself."

At the same time Hope laid off his New York and Hollywood publicists, Allan Kalmus and Frank Liberman, respectively, because he had acquired new publicity support connected with the Texaco deal. (Both Kalmus and Liberman returned to him in 1976, however.) The only staffer in the Hope organization not replaced at that time was Ward Grant, his personal public and media relations man, who was handed the thankless task of being the "punching bag" for the Hope show veterans who were on the way out the door. Grant was also the "information booth" for the changes being made and the new people being hired.

One of the wisest things "the owl"—Mort Lachman—did for Hope before he cleaned out his desk and moved over to become the producer of the enormously successful TV comedy series *All in the Family* was to advise the comedian not to tamper with the classic lines of Ogden Nash. It all had to do with a benefit that Tony's wife, Judy, was putting together for the Wellesley College Building Fund; she had had the good fortune of enlisting Arthur Fiedler, the conductor of the Boston Pops, to do a Pops night as a fund-raiser.

Equally gratifying was the yes she got from her father-in-law about making an appearance with the venerable maestro. When Hope asked, "What'll we do?" Fiedler sent him a copy of Ogden Nash's lyrics to Saint-Saens's *Carnival of the Animals*. Fiedler expected Hope would want to have his writers punch up the Nash verses to his own personal specifications. Hope did so and sent the manuscript over to Lachman, but he said, "Leave 'em alone. You can't improve on the best."

On May 5, Hope arrived in Boston with Dolores, Nora, and Kelly. Judy arrived with her two tots, Zachary, six, and Miranda, three. Miranda was scheduled to make her theatrical debut with her grandfather in a musical number, "You Must Have Been a Beautiful Baby."

To plug Hope's new commercial sponsor, and because Hope found out that Fiedler collected firemen's hats, Ward Grant called Chuck Gouret of Benton & Bowles and asked them to find an old firechief's helmet worn by Ed Wynn on the early *Texaco Star Theater* shows (the Texaco logo was a firehat). What they came up with instead was the hat worn by Steve McQueen in the film *The Towering Inferno*.

That night at Boston Symphony Hall turned out to be pure Hope gold. "I don't know how long Arthur Fiedler's been conducting," Hope told a responsive audience soon after his entrance, "but his first job was the victory party after the Battle of Bunker Hill."

For the *Carnival* narration, Hope sat on a high stool behind a music stand. He seemed to be enjoying the fun of the lyrics. He rolled the Nash word play like "totally turtlely torpor" off his lips with relish. That the performance was not taped for television (a decision Grant thinks was based on Hope's uneasiness with both venue and material) is unfortunate. Hope himself later regretted his decision. It was, however, audiotaped and has been broadcast more than once over Public Radio stations.

After the Saint-Saens piece, there was a Fiedler medley of songs from Hope movies and Broadway shows. Then Dolores was introduced and she sang in her appealingly throaty style, "On a Clear Day You Can See Forever." When tiny Miranda came out of the audience to sit on the steps leading up to centerstage, the three-year-old said, "I don't want to win any beauty prizes. I just want to be like you." Hope's double take fanned the audience's roar. Several times Miranda interrupted her grandfather to ask if she was going to be paid for this appearance. When he seemed to ignore her, she said calmly, "I'm not worried. Both my parents are lawyers."

The next morning, looking over the Boston newspaper coverage of the Pops event, he noticed there were several photos of Miranda and only one of himself. He turned to Ward Grant and said, "Remind me not to work with *her* again."

Later that year, Hope flexed his executive-producer muscles as promised for Texaco. In keeping with his contract it was a formidable production, but somehow everyone seemed to have forgotten the promises of eight months ago to produce very "special specials" with a "new look." *A Quarter Century of Bob Hope on Television* was indeed a solidly packed two-hour entertainment comprising segments with a total of 97 performers on black-and-white film and color tape as well as live studio appearances by superstars Bing Crosby, John Wayne, and Frank

Sinatra. Inevitably it was going to be an audience pleaser but in no way was it innovative. And it posed an inevitable question; Would Hope be able to give his shows a "new look"?

Hope was excited. "When you do a show like this it kills you to leave stuff out but you must. I spent two weeks reading through the old scripts and looking for the best of the eight hundred or so sketches we've performed over the years. Then, after we made the selections, there was the whole matter of clearances. I had to pay every writer and all the performers received a minimum salary."

And what performers he presented! Legendary stars like Maurice Chevalier, Bea Lillie, Ethel Merman, Jimmy Durante, Ernie Kovacs, Jack Benny, Gloria Swanson, Jimmy Cagney, and Ed Wynn; enduring stars like Dinah Shore, Rex Harrison, Mickey Rooney, Martha Raye, Betty Grable, Lana Turner, Joan Crawford, Lucille Ball, Steve Allen, Jack Paar, Barbra Streisand, William Holden, Phil Silvers, James Garner, Ginger Rogers, Fernandel, Ken Murray, Shirley MacLaine, Shelley Winters, Natalie Woods, Perry Como, Danny Thomas, Gina Lollobrigida, Fred MacMurray, Andy Williams, Sammy Davis, Jr., Dean Martin, Milton Berle, Carol Burnett—and more.

The risky part of such an historical parade is that it inevitably invites comparison with your current output. NBC was pleased as always that Hope would spend 20 hours or so being interviewed by national media and the advance press as well as the critical reviews were generally positive. Against NBC's wishes, Hope's production staff had authorized the finished program (minus the monologue, which was always taped at the last minute) for advanced viewing by the New York media.

John J. O'Connor of *The New York Times* in his telecast preview was as insightful as any critic in his appraisal of what Hope had selected as the best of his television work. After stating bluntly, "By any yardstick, Mr. Hope is an extraordinary figure in American show business," O'Connor lamented the evidence that the comic's "open courting of the establishment status quo" had weakened his ability to produce more pungent comedy:

> Some proof of this is on display, ironically in tonight's tribute. Almost invariably the material from the earlier TV years is superior stuff. It has more energy, zaniness and pure sass. His familiar routines with Bing Crosby are still marvelous. Too frequently, the later skits rely heavily on extraneous gimmicks, on silly drag costumes, on the mere presence of celebrity.
>
> Still, it can hardly be denied that Bob Hope is a performer of immense stature, an outstanding humanitarian and a very, very funny man. Tonight's highlights are dreadfully uneven, but there are enough good moments scattered throughout the two hours to demonstrate splendidly what all the fuss is about.

47

A Capital Affair

"I'm pretty sure I'm seventy-five. . . but I've lied to so many girls. . . Of course, they find out about one A.M.. . . Dolores, that's a joke!"

At age seventy-two, Hope finally got his high school diploma. The comedian already had 32 honorary degrees "from places I couldn't get into legitimately," and earlier in 1975 he had been made chancellor of Florida Southern College in Lakeland. But somehow no one had ever thought of awarding him an honorary secondary school diploma.

"Of course," said Hope, "I had to build the high school." Texaco executive Jack Williams was a loyal booster of the Hughen Center for Crippled Children in Port Arthur, Texas. After he successfully persuaded Hope to do a benefit to construct the nation's first high school for crippled teenagers, the Hughen officials and directors decided to name the new facility the Bob Hope High School for Crippled Children.

The morning after the benefit, Hope was pushing a ceremonial gold-plated shovel into the dirt to dig the new building's foundation, when the center's president, Claude Brown, surprised him with the school's first diploma. Hope turned to the crowd and offered, "Now that we've got a high school for these kids, what about a college? Could we make this an annual affair?" He got a tremendous hand from his audience, but the more skeptical among them frankly doubted they would ever see him again. They were wrong.

Hope returned to help Hughen three times. The first was to do another benefit and dedicate the opening of the high school. In 1982, he organized a six-state regional telethon and convinced 22 entertainment personalities to fly from Los Angeles to raise over $1 million for the center and the high school. The following year Bob and Dolores went back to Port Arthur to do a joint concert, at which time the center broke ground for the Dolores Hope Library.

Hope treasures that high school diploma, but when asked to name the most prestigious awards of his long and frequently honored career, he would invariably list two: the Congressional Gold Medal that Jack Kennedy handed him and the Sylvanus Thayer Award from West Point. That is, until the spring of 1976, when he eagerly added the honor that was conferred on him at the British embassy in Washington on July 1, 1976. Hope beamed as the British ambassador, Sir Peter Ramsbotham, told him he was commanded by Her Majesty Queen Elizabeth II to confer on him the Insignia of the Honorary Commander of the Order of the

British Empire. Sir Peter said the comedian was "regarded with enormous affection in Britain. Your services to British troops around the world during the Second World War, in particular, have never been forgotten by the British people. You have often appeared at royal command performances and are known to be a favorite of the Royal Family."

Also being so honored were Dr. Wallace Sterling, chancellor of Stanford University, and Eugene Ormandy, conductor of the Philadelphia Orchestra. An even bigger honor was conferred on Walter Annenberg, former ambassador to the Court of St. James, who was named a Knight of the British Empire.

The next day, in Washington, D.C., Hope introduced Gerald Ford at the Kennedy Center gala that was the capital's official kickoff of the nation's Bicentennial. Initially Hope had declined Ford's request because of a conflicting personal appearance. But the President offered to have an Air Force jet standing by to whisk the Hopes off in time to make his concert date if he would agree to open the gala. Who could refuse that?

In the fall, when the Thalians, a film industry women's auxiliary group, asked Hope, Crosby, and Lamour if they would consent to be the honorees of their glittering annual charity ball in Los Angeles, it seemed a good time to confirm persistent rumors that the three had reached an agreement that they would be reunited for the first time since 1962. Ben Starr had delivered each of them a script called *Road to Tomorrow*, which called for shooting locations in England, Saudi Arabia, and Moscow. At the time Hope said, "I prefer the title *The Road to the Fountain of Youth*, but in any case we play ourselves. It starts out with Bing and me taking our grandchildren to the airport, and meeting each other again after all these years. We tell each other how good we're looking at our age, and before you know it, we're on a plane to London and off on another mystery. Of course, along the way we bump into mother, Lamour." Crosby interjected, "We've got to get more lunacy into that script, Bob. When you've got two old guys, you've *got* to do something wild."

Lamour was cautious about all this. She had been badly burned in the *Road to Hong Kong* mess in 1961, but at least this time she was better prepared. She and husband, Bill Howard, had moved back to Los Angeles, and she was making a good living again doing television and musical comedy productions in regional theaters and summer stock. And, she reminded herself, this time she was being consulted from the start.

There were serious indications that the new *Road* picture would be shot in mid-1977 in London and produced by Sir Lew Grade. Crosby had already agreed to a series of summer concerts in Europe, kicking off the tour at the London Palladium. Meanwhile Hope agreed to help Bing celebrate his 50 years in show business at a gala tribute televised at Pasadena's Ambassador Auditorium in March. Twelve hundred of Bing's friends made up the audience that watched him sing his final song, alone on the stage. He bowed as the crowd gave him a standing ovation. (Hope and Crosby's other guest star, Pearl Bailey, had declined his invitation to close the show together and had retired to their dressing rooms, letting it be truly "Bing's night.")

As Crosby was leaving the stage, somehow he lost his footing and sagged into a prop wall, which masked a 15-foot-deep orchestra pit. Bing's weight was too much for the flimsy retainer and he crashed through to the pit below. His wife Kathryn gasped and rushed to where he had fallen. Bing was trying to get up, blood coming out of his cut forehead. As he was being helped out, neither of them realized that his injuries were more profound than they appeared. From his bed at Huntington Hospital, Crosby told Hope the next day, "I gotta change the act and get a new finish."

Bing's accident pushed the prospects of the *Road* filming further into 1977, and because his recovery was so much slower than expected, the picture had to be postponed indefinitely. Hope filled his suddenly empty schedule with playing golf and doing benefit golf tournaments he had previously turned down, as well as some media interviews and a few guest television appearances he had been putting off. He also managed to pick up his thirty-seventh, thirty-eighth, thirty-ninth, and fortieth honorary degrees from St. Anselm's, Benedictine, Western State, and Baldwin-Wallace colleges. In August, his seventh book, *The Road to Hollywood,* coauthored with the Associated Press's Bob Thomas, was published, and a fat book-promotion schedule followed with media interviews, book autographing, and talk-show appearances on both coasts.

Everywhere he went in August and September he managed to plug *The Road to Hollywood.* Inevitably in each interview there was a question about his relationship with Crosby. So "Old Dad's" name had been getting tossed around a lot that fall, when on October 14 the telephone rang in Bob's hotel suite in New York and he was told that Bing, in Spain for a concert date, had suffered a heart seizure following a golf game at Madrid's La Moreleja Club, and was dead. Hope was stupefied.

"My head just got so tight," he later said, "that it felt a little dangerous to me. So I lay down and rested, because the whole thing was such a shock, I didn't cry at all. I don't cry easily. I just felt that tightness."

Bob Thomas called Hope from Los Angeles for a comment, and Hope said, "I'm stunned. I'm supposed to go out to Morristown, New Jersey, tonight and do a show in memory of my old friend Hugh Davis who died a year ago, also of a heart attack.

"But I can't do it. I'm going to have to cancel. Do you know, Bob, that this is the first time I've ever had to do that? I just can't get funny tonight. It's just not in me. I'm going home." And that may have been the only time anyone ever heard Bob Hope say the words, "I'm going home."

He flew to Burbank's Lockheed Airport that afternoon in a private jet. He asked Bill Cosby to replace him at a Tucson, Arizona, engagement the following night. At home he was inundated with requests from the media for a statement.

At nearly two o'clock on Saturday morning, striding the periphery of his Toluca Lake estate under the stars, with Ward Grant at his side and his large snow-white Alsatians, Steele and Shadow, trotting along, Hope was searching for words that might convey his impressions of Bing. Finally, Hope stopped, turned, and headed for his office. He dictated to Grant: "The whole world loved Bing with a devotion that not only crossed international boundaries, but erased them. He made the world a single place and through his music, spoke to it in a language that everybody understands—the language of the heart. No matter where you were in the world, because of Bing, every Christmas was white. And because we had him with us—it will always seem a little whiter.

"The world put Bing on a pedestal. But somehow I don't think he ever really knew it. Bing asked the world, 'Going my way?' and we all were." Hope's voice slowed and he was quiet for a time. Then he started again, "Yesterday, a heart may have stopped, and a voice stilled, but the real melody Bing sang will linger on as long as there is a phonograph to be played—and a heart to be lifted."

Bob and Dolores were two of the 30 people Kathryn Crosby invited to mourn her husband at private services held in the chapel of the rectory at St. Paul the Apostle's at six o'clock in the morning of October 18. Kathryn had already informed the media that Bing had been emphatic in his instructions that only the closest of family and friends were to be present at his funeral.

Although Bob and Bing had performed and golfed together often in their Paramount years and had exchanged guest appearances on their TV shows through the 1950s and '60s, they were not especially close in the years of Crosby's second marriage and subsequent move to Hillsborough in northern California. But a peculiar intimacy had been rekindled, urged by Bing, in more recent years. The Crosbys had come to several of the Hope's more personal family occasions, and Bob and Dolores had gone up to spend Thanksgiving with the Crosbys a year or two ago. Bing had actually warmed to the idea of their planned "September Song" *Road* picture. Bing was not a warm or very friendly sort of man, but proof of how he had grown to regard Bob was perhaps best seen in his will, signed in 1977, which specified that Hope was to be at his burial. Dorothy Lamour's name was omitted in the will; consequently she was ignored by Kathryn and was deeply hurt, saying, "Bing and I were never as close as Bob and I, but we still went through a lot together. He may have forgotten that I was a headliner when he arrived at Paramount and I was able to help him."

In less than 10 days Hope was scheduled to present as part of his Texaco contract a TV show called *The Road to Hollywood*, designed to plug his new book and present highlights of his movie career from 1938 to 1972. It hit him the morning of Bing's funeral that he was going to scrap the format he had already developed—which was nearly complete—and substitute a new script that focused on the *Road* pictures and Bing's contributions to movies and television. It would be called *On the Road with Bing*, and, predictably, it turned out to be one of the most endearing and popular specials Hope ever produced.

When one world-famous figure dies, there is always an urgency to make sure that other living legends are shown adequate appreciation before time runs out. And by almost every measure possible—if one is to believe inscriptions on awards, photo captions, and tributes by colleagues and public figures—Hope seemed to have been ensconced already in the realm of the legendary.

Almost every national organization Hope had done benefits for had already begged his office for the privilege of helping him observe his seventy-fifth birthday, on May 29, 1978, in some significant way. But the prize for ingenuity should probably go to a man in Wampum, Pennsylvania, who had a different kind of dream. He wasn't influential or rich enough to organize a splashy party. He was dirt-poor, but he had a plan to alert the nation that it was soon to be Bob's birthday. He did have one claim to fame, according to the *Guinness Book of Records*— he was the "world champion hitchhiker." His name was DeVon Smith and in 1975 he had crisscrossed the nation collecting signatures on a huge "Happy Birthday, America" card, which he eventually was able to present to President Ford at the White House on July 4, 1976. In his *Guinness* entry it was claimed that he had traveled 11,000 miles to amass the 21,868 signatures for that Bicentennial card.

In the fall of 1977, Smith appeared one day in the editorial offices of the *Daily Trojan*, the University of Southern California's campus newspaper, announcing that he would like to begin his signature gathering for the Bob Hope birthday card then and there. The newspaper staff found him a bit "weird," but he spoke sensibly. He resembled a modern Johnny Appleseed, they thought, and so they gave him enough publicity to help him get over 1,000 signatures at USC with which to launch his hitchhiking tour.

"I'll be traveling about seventeen thousand miles a month for the next six or eight months to forty-nine other states," he said. "I hitchhike and sometimes sleep in Greyhound buses and eat one meal a day—breakfast—so I can get at least a hundred thousand people to sign 'Happy Birthday Bob.'"

DeVon proved to be resourceful. Before leaving for San Diego, he managed to get into a number of film studios where he found 35 movie and television personalities who became the first celebrities to sign the card.

Some of those same stars had been signed up to take part in quite a different kind of birthday salute on March 29, 1978—this one for Oscar. Howard Koch, president of the Academy of Motion Picture Arts and Sciences and producer of Hollywood's "big night," asked Hope if he would return to the role he had played so adroitly for so many years, master of ceremonies, for a whopping fiftieth-anniversary celebration. This would be Hope's seventeenth and final appearance as host of the awards.

The stage set for this motion picture extravaganza at the Dorothy Chandler Pavilion was a multilevel gold stairway emblazoned with the names of previous Oscar winners. As the curtains parted, standing at various levels of those stairs were some of the outstanding recipients of that highly coveted gold statuette through the years.

Backstage, in the hallway of the dressing-room area, traffic was heavy with people trying to get in to greet Hope, who spent most of his time going over his monologue material. Once responding to a knock, he got up and warmly squeezed the hand of Janet Gaynor, who had won her Oscar for best actress at the first ceremonies in 1928. Another who managed to hug him quickly was Debbie Reynolds just before she went onstage for her dance bit, which opened the show.

As Hope's name was announced and he stepped gingerly down the steep staircase (his eyes weren't quite as good at age 75), he smiled broadly as the cameras focused on the famous people he passed: Fred Astaire, Michael Caine, Kirk Douglas, Joan Fontaine, Greer Garson, Mark Hamill, Goldie Hawn, William Holden, Walter Matthau, Jack Nicholson, Gregory Peck, Eva Marie Saint, Maggie Smith, Barbara Stanwyck, Cecily Tyson, Jon Voight, Raquel Welch, and Natalie Wood. Hope said:

> Hey, can you believe this group? . . . All on the same stage at the same time? . . . It looks like a clearance sale at the Hollywood Wax Museum. . . Of all the Oscar winners, I'm the only one who had to show my American Express card to get onstage. . . Anyway, good evening and welcome to the real *Star Wars*. . .

Backstage buzz that night concerned whether the longtime feuding sisters Olivia de Havilland and Joan Fontaine would meet, and if so, whether they would speak to each other. On the stage, Vanessa Redgrave, who won that year's Oscar for best supporting actress in *Julia,* used her moment in the spotlight to blast "militant Zionist hoodlums" and to espouse her political views, which stirred up the audience. Hope held his tongue. There was no need to say what the audience also felt. But all in all it turned out to be a night of rich sentiment and memories.

Hope had the evening's last words, some of them directed to another legend, his Toluca Lake neighbor John Wayne, who had undergone open-heart surgery earlier that day. "Duke, we miss you tonight. We expect to see you amble out here in person next year, because nobody else can walk in John Wayne's boots."

In the tradition of his own television shows, he spoke the show's final serious birthday words: "The essence of our arts and sciences are dreams and hopes and faith in the future. That's why a half century is only a beginning." Then bringing the focus back to himself, he added: "Just want you to know, if the Academy wants me back here in another half century, I'm available."

Two months later to the day, another birthday celebration—Hope's seventy-fifth—was getting under way in Washington, D.C. It was happening there, first of all, because the USO wanted to salute Bob on behalf of the armed forces. Hope liked that idea, providing the occasion could become a fund-raiser for the proposed USO world headquarters in the capital. Of all the seventy-fifth birth-day proposals Hope had listened to during the previous year, this one made the most sense. Besides, the new headquarters would bear the name The Bob Hope USO Center, and in addition to office space and a theater the new complex would house a museum area displaying a segment of Hope's vast collection of GI memorabilia.

From that point on the birthday concept mushroomed. NBC and Texaco immediately saw the television production potential of a black-tie entertainment "roast" at the Kennedy Center. They envisioned a roster of big-name talent per-forming just for the comedian, and Hope would just sit back and enjoy it all as a spectator. James Lipton and Gerald Rafshoon were hired as executive producers and Bob Wynn was signed to produce and direct a three-hour "animated birthday card" headlined by Pearl Bailey, Lucille Ball, George Burns, Sammy Davis Jr., Redd Fox, Elliott Gould, Alan King, Dorothy Lamour, Carol Lawrence, Fred MacMurray, the Muppets, Donny and Marie Osmond, Telly Savalas, George C. Scott, Elizabeth Taylor, Danny Thomas, and John Wayne. Both Kathryn Crosby and Dolores Hope would have segments all their own, and the evening would have a national blessing given by President Jimmy Carter.

The two-day affair officially began at a luncheon hosted by congressional wives, followed by a white-tie reception with Jimmy and Rosalynn Carter and five hun-dred guests from Washington and Hollywood upper circles. Both national and local media people were in close pursuit as Bob and Dolores left the White House headed for Alexandria, Virginia, where the Hopes were throwing their own party to thank the crowd of celebrities appearing in the three-hour entertainment gala the next night at the Kennedy Center. Bob had arranged to take over Peter's Place, a fashionable dining spot owned by Dolores's sister's son, Peter Malatesta, a for-mer aide to Spiro Agnew.

Dolores's original list of 30 or 40 close friends and family had grown and grown and now had reached a tightly packed 210 and that did not include the corps of media people that Bob invited to sit down with them at the last minute for a lav-ish Italian meal. There was something warm and godfatherish about the whole scene, a marvelous clan gathering filled with all the love and deference for the patriarch.

George Murphy and Fred MacMurray were perhaps the only ones in the room besides Dolores who remembered Bob's cocky arrogance in those early Broadway days.

Dorothy Lamour could look back 35 years to their first *Road* trip together. She had come to Washington despite the recent death of her husband, Bill, because "nothing could have kept me away."

Five-star General Omar Bradley sat on the sidelines in his wheelchair next to General William Westmoreland and when he had the chance he reminded every-one how fast Hope had charged through Europe and North Africa during World War II.

Carrot-haired Lucille Ball and raucous Phyllis Diller were discussing Hope as their leading man as only two comediennes could. And the presence of people like Senator John Warner and his wife, the beauteous Elizabeth Taylor, emphasized Hope's intimacy with shakers and movers along the Potomac.

One of Bob's favorite comedians, Mark Russell, the only preplanned entertainer at that party, said it best when he got up to face the group. "Bob, some where tonight in Hollywood, California, there is a tourist from Alexandria, Virginia, wondering where all the stars are."

Around midnight, near the close of the dinner party, Hope, mellowed by a glass of Liebfraumilch, stood up to acknowledge the affection being offered him. He could not bring himself to be serious. Pearl Bailey had sung special lyrics that began "Hello, Bobby" to the tune of "Hello Dolly"; Dolores had sung "'S Wonderful" to him; Mayor Mann had presented Bob with the keys to Alexandria (to join the five hundred or so other city and town keys on display in Hope's trophy room); and Bob had been asked to cut the first of several special cakes that would be presented to him in the next 24 hours. After he tried to blow out some of the candles, he said, "I'm pretty sure I'm seventy-five. But I've lied to so many girls. Of course they always find out about one a.m.—Dolores!—that's a joke!" As a roar went through the room there was a Mona Lisa expression on Dolores's face and curious half smiles on other faces in the room.

If he could not show his emotions that night, it was quite a different story the next morning, when tears did well up and roll down past his famous nose and jaw. It was a portentous event, scheduled to begin at ten o'clock, and Hope, not quite awake at nine, asked Ward Grant, who was coordinating his Washington schedule, "Can't we change it to eleven?" Grant merely looked at his boss, thinking that when Congress decides to pay an uncommon tribute to an entertainer on the floor of the House, it's a momentous event; but when they plan to devote a full hour to this tribute, then somehow, Mr. Bob Hope, ten o'clock is not too early!

Just before ten, Bob and Dolores, Linda and Nora (without their husbands, because both women were in the process of legal separations), Tony and wife Judy, Kelly, the four grandchildren, and Bob's one remaining brother, Fred, with wife LaRue were ushered into VIP seats in the House gallery. Hope fully expected to hear a resolution passed commending his humanitarian acts, because this is what he had been told. He was certainly not prepared for the unconventional behavior that occurred during the next 50 minutes.

After the morning prayer, Speaker "Tip" O'Neill recognized Congressman Paul Findley of Illinois, who spoke in a stentorian, congressional voice: "Mister Speaker, today is the seventy-fifth birthday celebration of Bob Hope, the greatest humorist of this century. But we are not celebrating Mister Hope's humor today. Instead we are taking time to express our deep gratitude on behalf of the American people for his consistent willingness over the years to contribute countless hours serving his country and worthy charities." In his gallery seat Hope leaned forward to follow Findley's tribute:

He is a great physician. He has eased the pain of inflation and taxes, something no member of this House has ever done. He never hurt anyone, except when we laughed too hard. Christmas away from home, whether in the cold reaches of Germany during World War II, or the sweltering heat of Vietnam years later, was still enjoyable and memorable to millions of American men and women because Bob Hope was there. . .

Findley finally yielded the floor to Congressman Richard Schulze of Pennsylvania, who compared Hope to Adlai Stevenson's definition of patriotism, which is "the tranquil and steady dedication of a lifetime." The floor was then yielded to Jim Wright of Texas and then to several other members, Guyer of Ohio, Brademas of Indiana, Pettis of California, Oaker of Ohio, who got laughs by thanking Hope for "sticking by the Cleveland Indians through thick and thin." Findley then recognized Wydler of New York, who electrified the proceedings with the remark "I'm going to violate House rules and address a comment to our distinguished guest."

Speaker O'Neill spoke up quickly, "The gentleman is aware of the rules?"

"I am aware of the rules," replied Wydler. "On behalf of the people in my district, Bob, and of the people of America, just this one sentence sums up our feelings toward you, and that is, 'Thanks for the Memories.'" Sustained applause.

Claude Pepper of Florida looked up from his seat on the floor to Hope's gallery seat and said, "Bob, if you really want to endear yourself further to everybody in the House, just assure us before you leave that you will not run against any of us." That inspired shouts of "Hear, hear! Hear, hear!" throughout the gallery.

Then more words from Congressmen Wylie of Ohio, Sikes of Florida, McClory of Illinois, Harkin of Iowa, Montgomery of Mississippi, Rousselot of California, Glickman of Kansas, and Stratton of New York. Congressman Boland of Massachusetts reminded everyone that Dolores had just celebrated a birthday and everyone kept applauding until she stood.

The penultimate member to be recognized was Minority Whip Robert Michel, who broke the second and probably most strictly enforced House rule, no singing, by singing in a natural clear baritone:

Thanks for the memories,
Of places you have gone
To cheer our soldiers on,
The President sent Kissinger
But you sent Jill St. John
We thank you so much.
Seventy plus five is now your age, Bob,
We're glad to see you still on the stage, Bob,
We hope you make a decent living wage, Bob,

For the more you make,
The more you take!
Thanks for the memories. . .

The applause was interrupted by Findley's loud and urgent request that the House recognize Speaker O'Neill; his utter amazement at the preceding infractions of both rules and tradition in one of the nation's oldest institutions was perhaps one of Hope's finest accolades. The Speaker said, "I explain to our guests, particularly, that singing in the House, and speaking in a foreign language, are not customary in the House.

"Also, you may be interested to know that in my twenty-five years in Congress, and I know there are members senior to me here, never before have I ever witnessed anything of this nature.

"The rules say that nobody can be introduced from the gallery, and that rule cannot be waived. Presidents' wives and former Presidents merely sit there. I have seen distinguished visitors, who have come to the House, sit in the galleries, but never before have I seen anything compared to what is transpiring on the floor today. It is a show of appreciation, of love and affection to a great American, and I think it is a beautiful tribute."

O'Neill stopped for a moment, looked around at his colleagues, and said, "He is a fine American, he is a great American, he is an all-American. Happy Birthday, Bob."

The members stood and sang an unadulterated version of "Happy Birthday," and when they had finished, remained standing, looking up at him, applauding. Hope was standing, too, and his eyes glistened. Dolores, at his side, faced him applauding. Both Linda and Nora were crying, too. But they all were smiling and applauding—Tony, Judy, Kelly, Fred, LaRue, and the grandchildren. All in all, it isn't offered any citizen to have it much better than that.

48

Breaking China

"And let me tell you, I loved the Great Wall. Of course, I love anything as old as I am. . . "

Standing in front of his marble-topped, double-mirrored bathroom sink shaving, Bob Hope could easily say in June 1978 that he looked pretty good for a man his age, and he did. His jowls had not yet sagged, his eyes—despite the serious hemorrhaging behind his left one and four laser-type operations that followed—were still bright. He was still a few years away from the time when his right eye—the good one—would begin giving him the same trouble as his left.

His hair was thinning but he could still comb it from the front and hide the bald spot on top with a medium dark shade of hair coloring. He was vain. He frequently stopped to look at himself, and, as somebody cracked, "He never passed a mirror he didn't like." But the image that came back to him as he shaved still pleased him and he could still count on having some of the young lovelies—ex–beauty queens, aspiring actresses, and occasional flight attendants—willing to go to wherever he was appearing on the road to keep him company.

And what about that superglorious celebration in Washington! Not everybody gets to have two presidents and two first ladies as your party givers, along with the cream of Washington society and the likes of Elizabeth Taylor, John Wayne, George Burns, Lucille Ball, Pearl Bailey, and even Miss Piggy—wishing you well and singing your praises. Not everybody gets to experience this kind of outpouring of appreciation, but amid the accolades was there also a vague hint of eulogizing? In the inevitable summation of accomplishments was he being handed a national certificate to unlimited use of that rocking chair on the porch?

And, by the way, when America's lawmakers rose to their feet to honor him in an unprecedented, rule-shattering "happening" on their sacred House floor, how much of the rest of America—his stand-up comedian's live personal-appearance audience—did that represent? How did middle America really feel about him today?

Ward Grant had brought him a new book by British writer John Fisher entitled *Call Them Irreplaceable*—and pointed out that he, Bob Hope, was among an elite group of "legends" that included Noel Coward, Jack Benny, Judy Garland, Jimmy Durante, Al Jolson, Marlene Dietrich, Maurice Chevalier, and a few others. Seemingly unaffected, Hope waited as Grant began to read him Fisher's opening sentence: "It is disconcerting that at the age when entertainers of stature and durability become ripe for reassessment, Bob Hope should find his own achievement shrouded in the mist of his recent identification as a standard bearer for the American political right . . ." Grant waited for a response. "What do you think?"

"I think it's a shitty way of opening his story. But I think he may be right. What else does he say?"

"A lot of good stuff—spends a lot of time on your style, your comedy techniques, your screen characters, joking with presidents, traces your whole life right up to now."

"Does he take any more shots?"

"He talks about your army of writers but he also quotes your line 'It's like getting elected to office. You're going to get elected if you say the right things—but only if you say them right' and he spends a little time on your friendships with Nixon and Agnew. He quotes Groucho as saying, 'Hope's not a comedian, he just translates what others write for him.'"

"Groucho was always jealous. How does he end it?" asked Hope.

"He says that you are the one American entertainer who could run for the presidency and win. He calls you 'Yankee Doodle Dandy to the Silent Majority' and adds this, 'He is shrewd enough to know that as long as he holds that office he will somehow be above even the Presidency.' Pretty good. And there's a really great Hirschfeld drawing."

"Let me see. Yeah. We gotta use that."

Apparently to Hope a legend is still only as good as his latest legendary accomplishment, regardless of age, and so he must compulsively think of what's next for this 75-year-old life on the yellow brick road. But after all you've done, what will make them notice you this time?

Tape a show on the moon? Except the moon shuttle hasn't started running yet.

(Actually, Hope had already signed up at NASA to go on the first shuttle.) Or how about directing a film—he had often said in interviews that it was a lifetime goal. Aha! Perhaps he could finally receive some significant recognition for his body of cinematic work, which, God knows, a number of industry people (not to mention Hope himself) considered to be long overdue. "I think I did a couple of things that could have won an Oscar, like the Jimmy Walker role in *Beau James* and Eddie Foy. But they were never submitted."

Or, he could break yet another barrier, set yet another record by being the first American performer allowed to create an entertainment special for television in the People's Republic of China.

As matters turned out, the last two legendary accomplishments were both offered on a platter, and he grabbed them eagerly.

A little less than a year after his birthday salute in Washington, Hope received an invitation from the prestigious Film Society of Lincoln Center in New York City to be honored guest at a tribute to his film career, planned for spring of 1979.

This celebration of Hope's contribution to the art of cinema was the dream child of Film Society director Joanne Koch, who said, "I got the idea one night when I was watching a Dick Cavett–Woody Allen interview on PBS."

About that particular exchange with Allen, Cavett later said, "I steered the discussion around to Hope and recalled a private conversation with Woody years earlier, in which he had done an appreciative cadenza on Hope's greatness as a screen comic. Carefully separating Hope's screen work from Hope's TV shows (and political views), Allen praised him again in immaculately worded encomia, allowing how it would be fun to edit the body of Hope's film work into segments illustrating his admiration of Hope's screen talent in its many parts."

At Koch's urging, that is exactly what Allen did. He edited and narrated a 63-minute compilation of clips from 17 Hope films of the 1938–54 period, including cuts from five *Road* pictures and generous portions of *The Lemon Drop Kid*, *Monsieur Beaucaire*, *My Favorite Brunette*, *Son of Paleface*, and *Fancy Pants*. Allen titled the tribute *My Favorite Comedian*.

On May 7, Cavett, serving as master of ceremonies at the gala tribute, welcomed nearly three thousand movie industry, business, and political notables to

Lincoln Center's Avery Fisher Hall. He explained that although Woody Allen had been passionate about creating a film tribute and narrating it, he was unable to attend because such big events made him "break out in a rash." This caused many in the audience to look at each other in wonder; they were thinking it, and some actually voiced it petulantly, that if Hope's art of characterization had been such a touchstone for Allen, why wasn't he there. It didn't make much sense.

But Allen's narration was loud and clear, and during a Hope-Crosby camel scene from *Road to Morocco*, he confessed, "I saw this film in 1941 when I was only seven years old, but I knew from that moment on what I wanted to do with my life." When a scene from Hope's 1947 film *Where There's Life* came up, Woody commented, "A woman's man, a coward's coward and always brilliant." Allen added to his tribute a scene from one of his own films, *Love and Death,* to demonstrate specifically how Hope was a seminal influence on his own screen persona.

Cavett told the audience he shared with Allen a belief that it was time to correct an "artistic wrong" done to Hope by neglecting his talents as an actor. He suggested that Hope's film acting genius had been taken for granted because, like Rex Harrison, he "makes what is terribly difficult look so easy that it is underrated."

Hope was truly delighted as he came up from the audience to say a few words, and there was a note of nostalgia in his voice:

> I enjoyed it. I'd forgotten some of our crazy stunts. You know, when we'd get the *Road* scripts, I'd give them to the writers and they'd write things on the edge. I'd take them in to Bing and he'd go 'Oh, that's funny.' We wouldn't tell the director but we used to go on the stage and we'd ad-lib all this stuff and Lamour would just look at us. The crew would break up and our director would say, "Just tell me when to say stop."

Hope had not prepared a monologue and the audience seemed touched that they were hearing a different tone, one of pure reminiscence, not gags. Before he left the stage he couldn't resist one of his favorite Crosby stories: "You probably don't know that Bing snored. We were sharing a room together on some golf weekends. He'd wake up in the morning refreshed and would win all the marbles that day because I couldn't sleep. But I finally found a way to stop his snoring and get some sleep. Just before we'd go to bed I would kiss him right on the mouth. And Crosby would stay up the rest of the night just watching me." Most of the audience thought the joke hilarious but there were those who wished Hope had been less flippant and had kept on with stories relating to the art of moviemaking.

This tribute inspired a number of reevaluations of Hope's movie career, including one by *The New York Times* film critic Jeffrey Couchman, who esteemed Hope as a "first rate comic actor and a man worthy of a respected place in film history." He felt the reason Hope had never received the same critical acceptance afforded other film comics, such as Chaplin, W. C. Fields, and Groucho Marx, was that

Hope "never created a consistent character of grandiose proportions" or one easily caricatured.

Yet, one could argue successfully that no other film comic besides Chaplin, Fields, or Marx has sustained—through at least 30 films of his golden period—such a unified comic persona. Hope spoofed the same things they did—lechery, cowardice, vanity, greed, and all the other common targets of sterling comedy—but he did it without a duck walk, painted-on mustache, or funny hat. No tricks of voice, no dialects or ethnic characterizations—he was always and simply America's Everyman.

His dumb wise-guy, his reluctant hero, his bragging coward are all parts of your basic "wise fool," the oldest and most persistent comic type in American humor. When "Fearless Frazier" or "Chester" or "Ace" brags about his courage, his looks, his sexual powers, or his intellect, we laugh because we see our neighbor next door, or, more tellingly, we see our own braggadocio in him. When he takes a pratfall we know we're in for the same thing. His appeal, his traveling-salesman averageness is the reason why in the forties and fifties people flocked to see his movies. That's why television stations throughout the United States—and the world—still program them so frequently. And why Paramount in Hollywood still collects fan mail for him.

It's also probably a reason why China's Ministry of Culture asked Hope to conduct an acting seminar using some of his middle-period films when the comedian paid his historic visit there in 1979. *The Road to China* was not the last *Road* that Hope would present to American viewing audiences, but it was one of his most memorable. He waited longer for official sanction to take this road than he had for his hard-fought trip to Russia to film a TV program in 1957, and he paid dearly ($1,700,000, much of which was unrecoverable) for the privilege of taping a variety show on Chinese soil. That was more than any production company had paid for a television variety show anywhere.

Hope began badgering Henry Kissinger at private gatherings as early as 1973 about wanting to pull off a "first," and he promised to improve his Ping-Pong game if that would help. In early spring of 1979, the green light flashed when the State Department and Beijing's Ministry of Culture reached an agreement that gave him the best possible fortune cookie. Hope sobered at the enormity of his undertaking and asked Jim Lipton—the producer who had put together the three-hour birthday salute in Washington, D.C.—and his own daughter, Linda, whom he believed ready for her big production break, to act as co–executive producers, and Bob Wynn to produce and direct at the line level.

On Saturday, June 16, 1979, Bob and Dolores, Linda, Jim and Hedakai Lipton, two Hope writers, Gig Henry and Bob Mills, and a few very dependable staff and crew stepped off the plane at Beijing. It was not a typical Hope airport arrival with hordes of eager fans, a brass band, pompom girls, and a big news conference.

"There was a group of Japanese diplomats on our plane getting off when we did," said Dolores, "and we were pushed aside as the diplomats were greeted.

While they were bowing, we kind of sneaked around them and I turned to Bob and said, 'How does it feel to be ignored?' It was the first time in my memory of being with Bob when nobody looked at him. We had a lot of laughs about it."

Hope's anonymity continued, at least for the entire next week, while he helped Lipton and Linda scout locations in Beijing and Shanghai, while he and Dolores went shopping unrecognized along Liu Li Change, a winding alley of ramshackle shops with lace-curtained windows, and while he strolled through Tiananmen Square swinging his golf club. He was, of course, lionized by the U.S. embassy personnel when the Hopes dined with Ambassador Leonard Woodstock, and were waved at by some round-eyed tourists who spotted Bob when they were taken the 50 miles northwest of Beijing to walk along the Great Wall.

But all that changed when the stars of his variety show telecast flew in, including ballet superstar Mikhail Baryshnikov, the mimes Robert Shields and Lorene Yarnell, country singer Crystal Gale, soul singers Peaches and Herb, and the lovable Big Bird from *Sesame Street.* When they began taping at various legendary landmarks around Beijing, crowds gathered to gape and to follow them.

It was a rich and varied experience for Hope, and what he later showed his American viewers on that three-hour television special reflected it. In particular there were enormously clever acrobats and a funny Chinese comedian, plus Hope's reaction as he heard the translation. One particular segment, taped at famed Democracy Wall, was censored by the Chinese government. That piece of tape was smuggled out but was never used on the show.

Hope respected the Ministry of Culture's explicit caution that the comedian make no political references in his jokes. "In my monologue at the Wall," Hope explained, "I used the line 'I had one Mao-Tai and my head felt like the Gang of Four,' but the ministry asked me to take it out. So we changed it to 'I felt like my head was going through a cultural revolution,' but they snipped that for being too political."

Things were not always tranquil between Hope and Linda on the professional front, and it was on this trip that Hope had one of his stormiest fights with his producer-daughter. They differed usually not over artistic things but money. Hope accused her many times of overspending on production costs she thought were necessary to buy quality for his shows. At worst, Hope would fire her—and then hire her back. Their fight in China was so noisy and fierce that producer Bob Wynn had to step in and separate them.

The Hopes remained in China a month, the longest trip of any kind that Bob and Dolores had taken together in many, many years. It was an exotic adventure and they were captivated by almost everything they saw and did as they completed segment after segment of the three-hour show—everything, that is, except an excess of banqueting. "This place is a front for Alka-Seltzer," Hope said as he and Dolores would retreat from being wined and dined by their Chinese hosts in favor of a quiet evening of bread, butter, and milk in their hotel room.

Los Angeles Times television critic Cecil Smith, who could be described as one of the comedian's harshest as well as most perceptive arbiters through some 30 seasons of Hope TV specials, wrote an exceptionally full and detailed critical review of *Bob Hope on the Road to China*. He characterized the show as a "huge sprawling vaudeville" and was singularly impressed with Hope's vitality, especially the agility of a man his age in his dancing routines with Baryshnikov. He also observed that not all of Hope's urbane and topical jokes delighted the Chinese:

> Hope with that tentative grin on his face waited for the interpreter to finish like a little kid waiting for a balloon. When the audience laughed, he moved right on, when it didn't, he seemed at a loss. Eager as a young comic facing his first audience. At 76! With his money!

Smith's surprised tone suggests that he did not really know the quintessential Bob Hope, for whom laughter was the simplest of motivations. And that would be true for him at age 76 or 36 or 96—no difference. It was all about telling more jokes and getting more laughs (even though lately the writing quality had seemed inferior), about being at the front of the pack (this trip to China, for example, or the fact that in 1979, teenage readers of *Seventeen* magazine had voted him their most admired personality).

He was also motivated by money and loved being a successful commercial spokesman (Texaco had signed him once again to sell their products) and California Federal Savings Bank in 1980 hired him to be that institution's credibility figure for their radio and television advertising campaigns.

It was also about getting awards (in a single week in 1980, Hope was honored by the Catholics, the Jews, the Salvation Army, Motion Picture Pioneers, the Air National Guard, and the USO—for the umpteenth time), and about being immortalized (there were ongoing plans to open a Bob Hope Museum either on property the comedian owned across from NBC in Burbank or on land he had an option to buy in Orlando, Florida, or in the soon-to-be-built USO headquarters in Washington).

For Hope it was ultimately about staying power, what it took to keep his love affair with the American public alive. His ego surely got a boost two days before his seventy-eighth birthday when weekly *Variety* carried a story to the effect that Bob Hope's 30-year Nielson national audience ratings for his NBC television specials had just been released and he was declared the all-time champion. Their front-page headline story said in part that these figures represented an "unparalleled record of ratings achievement for a man of any age and none the less astonishing despite the fact that his appeal has begun to slide a bit in the past decade."

To test that appeal and find out just what kind of an audience draw he might attract in his own hometown, the comedian was invited to make his first live appearance before a paying audience in Los Angeles since he starred in *Roberta* at the old Philharmonic Auditorium in 1939. The event was held on Labor Day night in 1980 at Universal Studio's new Amphitheater, which already had gained a reputation for presenting high-visibility rock stars in concert. Diahann Carroll, backed by Les Brown's Band of Renown, performed a set of stylish vocals to warm up the huge crowd. They rose to their feet when Hope sauntered out, and they stayed up long enough for Hope to spot certain people who had shown up. He exclaimed, "Oh, my God," as he pointed to the visibly aging veteran comedian Ken Murray, who had helped bail him out at his first "Sunday night special" at the famed New York Palace in 1932. He also pointed out his *Roberta* costar and friend, Fred MacMurray, and his wife June Haver, at Eve Arden to whom he had sung "I Can't Get Started with You" in the *Ziegfeld Follies of 1936,* and also standing there and smiling up at him was *Road* costar Dorothy Lamour and fellow USO trouper Martha Raye.

Backstage, Frank Liberman, expert at his job of publicizing Hope in the entertainment media, started rattling off names from a three-page-long list of current film and television performers attending his first-night audience—but Hope stopped him before the end of the first page with "Isn't that great?"

Odds are that most of this eighties Hollywood crowd had never seen Hope live in concert. For them he was perhaps a true show business legend, but in real terms just the very funny co-star of a late-night-movie *Road* picture, and someone they only rarely bothered to catch on television. Odds are also that they were surprised by his energy, his soft-shoe dancing. In addition, for most of this crowd it was the first time they heard Dolores sing, and she drew a huge applause when she sang to Bob the Billy Joel lyrical "I Love You Just the Way You Are." The show drew respectable but not turn-away crowds for five nights.

When that engagement ended, Bob and Dolores, together with their friends the Clark Cliffords, the Stuart Symingtons, and the Alex Spanoses, took off across the Atlantic with several target destinations in mind. The first stop was Moscow, for Bob had been asked to entertain the American community in the Soviet capital; after the Soviet invasion of Afghanistan, U.S. diplomats and their families were feeling a bit "hangdog and lonely" due to the strain in relations between the two superpowers.

Ambassador Tom Watson threw a party at Spasso House for 380 people with Bob and Dolores providing the entertainment. Because it was an election year there was an especially big laugh for this joke: "Jimmy Carter is hoping brother Billy is born again—and comes back as Ronald Reagan's brother." And also again with "I was hoping Reagan would pick Charlton Heston for his vice-presidential running mate—we need a miracle—"

From Moscow they flew to London, changed planes, and went up to St. Andrews, a seaside resort in eastern Scotland on the North Sea famous for its golf courses and rich in history. They played golf every day that it didn't rain. The only thing that could pull them away from this particular holiday was their obligation to return to London in time for the opening round of the brand-new Bob Hope

British Classic, a golf tournament to benefit spastic children being played on a beautiful course at Epson, southwest of London in Surrey. The idea was good, and the attendance of both world-class professionals and a large ticket-buying gallery was impressive, but Hope had only lent his name to the event, not his experience of running a top tournament. It was announced as the first annual tournament, but mismanagement of funds left it in such a sorry condition that it only lasted two more years, a decided contrast to the enormously successful Hope Desert Classic.

During those two years, however, Hope had stipulated that his name could be used and he would play as long as the proceeds were split between two worthy causes, the original British beneficiary, which was the Stars Organization for Spastics, and something that Hope himself was increasingly interested in exploring, a new cultural center to be named after him in the suburban London town of Eltham, where he was born. He had learned that the Eltham Little Theatre might be a possible site for the center and that it was for sale; he designated 58,000 pounds of the tournament profits for that purpose.

Thrilled by this turn of events, the Eltham committee, headed by Jim Shepherd, called Hope on one September night at his London hotel and invited him and Dolores to come to see how the money could help make possible the Bob Hope Theatre project. They set a time for the visit and Shepherd put out a media alert. According to Shepherd and a local press notice, "The reception was overwhelming. The Hope car was mobbed on the forecourt and it became a struggle to get them safely into the theatre."

Hope was conducted to a side stairway to the stage and from there he announced to the theater partners, Eltham citizens who crowded in, as well as newspaper reporters and a battery of TV cameras, that he intended to get the project off the ground. He said, "And that's very important to me." In that confined space, the resulting applause and hurrahs were deafening.

Shepherd then suggested the Hopes might like to drive a short distance and take a look at 44 Craigton Road, and when Hope said yes, the media followed to capture the event as the current owners, John and Florence Ching, urging Bob and Dolores to come inside their neatly kept south London row house for tea, while a small crowd that had gathered in the street looked on curiously.

Bob had never lost that early sentimentality about his British roots. He liked to hear news about members of his family still living in England and especially about his cousins, Frank and Kathleen Symons. In 1982, when he learned they were to celebrate their golden anniversary, he gave them as a gift an all-expenses-paid trip to see as much of America as they wished on an open-ended airline ticket.

During the Symonses' trip, Bob and Dolores met them in Cleveland, where Hope was doing a benefit. On May 6, only 23 days from Hope's seventy-ninth birthday, they toured the city's recently renovated Palace Theater. Hope's eyes brightened when he told them how he, Frances Langford, and Jerry Colonna had played this house and "packed it to the rafters" in early June of 1943. The memories seemed to flood over him. Hope recalled a time around 1925 when his oldest brother, Ivor, had caught him in one of his Ohio tab show performances and gave him a two-word review, "You stink!" Then he described with his accustomed sneer the look of astonishment on Ivor's face with "eyes bugging out" when Hope showed him a check for $20,000, which he got for his shows there in 1943. "That was a lot of lettuce in those days," Hope said.

Later that day they drove up Euclid Avenue to East 105th so that he could show them where Uncle Frank's plumbing shop had been and the upstairs flat they had crowded into for their first weeks in Cleveland. Nearby in University Circle, four of them stood and looked up at the awe-inspiring façade of the historic Church of the Covenant at 10205 Euclid Avenue, which was Harry Hope's first stone-cutting job when he came to America in 1906.

Hope kept mouthing the words "Beautiful, beautiful" as they walked inside the church and were met by the minister, Reverend Albert Jeandheur. Hope looked at the walls and the ascending arches and marveled at how William Henry—or Harry, his dad—had worked here "lifting, chiseling and setting the massive stones." Hope was far from being the glib gagster when he reflected on the permanence of his father's skillful contribution, saying, "It's awfully great, I'll tell you that—yes—a masterpiece. This will be around a long time after I'm gone.

"We came to this church as kids. Mahm brought us here on Sunday mornings. We changed from being Episcopalian to Presbyterian because we liked the church so much. Every time I'm in Cleveland I drive past it and take a peek. Today, however, is the first time I've been inside since I left Cleveland and went on the road in 1924."

Rev. Jeandheur raised his arm to point out and admire the intricate carved stone work of the rose windows and also the hand-carved tableaus in the sanctuary. Hope stopped again and they heard him say over and over, "Beautiful, beautiful." It was difficult to tell in the half-light of the sanctuary whether there were tears glistening in Hope's eyes.

49

Bumps in the Road

"Being eighty-two is getting up in the middle of the night as many times as Bert Reynolds. But not for the same reason."

In the fall of 1983 there were other reasons for concern about those famous Hope eyes. During a rehearsal in New York for his November TV special, the comedian had difficulty seeing the cue cards being held up before him, and even after they enlarged the lettering by three or four inches, he still had trouble. Soon after, it was determined that his good eye, the right one, was now hemorrhaging and he was rushed to his ophthalmologist, Robert Ellsworth, at Cornell Medical Center. They decided on medication rather than laser treatment (a recently developed treatment) at this time, but cautioned the comedian against overworking and spending too much time in airplanes. Afterward Hope said: "This is caused by stupidity. It's caused by going too fast. Most of the time I think I'm about forty and I just fly, fly, fly." He was disappointed when his doctors forbade him to fly to Lebanon with a small USO group to entertain the American troops who had been called up and put in a dangerous stand-by position to wait out the latest Middle Eastern crisis.

Of course Hope did not slow down for long. He seemed in total denial concerning his eye problem. Imagining he was at least 10 or 15 years younger, he hit the road again. An examination of his official appointment calendar for 1983—and, mind you this is a man who is now 80—reveals that out of 365 available days he completed 174 engagements as a performer, which involved frequently flying across the country as well as the Atlantic Ocean to keep these dates. His office broke down the list: Hope produced six television specials, which means he was totally involved in days and hours of their direction, rehearsal, performance, and editing. He did 42 benefits, 86 paid personal appearances (at roughly $50,000 each), played in 14 golf tournaments where he usually entertained in some way, and made 11 guest shots on TV shows to entertain or to plug his own shows and 15 TV commercials for his sponsors.

Little wonder that less than a year after the right-eye crisis, Hope, in London again to play in the third and final Bob Hope British Classic, suffered more eye trauma and came back to Cornell Medical Center and Dr. Ellsworth for more treatments. But to no one's particular surprise, he decided after watching the news and talking to friends in Washington that the U.S. troops in Beirut needed a morale boost.

So for the first time since the Vietnam War, Hope finally got a chance to once more headline a USO show for his beloved GIs overseas. He chose for his troupe three attractive performers, Ann Jillian, Brooke Shields, and Kathie Lee Crosby. They were billeted on the USS *Guam* for performances on several ships of the Sixth Fleet in Haifa Bay. Hope was dismayed when he learned that owing to heavy security restriction, only he—and the news media that were covering him—would be allowed access to the Marines facility in Beirut, where 241 troops had been ambushed by terrorists and massacred.

When he arrived he was delighted to see his old friend the USO entertainer Johnny Grant, who was also on tour. Hope and Grant were only allowed to stay at the barracks site a short time because there was fighting between the Lebanese army and the rebels nearby. He did do a short monologue on closed-circuit TV for the American forces still stationed in the area and was flown back by Marine helicopter to the *Guam*. There seems to be no doubt that Hope felt that, despite his doctors' warnings, he had fulfilled a personal commitment, and the image transmitted by the news media to American readers and TV viewers was precisely *that*. Dolores, understandably, was not one bit happy about his further endangering his eyesight. But as usual, he had his own way.

Hope returned to the United States and continued his unrelenting travels to do personal appearances, benefits, and golf with a fierce declaration, "I don't think about my age. It's called keeping the excitement going. It makes your adrenaline pump and keeps you moving."

But the really unusual thing he did in the spring of 1984 was to slow down long enough to appear in a totally different role, this time as a professor. He decided to live up to the academic imprimatur of his 50-some honorary degrees, and appear as "Dr. Hope" in a classroom at his adopted Texas university, Southern Methodist. He agreed to show up for three days and conduct a symposium on the art, creation, and performance of comedy. Altogether there would be four seminars: "What Makes People Laugh"; "Standup Stage Routines"; "Comedy on Film"; and "How Comedy Has Changed over Thirty Years."

Of course, Hope was there chiefly to build an audience, and every ticket sold meant another $25 added to the Bob Hope Scholarship Fund. Hope had a good time. He showed no real depth of understanding of what makes people laugh, but when it came time to discuss the nature and characteristics of standup comedy, the structure and delivery of a monologue, and the value of "foxhole humor," Hope could not be matched, and being thought of as a humor guru gave him a real high—it appealed to his vanity.

In 1984 there was another instance of Hope's being honored for being an "outstanding humanitarian" and behaving somewhat ungratefully and ungraciously. One suspects that another celebrity might have displayed more sensitivity and better judgment than Hope did when he went to Florida that year to perform for the twenty-fourth time at the National Parkinson Foundation Ball in Miami.

As a thank-you for the many years he had helped them, the foundation had decided to rename the four-block street running in front of their headquarters Bob Hope Road. The comedian asked the foundation if they could possibly hold the ceremony the morning after his performance. They agreed and he said he could stop by before he went to the airport. Understandably they were offended by this apparent trivialization of their regard, but they accepted his conditions, and at 10:30 A.M., Miami Mayor Maurice Ferre handed Hope his proclamation and street sign while the engine of the comedian's white limo purred a few feet away.

Perhaps, to someone who already had so many things named for him, including a very long public road, Bob Hope Drive, linking several fashionable desert resort communities in Southern California, this tribute was nice but something he felt he could acknowledge on the run.

But the three honors that followed were of such consequence and national focus that Hope could not easily grab them and run. The first was intended to help celebrate his eighty-second birthday. The city of Washington in the District of Columbia notified the comedian that the national headquarters of the USO, to which he had devoted half his lifetime—would be dedicated to him. The very notion of having a building in the nation's capital with the Bob Hope name on it was something not many could expect.

But there was more to the story. At the time of his seventy-fifth birthday celebration, a major fund-raising effort was begun to raise big money for a new USO building, and it was hinted at the time that it would be named for Hope. But in the meantime the funds were both slow in coming and inadequate for new construction, so the committee ended up leasing four floors in a different building. This was something of a punctured balloon, and Hope was disappointed.

Moreover, he was alarmed to discover that someone somewhere (possibly on his own staff) had allowed the USO national committee to harbor other expectations. They assumed that one floor would be used to house the Bob Hope Museum. Hope said he had never agreed to this. He was considering options about where to place his huge cache of gifts, trophies, and artifacts from years of entertaining both at home and abroad. His hometown, Cleveland, Ohio, thought they deserved his museum.

Hope was still in talks with NBC in Burbank about the possibility of using land he owned across the street from the studios for an all-purpose building that could house his museum. Also, he had leased-to-buy property in Orlando, Florida, close to Disney World that he thought might be the most conspicuous. But he was resolute that no one except him or his family would have artistic and financial control over the museum.

Consequently, as flattered as he was to have his name on a new national headquarters, four floors at 601 Indiana Avenue, N.W., and a bust of himself at the entrance, it was not as he expected. Hope was further disappointed that President Reagan was in West Germany at the time and that Vice President George Bush, Secretary of Defense Caspar Weinberger, and D.C. Mayor Marion Berry would be doing the honors of dedicating the new building.

Of course there would be the usual crowd of congressmen, as well as ambassadors from South Korea and West Germany (nations that had contributed generously to the fund) and five busloads of servicemen and women. The ceremony was impressive and Hope felt touched by the effort of those who had contributed. All in all, despite the fact that his dear friend Alex Spanos had been instrumental in creating the new space, the project fell short of the original plans the USO had presented him.

The second important tribute was inclusion in the Kennedy Center Honors in December 1985 in Washington. Hope may have felt when he looked over the list of prior recipients that he had been overlooked too long, but considering that the only comedian honored before him was Danny Kaye, he could not be too unhappy. (Two years later, in 1987, he would be back here onstage at these same Honors paying tribute to his friend George Burns.)

Now, as he looked around the Kennedy Center Opera House with his eyes and ears both failing him, he was moved by the warmth coming from the Reagans sitting next to him in the presidential box. He was also nostalgic, thinking of the past, thinking also that now, none of the Hope brothers could be here to see this. His older brother Fred, the onetime butcher and Bob's partner in the meat-packing business, who had looked after him when he was a teenager, had just died of cancer. But Dolores, Linda, Tony, Judy, and Kelly and the grandchildren were sitting nearby.

This would be a good night. The other honorees included actress Irene Dunne, dancer-choreographer Merce Cunningham, opera singer Beverly Sills, and the composer-lyricist team of Alan J. Lerner and Frederick Loewe. Fritz Loewe was a Palm Springs neighbor and friend. When it was Hope's turn to be celebrated—the icing on his cake was the accolade given to him by Walter Cronkite, a man whom Hope deeply admired.

The third honor, which came a year later in November, was coveted by a song-and-dance man who felt he deserved to be mentioned prominently in the history of television.

Hope had never really gotten over the disappointment of not winning an Oscar as a performer (the others were honorary), so he was determined that his work as producer and principal performer in more than 500 television specials would not go unrecognized.

True, over the years many of his shows had won individual honors, like the Peabody Award, and had also set new ratings records. But Hope, a firm believer in the adage "No joke is as good as the one that follows," always had to top himself. So being singled out by a prestigious body of his peers like the Television Academy would help keep his career alive and give his agents a hot-ticket selling point for personal-appearance bookings.

That's why this honor, this night, was special. He was being inducted into the Television Academy's Hall of Fame, which included placement of a bronze statue in the courtyard of the new Academy building in North Hollywood, not far from his home in Toluca Lake. Important to him was the order of presentation of himself and the other new inductees—Johnny Carson, Jacques Cousteau, Leonard Goldenson, Jim Henson, Ernie Kovacs, and Eric Sevareid. Wanting to make sure he was the focal point of the evening, Hope had several of his staff working on Academy members to secure his preeminence in this group. He was delighted when Hank Rieger, a former president of the Academy and now publisher of *Emmy* magazine, called to assured him that his induction would come at the climax of the ceremony and his statuette would be presented by a previous inductee, Lucille Ball. All was well.

During this time Bob was also trying to finish a book, his first since *The Road to Hollywood*, written with Bob Thomas in 1977. In Augusta, Georgia, for the Masters Tournament, he had been talking with Bill Davis, founder of *Golf Digest*, who asked bluntly why he hadn't written about his lifetime compulsion about golf. Hope said that with a little help, he would. Davis suggested *Golf Digest* senior editor Dwayne Netland as a collaborator.

It wasn't easy. Netland flew to Los Angeles, Palm Springs, Columbus, Green Bay, St. Louis, and more cities pursuing his coauthor's "hectic spiral of tours, benefits, television specials and one-night stands." One of Hope's favorite golf quips was "After all, golf is my real profession. . . Entertainment is just a sidelight. . . I tell jokes to pay my green fees."

Hope lavished many hours of recollection and provided valuable access to hundreds of celebrities and golf professionals. He called his book *Bob Hope's Confessions of a Hooker: My Lifelong Love Affair with Golf.* It was a nonfiction bestseller and was translated into several languages, making abundantly clear just how much golf *had* contributed to Hope's celebrity, his health, and general well-being and, certainly, his relationships with U.S. presidents.

Hope would write one more book, *Don't Shoot, It's Only Me*, subtitled *Bob Hope's Comedy History of the United States*, written with Mel Shavelson, who had written the screenplays for a number of Hope movies, including *The Seven Little Foys* and *Beau James.* This was for Hope his valedictory on a lifetime of entertaining GIs and it was also a tip of the hat to all his costars, writers, and anyone to whom he might say, "Thanks for the memories."

In the book he describes a trip he took that he thought would be his final overseas Christmas show in December 1987, when the United States sent Navy ships and Air Force planes to the Middle East. The Ayatollah Khomeini had closed the Persian Gulf to oil shipments during Iran's war with Iraq. When things got tense in November, and with a lot of U.S. military personnel in the area, the Defense Department asked Hope to bring some entertainment to them for the holidays.

Hope signed up Kathie Lee Crosby, Barbara Eden, Ann Jillian, Brooke Shields, the Super Bowl Dancers, and Miss USA, Michelle Rogers, to go with him for eight days. En route to the Persian Gulf they did shows in Hawaii, Manila, and Cape Espiritu Santo. They did shows at a land base in Bahrain and on board the USS *Midway*, the USS *Kennedy*, and the USS *Okinawa*.

In his monologue his jokes seemed reminiscent of the World War II era: "Here we are in the north Arabian Sea aboard the *Midway*. . . I think this is appropriate—the oldest aircraft carrier meets the oldest operational comedian. . . I knew this carrier was old when someone poured my Geritol into the fuel tanks . . ." Of this strange military effort, which American public opinion was questioning, Hope said: "Jokes couldn't make it go away, but we could do a little to help the men endure the heat and boredom of another nonwar."

Hope allows himself a bit of sentimentality near the close of *Don't Shoot, It's Only Me* when he writes about rediscovering his show business roots in a highly touted, big comedy show in New York. "Everything in my life seemed to come full circle on October 2, 1989. I went back to where it all began: vaudeville. . . Almost fourteen thousand people showed up in Madison Square Garden to see two guys whose ages added up to 179 years do a live act, which I guess a lot of the audience came to see if we could prove." The other guy onstage with him for nearly three hours was a nonagenarian song-and-dance man seven years his senior—the irrepressible, cigar-smoking George Burns.

> As we stood out there, two lonely figures in the glare of the spotlights, I felt lucky to have the best ninety-year-old tap dancer in the business as my partner. We had only to look at each other to see all those years of one-night stands in places like Williamsport, Pennsylvania, and Hamtract, Michigan, when we both learned to cook hash over a hot plate in our dressing room and wondered if we'd eat again tomorrow.

And Hope and Burns knew only too well this was not 1923; they were not on the Gus Sun Time Circuit. Hope says, "This wasn't an audience we faced in Madison Square Garden; it was a jury. These weren't GIs grateful for any kind of free entertainment, but New Yorkers only half a mile from Broadway. Go ahead, we could almost hear them saying—lay an egg, with two old yolks."

Bob and George were joined by a couple of beauty queens as foils for their sexual innuendoes, and Dionne Warwick came out several times to sing. Burns did nearly an hour alone onstage as "a stand-up comedian sitting down," and because he was playing in the round, he rotated his chair to make contact with the whole audience. Hope's monologue touched on the high price of New York theatergoing: "And I can't believe the ticket prices. When I was doing *Roberta* on Broadway if you paid that kind of money you owned a piece of the show. . . *and* the leading lady. . . Our tickets are nothing like that. George and I figured you should be able to tour these two old monuments for about the same price as they charge for the Statue of Liberty. . . "

For their finale, the two comedians dipped into vaudeville for one of the most beloved acts in show business history, George Burns and Grace Allen—with Hope playing Gracie. At the close, they danced "Tea for Two" together and George said, "Say good night, Gracie." Hope said, "Good night, Gracie." The two walked offstage arm in arm, and the audience stood up and cheered.

Critics were in favor. The people's newspaper, the New York *Daily News*, said, "George and Bob gave a show to remember." *Variety* said that it was "a fun-filled evening that failed to fill a lot of seats." True, it wasn't a complete sellout, but 14,000 made up a good-looking and good-sounding house. There were offers to take this show elsewhere in the nation, but George didn't feel he could do it, and Hope had commitments.

Spoofing about his age—and aging—as he had just done in front of 14,000 people in Madison Square Garden was acceptable to Hope just as long as he could feel that he was relatively immune from the stigma of "old age." Bob Thomas was able to report to his Associated Press readers about this time: "Hope's face seems little changed. The skin is smooth and tanned from daily golf, the voice is strong and clear."

But the reality check came each time a valued contemporary—someone even a bit younger, perhaps—would die, and he was forced to grapple with his own mortality. Such was the case when Lucille Ball died from cardiac arrest in 1989 when only 77. She had been important in his entertainment life, she was his "favorite redhead," and he considered her a friend as well as leading lady. She costarred with him in four films, including two regarded as among his best, *Sorrowful Jones* and *Facts of Life*, as well as being his frequent blockbusting guest in television specials and at major industry benefit shows.

Sitting at Forest Lawn Cemetery as part of a group of mourners who were close family, Hope preferred to remember his and Lucille's craziness together and he particularly liked the moment in an early TV appearance when he said, "Lucy, if you didn't do comedy, what would you like to do?" She had fired back, "Probably what you're doing." He told a reporter as he left the grave site, "God, she was something, wasn't she? I always had a great time with her. I just loved her." And she loved Hope—enough to scold him once, and he never forgot: "Why don't you grow up and stop chasing around?"

In 1990, Hope still had plenty of vitality, enough at least to do three or four TV specials a season. One, for example, had been planned to be taped in Berlin and Moscow to help celebrate the collapse of the Iron Curtain. He called that one *Bob Hope's U.S.O. Road to the Berlin Wall and Moscow*. It wasn't memorable, despite some great singing by Rosemary Clooney, Dolores Hope, and LaToya Jackson, and the usual mugging by Hope and Brooke Shields.

Later that year, however, was a different matter because it would probably be Hope's very last opportunity to make a Christmas journey to entertain American GIs. In August, Saddam Hussein sent his Iraqi army against Kuwait; the United Nations said: Stop. But Saddam refused to yield and a NATO force called "Operation Desert Shield" was formed.

Hope called George Bush in the White House and asked him if he could do a show for the combined troops there. Bush called Secretary of Defense Dick Cheney and told him to give Hope what he wanted. Hope wanted a Lockheed Starlifter like the one he had had during the Vietnam War because he was planning a full-scale show, not just a hand-shaking tour. So he decided it was appropriate for this last big overseas show that Dolores be the headliner, along with Ann Jillian, Marie Osmond, the Pointer Sisters, and Johnny Bench.

By any standards, this one was not easy. There were so many restrictions. Hope's jokes were monitored by the State Department to avoid offending the Saudis. There was intense security about everything they planned and did, and for the first time in Hope's memory, the media was restricted from covering the shows. Responding to news reporters' howls about the coverage blackout, Hope said it didn't come from him. "Did I ever say keep the press away. I live for the press." And nobody doubted that.

Because in Saudi Arabia national custom prescribes that women must be veiled in public, Ann Jillian, Marie Osmond, and the Pointer Sisters were left out of

Hope's Christmas Eve show in that country. Dolores, however, was allowed to sing "White Christmas." As Hope was leaving the show site, he asked in a generic way, "Where are you guys from?" And the group standing around him said, "Twenty-nine Palms, California." Hope said, "I came all this way when I could have stayed home and invited you to my house."

In fact, he did invite those Marines—350 of them—to come to his Palm Springs house for Easter Sunday brunch. He also invited everyone who had been part of his Desert Shield shows to join the Marines there. He called it "Bob Hope's Yellow Ribbon Party." On the telecast of that brunch party, Bob Hope began to look his age.

Media inquiries to Ward Grant's public relations office about Hope's health were frequent and occasionally there was a wild rumor about Hope's death that had to be quashed. Perhaps the comedian would have preferred to be among the missing right around early 1991. It was then that Grant called down to Palm Springs to alert Hope about a series of "tell all" articles being written by his former secretary Jan King and being published weekly in the scandal-loving tabloid *The Globe*. King had been hired by Hope in the early sixties to take care of an overload of secretarial work when he opened a second office at Universal Studios to handle his Chrysler show obligations.

King was a statuesque blonde (the Swedish variety), a onetime model, and a story editor at NBC when they met. She was definitely Hope's type for amorous pursuit, but King always insisted that a liaison never occurred, although Bob once tried. But she observed a great deal, kept notes, and was loyally discreet. Furthermore, in recent years when she was no longer working directly for him, she and her mother lived as tenants on one of Hope's properties in Palm Springs.

She was fond of telling people that one day she would write a book about her famous employer. At one point she asked Hope for a retirement package and he refused. So she decided to write a sort of memoir focusing on Hope's "hidden side." She sold her story to be published as a series in supermarket tabloid *The Globe*. In these articles she called him a penny-pincher and said he was mean to his writers and others. More damning, she offered in very explicit terms names, places, and dates of Hope's infidelities.

The Globe had a large readership, but it was not a morning newspaper tossed on the lawn, nor were its contents normally discussed on radio or television news. The mainstream news media ordinarily stayed clear of tabloid sensationalism. In fact, the image of Hope that King painted was not really that far from the one Hope had been humorously portraying in films and television.

But King's work was seminal, and it was followed, less than two years later, by a book that expanded on the *Globe* article. It was an exploitative, lazily researched literary effort whose material was largely lifted from previous documented biographies, including this one. Called *The Secret Life of Bob Hope*, it was written by Groucho's son, Arthur Marx, who some years earlier, with a partner, Bob Fisher, had written three of Hope's final mediocre-to-bad films.

Marx's personal association with the comedian was limited and relatively brief, and he chose to focus on the dark side of the comedian, a bitter effort in which he devoted an inordinate space to detailing sexual escapades, making, for example, 27 separate references to Jan King's angry revelations. On the book jacket, the publisher states that "Groucho Marx insisted that Hope wasn't funny but rather a translator of funny lines written by his writers." One of those writers, since deceased, said, "I didn't know that Frank Sinatra and Judy Garland wrote all the tunes and lyrics they sang."

Five years later, Lawrence J. Quirk wrote a book called *The Road Well Traveled* whose dust jacket asked these provocative questions: "Why did Bob Hope become so identified with sponsoring the Vietnamese War? What's the real scoop on his relationship with Bing Crosby? How far astray did Hope's oversexed nature lead him from the marriage he successfully maintained with Dolores for over sixty years?"

There are no surprises in Quirk's answers to these, but at least he furnishes a "selective bibliography" and his sources are for the most part substantive.

The most curious part of this volume is the inordinate time the author spends trying to connect Hope in some way—in any way he can—with homosexuality. Quirk quotes director George Cukor, for example, in naming Hope's second dancing partner George Byrne as a confirmed homosexual. He speculates about Hope's writer-friend Fred Williams's sexual orientation. In a much longer section, he relates the story of the hackles raised among gay activists after Hope told and apologized for telling an AIDS-related joke. The comedian admitted it was in poor taste and soon afterward cut some public service spots denouncing antihomosexual prejudice and violence. Nevertheless, Quirk's tone is insinuating when he writes "and then there was his own vulnerability."

Perhaps the bumpiest stretch on Hope's road to retirement was the seemingly never-ending story, hashed and rehashed in the media, of the sale of his vast real estate holding known as the Jordan Ranch (once owned by Jim "Fibber McGee" and Mollie Jordan) to an East Coast developer. He knew that the Potomac Investment Associates of Gaithersburg, Maryland, who had worked for the Professional Golf Association, wanted to build a PGA Tour course and an upscale housing community on Hope's 2,324-acre Jordan Ranch. From the first announcement there were wails of protest from Santa Monica Mountains environmentalists, notably Save Open Space and the Wilderness Society. They thought Hope should not sell but instead donate his land to the National Park Service because it abutted Cheseborough Canyon Park. To them, putting a development so close to the unspoiled park was not acceptable.

Then negotiations began for Hope to swap land with the National Park Service to both mollify environmentalists and satisfy the developers as long as the project was down-sized. Everyone agreed. But then, a new, very different venture was announced by the Ahmanson Land Company, which owned 5,400 acres nearby and wanted to create a similar golf community. The red flags went up immediately. All deals were off. More newspaper headlines.

Then a new suggestion was made and a deal offered for the Park Service to buy at fair market value Hope's land to protect the rest of the park and recreation area. Hope agreed, and when the deal was announced, nine lawsuits were filed to halt the Ahmanson Land Company project. Hope then backed out, claiming he would never ever see his money. All this time the media were clearly in step with the environmentalists, and Hope had to contend with protests, including one well-publicized group of picketers who gathered in front of the Toluca Lake estate.

In preparation to meet the protesters, Ward Grant set up two long tables with tablecloths from which to serve soft drinks in recyclable cans. First the protesters, headed by Dick Van Dyke's son, went to the wrong address across the road and were beckoned to come over to the Hope house. They all had a drink and deposited their cans in a recyclables bin and one commented quietly, "You did well. But this soda is full of impurities. You would have been better to provide us with pure juices in cardboard cartons." Grant smiled and said "Thank you," and under his breath added, "You no good son-of-a-bitch." They left a letter for Hope and went away.

Next, the National Park Service notified Hope they wanted to buy Jordan Ranch and another parcel for about $20 million. Hope let their deadline for the offer go by, and finally the Park Service came back with a better offer—at less than best market value—for just Jordan Ranch, and Hope felt right about selling. A lot of ugly things had been said about him by the environmentalists and a few of the Ventura County supervisors, but in the end he donated a generous parcel of land to the Santa Monica Mountain Conservancy.

The subject of Hope's net worth has been a favorite one with both entertainment columnists and business writers for many years. In 1966, *Time* magazine estimated Hope's wealth to be somewhere around a half a billion, to which the comedian—just back from a Southeast Asia Christmas trip—said, "If I had that kind of money, I wouldn't have to go to Vietnam—I'd send for it." And when *Fortune* reported in 1968 his income at $200 million, he quipped, "When Dolores read that, she started tearing up the mattresses."

Joking aside, figuring up his true worth was always a matter of speculation anyway, because only Hope knew what he owned in terms of real property as well as what he could expect if it were offered on the market. He would refer to himself as "property poor" and whenever someone suggested that a certain piece of his real estate holdings was worth $50 million, he'd say, "You want it for that? Show me your money and it's yours."

Hope's wealth had begun to accumulate faster when he and Bing struck oil in Texas in the early fifties. Each had invested $100,000 and after their well gushed black gold, Hope sold his shares in the Kelly-Snyder Oil Company in 1954. A Bank of America financial adviser at the comedian's Toluca Lake branch counseled him to buy land in Ventura County just beyond the Los Angeles County line. Hope did just that and what he bought for $500 an acre in the fifties is worth more like $10,000 an acre in the nineties.

In the sixties Hope got $25,000 a night for a personal appearance, but more recently he was asking for $50,000 to $75,000 and getting it. One might speculate that in a given year, if he did 75 to 80 paid engagements (out of a total of 150 appearances of various kinds), he might gross somewhere near $5 million. In addition, his television show income goes through Hope Enterprises and that amounts to somewhere between $1 million and $2 million. A conservative estimate, then, would be that his annual income in the nineties could be close to $7 million. And that wouldn't include his investment portfolio or his separate commercial contracts.

Not bad for an immigrant kid from Cleveland who sold newspapers on that windy southwest grocery corner of Euclid Avenue and 105th.

50

Icon in Cyberspace

"I can't quit show business. I have a government to support."

It was ironic that while NBC was dedicating its Burbank studios to Bob Hope in honor of his ninetieth birthday and, incidentally, over 50 years of making big money from their partnership, his current contract with them was in doubt. NBC had weighed the truth that Hope's ratings were not what they had once been. Critics had not been kind to some of his recent specials. They could not quarrel with the attention he had received for his ninetieth-birthday salute on the network or all the concurrent publicity. What should they do?

Tawny Little, a popular anchor for Channel 9 news in Los Angeles, asked in her nightly ten o'clock spot, "Has NBC abandoned Hope? On the eve of its three-hour prime-time tribute to Hope, the network is trying to diffuse reports that it's about to tell the legendary comedian, thanks for the memories."

When the *New York Post* got wind of it they ran a banner headline NO HOPE FOR NBC; when they telephoned the Hope house they got connected. "Was it true?" the reporter asked him. "Have they renewed your contract?"

"Nope," answered Hope. "I'm not signed for next year. I'm a freelancer. I'm wide open."

"Don't you usually do three or four specials a year?"

"I may not have another one. This could be my last show," answered Hope.

An NBC spokesman responded to the *Post*'s queries with a statement: "This is the time we renegotiate Bob Hope's contract, and we have not concluded the process."

When the *Post* called Linda Hope, Bob's executive producer, she said, "I'm surprised because Dad has always been locked into next season by this time. I know they're hedging right now and our lawyers are talking with the network. But NBC hasn't committed one way or another. I think they're waiting to see the ratings from our big show tomorrow night."

Apparently network officials had complained to Linda that the Hope format was tired and didn't appeal to a youthful audience. Linda said she was willing to revamp, restyle, and bring the Hope shows into the twenty-first century.

"In the old days," she recalled, "they [NBC] looked after employees. But those values, like loyalty, that used to be prized so highly are disappearing. The only thing that matters is the bottom line. They've been on this youth kick lately and that hasn't always proved successful."

After the impressively high ratings were logged for the Hope birthday special, NBC responded very quickly and signed Hope for two more seasons of four specials each. Actually, the show won an Emmy, and that further reinforced NBC's decision, but it also meant that Linda had to be even more forceful and inventive than ever in using existing footage to produce those final eight shows. The once tightly wound clock that was her dad was slowly winding down. Basically all she could do was hope he could deliver a monologue at half his usual speed to front a show full of clips from previous specials and entertainment documentaries.

And that had to be good enough. Linda would explain that her father was really too set in his ways to change much; for him, what had worked well in the past had to work again. Like some jokes. You just need to change a few things but the structure of the joke always works. Gene Perret, a Hope gag writer for 25 years, said that Hope always knew when a joke would work, and after all these years he still hadn't changed his mode of operation except for one thing: fax.

"God bless fax," Perret said. "Bob is anti-anything new. He likes his way of doing things. Then one day he was on the road and a hotel bellboy delivered jokes that had arrived by fax. Bob said, 'Wow! how long has this been going on?' He then announced he was going home and would install a fax machine and that I should install one, too. But when I got home I called his office anyway because I had been through the business of 'trying new things' before with him. But he really did [install the fax], and then I did, and life has been easier since."

In 1995, Hope decided that when his current contract with NBC expired he would not press for renewal. And NBC was relieved. His body hadn't given out, but he was having increasing difficulty seeing the already greatly enlarged cues and hearing what the director and technicians on the floor were saying to him. Linda had once talked him into working with a special hearing device that allowed him to hear the director or her giving cues, but it confused him. Once when she was feeding him a joke line, he snapped—and everyone heard—"I know that one, Linda."

He needed to have the flexibility to decide whether and when he would do television, or continue to do an occasional personal appearance or write more books.

Hope's final TV special for NBC provided an opportunity to mount a collage of live, taped, and filmed recollections and experiences with the 11 U.S. presidents he had entertained and with whom he had played golf. It also provided an opportunity for him to do some valuable cross plugging for a book that he and Ward Grant had put together of favorite stories and jokes inspired by the presidents. They were calling their book *Dear Prez, I Wanna Tell Ya!* and to their surprise, and great satisfaction, within a few weeks after publication it made its way to the top of the best-seller list for nonfiction. And that managed to boost Hope's sagging spirits caused by his slowdown.

The TV special, called *Laughing with the Presidents*, was cohosted by actor Tony Danza with appearances by President Bill Clinton and First Lady Hillary, George and Barbara Bush, Gerald and Betty Ford, and David and Julie Nixon Eisenhower and from Hollywood, Don Johnson, Naomi Judd, Ann-Margret, and Tom Selleck.

When it came time to publicize the show, Hope was willing to do his accustomed telephone interviews and a few face-to-face ones with syndicated writers. Then NBC suggested that the show might get an extra shot of promotion in a very new medium—the Internet. Chat rooms were a relatively new phenomenon, and NBC had the idea that Hope could get on-line and talk with his fans wherever they might be found.

Mike Mannarino, director of NBC's Interactive Promotion Department, was called in to set up all the special computer equipment needed at the Palm Springs house. Hope was interested because it sounded so easy, and he agreed to spend three hours with the team NBC sent down from Burbank a few days before the TV special. Once Hope was on-line and signed into the cyberspace chat room, the questions came up on the screen from individuals and groups who had gathered to talk to him at sites all over the world. They asked mostly about his films, and Hope adroitly managed to steer them toward the TV special by his Internet responses.

However, as easy as it sounded, it wasn't easy for him. "This is difficult," he said. "I can't tell if they're laughing." And almost immediately the responses came in, "We're laughing."

"You're kidding," Hope said. "But I can't hear it. And for a guy like me, I have to hear the sound of laughter. It's in my blood."

Later Mannarino said, "Hope was amazed that he was interacting with people who wanted to talk to him from all parts of the world—Russia, New Zealand, South America. It was fun to watch his face react to being on the World Wide Web. I heard one of the NBC guys say in a kind of lowered voice, 'An icon in cyberspace.' To be truthful, there was a common perception among us that his core fan base would probably not be on-line. But he proved us wrong—there were many seniors as well as other ages represented. His fan base is timeless."

It would be against Hope's nature to be sentimental about the close of an era, so he decided on a bit of sardonic humor in his public farewell to NBC. He took a full-page ad in the *Los Angeles Times* and in the much-read trade papers *Variety* and *Hollywood Reporter* to announce his new status:

> Guess what? I've decided to become a FREE AGENT! So watch out, Michael Jordan! I've enjoyed 60 memorable years with NBC. I started before the peacock and he wound up taking my parking space!
>
> On Saturday, November 23rd, I do my final special, "Laughing with the Presidents," and I hope you'll join me. After all, your loyalty and laughs have kept me in business.
>
> My thanks to NBC for making it possible to be part of your lives all these years. It's been a great ride. Now, caddy, hand me my seven-iron. I'm going to put one right up on the green—unless a twelve-year-old Yankee fan sticks his glove out and ruins my shot.

As it turned out, Hope would never again put on makeup for the television cameras. He did, however, devote some time to helping Hope Enterprises film editor Jim Hardy prepare a series of videotapes to be marketed worldwide that captured the "best of" Hope's TV specials and Christmas shows, highlights of his USO tours, and his golfing experiences with Bing Crosby and several presidents.

Since Hope now was not performing much—was doing a lot less of everything, including golf—he was seen more often around his two residential milieus of Toluca Lake and Palm Springs. He slept late, as always, and sometimes asked his valet-companion, J. Dennis Paulin (whom he called simply J.), who took exceptionally good care of him, to take him for a ride or a walk. Hope would be spotted at Starbucks having a caffé latte, and because his sight and hearing were poor he often failed to react when people greeted him. This resulted in thoughtless claims that he had "lost it."

Both of the sometimes reckless mid-'90s biographies written about Hope seem to depict him as some kind of witless King Lear stumbling around with eyes "red-rimmed and swollen" and wild wispy hair. Certainly in 1998, Hope at 95 did not look as aware as he did when he was 90, because the aging process had of course progressed—but his innate fastidiousness and the exquisite care he was receiving from both Dolores and J. meant that he always looked neat and fashionable.

In 1997, Bob accompanied Dolores to Hollywood Boulevard when she received her star on the Walk of Fame and the news shots taken at that time show the comedian being helped from the car with a concerned, troubled expression on his face. J. explained that Bob wasn't feeling well that day but had insisted on going to the ceremony. His expressions suggested acute discomfort.

Shortly afterward, there appeared on the cover of the May 20, 1997, issue of *National Inquirer* inch-and-a-half-high headlines screaming BOB HOPE'S TRAGIC LAST DAYS with a close-up color photograph of his contorted face and slightly bloodshot eyes. Inside the story screamed another headline, BOB HOPE'S BRAVE

LAST GOOD-BYE. But the story was less grave. It quoted the usual "insider," who speaks of his altered looks, stooped walk, and thinner hair, and suggested that Hope was not always as alert as he once had been. But the insider also said, "I saw him at a dinner honoring orchestra leader Les Brown. Dolores got up and sang. She asked Bob to get up and sing 'De-Lovely' with her and to everyone's amazement he did just that. He did the routine perfectly! He's just an old show business warhorse. When the spotlight hits him, he can still turn it on."

June 1997 until the fall of 1998 was undeniably a period of time when he had to "turn it on," at least enough times to respond to a remarkable series of events. On June 3, Ward Grant sent a message to Hope that the U.S. House of Representatives had passed a resolution conferring on the comedian the status of an "Honorary Veteran of the U.S. Armed Forces"; very important, he was the first individual to be so honored. The Senate passed the resolution on September 9, when it was immediately forwarded to the White House.

Clinton decided that he would like to have Bob and his family in the Oval Office for a ceremonial signing of Resolution 75 but not without Hope's having the pleasure of being saluted by the full membership of Congress. So when a date could be arranged, October 29, Dolores gathered a delegation of Hopes—Linda and son Andrew, Tony and his new wife, Paula, Kelly—and some close friends who flew to Washington and were seated proudly in the front row at the Capitol Rotunda. Behind them were rows upon rows of Congressmen and -women, cabinet members, Pentagon brass, and representatives of the enlisted men and women of the armed forces. A color guard and the U.S. Army Band were on hand. Bob and Dolores were invited to a small stage where congressional leaders Newt Gingrich, Richard Gephardt, Strom Thurmond, Trent Lott, Tom Daschle, Bob Stump, Lane Evans, and John D. Rockefeller IV greeted them. Also standing there busting with pride was USO president General Carl E. Mundy, Jr., who had been very instrumental in bringing about this honor. The joint resolution was read aloud and Hope was moved to tears. Dolores squeezed his hand and stepped to the microphone, saying, "Bob wants you all to hear what he has to say: 'I've been given many awards in my lifetime, but to be numbered among the men and women I admire most is the greatest honor I have ever received.'"

That ceremony lasted less than an hour and then Dolores took Bob and their guests to lunch at the Jockey Club. Next day, the Hope family and close friends gathered again, this time to be taken in limos to the White House and into the Oval Office, where Bill Clinton signed the resolution into law. Hope said he couldn't be funny about this honor, only grateful. He presented the President with a special golf putter, with a caricature of himself in the hosel and autographed on the back of the blade. The two then proceeded to have a putting match in the Oval Office. In the afternoon, he was driven to the Vietnam Wall and he stood alone in front of it for a longer period than anyone around him believed he would.

A few months later, in February, British Prime Minister Tony Blair came to Washington for three days of talks with President Clinton. At a banquet held in his honor he announced that he had permission from Queen Elizabeth to relay the message that as part of her 1999 honors list she was naming Hope Knight Commander of the Most Excellent Order of the British Empire, "in recognition of his contributions to film, to song, and to the entertainment of troops in the past." This honor had previously been conferred on only two other Americans—André Previn and John Paul Getty II.

Hope was in Palm Springs at the time. That night he received a telephone call from a Washington reporter for the British newspaper *The Guardian*, who asked him for his reaction. He thought a moment before responding: "I am speechless. Seventy years of ad-lib material and I'm speechless." He thought a bit longer. "What an honor—and what a surprise for a boy born in England, raised in Cleveland and schooled in vaudeville. Where are my writers when I need them! If Mahm could see me now."

"Will you be going to London for this?"

"Oh, I'm not sure. We'll have to let you know." And before he hung up he said, "By the way, would you happen to know if I have to give up my CBE [Commander of the Order of the British Empire] that her majesty gave me in 1976?"

"That one I don't know," the reporter said, "but if I find out I'll call you."

Also going on at this time was the final decision stage of a process that had been vaguely in the works for several years concerning the whole matter of the comedian's legacy. Bob and Dolores had finally agreed that his personal papers, extensive joke files, photos, and original radio and television programs should not be put in a Hope Museum but rather in a special room of the Library of Congress. In discussions with James H. Billington, the congressional librarian, it was determined that the gallery, to be in the Thomas Jefferson Building, should be called the Bob Hope Gallery of American Entertainment. The Hopes offered to donate $3.5 million for construction and maintenance, and they chose May 19, 1998, as the date for formalizing the gift in Washington.

Dolores thought that if Bob was to be in Washington for the library event, why not try to combine his receiving the knighthood in the same trip. All parties agreed, so they picked Sunday, May 17. Dolores once again gathered up her children and grandchildren and some close friends and all were invited to watch British Ambassador Sir Christopher Meyer place the ribbon holding the KBE cross over Hope's head and on his shoulders. There was restrained applause and good food.

On Monday night, the Hope entourage went out to dinner at Goldoni's restaurant and Hope felt spry enough to lead his table in "Happy Birthday" when he learned that another diner was celebrating his natal day. But he might have overdone things, because he begged off the following night, when he was supposed to be at his own candlelit birthday party, a banquet thrown in the ornate Great Hall of the Library of Congress to honor his generous endowment of the Bob Hope Gallery. Dolores attended the dinner in his place, and apologized for Bob's absence and said she was glad her husband's comedy material would be "in safe-keeping here. . . and made available for the American people to enjoy. . . though I will miss the dusting." Librarian Billington said he had given Hope a tour the day before, and when he was shown the Gutenberg Bible he cracked, "That's great, but who wrote the music?"

Two days later they went to New York, where Dolores appeared with Rosemary Clooney at the Rainbow and Stars cabaret. They celebrated Dolores's birthday, May 27, quietly and went with the Spanos for a few days of fishing in Maryland, where they stayed at the home of their close friend Laura Mako before heading back to Toluca Lake for Bob's ninety-fifth birthday party, which was intimate and quiet. On Saturday, May 30, the Hopes were the grand marshals of the Toluca Lake seventy-fifth anniversary parade.

As if those weren't honors enough, there were still two more to come. On June 10, at the Hopes' parish church, St. Charles Borromeo, with Cardinal Roger Mahoney of the Los Angeles Archdiocese officiating on behalf of Pope John Paul II, Bob and Dolores received the "highest honors the Holy Father can confer," he as Knight Commander and she as Dame of the Order of St. Gregory the Great (Hope had quipped: "If you're married to a Catholic, you're one whether you want to be or not"). Mahoney told Dolores she was one of four women in the world to receive her honor. And for Hope, this was his second knighthood of the year. Chances are Dolores was more happy about this one. (Since that time Bob has converted to Catholicism.)

It was at about this time that Don Mischer, who was producing the Fiftieth Annual Emmy Awards ceremony for the Academy of Television Arts and Sciences, called Linda Hope to ask if she thought her father would be able to make an appearance on Sunday, September 13, at the Shrine Auditorium in downtown Los Angeles. The question was put to Dolores, who then put it to Bob. He liked the idea, but everyone wanted to know how he would be presented.

Mischer said the academy wanted to pay tribute to three giants of the last 50 years of television. They had selected Hope, Milton Berle, and Sid Caesar, and the plan was, early in the telecast, to cut away from a commercial and have the camera come in on the three seated centerstage in director's chairs. Good idea, Dolores said, and Bob agreed. But the reality was that Bob by now needed special handling; he walked slowly and would need someone to assist him on and off the stage.

Hope seemed to enjoy it all—the ride to the Shrine, the dressing room crowded with his own people (Linda, Ward, J., and a hairdresser), and being with Caesar, 76, ("I think he might be the funniest of them all," Hope told J. one day) and his old, old friend Berle, now 90. One of the stage managers was standing by to cue them. He was clearly thrilled to have this assignment with these three pioneers. He proudly told them that they would be watched tonight by 700 million viewers in 92 countries.

When they were called, Berle and Caesar took charge of Hope and led him slowly to centerstage. As they approached, there was only one chair and they guided Hope to it. Then the two comedians stood on either side, each with a hand on Bob's shoulder. Between them they decided not to sit, to let Hope be enthroned. It was touching and highly emotional. The crowd of six thousand—television actors, directors, producers, writers, and all sorts of technical people—rose to their feet in what was probably the longest ovation in the academy's history.

FADE OUT: I'M STILL HERE

"I'm getting faster at ninety-five. After I hit my tee shot, it doesn't take me nearly as long to walk to the ball."

It was just past three o'clock in the afternoon of June 5, 1998, when an aide in the office of Majority Leader Dick Armey was surfing the Internet and saw a headline apparently from the Associated Press that was numbing. She printed it out and took it to her boss in the House. At that time Congressman Bob Stump was speaking on the floor and Armey interrupted him, and together they had a short discussion. Then Stump proceeded to announce to his colleagues in the House in a dark and solemn voice, "It is with great sadness that I announce that Bob Hope is dead."

The announcement was carried live on C-Span. Meanwhile other news media, not willing to accept the bulletin without verification, telephoned Hope Enterprises in Toluca Lake and reached Linda Hope. "Somebody goofed somewhere," she said. "My dad is having breakfast right now." Very quickly, Congress was advised it had no cause for mourning and the error was traced. The Associated Press periodically updates its obituaries and its most recent version on Hope was somehow—don't ask how—inadvertently released by Internet news handlers. There were a lot of red faces.

According to Linda, Bob had a good laugh and, sounding like a refrain from Stephen Sondheim's *Follies*, said, "I'm still here, at least the last time I felt." In fact, Hope's public relations aide, Ward Grant, reveals that his office receives a serious call every few days from some source seeking to verify that Hope is still alive. If he visits a doctor or goes to a hospital for a checkup, the media death-watch team is alerted. And elsewhere, among the nation's vast news networks, there sits a legion of city editors, editorial writers, feature writers, television critics, gossip columnists, and sports writers who have had—or never had—any personal acquaintance with, or feelings about, this icon, and yet they will hit their keyboards running when it is time. That's the way it is in a nation addicted to celebrity.

How much of Hope's total celebrity still lingers in his own mind is of course questionable. At his age he might not still be feeling the same need for applause—but that, too, is questionable. With Hope it always was about the audience and their laughs. Without them it would be nothing.

Hope's most recent head writer, Gene Perret, underscores that point with this story: "He was appearing somewhere when he was about ninety and he wasn't feeling well that day. Someone told him he could just tell the audience that, because they wouldn't mind at his age. I was told he straightened up and snapped, 'You don't want sympathy out there. You want laughs.'"

In an earlier instance, Hope took Dolores and the kids away for a much-needed, much-deserved holiday fishing in the Northwest, and suddenly returned to Toluca Lake and called his writers. "What happened?" asked Norm Sullivan. Hope joked on the square, "Fish don't applaud." He had learned profound respect for those whose applause had catapulted him from vaudeville to Broadway to radio and movies and to those enormous military and movie-house audiences that made him a legend. A tempting way to characterize Hope would be "What you see is what you get," but that's too simple. It suggests that there was nothing interesting behind Hope's 65-year marathon of multimedia entertaining or the genesis of his comic persona.

There's always the old psychoanalytic approach, which would seek to distinguish between Hope's ego and his superego and then trying to locate the id. Three recent biographers seem to believe they have found paydirt in the dark side, as one terms it, the "secret life" of the comedian. They titter over the discovery that he was mean to his writers and that he had a previously undisclosed first marriage, and they quote liberally from misleading headlines of the tabloid press, relishing the sensational revelations of two former secretaries whose agendas for telling tales are shadowy.

In telling and assessing any life, one is obligated to try for the essence. And after recounting the extraordinary ways Hope chose to live that life, by sifting through the narratives, observations, and confessions and weighing the significant detours and opportunities that mapped the roads he took, there remains the question: What has his life meant to his family? To his friends and colleagues? To the public? What impact did the life make on the history of entertainment, on a better understanding of humor and of stand-up comedy? How will he be remembered?

Essentially Hope was a rover. From his beginnings to the close of the millennium he had a compulsion to be on the move. And more than most, Leslie Towns Hope needed to be noticed and loved. That restlessness and drive to perform led him to a seminal training experience in a traveling tabloid troupe where he honed a few other lifelong traits: to be adaptable, versatile, and persevering. He also learned how to nurture his driving ambition. Appealingly virile, and with an unusually active libido, he fed his ego with both applause and sex.

Who can guess Hope's impact on American entertainment without considering his evolution as a monologuist. Learning to be the century's most famous stand-up comic was full of risks, but Hope seemed fearless. When agent Charlie Hogan saved the young entertainer from starvation by booking him in a tough Chicago neighborhood vaudeville theater, Hope's survival was on the line. To win that audience he developed a brash and impudent stage personality. He learned quickly and painfully that when you are working the same audience night after night, survival depends on how you freshen your jokes—and, of course, that would become a lifelong concern. He developed a shotgun delivery, which became his genius touch and something that could even "save" inferior jokes. He learned the value of a stage wait and found a degree of subtlety appropriate to his audience. These are the concerns of today's talk-show hosts.

Hope put his personal stamp on the classic vaudeville monologue and made it the twentieth-century model for all subsequent stand-up acts. It was about time and timing. Time had to do with the fact that he was getting his ideas from the daily newspapers; timing had to do with tempo and pauses. It was as much the way he delivered his gags as what they contained. He discovered that jokes based on today's headlines could break up an audience—but not *all* audiences. Context was important; so was subtlety, and so was being fresh. Jay Leno says, "He always had fresh jokes. If he were still performing, he'd be doing material about rap music."

His style gained him enough attention to merit chances to appear in Broadway musicals, on network radio, and eventually in motion pictures. Fifteen years of apprenticeship before live audiences had led to an uncommon performance sophistication and mastery of his art. There was one serious side effect, however—an increasing need for applause.

Hope's jibes were snappy, subtle, and nonlethal; his style was original and different from the normal radio fare of situation comedy. By 1940, Hope's ambition and hard work and spark of genius resulted in such exposure and resultant popularity from movies and his radio show that he won laurels as the "nation's No. 1 entertainer" and earned clear admittance into an elite circle of top American comedians.

Originating his entertainment at military sites during World War II, indeed for the remainder of his active life as a performer, established his image as "defender of the defenders." Chiefly he functioned in this "clown-hero" role as a link between the normative carefree American way of life and the harsh realities of wartime or the fear of attack during the stand-off with the Soviet Union. Hope was a comic escape hatch for the tensions of loneliness and fear, the petty irritations of tinned rations, mosquitoes, jungle rot, the blazing heat of Africa, the subzero cold of the Arctic, factors that can be paramount considerations under military conditions. By bringing laughter to the troops, and by his constant reminder, through radio and television broadcasts, to the general public of the soldier's sacrifice, Hope made an effort to amalgamate and unify both publics. Consequently, to a vast following he became identified with the soldier and to millions he appeared heroic. It was to become the most enduring image of his life.

Enhanced by his peripatetic wartime feats, the impression of Hope that pervaded the remainder of the 1940s and the 1950s was that of a hard-driving, fast-moving, updated Yankee peddler, an impudent opportunist who aggressively courted the popular mind with comic commentary. Hope's 25 film roles over a

15-year period between 1942 and 1957 were remarkable for their freshness, and these will probably remain in circulation and be watched for decades to come, longer and more than any other examples of his comedic power.

NBC's late-night talk show host, Conan O'Brien, said, "I don't think a lot of people in my generation saw his best work. . . If you go back and look at the movies. . . like *Son of Paleface* or any of the *Road* movies, you're just amazed at his talent. He was so smooth and so precise."

Hope drummed a consistent beat for a broadly conceived American march, concentrating his efforts largely on reflecting the insignia of the nation's popular culture. Hope was perhaps his most ingenious at this time, speaking like an average-looking, average-speaking traveling salesman. O'Brien also said, "I think he was the first guy to master the fast-talking coward, the cowardly wise guy, the one who has a lot of bravado but when the tough guy sneaks up behind him, he's suddenly saying, 'Oh, you've been working out, haven't you?'"

The staccato approach of early radio was softened for television, and as he gradually matured from perennial sophomore to a more astute observer, his monologues attempted to keep pace with America's growing awareness of her place in a world society. Hope's jokes in this period made references that ranged beyond fads and foibles to include topics about government programs and matters of national and international urgency, including science and technology and social welfare. His persona approached the status of the popular oracle.

Hope played "court jester" to important people in the entertainment world, to politicians, and to presidents. It was especially ingratiating to Mr. and Mrs. Average Consumer when Hope as the popularly accepted wisecracker for whom any topic was fair game was overheard being impertinent to the leaders of industry about their public behavior and decision making.

His roasting of film industry giants especially at Academy Award ceremonies became opportunities to rib the gloss of movie image making. His frequent lampoons of local and national politics were tart and timely, but largely limited to the superficial markings of political figures. Hope's more incisive efforts of satire in the 1950s were his jabs at the red-baiting tactics of Senator McCarthy, America's second-place standing in the missile and space races, and the nation's dollar diplomacy. Hope's approach to comic White House counseling took different forms, from respect for Roosevelt to indecision about Truman to an unabashed liking for Eisenhower up to and including his classic jester approach toward both Kennedy and Johnson. The presidency was, undeniably, Hope's favorite target.

Hope's mythic image as devoted advocate of the American soldier was fixed even more securely as a result of his repeated visits to the troops engaged in the much-debated, hotly contested national trauma, Vietnam. Hope's humor for the enjoyment of the GIs of the revolutionary 1960s was more sophisticated than it had been in World War II. His jokes not only supposed someone more informed, but also a combatant who understood that he or she was embroiled in ideological conflicts that were not entirely clear-cut or supportable. As a patriot, Hope preached loyalty, in spite of American internal wrangling and guilty agonizing over Vietnam, and his efforts extended beyond his eloquent and simplistic defense of the nation's "commitment" position to fervently sentimental and probably influential public appearances, media statements, and homely speeches in support of national unity. He was accused of being a "publicist" for Vietnam.

Although there was still respect, it generally appeared that his strong nationalistic voice had been blunted by his partisan one. But Hope had convictions and he stuck by them. Those who love comparing Hope to Will Rogers should remember that Rogers's staunch isolationist stance after World War I and his active campaigning against the League of Nations in the early 1920s were also criticized. Rogers is thought by some historians to have done a disservice to his country. Some of Hope's associates, friends in high places, and writers felt that he betrayed the public's faith in his role as a popular oracle.

As Vietnam faded into a bad memory, and the nation became more fragmented than at any other time since the Civil War, Hope resumed an almost driven schedule of engagements, personal appearances, and benefits. Where his widest public appeal had been, he was less active. He did only a handful of television specials a year. In some of these he tried to be innovative, but the best of them were reassembled from film clips of past popular shows.

The most pervasive image of Hope during his mature period (1962–1975) was that of a national institution, with component images as entrepreneur, as highly honored member of society, as an establishment figure who clung to the values in society that had created his fame. Hope's humor was seen as a highly regarded, effortlessly mass-produced phenomenon. The comedian had moved from fast-moving drummer to executive figure, entirely in control of his seemingly limitless energy and capacity for performing and promoting a multiplicity of humor enterprises.

Hope also appeared to the public gaze as generous benefactor, chiefly demonstrated by his frequent performances for worthy causes, by his donations to universities and hospitals, and particularly by his creating the Eisenhower Medical Center. He also appeared to the public as a "national treasure" as a result of the honors, awards, and gratuitous expressions of respect he received—the Congressional Gold Medal, 51 honorary degrees from colleges and universities, and numerous public buildings and streets named after him.

The legend had become an icon. And as it did his focus turned from his professional life to his private one, mostly centering on Dolores, his faithful wife of 64 years. For many of those years the media had raised questions about how happy the Hope marriage might or might not be in the face of his frequent absences from home, not only from wife and homemaker but also from his four adopted children, Linda, Tony, Nora, and Kelly.

It didn't take much imagination to suspect that Dolores and Bob needed to have a deep understanding, a very special relationship, to bear both the long and short separations, and for her to endure the rumors and even the evidence of her husband's wandering eye. When she had doubts and needed advice she turned to the Church and her faith. Divorce to a devout Roman Catholic like Dolores would be a nonsubject, and as it turned out her trust in the substance of their marriage was well founded. Bob came home, as always, to her.

At 95, when Hope was asked by *USA Today* reporter Kurt Jensen, "How has Dolores changed your life?" the comedian replied, "From the beginning, sixty-four years ago, she's been my stability." And the opinion of many of the people who were around the comedian the longest is that that seems to be the absolute truth. No matter how much or how many times Hope was persuaded by his urges to violate his marriage vows, he came home to Dolores. When he was away from home, wherever that might be, she remained connected to him, and she knew it. He telephoned her almost the instant that he arrived in whatever place he was staying on those many trips away from her. At 83, she was starting a new life, feeling at last that it was her turn to be heard and even to resume her career. She was encouraged by Bob and her daughter Linda to pick a set of favorite songs, hire an arranger, and record an album. She did, and for Hope insiders there was particular interest in noting what material she chose to record. After she made the decision to include "their song," the one that Dolores was singing when Bob walked into the Vogue Club in 1934, "It's Only a Paper Moon," the bets were on that she would include other lyrics that matched her carefully chosen album title, *Now and Then*.

The durable feeling of love Dolores had for Bob, which clearly endured the tough times they went through, was defined in the tune "Come In from the Rain," which she sings perhaps more fervently and insightfully than any other. The song's lyrics reverberate with significance: "There's no right or wrong/I'm not here to blame/I just want to be the one/To keep you from the rain."

By 1999 Dolores had cut five compact disc albums of tunes (the most recent titled *Cheek to Cheek*), and she seems to enjoy telling people, "I'll be ninety this year, and my career is just beginning." Her several well-received solo appearances in cabaret concerts and her role as true matriarch of her family (and finally in full control of family interests) have been marvelous for her self-esteem. She knows that Bob feels cut off from the world now and that he must experience the loneliness and estrangement of one past his prime, not able to be "on." She is now Bob's eyes and ears, head nurse and loving friend on duty. "He's doing fine," she reports, "really fine, thank God. He can still hit the golf ball. It's amazing. He walks and he sees. He can see sunsets and the beautiful hills and flowers. God is good, because he doesn't complain except when it comes to doing mild calisthenics—then he's stubborn. But he's never nasty. He loves music, he loves riding in the car and listening to tapes. He's really very quiet and not unhappy." She might have added that sometimes he grumbles, "I'm not through yet" and adds, "and I'll have a few routines on the way to the big divot."

Dolores has also found ways to involve the children—at least the ones that want to be involved—in family life. All four are protected financially with seven-figure trust funds, which Dolores demanded be set up in the late 1940s, when Hope's income began to soar.

Linda, who has confessed that she used to take her father for granted and was "blown away" when she examined the quality of his life's output, also said more recently she thought his potential as a "great actor" was never fulfilled, and she regrets this both for him (the Oscar he desperately wanted and never got) and for posterity. She enjoys knowing that film critics such as John McDonough of the *Chicago Tribune* and even academics such as Jeanine Basinger, professor of film studies at Wesleyan University, have begun to analyze the "aesthetics" of Hope's movies—something the comedian would probably not have tried to comprehend.

McDonough feels that when Hope broke the medium's most fundamental power of illusion by breaking through the fourth wall, speaking to the audience and "betraying the unspoken basis of the film-audience partnership" he became a "postmodern." Basinger says, "His best films—and there are many—are genuinely great films. But he never presents himself as serious. While we probe the aesthetics of all this, he just knocks it off."

Linda's job has been keeper of the flame. She maintains the profitability of Hope Enterprises, which still markets the Hope image in her father's books, videotapes of performance excerpts, and other souvenir items. She said wistfully to John Lahr, who wrote a highly publicized profile of the comedian for *The New Yorker* in December 1998, "I don't feel that I really know him. That's a kind of sadness for me because I would have liked to know him better."

Tony is probably the Hope who had the most difficulty growing up in the shadow of his father. After finishing law school, he tried show business for a time and even tried using another name to establish his own identity, but he soon returned to Tony Hope. He ran for public office in 1986, even got some support from his father in campaigning, but his chances were doomed when his opponent found out that Tony hadn't voted in the last two elections and spread the word. Tony, divorced from Judy and remarried, has returned to a successful law practice in Washington, D.C.

Nora, now 54 and living in Northern California, has distanced herself from her family. After her marriage to Sam McCullough, a college administrator, ended, she married Bruce Somers (former husband of Suzanne Somers). For years supposed by many to be especially close to her father, Nora now has chosen to concentrate on her own life. Nora's daughter, Alicia, lives in Northern California.

Kelly, the second son and the same age as Nora, lives in Oakland, California, and is yet unmarried. He is a freelance photographer and the most dependable cheerleader for the legend and icon status of his father. He can be counted on to show up for every honor and award, for every holiday and occasion where he feels useful.

There are four grandchildren. Linda's son, Andrew Lande, is a writer who recently has published *The Cigar Connoisseur*, written with his father, Nathaniel.

Andrew is also credited with writing *The Bob Hope World War II* video as well as other Hope Enterprises projects and is pursuing a career in marketing.

Tony Hope's children, Zachary and Miranda, both have made a stab at show business. Zachary, after getting degrees from Harvard and Berkeley, accepted several encouraging acting assignments but now is pursuing a career in marketing. Miranda, once involved in legitimate theater in Washington, D.C., as both actor and director, is now teaching and is married to Andrew Smith.

Hope is often asked these days how he wants to be remembered, to which he invariably responds, "For a laugh, of course. Maybe two or three." He could not, or would not, respond in the language of a number of thoughtful critics: that the legacy of Bob Hope's career is that he is the most versatile entertainer of our time and that his humor—especially his monologues—has, uniquely, mirrored the history of the past century.

Perhaps it was Tony (also quoted in the Lahr piece) who said it best—that his father had "discovered a formula for comedy that was better than what anyone else was doing, and he sought to expand it. He put together a machine that spread the word to ninety percent of the globe that when you said 'ad-lib' or 'stand-up' you meant Bob Hope or a cheap imitation of him."

In the winter of 1999, this author was invited to be among a small circle of people around Hope when he made a rare public appearance. Dolores and J. Paulin brought him down from the Palm Springs mountaintop home to take part in the opening ceremonies of the Bob Hope Desert Classic. He was scheduled to arrive at the Bermuda Dunes Country Club course at 9:30 A.M., and when the recreational-type van pulled up he was carefully helped out and into a golf cart. Someone said loudly to him that I was standing next to his cart and when I leaned in to greet him, he squeezed my wrist. He looked serene and he had a fixed smile as the cart, just ahead of the one Dolores was riding in, edged slowly through a dense gallery crowd with people calling out, "Hi, Bob!" and applauding the procession toward the tenth tee.

When the gallery spotted him arriving on the tee, they cheered but were quickly hushed into silence because a golfer was teeing off. He sat and waited silently, if a bit mystified, for directions. While he waited Arnold Palmer came up to his electric cart, leaned close to his ear, and spoke to him. Hope smiled and nodded.

Then the large gallery reacted and applauded as basketball superstars Michael Jordan and Charles Barkley arrived on the tee. Ward Grant stepped up, and J. helped Hope out of the cart and over to the two giant athletes; then Grant pushed a basketball under each of Hope's arms as he stood flanked by the other two. "We have a lot of press now. Smile!" Flashes and clicking shutters came from both nearby media and the enthusiastic gallery.

Hope smiled broadly, trying to be involved. The media had been told that he would hit a ball or two. Hope was escorted to the men's tee and was handed a three-wood. J. helped him to a position and Bob did the rest. He missed the first swing, turned to the gallery, and said as loud as he could, "Practice shot!" Lots of laughter and applause. Then he swung a second time and the ball went out straight for a 150-yard drive. Much applause.

As he turned to be helped back to his cart, three young and very pretty girls in white miniskirts whose white sweaters spelled out HOPE DESERT CLASSIC when the girls stood together were called over to meet him. Cameras clicked and videotape rolled, and as the girls started to get into posing position, a perky blonde with CLASSIC on her chest came up very close to him and purred, "Hello, Mr. Hope." Bob, looking her over slowly, said back to her, "Hello, doll." Where there's life. . .

ACKNOWLEDGMENTS

The debt owed to those who helped shape this telling of Bob Hope's life is enormous. Although twenty years of association with Hope and some focused interviews with him made the research easier, it would not have been possible without help from his family, his lifelong friends, and numerous associates who shared impressions and valuable insights. This applies to the first edition (1982) as well as this revised and updated edition celebrating Hope's 100th birthday.

The fact that a number of my interviewees are no longer with us does not diminish in any degree the weight of my sincere gratitude. I'm thankful to have reached so many of them in time.

Sifting through thousands of bits of data concerning this most public of men, I encountered more than one version of certain episodes in his life, and when variance appeared I allowed conversations and interviews with Hope to predominate.

When I credit beginnings, it was my late parents Winnie and Lloyd who used to say, sometimes in chorus, "You ought to write a book!" Their lives and their love and confidence were matchless gifts. I hope they approve.

But more concretely, these are my tributes:

To NBC's West Coast publicity chief Casey Shawhan who greeted me that August morning in 1959 with these surprising words: "Welcome to Tinsel Town, Bill—the good news is I've assigned you to work with Bob Hope."

To three colleagues at the University of Southern California—Walter Fisher, Theodore Kruglak, and Kenneth Owler Smith—who guided the doctoral thesis, *Bob Hope and the Popular Oracle Tradition in American Humor*, from which this book grew.

To Fred Hope for illuminating his brother's family relationships, and to Wyn Hope for sharing her husband Jim's book, *Mother Had Hopes*.

To Mildred Rosequist Brod, who offered most liberally her memories and memorabilia of the early Cleveland years; Charles Cirillo and Charley Cooley for reliving so vividly what life was like in the vaudeville era; Alan Calm, Eve Arden,

George Murphy, Fred MacMurray, and Fred de Cordova for recalling Hope's Broadway years; Jerry Colonna and Frances Langford for their memories of the radio shows and wartime trouping; Dorothy Lamour for being such a good friend as well as the observant "girl in the middle" along those several *Roads*; Marjorie Hughes, whose sage counsel and acute perception improved my judgement; Mildred MacArthur Serrano for her recollections of significant moments in the Hope family life; and to generous and talented Johnny Grant for more help over the past forty years than he or I could put into words.

To these among Hope's close professional associates: producer-writer Mort Lachman and veteran Hope writers Lester White and Charlie Lee, who offered incomparable portraitures of the man over an extended period of time; and to Ward Grant most particularly and most gratefully. It was he who opened countless windows and doors to the people and events in Hope's life over the past twenty-five years, and whose memory associations and acuity in commanding detail have been simply phenomenal.

To a host of entertainment writers and critics—especially Hollywood observers Army Archerd, Jim Bacon, Vernon Scott, and Bob Thomas, as well as from around the country Shirley Eder, Vince Flaherty, Kay Gardella, Ann Hodges, Irv Kupcinet, and Earl Wilson—who have so intelligently and perceptively followed his career.

To so many others, but chiefly these who never flinched at how many times I came back for help: Mark Anthony, Paul Bailey, Herb Ball, Les Brown, Norma Brown, Sil Caranchini, Frank Carroll, Ann Charles, Mary Davis, Denis Goodwin, Nancy Gordon, Gig Henry, Robert Hussey, Allan Kalmus, Sam Kaufman, Maggie Klier, Elliott Kozak, Betty Lanigan, Bill Larkin, Frank Liberman, Barney McNulty, Howard Miller, Joe Morella, Onnie Morrow, Gary Null, Johnny Pawlek, Paul Pepe, Jerry Raboy, Henry Rieger, Joe and Barbara Saltzman, Jimmy Saphier, Dee Shidler, Marjorie Thayer, Lady Carolyn Townshend, and Earl Ziegler.

To Gilbert Parker for his vision, my agent Robert Lescher for his continuing confidence, and Diane Reverand, who superbly edited the 1982 publication.

For this revised and updated manuscript, I give unstinting credit and never-ending thanks to the elegance of Jane Centofante's wise editorial counsel that truly enabled this final version. In closing, my gratitude to Da Capo's John Radziewicz, Dan O'Neil, and Fred Francis, and their skillful team who straightened out sentences and repaired fractured meanings that now, of course, make perfect sense.

My heartfelt thanks to all.

FILMOGRAPHY

Short Comedies

Going Spanish (Educational Films, 1934) Cast: Bob Hope and Leah Ray. Directed by Al Christe. Screenplay by William Watson and Art Jarrett.

Paree, Paree (Warner Bros., 1934) Cast: Bob Hope (as Peter Forbes), Dorothy Stone, Charles Collins, Lorraine Collier, Billie Leonard. Directed by Roy Mack. Screenplay by Cyrus Wood based on a musical *Fifty Million Frenchmen* by Herbert Fields, E. Ray Goetz, and Cole Porter.

The Old Grey Mayor (Warner Bros., 1935) Cast: Bob Hope, Ruth Blasco, Lionel Stander, Sam Wren, George Watts. Directed by Lloyd French. Screenplay by Herman Ruby.

Watch the Birdie (Warner Bros., 1935) Cast: Bob Hope, Neil O'Day, Arline Dintz, Marie Nordstrom, George Watts. Directed by Lloyd French. Screenplay by Dolph Singer and Jack Henley.

Double Exposure (Warner Bros., 1935) Cast: Bob Hope, Johnny Berkes, Jules Epailley, Loretta Sayers. Directed by Lloyd French. Screenplay by Burnet Hershey and Jack Henley.

Calling All Tars (Warner Bros., 1936) Cast: Bob Hope, Johnny Berkes, Oscar Ragland. Directed by Lloyd French. Screenplay by Jack Henley and Burnet Hershey.

Shop Talk (Warner Bros., 1936) Cast: Bob Hope. Directed by Lloyd French. Screenplay by Burnet Hershey and Jack Henley.

Feature Films

The Big Broadcast of 1938 (Paramount, 1938) Cast: Bob Hope (as Buzz Fielding), W.C. Fields, Martha Raye, Dorothy Lamour, Shirley Ross, Lynn Overland, Ben

Blue, Leif Erikson, Grace Bradley, Rufe Davis, Kirsten Flagstad, Tito Guizar, Lionel Pape, Dorothy Howe, Russell Hicks, Leonid Kinskey, Patricia ("Honey Chile") Wilder, Shep Fields and his orchestra. Directed by Mitchell Leisen. Produced by Harlan Thompson. Screenplay by Walter De Leon, Francis Martin, and Ken Englund, based on a story by Frederick Hazlitt Brennan, adapted by Howard Lindsay and Russell Crouse.

College Swing (Paramount, 1938) Cast: Bob Hope (as Bub Brady), Gracie Allen, George Burns, Martha Raye, Edward Everett Horton, Florence George, Ben Blue, Betty Grable, Jackie Coogan, John Payne, Cecil Cunningham, Robert Cummings, Jerry Colonna, Tully Marshall. Directed by Raoul Walsh. Produced by Lewis Gensler. Screenplay by Walter De Leon and Francis Martin, adaptation by Frederick Hazlitt Brennan of an idea by Ted Lesser.

Give Me a Sailor (Paramount, 1938) Cast: Bob Hope (as Jim Brewster), Martha Raye, Betty Grable, Jack Whiting, Clarence Kolb, Nana Bryant, Emerson Treacy, Kathleen Lockhart, Bonnie Jean Churchill, Ralph Sanford, Edward Earle. Directed by Elliott Nugent. Produced by Jeff Lazarus. Screenplay by Doris Anderson and Frank Butler, based on a play by Anne Nichols.

Thanks for the Memory (Paramount, 1938) Cast: Bob Hope (as Steve Merrick), Shirley Ross, Charles Butterworth, Otto Kruger, Hedda Hopper, Laura Hope Crews, Emma Dunn, Roscoe Karns, Eddie "Rochester" Anderson, Edward Gargan, Jack Norton, Patricia ("Honey Chile") Wilder, William Collier, Sr. Directed by George Archinbaud. Produced by Mel Shauer (associate). Screenplay by Lynn Starling, based on Albert Hackett and France Goodrich's play *Up Pops The Devil.*

Never Say Die (Paramount, 1939) Cast: Bob Hope (as John Kidley), Martha Raye, Ernest Cossart, Paul Harvey, Siegfried Rumann, Andy Devine, Alan Mowbray. Directed by Elliot Nugent. Produced by Paul Jones. Screenplay by Don Hartman, Frank Butler, and Preston Sturges, based on the play by William H. Post.

Some Like It Hot (Renamed *Rhythm Romance*) (Paramount, 1939) Cast: Bob Hope (as Nicky Nelson), Shirley Ross, Gene Krupa and Orchestra, Una Merkel, Rufe Davis, Bernard Nedell, Wayne "Tiny" Whitt, Harry Barn, Frank Sully, Clarence H. Wilson, Dudley Dickerson, Richard Denning, Pat West, Lillian Fitzgerald, Sam Ash. Directed by George Archinbaud. Produced by William C. Thomas (associate). Screenplay by Lewis R. Foster and Wilkie C. Mahoney, based on the play by Ben Hecht and Gene Fowler.

The Cat and the Canary (Paramount, 1939) Cast: Bob Hope (as Wally Hampton), Paulette Goddard, John Beal, Douglass Montgomery, Gale Sondergaard, Nydia Westman, George Zucco, Willard Robertson, Elizabeth Patterson. Directed by Elliot Nugent. Produced by Arthur Hornblow, Jr. Screenplay by Walter De Leon and Lynn Starling, based on the John Willard play.

Road to Singapore (Paramount, 1940) Cast: Bob Hope (as Ace Lannigan), Bing Crosby, Dorothy Lamour, Anthony Quinn, Charles Coburn, Jerry Colonna.

Directed by Victor Schertzinger. Produced by Harlan Thompson. Screenplay by Frank Butler and Don Hartman, based on a story by Harry Hervey.

The Ghost Breakers (Paramount, 1940) Cast: Bob Hope (as Larry Lawrence), Paulette Goddard, Richard Carlson, Anthony Quinn, Paul Lukas, Willie Best, Pedro De Cordoba. Directed by George Marshall. Produced by Arthur Hornblow, Jr. Screenplay by Walter De Leon, based on the play by Paul Dickey and Charles W. Goddard.

Road to Zanzibar (Paramount, 1941) Cast: Bob Hope (as Fearless Hubert Frazier), Bing Crosby, Dorothy Lamour, Una Merkel, Eric Blore, Luis Alberni, Joan Marsh, Douglas Dumbrille, Iris Adrian, Noble Johnson. Directed by Victor Schertzinger. Produced by Paul Jones. Screenplay by Frank Butler and Don Hartman, based on the story "Find Colonel Fawcett" by Don Hartman and Sy Bartlett.

Caught in the Draft (Paramount, 1941) Cast: Bob Hope (as Don Bolton), Dorothy Lamour, Lynne Overman, Eddie Bracken, Clarence Kolb, Paul Hurst, Phyllis Ruth, Irving Bacon, Arthur Loft, Edgar Dearing. Directed by David Butler. Produced by B. G. DeSylva. Screenplay by Harry Tugend with additional dialogue by Wilkie C. Mahoney.

Nothing but the Truth (Paramount, 1941) Cast: Bob Hope (as Steve Bennett), Paulette Goddard, Edward Arnold, Leif Erikson, Helen Vinson, Willie Best, Glenn Anders, Grant Mitchell, Catherine Doucet, Clarence Kolb. Directed by Elliott Nugent. Produced by Arthur Hornblow, Jr. Screenplay by Don Hartman and Ken Englund, from the play by James Montgomery based on the novel by Frederic S. Isham.

Louisiana Purchase (Paramount, 1941) Cast: Bob Hope (as Jim Taylor), Victor Moore, Vera Zorina, Irene Bordoni, Dona Drake, Raymond Walburn, Maxie Rosenbloom, Phyllis Ruth, Frank Albertson, Donald MacBride, Jack Norton, Barbara Britton, Margaret Hayes, Jean Wallace, Dave Willock. Directed by Irving Cummings. Produced by Harold Wilson (associate). Screenplay by Jerome Chodorov and Joseph Fields, from the musical comedy by Morrie Ryskind based on a story by B.G. DeSylva.

My Favorite Blonde (Paramount, 1942) Cast: Bob Hope (as Larry Haines), Madeleine Carroll, Gale Sondergaard, George Zucco, Victor Varconi, Edward Gargan, Dooley Wilson, Isabel Randolph, Monte Blue, Minerva Urecal. Directed by Sidney Lanfield. Produced by Paul Jones (associate). Screenplay by Don Hartman and Frank Butler, based on the story by Melvin Frank and Norman Panama.

Road to Morocco (Paramount, 1942) Cast: Bob Hope (as Turkey Jackson), Bing Crosby, Dorothy Lamour, Anthony Quinn, Dona Drake, Mikhail Rasumny, Laura La Plante, Yvonne De Carlo, Monte Blue. Directed by David Butler. Produced by Paul Jones (associate). Screenplay by Frank Butler and Don Hartman.

They Got Me Covered (Goldwyn–RKO, 1943) Cast: Bob Hope (as Robert Kittredge), Dorothy Lamour, Lenore Aubert, Otto Preminger, Eduardo Ciannelli,

Florence Bates, Marion Martin, Donald Meek, Walter Catlett, Philip Ahn, John Abbott, Mary Treen. Directed by David Butler. Produced by Samuel Goldwyn. Screenplay by Harry Kurnitz, based on the story by Leonard Q. Ross and Leonard Spigelgass.

Let's Face It (Paramount, 1943) Cast: Bob Hope (as Jerry Walker), Betty Hutton, Zasu Pitts, Phyllis Povah, Eve Arden, Dave Willock, Raymond Walburn, Marjorie Weaver, Dona Drake, Arthur Loft, Joseph Sawyer. Directed by Sidney Lanfield. Produced by Fred Kohlmar (associate). Screenplay by Harry Tugend, based on a musical play by Herbert Fields, Dorothy Fields, and Cole Porter suggested by a play by Norma Mitchell and Russell G. Medcraft.

The Princess and the Pirate (Goldwyn–RKO, 1944) Cast: Bob Hope (as Sylvester the Great), Virginia Mayo, Walter Brennan, Walter Slezak, Victor McLaglen, Marc Lawrence, Hugo Haas, Maude Eburne, Mike Mazurki, Bing Crosby (guest bit). Directed by David Butler. Produced by Samuel Goldwyn. Screenplay by Don Hartman, Melville Shavelson, and Everett Freeman, adapted by Allen Boretz and Curtis Kenyon from a story by Sy Bartlett.

Road to Utopia (Paramount, 1946) Cast: Bob Hope (as Chester Hooton), Bing Crosby, Dorothy Lamour, Hillary Brooke, Douglas Dumbrille, Jack LaRue, Robert Barrat, Nestor Paiva, Robert Benchley (narrator). Directed by Hal Walker. Produced by Paul Jones. Screenplay by Norman Panama and Melvin Frank.

Monsieur Beaucaire (Paramount, 1946) Cast: Bob Hope (as Monsieur Beaucaire), Joan Caulfield, Patric Knowles, Marjorie Reynolds, Cecil Kellaway, Joseph Schildkraut, Reginald Owen, Constance Collier, Hillary Brooke, Mary Nash, Douglas Dumbrille. Directed by George Marshall. Produced by Paul Jones. Screenplay by Melvin Frank and Norman Panama, based on Booth Tarkington's novel.

My Favorite Brunette (Paramount, 1947) Cast: Bob Hope (as Ronnie Jackson), Dorothy Lamour, Peter Lorre, Lon Chaney, Jr., John Hoyt, Charles Dingle, Frank Puglia, Ann Doran, Willard Robertson, Bing Crosby (guest bit). Directed by Elliott Nugent. Produced by Daniel Dare. Screenplay by Edmund Beloin and Jack Rose.

Where There's Life (Paramount, 1947) Cast: Bob Hope (as Michael Valentine), Signe Hasso, William Bendix, George Coulouris, George Zucco, John Alexander, Denis Hoey, Joseph Vitale, Harry Von Zell. Directed by Sidney Lanfield. Produced by Paul Jones. Screenplay by Allen Boretz and Melville Shavelson, based on a story by Shavelson.

Road to Rio (Paramount, 1948) Cast: Bob Hope (as Hot Lips Barton), Bing Crosby, Dorothy Lamour, Gale Sondergaard, Frank Faylen, Joseph Vitak, Frank Puglia, Nestor Paiva, Jerry Colonna, The Wiere Brothers, The Andrews Sisters, Tan Van Brunt. Directed by Norman Z. McLeod. Produced by Daniel Dare. Screenplay by Edmund Beloin and Jack Rose.

The Paleface (Paramount, 1948) Cast: Bob Hope (as Painless Peter Potter), Jane Russell, Robert Armstrong, Iris Adrian, Robert Watson, Jack Scud, Joseph Vitale,

Charles Trowbridge, Clem Bevans, Jeff York, Stanley Adams, Iron Eyes Cody. Directed by Norman Z. McLeod. Produced by Robert L. Welch. Screenplay by Edmund Hartmann and Frank Tashlin, with additional dialogue by Jack Rose.

Sorrowful Jones (Paramount, 1949) Cast: Bob Hope (as Sorrowful Jones), Lucille Ball, Mary Jane Saunders, William Demarest, Bruce Cabot, Thomas Gomez, Tom Pedi, Paul Lees. Directed by Sidney Lanfield. Produced by Robert L. Welch. Screenplay by Melville Shavelson, Edmund Hartmann, and Jack Rose, based on the Damon Runyon play.

The Great Lover (Paramount, 1949) Cast: Bob Hope (as Freddie Hunter), Rhonda Fleming, Roland Young, Roland Culver, Richard Lyon, Jerry Hunter, Jackie Jackson, Karl Wright, George Reeves, Jim Backus, Sig Arno. Directed by Alexander Hall. Produced by Edmund Beloin. Screenplay by Edmund Beloin, Melville Shavelson, and Jack Rose.

Fancy Pants (Paramount, 1950) Cast: Bob Hope (as Humphrey), Lucille Ball, Bruce Cabot, Jack Kirkwood, Lea Pennman, Hugh French, Eric Blore, Joseph Vitale, John Alexander, Norma Varden, Colin Keith-Johnston, Ida Moore. Directed by George Marshall. Produced by Robert Welch. Screenplay by Edmund Hartmann and Robert O'Brien, based on Harry Leon Wilson's novel *Ruggles of Red Gap*.

The Lemon Drop Kid (Paramount, 1951) Cast: Bob Hope (as The Lemon Drop Kid), Marilyn Maxwell, Lloyd Nolan, Jane Darwell, Andrea King, Fred Clark, Jay C. Flippen, William Frawley, Harry Bellaver, Sid Melton, Ida Moore. Directed by Sidney Lanfield. Produced by Robert L. Welch. Screenplay by Frank Tashlin, Edmund Hartmann, and Robert O'Brien. With additional dialogue by Irving Elinson, adaptation by Edmund Beloin of the Damon Runyon short story.

My Favorite Spy (Paramount, 1951) Cast: Bob Hope (as Peanuts White), Hedy Lamarr, Francis L. Sullivan, Arnold Moss, Stephen Chase, John Archer, Morris Ankrum, Luis Van Rooten. Directed by Norman Z. McLeod. Produced by Paul Jones. Screenplay by Edmund Hartmann and Jack Sher.

Son of Paleface (Paramount, 1952) Cast: Bob Hope (as Junior), Jane Russell, Roy Rogers, Bill Williams, Lloyd Corrigan, Paul E. Burns, Douglas Dumbrille, Harry Von Zell, Iron Eyes Cody. Directed by Frank Tashlin. Produced by Robert Welch. Screenplay by Frank Tashlin, Robert L. Welch, and Joseph Quillan.

Road to Bali (Paramount, 1952) Cast: Bob Hope (as Harold Gridley), Bing Crosby, Dorothy Lamour, Murvyn Vye, Ralph Moody, Peter Coe, Leon Askin; and as guests: Bob Crosby, Humphrey Bogart (in a clip from *The African Queen),* Jane Russell, Dean Martin, Jerry Lewis. Directed by Hal Walker. Produced by Harry Tugend. Screenplay by Frank Butler, Hal Kanter, and William Morrow, based on a story by Frank Butler and Harry Tugend.

Off Limits (Paramount, 1953) Cast: Bob Hope (as Wally Hogan), Mickey Rooney, Marilyn Maxwell, Eddie Mayehoff, Stanley Clements, Marvin Miller, John Ridgely, Carolyn Jones. Directed by George Marshall. Produced by Harry Tugend. Screenplay by Hal Kanter and Jack Sher.

Here Come the Girls (Paramount, 1953) Cast: Bob Hope (as Stanley Snodgrass), Tony Martin, Arlene Dahl, Rosemary Clooney, Millard Mitchell, William Demarest, Fred Clark, Robert Strauss. Directed by Claude Binyon. Produced by Paul Jones. Screenplay by Edmund Hartmann (his story) and Hal Kanter.

Casanova's Big Night (Paramount, 1954) Cast: Bob Hope (as Pippo Poppolin), Joan Fontaine, Audrey Dalton, Basil Rathbone, Arnold Moss, John Carradine, Hope Emerson. Directed by Norman Z. McLeod. Produced by Paul Jones. Screenplay by Hal Kanter and Edmund Hartmann, based on a story by Aubrey Wisberg.

The Seven Little Foys (Paramount, 1955) Cast: Bob Hope (as Eddie Foy), Milly Vitale, George Tobias, Angela Clarke, Richard Shannon, Billy Gray, Lydia Reed, Linda Bennett, Jimmy Baird, James Cagney (as George M. Cohan). Directed by Melville Shavelson. Produced by Jack Rose. Screenplay by Melville Shavelson and Jack Rose.

That Certain Feeling (Paramount, 1956) Cast: Bob Hope (as Francis X. Digman), Eva Marie Saint, George Sanders, Pearl Bailey, David Lewis, Al Capp, Jerry Mathers, Florenz Ames. Directed by Norman Panama. Produced by Norman Panama and Melvin Frank. Screenplay by Norman Panama, Melvin Frank, I.A.L. Diamond, and William Altman, based on the play *King of Hearts* by Jean Kerr and Eleanor Brooke.

The Iron Petticoat (Metro-Goldwyn-Mayer, 1956) Cast: Bob Hope (as Chuck Lockwood), Katharine Hepburn, Noelle Middleton, James Robertson Justice, Robert Helpmann, David Kossoff, Alan Giggord, Alexander Gauge. Directed by Ralph Thomas. Produced by Betty Box. Screenplay by Ben Hecht.

Beau James (Paramount, 1957) Cast: Bob Hope (as Jimmy Walker), Vera Miles, Alexis Smith, Paul Douglas, Darren McGavin, Joseph Mantell, Jimmy Durante (as himself), Walter Catlett. Directed by Melville Shavelson. Produced by Jack Rose. Screenplay by Jack Rose and Melville Shavelson, based on *Beau James,* the biography of James Walker by Gene Fowler.

Paris Holiday (United Artists, 1958) Cast: Bob Hope (as Robert Leslie), Fernandel, Anita Ekberg, Martha Hyer, Preston Sturges, Andre Morell, Alan Gifford. Directed by Gerg Oswald. Produced by Robert Hope. Screenplay by Edmund Beloin and Dean Riesner, based on a story by Robert Hope.

Alias Jesse James (United Artists, 1959) Cast: Bob Hope (as Milford Farnsworth), Rhonda Fleming, Wendell Corey, Jim Davis, Gloria Talbot, Will Wright, Mary Young; and as guests: James Arness, Ward Bond, Gary Cooper, Bing Crosby, Gail Davis, Jay Silverheels, Hugh O'Brian, Fess Parker, Roy Rogers. Directed by Norman Z. McLeod. Executive Producer, Bob Hope. Produced by Jack Hope. Screenplay by William Bowers and Daniel D. Beauchamp, based on a story by Robert St. Aubrey and Bert Lawrence.

The Facts of Life (United Artists, 1960) Cast: Bob Hope (as Larry Gilbert), Lucille Ball, Ruth Hussey, Don Defore, Louis Nye, Philip Ober, Marianne Stewart, Peter

Leeds, Louise Beavers, Robert F. Simon, Mike Mazurki. Directed by Melvin Frank. Produced by Norman Panama. Screenplay by Norman Panama and Melvin Frank.

Bachelor in Paradise (Metro-Goldwyn-Mayer, 1961) Cast: Bob Hope (as Adam J. Niles), Lana Turner, Janis Paige, Jim Hutton, Paula Prentiss, Don Porter, Virginia Grey, John McGiver, Florence Sundstrom, Clinton Sundberg. Directed by Jack Arnold. Produced by Ted Richmond. Screenplay by Valentine Davies and Hal Kanter, based on a story by Vera Caspary.

Road to Hong Kong (United Artists, 1962) Cast: Bob Hope (as Chester Babcock), Bing Crosby, Dorothy Lamour, Joan Collins, Robert Morley; and as guests: Peter Sellers, Frank Sinatra, Dean Martin, David Niven, Zsa Zsa Gabor, Dave King, Jerry Colonna. Directed by Norman Panama. Produced by Melvin Frank. Screenplay by Norman Panama and Melvin Frank.

Critic's Choice (Warner Bros., 1963) Cast: Bob Hope (as Parker Ballantine), Lucille Ball, Marilyn Maxwell, Rip Torn, Jessie Royce Landis, Jim Backus, Rick Kellman, Dorothy Green, Marie Windsor, Jerome Cowan, Lurene Tuttle, Stanley Adams. Directed by Don Weis. Produced by Frank P. Rosenberg. Screenplay by Jack Sher, based on the Ira Levin play.

Call Me Bwana (United Artists, 1963) Cast: Bob Hope (as Matt Merriwether), Anita Ekberg, Edie Adams, Lionel Jeffries, Percy Herbert. Directed by Gordon Douglas. Produced by Albert R. Broccoli. Screenplay by Nate Monaster and Johanna Harwood.

A Global Affair (Metro-Goldwyn-Mayer, 1964) Cast: Bob Hope (as Frank Larrimore), Lilo Pulver, Michele Mercier, Elga Andersen. Directed by Jack Arnold. Produced by Hall Bartlett. Screenplay by Arthur Marx, Bob Fisher, and Charles Lederer, based on a story by Eugene Vale.

I'll Take Sweden (United Artists, 1965) Cast: Bob Hope (as Bob Holcomb), Tuesday Weld, Dina Merrill, Frankie Avalon, Jeremy Slate, Rosemarie Frankland. Directed by Frederick De Cordova. Produced by Edward Small. Screenplay by Nat Perrin, Bob Fisher, and Arthur Marx.

Boy, Did I Get a Wrong Number! (United Artists, 1966) Cast: Bob Hope (as Tom Meade), Elke Sommer, Phyllis Diller, Cesare Danova, Marjorie Lord, Kelly Thordsen, Benny Baker, Terry Burnham, Joyce Jameson, Harry Von Zell. Directed by George Marshall. Produced by Edward Small. Screenplay by Burt Styler, Albert E. Lewin, and George Kennett, based on a story by George Beck.

Eight on the Lam (United Artists, 1967) Cast: Bob Hope (as Henry Dimsdale), Phyllis Diller, Jonathan Winters, Shirley Eaton, Jill St. John, Stacey Maxwell, Kevin Brody, Glenn Gilger, Debi Storm, Michael Freeman, Austin Willis, Peter Leeds, and Hope's grandchildren—Avis and Robert Hope. Directed by George Marshall. Produced by Bill Lawrence (associate). Screenplay by Albert E. Lewin, Burt Styler, and (also story) Bob Fisher and Arthur Marx.

The Private Navy of Sgt. O'Farrell (United Artists, 1968) Cast: Bob Hope (as Master Sergeant Dan O'Farrell), Phyllis Diller, Jeffrey Hunter, Gina Lollobrigida, Mylene Demongeot, Henry Wilcoxon, William Wellman, Jr. Directed by Frank Tashlin. Produced by John Beck. Screenplay by Frank Tashlin, based on a story by John L. Greene and Robert M. Fresco.

How to Commit Marriage (Cinerama, 1969) Cast: Bob Hope (as Frank Benson), Jane Wyman, Jackie Gleason, Maureen Arthur, Tina Louise, Leslie Nielsen, Paul Stewart, Irwin Corey. Directed by Norman Panama. Produced by Bill Lawrence. Screenplay by Ben Starr and Michael Kanin.

Cancel My Reservation (Warner Bros., 1972) Cast: Bob Hope (as Dan Bartlett), Eva Marie Saint, Ralph Bellamy, Forrest Tucker, Keenan Wynn, Doodles Weaver, Betty Ann Carr, Henry Darrow, Chief Dan George, Anne Archer. Directed by Paul Bogart. Executive Producer, Bob Hope. Produced by Gordon Oliver. Screenplay by Arthur Marx and Robert Fisher.

Appearances, Cameos, Documentaries

Don't Hook Now (Paramount, 1938) Filmed golf tournament. Bob Hope as himself with Bing Crosby. Directed by Herbert Poleise.

Star Spangled Rhythm (Paramount, 1942) Feature film. Cast: Bob Hope (as himself, Master of Ceremonies), Eddie Bracken, Victor Moore, Betty Hutton, Anne Revere, Walter Abel, William Bendix, MacDonald Carey, Walter Catlett, Jerry Colonna, Bing Crosby, Gary Crosby, Edgar Dearing, Cecil B. De Mille, Dona Drake, Katherine Dunham, Edward Fielding, Paulette Goddard, Eddie Johnson, Johnny Johnston, William Haade, Susan Hayward, Sterling Holloway, Maynard Holmes, Alan Ladd, Veronica Lake, Gil Lamb, Dorothy Lamour, Fred MacMurray, Mary Martin, James Millican, Ray Milland, Ralph Murphy, Lynne Overman, Dick Powell, Marjorie Reynolds, Eddie "Rochester" Anderson, Betty Rhodes, Preston Sturges, Franchot Tone, Arthur Treacher, Ernest Truex, Walter Whal, Vera Zorina, the Golden Gate Quartet, Slim and Sam. Directed by George Marshall. Produced by Joseph Sistrom (associate). Screenplay by Harry Tugend.

Welcome to Britain (Strand-M.O.I., 1943) A guide to British institutions and behavior for U.S. troops stationed in England. Cast: Bob Hope (as himself), Felix Aylmer, Carla Lehmann, Beatrice Lillie, Burgess Meredith, Johnny Schofield, Beatrice Varley. Directed by Anthony Asquith with Burgess Meredith.

All Star Bond Rally (20th Century-Fox, 1945) One-reel variety show for the U.S. Government–War Activities Committee and U.S. Treasury Department. Cast: Bob Hope (as himself, singing "Buy Buy Bonds"), Jeanne Crain, Bing Crosby, Linda Darnell, Betty Grable, Harpo Marx, Frank Sinatra, Fibber McGee and Molly, Harry James and his orchestra. Directed by Michael Audley.

Hollywood Victory Caravan (Paramount, 1945) Two-reel variety show for U.S. Government. Cast: Bob Hope (as himself), Robert Benchley, Humphrey Bogart,

Bing Crosby, William Demarest, Dona Drake, Betty Hutton, Alan Ladd, Diana Lynn, Franklin Pangborn, Olga San Juan, Barbara Stanwyck, Carmen Cavallaro. Directed by William Russell. Screenplay by Melville Shavelson.

Variety Girl (Paramount, 1947) Feature film–Variety Show in tribute to the Variety Clubs of America. Cast: Bob Hope (as himself), Mary Hatcher, Olga San Juan, DeForrest Kelly, Neila Walker, Torben Meyer, Jack Norton, Bing Crosby, Gary Cooper, Paulette Goddard, Alan Ladd, Veronica Lake, Dorothy Lamour, Burt Lancaster, Ray Milland, Robert Preston, Gail Russell, Barbara Stanwyck, Billy De Wolfe. Directed by George Marshall. Screenplay by Edmund Hartmann, Frank Tashlin, Robert Welch, and Monte Brice.

The Greatest Show on Earth (Paramount, 1952) Feature film. Bob Hope (unbilled cameo as part of the audience in one scene). Directed by Cecil B. De Mille.

Scared Stiff (Paramount, 1953) Feature film–remake of *Ghost Breakers*. Bob Hope (unbilled walk-on–cameo). Directed by George Marshall.

Showdown at Ulcer Gulch (Saturday Evening Post, 1958) Promotional film. Bob Hope (unbilled cameo).

Five Pennies (Paramount, 1959) Feature film. Cast: Bob Hope (as himself, as guest), Danny Kaye, Barbara Bel Geddes, Tuesday Weld, Harry Guardino, Louis Armstrong, Bob Crosby, Susan Gordon, Ray Daley, Richard Shavelson. Directed by Melville Shavelson. Screenplay by Melville Shavelson and Jack Rose.

The Sound of Laughter (Union Film Release, 1963) Feature-length documentary of comedy scenes from early talkies. Bob Hope and Leah Ray in scene from *Going Spanish*. Directed and compiled by John O'Shaughnessy. Narration by Fred Saidy, spoken by Ed Wynn.

The Oscar (Paramount, 1966) Feature film. Bob Hope (as himself) in one scene as Master of Ceremonies of Academy Awards presentation. Directed by Russell Rouse.

The Muppet Movie (Sir Lew Grade, 1979) Feature film. Bob Hope in cameo as the ice cream man. Created by Jim Henson. Directed by James Frawley.

BIBLIOGRAPHY

Adams, Cindy. "Thanks for the Memories." *Ladies Home Journal,* December, 1987.

Adams, Joey. *Here's to the Friars: The Heart of Show Business.* New York: Crown, 1976.

Allen, Steve. *The Funny Men.* New York: Simon and Schuster, 1956.

Anderson, John Murray. *Out Without My Rubbers.* New York: Library Publishers, 1954.

Arden, Eve. *The Three Phases of Eve.* New York: St. Martin's Press, 1985.

Bandler, Michael. "Mr. Hope Goes to Washington." *Modern Maturity,* November, 1978.

Barthel, Joan. "Bob Hope." *Life,* January 29, 1971.

Bell, Joseph N. "Bob Hope's Scrapbook: Thanks for the Memories." *Good Housekeeping,* January, 1974.

Berle, Milton. *B.S. I Love You.* New York: McGraw Hill, 1988.

Berle, Milton, with Haskel Frankel. *Milton Berle: An Autobiography.* New York: Delacorte, 1974.

Buxton, Frank and Bill Owen. *The Big Broadcast: 1920–1950.* New York: Viking Press, 1972.

Cahill, Tim. "Bob Hope." *Rolling Stone,* March, 1980.

Carroll, Carroll. *None of Your Business.* New York: Cowles, 1970.

Carter, E. Graydon. "America's Greatest Hope." *Family Weekly,* May 26, 1985.

Crosby, Bing, as told to Pete Martin. *Call Me Lucky.* New York: Simon and Schuster, 1953.

Eels, George. *Cole Porter: The Life That Late He Led.* New York: G. P. Putnam's Sons, 1967.

Faith, William Robert. *Bob Hope and the Popular Oracle Tradition in American Humor.* (Doctoral Dissertation) Los Angeles, CA: University of Southern California, 1976.

Faith, William Robert. *Bob Hope: A Life in Comedy.* New York: G. P. Putnam's Sons, 1982.

Fein, Irving. *Jack Benny: An Intimate Biography*. New York: G. P. Putnam's Sons, 1976.

Fisher, John. *Call Them Irreplaceable*. New York: Stein and Day, 1976.

Fowler, Gene. *Schnozzola*. New York: Viking, 1951.

French, William. "From Gags to Riches." Unpublished manuscript, n.d.

"The Future Still Hopeful." *TV Guide,* May 23, 1958.

Gilbert, Douglas. *American Vaudeville: Its Life and Times*. New York: Dover Publications, 1968.

Gordon, Max and Lewis Funke. *Max Gordon Presents*. New York: Geis, 1963.

Harris, Warren G. *Lucy and Desi*. New York: Simon and Schuster, 1991.

Hickey, Neil. "Bob Hope Turns Serious." (Part 1) *TV Guide*, January 19, 1977.

_____. "Bob Hope Turns Serious." (Part 2) *TV Guide*, January 26, 1977.

Hope, Bob. *Five Women I Love*. New York: Doubleday, 1966.

_____. *I Never Left Home*. New York: Simon and Schuster, 1944.

_____. *I Owe Russia $1200*. New York: Doubleday, 1963.

_____. *So This is Peace*. New York: Simon and Schuster, 1946.

_____. *They Got Me Covered*. Hollywood: Bob Hope Enterprise, 1941.

Hope, Bob, with Ward Grant. *Dear Prez, I Wanna Tell Ya. A Presidential Jokebook*. Santa Monica, CA: General Publishing: 1996.

_____. *I Was There*. Burbank, CA: Hope Enterprises, 1995.

_____. *Bob Hope and His Friends*. Denver, CO: King of Comedy Associates, 1979.

Hope Bob, as told to Eleanor Harris. "My Favorite Mother-in-Law." *McCall's,* October 1955.

Hope, Bob, as told to Pete Martin. *Bob Hope's Own Story: Have Tux, Will Travel*. New York: Simon and Schuster, 1954.

_____. *The Last Christmas Show*. New York: Doubleday, 1974.

Hope, Bob, as told to Dwayne Netland. *Bob Hope's Confessions of a Hooker: My Lifelong Love Affair With Golf*. New York: Doubleday, 1985.

Hope, Bob, with Melville Shavelson. *Don't Shoot, It's Only Me*. New York: G. P. Putnam's Sons, 1990.

Hope, Bob and Bob Thomas. *The Road to Hollywood*. New York: Doubleday, 1977.

Hope, Dolores. "My Life is Full of Hope." *Woman's Home Companion*, November, 1953.

Hope, James. *Mother Had Hopes*. Unpublished manuscript, 1962.

"Hope for Housewives." *Newsweek*, December 15, 1952.

"Hope for Humanity." *Time*, September 20, 1943.

Hotchner, A. E. *Doris Day, Her Own Words*. New York: Morrow, 1976.

Jennings, C. Robert. "On the Road with the All-American Funny Man." *Today*, July 2, 1972.

_____. "This is Bob (Legend in His Own Time) Hope." *West*, May 14, 1972.

Johnson, Tom. "Hope's Last Road Show." *Los Angeles Magazine,* March, 1991.

Kalb, Marvin and Bernard Kalb. *Kissinger*. Boston: Little and Brown, 1974.

Lahr, John. *Notes on a Cowardly Lion*. New York: Knopf, 1969.

Lamour, Dorothy, as told to Dick McInnes. *My Side of the Road*. New Jersey: Prentice Hall, 1980.

Lukas, J. Anthony. "This is Bob (Politician-Patriot-Publicist) Hope." *The New York Times Magazine*, October, 1970.

Merman, Ethel, and Pete Martin. *Who Could Ask For Anything More?* New York: Doubleday, 1955.

Merman, Ethel, with George Eels. *Merman: An Autobiography*. New York: Simon and Schuster, 1978.

Morella, Joe, Edward Z. Epstein and Eleanor Clark. *The Amazing Careers of Bob Hope*. New York: Arlington House, 1973.

Murphy, George, with Victor Lasky. *Say, Didn't You Used to Be George Murphy?* New York: Bartholomew, 1970.

Nattin, Pete. "I Call on Bob Hope." *Saturday Evening Post,* April 26, 1958.

Osborne, Robert. *50 Golden Years of Oscar: The Official History of the Academy of Motion Picture Arts and Sciences*. La Habra: ESE California, 1978.

Quirk, Lawrence J. *The Road Well-Traveled*. New York: Applause, 1998.

Richman, Harry. *A Hell of a Life*. New York: Duell, Sloan and Pearce, 1956.

Rochlin, Margy. "Funny Man." *Los Angeles Times Magazine,* February 1, 1987.

Rosten, Leo. "Gags to Riches." *Look,* September 24, 1953.

Russell, Jane. *Jane Russell: An Autobiography*. New York: Franklin Watts, 1985.

Schallert, Lisa. "Bob Hope—Soldier in Civvies." *Photoplay,* November 1943.

Scott, Vernon. "What Makes Bob Hope Run?" *United Press International,* November 17, 1973.

Spitzer, Marian. *The Palace*. New York: Atheneum, 1969.

Stagg, Jerry. *The Brothers Shubert*. New York: Random House, 1968.

Streete, Horton. "Have Tux, Will Travel and That's What Bob Hope Did With That Blonde." *Confidential,* July 1956.

Thomas, Bob. *Winchell*. New York: Doubleday, 1971.

Thompson, Charles. *Bob Hope: Portrait of a Superstar*. New York: St. Martin's, 1980.

_____. *The Complete Crosby*. London: W.H. Allen, 1978.

Torrence, Bruce. *Hollywood: The First 100 Years*. Hollywood: Hollywood Chamber of Commerce and Fiske Enterprises, 1979.

Trescott, Pamela. *Bob Hope: A Comic Life*. Atlanta: Acropolis, 1985.

Whitney, Dwight. "Bob Hope: An American Institution." *TV Guide*, January 15, 1964.

SOURCE NOTES

In addition to personal interviews and conversations with Bob Hope, interviews and conversations with many people who have been and are still associated with him, quotations and notations from the comedian's several autobiographical writings, and hundreds of media accounts, there are three essential sources of data underpinning this life story that are referred to frequently during these end notes. They are:

Bob Hope Joke Files (BHJF), containing many, many thousands of jokes filed chronologically by show and cross-filed by subject matter in two vaults in the comedian's Toluca Lake office. Included is comedy material from vaudeville, radio scripts, films, personal appearance routines, and benefit monologues dating from the 1920s to the present, as well as scripts from military entertaining in World War II, Korea, Vietnam, and Desert Storm and from his television shows from 1950 to 1995.

Bob Hope Personal Files (BHPF), also based in his Toluca Lake office, include his correspondence and his professional and business records covering the last sixty years.

Hope Enterprises Public Relations Files (HEPRF), located at a separate office in Toluca Lake, include fact sheets, biographies, correspondence, press clippings, scrapbooks, and photographs that document the comedian's professional and personal activities from 1938 to the present.

The critical/analytic and empirical studies and their findings conducted during the writing of the Faith Ph.D. dissertation *Bob Hope and the Popular Oracle Tradition in American Humor* (BHPOT) were important in tracing the developments in Hope's comedic life, i.e., Brash and Impudent, Clown Hero, Comic Drummer, et al., and defining the nature and characteristics of Hope's humor.

Cue-In: Ninety in the Sun

Materials for this introductory section of the book come from NBC Burbank Studio files and from this writer's observations and conversations as a guest at NBC's taping of *Bob Hope: The First Ninety Years*. Ward Grant provided details of the Hope meeting with President Clinton and the videotape of Dolores Hope's backyard birthday party.

The Patrick MacDonald, Eirik Knutzen, John McDonough, Bob Thomas, and John Stanley interviews were taken from the HEPRF.

Jolly Follies

In Chapter 1, both baptismal records and the efforts of Sue P. McKean and Kendall H. Williams, Research International, Salt Lake City, give clear proof that Avis's family name and Bob's middle name is Towns, not Townes as erroneously recorded in the autobiographical *Bob Hope's Own Story: Have Tux, Will Travel*. In Chapter 2, the early Cleveland, Ohio, years are recreated through interviews with Hope family members, with Mildred Rosequist Brod, and with several of Hope's childhood friends. Invaluable was the unpublished manuscript *Mother Had Hopes* by James Hope, based in part on late-night conversations with his mother Avis in the kitchen of their Cleveland home between 1910 and 1915 (courtesy of Wyn Hope). In Chapters 3, 4, and 5, details of Hope's years in tab shows and on various vaudeville stages have been derived from interviews with Mildred Rosequist Brod, Charley Cooley, and Charlie Cirillo. Essential were Hope's personal scrapbooks (BHPF) and scrapbooks kept by Frank Maley, manager of Hurley's *Jolly Follies,* loaned by one of Maley's relatives, Don Mattticks of Lubbock, Texas.

Brash and Impudent

Chapters 6–14 lean heavily on Hope's own recollections, as well as on interviews with Eve Arden, Charley Cooley, Charlie Cirillo, Alan Calm, and Fred DeCordova, with additional materials from BHJF and BHPF. In Chapter 7, Marion Spitzer's authoritative *The Palace* reports: "Neither in the Palace record book nor in Bob's own book (*Have Tux, Will Travel*) is there a definite date given for his appearance there as a single. The only reference is to Bob Hope as part of *Antics of 1931*." Odd, because the *New York Times* review of February 11, 1931 (HEPRF), describes both his single act and his part in the *Antics* afterpiece, and the newspaper advertising for the week carries the name "Bob Hope" in the same size type as headliner Bea Lillie (BHPF). Details of Hope's Broadway years in Chapters 8, 9, 10, 11, 12, and 13 are enhanced by anecdotes or observations by Dolores Hope and in books by and about John Murray Anderson, Milton Berle, Bing Crosby, Jimmy Durante, Ethel Merman, George Murphy, Cole Porter, Harry Richman, and the Shuberts.

Hooray for Hollywood

In writing Chapters 15–19, interviews with Dolores Hope, Dorothy Lamour, James Saphier, and Mildred MacArthur Serrano and Rita Millar Sigmund have been key in discerning the attitudes and activities surrounding the Hopes' arrival in Hollywood and efforts to more fully develop his new career directions. Particular insights came from the Morella, Epstein, and Clark *The Amazing Careers of Bob Hope*, William French's unpublished "From Gags to Riches" (BHPF), and information acquired from The Museum of the Sea, *Queen Mary*, Long Beach. The joke files (BHJF) and the analyses of the early radio monologues (BHPOT) were especially valuable resources.

Clown Hero

For Chapters 20–24, evidence of Hope's soldier-in-greasepaint role during World War II was vividly captured by journalists like Ernie Pyle and John Steinbeck (BHPF, HEPRF). There were the important contributions of Carroll Carroll, who guided Hope through two books about his experiences in the European and South Pacific theaters of the war. Valuable input came also from eyewitness accounts in an extraordinary *Time* cover story (HEPRF) attempting to characterize Hope's persona and the nature of his foxhole humor. The Hope office files (BHJF, BHPF, HEPRF), the analysis of his wartime monologues (BHPOT), and the comedian's wartime memorabilia proved indispensable.

Comic Drummer

In Chapter 25, Fred Hope was a reliable resource for insights on how the comedian was dealing with celebrity and his rapidly accumulating wealth, and particularly on Bob's familial relationships and his business arrangements with Ivor, Fred, and Jack. Wyn Hope shed light on other aspects of Hope family intimacies, especially the longstanding rivalry between Bob and brother Jim. For Chapters 26–30, Larry Gelbart, Charlie Lee, Doris Day, Les Brown, and James Saphier provided incisive clues as to how Hope managed to juggle movies, radio, personal appearances, benefits, and GI entertaining so energetically. Several of Hope's associates, with promises of anonymity, discussed the comedian's tendency to womanize.

Court Jester

Chapters 31–36 have made optimal use of an empirical study (Content Analysis of Bob Hope's Radio and Television Monologues, 1938–1973, BHJF) conducted by journalism graduate students of the University of Southern California. The study's purpose was to determine the nature and characteristics of his humor as a monologist and to discover to what extent he belongs to the tradition of the popular oracle in American humor. The study found that during the years 1952 to 1963, as in no other period of his long career, political subject matter played a dominant role. His humor focused heavily on both the person and administration of Presidents Eisenhower and Kennedy. Hope involved himself more intensely in the issues of the period, i.e., McCarthyism, the space race, the Peace Corps, and the Cold War. Hope's professional associates as well as outside critics agree that he may have met, perhaps, but never surpassed the quality of comedic accomplishments of this particular decade. This writer's eyewitness accounts concerning Hope are circa August 1959, when NBC hired me as media coordinator for *The Bob Hope Show* and assigned me to accompany the comedian on that year's USO Christmas tour of Alaska.

The Patriot

The resources for Chapters 37–40 lie in the heavy media response to Hope's decision to place himself as the preeminent entertainer of the fighting forces in Vietnam (BHJF, BHPF, HEPRF). In 1963, my position as media and public relations director for Hope Enterprises required immersion in Hope's personal and public life. A large segment of my responsibility lay in traveling with him throughout the United States for personal appearances and benefit performances, as well as managing the public relations for his USO Christmas tours. Clearly this role cast me as a central ingredient in most of the events and encounters with the political, military, and industry leaders, as well as the entertainment figures related herein.

The Loyalist

In Chapters 41–45, important sources are interviews with Bob Hope, Mort Lachman, General Rosy O'Donnell, and Howard Miller about the issues surrounding the strung-out Vietnam conflict, the growing tide of antiwar unrest, and accusations that Hope had lost touch with American youth. Concerning two of the most significant media stories of these years—the Anthony J. Lucas piece in *The New York Times Magazine* and Joan Barthel's *Life* cover story—it seemed clear to a wide circle of neutral observers that neither journalist had any intention of reporting objectively. The volatility of this period and the heat of its issues are faithfully collected in bulging Hope office files (BHJF, BHPF, HEPRF).

Legend to Icon

Sources for Chapters 46–50 include interviews with Mort Lachman, Marjorie Hughes, Dorothy Lamour, Linda Hope, and Ward Grant for a deeper understanding of both the lows and highs of Hope's autumnal years, marked as they have been by the deaths of close associates and friends, but also filled with some outstanding achievements and honors. This writer had ended his full-time employment with Hope Enterprises, but was still employed as a consultant on the Bob Hope Museum project, which allowed continued access to correspondence, business documents, joke files, television specials, personal appearances, benefits, and media clippings (BHJF, BHPF, HEPRF).

Fade Out: I'm Still Here

The sources for this final segment consist of all preceding materials, as well as additional findings from *Bob Hope and the Popular Oracle Tradition in American Humor*, the critical assessments of which Hope respected when the dissertation was accepted by USC in 1976. Meeting him in a hallway of his Toluca Lake home one afternoon, I said, "Now, Bob, you're going to have to call me Doctor Faith." And Bob said, "Then you'll have to call me Doctor, Doctor, Doctor, Doctor, Doctor. . . ." (He now has fifty-four honorary doctoral degrees from colleges and universities.) (BHPF)

INDEX